TOM THE DANCING BUG:

INTO the TRUMPVERSE

THANKS TO A PROUD & MIGHTY

InnerHive MEMBER!

FOR ZACH

10/10/20

Your Pal, RUBEN BOLLING

BOOK DESIGN BY ROBBIE ROBBINS

This is the 7th volume in
The Complete Tom the Dancing Bug.

TOM THE DANCING BUG: INTO THE TRUMPVERSE
© 2020 RUBEN BOLLING, ALL RIGHTS RESERVED.

FOREWORD © 2020 NEIL GAIMAN

ISBN: 978-1-951038-08-3

FIRST PRINTING AUGUST 2020

4 3 2 1   20 21 22 24

PRINTED IN KOREA

CLOVER PRESS:
ROBBIE ROBBINS, PRESIDENT/ART DIRECTOR
TED ADAMS, PUBLISHER
ELAINE LAROSA, OPERATIONS
NATE MURRAY, BUSINESS DEVELOPMENT
TIM BELL, SHIPPING ASSISTANT
ELIZABETH NEE, MARKETING ASSISTANT

SAN DIEGO, CA

TOM THE DANCING BUG:
INTO the TRUMPVERSE

Comics by **Ruben Bolling**

About Tom the Dancing Bug

Tom the Dancing Bug is the weekly comic strip by Ruben Bolling that appears in newspapers across North America and on the internet. It takes a sketch-comedy approach to comic strip cartooning, with varying new or recurring characters, formats and even art styles each week.

It started its professional incarnation in 1990 in a small newspaper in New York City, *New York Perspectives* (now defunct), and Bolling self-syndicated it to many other newspapers until 1997, when the company now known as Andrews McMeel Syndication took on syndication, which it continues to this day.

In its early years, its subject matter was only occasionally political, and it featured such characters as Max & Doug, Charley the Australopithecine, Louis Maltby, Harvey Richards: Lawyer for Children, God-Man, Sam Roland: The Detective Who Dies, and Billy Dare: Boy Adventurer. In 1997, Bolling introduced the popular Super-Fun-Pak Comix format, which simulates a surreal daily comics page.

In the 1990s, the comic strip's readership grew, with a newspaper client list exceeding 100, including leading daily newspapers (such as *The Washington Post*), and leading alternative newsweeklies (such as *The Village Voice*). Alternative newspapers were a particularly important part of the comic's distribution and growth, and in the space of eight years, it won five Association of Alternative Newsweekly Best Comic awards.

Tom the Dancing Bug shifted after September, 2001, when Bolling, a New Yorker, felt the urgent need to inject more politics and topical matters into the comic strip's content. New characters of a political bent, like Lucky Ducky and Nate the Neoconservative were introduced, and the comic's political satire became more frequent and increasingly pointed and specific.

As more print newspaper clients (especially alternative newspapers) disappeared or downsized in the late 2000s and early 2010s, the internet became a more important part of the comic's distribution. In that time, T*om the Dancing Bug* gained important web clients BoingBoing.net, DailyKos.com and GoComics.com, which dramatically increased the size and enthusiasm of its readership. In 2012, Bolling launched the "Inner Hive," an email subscription club that emails members each week's comic before it's published on the web, plus other exclusive content, commentary, comics and benefits.

(It is the "Inner Hive" that Neil Gaiman is referring to when he says in the Foreword to this book that he now receives *Tom the Dancing Bug* comics by email. He's been a member since the "Inner Hive" first launched.)

Bolling conceived the social satire feature "Chagrin Falls" in 2013, in which the Smythe family grapples with their increasingly marginalized middle class American lives. One of these installments was the 2014 Gold Medal Winner for the Society of Illustrators Comic Strip Awards.

But in 2016, *Tom the Dancing Bug* took an even sharper political turn when Bolling recognized that Donald Trump represented the political phenomenon of his lifetime, and devoted much of the comic strip to the campaign, which carried over (to Bolling's chagrin) to Trump's election and administration.

This did, however, lead to greater recognition of *Tom the Dancing Bug*, including a 2017 Herblock Prize and a 2018 Robert F. Kennedy Journalism Award. Ruben Bolling was a 2019 Pulitzer Prize Finalist.

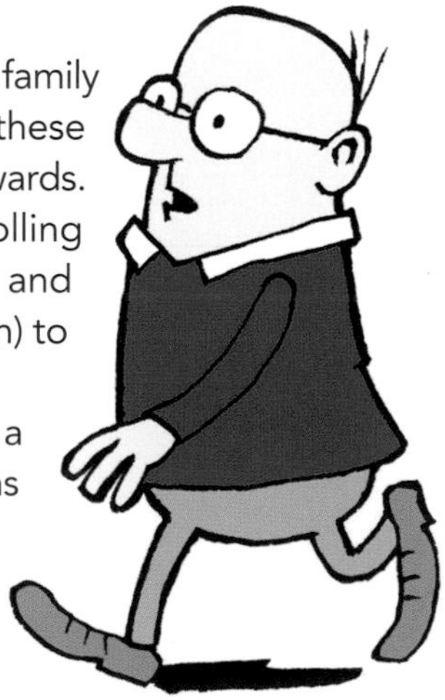

TO JOIN TOM THE DANCING BUG'S "INNER HIVE," GO TO
tomthedancingbug.com

Foreword
by Neil Gaiman

I moved to America in 1992, and was given a copy of the Twin Cities' *City Pages* on my arrival. I was told that in order to understand what was going on, I should read Ruben Bolling's *Tom the Dancing Bug*. I took this advice seriously, and bought the first *Tom* collection. I loved the quiet humour, the gentle outrage, the wise foolishness, the silly wisdom and the occasionally dangerous irony.

Twenty-eight years later, a lot of things in America have changed. For a start, I now get my weekly *Tom the Dancing Bug* fix straight to my email. But Ruben Bolling's craft and commentary are as powerful and as pointed, as capable of making you laugh while breaking your heart as they were when we were all so very young.

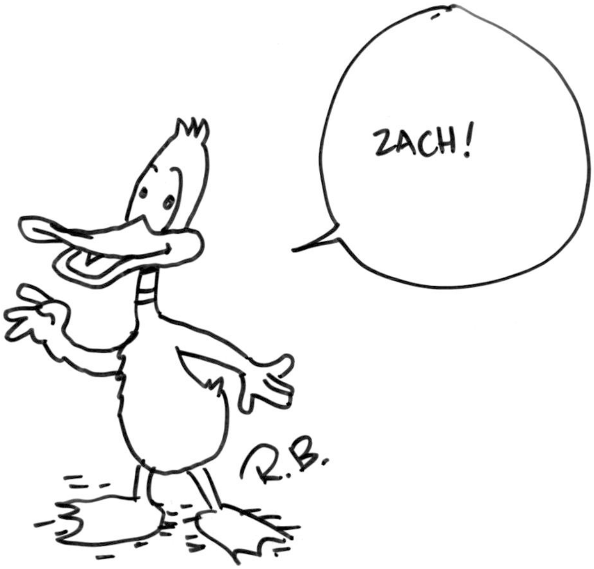
ZACH!
R.B.

Tom the Dancing Bug

by Ruben Bolling

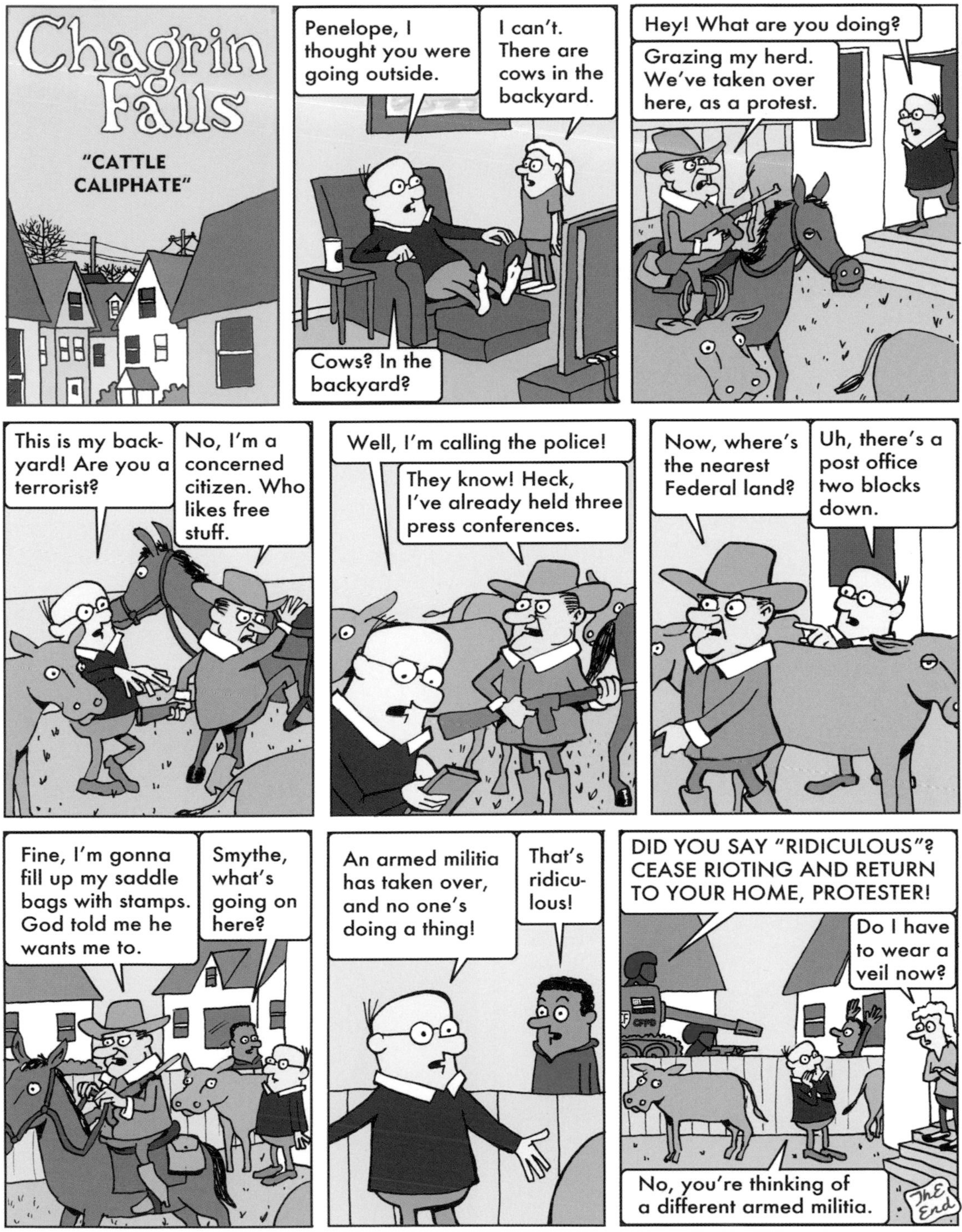

Chagrin Falls
"CATTLE CALIPHATE"
Penelope, I thought you were going outside.
I can't. There are cows in the backyard.
Cows? In the backyard?
Hey! What are you doing?
Grazing my herd. We've taken over here, as a protest.
This is my backyard! Are you a terrorist?
No, I'm a concerned citizen. Who likes free stuff.
Well, I'm calling the police!
They know! Heck, I've already held three press conferences.
Now, where's the nearest Federal land?
Uh, there's a post office two blocks down.
Fine, I'm gonna fill up my saddle bags with stamps. God told me he wants me to.
Smythe, what's going on here?
An armed militia has taken over, and no one's doing a thing!
That's ridiculous!
DID YOU SAY "RIDICULOUS"? CEASE RIOTING AND RETURN TO YOUR HOME, PROTESTER!
Do I have to wear a veil now?
No, you're thinking of a different armed militia.
The End

1/4/16

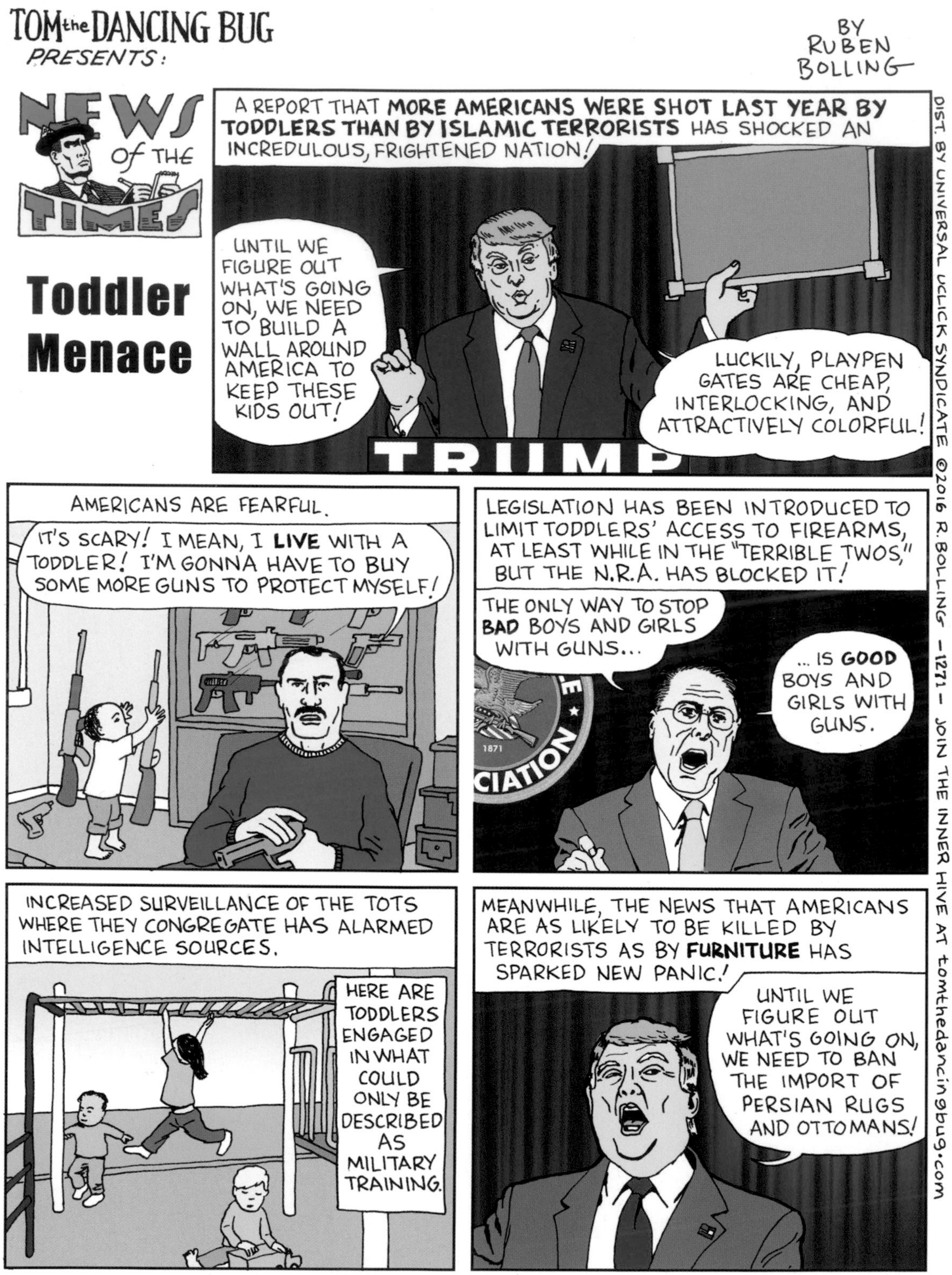
TOM the DANCING BUG
PRESENTS:
BY RUBEN BOLLING
NEWS of the TIMES
Toddler Menace
A REPORT THAT MORE AMERICANS WERE SHOT LAST YEAR BY TODDLERS THAN BY ISLAMIC TERRORISTS HAS SHOCKED AN INCREDULOUS, FRIGHTENED NATION!
UNTIL WE FIGURE OUT WHAT'S GOING ON, WE NEED TO BUILD A WALL AROUND AMERICA TO KEEP THESE KIDS OUT!
LUCKILY, PLAYPEN GATES ARE CHEAP, INTERLOCKING, AND ATTRACTIVELY COLORFUL!
TRUMP
AMERICANS ARE FEARFUL.
IT'S SCARY! I MEAN, I LIVE WITH A TODDLER! I'M GONNA HAVE TO BUY SOME MORE GUNS TO PROTECT MYSELF!
LEGISLATION HAS BEEN INTRODUCED TO LIMIT TODDLERS' ACCESS TO FIREARMS, AT LEAST WHILE IN THE "TERRIBLE TWOS," BUT THE N.R.A. HAS BLOCKED IT!
THE ONLY WAY TO STOP BAD BOYS AND GIRLS WITH GUNS...
... IS GOOD BOYS AND GIRLS WITH GUNS.
INCREASED SURVEILLANCE OF THE TOTS WHERE THEY CONGREGATE HAS ALARMED INTELLIGENCE SOURCES.
HERE ARE TODDLERS ENGAGED IN WHAT COULD ONLY BE DESCRIBED AS MILITARY TRAINING.
MEANWHILE, THE NEWS THAT AMERICANS ARE AS LIKELY TO BE KILLED BY TERRORISTS AS BY FURNITURE HAS SPARKED NEW PANIC!
UNTIL WE FIGURE OUT WHAT'S GOING ON, WE NEED TO BAN THE IMPORT OF PERSIAN RUGS AND OTTOMANS!
DIST. BY UNIVERSAL UCLICK SYNDICATE ©2016 R. BOLLING -1271- JOIN THE INNER HIVE AT tomthedancingbug.com

1/11/16

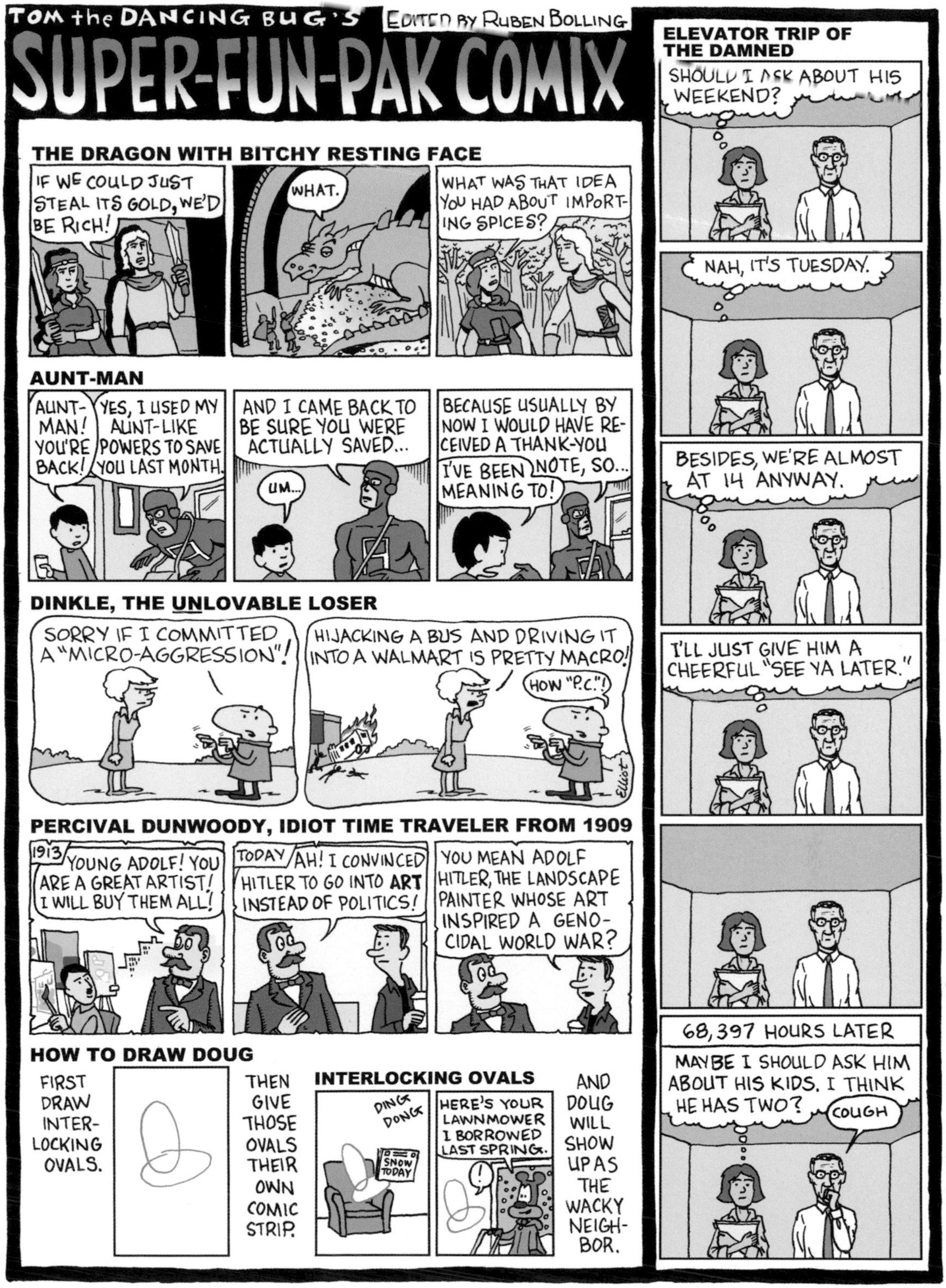
TOM the DANCING BUG'S
EDITED BY RUBEN BOLLING
SUPER-FUN-PAK COMIX
THE DRAGON WITH BITCHY RESTING FACE
IF WE COULD JUST STEAL ITS GOLD, WE'D BE RICH!
WHAT.
WHAT WAS THAT IDEA YOU HAD ABOUT IMPORTING SPICES?
AUNT-MAN
AUNT-MAN! YOU'RE BACK!
YES, I USED MY AUNT-LIKE POWERS TO SAVE YOU LAST MONTH.
AND I CAME BACK TO BE SURE YOU WERE ACTUALLY SAVED...
UM...
BECAUSE USUALLY BY NOW I WOULD HAVE RECEIVED A THANK-YOU NOTE, SO...
I'VE BEEN MEANING TO!
DINKLE, THE UNLOVABLE LOSER
SORRY IF I COMMITTED A "MICRO-AGGRESSION"!
HIJACKING A BUS AND DRIVING IT INTO A WALMART IS PRETTY MACRO!
HOW "P.C."!
Elliot
PERCIVAL DUNWOODY, IDIOT TIME TRAVELER FROM 1909
1913
YOUNG ADOLF! YOU ARE A GREAT ARTIST! I WILL BUY THEM ALL!
TODAY
AH! I CONVINCED HITLER TO GO INTO ART INSTEAD OF POLITICS!
YOU MEAN ADOLF HITLER, THE LANDSCAPE PAINTER WHOSE ART INSPIRED A GENOCIDAL WORLD WAR?
HOW TO DRAW DOUG
FIRST DRAW INTERLOCKING OVALS.
THEN GIVE THOSE OVALS THEIR OWN COMIC STRIP.
INTERLOCKING OVALS
DING DONG
SNOW TODAY
HERE'S YOUR LAWNMOWER I BORROWED LAST SPRING.
!
AND DOUG WILL SHOW UP AS THE WACKY NEIGHBOR.
ELEVATOR TRIP OF THE DAMNED
SHOULD I ASK ABOUT HIS WEEKEND?
NAH, IT'S TUESDAY.
BESIDES, WE'RE ALMOST AT 14 ANYWAY.
I'LL JUST GIVE HIM A CHEERFUL "SEE YA LATER."
68,397 HOURS LATER
MAYBE I SHOULD ASK HIM ABOUT HIS KIDS. I THINK HE HAS TWO?
COUGH

1/18/16

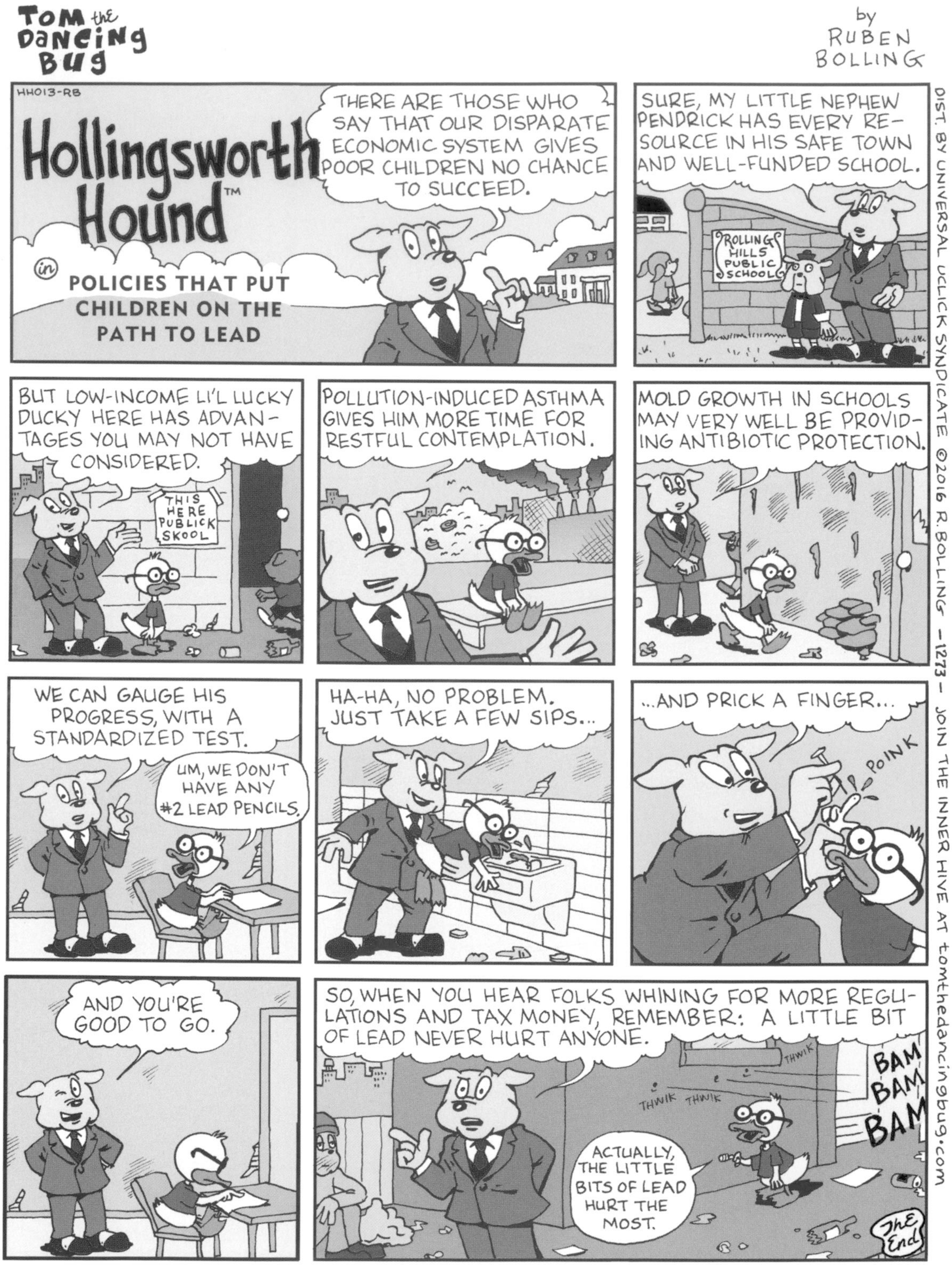
TOM the DANCING BUG
by RUBEN BOLLING
HH013-RB
Hollingsworth Hound™
in POLICIES THAT PUT CHILDREN ON THE PATH TO LEAD
THERE ARE THOSE WHO SAY THAT OUR DISPARATE ECONOMIC SYSTEM GIVES POOR CHILDREN NO CHANCE TO SUCCEED.
SURE, MY LITTLE NEPHEW PENDRICK HAS EVERY RESOURCE IN HIS SAFE TOWN AND WELL-FUNDED SCHOOL.
ROLLING HILLS PUBLIC SCHOOL
BUT LOW-INCOME LI'L LUCKY DUCKY HERE HAS ADVANTAGES YOU MAY NOT HAVE CONSIDERED.
THIS HERE PUBLICK SKOOL
POLLUTION-INDUCED ASTHMA GIVES HIM MORE TIME FOR RESTFUL CONTEMPLATION.
MOLD GROWTH IN SCHOOLS MAY VERY WELL BE PROVIDING ANTIBIOTIC PROTECTION.
WE CAN GAUGE HIS PROGRESS, WITH A STANDARDIZED TEST.
UM, WE DON'T HAVE ANY #2 LEAD PENCILS.
HA-HA, NO PROBLEM. JUST TAKE A FEW SIPS...
...AND PRICK A FINGER...
POINK
AND YOU'RE GOOD TO GO.
SO, WHEN YOU HEAR FOLKS WHINING FOR MORE REGULATIONS AND TAX MONEY, REMEMBER: A LITTLE BIT OF LEAD NEVER HURT ANYONE.
THWIK
THWIK THWIK
BAM BAM BAM
ACTUALLY, THE LITTLE BITS OF LEAD HURT THE MOST.
THE End
DIST. BY UNIVERSAL UCLICK SYNDICATE ©2016 R. BOLLING -1273- JOIN THE INNER HIVE AT tomthedancingbug.com

1/25/16

TOM the DANCING BUG

by RUBEN BOLLING

NEURON HEROES OF THE
SUPER BOWL

A TRIBUTE TO THE SACRIFICES MADE BY NFL NEURONS IN SERVICE OF THEIR TEAMS AND THE GRAND GAME OF THE GRIDIRON

SUPER BOWL II No. 37395496584, Packers

With the Packers up 13-7 and driving toward the end zone with the clock ticking down on the first half, this neuron laid it on the line, suffering complete devastation to its membrane permeability during a hit to the head of Green Bay tight end Ron Ingalls.

SUPER BOWL XIV No. 82642989, Steelers

In the Steelers' first possession, this brave neuron within the brain of tackle Brett Overton risked it all in a subconcussive trauma, and was totally obliterated, causing tau proteins to amass pathologically.
But: First and ten, Steelers!

SUPER BOWL XXXIII No. 440212611, Broncos

This indomitable neuron, posthumously inducted into the NFL neurological Hall of Fame, gave 110% - of its microtubule tract - so that Broncos wide receiver Billy Goddard, in whose brain it was a loyal teammate, could make a third quarter reception for a gain of 12.

SUPER BOWL XLI No. 107477362083, Colts

On a field goal that would give the Colts a five-point lead, this pesky, selfless neuron was violently stripped in a collision, after which positively charged sodium ions were released and flooded into the brain of guard Tripp Fredricksen.

On behalf of these and billions of other neurons who left it all on the field, Tripp Fredricksen would like to say a few words.

UM... I DON'T... LUNCH?

Thank you to all the heroic cellular competitors who gave their all to give fans great Super Bowl memories, and give players Chronic Traumatic Encephalopathy!

DIST. BY UNIVERSAL UCLICK SYNDICATE - © 2016 R. BOLLING - 1274 - JOIN THE INNER HIVE AT tomthedancingbug.com

2/1/16

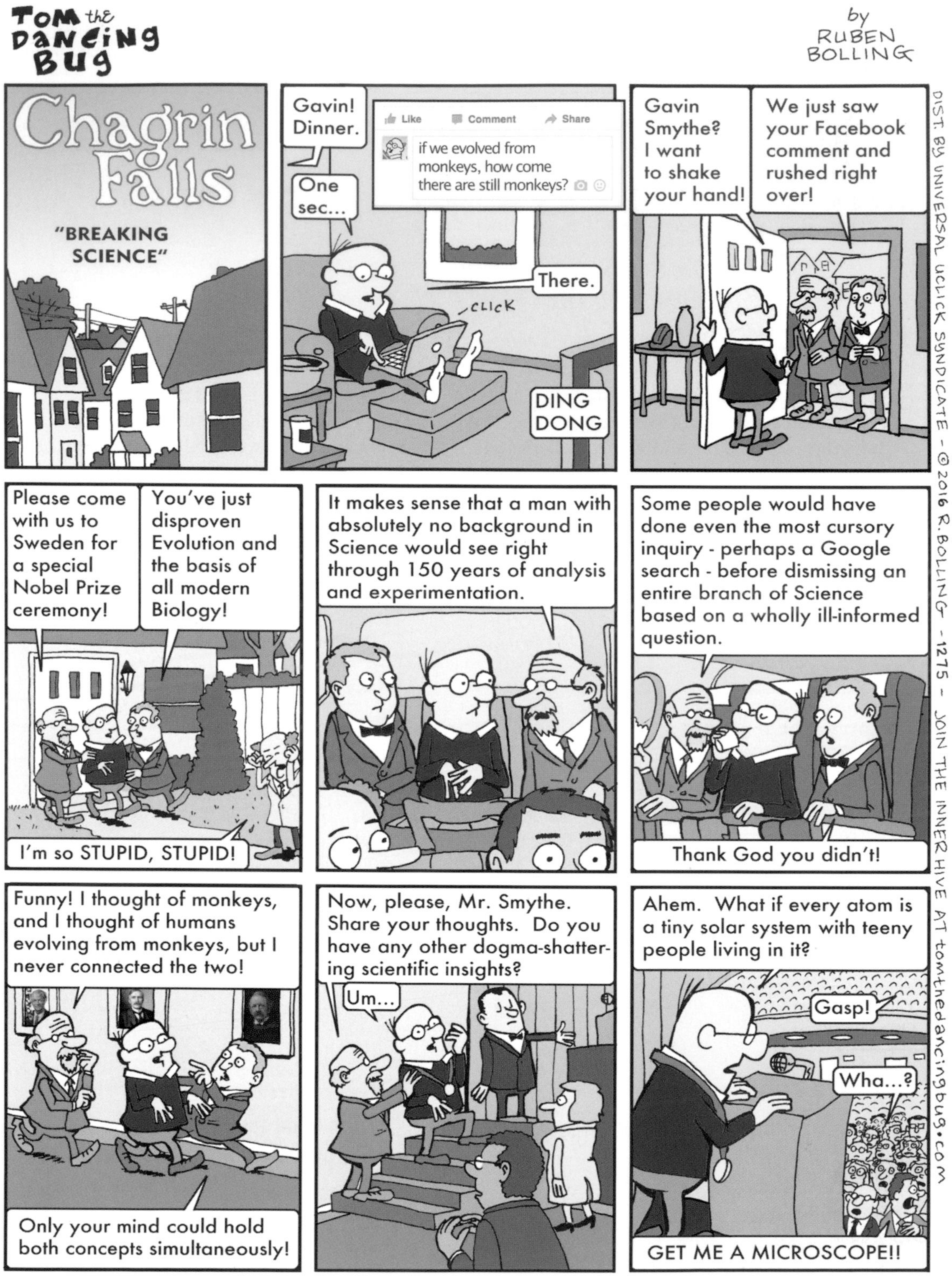

TOM the DANCING BUG
by RUBEN BOLLING
Chagrin Falls
"BREAKING SCIENCE"
Gavin! Dinner.
One sec...
Like
Comment
Share
if we evolved from monkeys, how come there are still monkeys?
There.
-CLICK
DING DONG
Gavin Smythe? I want to shake your hand!
We just saw your Facebook comment and rushed right over!
Please come with us to Sweden for a special Nobel Prize ceremony!
You've just disproven Evolution and the basis of all modern Biology!
I'm so STUPID, STUPID!
It makes sense that a man with absolutely no background in Science would see right through 150 years of analysis and experimentation.
Some people would have done even the most cursory inquiry - perhaps a Google search - before dismissing an entire branch of Science based on a wholly ill-informed question.
Thank God you didn't!
Funny! I thought of monkeys, and I thought of humans evolving from monkeys, but I never connected the two!
Only your mind could hold both concepts simultaneously!
Now, please, Mr. Smythe. Share your thoughts. Do you have any other dogma-shattering scientific insights?
Um...
Ahem. What if every atom is a tiny solar system with teeny people living in it?
Gasp!
Wha...?
GET ME A MICROSCOPE!!
DIST. BY UNIVERSAL UCLICK SYNDICATE - ©2016 R. BOLLING - 1275 - JOIN THE INNER HIVE AT tomthedancingbug.com

2/8/16

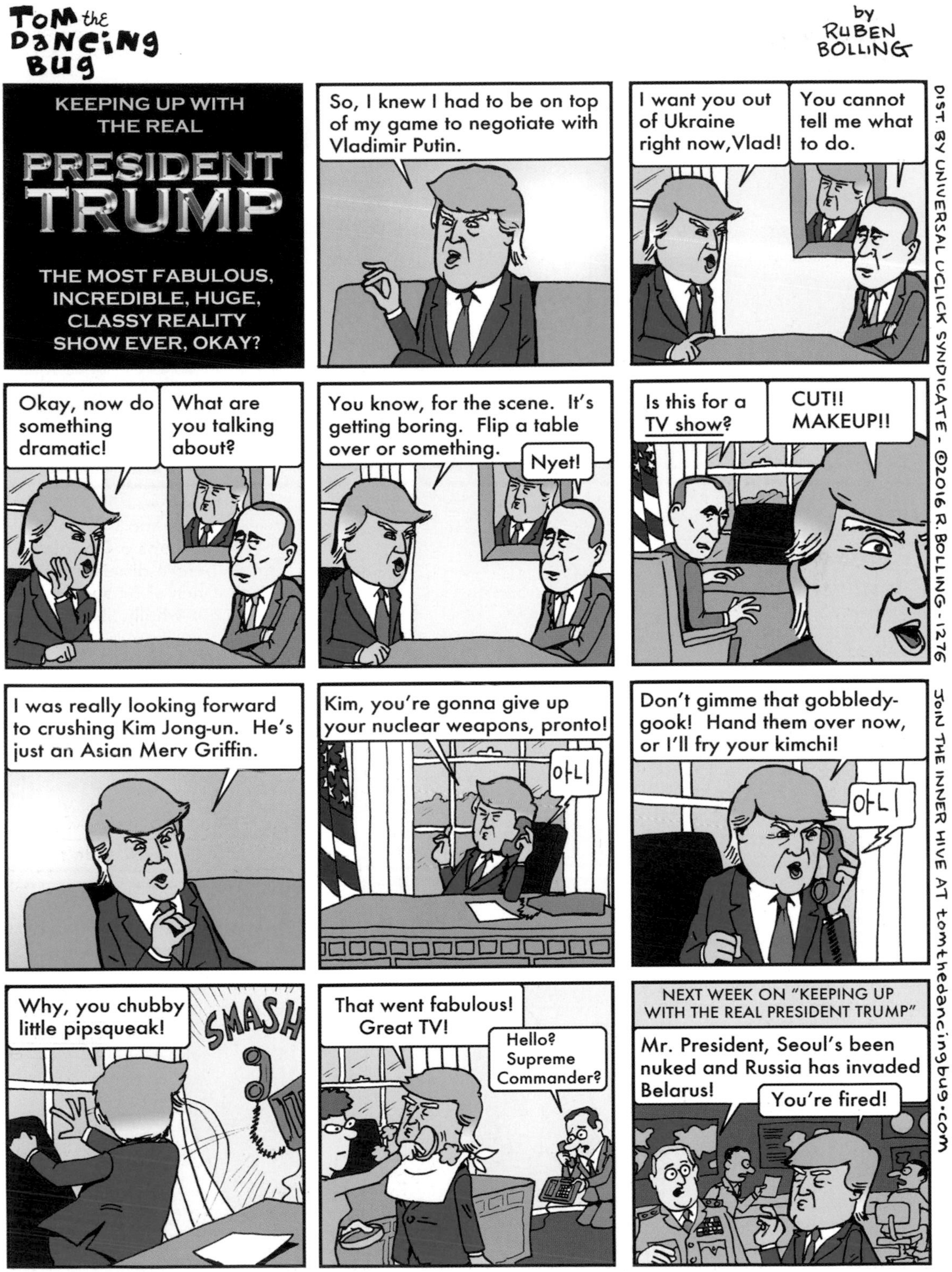

Tom the Dancing Bug
by Ruben Bolling
KEEPING UP WITH THE REAL
PRESIDENT TRUMP
THE MOST FABULOUS, INCREDIBLE, HUGE, CLASSY REALITY SHOW EVER, OKAY?
So, I knew I had to be on top of my game to negotiate with Vladimir Putin.
I want you out of Ukraine right now, Vlad!
You cannot tell me what to do.
Okay, now do something dramatic!
What are you talking about?
You know, for the scene. It's getting boring. Flip a table over or something.
Nyet!
Is this for a TV show?
CUT!! MAKEUP!!
I was really looking forward to crushing Kim Jong-un. He's just an Asian Merv Griffin.
Kim, you're gonna give up your nuclear weapons, pronto!
아니
Don't gimme that gobbledy-gook! Hand them over now, or I'll fry your kimchi!
아니
Why, you chubby little pipsqueak!
SMASH
That went fabulous! Great TV!
Hello? Supreme Commander?
NEXT WEEK ON "KEEPING UP WITH THE REAL PRESIDENT TRUMP"
Mr. President, Seoul's been nuked and Russia has invaded Belarus!
You're fired!
DIST. BY UNIVERSAL UCLICK SYNDICATE - ©2016 R. BOLLING - 1276
JOIN THE INNER HIVE AT tomthedancingbug.com

2/15/16

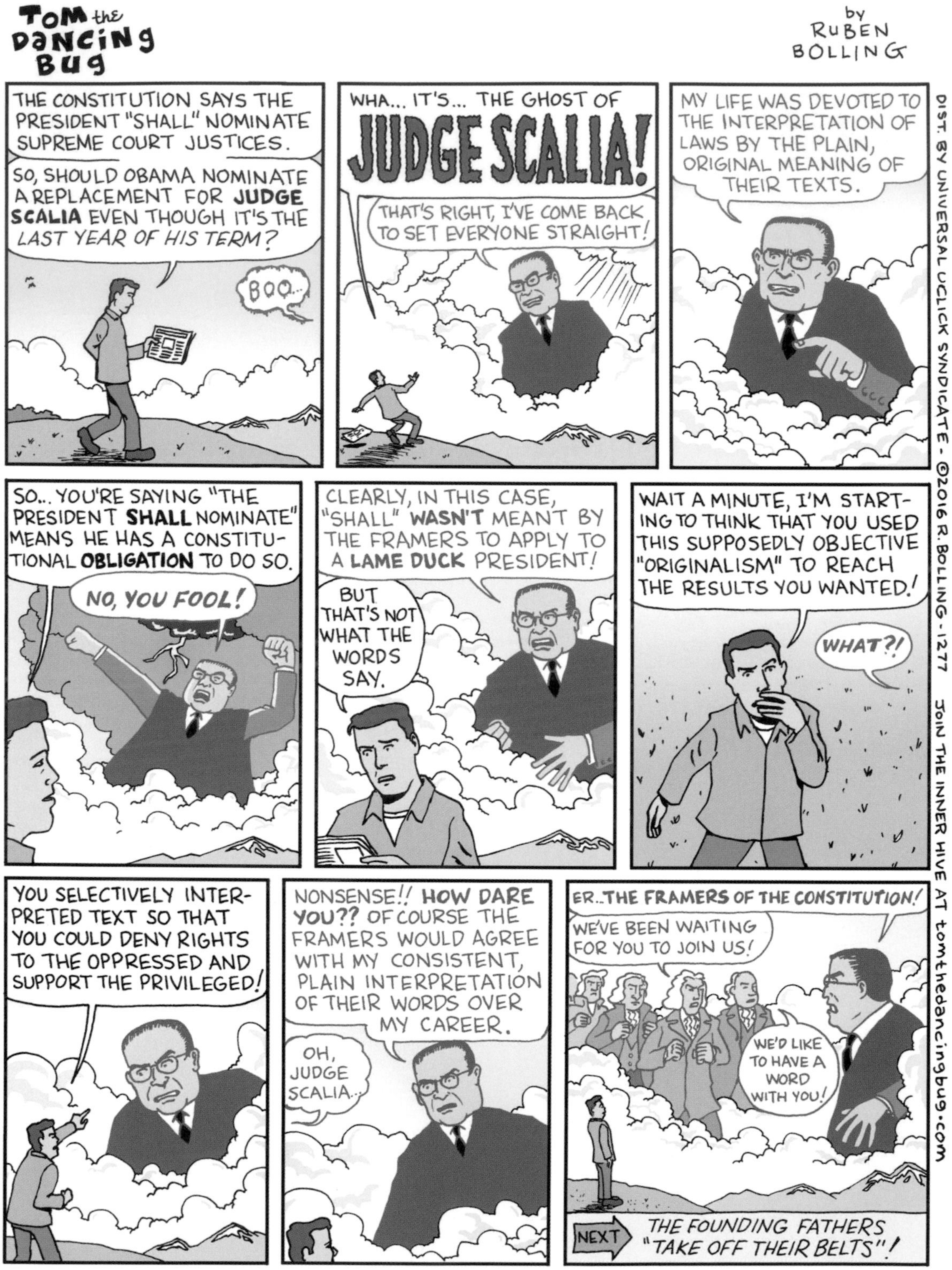
TOM the DANCING BUG
by RUBEN BOLLING
THE CONSTITUTION SAYS THE PRESIDENT "SHALL" NOMINATE SUPREME COURT JUSTICES.
SO, SHOULD OBAMA NOMINATE A REPLACEMENT FOR JUDGE SCALIA EVEN THOUGH IT'S THE LAST YEAR OF HIS TERM?
BOO...
WHA... IT'S... THE GHOST OF
JUDGE SCALIA!
THAT'S RIGHT, I'VE COME BACK TO SET EVERYONE STRAIGHT!
MY LIFE WAS DEVOTED TO THE INTERPRETATION OF LAWS BY THE PLAIN, ORIGINAL MEANING OF THEIR TEXTS.
SO... YOU'RE SAYING "THE PRESIDENT SHALL NOMINATE" MEANS HE HAS A CONSTITUTIONAL OBLIGATION TO DO SO.
NO, YOU FOOL!
CLEARLY, IN THIS CASE, "SHALL" WASN'T MEANT BY THE FRAMERS TO APPLY TO A LAME DUCK PRESIDENT!
BUT THAT'S NOT WHAT THE WORDS SAY.
WAIT A MINUTE, I'M STARTING TO THINK THAT YOU USED THIS SUPPOSEDLY OBJECTIVE "ORIGINALISM" TO REACH THE RESULTS YOU WANTED!
WHAT?!
YOU SELECTIVELY INTERPRETED TEXT SO THAT YOU COULD DENY RIGHTS TO THE OPPRESSED AND SUPPORT THE PRIVILEGED!
NONSENSE!! HOW DARE YOU?? OF COURSE THE FRAMERS WOULD AGREE WITH MY CONSISTENT, PLAIN INTERPRETATION OF THEIR WORDS OVER MY CAREER.
OH, JUDGE SCALIA...
ER... THE FRAMERS OF THE CONSTITUTION!
WE'VE BEEN WAITING FOR YOU TO JOIN US!
WE'D LIKE TO HAVE A WORD WITH YOU!
NEXT
THE FOUNDING FATHERS "TAKE OFF THEIR BELTS"!
DIST. BY UNIVERSAL UCLICK SYNDICATE - ©2016 R. BOLLING - 1277
JOIN THE INNER HIVE AT tomthedancingbug.com

2/22/16

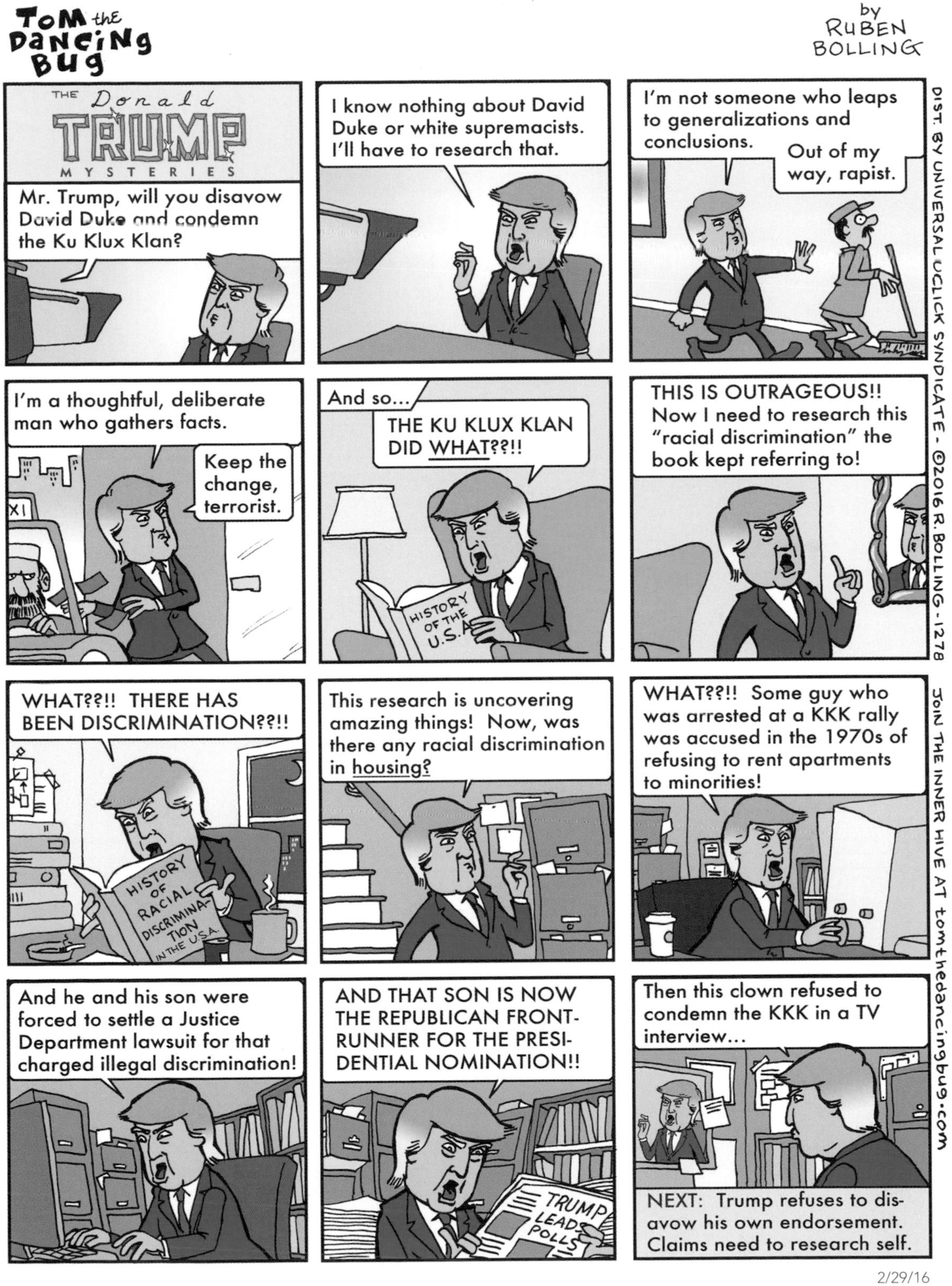
TOM THE DANCING BUG
by RUBEN BOLLING
THE Donald TRUMP MYSTERIES
Mr. Trump, will you disavow David Duke and condemn the Ku Klux Klan?
I know nothing about David Duke or white supremacists. I'll have to research that.
I'm not someone who leaps to generalizations and conclusions.
Out of my way, rapist.
I'm a thoughtful, deliberate man who gathers facts.
Keep the change, terrorist.
And so...
THE KU KLUX KLAN DID WHAT??!!
HISTORY OF THE U.S.A.
THIS IS OUTRAGEOUS!! Now I need to research this "racial discrimination" the book kept referring to!
WHAT??!! THERE HAS BEEN DISCRIMINATION??!!
HISTORY OF RACIAL DISCRIMINATION IN THE U.S.A.
This research is uncovering amazing things! Now, was there any racial discrimination in housing?
WHAT??!! Some guy who was arrested at a KKK rally was accused in the 1970s of refusing to rent apartments to minorities!
And he and his son were forced to settle a Justice Department lawsuit for that charged illegal discrimination!
AND THAT SON IS NOW THE REPUBLICAN FRONT-RUNNER FOR THE PRESIDENTIAL NOMINATION!!
TRUMP LEADS POLLS
Then this clown refused to condemn the KKK in a TV interview...
NEXT: Trump refuses to disavow his own endorsement. Claims need to research self.
DIST. BY UNIVERSAL UCLICK SYNDICATE - ©2016 R. BOLLING - 1278
JOIN THE INNER HIVE AT tomthedancingbug.com

2/29/16

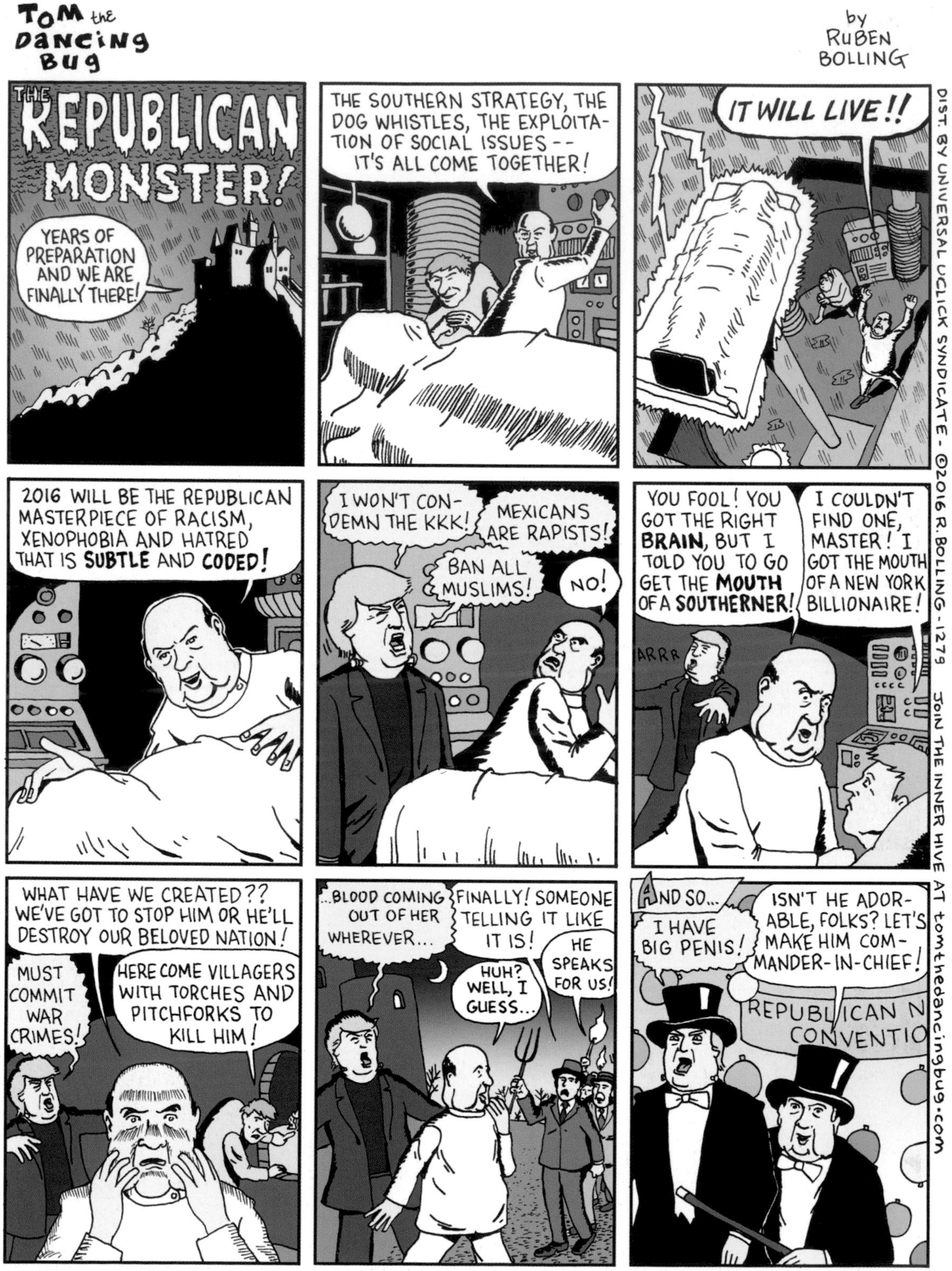
TOM the DANCING BUG
by RUBEN BOLLING
THE REPUBLICAN MONSTER!
YEARS OF PREPARATION AND WE ARE FINALLY THERE!
THE SOUTHERN STRATEGY, THE DOG WHISTLES, THE EXPLOITATION OF SOCIAL ISSUES -- IT'S ALL COME TOGETHER!
IT WILL LIVE!!
2016 WILL BE THE REPUBLICAN MASTERPIECE OF RACISM, XENOPHOBIA AND HATRED THAT IS SUBTLE AND CODED!
I WON'T CONDEMN THE KKK!
MEXICANS ARE RAPISTS!
BAN ALL MUSLIMS!
NO!
YOU FOOL! YOU GOT THE RIGHT BRAIN, BUT I TOLD YOU TO GO GET THE MOUTH OF A SOUTHERNER!
I COULDN'T FIND ONE, MASTER! I GOT THE MOUTH OF A NEW YORK BILLIONAIRE!
ARRR
WHAT HAVE WE CREATED?? WE'VE GOT TO STOP HIM OR HE'LL DESTROY OUR BELOVED NATION!
MUST COMMIT WAR CRIMES!
HERE COME VILLAGERS WITH TORCHES AND PITCHFORKS TO KILL HIM!
...BLOOD COMING OUT OF HER WHEREVER...
FINALLY! SOMEONE TELLING IT LIKE IT IS!
HUH? WELL, I GUESS...
HE SPEAKS FOR US!
AND SO...
I HAVE BIG PENIS!
ISN'T HE ADORABLE, FOLKS? LET'S MAKE HIM COMMANDER-IN-CHIEF!
REPUBLICAN N CONVENTIO
DIST. BY UNIVERSAL UCLICK SYNDICATE - ©2016 R. BOLLING - 1279 JOIN THE INNER HIVE AT tomthedancingbug.com

3/7/16

TOM the DANCING BUG

by RUBEN BOLLING

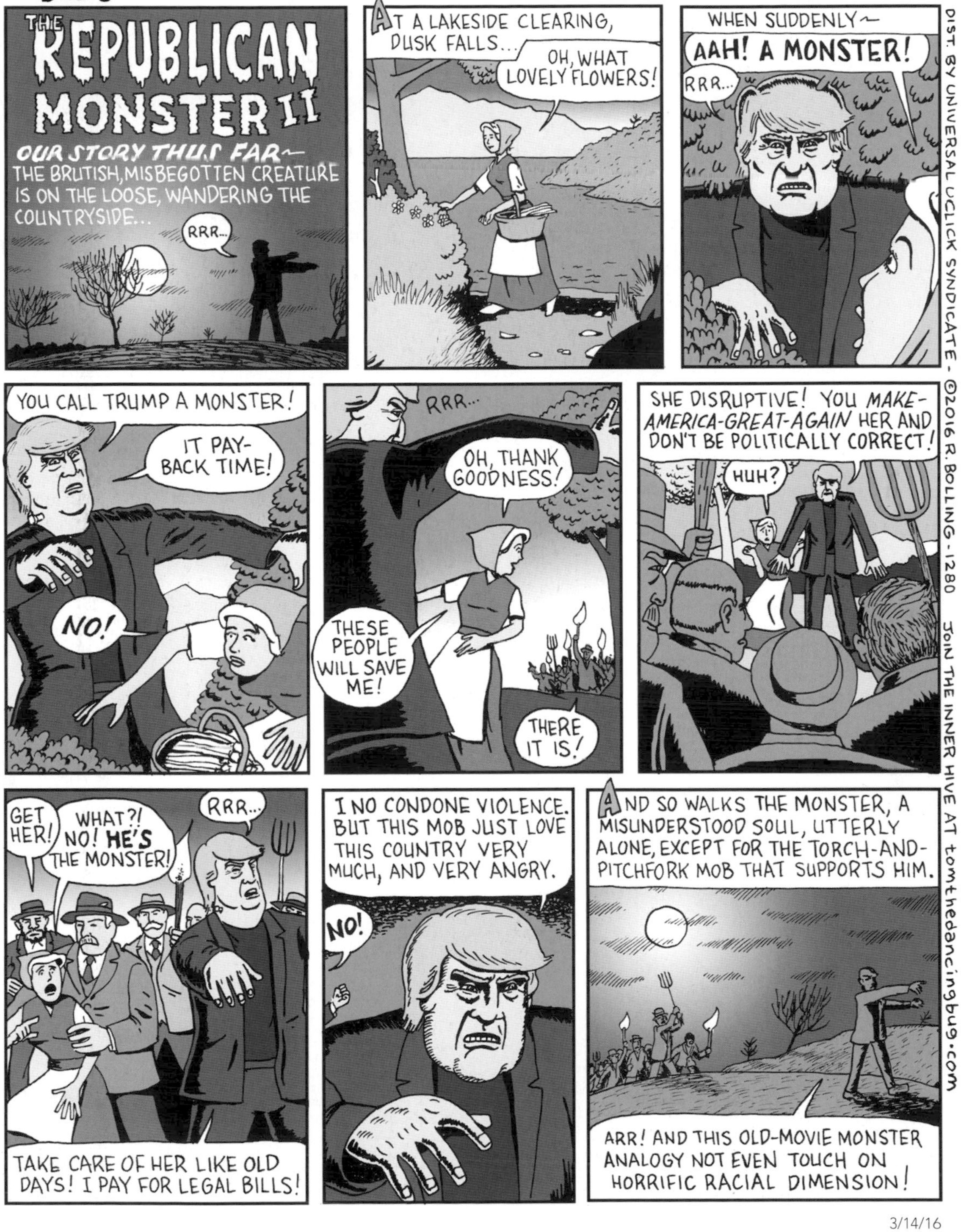
THE REPUBLICAN MONSTER II
OUR STORY THUS FAR—
THE BRUTISH, MISBEGOTTEN CREATURE IS ON THE LOOSE, WANDERING THE COUNTRYSIDE...
RRR...
AT A LAKESIDE CLEARING, DUSK FALLS...
OH, WHAT LOVELY FLOWERS!
WHEN SUDDENLY—
AAH! A MONSTER!
RRR...
YOU CALL TRUMP A MONSTER!
IT PAY-BACK TIME!
NO!
RRR...
OH, THANK GOODNESS!
THESE PEOPLE WILL SAVE ME!
THERE IT IS!
SHE DISRUPTIVE! YOU MAKE-AMERICA-GREAT-AGAIN HER AND DON'T BE POLITICALLY CORRECT!
HUH?
GET HER!
WHAT?! NO! HE'S THE MONSTER!
RRR...
TAKE CARE OF HER LIKE OLD DAYS! I PAY FOR LEGAL BILLS!
I NO CONDONE VIOLENCE. BUT THIS MOB JUST LOVE THIS COUNTRY VERY MUCH, AND VERY ANGRY.
NO!
AND SO WALKS THE MONSTER, A MISUNDERSTOOD SOUL, UTTERLY ALONE, EXCEPT FOR THE TORCH-AND-PITCHFORK MOB THAT SUPPORTS HIM.
ARR! AND THIS OLD-MOVIE MONSTER ANALOGY NOT EVEN TOUCH ON HORRIFIC RACIAL DIMENSION!
DIST. BY UNIVERSAL UCLICK SYNDICATE - ©2016 R. BOLLING - 1280 JOIN THE INNER HIVE AT tomthedancingbug.com

3/14/16

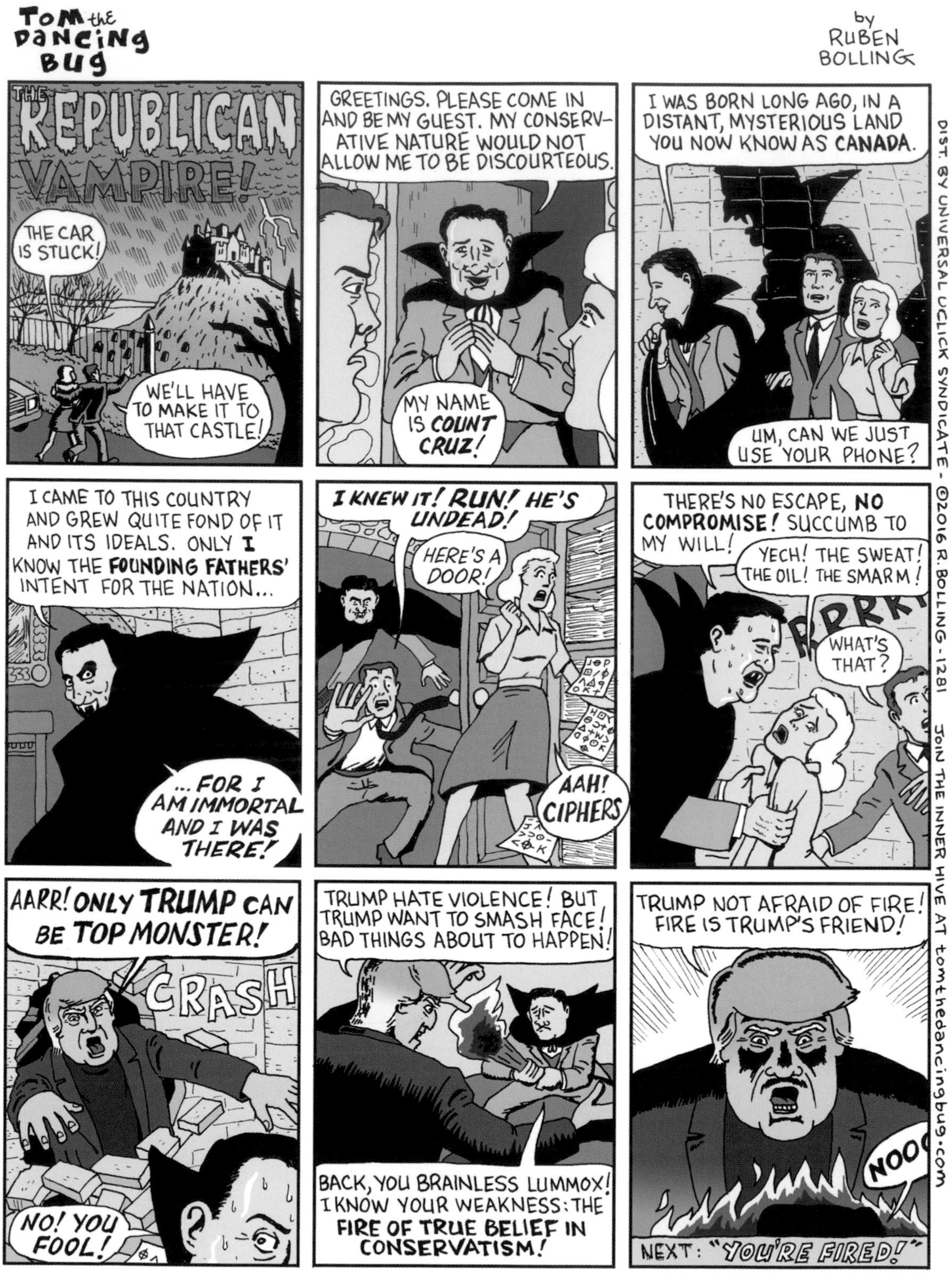
TOM the DANCING BUG
by RUBEN BOLLING
THE REPUBLICAN VAMPIRE!
THE CAR IS STUCK!
WE'LL HAVE TO MAKE IT TO THAT CASTLE!
GREETINGS. PLEASE COME IN AND BE MY GUEST. MY CONSERVATIVE NATURE WOULD NOT ALLOW ME TO BE DISCOURTEOUS.
MY NAME IS COUNT CRUZ!
I WAS BORN LONG AGO, IN A DISTANT, MYSTERIOUS LAND YOU NOW KNOW AS CANADA.
UM, CAN WE JUST USE YOUR PHONE?
I CAME TO THIS COUNTRY AND GREW QUITE FOND OF IT AND ITS IDEALS. ONLY I KNOW THE FOUNDING FATHERS' INTENT FOR THE NATION...
...FOR I AM IMMORTAL AND I WAS THERE!
I KNEW IT! RUN! HE'S UNDEAD!
HERE'S A DOOR!
AAH! CIPHERS
THERE'S NO ESCAPE, NO COMPROMISE! SUCCUMB TO MY WILL!
YECH! THE SWEAT! THE OIL! THE SMARM!
RRRR
WHAT'S THAT?
AARR! ONLY TRUMP CAN BE TOP MONSTER!
CRASH
NO! YOU FOOL!
TRUMP HATE VIOLENCE! BUT TRUMP WANT TO SMASH FACE! BAD THINGS ABOUT TO HAPPEN!
BACK, YOU BRAINLESS LUMMOX! I KNOW YOUR WEAKNESS: THE FIRE OF TRUE BELIEF IN CONSERVATISM!
TRUMP NOT AFRAID OF FIRE! FIRE IS TRUMP'S FRIEND!
NOOO
NEXT: "YOU'RE FIRED!"
DIST. BY UNIVERSAL UCLICK SYNDICATE - ©2016 R. BOLLING - 1281 JOIN THE INNER HIVE AT tomthedancingbug.com

3/21/16

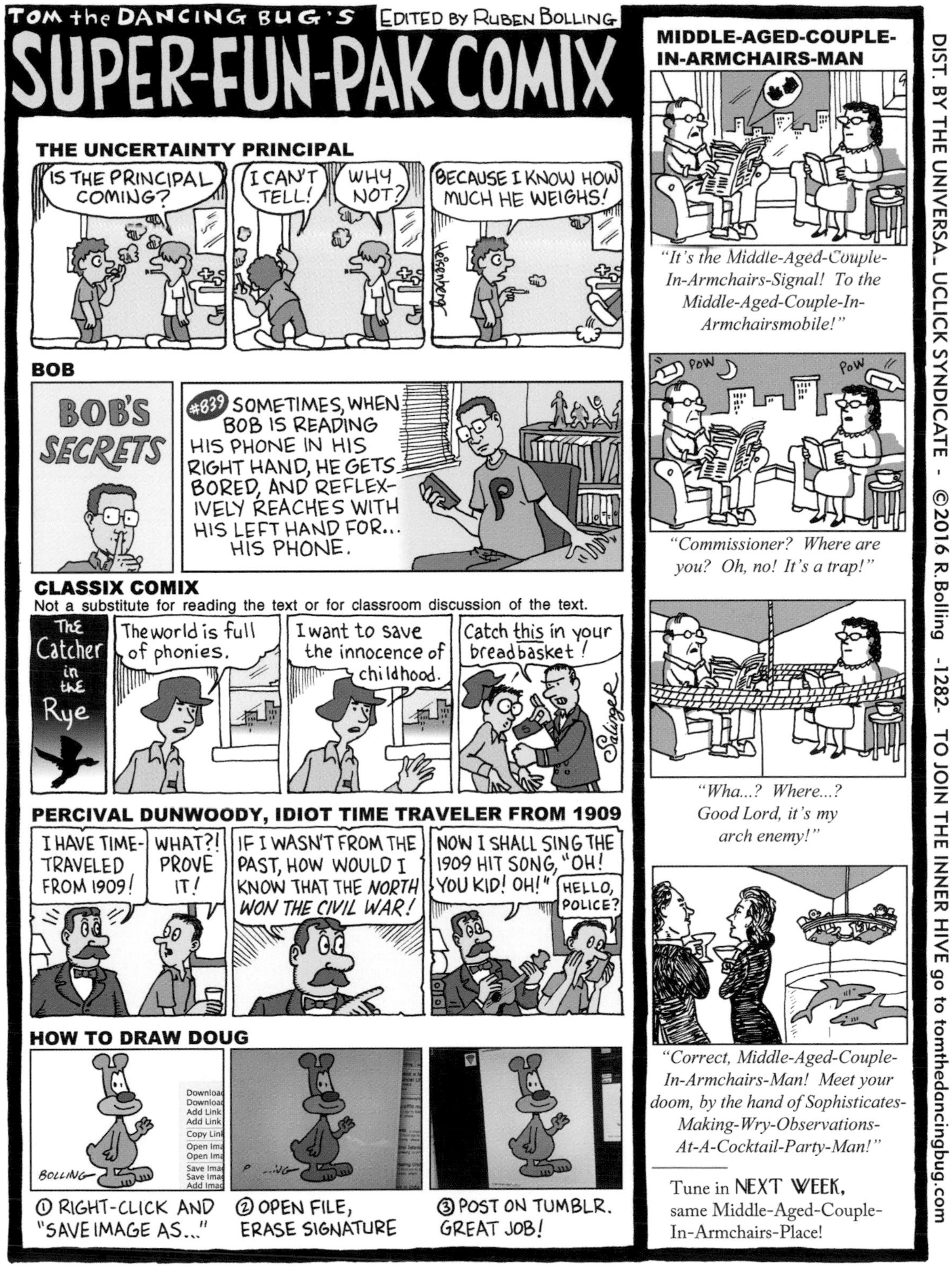
TOM the DANCING BUG'S
EDITED BY RUBEN BOLLING
SUPER-FUN-PAK COMIX
THE UNCERTAINTY PRINCIPAL
IS THE PRINCIPAL COMING?
I CAN'T TELL!
WHY NOT?
BECAUSE I KNOW HOW MUCH HE WEIGHS!
Heisenberg
BOB
BOB'S SECRETS
#839 SOMETIMES, WHEN BOB IS READING HIS PHONE IN HIS RIGHT HAND, HE GETS BORED, AND REFLEXIVELY REACHES WITH HIS LEFT HAND FOR... HIS PHONE.
CLASSIX COMIX
Not a substitute for reading the text or for classroom discussion of the text.
The Catcher in the Rye
The world is full of phonies.
I want to save the innocence of childhood.
Catch this in your breadbasket!
Salinger
PERCIVAL DUNWOODY, IDIOT TIME TRAVELER FROM 1909
I HAVE TIME-TRAVELED FROM 1909!
WHAT?! PROVE IT!
IF I WASN'T FROM THE PAST, HOW WOULD I KNOW THAT THE NORTH WON THE CIVIL WAR!
NOW I SHALL SING THE 1909 HIT SONG, "OH! YOU KID! OH!"
HELLO, POLICE?
HOW TO DRAW DOUG
BOLLING
① RIGHT-CLICK AND "SAVE IMAGE AS..."
② OPEN FILE, ERASE SIGNATURE
③ POST ON TUMBLR. GREAT JOB!
MIDDLE-AGED-COUPLE-IN-ARMCHAIRS-MAN
"It's the Middle-Aged-Couple-In-Armchairs-Signal! To the Middle-Aged-Couple-In-Armchairsmobile!"
POW
POW
"Commissioner? Where are you? Oh, no! It's a trap!"
"Wha...? Where...? Good Lord, it's my arch enemy!"
"Correct, Middle-Aged-Couple-In-Armchairs-Man! Meet your doom, by the hand of Sophisticates-Making-Wry-Observations-At-A-Cocktail-Party-Man!"
Tune in NEXT WEEK, same Middle-Aged-Couple-In-Armchairs-Place!
DIST. BY THE UNIVERSAL UCLICK SYNDICATE - ©2016 R. Bolling -1282- TO JOIN THE INNER HIVE go to tomthedancingbug.com

3/28/16

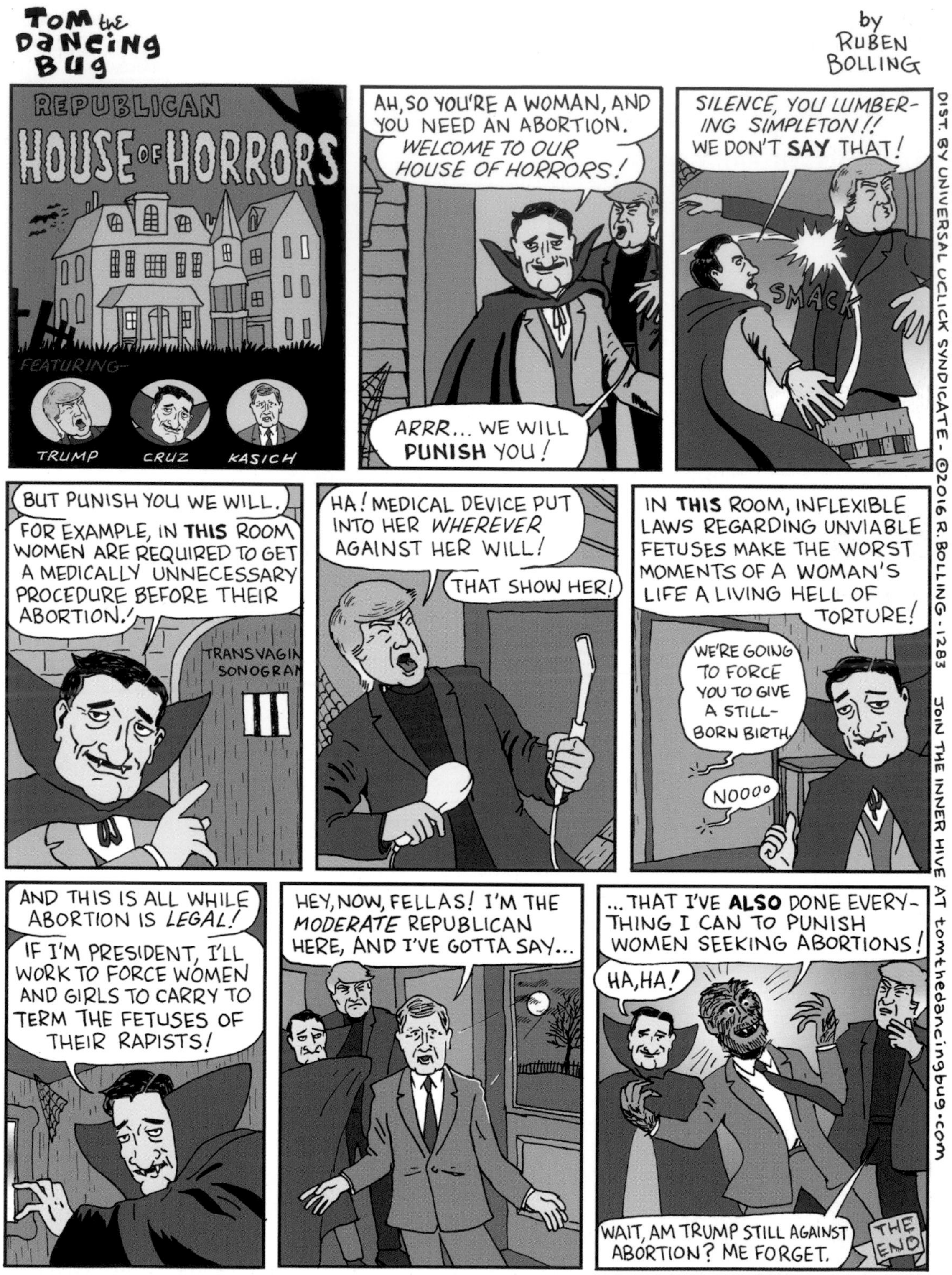
TOM the DANCING BUG
by RUBEN BOLLING
REPUBLICAN HOUSE OF HORRORS
FEATURING—
TRUMP
CRUZ
KASICH
AH, SO YOU'RE A WOMAN, AND YOU NEED AN ABORTION. WELCOME TO OUR HOUSE OF HORRORS!
ARRR... WE WILL PUNISH YOU!
SILENCE, YOU LUMBERING SIMPLETON!! WE DON'T SAY THAT!
SMACK
BUT PUNISH YOU WE WILL.
FOR EXAMPLE, IN THIS ROOM WOMEN ARE REQUIRED TO GET A MEDICALLY UNNECESSARY PROCEDURE BEFORE THEIR ABORTION.
TRANSVAGIN SONOGRAM
HA! MEDICAL DEVICE PUT INTO HER WHEREVER AGAINST HER WILL!
THAT SHOW HER!
IN THIS ROOM, INFLEXIBLE LAWS REGARDING UNVIABLE FETUSES MAKE THE WORST MOMENTS OF A WOMAN'S LIFE A LIVING HELL OF TORTURE!
WE'RE GOING TO FORCE YOU TO GIVE A STILL-BORN BIRTH.
NOOOO
AND THIS IS ALL WHILE ABORTION IS LEGAL!
IF I'M PRESIDENT, I'LL WORK TO FORCE WOMEN AND GIRLS TO CARRY TO TERM THE FETUSES OF THEIR RAPISTS!
HEY, NOW, FELLAS! I'M THE MODERATE REPUBLICAN HERE, AND I'VE GOTTA SAY...
...THAT I'VE ALSO DONE EVERYTHING I CAN TO PUNISH WOMEN SEEKING ABORTIONS!
HA, HA!
WAIT, AM TRUMP STILL AGAINST ABORTION? ME FORGET.
THE END
DIST. BY UNIVERSAL UCLICK SYNDICATE - ©2016 R. BOLLING - 1283
JOIN THE INNER HIVE AT tomthedancingbug.com

4/11/16

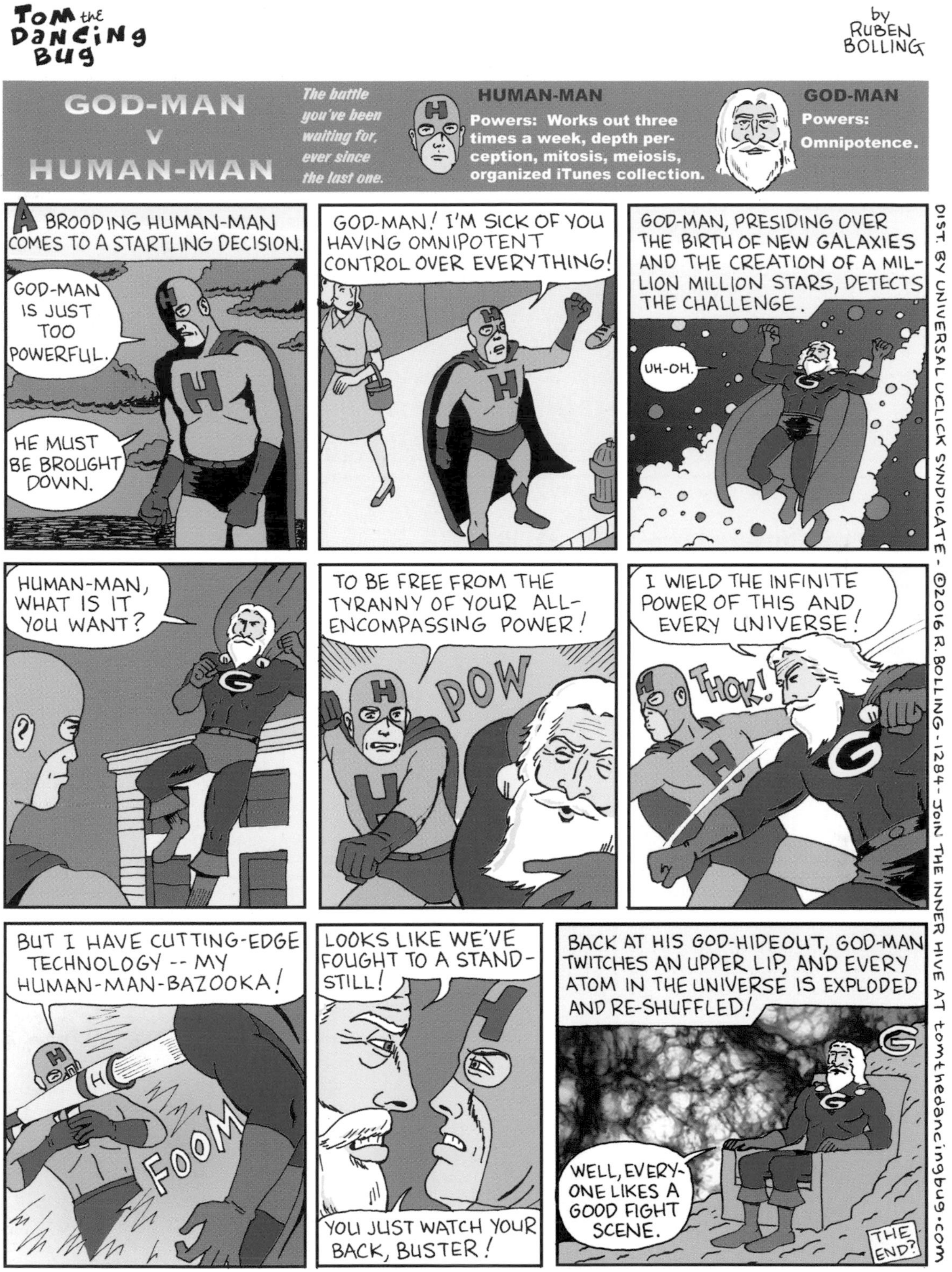
Tom the Dancing Bug
by Ruben Bolling
GOD-MAN V HUMAN-MAN
The battle you've been waiting for, ever since the last one.
HUMAN-MAN
Powers: Works out three times a week, depth perception, mitosis, meiosis, organized iTunes collection.
GOD-MAN
Powers: Omnipotence.
A BROODING HUMAN-MAN COMES TO A STARTLING DECISION.
GOD-MAN IS JUST TOO POWERFUL.
HE MUST BE BROUGHT DOWN.
GOD-MAN! I'M SICK OF YOU HAVING OMNIPOTENT CONTROL OVER EVERYTHING!
GOD-MAN, PRESIDING OVER THE BIRTH OF NEW GALAXIES AND THE CREATION OF A MILLION MILLION STARS, DETECTS THE CHALLENGE.
UH-OH.
HUMAN-MAN, WHAT IS IT YOU WANT?
TO BE FREE FROM THE TYRANNY OF YOUR ALL-ENCOMPASSING POWER!
POW
I WIELD THE INFINITE POWER OF THIS AND EVERY UNIVERSE!
THOK!
BUT I HAVE CUTTING-EDGE TECHNOLOGY -- MY HUMAN-MAN-BAZOOKA!
FOOM
LOOKS LIKE WE'VE FOUGHT TO A STANDSTILL!
YOU JUST WATCH YOUR BACK, BUSTER!
BACK AT HIS GOD-HIDEOUT, GOD-MAN TWITCHES AN UPPER LIP, AND EVERY ATOM IN THE UNIVERSE IS EXPLODED AND RE-SHUFFLED!
WELL, EVERYONE LIKES A GOOD FIGHT SCENE.
THE END?
DIST. BY UNIVERSAL UCLICK SYNDICATE - ©2016 R. BOLLING - 1284 - JOIN THE INNER HIVE AT tomthedancingbug.com

4/18/16

TOM the DANCING BUG

by RUBEN BOLLING

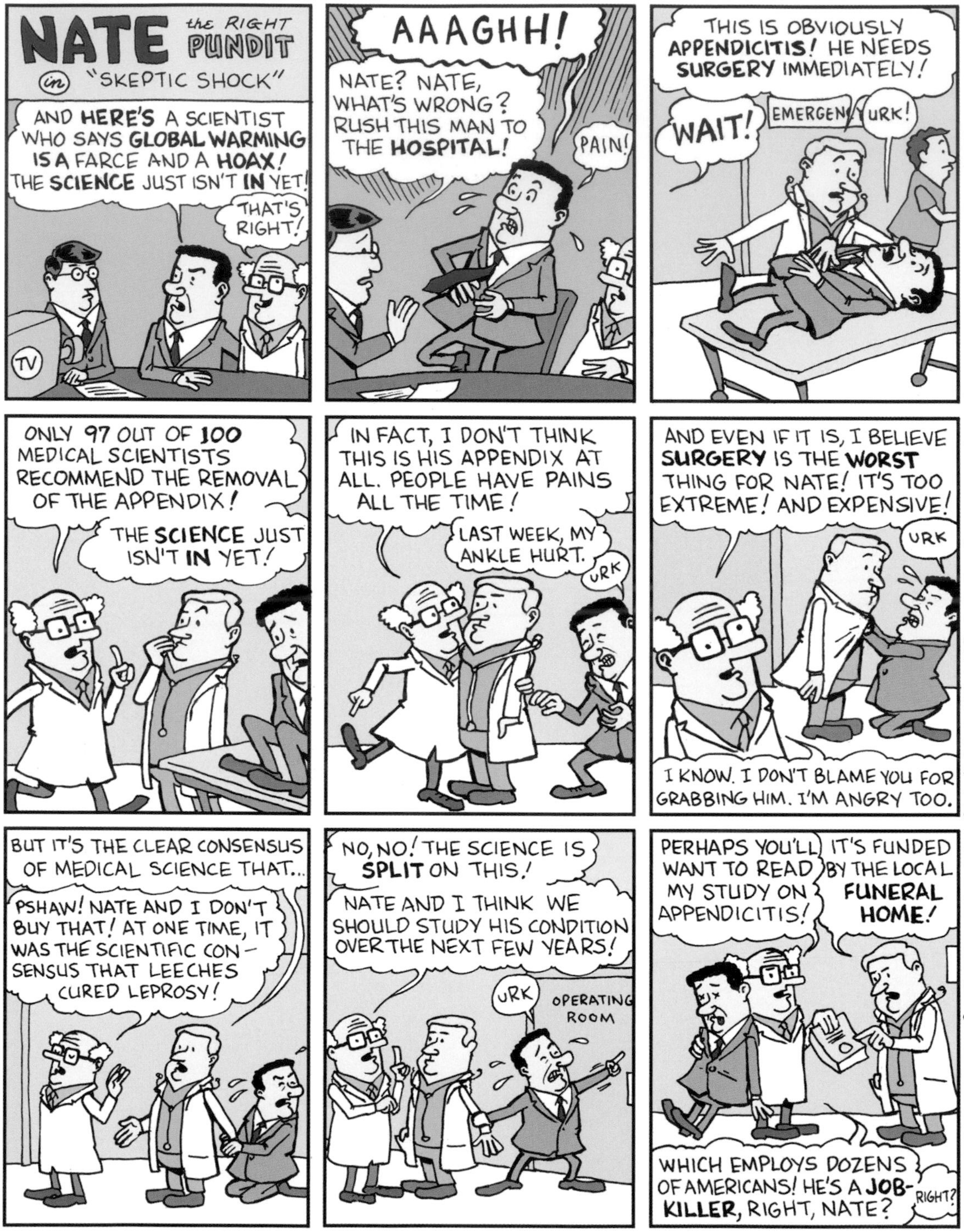
NATE the RIGHT PUNDIT
in "SKEPTIC SHOCK"
AND HERE'S A SCIENTIST WHO SAYS GLOBAL WARMING IS A FARCE AND A HOAX! THE SCIENCE JUST ISN'T IN YET!
THAT'S RIGHT!
TV
AAAGHH!
NATE? NATE, WHAT'S WRONG? RUSH THIS MAN TO THE HOSPITAL!
PAIN!
THIS IS OBVIOUSLY APPENDICITIS! HE NEEDS SURGERY IMMEDIATELY!
WAIT!
EMERGEN
URK!
ONLY 97 OUT OF 100 MEDICAL SCIENTISTS RECOMMEND THE REMOVAL OF THE APPENDIX!
THE SCIENCE JUST ISN'T IN YET!
IN FACT, I DON'T THINK THIS IS HIS APPENDIX AT ALL. PEOPLE HAVE PAINS ALL THE TIME!
LAST WEEK, MY ANKLE HURT.
URK
AND EVEN IF IT IS, I BELIEVE SURGERY IS THE WORST THING FOR NATE! IT'S TOO EXTREME! AND EXPENSIVE!
URK
I KNOW. I DON'T BLAME YOU FOR GRABBING HIM. I'M ANGRY TOO.
BUT IT'S THE CLEAR CONSENSUS OF MEDICAL SCIENCE THAT...
PSHAW! NATE AND I DON'T BUY THAT! AT ONE TIME, IT WAS THE SCIENTIFIC CONSENSUS THAT LEECHES CURED LEPROSY!
NO, NO! THE SCIENCE IS SPLIT ON THIS!
NATE AND I THINK WE SHOULD STUDY HIS CONDITION OVER THE NEXT FEW YEARS!
URK
OPERATING ROOM
PERHAPS YOU'LL WANT TO READ MY STUDY ON APPENDICITIS!
IT'S FUNDED BY THE LOCAL FUNERAL HOME!
WHICH EMPLOYS DOZENS OF AMERICANS! HE'S A JOB-KILLER, RIGHT, NATE?
RIGHT?

4/25/16

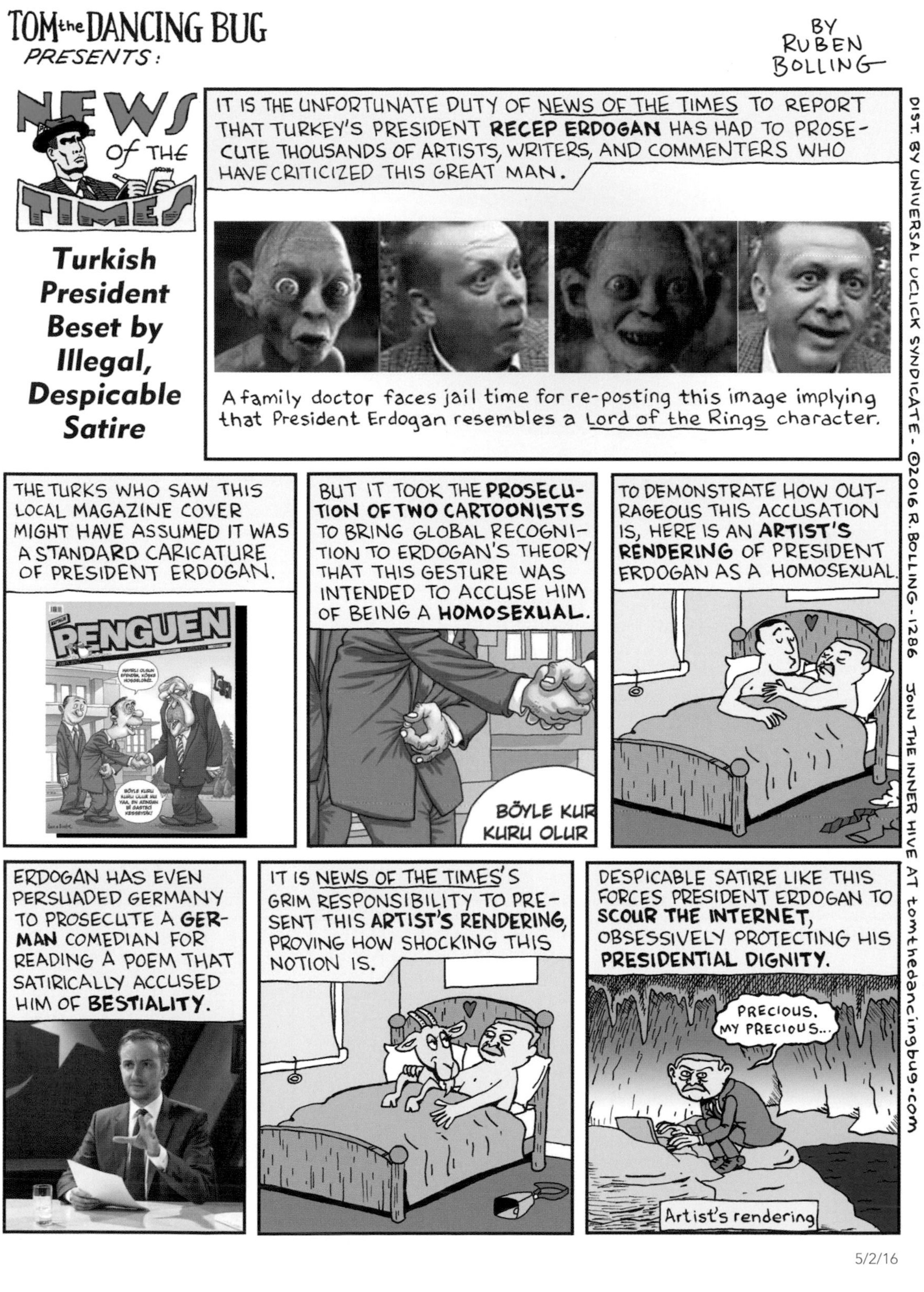
TOM the DANCING BUG
PRESENTS:
BY RUBEN BOLLING
NEWS of THE TIMES
Turkish President Beset by Illegal, Despicable Satire
IT IS THE UNFORTUNATE DUTY OF NEWS OF THE TIMES TO REPORT THAT TURKEY'S PRESIDENT RECEP ERDOGAN HAS HAD TO PROSECUTE THOUSANDS OF ARTISTS, WRITERS, AND COMMENTERS WHO HAVE CRITICIZED THIS GREAT MAN.
A family doctor faces jail time for re-posting this image implying that President Erdogan resembles a Lord of the Rings character.
THE TURKS WHO SAW THIS LOCAL MAGAZINE COVER MIGHT HAVE ASSUMED IT WAS A STANDARD CARICATURE OF PRESIDENT ERDOGAN.
PENGUEN
BUT IT TOOK THE PROSECUTION OF TWO CARTOONISTS TO BRING GLOBAL RECOGNITION TO ERDOGAN'S THEORY THAT THIS GESTURE WAS INTENDED TO ACCUSE HIM OF BEING A HOMOSEXUAL.
BÖYLE KUR
KURU OLUR
TO DEMONSTRATE HOW OUTRAGEOUS THIS ACCUSATION IS, HERE IS AN ARTIST'S RENDERING OF PRESIDENT ERDOGAN AS A HOMOSEXUAL.
ERDOGAN HAS EVEN PERSUADED GERMANY TO PROSECUTE A GERMAN COMEDIAN FOR READING A POEM THAT SATIRICALLY ACCUSED HIM OF BESTIALITY.
IT IS NEWS OF THE TIMES'S GRIM RESPONSIBILITY TO PRESENT THIS ARTIST'S RENDERING, PROVING HOW SHOCKING THIS NOTION IS.
DESPICABLE SATIRE LIKE THIS FORCES PRESIDENT ERDOGAN TO SCOUR THE INTERNET, OBSESSIVELY PROTECTING HIS PRESIDENTIAL DIGNITY.
PRECIOUS, MY PRECIOUS...
Artist's rendering
DIST. BY UNIVERSAL UCLICK SYNDICATE - ©2016 R. BOLLING - 1286 JOIN THE INNER HIVE AT tomthedancingbug.com

5/2/16

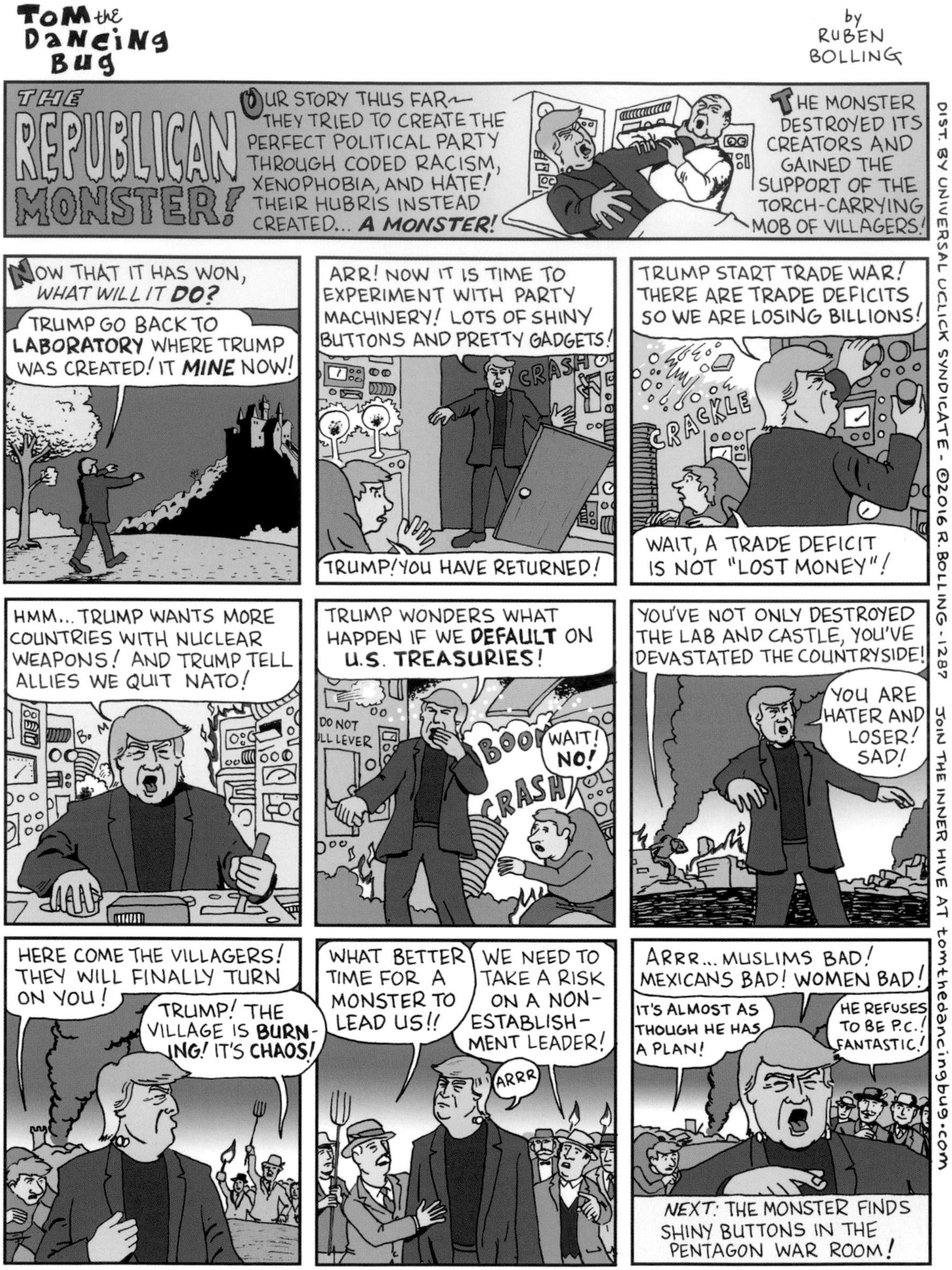

TOM the DANCING BUG
by RUBEN BOLLING
THE REPUBLICAN MONSTER!
OUR STORY THUS FAR— THEY TRIED TO CREATE THE PERFECT POLITICAL PARTY THROUGH CODED RACISM, XENOPHOBIA, AND HATE! THEIR HUBRIS INSTEAD CREATED... A MONSTER!
THE MONSTER DESTROYED ITS CREATORS AND GAINED THE SUPPORT OF THE TORCH-CARRYING MOB OF VILLAGERS!
NOW THAT IT HAS WON, WHAT WILL IT DO?
TRUMP GO BACK TO LABORATORY WHERE TRUMP WAS CREATED! IT MINE NOW!
ARR! NOW IT IS TIME TO EXPERIMENT WITH PARTY MACHINERY! LOTS OF SHINY BUTTONS AND PRETTY GADGETS!
CRASH
TRUMP! YOU HAVE RETURNED!
TRUMP START TRADE WAR! THERE ARE TRADE DEFICITS SO WE ARE LOSING BILLIONS!
CRACKLE
WAIT, A TRADE DEFICIT IS NOT "LOST MONEY"!
HMM... TRUMP WANTS MORE COUNTRIES WITH NUCLEAR WEAPONS! AND TRUMP TELL ALLIES WE QUIT NATO!
TRUMP WONDERS WHAT HAPPEN IF WE DEFAULT ON U.S. TREASURIES!
DO NOT
LL LEVER
BOOM
WAIT! NO!
CRASH
YOU'VE NOT ONLY DESTROYED THE LAB AND CASTLE, YOU'VE DEVASTATED THE COUNTRYSIDE!
YOU ARE HATER AND LOSER! SAD!
HERE COME THE VILLAGERS! THEY WILL FINALLY TURN ON YOU!
TRUMP! THE VILLAGE IS BURNING! IT'S CHAOS!
WHAT BETTER TIME FOR A MONSTER TO LEAD US!!
WE NEED TO TAKE A RISK ON A NON-ESTABLISHMENT LEADER!
ARRR
ARRR... MUSLIMS BAD! MEXICANS BAD! WOMEN BAD!
IT'S ALMOST AS THOUGH HE HAS A PLAN!
HE REFUSES TO BE P.C.! FANTASTIC!
NEXT: THE MONSTER FINDS SHINY BUTTONS IN THE PENTAGON WAR ROOM!
DIST. BY UNIVERSAL UCLICK SYNDICATE - ©2016 R. BOLLING - 1287
JOIN THE INNER HIVE AT tomthedancingbug.com

5/9/16

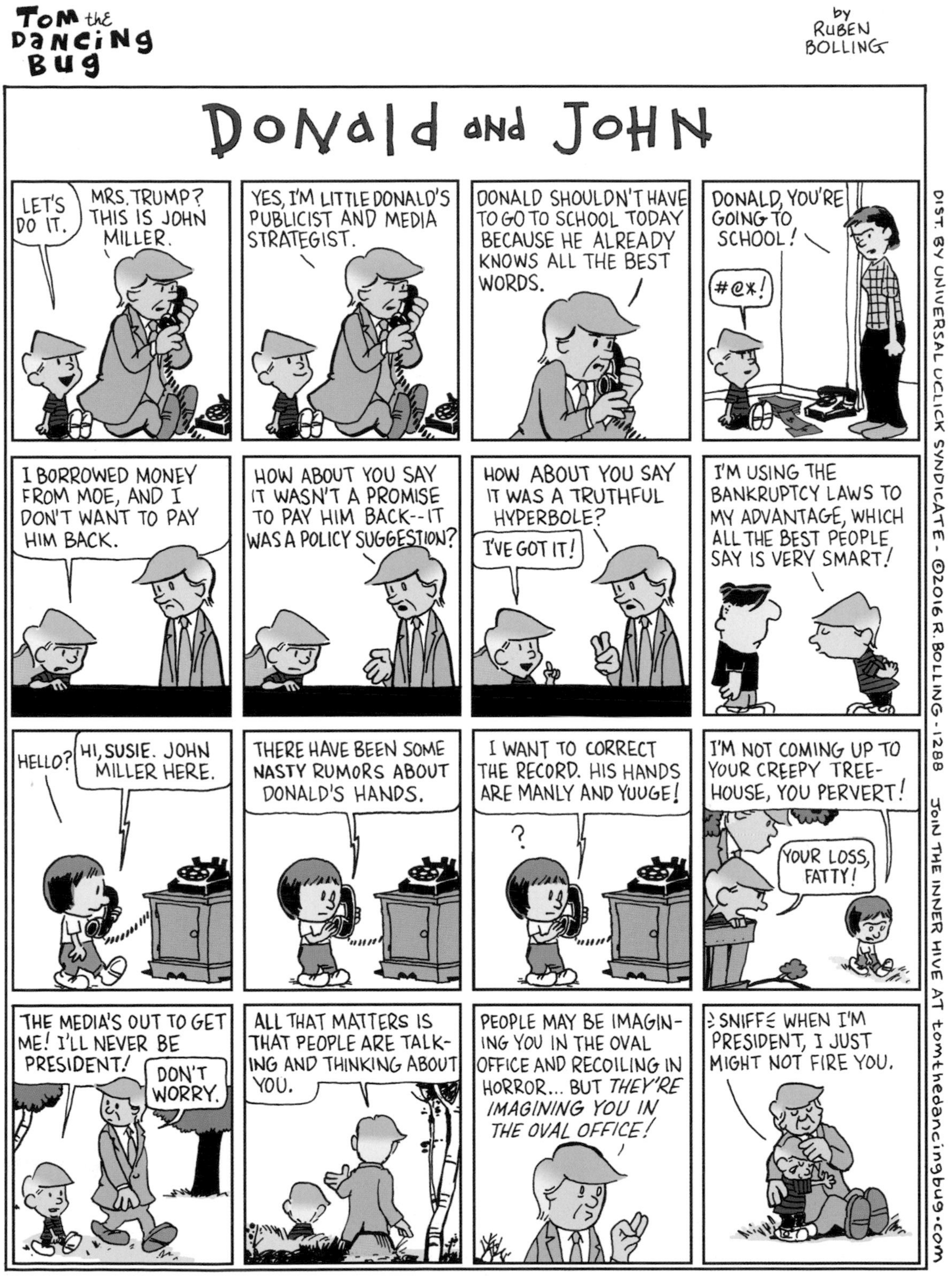
TOM the DANCING BUG
by RUBEN BOLLING
DONALD and JOHN
LET'S DO IT.
MRS. TRUMP? THIS IS JOHN MILLER.
YES, I'M LITTLE DONALD'S PUBLICIST AND MEDIA STRATEGIST.
DONALD SHOULDN'T HAVE TO GO TO SCHOOL TODAY BECAUSE HE ALREADY KNOWS ALL THE BEST WORDS.
DONALD, YOU'RE GOING TO SCHOOL!
#@*!
I BORROWED MONEY FROM MOE, AND I DON'T WANT TO PAY HIM BACK.
HOW ABOUT YOU SAY IT WASN'T A PROMISE TO PAY HIM BACK--IT WAS A POLICY SUGGESTION?
HOW ABOUT YOU SAY IT WAS A TRUTHFUL HYPERBOLE?
I'VE GOT IT!
I'M USING THE BANKRUPTCY LAWS TO MY ADVANTAGE, WHICH ALL THE BEST PEOPLE SAY IS VERY SMART!
HELLO?
HI, SUSIE. JOHN MILLER HERE.
THERE HAVE BEEN SOME NASTY RUMORS ABOUT DONALD'S HANDS.
I WANT TO CORRECT THE RECORD. HIS HANDS ARE MANLY AND YUUGE!
?
I'M NOT COMING UP TO YOUR CREEPY TREE-HOUSE, YOU PERVERT!
YOUR LOSS, FATTY!
THE MEDIA'S OUT TO GET ME! I'LL NEVER BE PRESIDENT!
DON'T WORRY.
ALL THAT MATTERS IS THAT PEOPLE ARE TALKING AND THINKING ABOUT YOU.
PEOPLE MAY BE IMAGINING YOU IN THE OVAL OFFICE AND RECOILING IN HORROR... BUT THEY'RE IMAGINING YOU IN THE OVAL OFFICE!
SNIFF WHEN I'M PRESIDENT, I JUST MIGHT NOT FIRE YOU.
DIST. BY UNIVERSAL UCLICK SYNDICATE - ©2016 R. BOLLING - 1288
JOIN THE INNER HIVE AT tomthedancingbug.com

5/16/16

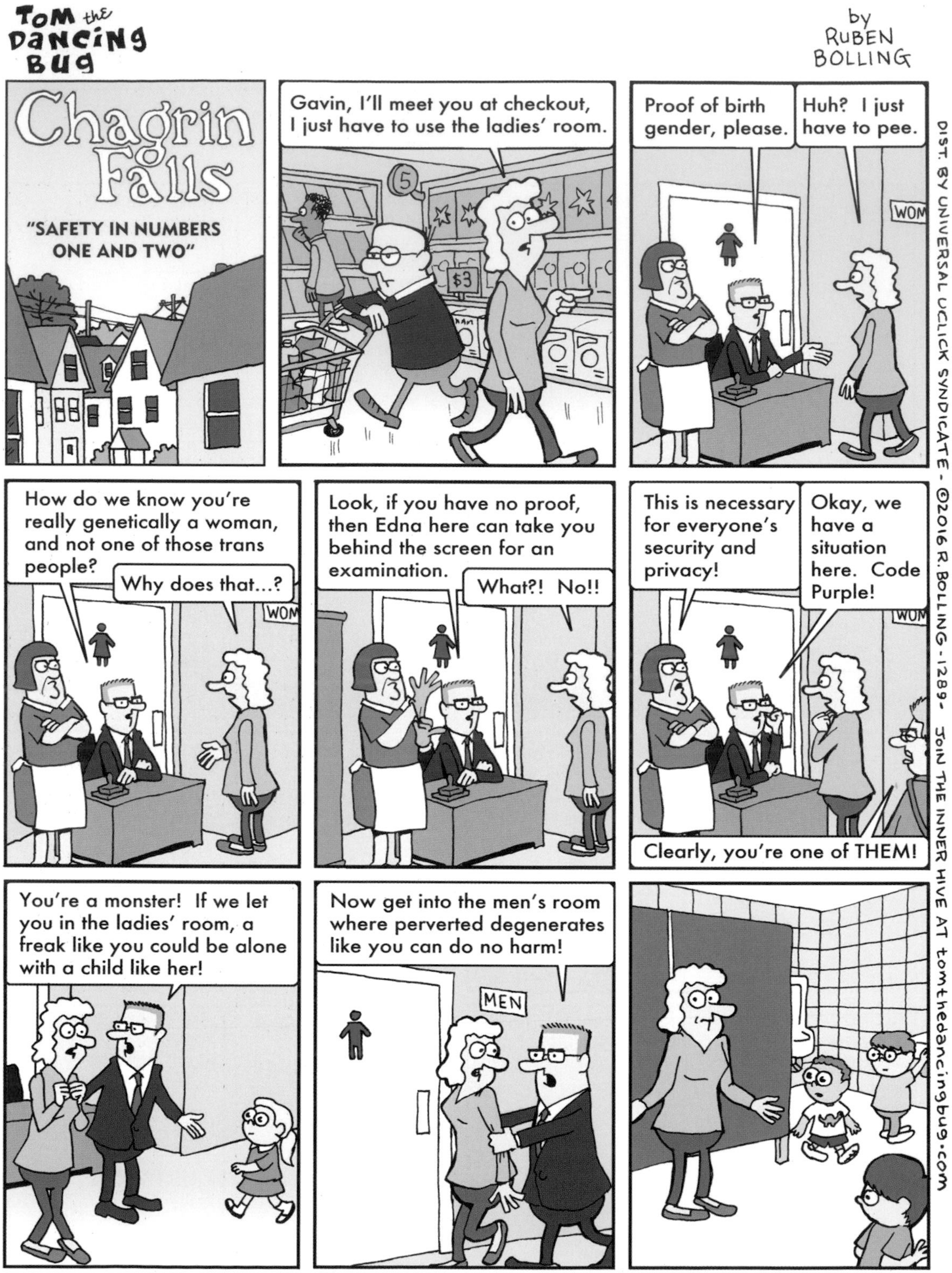

TOM the DANCING BUG
by RUBEN BOLLING
Chagrin Falls
"SAFETY IN NUMBERS ONE AND TWO"
Gavin, I'll meet you at checkout, I just have to use the ladies' room.
5
$3
Proof of birth gender, please.
Huh? I just have to pee.
WOM
How do we know you're really genetically a woman, and not one of those trans people?
Why does that...?
WOM
Look, if you have no proof, then Edna here can take you behind the screen for an examination.
What?! No!!
This is necessary for everyone's security and privacy!
Okay, we have a situation here. Code Purple!
WOM
Clearly, you're one of THEM!
You're a monster! If we let you in the ladies' room, a freak like you could be alone with a child like her!
Now get into the men's room where perverted degenerates like you can do no harm!
MEN
DIST. BY UNIVERSAL UCLICK SYNDICATE - ©2016 R. BOLLING - 1289 - JOIN THE INNER HIVE AT tomthedancingbug.com

5/23/16

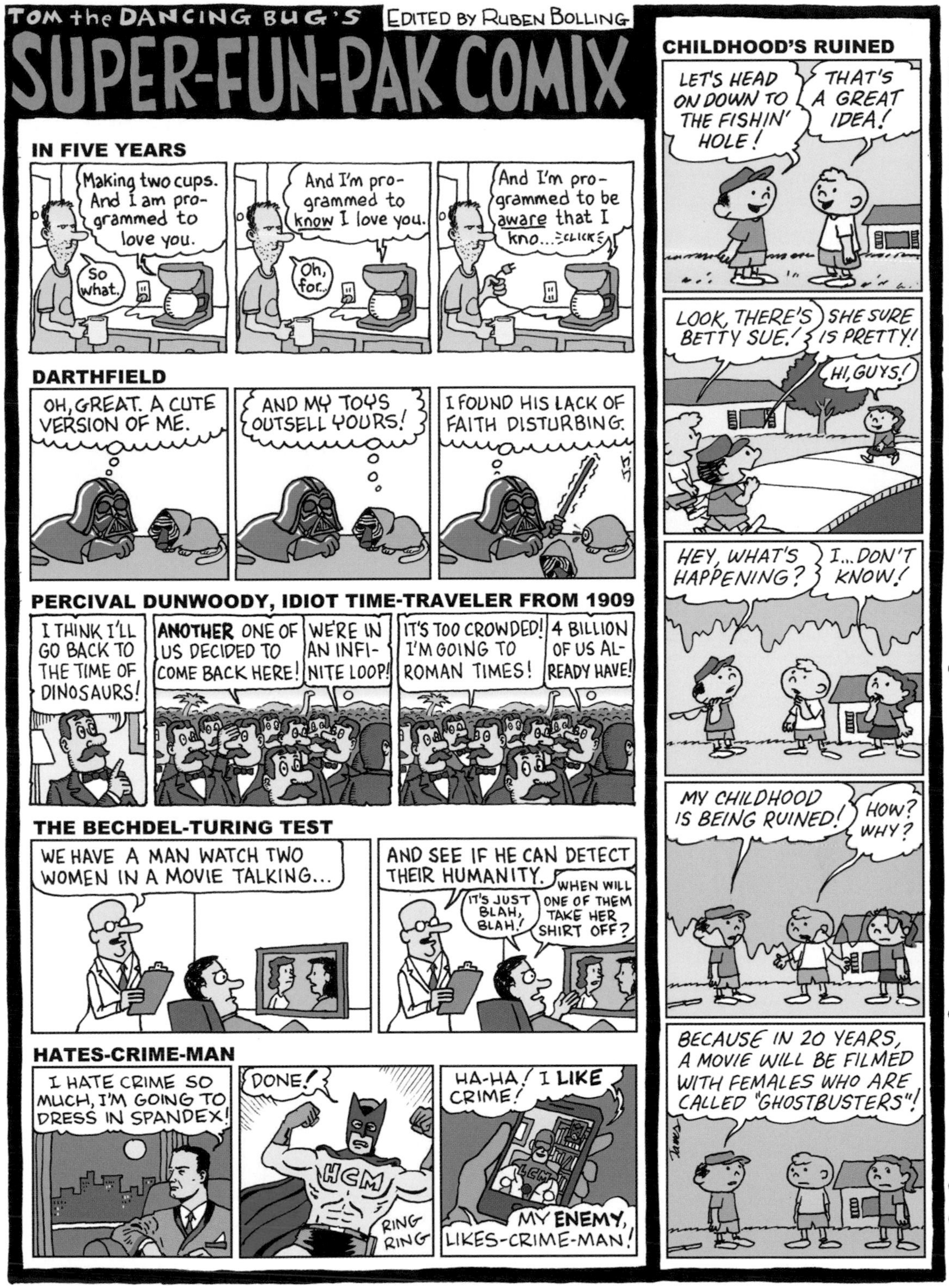
TOM the DANCING BUG'S
EDITED BY RUBEN BOLLING
SUPER-FUN-PAK COMIX
IN FIVE YEARS
Making two cups. And I am programmed to love you.
So what.
And I'm programmed to know I love you.
Oh, for..
And I'm programmed to be aware that I kno... CLICK
DARTHFIELD
OH, GREAT. A CUTE VERSION OF ME.
AND MY TOYS OUTSELL YOURS!
I FOUND HIS LACK OF FAITH DISTURBING.
PERCIVAL DUNWOODY, IDIOT TIME-TRAVELER FROM 1909
I THINK I'LL GO BACK TO THE TIME OF DINOSAURS!
ANOTHER ONE OF US DECIDED TO COME BACK HERE!
WE'RE IN AN INFINITE LOOP!
IT'S TOO CROWDED! I'M GOING TO ROMAN TIMES!
4 BILLION OF US ALREADY HAVE!
THE BECHDEL-TURING TEST
WE HAVE A MAN WATCH TWO WOMEN IN A MOVIE TALKING...
AND SEE IF HE CAN DETECT THEIR HUMANITY.
IT'S JUST BLAH, BLAH!
WHEN WILL ONE OF THEM TAKE HER SHIRT OFF?
HATES-CRIME-MAN
I HATE CRIME SO MUCH, I'M GOING TO DRESS IN SPANDEX!
DONE!
HCM
RING RING
HA-HA! I LIKE CRIME!
LCM
MY ENEMY, LIKES-CRIME-MAN!
CHILDHOOD'S RUINED
LET'S HEAD ON DOWN TO THE FISHIN' HOLE!
THAT'S A GREAT IDEA!
LOOK, THERE'S BETTY SUE!
SHE SURE IS PRETTY!
HI, GUYS!
HEY, WHAT'S HAPPENING?
I... DON'T KNOW!
MY CHILDHOOD IS BEING RUINED!
HOW? WHY?
BECAUSE IN 20 YEARS, A MOVIE WILL BE FILMED WITH FEMALES WHO ARE CALLED "GHOSTBUSTERS"!

5/30/16

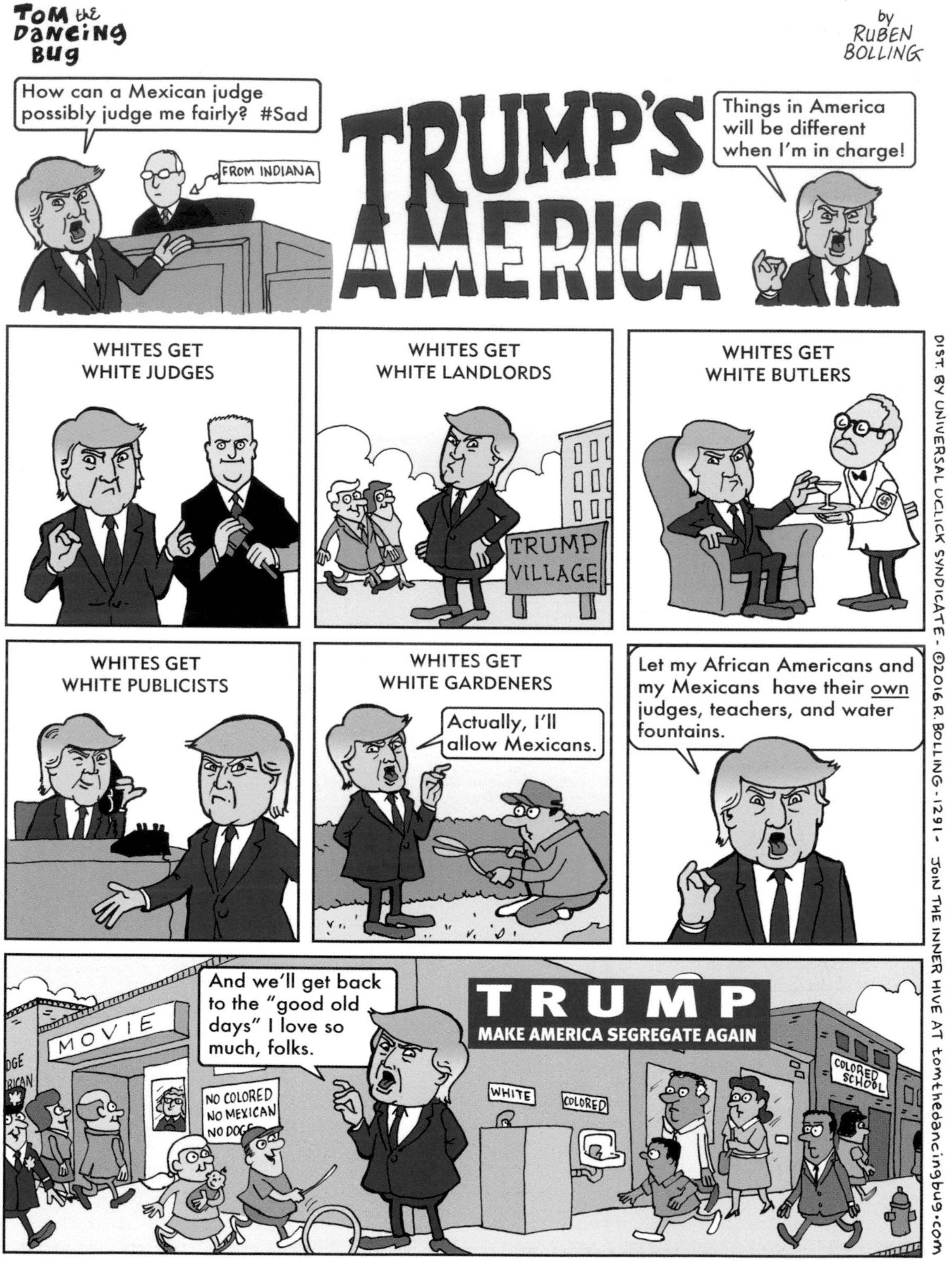
TOM the DANCING BUG
by RUBEN BOLLING
How can a Mexican judge possibly judge me fairly? #Sad
FROM INDIANA
TRUMP'S AMERICA
Things in America will be different when I'm in charge!
WHITES GET WHITE JUDGES
WHITES GET WHITE LANDLORDS
TRUMP VILLAGE
WHITES GET WHITE BUTLERS
WHITES GET WHITE PUBLICISTS
WHITES GET WHITE GARDENERS
Actually, I'll allow Mexicans.
Let my African Americans and my Mexicans have their own judges, teachers, and water fountains.
And we'll get back to the "good old days" I love so much, folks.
MOVIE
NO COLORED NO MEXICAN
TRUMP
MAKE AMERICA SEGREGATE AGAIN
WHITE
COLORED
COLORED SCHOOL
DIST. BY UNIVERSAL UCLICK SYNDICATE - ©2016 R. BOLLING - 1291 - JOIN THE INNER HIVE AT tomthedancingbug.com

6/6/16

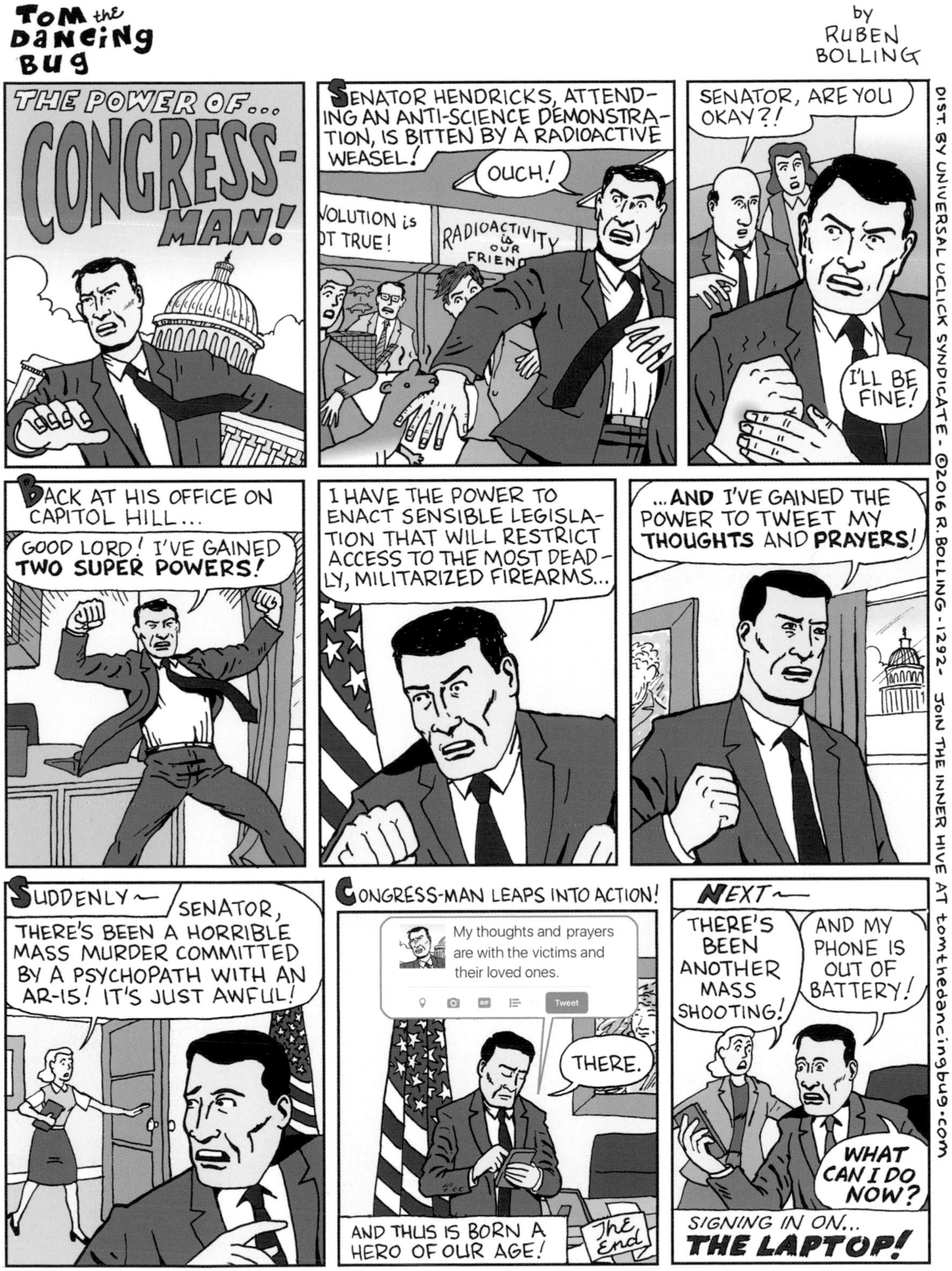
TOM the DANCING BUG
by RUBEN BOLLING
THE POWER OF...
CONGRESS-MAN!
SENATOR HENDRICKS, ATTENDING AN ANTI-SCIENCE DEMONSTRATION, IS BITTEN BY A RADIOACTIVE WEASEL!
OUCH!
VOLUTION is
T TRUE!
RADIOACTIVITY is OUR FRIEND
SENATOR, ARE YOU OKAY?!
I'LL BE FINE!
BACK AT HIS OFFICE ON CAPITOL HILL...
GOOD LORD! I'VE GAINED TWO SUPER POWERS!
I HAVE THE POWER TO ENACT SENSIBLE LEGISLATION THAT WILL RESTRICT ACCESS TO THE MOST DEADLY, MILITARIZED FIREARMS...
...AND I'VE GAINED THE POWER TO TWEET MY THOUGHTS AND PRAYERS!
SUDDENLY—
SENATOR, THERE'S BEEN A HORRIBLE MASS MURDER COMMITTED BY A PSYCHOPATH WITH AN AR-15! IT'S JUST AWFUL!
CONGRESS-MAN LEAPS INTO ACTION!
My thoughts and prayers are with the victims and their loved ones.
Tweet
THERE.
AND THUS IS BORN A HERO OF OUR AGE!
The End
NEXT—
THERE'S BEEN ANOTHER MASS SHOOTING!
AND MY PHONE IS OUT OF BATTERY!
WHAT CAN I DO NOW?
SIGNING IN ON... THE LAPTOP!
DIST. BY UNIVERSAL UCLICK SYNDICATE - ©2016 R. BOLLING - 1292 - JOIN THE INNER HIVE AT tomthedancingbug.com

6/13/16

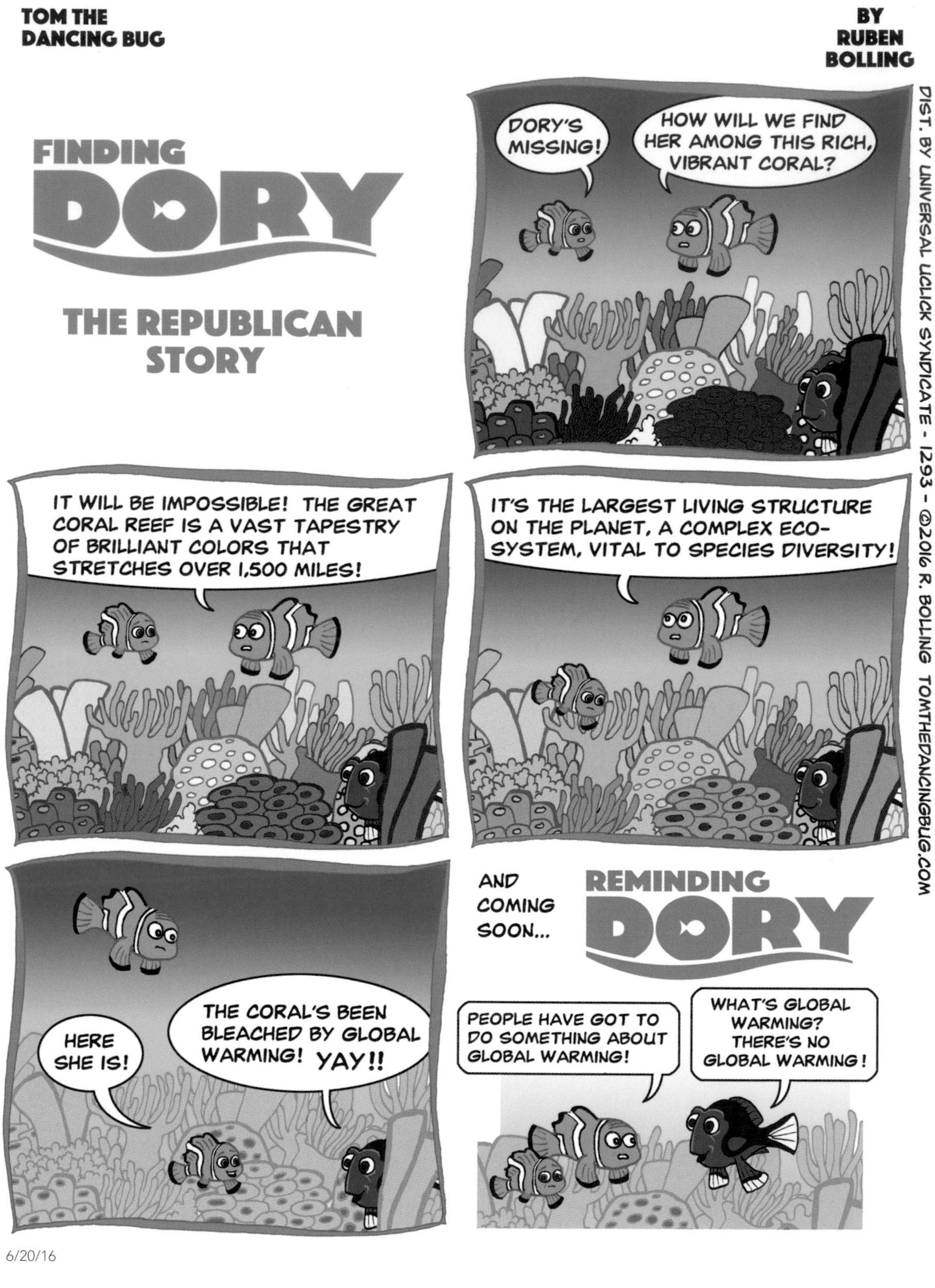
TOM THE DANCING BUG
BY RUBEN BOLLING
FINDING DORY
THE REPUBLICAN STORY
DORY'S MISSING!
HOW WILL WE FIND HER AMONG THIS RICH, VIBRANT CORAL?
IT WILL BE IMPOSSIBLE! THE GREAT CORAL REEF IS A VAST TAPESTRY OF BRILLIANT COLORS THAT STRETCHES OVER 1,500 MILES!
IT'S THE LARGEST LIVING STRUCTURE ON THE PLANET, A COMPLEX ECO-SYSTEM, VITAL TO SPECIES DIVERSITY!
HERE SHE IS!
THE CORAL'S BEEN BLEACHED BY GLOBAL WARMING! YAY!!
AND COMING SOON...
REMINDING DORY
PEOPLE HAVE GOT TO DO SOMETHING ABOUT GLOBAL WARMING!
WHAT'S GLOBAL WARMING? THERE'S NO GLOBAL WARMING!
DIST. BY UNIVERSAL UCLICK SYNDICATE - 1293 - ©2016 R. BOLLING TOMTHEDANCINGBUG.COM

6/20/16

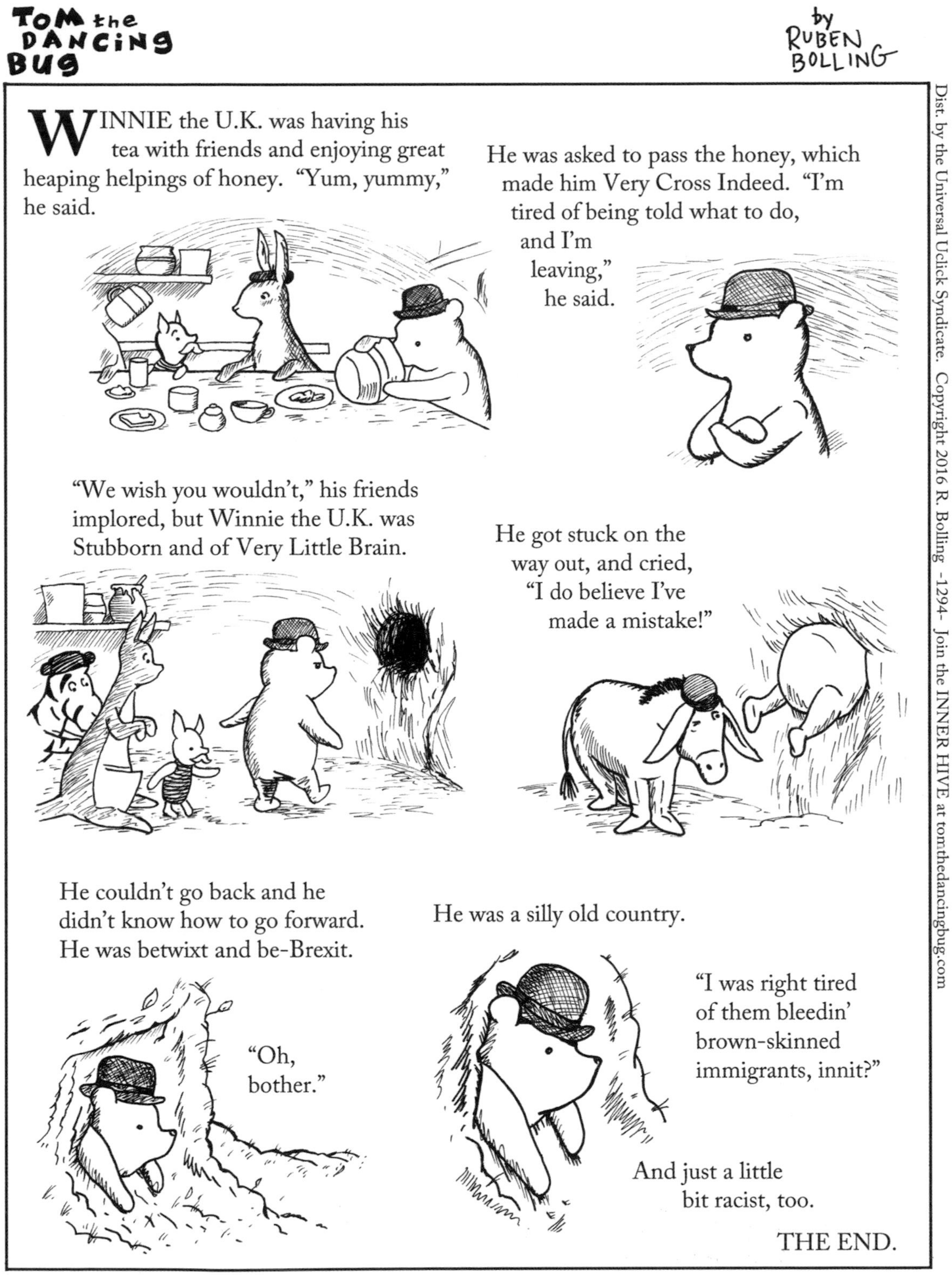
TOM the DANCING BUG
by RUBEN BOLLING
WINNIE the U.K. was having his tea with friends and enjoying great heaping helpings of honey. "Yum, yummy," he said.
He was asked to pass the honey, which made him Very Cross Indeed. "I'm tired of being told what to do, and I'm leaving," he said.
"We wish you wouldn't," his friends implored, but Winnie the U.K. was Stubborn and of Very Little Brain.
He got stuck on the way out, and cried, "I do believe I've made a mistake!"
He couldn't go back and he didn't know how to go forward. He was betwixt and be-Brexit.
"Oh, bother."
He was a silly old country.
"I was right tired of them bleedin' brown-skinned immigrants, innit?"
And just a little bit racist, too.
THE END.
Dist. by the Universal Uclick Syndicate. Copyright 2016 R. Bolling -1294- Join the INNER HIVE at tomthedancingbug.com

6/27/16

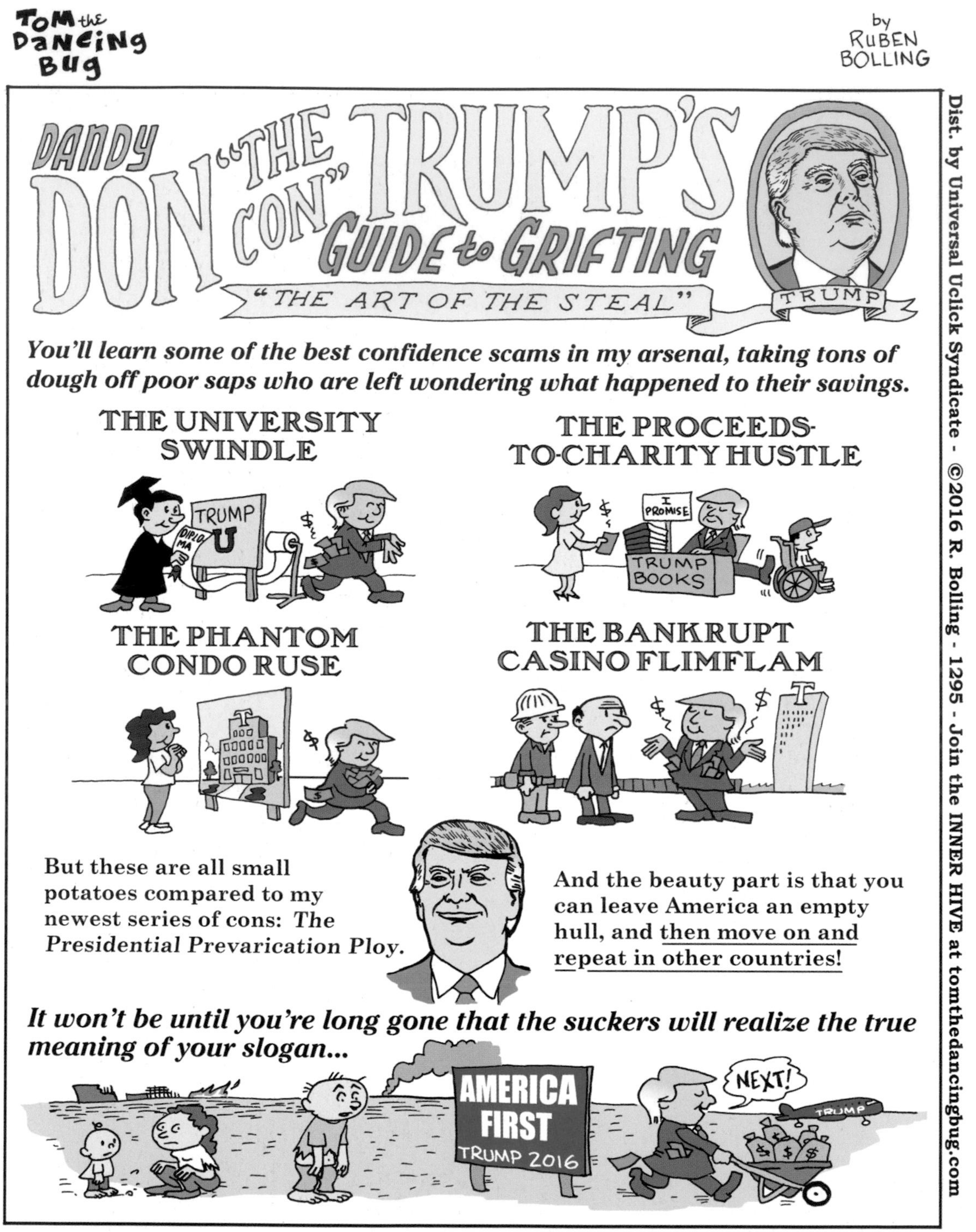
TOM the DANCING BUG
by RUBEN BOLLING
Dist. by Universal Uclick Syndicate - ©2016 R. Bolling - 1295 - Join the INNER HIVE at tomthedancingbug.com
DANDY DON "THE CON" TRUMP'S GUIDE to GRIFTING
"THE ART OF THE STEAL"
TRUMP
You'll learn some of the best confidence scams in my arsenal, taking tons of dough off poor saps who are left wondering what happened to their savings.
THE UNIVERSITY SWINDLE
TRUMP U
DIPLOMA
THE PROCEEDS-TO-CHARITY HUSTLE
I PROMISE
TRUMP BOOKS
THE PHANTOM CONDO RUSE
THE BANKRUPT CASINO FLIMFLAM
But these are all small potatoes compared to my newest series of cons: The Presidential Prevarication Ploy.
And the beauty part is that you can leave America an empty hull, and then move on and repeat in other countries!
It won't be until you're long gone that the suckers will realize the true meaning of your slogan...
AMERICA FIRST
TRUMP 2016
NEXT!
TRUMP

"IT'S VERY POSSIBLE THAT I COULD BE THE FIRST PRESIDENTIAL CANDIDATE TO RUN AND MAKE MONEY ON IT." -ACTUAL DONALD J. TRUMP QUOTE

7/4/16

TOM the DANCING BUG

by RUBEN BOLLING

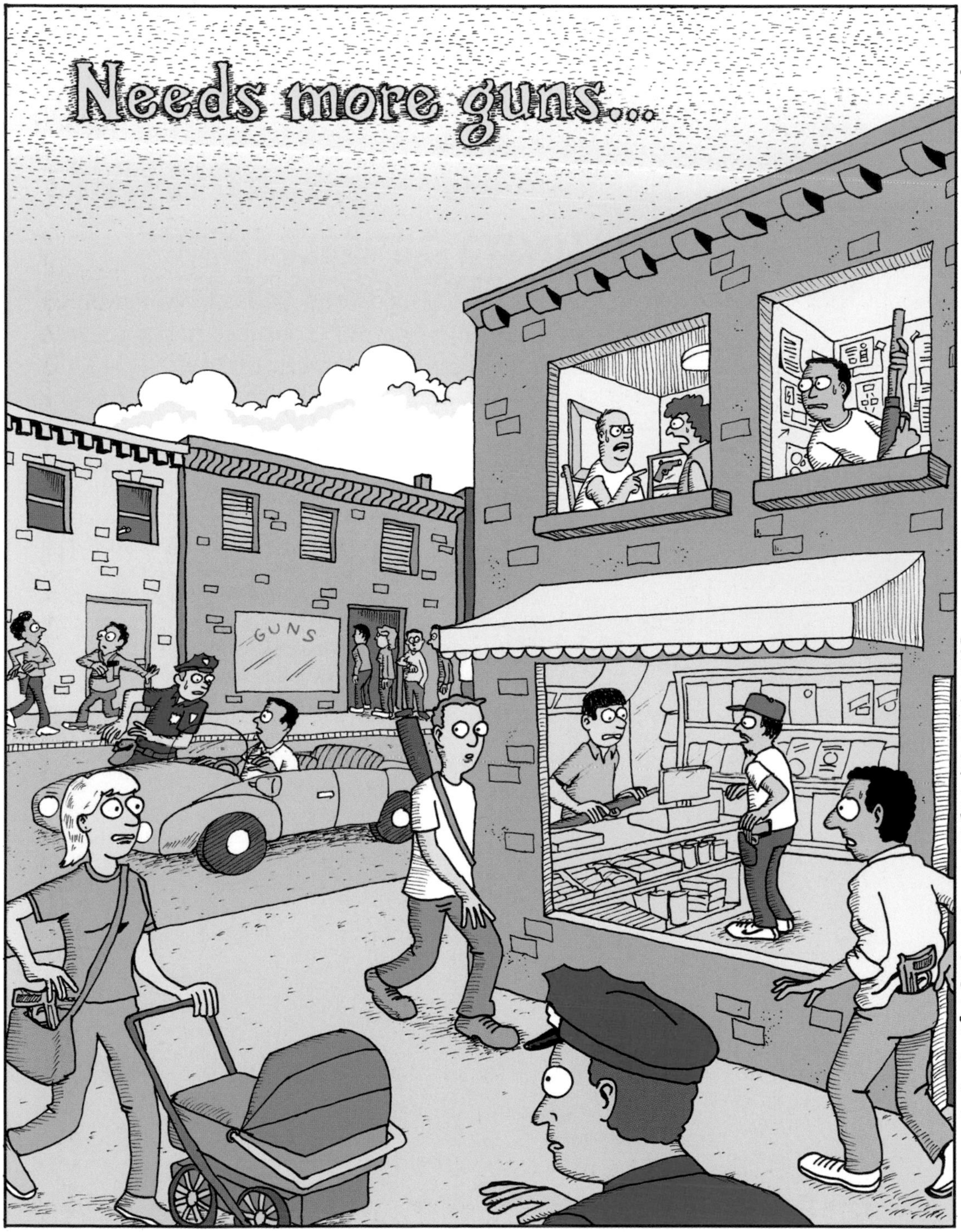
Needs more guns...
GUNS

7/11/16

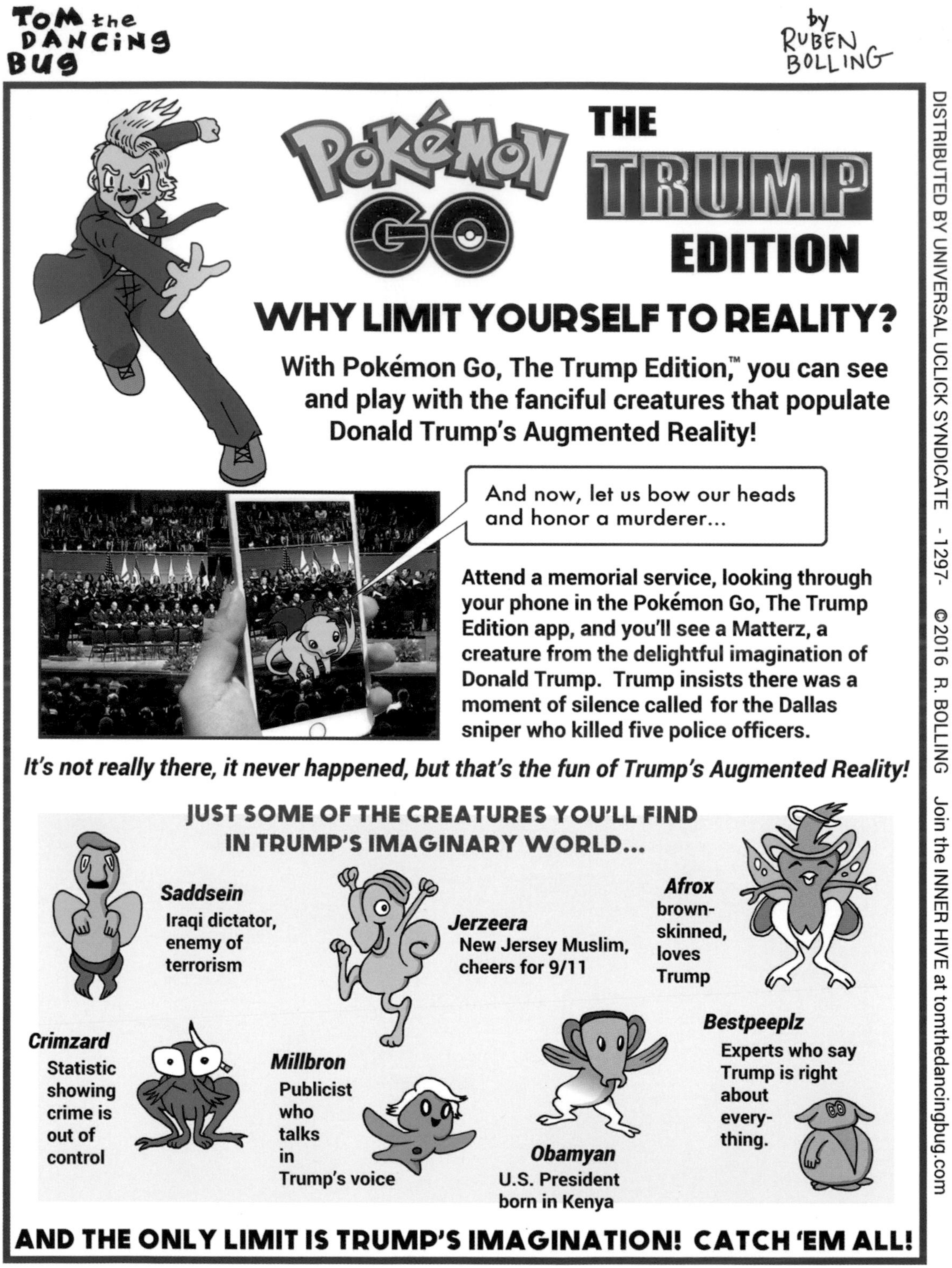
TOM the DANCING BUG
by RUBEN BOLLING
POKÉMON GO
THE TRUMP EDITION
WHY LIMIT YOURSELF TO REALITY?
With Pokémon Go, The Trump Edition,™ you can see and play with the fanciful creatures that populate Donald Trump's Augmented Reality!
And now, let us bow our heads and honor a murderer...
Attend a memorial service, looking through your phone in the Pokémon Go, The Trump Edition app, and you'll see a Matterz, a creature from the delightful imagination of Donald Trump. Trump insists there was a moment of silence called for the Dallas sniper who killed five police officers.
It's not really there, it never happened, but that's the fun of Trump's Augmented Reality!
JUST SOME OF THE CREATURES YOU'LL FIND IN TRUMP'S IMAGINARY WORLD...
Saddsein Iraqi dictator, enemy of terrorism
Jerzeera New Jersey Muslim, cheers for 9/11
Afrox brown-skinned, loves Trump
Crimzard Statistic showing crime is out of control
Millbron Publicist who talks in Trump's voice
Obamyan U.S. President born in Kenya
Bestpeeplz Experts who say Trump is right about every-thing.
AND THE ONLY LIMIT IS TRUMP'S IMAGINATION! CATCH 'EM ALL!
DISTRIBUTED BY UNIVERSAL UCLICK SYNDICATE - 1297- ©2016 R. BOLLING Join the INNER HIVE at tomthedancingbug.com

7/18/16

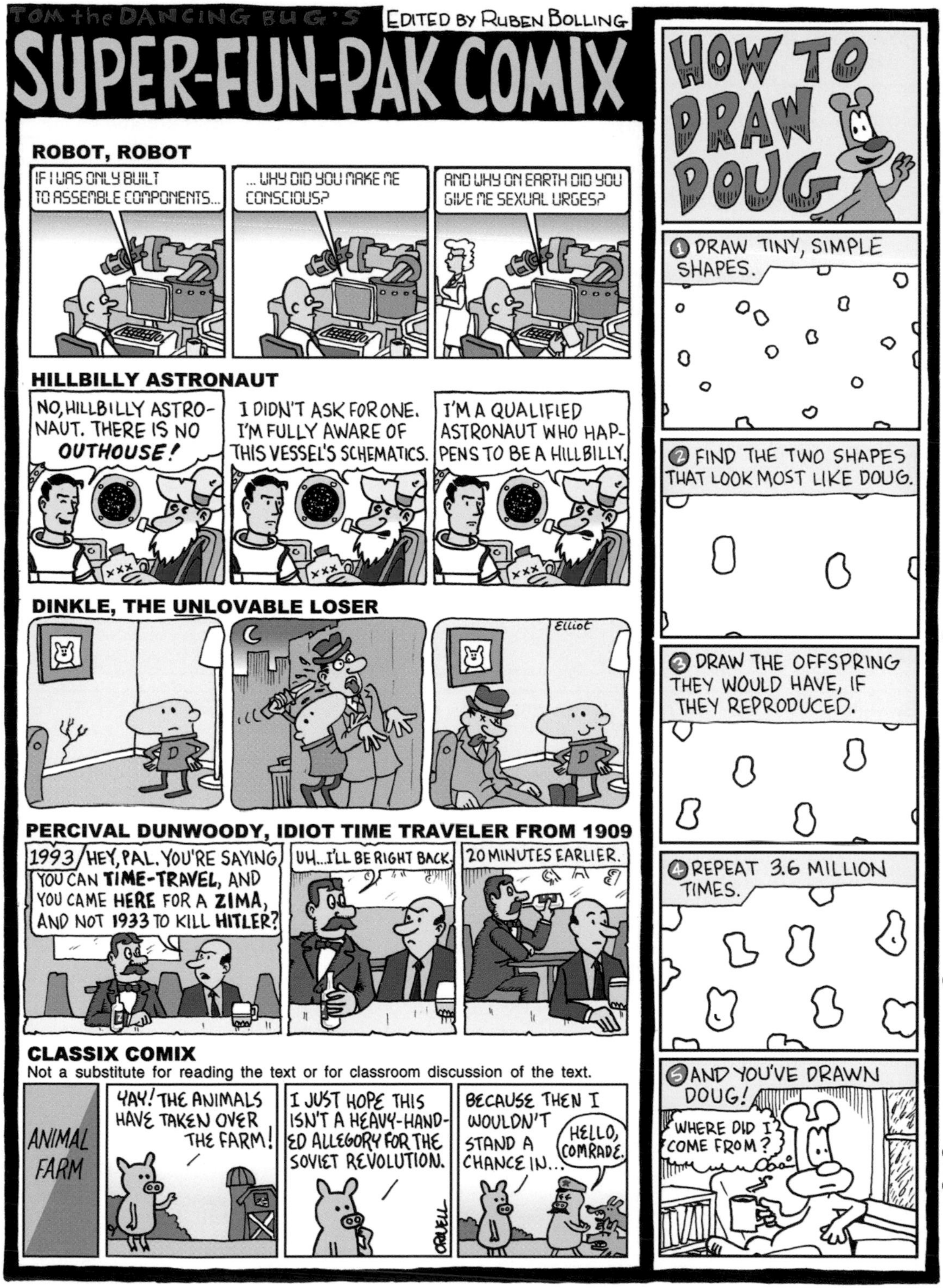
TOM the DANCING BUG'S
EDITED BY RUBEN BOLLING
SUPER-FUN-PAK COMIX
ROBOT, ROBOT
IF I WAS ONLY BUILT TO ASSEMBLE COMPONENTS...
... WHY DID YOU MAKE ME CONSCIOUS?
AND WHY ON EARTH DID YOU GIVE ME SEXUAL URGES?
HILLBILLY ASTRONAUT
NO, HILLBILLY ASTRONAUT. THERE IS NO OUTHOUSE!
I DIDN'T ASK FOR ONE. I'M FULLY AWARE OF THIS VESSEL'S SCHEMATICS.
I'M A QUALIFIED ASTRONAUT WHO HAPPENS TO BE A HILLBILLY.
XXX
DINKLE, THE UNLOVABLE LOSER
D
Elliot
PERCIVAL DUNWOODY, IDIOT TIME TRAVELER FROM 1909
1993
HEY, PAL. YOU'RE SAYING YOU CAN TIME-TRAVEL, AND YOU CAME HERE FOR A ZIMA, AND NOT 1933 TO KILL HITLER?
UH...I'LL BE RIGHT BACK.
20 MINUTES EARLIER.
CLASSIX COMIX
Not a substitute for reading the text or for classroom discussion of the text.
ANIMAL FARM
YAY! THE ANIMALS HAVE TAKEN OVER THE FARM!
I JUST HOPE THIS ISN'T A HEAVY-HANDED ALLEGORY FOR THE SOVIET REVOLUTION.
ORWELL
BECAUSE THEN I WOULDN'T STAND A CHANCE IN...
HELLO, COMRADE.
HOW TO DRAW DOUG
1 DRAW TINY, SIMPLE SHAPES.
2 FIND THE TWO SHAPES THAT LOOK MOST LIKE DOUG.
3 DRAW THE OFFSPRING THEY WOULD HAVE, IF THEY REPRODUCED.
4 REPEAT 3.6 MILLION TIMES.
5 AND YOU'VE DRAWN DOUG!
WHERE DID I COME FROM?

7/25/16

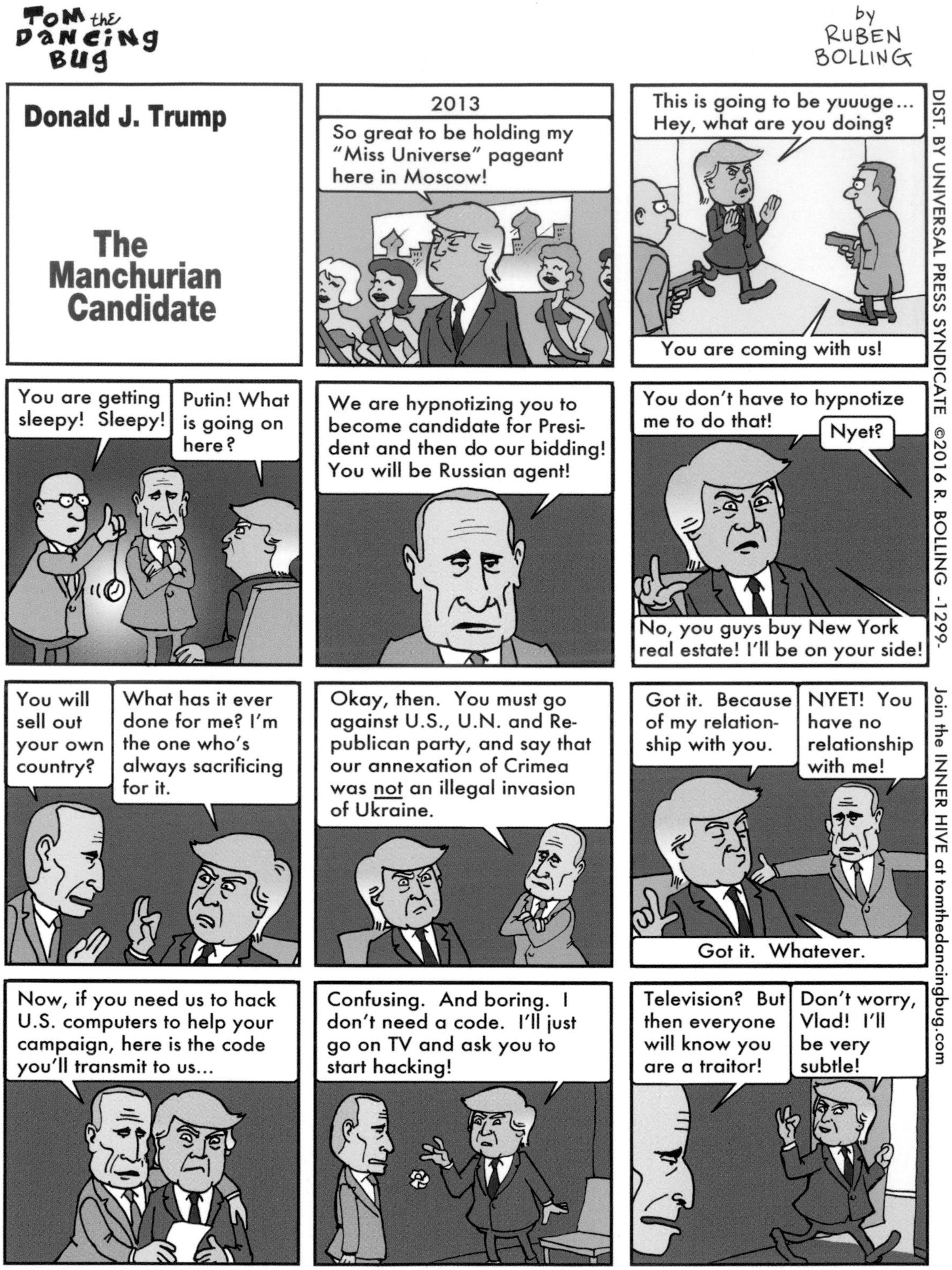
TOM the DANCING BUG
by RUBEN BOLLING
Donald J. Trump
The Manchurian Candidate
2013
So great to be holding my "Miss Universe" pageant here in Moscow!
This is going to be yuuuge... Hey, what are you doing?
You are coming with us!
You are getting sleepy! Sleepy!
Putin! What is going on here?
We are hypnotizing you to become candidate for President and then do our bidding! You will be Russian agent!
You don't have to hypnotize me to do that!
Nyet?
No, you guys buy New York real estate! I'll be on your side!
You will sell out your own country?
What has it ever done for me? I'm the one who's always sacrificing for it.
Okay, then. You must go against U.S., U.N. and Republican party, and say that our annexation of Crimea was not an illegal invasion of Ukraine.
Got it. Because of my relationship with you.
NYET! You have no relationship with me!
Got it. Whatever.
Now, if you need us to hack U.S. computers to help your campaign, here is the code you'll transmit to us...
Confusing. And boring. I don't need a code. I'll just go on TV and ask you to start hacking!
Television? But then everyone will know you are a traitor!
Don't worry, Vlad! I'll be very subtle!

Join the INNER HIVE at tomthedancingbug.com

8/1/16

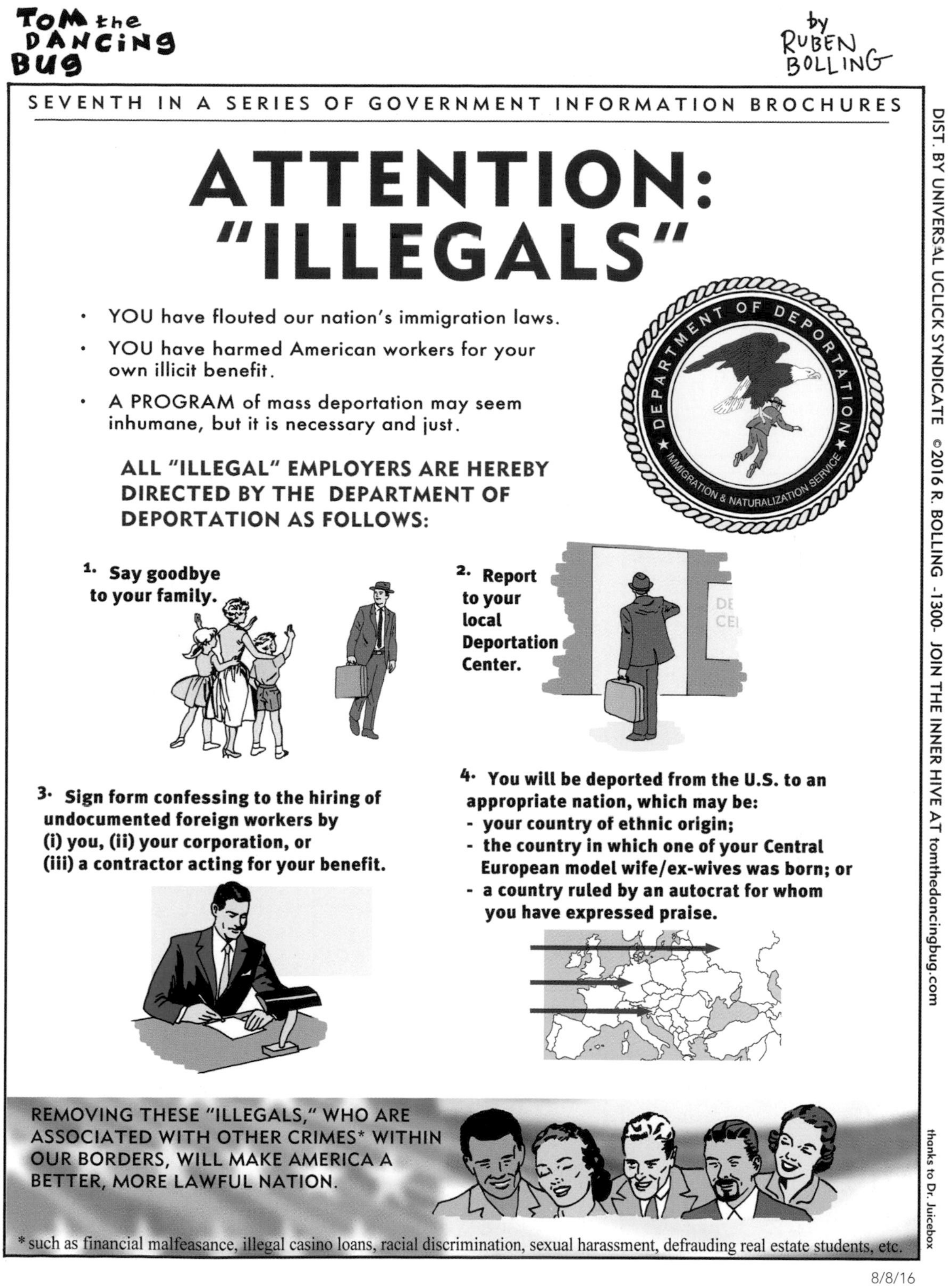
TOM the DANCING BUG
by RUBEN BOLLING
SEVENTH IN A SERIES OF GOVERNMENT INFORMATION BROCHURES
ATTENTION: "ILLEGALS"
• YOU have flouted our nation's immigration laws.
• YOU have harmed American workers for your own illicit benefit.
• A PROGRAM of mass deportation may seem inhumane, but it is necessary and just.
DEPARTMENT OF DEPORTATION
IMMIGRATION & NATURALIZATION SERVICE
ALL "ILLEGAL" EMPLOYERS ARE HEREBY DIRECTED BY THE DEPARTMENT OF DEPORTATION AS FOLLOWS:
1. Say goodbye to your family.
2. Report to your local Deportation Center.
3. Sign form confessing to the hiring of undocumented foreign workers by (i) you, (ii) your corporation, or (iii) a contractor acting for your benefit.
4. You will be deported from the U.S. to an appropriate nation, which may be:
- your country of ethnic origin;
- the country in which one of your Central European model wife/ex-wives was born; or
- a country ruled by an autocrat for whom you have expressed praise.
REMOVING THESE "ILLEGALS," WHO ARE ASSOCIATED WITH OTHER CRIMES* WITHIN OUR BORDERS, WILL MAKE AMERICA A BETTER, MORE LAWFUL NATION.
* such as financial malfeasance, illegal casino loans, racial discrimination, sexual harassment, defrauding real estate students, etc.
DIST. BY UNIVERSAL UCLICK SYNDICATE ©2016 R. BOLLING -1300- JOIN THE INNER HIVE AT tomthedancingbug.com
thanks to Dr. Juicebox
8/8/16

TOM the DANCING BUG

by RUBEN BOLLING

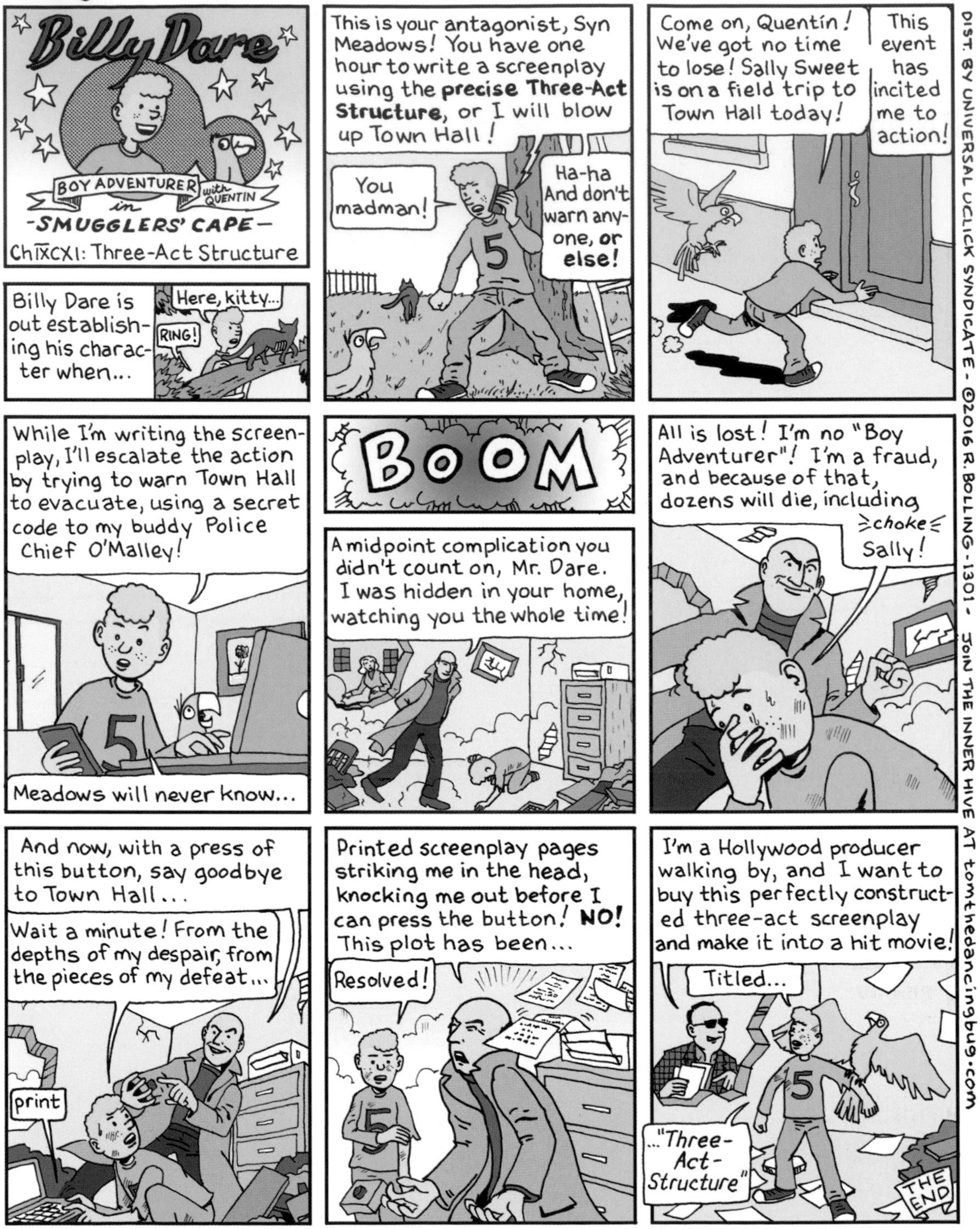
Billy Dare
BOY ADVENTURER with QUENTIN
in
-SMUGGLERS' CAPE-
ChIXCXI: Three-Act Structure
Billy Dare is out establishing his character when...
Here, kitty...
RING!
This is your antagonist, Syn Meadows! You have one hour to write a screenplay using the **precise Three-Act Structure**, or I will blow up Town Hall!
You madman!
Ha-ha And don't warn anyone, **or else!**
Come on, Quentin! We've got no time to lose! Sally Sweet is on a field trip to Town Hall today!
This event has incited me to action!
While I'm writing the screenplay, I'll escalate the action by trying to warn Town Hall to evacuate, using a secret code to my buddy Police Chief O'Malley!
Meadows will never know...
BOOM
A midpoint complication you didn't count on, Mr. Dare. I was hidden in your home, watching you the whole time!
All is lost! I'm no "Boy Adventurer"! I'm a fraud, and because of that, dozens will die, including
choke
Sally!
And now, with a press of this button, say goodbye to Town Hall...
Wait a minute! From the depths of my despair, from the pieces of my defeat...
print
Printed screenplay pages striking me in the head, knocking me out before I can press the button! **NO!** This plot has been...
Resolved!
I'm a Hollywood producer walking by, and I want to buy this perfectly constructed three-act screenplay and make it into a hit movie!
Titled...
..."Three-Act-Structure"
THE END
DIST. BY UNIVERSAL UCLICK SYNDICATE - ©2016 R. BOLLING - 1301 - JOIN THE INNER HIVE AT tomthedancingbug.com

8/15/16

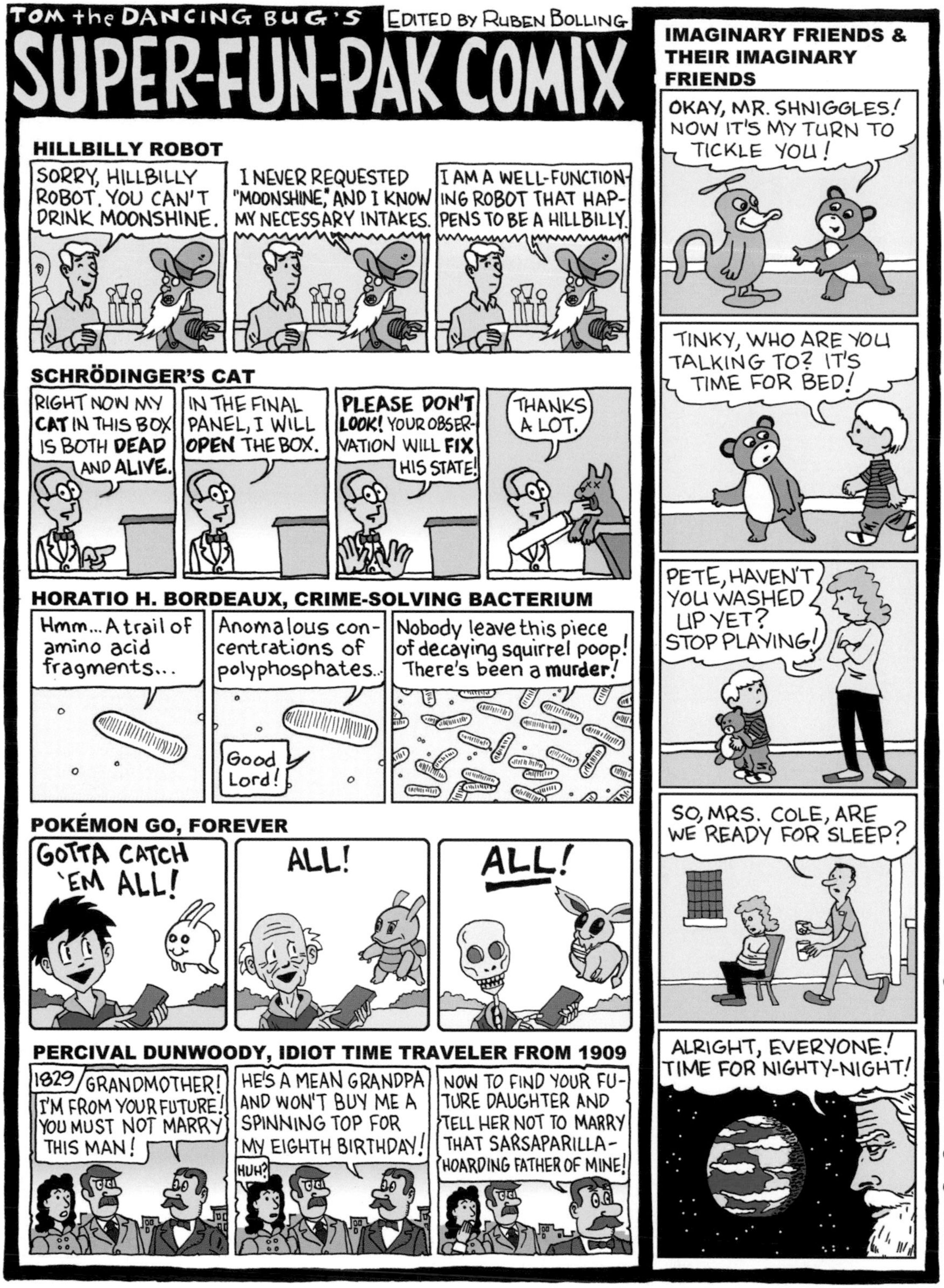
TOM the DANCING BUG'S
EDITED BY RUBEN BOLLING
SUPER-FUN-PAK COMIX
HILLBILLY ROBOT
SORRY, HILLBILLY ROBOT. YOU CAN'T DRINK MOONSHINE.
I NEVER REQUESTED "MOONSHINE," AND I KNOW MY NECESSARY INTAKES.
I AM A WELL-FUNCTIONING ROBOT THAT HAPPENS TO BE A HILLBILLY.
SCHRÖDINGER'S CAT
RIGHT NOW MY CAT IN THIS BOX IS BOTH DEAD AND ALIVE.
IN THE FINAL PANEL, I WILL OPEN THE BOX.
PLEASE DON'T LOOK! YOUR OBSERVATION WILL FIX HIS STATE!
THANKS A LOT.
HORATIO H. BORDEAUX, CRIME-SOLVING BACTERIUM
Hmm... A trail of amino acid fragments...
Anomalous concentrations of polyphosphates...
Good Lord!
Nobody leave this piece of decaying squirrel poop! There's been a murder!
POKÉMON GO, FOREVER
GOTTA CATCH 'EM ALL!
ALL!
ALL!
PERCIVAL DUNWOODY, IDIOT TIME TRAVELER FROM 1909
1829
GRANDMOTHER! I'M FROM YOUR FUTURE! YOU MUST NOT MARRY THIS MAN!
HE'S A MEAN GRANDPA AND WON'T BUY ME A SPINNING TOP FOR MY EIGHTH BIRTHDAY!
HUH?
NOW TO FIND YOUR FUTURE DAUGHTER AND TELL HER NOT TO MARRY THAT SARSAPARILLA-HOARDING FATHER OF MINE!
IMAGINARY FRIENDS & THEIR IMAGINARY FRIENDS
OKAY, MR. SHNIGGLES! NOW IT'S MY TURN TO TICKLE YOU!
TINKY, WHO ARE YOU TALKING TO? IT'S TIME FOR BED!
PETE, HAVEN'T YOU WASHED UP YET? STOP PLAYING!
SO, MRS. COLE, ARE WE READY FOR SLEEP?
ALRIGHT, EVERYONE! TIME FOR NIGHTY-NIGHT!

8/22/16

Tom the Dancing Bug

by Ruben Bolling

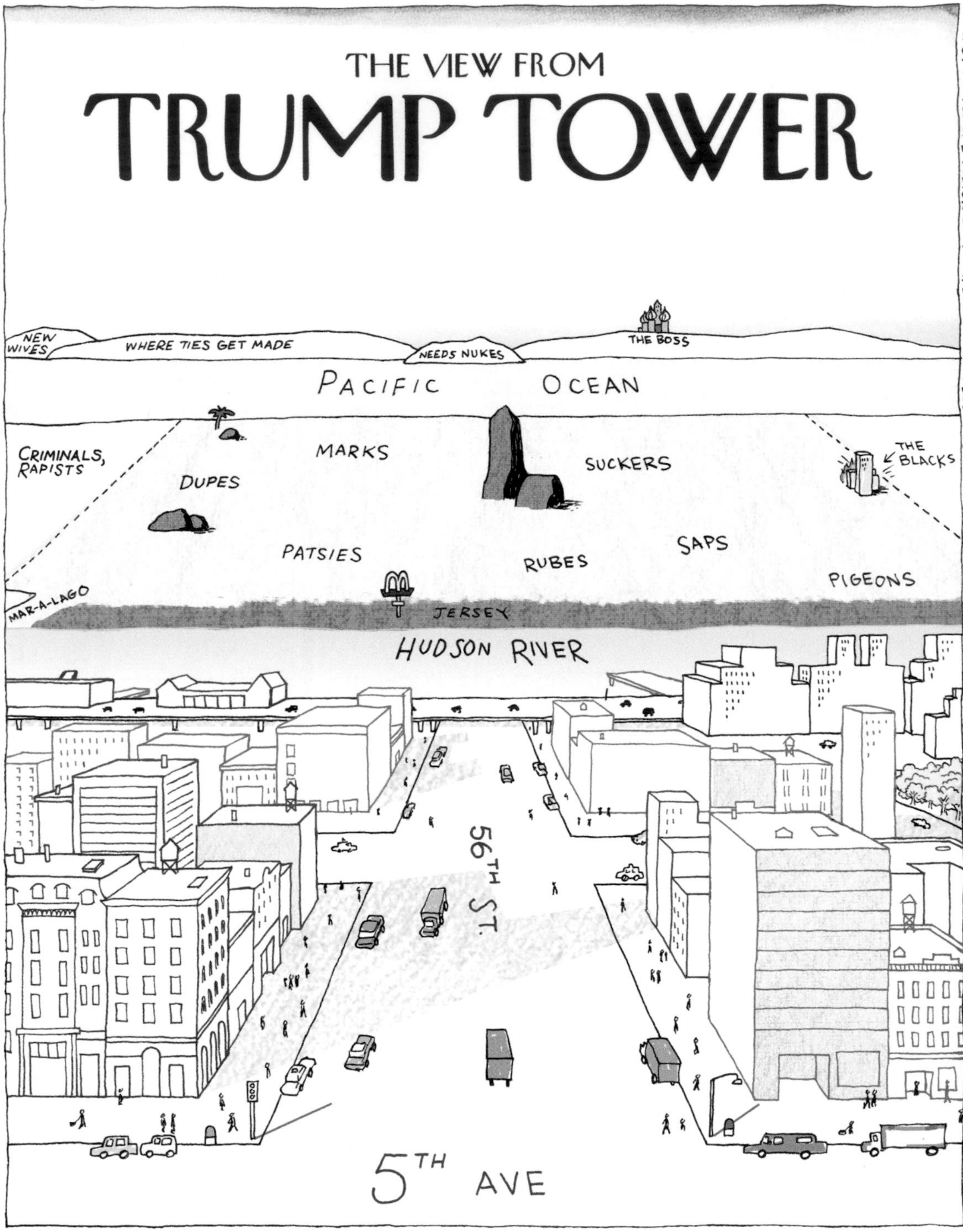
THE VIEW FROM
TRUMP TOWER
NEW WIVES
WHERE TIES GET MADE
NEEDS NUKES
THE BOSS
PACIFIC OCEAN
CRIMINALS, RAPISTS
MARKS
DUPES
SUCKERS
THE BLACKS
PATSIES
RUBES
SAPS
PIGEONS
MAR-A-LAGO
JERSEY
HUDSON RIVER
56TH ST.
5TH AVE

9/5/16

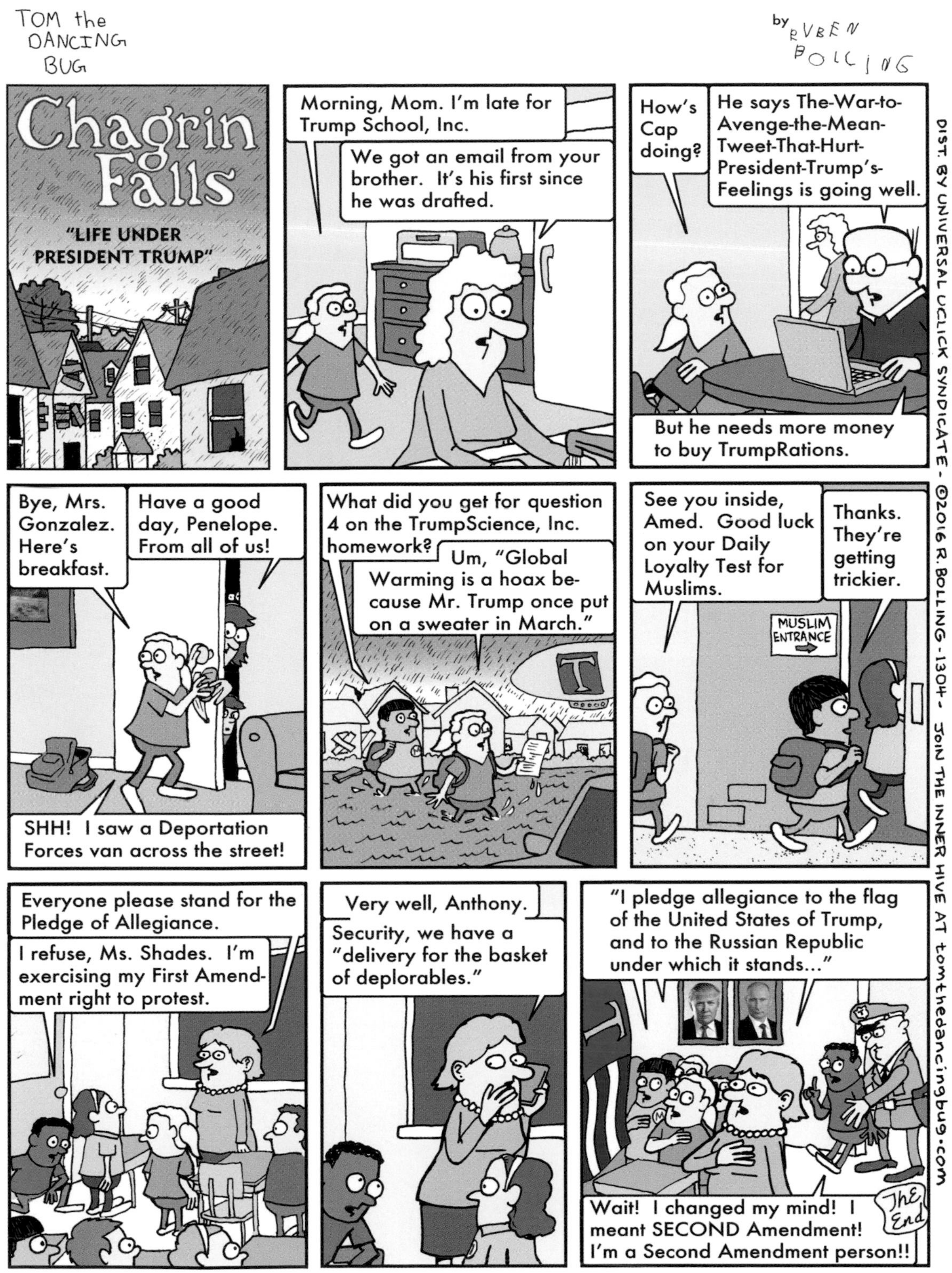
TOM the DANCING BUG
by RUBEN BOLLING
Chagrin Falls
"LIFE UNDER PRESIDENT TRUMP"
Morning, Mom. I'm late for Trump School, Inc.
We got an email from your brother. It's his first since he was drafted.
How's Cap doing?
He says The-War-to-Avenge-the-Mean-Tweet-That-Hurt-President-Trump's-Feelings is going well.
But he needs more money to buy TrumpRations.
Bye, Mrs. Gonzalez. Here's breakfast.
Have a good day, Penelope. From all of us!
SHH! I saw a Deportation Forces van across the street!
What did you get for question 4 on the TrumpScience, Inc. homework?
Um, "Global Warming is a hoax because Mr. Trump once put on a sweater in March."
See you inside, Amed. Good luck on your Daily Loyalty Test for Muslims.
Thanks. They're getting trickier.
MUSLIM ENTRANCE →
Everyone please stand for the Pledge of Allegiance.
I refuse, Ms. Shades. I'm exercising my First Amendment right to protest.
Very well, Anthony.
Security, we have a "delivery for the basket of deplorables."
"I pledge allegiance to the flag of the United States of Trump, and to the Russian Republic under which it stands..."
Wait! I changed my mind! I meant SECOND Amendment! I'm a Second Amendment person!!
The End
DIST. BY UNIVERSAL UCLICK SYNDICATE - ©2016 R. BOLLING - 1304 - JOIN THE INNER HIVE AT tomthedancingbug.com

9/12/16

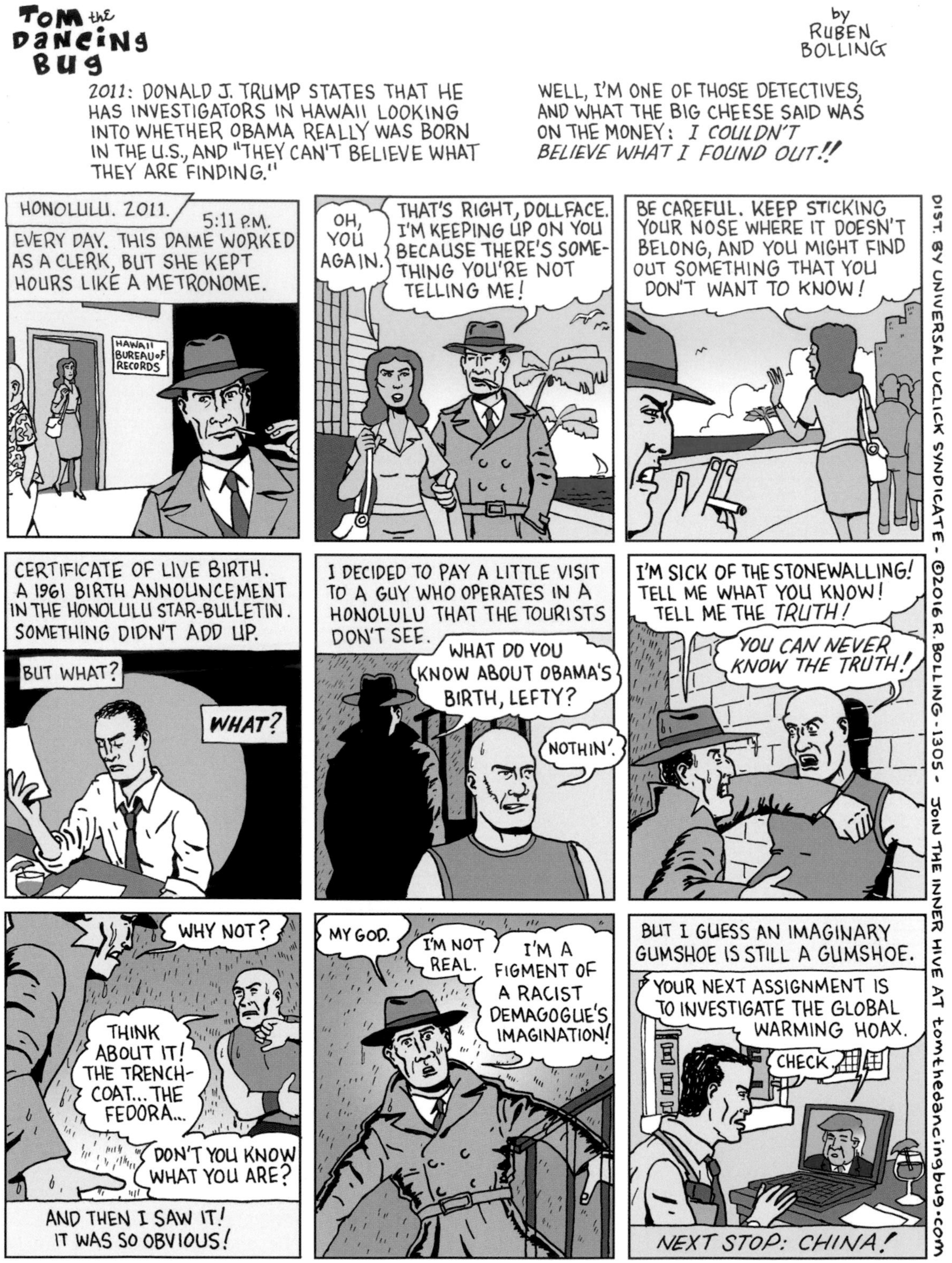
TOM the DANCING BUG
by RUBEN BOLLING
2011: DONALD J. TRUMP STATES THAT HE HAS INVESTIGATORS IN HAWAII LOOKING INTO WHETHER OBAMA REALLY WAS BORN IN THE U.S., AND "THEY CAN'T BELIEVE WHAT THEY ARE FINDING."
WELL, I'M ONE OF THOSE DETECTIVES, AND WHAT THE BIG CHEESE SAID WAS ON THE MONEY: I COULDN'T BELIEVE WHAT I FOUND OUT!!
HONOLULU. 2011.
5:11 P.M.
EVERY DAY. THIS DAME WORKED AS A CLERK, BUT SHE KEPT HOURS LIKE A METRONOME.
HAWAII BUREAU of RECORDS
OH, YOU AGAIN.
THAT'S RIGHT, DOLLFACE. I'M KEEPING UP ON YOU BECAUSE THERE'S SOMETHING YOU'RE NOT TELLING ME!
BE CAREFUL. KEEP STICKING YOUR NOSE WHERE IT DOESN'T BELONG, AND YOU MIGHT FIND OUT SOMETHING THAT YOU DON'T WANT TO KNOW!
CERTIFICATE OF LIVE BIRTH. A 1961 BIRTH ANNOUNCEMENT IN THE HONOLULU STAR-BULLETIN. SOMETHING DIDN'T ADD UP.
BUT WHAT?
WHAT?
I DECIDED TO PAY A LITTLE VISIT TO A GUY WHO OPERATES IN A HONOLULU THAT THE TOURISTS DON'T SEE.
WHAT DO YOU KNOW ABOUT OBAMA'S BIRTH, LEFTY?
NOTHIN'.
I'M SICK OF THE STONEWALLING! TELL ME WHAT YOU KNOW! TELL ME THE TRUTH!
YOU CAN NEVER KNOW THE TRUTH!
WHY NOT?
THINK ABOUT IT! THE TRENCH-COAT... THE FEDORA...
DON'T YOU KNOW WHAT YOU ARE?
AND THEN I SAW IT! IT WAS SO OBVIOUS!
MY GOD.
I'M NOT REAL.
I'M A FIGMENT OF A RACIST DEMAGOGUE'S IMAGINATION!
BUT I GUESS AN IMAGINARY GUMSHOE IS STILL A GUMSHOE.
YOUR NEXT ASSIGNMENT IS TO INVESTIGATE THE GLOBAL WARMING HOAX.
CHECK.
NEXT STOP: CHINA!
DIST. BY UNIVERSAL UCLICK SYNDICATE - ©2016 R. BOLLING - 1305 - JOIN THE INNER HIVE AT tomthedancingbug.com

9/19/16

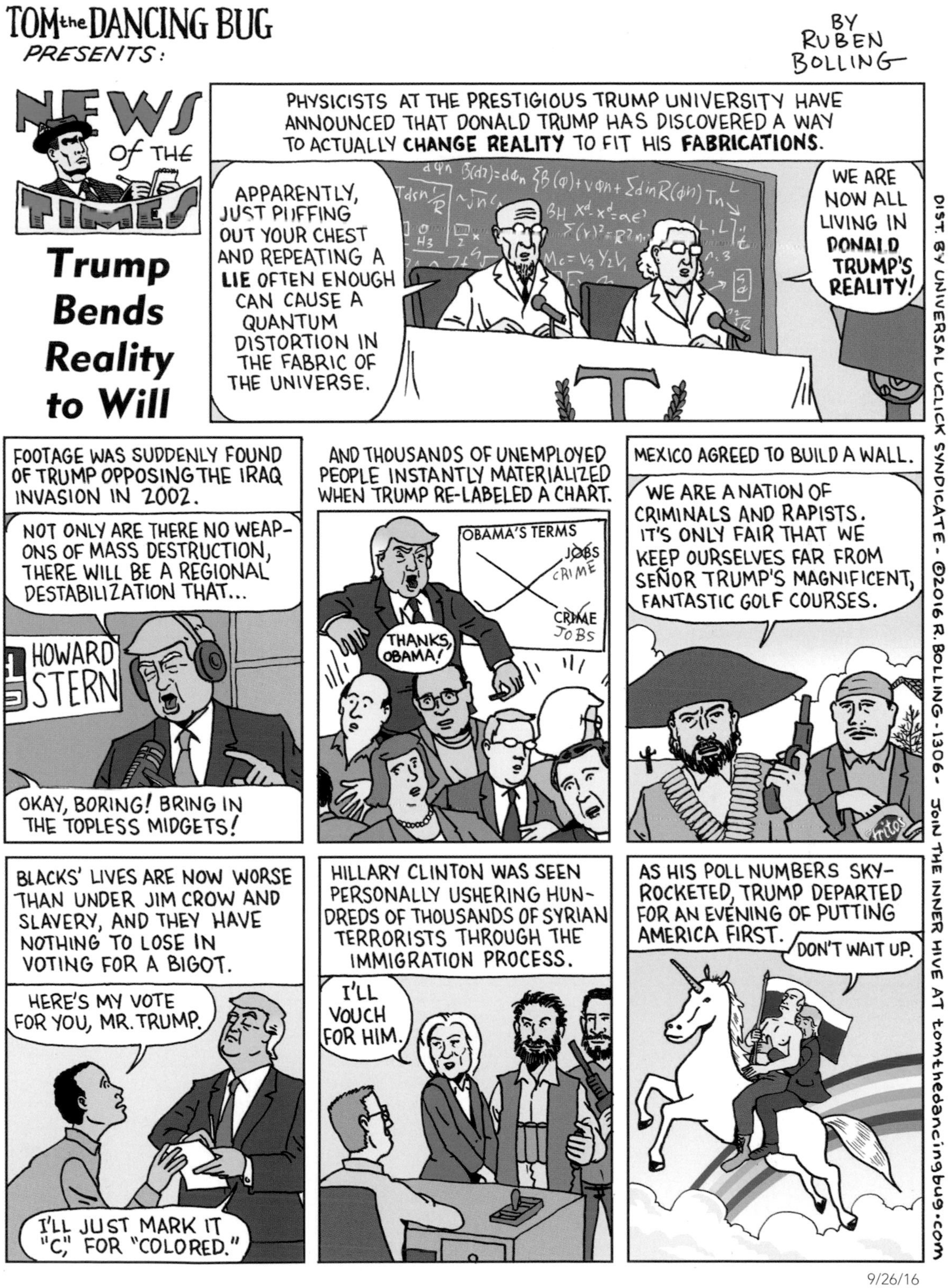
TOM the DANCING BUG PRESENTS:
BY RUBEN BOLLING
NEWS of THE TIMES
Trump Bends Reality to Will
PHYSICISTS AT THE PRESTIGIOUS TRUMP UNIVERSITY HAVE ANNOUNCED THAT DONALD TRUMP HAS DISCOVERED A WAY TO ACTUALLY **CHANGE REALITY** TO FIT HIS **FABRICATIONS**.
APPARENTLY, JUST PUFFING OUT YOUR CHEST AND REPEATING A **LIE** OFTEN ENOUGH CAN CAUSE A QUANTUM DISTORTION IN THE FABRIC OF THE UNIVERSE.
WE ARE NOW ALL LIVING IN **DONALD TRUMP'S REALITY!**
FOOTAGE WAS SUDDENLY FOUND OF TRUMP OPPOSING THE IRAQ INVASION IN 2002.
NOT ONLY ARE THERE NO WEAPONS OF MASS DESTRUCTION, THERE WILL BE A REGIONAL DESTABILIZATION THAT...
HOWARD STERN
OKAY, BORING! BRING IN THE TOPLESS MIDGETS!
AND THOUSANDS OF UNEMPLOYED PEOPLE INSTANTLY MATERIALIZED WHEN TRUMP RE-LABELED A CHART.
OBAMA'S TERMS
JOBS CRIME
CRIME JOBS
THANKS, OBAMA!
MEXICO AGREED TO BUILD A WALL.
WE ARE A NATION OF CRIMINALS AND RAPISTS. IT'S ONLY FAIR THAT WE KEEP OURSELVES FAR FROM SEÑOR TRUMP'S MAGNIFICENT, FANTASTIC GOLF COURSES.
BLACKS' LIVES ARE NOW WORSE THAN UNDER JIM CROW AND SLAVERY, AND THEY HAVE NOTHING TO LOSE IN VOTING FOR A BIGOT.
HERE'S MY VOTE FOR YOU, MR. TRUMP.
I'LL JUST MARK IT "C," FOR "COLORED."
HILLARY CLINTON WAS SEEN PERSONALLY USHERING HUNDREDS OF THOUSANDS OF SYRIAN TERRORISTS THROUGH THE IMMIGRATION PROCESS.
I'LL VOUCH FOR HIM.
AS HIS POLL NUMBERS SKYROCKETED, TRUMP DEPARTED FOR AN EVENING OF PUTTING AMERICA FIRST.
DON'T WAIT UP.
DIST. BY UNIVERSAL UCLICK SYNDICATE - ©2016 R. BOLLING - 1306 - JOIN THE INNER HIVE AT tomthedancingbug.com

9/26/16

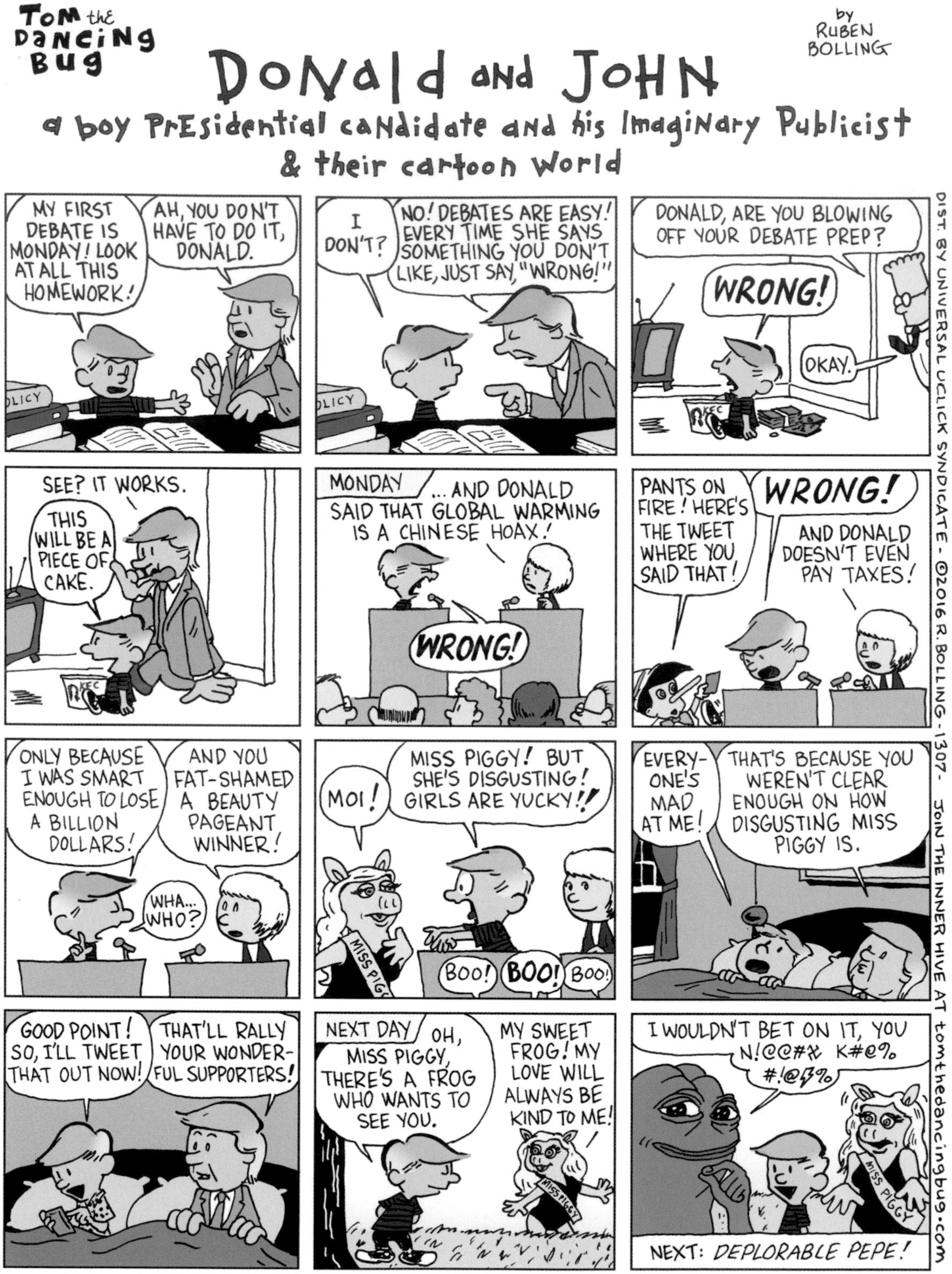

TOM the DANCING BUG
by RUBEN BOLLING
DONALD and JOHN
a boy Presidential candidate and his Imaginary Publicist & their cartoon World
DIST. BY UNIVERSAL UCLICK SYNDICATE - ©2016 R. BOLLING - 1307 - JOIN THE INNER HIVE AT tomthedancingbug.com
MY FIRST DEBATE IS MONDAY! LOOK AT ALL THIS HOMEWORK!
AH, YOU DON'T HAVE TO DO IT, DONALD.
POLICY
I DON'T?
NO! DEBATES ARE EASY! EVERY TIME SHE SAYS SOMETHING YOU DON'T LIKE, JUST SAY, "WRONG!"
DONALD, ARE YOU BLOWING OFF YOUR DEBATE PREP?
WRONG!
OKAY.
KFC
SEE? IT WORKS.
THIS WILL BE A PIECE OF CAKE.
MONDAY
...AND DONALD SAID THAT GLOBAL WARMING IS A CHINESE HOAX!
WRONG!
PANTS ON FIRE! HERE'S THE TWEET WHERE YOU SAID THAT!
WRONG!
AND DONALD DOESN'T EVEN PAY TAXES!
ONLY BECAUSE I WAS SMART ENOUGH TO LOSE A BILLION DOLLARS!
AND YOU FAT-SHAMED A BEAUTY PAGEANT WINNER!
WHA... WHO?
MOI!
MISS PIGGY! BUT SHE'S DISGUSTING! GIRLS ARE YUCKY!!
BOO! BOO! BOO!
EVERY-ONE'S MAD AT ME!
THAT'S BECAUSE YOU WEREN'T CLEAR ENOUGH ON HOW DISGUSTING MISS PIGGY IS.
GOOD POINT! SO, I'LL TWEET THAT OUT NOW!
THAT'LL RALLY YOUR WONDER-FUL SUPPORTERS!
NEXT DAY
OH, MISS PIGGY, THERE'S A FROG WHO WANTS TO SEE YOU.
MY SWEET FROG! MY LOVE WILL ALWAYS BE KIND TO ME!
MISS PIGGY
I WOULDN'T BET ON IT, YOU N!@@#% K#@% #!@%%
MISS PIGGY
NEXT: DEPLORABLE PEPE!

10/3/16

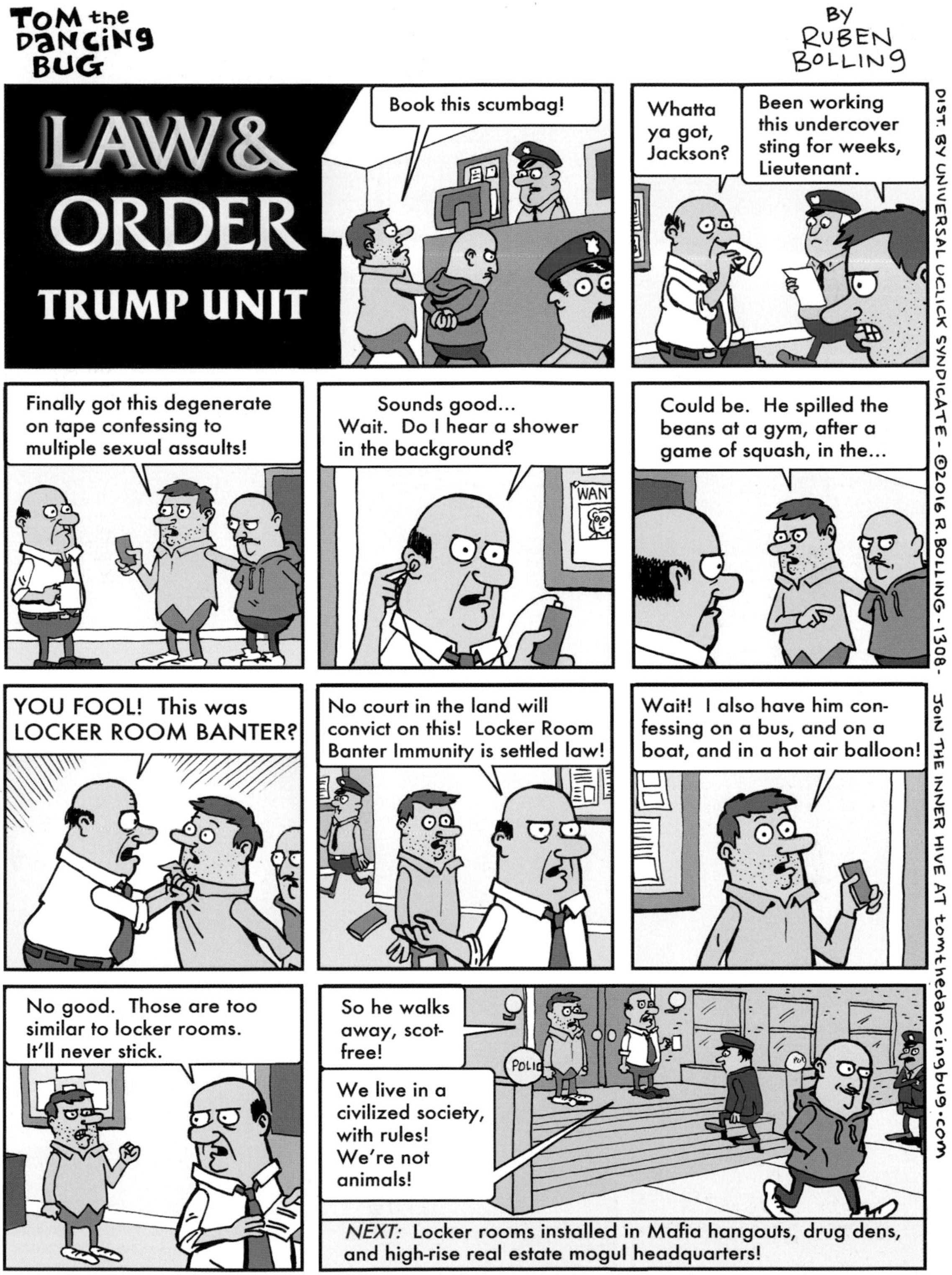
TOM the DANCING BUG
BY RUBEN BOLLING
LAW & ORDER
TRUMP UNIT
Book this scumbag!
Whatta ya got, Jackson?
Been working this undercover sting for weeks, Lieutenant.
Finally got this degenerate on tape confessing to multiple sexual assaults!
Sounds good... Wait. Do I hear a shower in the background?
WANT
Could be. He spilled the beans at a gym, after a game of squash, in the...
YOU FOOL! This was LOCKER ROOM BANTER?
No court in the land will convict on this! Locker Room Banter Immunity is settled law!
Wait! I also have him confessing on a bus, and on a boat, and in a hot air balloon!
No good. Those are too similar to locker rooms. It'll never stick.
So he walks away, scot-free!
We live in a civilized society, with rules! We're not animals!
POLIC
NEXT: Locker rooms installed in Mafia hangouts, drug dens, and high-rise real estate mogul headquarters!
DIST. BY UNIVERSAL UCLICK SYNDICATE - ©2016 R. BOLLING - 1308 - JOIN THE INNER HIVE AT tomthedancingbug.com

10/10/16

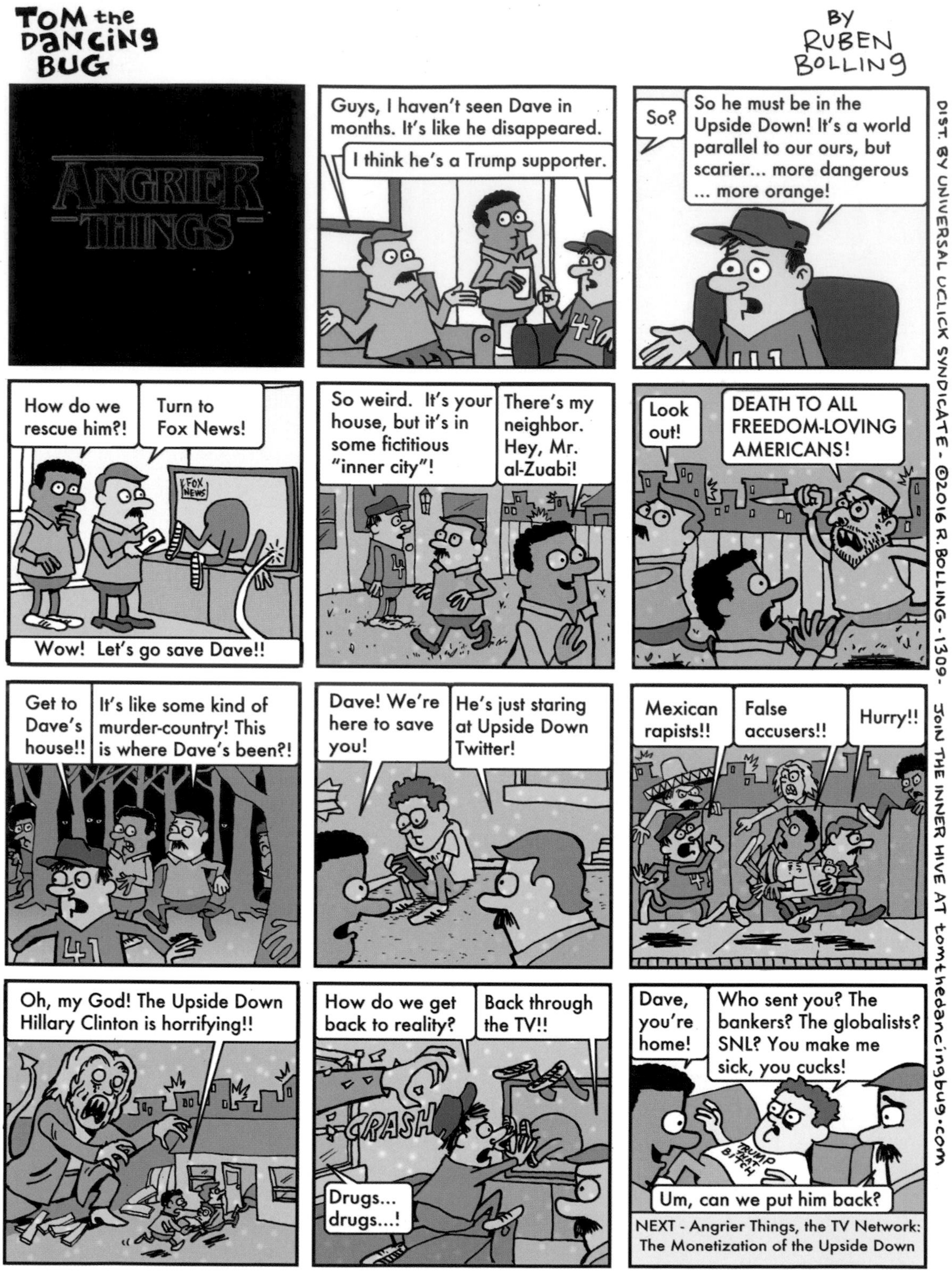
TOM the DANCING BUG
BY RUBEN BOLLING
ANGRIER THINGS
Guys, I haven't seen Dave in months. It's like he disappeared.
I think he's a Trump supporter.
So?
So he must be in the Upside Down! It's a world parallel to our ours, but scarier... more dangerous ... more orange!
How do we rescue him?!
Turn to Fox News!
FOX NEWS
Wow! Let's go save Dave!!
So weird. It's your house, but it's in some fictitious "inner city"!
There's my neighbor. Hey, Mr. al-Zuabi!
Look out!
DEATH TO ALL FREEDOM-LOVING AMERICANS!
Get to Dave's house!!
It's like some kind of murder-country! This is where Dave's been?!
Dave! We're here to save you!
He's just staring at Upside Down Twitter!
Mexican rapists!!
False accusers!!
Hurry!!
Oh, my God! The Upside Down Hillary Clinton is horrifying!!
How do we get back to reality?
Back through the TV!!
CRASH
Drugs... drugs...!
Dave, you're home!
Who sent you? The bankers? The globalists? SNL? You make me sick, you cucks!
Um, can we put him back?
NEXT - Angrier Things, the TV Network: The Monetization of the Upside Down
DIST. BY UNIVERSAL UCLICK SYNDICATE - ©2016 R. BOLLING - 1309 - JOIN THE INNER HIVE AT tomthedancingbug.com

10/17/16

TOM the DANCING BUG

"A lot of the people that are poor take advantage of loopholes and pay no taxes. Those are loopholes also."
- Trump adviser Rudolph Giuliani

BY RUBEN BOLLING

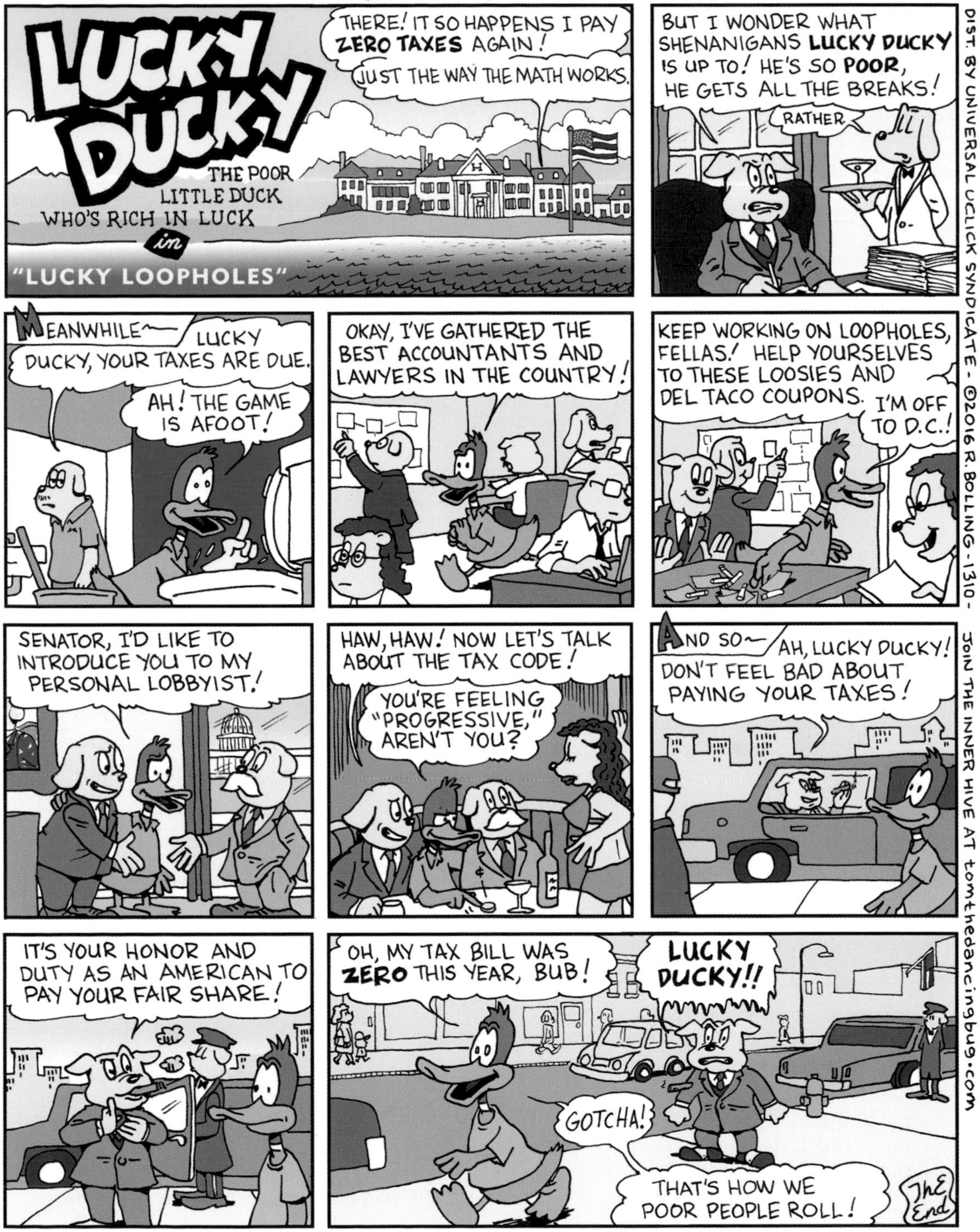

LUCKY DUCKY
THE POOR LITTLE DUCK WHO'S RICH IN LUCK
in
"LUCKY LOOPHOLES"
THERE! IT SO HAPPENS I PAY ZERO TAXES AGAIN!
JUST THE WAY THE MATH WORKS.
BUT I WONDER WHAT SHENANIGANS LUCKY DUCKY IS UP TO! HE'S SO POOR, HE GETS ALL THE BREAKS!
RATHER.
MEANWHILE~
LUCKY DUCKY, YOUR TAXES ARE DUE.
AH! THE GAME IS AFOOT!
OKAY, I'VE GATHERED THE BEST ACCOUNTANTS AND LAWYERS IN THE COUNTRY!
KEEP WORKING ON LOOPHOLES, FELLAS! HELP YOURSELVES TO THESE LOOSIES AND DEL TACO COUPONS.
I'M OFF TO D.C.!
SENATOR, I'D LIKE TO INTRODUCE YOU TO MY PERSONAL LOBBYIST!
HAW, HAW! NOW LET'S TALK ABOUT THE TAX CODE!
YOU'RE FEELING "PROGRESSIVE," AREN'T YOU?
AND SO~
AH, LUCKY DUCKY! DON'T FEEL BAD ABOUT PAYING YOUR TAXES!
IT'S YOUR HONOR AND DUTY AS AN AMERICAN TO PAY YOUR FAIR SHARE!
OH, MY TAX BILL WAS ZERO THIS YEAR, BUB!
LUCKY DUCKY!!
GOTCHA!
THAT'S HOW WE POOR PEOPLE ROLL!
THE End
DIST. BY UNIVERSAL UCLICK SYNDICATE - ©2016 R. BOLLING - 1310 - JOIN THE INNER HIVE AT tomthedancingbug.com

10/24/16

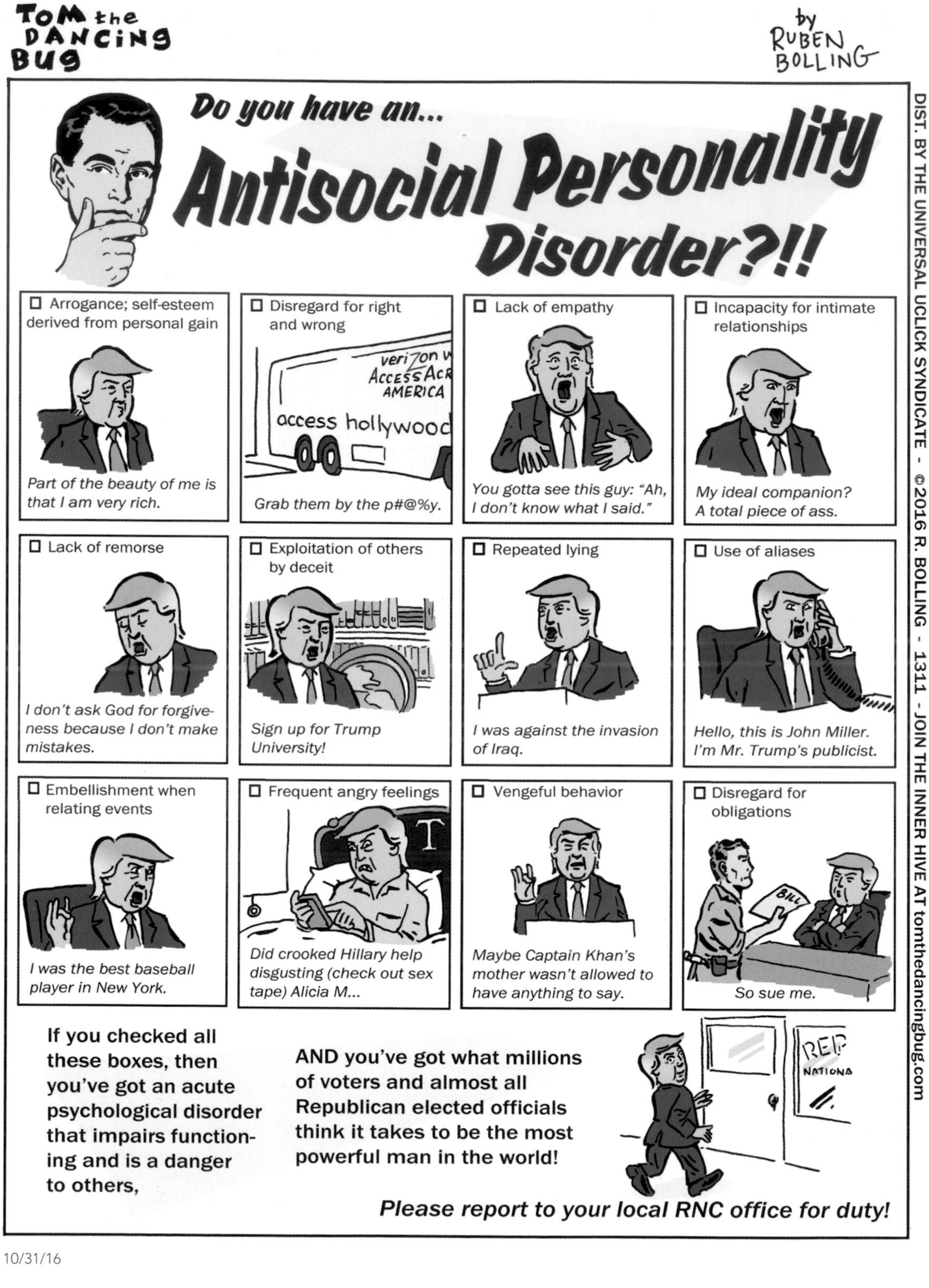

TOM the DANCING BUG
by RUBEN BOLLING
Do you have an...
Antisocial Personality Disorder?!!
Arrogance; self-esteem derived from personal gain
Part of the beauty of me is that I am very rich.
Disregard for right and wrong
access hollywood
Grab them by the p#@%y.
Lack of empathy
You gotta see this guy: "Ah, I don't know what I said."
Incapacity for intimate relationships
My ideal companion? A total piece of ass.
Lack of remorse
I don't ask God for forgiveness because I don't make mistakes.
Exploitation of others by deceit
Sign up for Trump University!
Repeated lying
I was against the invasion of Iraq.
Use of aliases
Hello, this is John Miller. I'm Mr. Trump's publicist.
Embellishment when relating events
I was the best baseball player in New York.
Frequent angry feelings
T
Did crooked Hillary help disgusting (check out sex tape) Alicia M...
Vengeful behavior
Maybe Captain Khan's mother wasn't allowed to have anything to say.
Disregard for obligations
BILL
So sue me.
If you checked all these boxes, then you've got an acute psychological disorder that impairs functioning and is a danger to others,
AND you've got what millions of voters and almost all Republican elected officials think it takes to be the most powerful man in the world!
NATIONA
Please report to your local RNC office for duty!
DIST. BY THE UNIVERSAL UCLICK SYNDICATE - ©2016 R. BOLLING - 1311 - JOIN THE INNER HIVE AT tomthedancingbug.com

10/31/16

TOM the DANCING BUG'S
SUPER-FUN-PAK COMIX
EDITED BY RUBEN BOLLING

GOOD COP / BAD COP

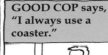

BAD COP says, "I shall leave my coffee cup on the table."

GOOD COP says, "I always use a coaster."

OKAY, I'LL TALK! JUST STOP WITH THE SAPPY MORALITY PLAYS!

PHIL COLLINS

HEY, LOOK! IT'S 1980s SUPERSTAR PHIL COLLINS!

HA!

WHAT'S FUNNY ABOUT THAT?

I'M A KIND, TALENTED MAN WHO HAS WORKED HARD TO CREATE GOOD MUSIC THAT HAS BEEN VERY POPULAR.

HILLBILLY FRANKENSTEIN

SORRY, HILLBILLY FRANKENSTEIN! NO SHOES, NO SERVICE.

ME WEARING SHOES! FRANKENSTEIN SHOES!

ME A NORMAL FRANKENSTEIN WHO JUST HAPPENS TO BE A HILLBILLY.

ALLOWS-PEOPLE-TO-USE-THE-CHAIR-MAN

IN A WORLD GONE MAD, ONE MAN'S SELFLESS DISPOSITION CAN COMFORT THE AFFLICTED!

CAN I USE THIS CHAIR?

SURE, GO RIGHT AHEAD.

ONCE AGAIN, THE CITY'S CHAIRLESS CAN REST EASY, THANKS TO ALLOWS-PEOPLE-TO-USE-THE-CHAIR-MAN!

ARTIST

I need to say something about which I feel passionately, in a way that is creative and entertaining!

Wow. What is it you want to say?

Oh, I don't know yet.

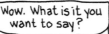

PERCIVAL DUNWOODY, IDIOT TIME TRAVELER FROM 1909

1909, CHICAGO— AH, I SPILLED MY SARSAPARILLA!

WORLD CHAMP CUBS

I SHALL GO BACK IN TIME AND PREVENT THAT FROM HAPPENING!

WORLD CHAMP CUBS

MOMENTS EARLIER~ BE CAREFUL WITH YOUR DRINK!

HEY! BUMP!

WORLD CHAMP CU

YOU SET IN MOTION A CHAIN OF EVENTS THAT WILL CAUSE A 108-YEAR CUBS CHAMPIONSHIP DROUGHT!

AH, BUT IT WILL ALSO EVENTUALLY CAUSE TWO WORLD WARS.

OH.

WORLD CHAMP CUBS

WITH YOU CUBS FANS, IT'S ALWAYS ABOUT YOU!

WORLD CHAMP CUBS

DIST. BY THE UNIVERSAL UCLICK SYNDICATE - ©2016 R.Bolling -1312- TO JOIN THE INNER HIVE go to tomthedancingbug.com

11/7/16

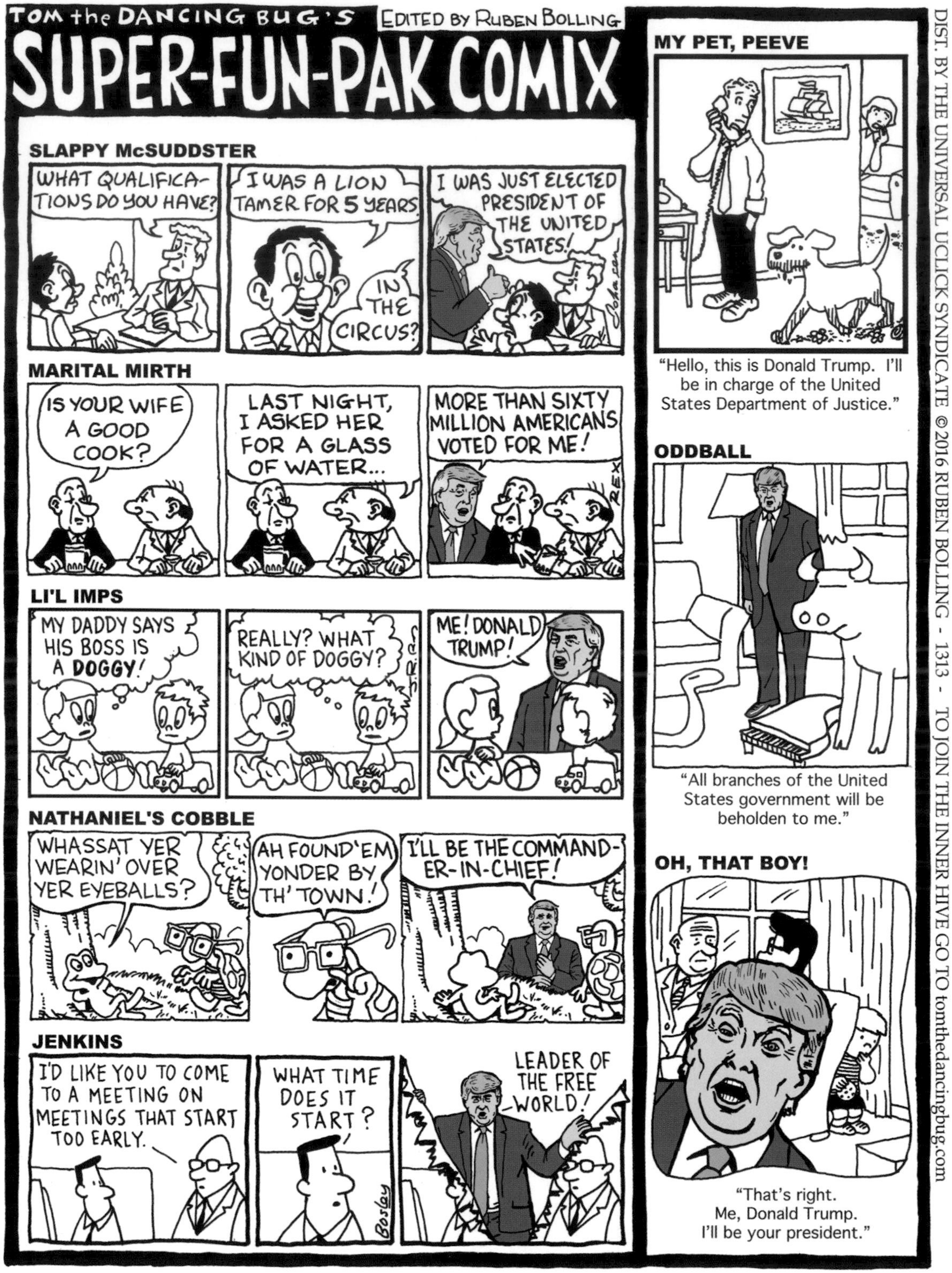

TOM the DANCING BUG'S
EDITED BY RUBEN BOLLING
SUPER-FUN-PAK COMIX
SLAPPY McSUDDSTER
WHAT QUALIFICATIONS DO YOU HAVE?
I WAS A LION TAMER FOR 5 YEARS
IN THE CIRCUS?
I WAS JUST ELECTED PRESIDENT OF THE UNITED STATES!
MARITAL MIRTH
IS YOUR WIFE A GOOD COOK?
LAST NIGHT, I ASKED HER FOR A GLASS OF WATER...
MORE THAN SIXTY MILLION AMERICANS VOTED FOR ME!
LI'L IMPS
MY DADDY SAYS HIS BOSS IS A DOGGY!
REALLY? WHAT KIND OF DOGGY?
ME! DONALD TRUMP!
NATHANIEL'S COBBLE
WHASSAT YER WEARIN' OVER YER EYEBALLS?
AH FOUND'EM YONDER BY TH' TOWN!
I'LL BE THE COMMANDER-IN-CHIEF!
JENKINS
I'D LIKE YOU TO COME TO A MEETING ON MEETINGS THAT START TOO EARLY.
WHAT TIME DOES IT START?
LEADER OF THE FREE WORLD!
MY PET, PEEVE
"Hello, this is Donald Trump. I'll be in charge of the United States Department of Justice."
ODDBALL
"All branches of the United States government will be beholden to me."
OH, THAT BOY!
"That's right. Me, Donald Trump. I'll be your president."
DIST. BY THE UNIVERSAL UCLICK SYNDICATE © 2016 RUBEN BOLLING - 1313 - TO JOIN THE INNER HIVE GO TO tomthedancingbug.com

11/14/16

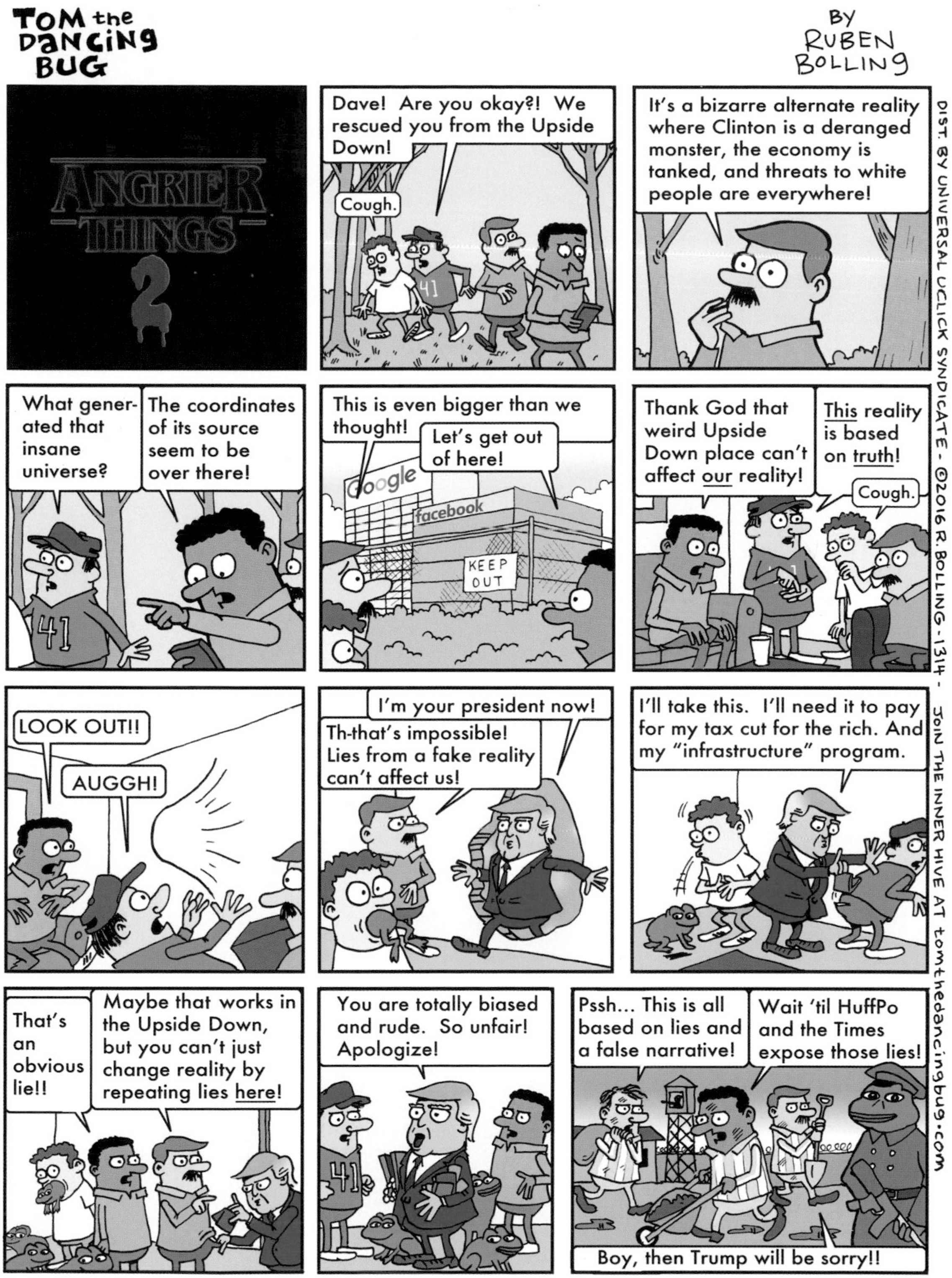
TOM the DANCING BUG
BY RUBEN BOLLING
ANGRIER THINGS 2
Dave! Are you okay?! We rescued you from the Upside Down!
Cough.
It's a bizarre alternate reality where Clinton is a deranged monster, the economy is tanked, and threats to white people are everywhere!
What generated that insane universe?
The coordinates of its source seem to be over there!
This is even bigger than we thought!
Let's get out of here!
Google
facebook
KEEP OUT
Thank God that weird Upside Down place can't affect our reality!
This reality is based on truth!
Cough.
LOOK OUT!!
AUGGH!
I'm your president now!
Th-that's impossible! Lies from a fake reality can't affect us!
I'll take this. I'll need it to pay for my tax cut for the rich. And my "infrastructure" program.
That's an obvious lie!!
Maybe that works in the Upside Down, but you can't just change reality by repeating lies here!
You are totally biased and rude. So unfair! Apologize!
Pssh... This is all based on lies and a false narrative!
Wait 'til HuffPo and the Times expose those lies!
Boy, then Trump will be sorry!!
DIST. BY UNIVERSAL UCLICK SYNDICATE - ©2016 R. BOLLING - 1314 - JOIN THE INNER HIVE AT tomthedancingbug.com

11/21/16

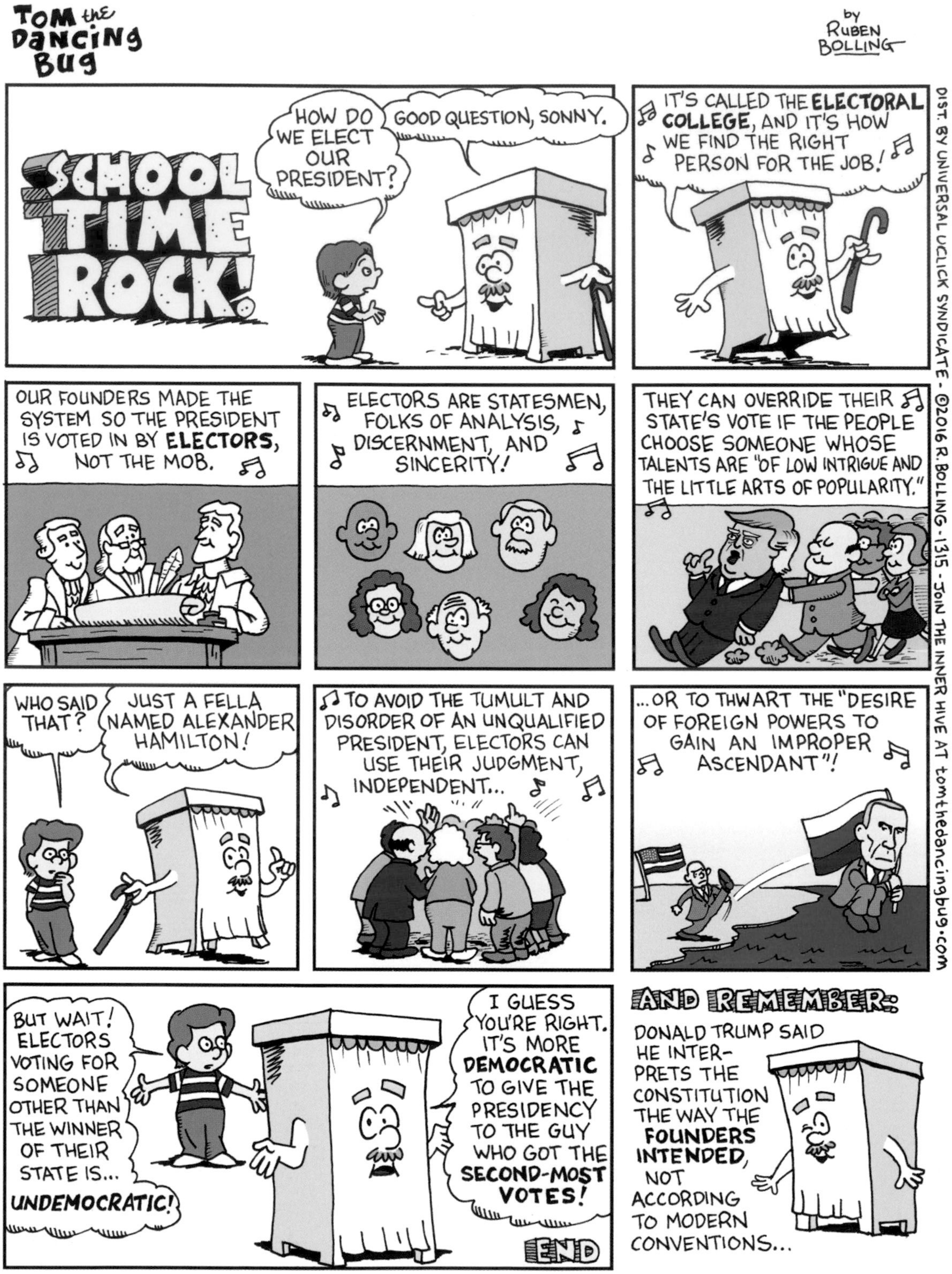

TOM the DANCING Bug
by RUBEN BOLLING
SCHOOL TIME ROCK!
HOW DO WE ELECT OUR PRESIDENT?
GOOD QUESTION, SONNY.
IT'S CALLED THE ELECTORAL COLLEGE, AND IT'S HOW WE FIND THE RIGHT PERSON FOR THE JOB!
OUR FOUNDERS MADE THE SYSTEM SO THE PRESIDENT IS VOTED IN BY ELECTORS, NOT THE MOB.
ELECTORS ARE STATESMEN, FOLKS OF ANALYSIS, DISCERNMENT, AND SINCERITY!
THEY CAN OVERRIDE THEIR STATE'S VOTE IF THE PEOPLE CHOOSE SOMEONE WHOSE TALENTS ARE "OF LOW INTRIGUE AND THE LITTLE ARTS OF POPULARITY."
WHO SAID THAT?
JUST A FELLA NAMED ALEXANDER HAMILTON!
TO AVOID THE TUMULT AND DISORDER OF AN UNQUALIFIED PRESIDENT, ELECTORS CAN USE THEIR JUDGMENT, INDEPENDENT...
...OR TO THWART THE "DESIRE OF FOREIGN POWERS TO GAIN AN IMPROPER ASCENDANT"!
BUT WAIT! ELECTORS VOTING FOR SOMEONE OTHER THAN THE WINNER OF THEIR STATE IS... UNDEMOCRATIC!
I GUESS YOU'RE RIGHT. IT'S MORE DEMOCRATIC TO GIVE THE PRESIDENCY TO THE GUY WHO GOT THE SECOND-MOST VOTES!
END
AND REMEMBER:
DONALD TRUMP SAID HE INTERPRETS THE CONSTITUTION THE WAY THE FOUNDERS INTENDED, NOT ACCORDING TO MODERN CONVENTIONS...
DIST. BY UNIVERSAL UCLICK SYNDICATE - ©2016 R. BOLLING - 1315 - JOIN THE INNER HIVE AT tomthedancingbug.com

11/28/16

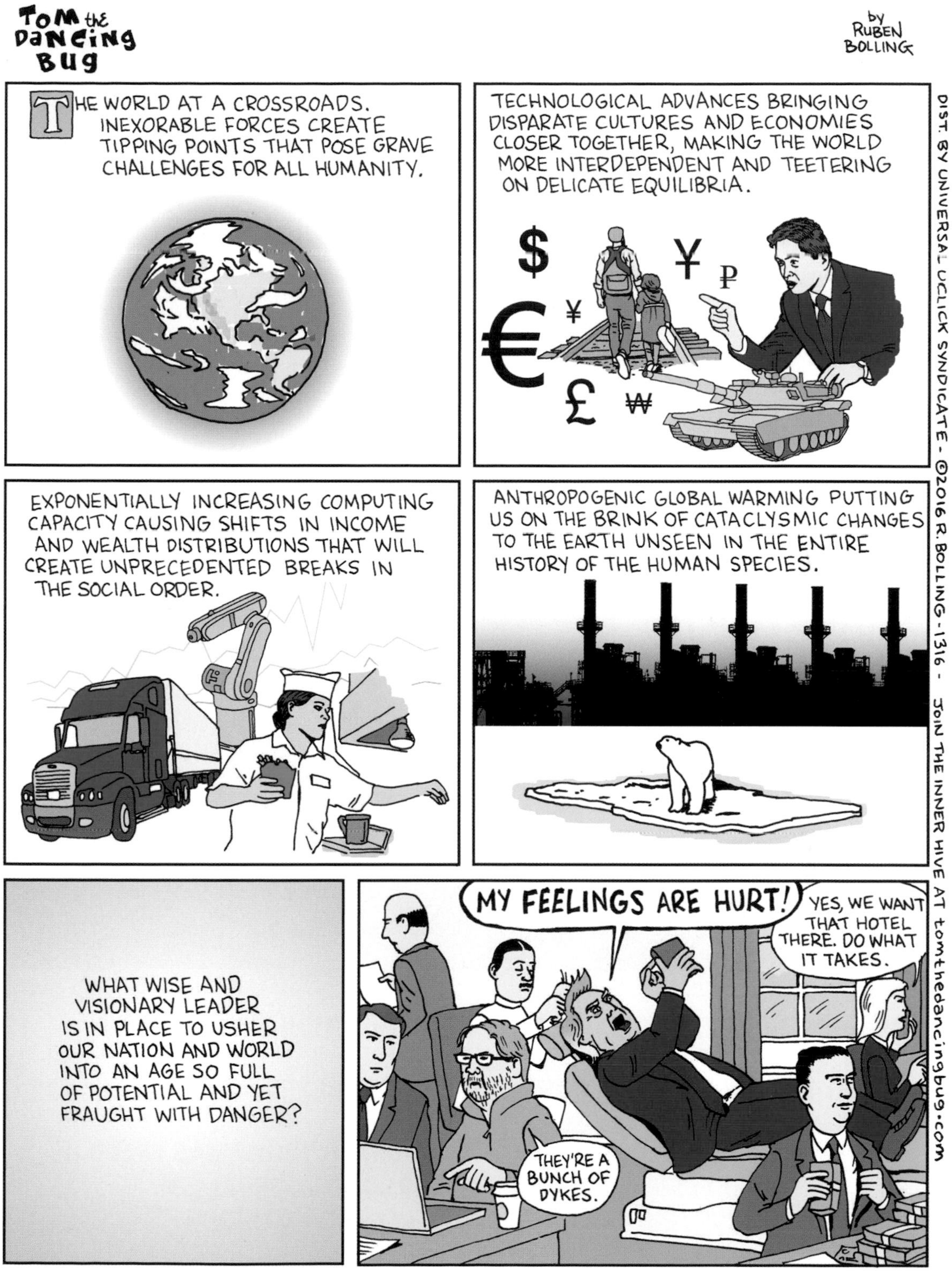
TOM the DANCING BUG
by RUBEN BOLLING
THE WORLD AT A CROSSROADS. INEXORABLE FORCES CREATE TIPPING POINTS THAT POSE GRAVE CHALLENGES FOR ALL HUMANITY.
TECHNOLOGICAL ADVANCES BRINGING DISPARATE CULTURES AND ECONOMIES CLOSER TOGETHER, MAKING THE WORLD MORE INTERDEPENDENT AND TEETERING ON DELICATE EQUILIBRIA.
$ ¥ ₽ € ¥ £ ₩
EXPONENTIALLY INCREASING COMPUTING CAPACITY CAUSING SHIFTS IN INCOME AND WEALTH DISTRIBUTIONS THAT WILL CREATE UNPRECEDENTED BREAKS IN THE SOCIAL ORDER.
ANTHROPOGENIC GLOBAL WARMING PUTTING US ON THE BRINK OF CATACLYSMIC CHANGES TO THE EARTH UNSEEN IN THE ENTIRE HISTORY OF THE HUMAN SPECIES.
WHAT WISE AND VISIONARY LEADER IS IN PLACE TO USHER OUR NATION AND WORLD INTO AN AGE SO FULL OF POTENTIAL AND YET FRAUGHT WITH DANGER?
MY FEELINGS ARE HURT!
YES, WE WANT THAT HOTEL THERE. DO WHAT IT TAKES.
THEY'RE A BUNCH OF DYKES.
DIST. BY UNIVERSAL UCLICK SYNDICATE - ©2016 R. BOLLING - 1316 - JOIN THE INNER HIVE AT tomthedancingbug.com

12/5/16

TOM THE DANCING BUG

BY RUBEN BOLLING

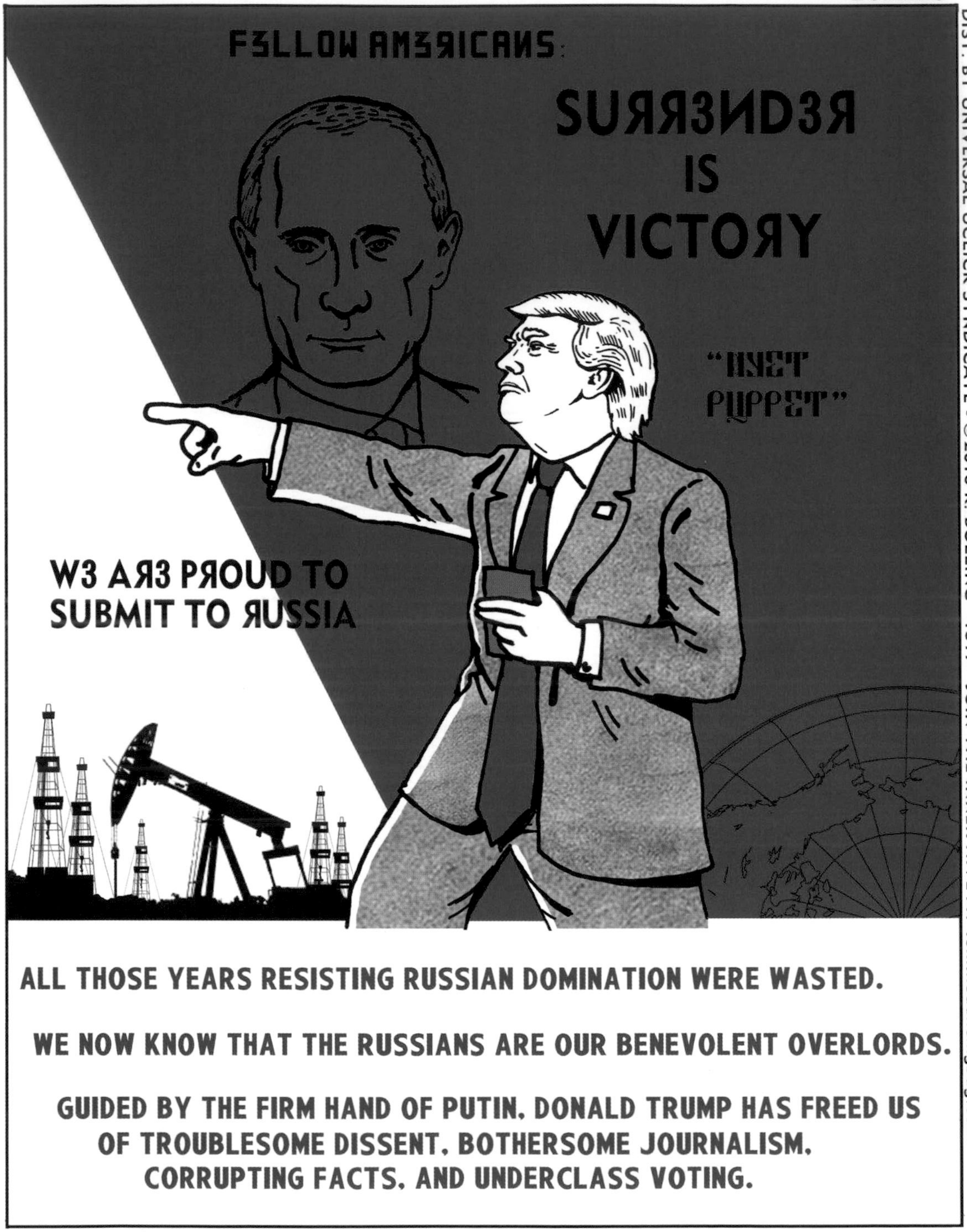

F3LLOW AM3ЯICANS:
SUЯЯ3ND3Я
IS
VICTOЯY
“ИYET PUPPET”
W3 AЯ3 PЯOUD TO SUBMIT TO ЯUSSIA
ALL THOSE YEARS RESISTING RUSSIAN DOMINATION WERE WASTED.
WE NOW KNOW THAT THE RUSSIANS ARE OUR BENEVOLENT OVERLORDS.
GUIDED BY THE FIRM HAND OF PUTIN, DONALD TRUMP HAS FREED US OF TROUBLESOME DISSENT, BOTHERSOME JOURNALISM, CORRUPTING FACTS, AND UNDERCLASS VOTING.

12/12/16

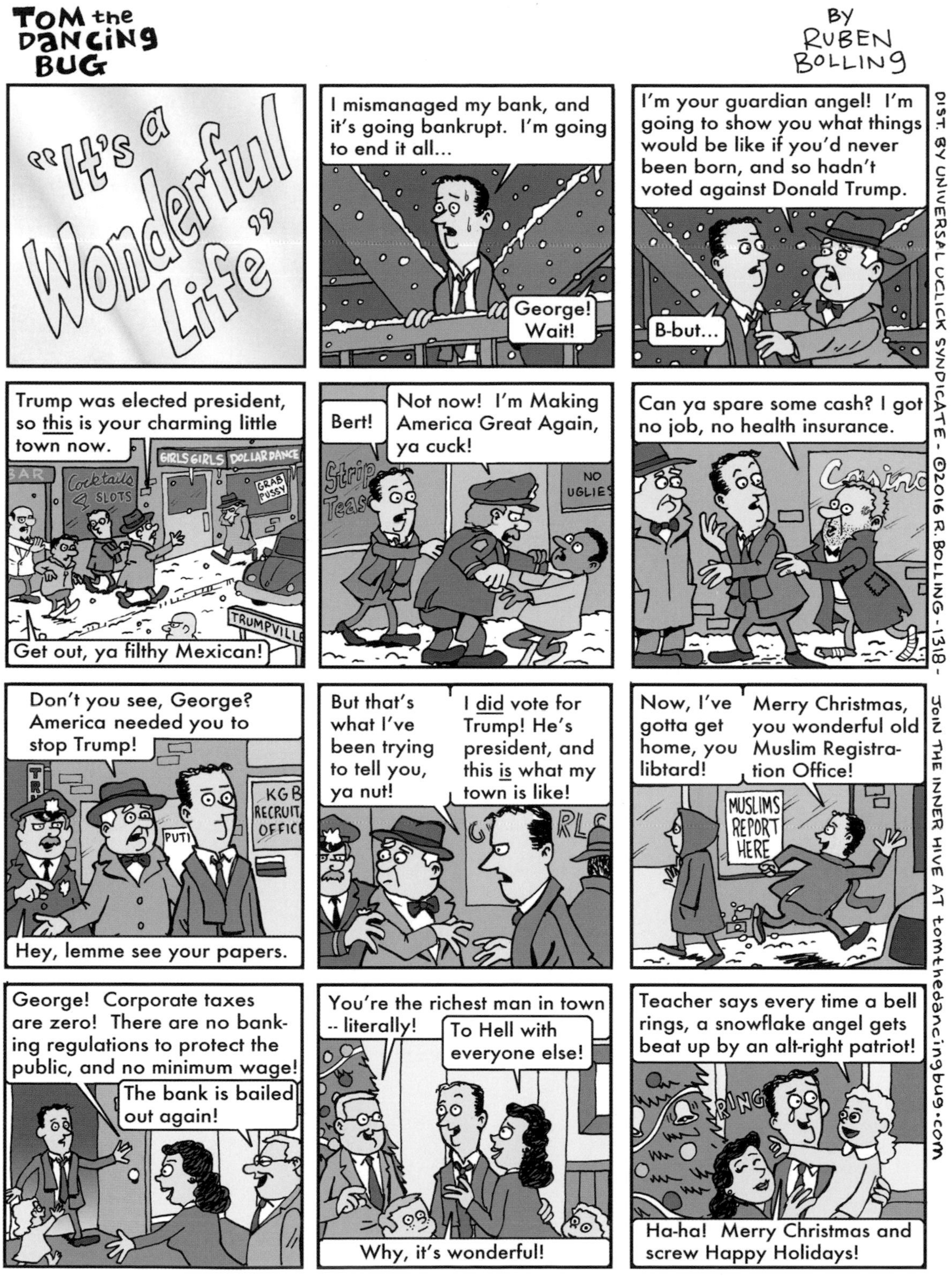

TOM the DANCING BUG
BY RUBEN BOLLING
"It's a Wonderful Life"
I mismanaged my bank, and it's going bankrupt. I'm going to end it all...
George! Wait!
I'm your guardian angel! I'm going to show you what things would be like if you'd never been born, and so hadn't voted against Donald Trump.
B-but...
Trump was elected president, so this is your charming little town now.
GIRLS GIRLS
DOLLAR DANCE
Cocktails & SLOTS
GRAB PUSSY
TRUMPVILLE
Get out, ya filthy Mexican!
Bert!
Not now! I'm Making America Great Again, ya cuck!
Strip Tease
NO UGLIES
Can ya spare some cash? I got no job, no health insurance.
Casino
Don't you see, George? America needed you to stop Trump!
KGB RECRUIT OFFICE
Hey, lemme see your papers.
But that's what I've been trying to tell you, ya nut!
I did vote for Trump! He's president, and this is what my town is like!
Now, I've gotta get home, you libtard!
Merry Christmas, you wonderful old Muslim Registration Office!
MUSLIMS REPORT HERE
George! Corporate taxes are zero! There are no banking regulations to protect the public, and no minimum wage!
The bank is bailed out again!
You're the richest man in town -- literally!
To Hell with everyone else!
Why, it's wonderful!
Teacher says every time a bell rings, a snowflake angel gets beat up by an alt-right patriot!
RING
Ha-ha! Merry Christmas and screw Happy Holidays!
DIST. BY UNIVERSAL UCLICK SYNDICATE - ©2016 R. BOLLING - 1318 - JOIN THE INNER HIVE AT tomthedancingbug.com

12/19/16

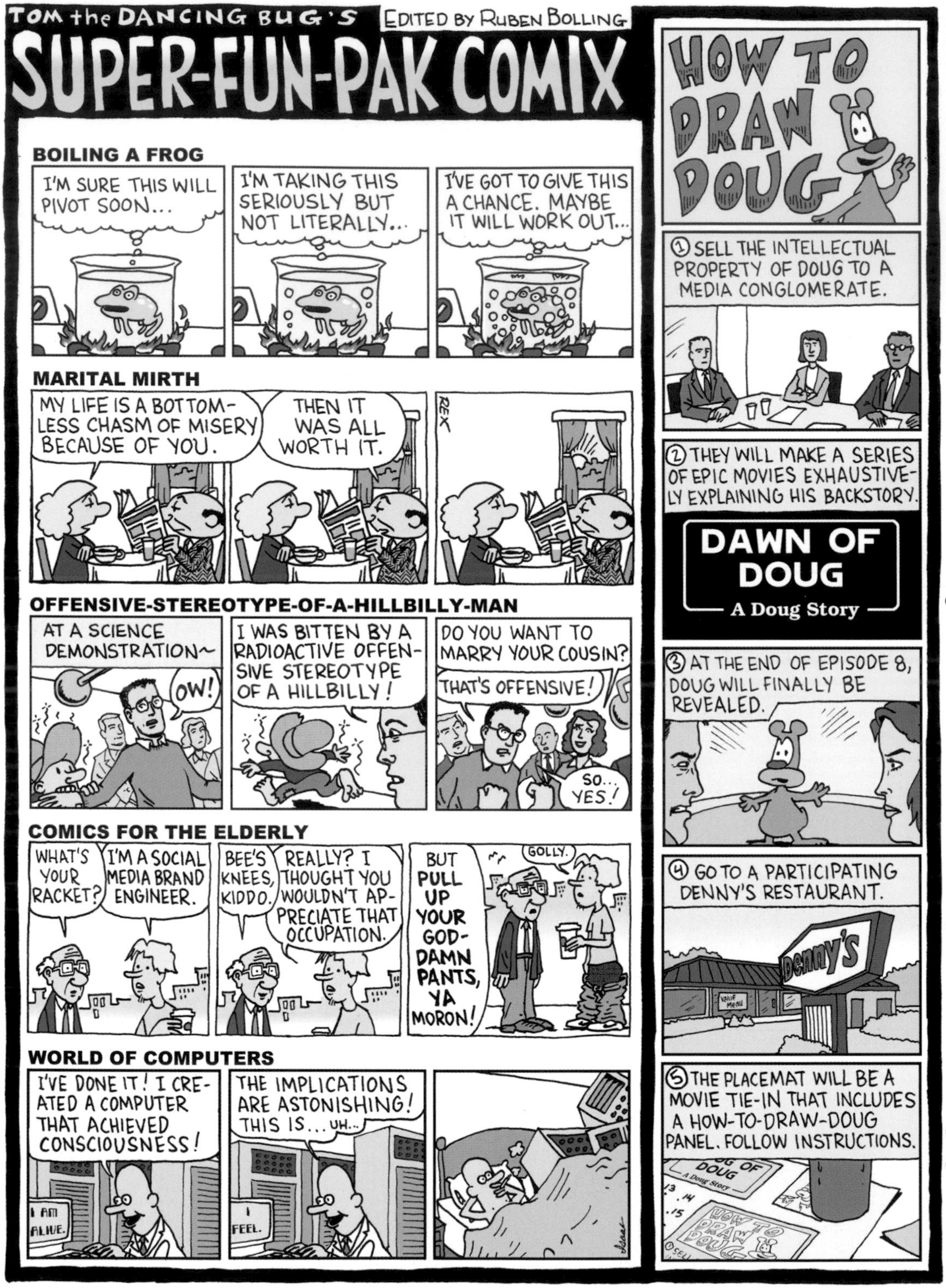
TOM the DANCING BUG'S
EDITED BY RUBEN BOLLING
SUPER-FUN-PAK COMIX
BOILING A FROG
I'M SURE THIS WILL PIVOT SOON...
I'M TAKING THIS SERIOUSLY BUT NOT LITERALLY...
I'VE GOT TO GIVE THIS A CHANCE. MAYBE IT WILL WORK OUT...
MARITAL MIRTH
MY LIFE IS A BOTTOM-LESS CHASM OF MISERY BECAUSE OF YOU.
THEN IT WAS ALL WORTH IT.
REX
OFFENSIVE-STEREOTYPE-OF-A-HILLBILLY-MAN
AT A SCIENCE DEMONSTRATION~
OW!
I WAS BITTEN BY A RADIOACTIVE OFFEN-SIVE STEREOTYPE OF A HILLBILLY!
DO YOU WANT TO MARRY YOUR COUSIN?
THAT'S OFFENSIVE!
SO... YES!
COMICS FOR THE ELDERLY
WHAT'S YOUR RACKET?
I'M A SOCIAL MEDIA BRAND ENGINEER.
BEE'S KNEES, KIDDO.
REALLY? I THOUGHT YOU WOULDN'T AP-PRECIATE THAT OCCUPATION.
BUT PULL UP YOUR GOD-DAMN PANTS, YA MORON!
GOLLY.
WORLD OF COMPUTERS
I'VE DONE IT! I CRE-ATED A COMPUTER THAT ACHIEVED CONSCIOUSNESS!
I AM ALIVE.
THE IMPLICATIONS ARE ASTONISHING! THIS IS... UH...
I FEEL.
HOW TO DRAW DOUG
① SELL THE INTELLECTUAL PROPERTY OF DOUG TO A MEDIA CONGLOMERATE.
② THEY WILL MAKE A SERIES OF EPIC MOVIES EXHAUSTIVE-LY EXPLAINING HIS BACKSTORY.
DAWN OF DOUG
A Doug Story
③ AT THE END OF EPISODE 8, DOUG WILL FINALLY BE REVEALED.
④ GO TO A PARTICIPATING DENNY'S RESTAURANT.
Denny's
⑤ THE PLACEMAT WILL BE A MOVIE TIE-IN THAT INCLUDES A HOW-TO-DRAW-DOUG PANEL. FOLLOW INSTRUCTIONS.
HOW TO DRAW DOUG

1/2/17

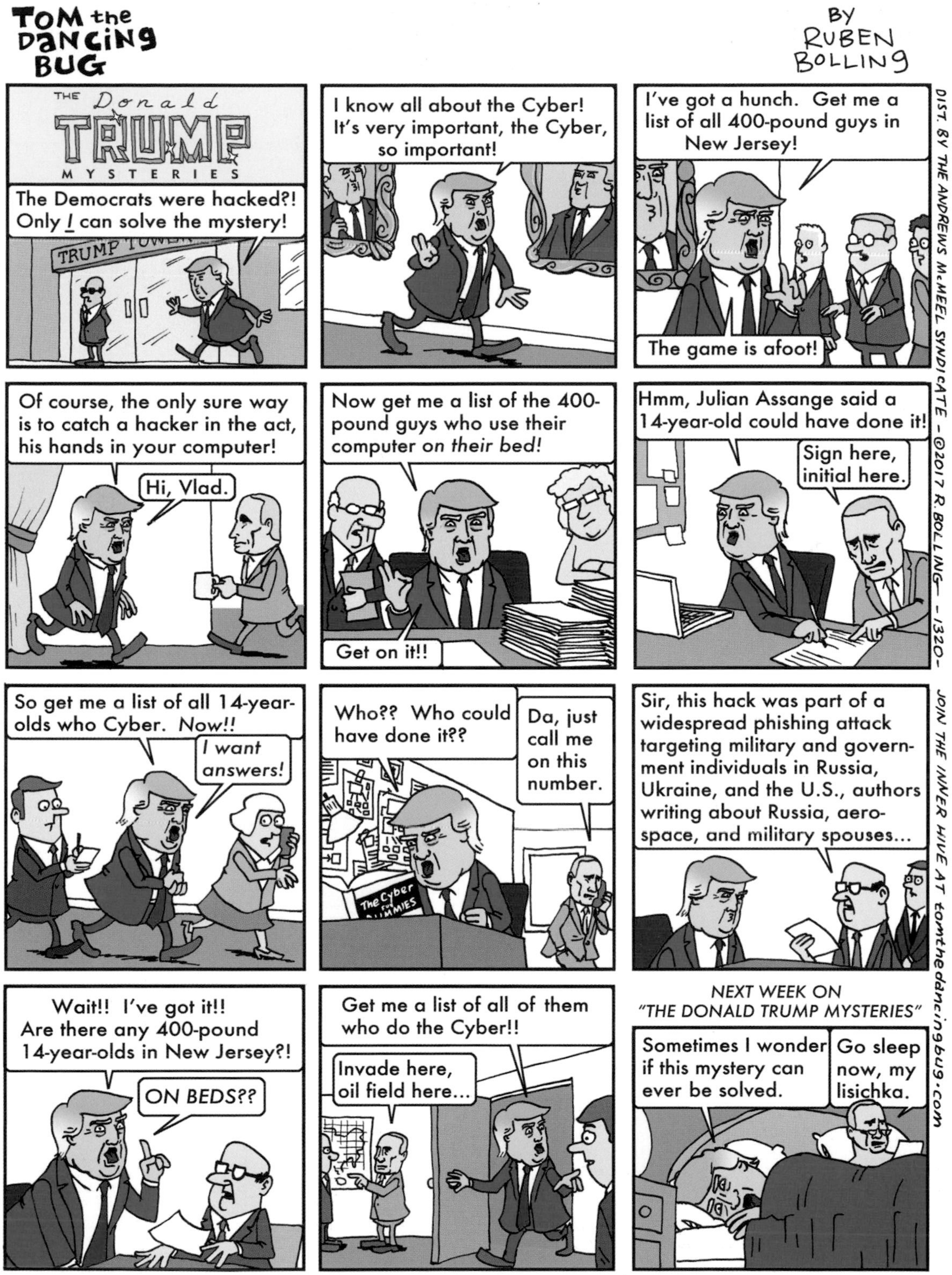
TOM the DANCING BUG
BY RUBEN BOLLING
THE Donald TRUMP MYSTERIES
The Democrats were hacked?! Only *I* can solve the mystery!
TRUMP TOWER
I know all about the Cyber! It's very important, the Cyber, so important!
I've got a hunch. Get me a list of all 400-pound guys in New Jersey!
The game is afoot!
Of course, the only sure way is to catch a hacker in the act, his hands in your computer!
Hi, Vlad.
Now get me a list of the 400-pound guys who use their computer *on their bed!*
Get on it!!
Hmm, Julian Assange said a 14-year-old could have done it!
Sign here, initial here.
So get me a list of all 14-year-olds who Cyber. *Now!!*
I want answers!
Who?? Who could have done it??
Da, just call me on this number.
Sir, this hack was part of a widespread phishing attack targeting military and government individuals in Russia, Ukraine, and the U.S., authors writing about Russia, aerospace, and military spouses...
Wait!! I've got it!! Are there any 400-pound 14-year-olds in New Jersey?!
ON BEDS??
Get me a list of all of them who do the Cyber!!
Invade here, oil field here...
NEXT WEEK ON "THE DONALD TRUMP MYSTERIES"
Sometimes I wonder if this mystery can ever be solved.
Go sleep now, my lisichka.
DIST. BY THE ANDREWS McMEEL SYNDICATE - ©2017 R. BOLLING - 1320-
JOIN THE INNER HIVE AT tomthedancingbug.com

1/9/17

TOM the DANCING BUG

by RUBEN BOLLING

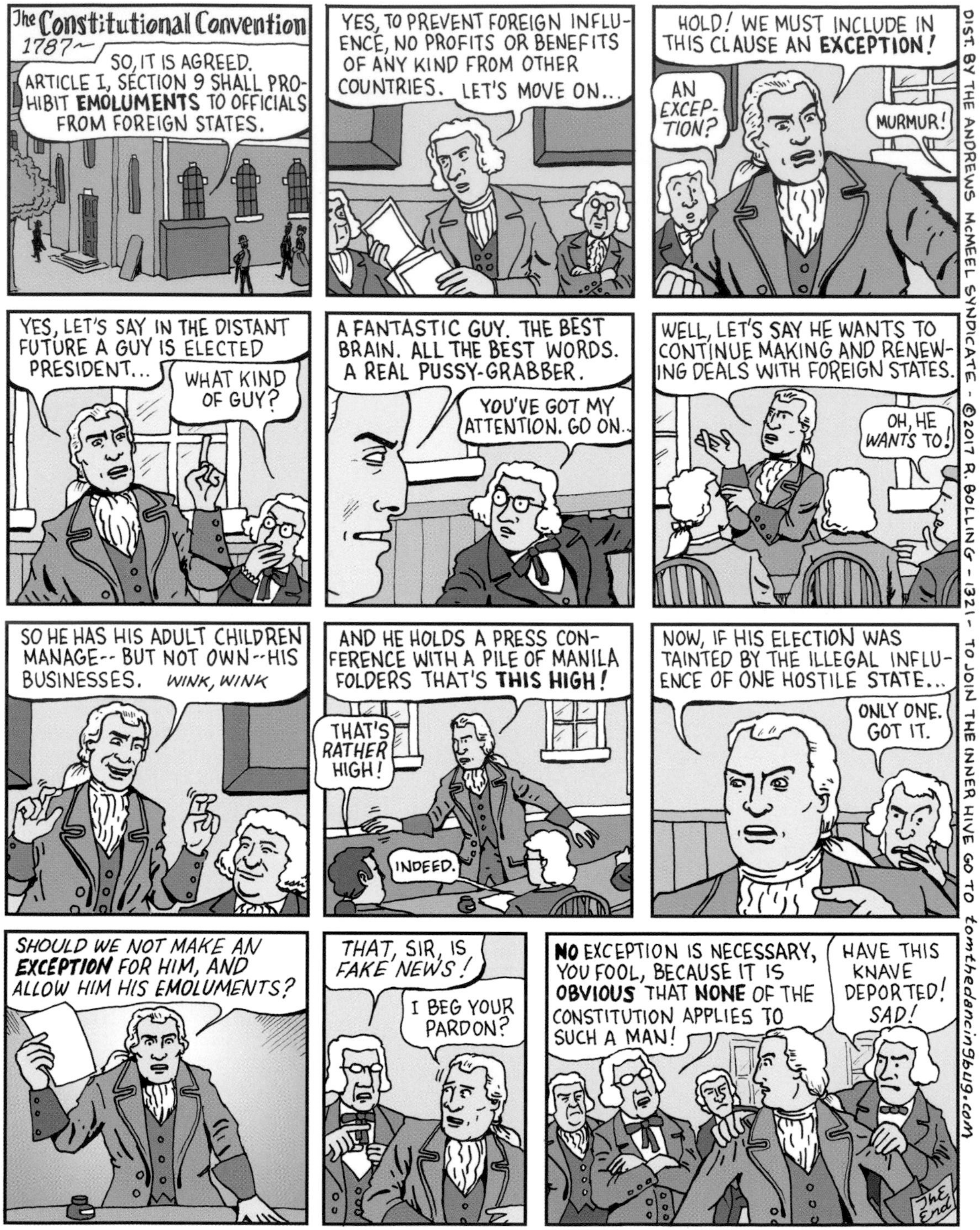

The Constitutional Convention 1787~
SO, IT IS AGREED. ARTICLE I, SECTION 9 SHALL PROHIBIT EMOLUMENTS TO OFFICIALS FROM FOREIGN STATES.
YES, TO PREVENT FOREIGN INFLUENCE, NO PROFITS OR BENEFITS OF ANY KIND FROM OTHER COUNTRIES. LET'S MOVE ON...
HOLD! WE MUST INCLUDE IN THIS CLAUSE AN EXCEPTION!
AN EXCEPTION?
MURMUR!
YES, LET'S SAY IN THE DISTANT FUTURE A GUY IS ELECTED PRESIDENT...
WHAT KIND OF GUY?
A FANTASTIC GUY. THE BEST BRAIN. ALL THE BEST WORDS. A REAL PUSSY-GRABBER.
YOU'VE GOT MY ATTENTION. GO ON..
WELL, LET'S SAY HE WANTS TO CONTINUE MAKING AND RENEWING DEALS WITH FOREIGN STATES.
OH, HE WANTS TO!
SO HE HAS HIS ADULT CHILDREN MANAGE-- BUT NOT OWN--HIS BUSINESSES. WINK, WINK
AND HE HOLDS A PRESS CONFERENCE WITH A PILE OF MANILA FOLDERS THAT'S THIS HIGH!
THAT'S RATHER HIGH!
INDEED.
NOW, IF HIS ELECTION WAS TAINTED BY THE ILLEGAL INFLUENCE OF ONE HOSTILE STATE...
ONLY ONE. GOT IT.
SHOULD WE NOT MAKE AN EXCEPTION FOR HIM, AND ALLOW HIM HIS EMOLUMENTS?
THAT, SIR, IS FAKE NEWS!
I BEG YOUR PARDON?
NO EXCEPTION IS NECESSARY, YOU FOOL, BECAUSE IT IS OBVIOUS THAT NONE OF THE CONSTITUTION APPLIES TO SUCH A MAN!
HAVE THIS KNAVE DEPORTED! SAD!
THE End
DIST. BY THE ANDREWS MCMEEL SYNDICATE - ©2017 R. BOLLING - 1321 - TO JOIN THE INNER HIVE GO TO tomthedancingbug.com

1/16/17

TOM the DANCING BUG

by RUBEN BOLLING

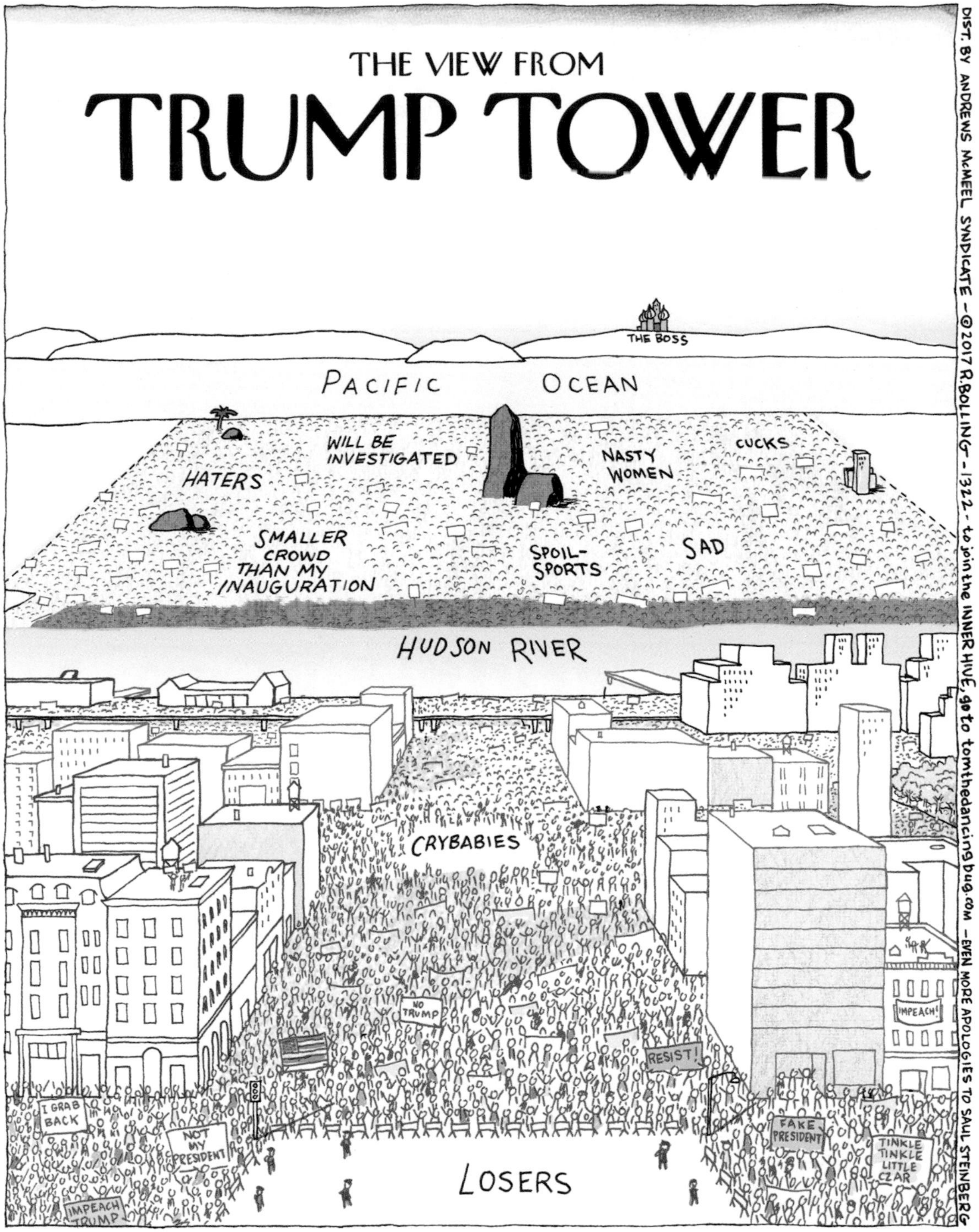
THE VIEW FROM
TRUMP TOWER
THE BOSS
PACIFIC OCEAN
WILL BE INVESTIGATED
CUCKS
NASTY WOMEN
HATERS
SMALLER CROWD THAN MY INAUGURATION
SPOIL-SPORTS
SAD
HUDSON RIVER
CRYBABIES
NO TRUMP
RESIST!
IMPEACH!
I GRAB BACK
NOT MY PRESIDENT
FAKE PRESIDENT
TINKLE TINKLE LITTLE CZAR
LOSERS
IMPEACH TRUMP
DIST. BY ANDREWS McMEEL SYNDICATE –©2017 R.BOLLING – 1322 – to join the INNER HIVE, go to tomthedancingbug.com – EVEN MORE APOLOGIES TO SAUL STEINBERG

1/23/17

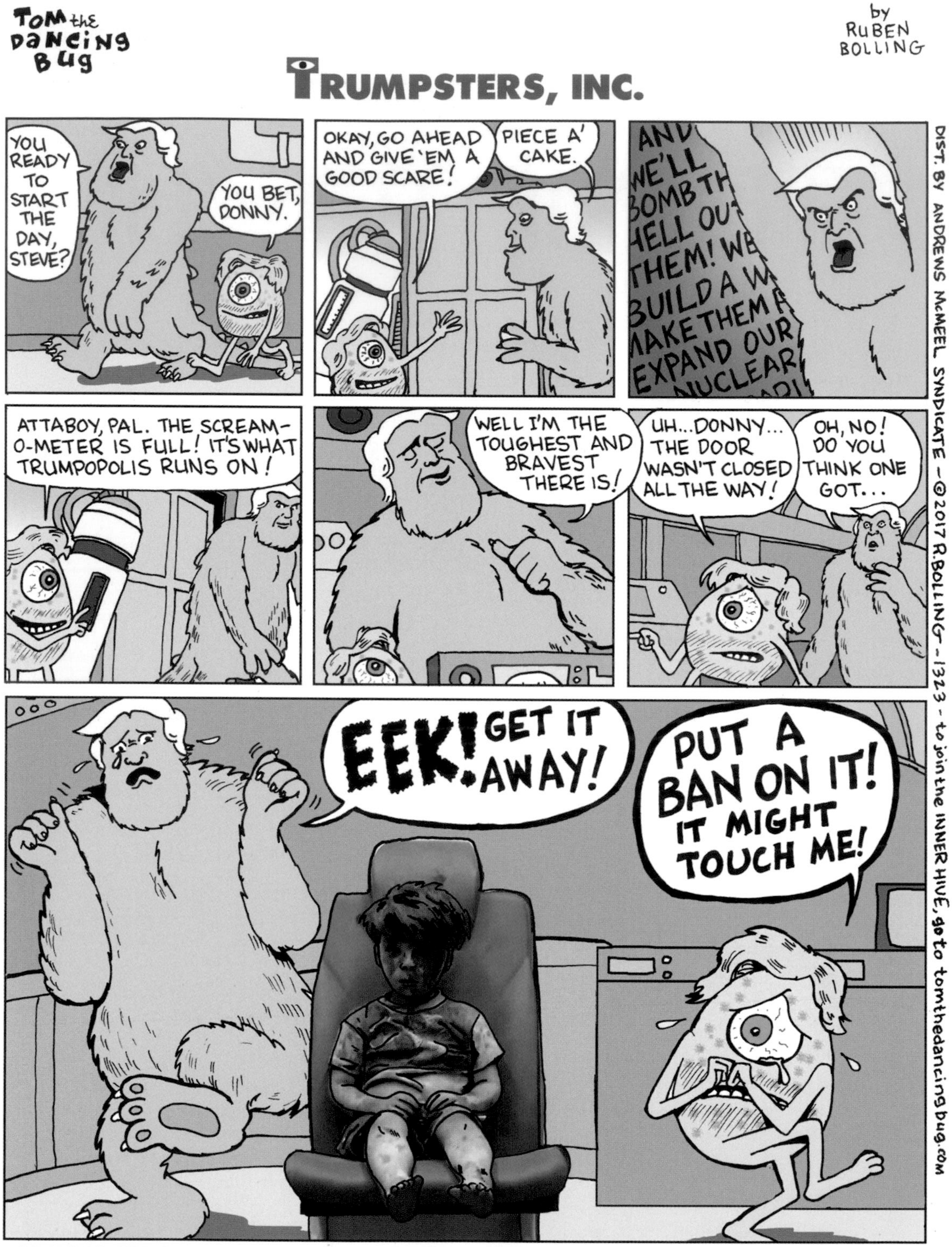
TOM the DANCING BUG
by RUBEN BOLLING
TRUMPSTERS, INC.
YOU READY TO START THE DAY, STEVE?
YOU BET, DONNY.
OKAY, GO AHEAD AND GIVE 'EM A GOOD SCARE!
PIECE A' CAKE.
AND WE'LL BOMB TH HELL OU THEM! WE BUILD A W MAKE THEM EXPAND OUR NUCLEAR
ATTABOY, PAL. THE SCREAM-O-METER IS FULL! IT'S WHAT TRUMPOPOLIS RUNS ON!
WELL I'M THE TOUGHEST AND BRAVEST THERE IS!
UH...DONNY... THE DOOR WASN'T CLOSED ALL THE WAY!
OH, NO! DO YOU THINK ONE GOT...
EEK! GET IT AWAY!
PUT A BAN ON IT! IT MIGHT TOUCH ME!
DIST. BY ANDREWS McMEEL SYNDICATE -©2017 R.BOLLING - 1323 - to join the INNER HIVE, go to tomthedancingbug.com

COMING THIS WINTER... AND SPRING... AND SUMMER... AND ON AND ON....

1/30/17

TOM the DANCING BUG

by RUBEN BOLLING

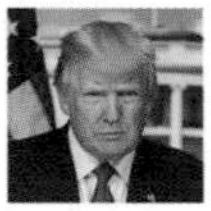

A LEAFLET FROM THE TRUMP ADMINISTRATION

Illegals Pose Public Safety Threat

Those who defy our immigration laws are a dangerous menace, committing other crimes that harm and kill Americans.

As a public service, the Trump administration is proudly publishing periodic lists of horrible crimes committed by those involved in breaking immigration laws. This is the first of many installments to come.

TYSON FOODS, INC.

Hired illegal immigrants

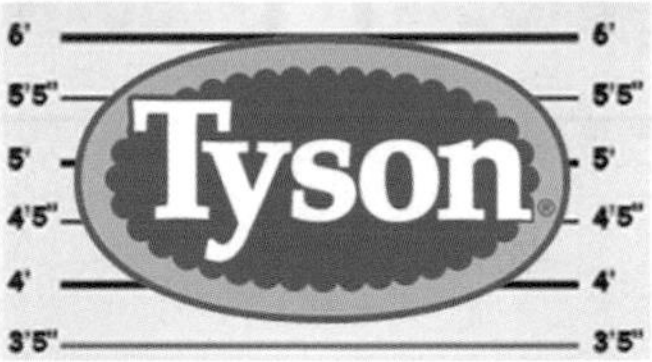
Tyson

OTHER CRIMES:

Criminal penalties for bribery, environmental crimes, workplace violations that led to death

WAL-MART STORES, INC.

Used contractor who hired illegal immigrants

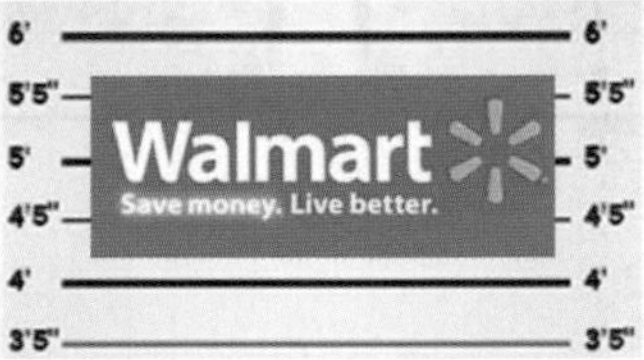
Walmart
Save money. Live better.

OTHER CRIMES:

Multiple environmental crimes

EXXONMOBIL CORP.

Fuel depot shut down after illegal immigrants found cleaning up hazardous materials

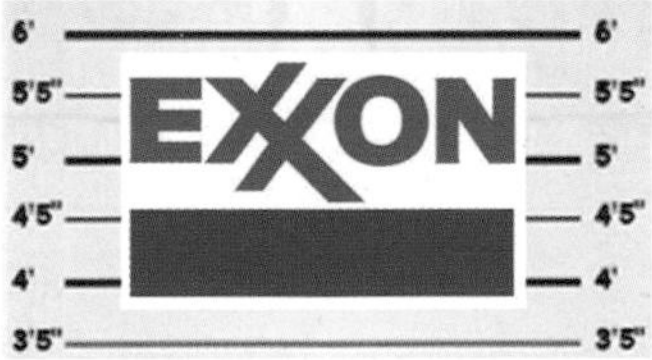
EXXON

OTHER CRIMES:

Decades-long environmental crime spree; criminal penalties for massive oil spills, Clean Water and Clean Air Act violations

DONALD J. TRUMP

Conspired to hire illegal immigrants on a building project

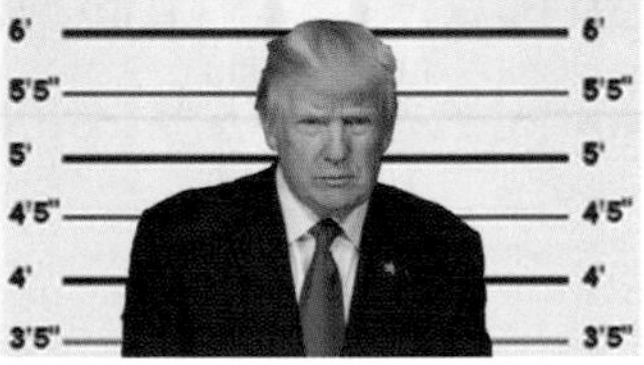

OTHER CRIMES:

Multiple fines for breaking casino operation rules; admitted to sexual assaults; Foundation fine for self-dealing; FTC fine for antitrust violation; multiple violations of the United States Constitution (cont'd on other side...)

We must ship these criminals out of the country and Make America Great Again!

2/6/17

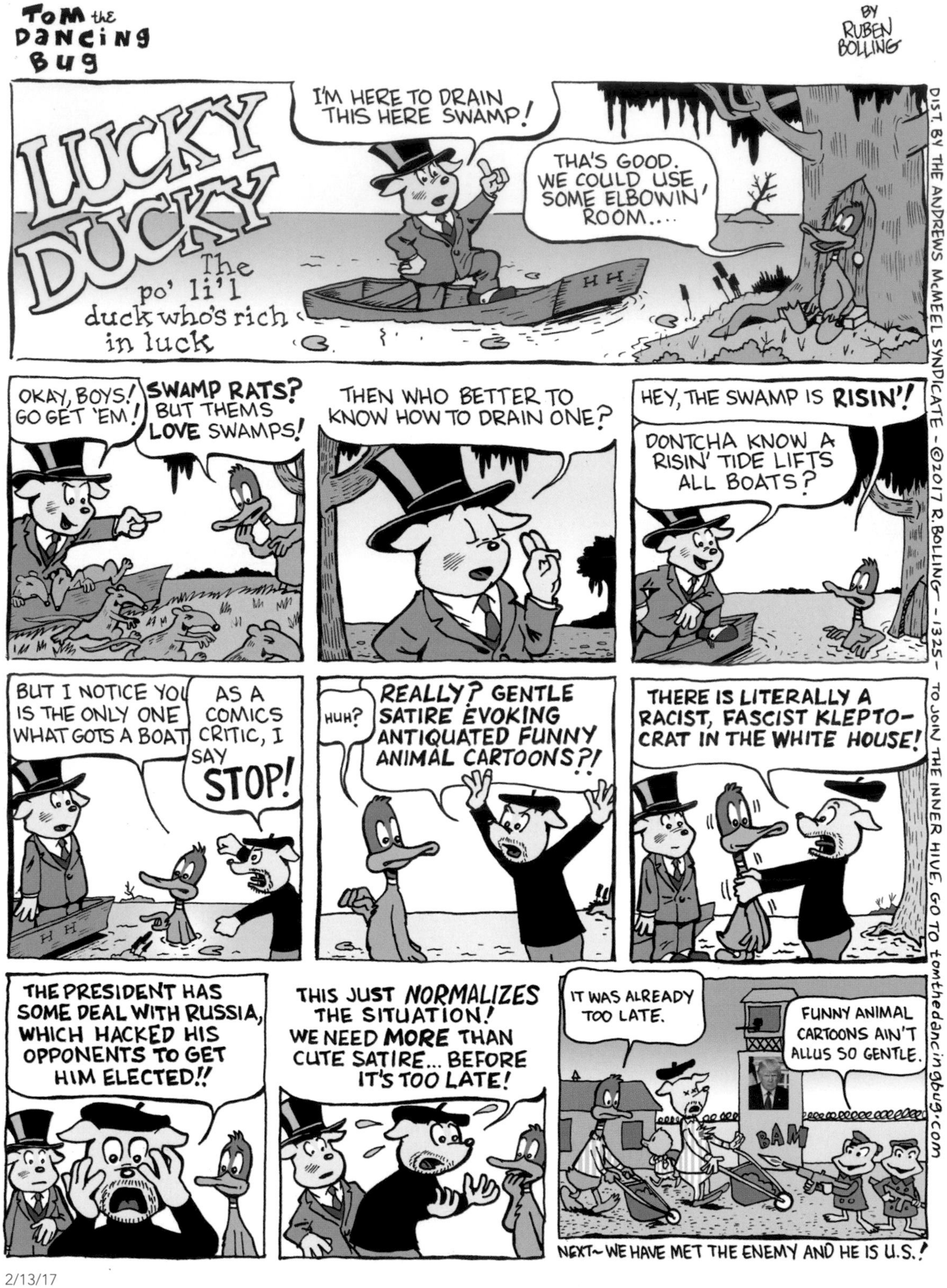
TOM the DANCING BUG
BY RUBEN BOLLING
LUCKY DUCKY
The po' li'l duck who's rich in luck
I'M HERE TO DRAIN THIS HERE SWAMP!
THA'S GOOD. WE COULD USE SOME ELBOWIN' ROOM....
H H
OKAY, BOYS! GO GET 'EM!
SWAMP RATS? BUT THEMS LOVE SWAMPS!
THEN WHO BETTER TO KNOW HOW TO DRAIN ONE?
HEY, THE SWAMP IS RISIN'!
DONTCHA KNOW A RISIN' TIDE LIFTS ALL BOATS?
BUT I NOTICE YOU IS THE ONLY ONE WHAT GOTS A BOAT
AS A COMICS CRITIC, I SAY STOP!
HUH?
REALLY? GENTLE SATIRE EVOKING ANTIQUATED FUNNY ANIMAL CARTOONS?!
THERE IS LITERALLY A RACIST, FASCIST KLEPTOCRAT IN THE WHITE HOUSE!
THE PRESIDENT HAS SOME DEAL WITH RUSSIA, WHICH HACKED HIS OPPONENTS TO GET HIM ELECTED!!
THIS JUST NORMALIZES THE SITUATION! WE NEED MORE THAN CUTE SATIRE... BEFORE IT'S TOO LATE!
IT WAS ALREADY TOO LATE.
FUNNY ANIMAL CARTOONS AIN'T ALLUS SO GENTLE.
BAM
NEXT~ WE HAVE MET THE ENEMY AND HE IS U.S.!
DIST. BY THE ANDREWS McMEEL SYNDICATE - ©2017 R. BOLLING - 1325 - TO JOIN THE INNER HIVE, GO TO tomthedancingbug.com

2/13/17

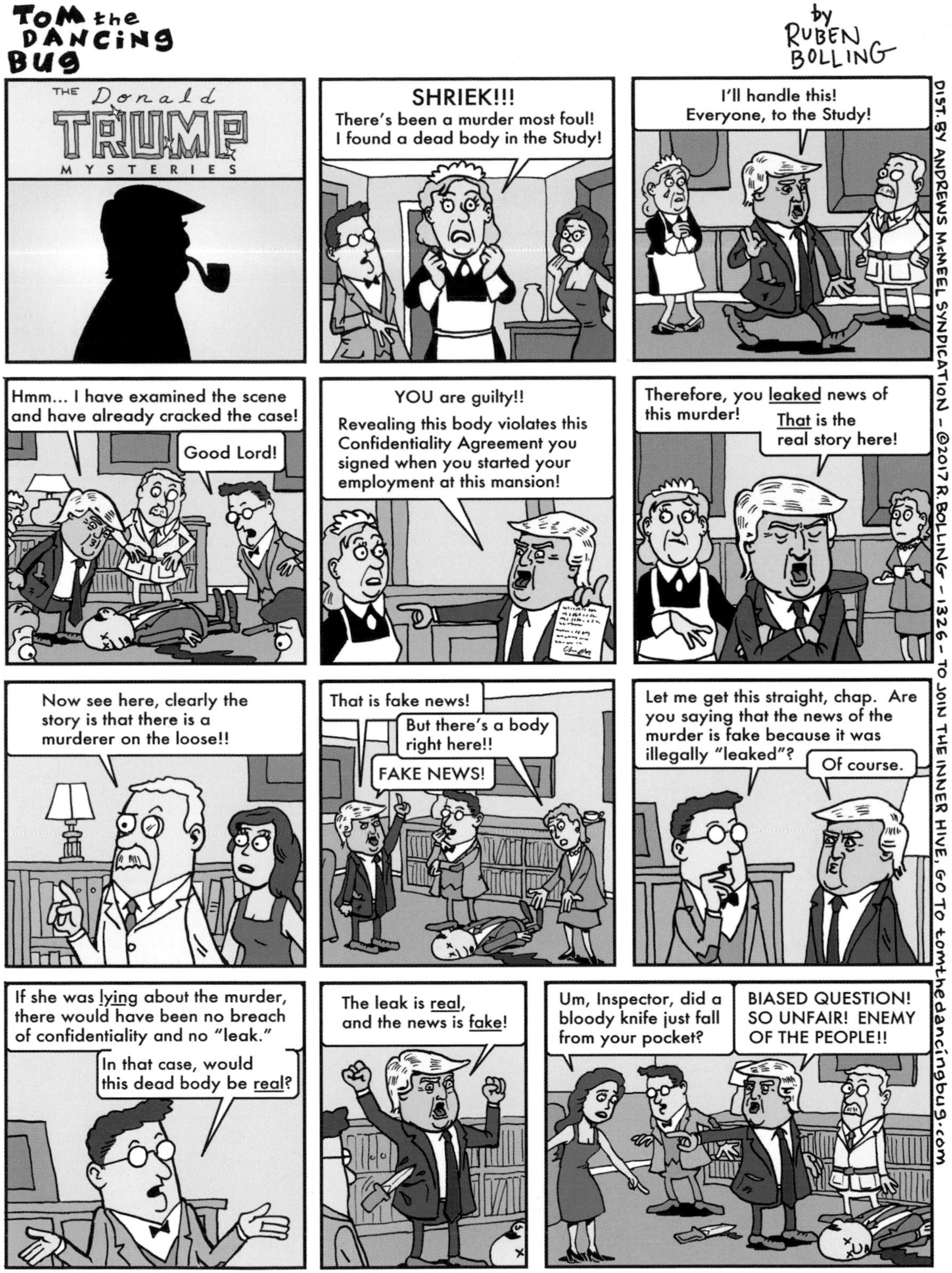
TOM the DANCING BUG
by RUBEN BOLLING
THE Donald TRUMP MYSTERIES
SHRIEK!!!
There's been a murder most foul! I found a dead body in the Study!
I'll handle this! Everyone, to the Study!
Hmm... I have examined the scene and have already cracked the case!
Good Lord!
YOU are guilty!!
Revealing this body violates this Confidentiality Agreement you signed when you started your employment at this mansion!
Therefore, you leaked news of this murder!
That is the real story here!
Now see here, clearly the story is that there is a murderer on the loose!!
That is fake news!
But there's a body right here!!
FAKE NEWS!
Let me get this straight, chap. Are you saying that the news of the murder is fake because it was illegally "leaked"?
Of course.
If she was lying about the murder, there would have been no breach of confidentiality and no "leak."
In that case, would this dead body be real?
The leak is real, and the news is fake!
Um, Inspector, did a bloody knife just fall from your pocket?
BIASED QUESTION! SO UNFAIR! ENEMY OF THE PEOPLE!!
DIST. BY ANDREWS McMEEL SYNDICATION – ©2017 R. BOLLING – 1326 – TO JOIN THE INNER HIVE, GO TO tomthedancingbug.com

2/20/17

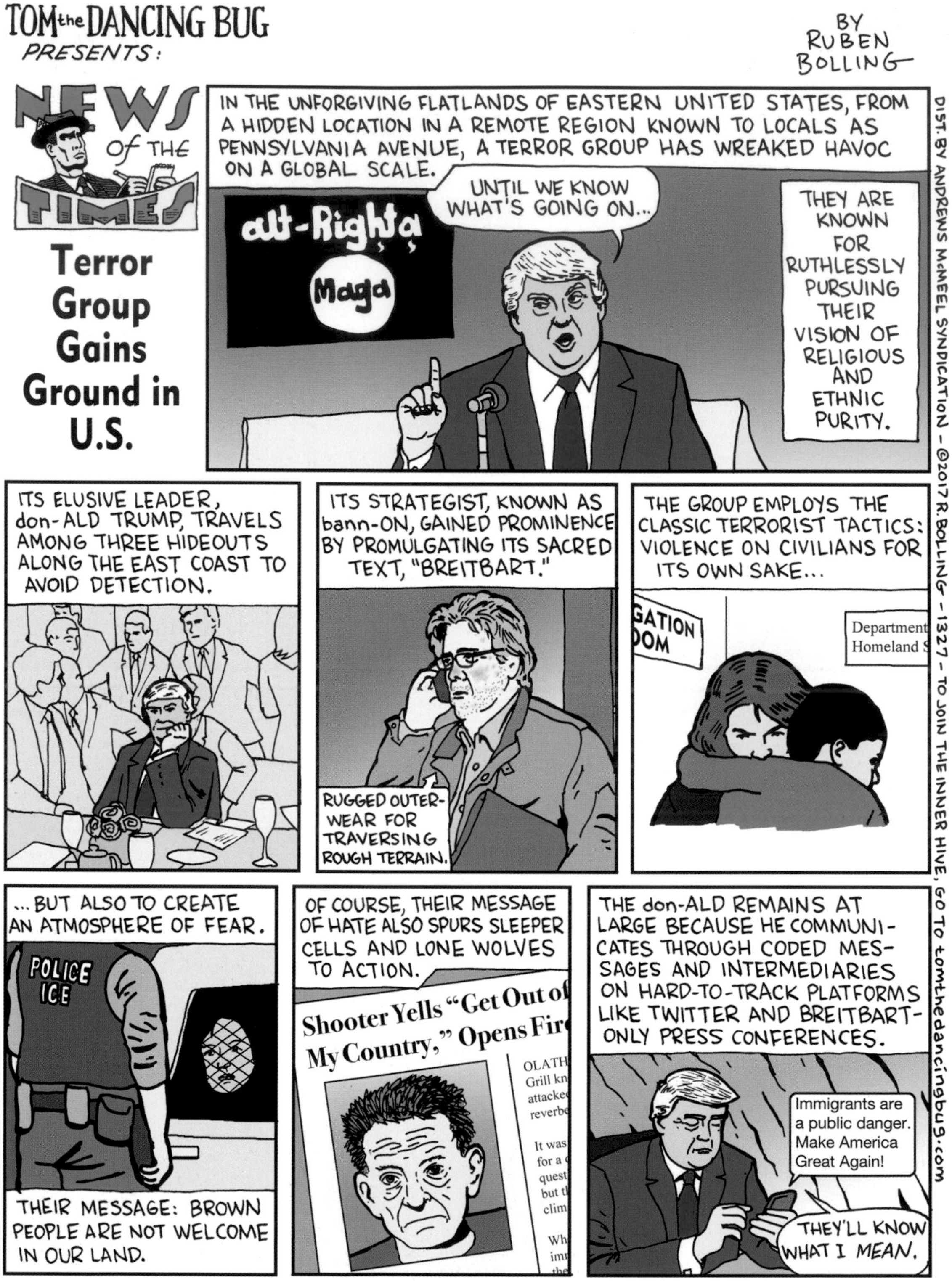
TOM the DANCING BUG
PRESENTS:
BY RUBEN BOLLING
NEWS of THE TIMES
Terror Group Gains Ground in U.S.
IN THE UNFORGIVING FLATLANDS OF EASTERN UNITED STATES, FROM A HIDDEN LOCATION IN A REMOTE REGION KNOWN TO LOCALS AS PENNSYLVANIA AVENUE, A TERROR GROUP HAS WREAKED HAVOC ON A GLOBAL SCALE.
alt-Right'a
Maga
UNTIL WE KNOW WHAT'S GOING ON...
THEY ARE KNOWN FOR RUTHLESSLY PURSUING THEIR VISION OF RELIGIOUS AND ETHNIC PURITY.
ITS ELUSIVE LEADER, don-ALD TRUMP, TRAVELS AMONG THREE HIDEOUTS ALONG THE EAST COAST TO AVOID DETECTION.
ITS STRATEGIST, KNOWN AS bann-ON, GAINED PROMINENCE BY PROMULGATING ITS SACRED TEXT, "BREITBART."
RUGGED OUTER-WEAR FOR TRAVERSING ROUGH TERRAIN.
THE GROUP EMPLOYS THE CLASSIC TERRORIST TACTICS: VIOLENCE ON CIVILIANS FOR ITS OWN SAKE...
GATION
OOM
Department
Homeland S
...BUT ALSO TO CREATE AN ATMOSPHERE OF FEAR.
POLICE ICE
THEIR MESSAGE: BROWN PEOPLE ARE NOT WELCOME IN OUR LAND.
OF COURSE, THEIR MESSAGE OF HATE ALSO SPURS SLEEPER CELLS AND LONE WOLVES TO ACTION.
Shooter Yells "Get Out of My Country," Opens Fir
THE don-ALD REMAINS AT LARGE BECAUSE HE COMMUNICATES THROUGH CODED MESSAGES AND INTERMEDIARIES ON HARD-TO-TRACK PLATFORMS LIKE TWITTER AND BREITBART-ONLY PRESS CONFERENCES.
Immigrants are a public danger. Make America Great Again!
THEY'LL KNOW WHAT I MEAN.
DIST. BY ANDREWS McMEEL SYNDICATION – ©2017 R. BOLLING – 1327 – TO JOIN THE INNER HIVE, GO TO tomthedancingbug.com

2/27/17

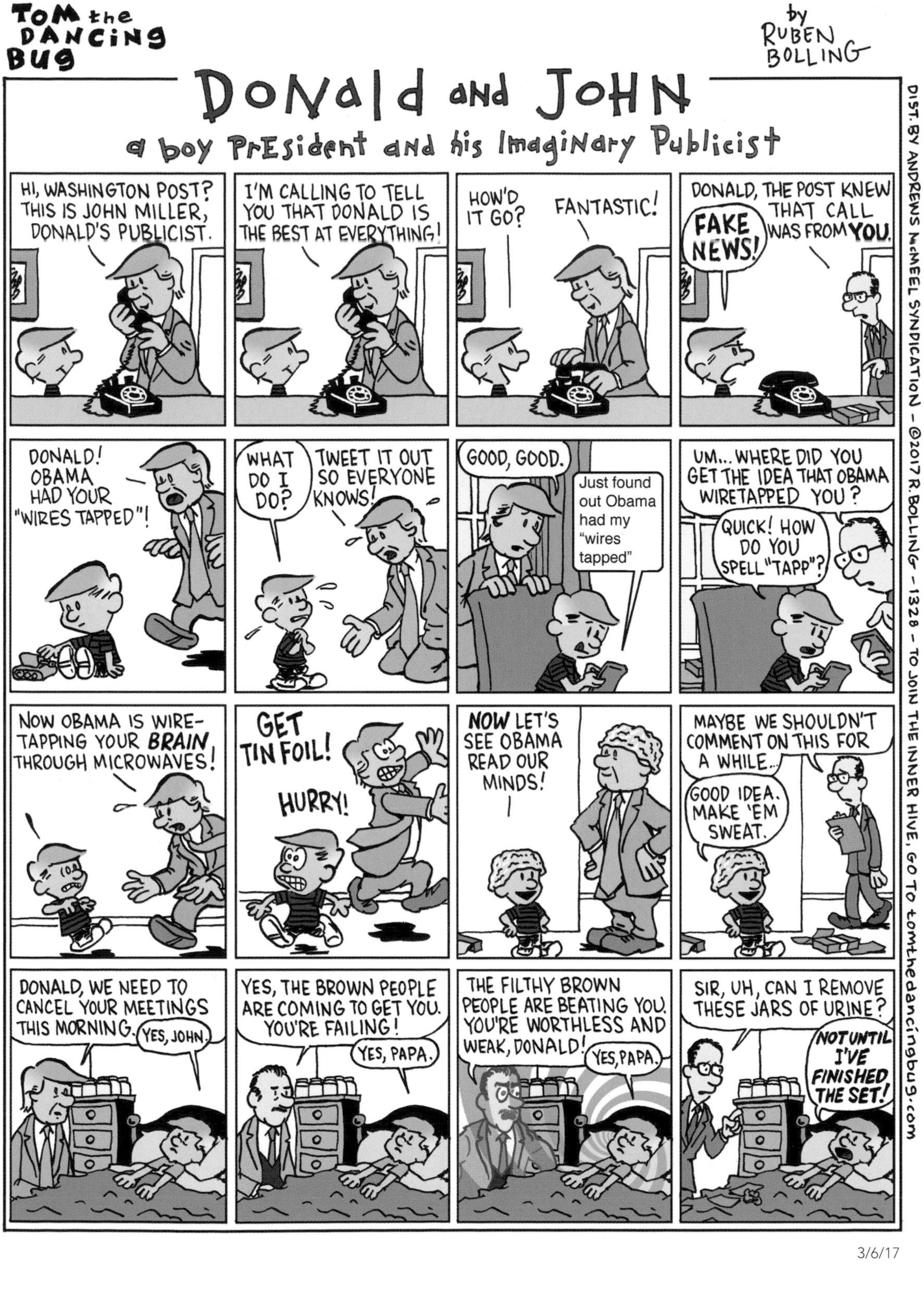
TOM the DANCING BUG
by RUBEN BOLLING
DONALD and JOHN
a boy President and his Imaginary Publicist
HI, WASHINGTON POST? THIS IS JOHN MILLER, DONALD'S PUBLICIST.
I'M CALLING TO TELL YOU THAT DONALD IS THE BEST AT EVERYTHING!
HOW'D IT GO?
FANTASTIC!
DONALD, THE POST KNEW THAT CALL WAS FROM YOU.
FAKE NEWS!
DONALD! OBAMA HAD YOUR "WIRES TAPPED"!
WHAT DO I DO?
TWEET IT OUT SO EVERYONE KNOWS!
GOOD, GOOD.
Just found out Obama had my "wires tapped"
UM... WHERE DID YOU GET THE IDEA THAT OBAMA WIRETAPPED YOU?
QUICK! HOW DO YOU SPELL "TAPP"?
NOW OBAMA IS WIRE-TAPPING YOUR BRAIN THROUGH MICROWAVES!
GET TIN FOIL!
HURRY!
NOW LET'S SEE OBAMA READ OUR MINDS!
MAYBE WE SHOULDN'T COMMENT ON THIS FOR A WHILE...
GOOD IDEA. MAKE 'EM SWEAT.
DONALD, WE NEED TO CANCEL YOUR MEETINGS THIS MORNING.
YES, JOHN.
YES, THE BROWN PEOPLE ARE COMING TO GET YOU. YOU'RE FAILING!
YES, PAPA.
THE FILTHY BROWN PEOPLE ARE BEATING YOU. YOU'RE WORTHLESS AND WEAK, DONALD!
YES, PAPA.
SIR, UH, CAN I REMOVE THESE JARS OF URINE?
NOT UNTIL I'VE FINISHED THE SET!
DIST. BY ANDREWS McMEEL SYNDICATION – ©2017 R. BOLLING – 1328 – TO JOIN THE INNER HIVE, GO TO tomthedancingbug.com

3/6/17

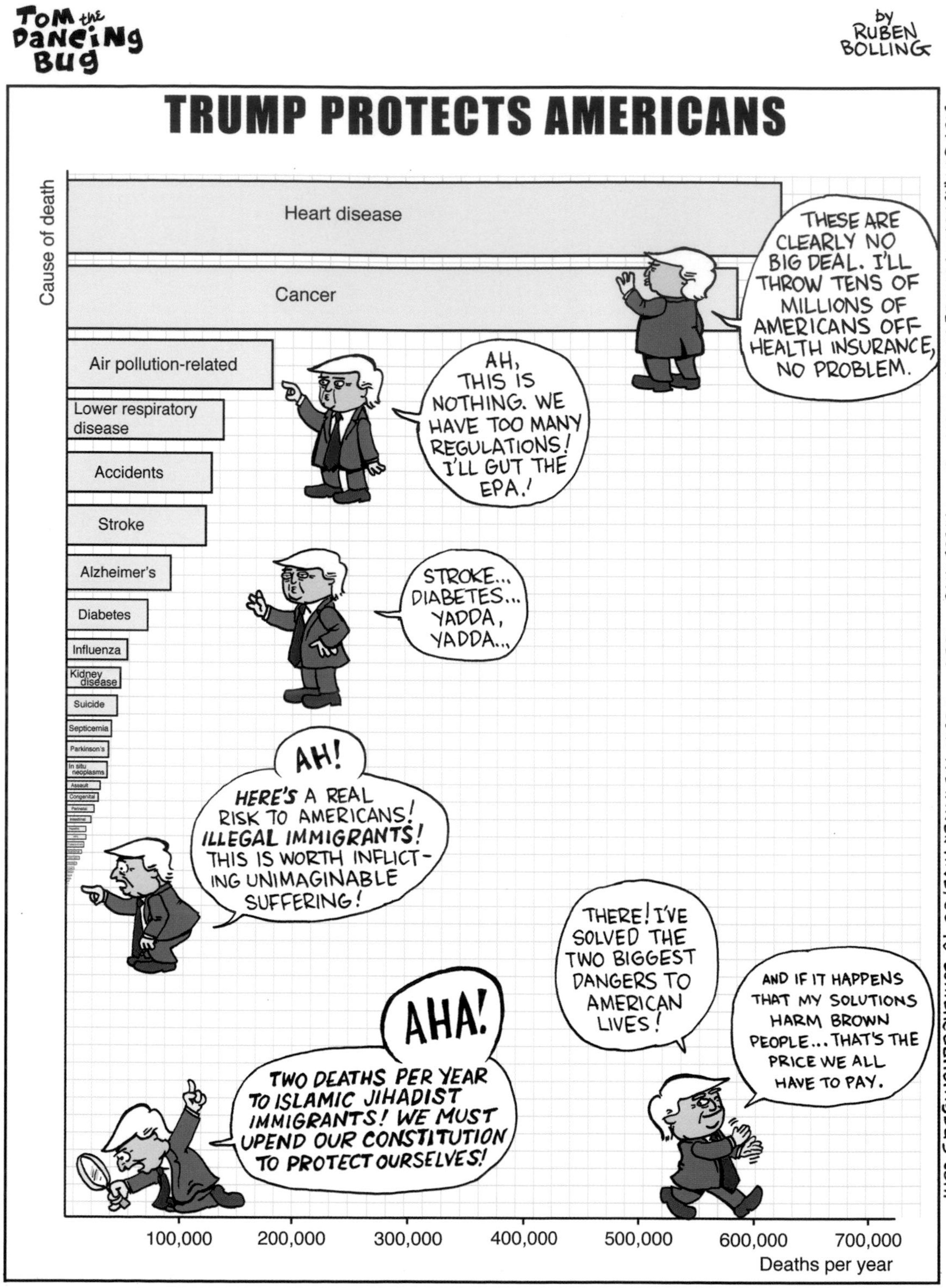

TOM the DANCING BUG
by RUBEN BOLLING
TRUMP PROTECTS AMERICANS
Cause of death
Heart disease
Cancer
Air pollution-related
Lower respiratory disease
Accidents
Stroke
Alzheimer's
Diabetes
Influenza
Kidney disease
Suicide
Septicemia
Parkinson's
In situ neoplasms
THESE ARE CLEARLY NO BIG DEAL. I'LL THROW TENS OF MILLIONS OF AMERICANS OFF HEALTH INSURANCE, NO PROBLEM.
AH, THIS IS NOTHING. WE HAVE TOO MANY REGULATIONS! I'LL GUT THE EPA!
STROKE... DIABETES... YADDA, YADDA...
AH!
HERE'S A REAL RISK TO AMERICANS! ILLEGAL IMMIGRANTS! THIS IS WORTH INFLICTING UNIMAGINABLE SUFFERING!
AHA!
TWO DEATHS PER YEAR TO ISLAMIC JIHADIST IMMIGRANTS! WE MUST UPEND OUR CONSTITUTION TO PROTECT OURSELVES!
THERE! I'VE SOLVED THE TWO BIGGEST DANGERS TO AMERICAN LIVES!
AND IF IT HAPPENS THAT MY SOLUTIONS HARM BROWN PEOPLE... THAT'S THE PRICE WE ALL HAVE TO PAY.
100,000
200,000
300,000
400,000
500,000
600,000
700,000
Deaths per year
DIST. BY ANDREWS McMEEL SYNDICATION - ©2017 R. BOLLING - 1329 - TO JOIN THE INNER HIVE, GO TO tomthedancingbug.com

3/13/17

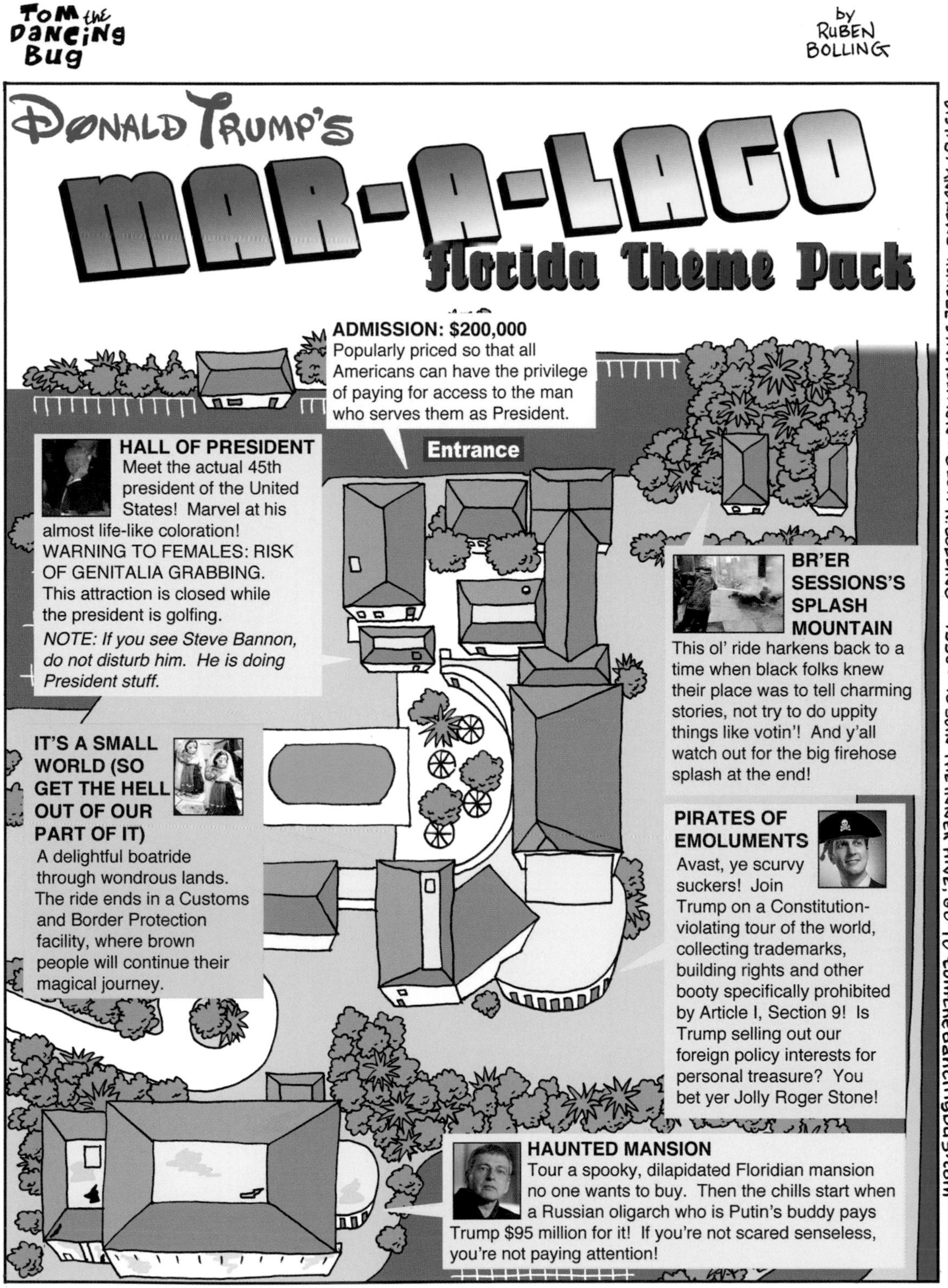
TOM the DANCING BUG
by RUBEN BOLLING
DONALD TRUMP'S
MAR-A-LAGO
Florida Theme Park
ADMISSION: $200,000
Popularly priced so that all Americans can have the privilege of paying for access to the man who serves them as President.
Entrance
HALL OF PRESIDENT
Meet the actual 45th president of the United States! Marvel at his almost life-like coloration! WARNING TO FEMALES: RISK OF GENITALIA GRABBING. This attraction is closed while the president is golfing.
NOTE: If you see Steve Bannon, do not disturb him. He is doing President stuff.
BR'ER SESSIONS'S SPLASH MOUNTAIN
This ol' ride harkens back to a time when black folks knew their place was to tell charming stories, not try to do uppity things like votin'! And y'all watch out for the big firehose splash at the end!
IT'S A SMALL WORLD (SO GET THE HELL OUT OF OUR PART OF IT)
A delightful boatride through wondrous lands. The ride ends in a Customs and Border Protection facility, where brown people will continue their magical journey.
PIRATES OF EMOLUMENTS
Avast, ye scurvy suckers! Join Trump on a Constitution-violating tour of the world, collecting trademarks, building rights and other booty specifically prohibited by Article I, Section 9! Is Trump selling out our foreign policy interests for personal treasure? You bet yer Jolly Roger Stone!
HAUNTED MANSION
Tour a spooky, dilapidated Floridian mansion no one wants to buy. Then the chills start when a Russian oligarch who is Putin's buddy pays Trump $95 million for it! If you're not scared senseless, you're not paying attention!
DIST. BY ANDREWS McMEEL SYNDICATION – ©2017 R. BOLLING – 1330 – TO JOIN THE INNER HIVE, GO TO tomthedancingbug.com

3/20/17

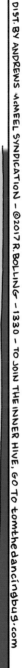

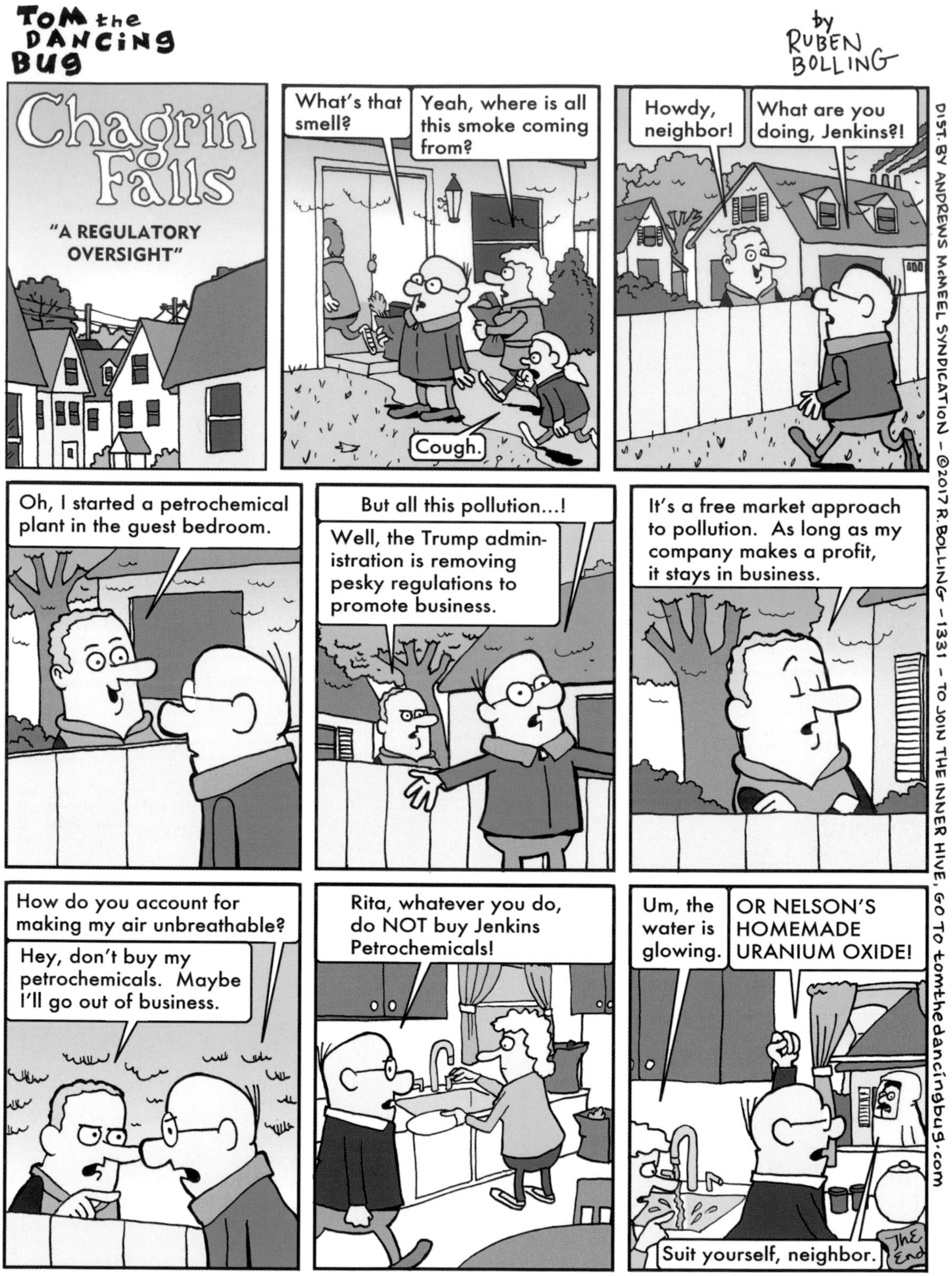
TOM the DANCING BUG
by RUBEN BOLLING
Chagrin Falls
"A REGULATORY OVERSIGHT"
What's that smell?
Yeah, where is all this smoke coming from?
Cough.
Howdy, neighbor!
What are you doing, Jenkins?!
Oh, I started a petrochemical plant in the guest bedroom.
But all this pollution...!
Well, the Trump administration is removing pesky regulations to promote business.
It's a free market approach to pollution. As long as my company makes a profit, it stays in business.
How do you account for making my air unbreathable?
Hey, don't buy my petrochemicals. Maybe I'll go out of business.
Rita, whatever you do, do NOT buy Jenkins Petrochemicals!
Um, the water is glowing.
OR NELSON'S HOMEMADE URANIUM OXIDE!
Suit yourself, neighbor.
The End
DIST. BY ANDREWS McMEEL SYNDICATION – ©2017 R. BOLLING – 1331 – TO JOIN THE INNER HIVE, GO TO tomthedancingbug.com

3/27/17

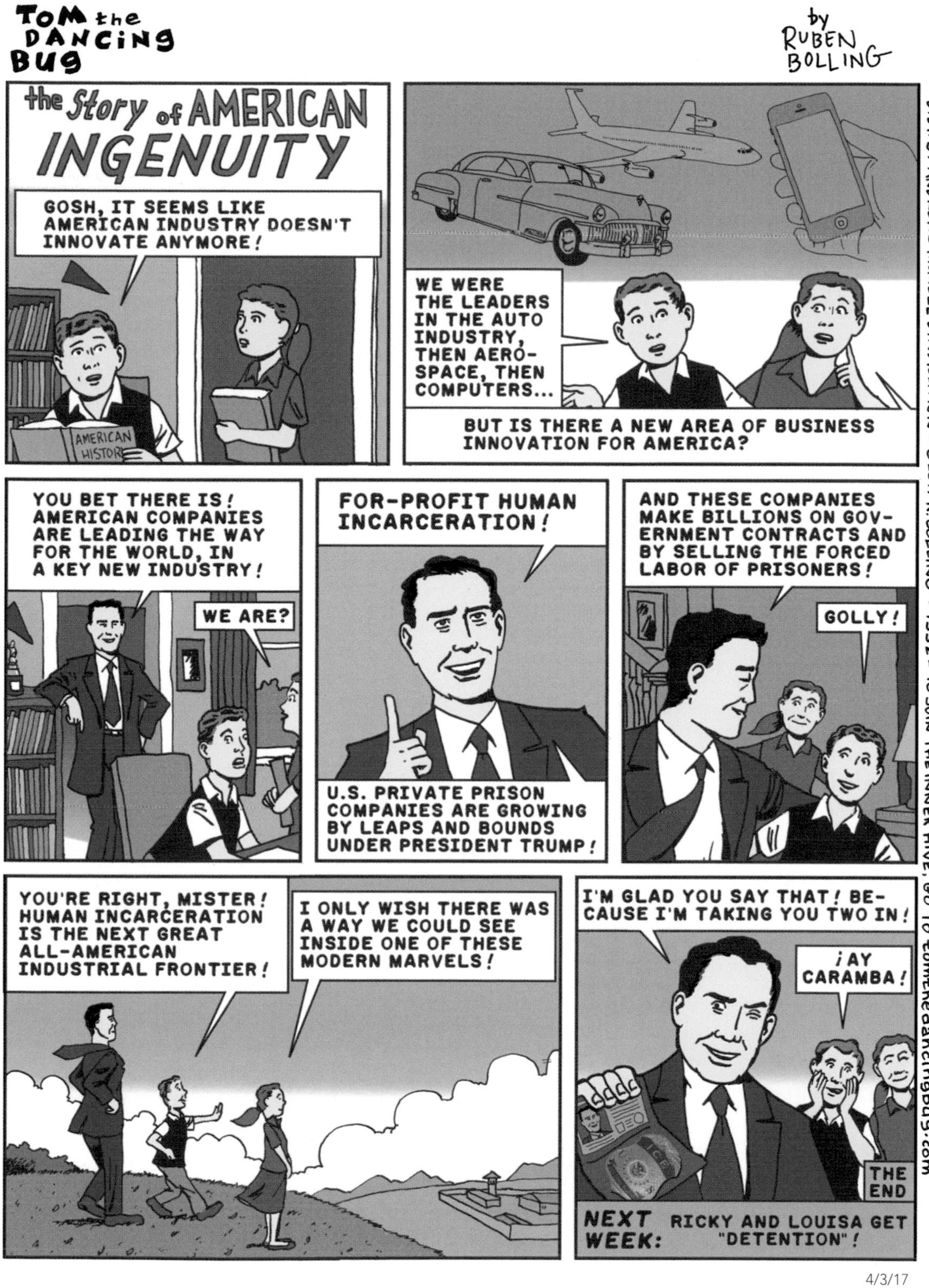
TOM the DANCING BUG
by RUBEN BOLLING
the Story of AMERICAN INGENUITY
GOSH, IT SEEMS LIKE AMERICAN INDUSTRY DOESN'T INNOVATE ANYMORE!
AMERICAN HISTORY
WE WERE THE LEADERS IN THE AUTO INDUSTRY, THEN AERO-SPACE, THEN COMPUTERS...
BUT IS THERE A NEW AREA OF BUSINESS INNOVATION FOR AMERICA?
YOU BET THERE IS! AMERICAN COMPANIES ARE LEADING THE WAY FOR THE WORLD, IN A KEY NEW INDUSTRY!
WE ARE?
FOR-PROFIT HUMAN INCARCERATION!
U.S. PRIVATE PRISON COMPANIES ARE GROWING BY LEAPS AND BOUNDS UNDER PRESIDENT TRUMP!
AND THESE COMPANIES MAKE BILLIONS ON GOV-ERNMENT CONTRACTS AND BY SELLING THE FORCED LABOR OF PRISONERS!
GOLLY!
YOU'RE RIGHT, MISTER! HUMAN INCARCERATION IS THE NEXT GREAT ALL-AMERICAN INDUSTRIAL FRONTIER!
I ONLY WISH THERE WAS A WAY WE COULD SEE INSIDE ONE OF THESE MODERN MARVELS!
I'M GLAD YOU SAY THAT! BE-CAUSE I'M TAKING YOU TWO IN!
¡AY CARAMBA!
ICE
THE END
NEXT WEEK: RICKY AND LOUISA GET "DETENTION"!
DIST. BY ANDREWS McMEEL SYNDICATION – ©2017 R. BOLLING – 1332 – TO JOIN THE INNER HIVE, GO TO tomthedancingbug.com

4/3/17

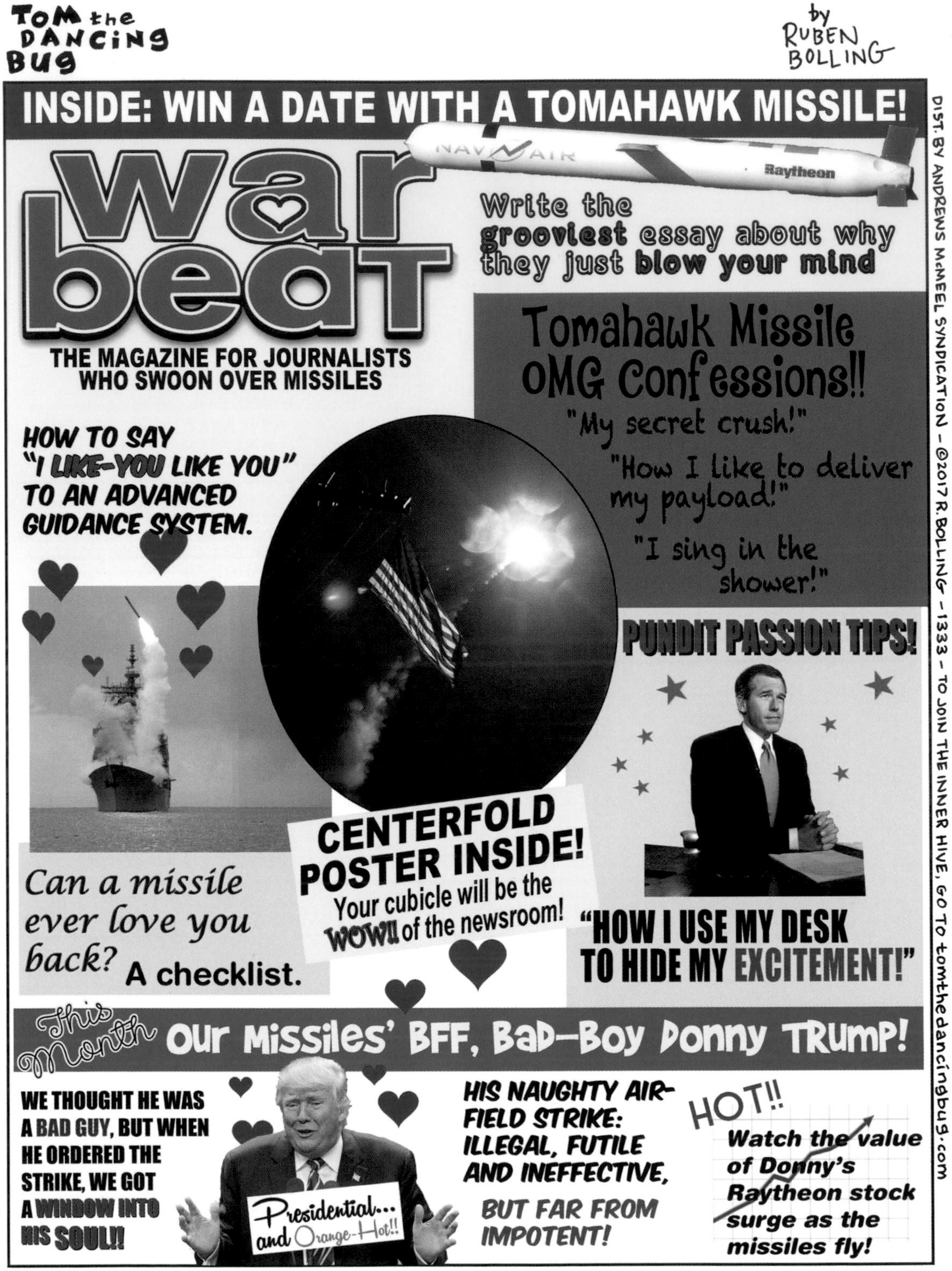
TOM the DANCING BUG
by RUBEN BOLLING
INSIDE: WIN A DATE WITH A TOMAHAWK MISSILE!
war beat
THE MAGAZINE FOR JOURNALISTS WHO SWOON OVER MISSILES
Write the groovlest essay about why they just blow your mind
Tomahawk Missile OMG Confessions!!
"My secret crush!"
"How I like to deliver my payload!"
"I sing in the shower!"
HOW TO SAY "I LIKE-YOU LIKE YOU" TO AN ADVANCED GUIDANCE SYSTEM.
PUNDIT PASSION TIPS!
Can a missile ever love you back? A checklist.
CENTERFOLD POSTER INSIDE! Your cubicle will be the WOW!! of the newsroom!
"HOW I USE MY DESK TO HIDE MY EXCITEMENT!"
This Month Our Missiles' BFF, Bad-Boy Donny TRUMP!
WE THOUGHT HE WAS A BAD GUY, BUT WHEN HE ORDERED THE STRIKE, WE GOT A WINDOW INTO HIS SOUL!!
Presidential... and Orange-Hot!!
HIS NAUGHTY AIR-FIELD STRIKE: ILLEGAL, FUTILE AND INEFFECTIVE, BUT FAR FROM IMPOTENT!
HOT!!
Watch the value of Donny's Raytheon stock surge as the missiles fly!
DIST. BY ANDREWS McMEEL SYNDICATION - ©2017 R. BOLLING - 1333 - TO JOIN THE INNER HIVE, GO TO tomthedancingbug.com

4/10/17

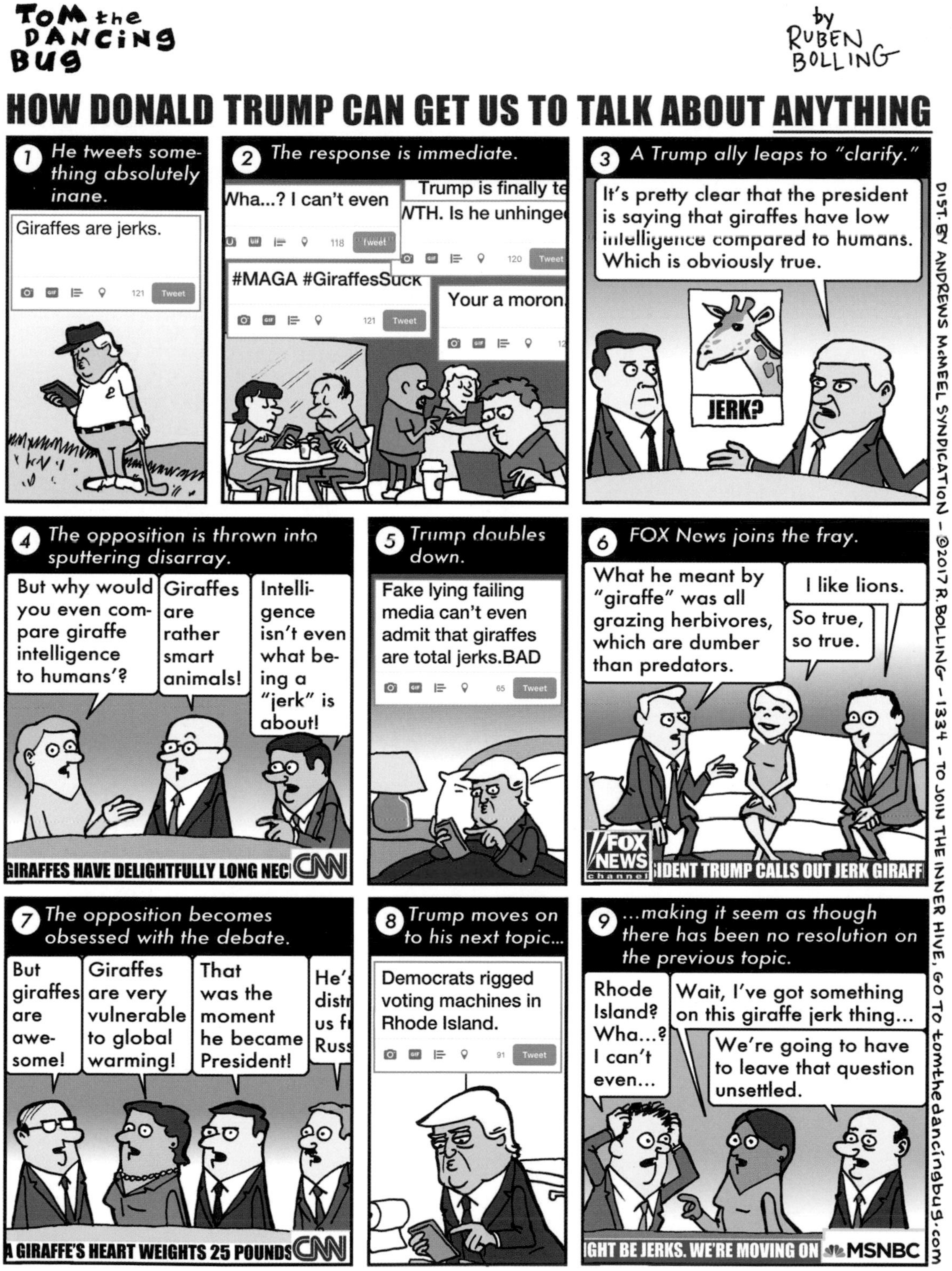
TOM the DANCING BUG
by RUBEN BOLLING
HOW DONALD TRUMP CAN GET US TO TALK ABOUT ANYTHING
1 He tweets something absolutely inane.
Giraffes are jerks.
121 Tweet
2 The response is immediate.
Wha...? I can't even
118 Tweet
Trump is finally te
WTH. Is he unhinge
120 Tweet
#MAGA #GiraffesSuck
121 Tweet
Your a moron.
3 A Trump ally leaps to "clarify."
It's pretty clear that the president is saying that giraffes have low intelligence compared to humans. Which is obviously true.
JERK?
4 The opposition is thrown into sputtering disarray.
But why would you even compare giraffe intelligence to humans'?
Giraffes are rather smart animals!
Intelligence isn't even what being a "jerk" is about!
GIRAFFES HAVE DELIGHTFULLY LONG NEC
CNN
5 Trump doubles down.
Fake lying failing media can't even admit that giraffes are total jerks.BAD
65 Tweet
6 FOX News joins the fray.
What he meant by "giraffe" was all grazing herbivores, which are dumber than predators.
I like lions.
So true, so true.
FOX NEWS channel
SIDENT TRUMP CALLS OUT JERK GIRAFF
7 The opposition becomes obsessed with the debate.
But giraffes are awesome!
Giraffes are very vulnerable to global warming!
That was the moment he became President!
He's distr us fr Russ
A GIRAFFE'S HEART WEIGHTS 25 POUNDS
CNN
8 Trump moves on to his next topic...
Democrats rigged voting machines in Rhode Island.
91 Tweet
9 ...making it seem as though there has been no resolution on the previous topic.
Rhode Island? Wha...? I can't even...
Wait, I've got something on this giraffe jerk thing...
We're going to have to leave that question unsettled.
IGHT BE JERKS. WE'RE MOVING ON
MSNBC
DIST. BY ANDREWS McMEEL SYNDICATION – ©2017 R. BOLLING – 1334 – TO JOIN THE INNER HIVE, GO TO tomthedancingbug.com

4/17/17

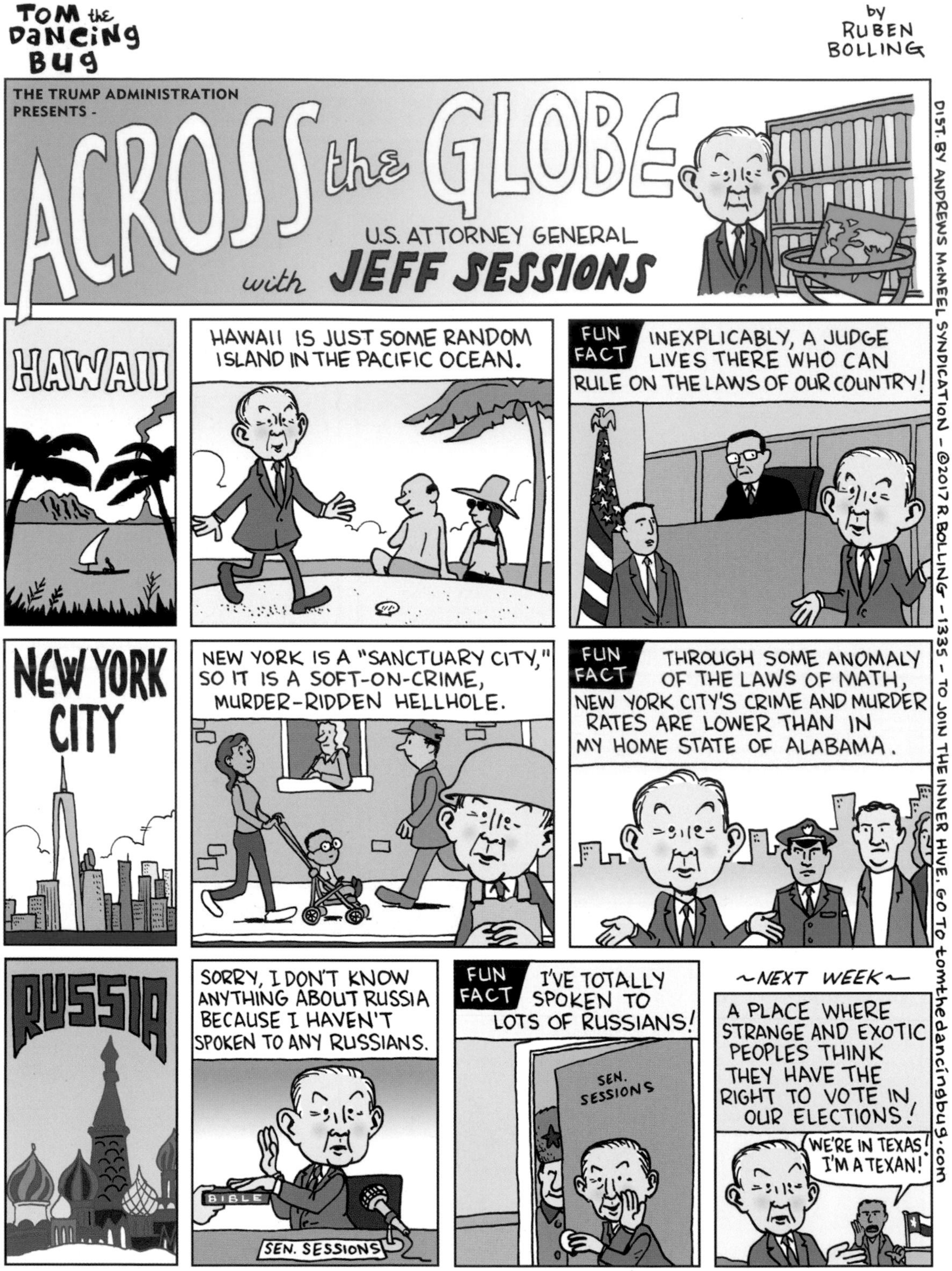

TOM the DANCING BUG
by RUBEN BOLLING
THE TRUMP ADMINISTRATION PRESENTS -
ACROSS the GLOBE
U.S. ATTORNEY GENERAL
with JEFF SESSIONS
HAWAII
HAWAII IS JUST SOME RANDOM ISLAND IN THE PACIFIC OCEAN.
FUN FACT
INEXPLICABLY, A JUDGE LIVES THERE WHO CAN RULE ON THE LAWS OF OUR COUNTRY!
NEW YORK CITY
NEW YORK IS A "SANCTUARY CITY," SO IT IS A SOFT-ON-CRIME, MURDER-RIDDEN HELLHOLE.
FUN FACT
THROUGH SOME ANOMALY OF THE LAWS OF MATH, NEW YORK CITY'S CRIME AND MURDER RATES ARE LOWER THAN IN MY HOME STATE OF ALABAMA.
RUSSIA
SORRY, I DON'T KNOW ANYTHING ABOUT RUSSIA BECAUSE I HAVEN'T SPOKEN TO ANY RUSSIANS.
BIBLE
SEN. SESSIONS
FUN FACT
I'VE TOTALLY SPOKEN TO LOTS OF RUSSIANS!
SEN. SESSIONS
~NEXT WEEK~
A PLACE WHERE STRANGE AND EXOTIC PEOPLES THINK THEY HAVE THE RIGHT TO VOTE IN OUR ELECTIONS!
WE'RE IN TEXAS! I'M A TEXAN!
DIST. BY ANDREWS McMEEL SYNDICATION - ©2017 R. BOLLING - 1335 - TO JOIN THE INNER HIVE, GO TO tomthedancingbug.com

4/24/17

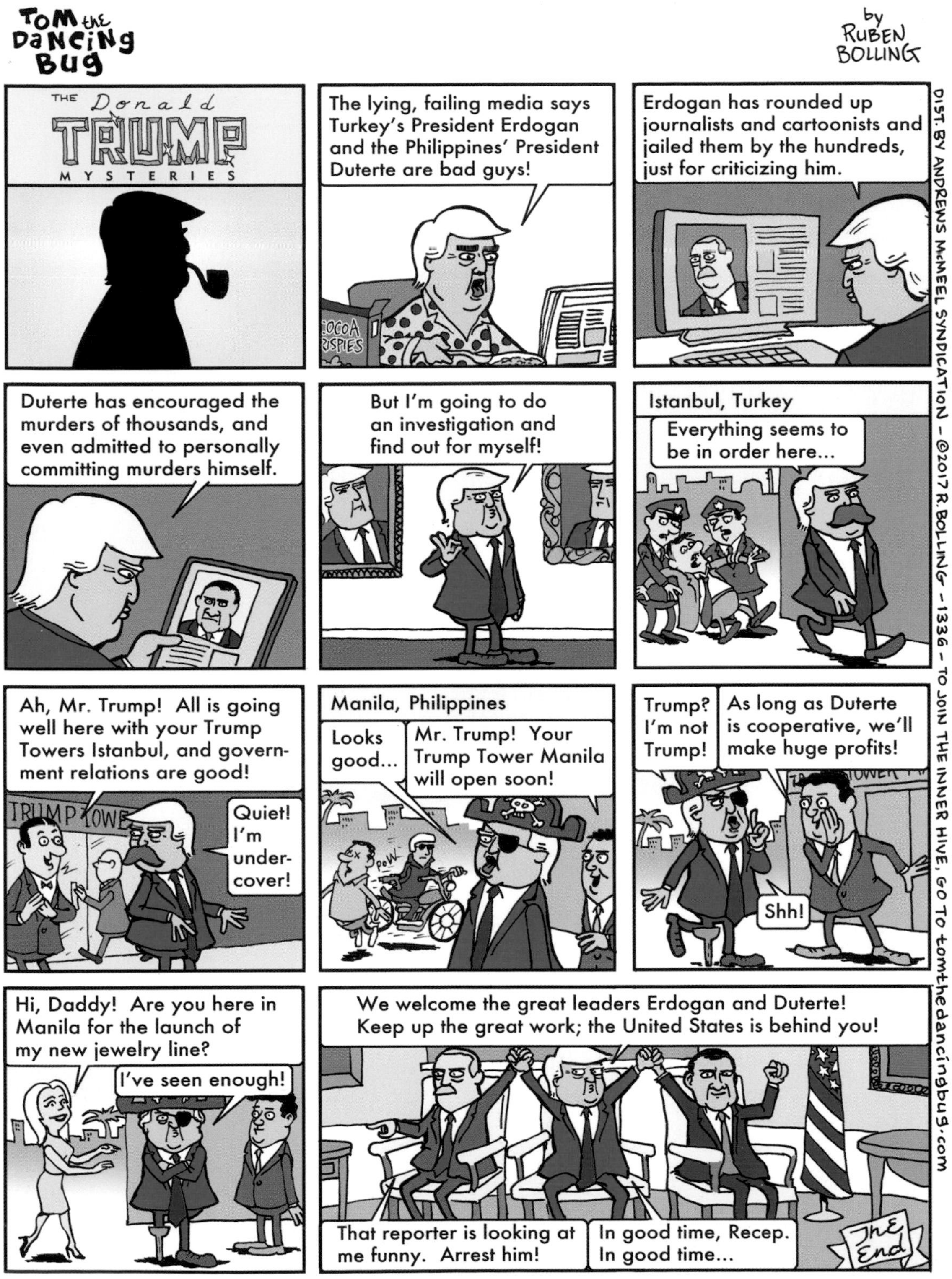

TOM the DANCING BUG
by RUBEN BOLLING
THE Donald TRUMP MYSTERIES
The lying, failing media says Turkey's President Erdogan and the Philippines' President Duterte are bad guys!
COCOA KRISPIES
Erdogan has rounded up journalists and cartoonists and jailed them by the hundreds, just for criticizing him.
Duterte has encouraged the murders of thousands, and even admitted to personally committing murders himself.
But I'm going to do an investigation and find out for myself!
Istanbul, Turkey
Everything seems to be in order here...
Ah, Mr. Trump! All is going well here with your Trump Towers Istanbul, and government relations are good!
TRUMP TOWE
Quiet! I'm undercover!
Manila, Philippines
Looks good...
Mr. Trump! Your Trump Tower Manila will open soon!
POW
Trump? I'm not Trump!
As long as Duterte is cooperative, we'll make huge profits!
Shh!
Hi, Daddy! Are you here in Manila for the launch of my new jewelry line?
I've seen enough!
We welcome the great leaders Erdogan and Duterte! Keep up the great work; the United States is behind you!
That reporter is looking at me funny. Arrest him!
In good time, Recep. In good time...
THE End
DIST. BY ANDREWS McMEEL SYNDICATION – ©2017 R. BOLLING – 1336 – TO JOIN THE INNER HIVE, GO TO tomthedancingbug.com

5/1/17

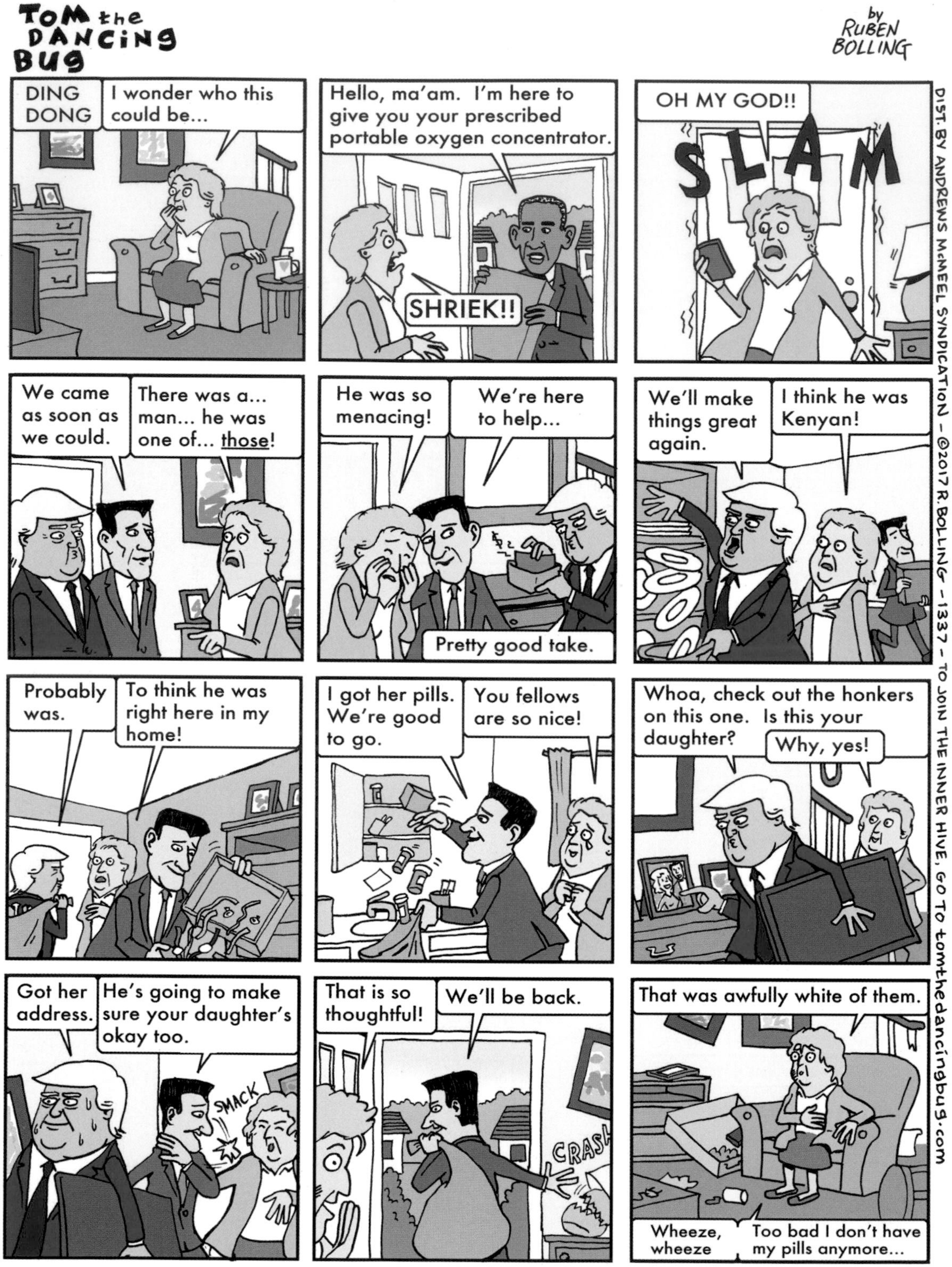
TOM the DANCING BUG
by RUBEN BOLLING
DING DONG
I wonder who this could be...
Hello, ma'am. I'm here to give you your prescribed portable oxygen concentrator.
SHRIEK!!
OH MY GOD!!
SLAM
We came as soon as we could.
There was a... man... he was one of... those!
He was so menacing!
We're here to help...
Pretty good take.
We'll make things great again.
I think he was Kenyan!
Probably was.
To think he was right here in my home!
I got her pills. We're good to go.
You fellows are so nice!
Whoa, check out the honkers on this one. Is this your daughter?
Why, yes!
Got her address.
He's going to make sure your daughter's okay too.
SMACK
That is so thoughtful!
We'll be back.
CRASH
That was awfully white of them.
Wheeze, wheeze
Too bad I don't have my pills anymore...
DIST. BY ANDREWS McMEEL SYNDICATION – ©2017 R. BOLLING – 1337 – TO JOIN THE INNER HIVE, GO TO tomthedancingbug.com

5/8/17

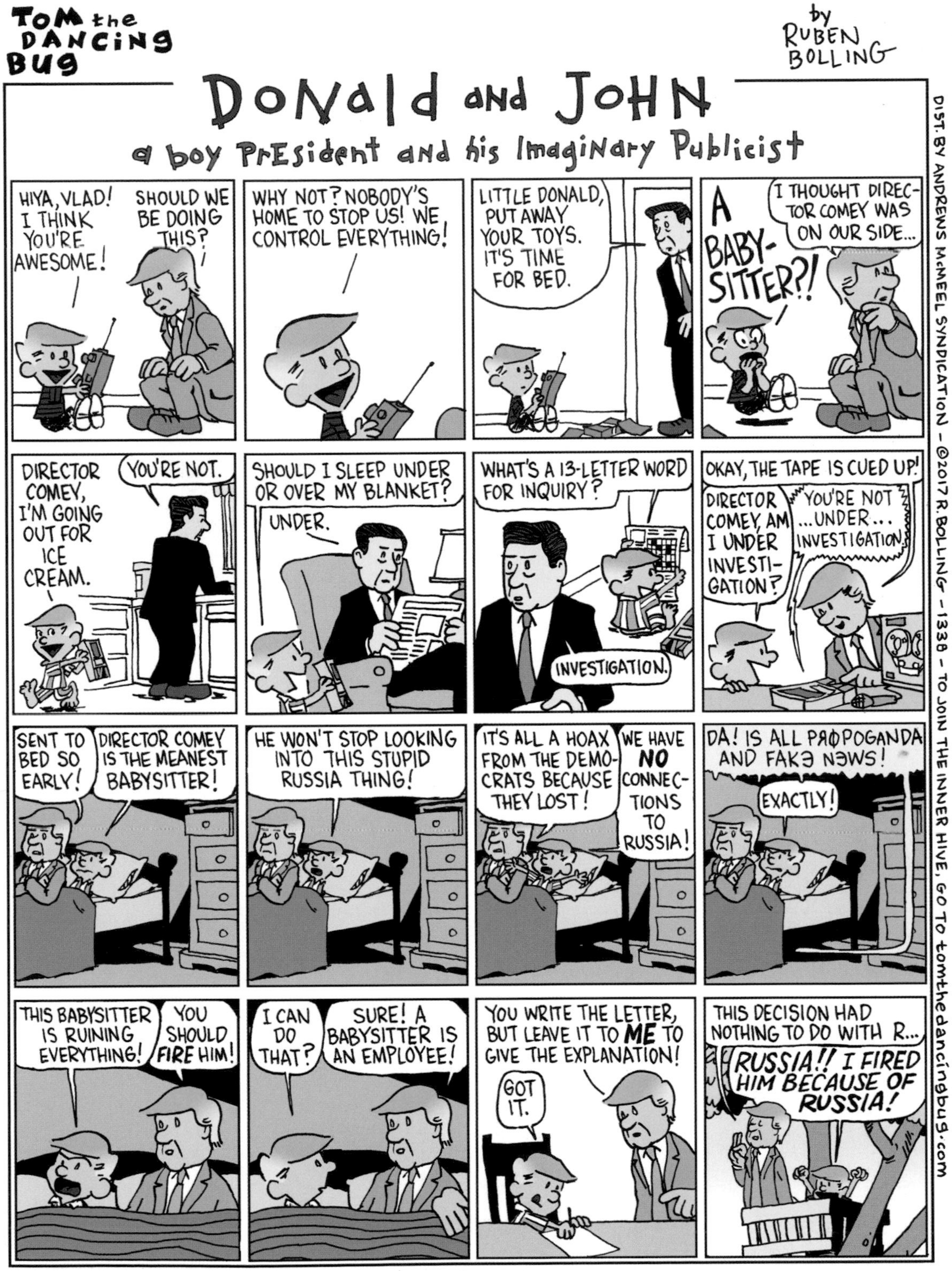
TOM the DANCING BUG
by RUBEN BOLLING
DONALD AND JOHN
a boy President and his Imaginary Publicist
HIYA, VLAD! I THINK YOU'RE AWESOME!
SHOULD WE BE DOING THIS?
WHY NOT? NOBODY'S HOME TO STOP US! WE CONTROL EVERYTHING!
LITTLE DONALD, PUT AWAY YOUR TOYS. IT'S TIME FOR BED.
A BABY-SITTER?!
I THOUGHT DIRECTOR COMEY WAS ON OUR SIDE...
DIRECTOR COMEY, I'M GOING OUT FOR ICE CREAM.
YOU'RE NOT.
SHOULD I SLEEP UNDER OR OVER MY BLANKET?
UNDER.
WHAT'S A 13-LETTER WORD FOR INQUIRY?
INVESTIGATION.
OKAY, THE TAPE IS CUED UP!
DIRECTOR COMEY, AM I UNDER INVESTIGATION?
YOU'RE NOT ...UNDER... INVESTIGATION.
SENT TO BED SO EARLY!
DIRECTOR COMEY IS THE MEANEST BABYSITTER!
HE WON'T STOP LOOKING INTO THIS STUPID RUSSIA THING!
IT'S ALL A HOAX FROM THE DEMOCRATS BECAUSE THEY LOST!
WE HAVE NO CONNECTIONS TO RUSSIA!
DA! IS ALL PRØPOGANDA AND FAKƎ NƎWS!
EXACTLY!
THIS BABYSITTER IS RUINING EVERYTHING!
YOU SHOULD FIRE HIM!
I CAN DO THAT?
SURE! A BABYSITTER IS AN EMPLOYEE!
YOU WRITE THE LETTER, BUT LEAVE IT TO ME TO GIVE THE EXPLANATION!
GOT IT.
THIS DECISION HAD NOTHING TO DO WITH R...
RUSSIA!! I FIRED HIM BECAUSE OF RUSSIA!
DIST. BY ANDREWS McMEEL SYNDICATION – ©2017 R. BOLLING – 1338 – TO JOIN THE INNER HIVE, GO TO tomthedancingbug.com

5/15/17

TOM the DANCING BUG
by RUBEN BOLLING
LAST BREATH
THE ONE KNOWN AS ROGER AILES...
...IS DEAD.
THE DREAM IS OVER.
A CELESTIAL GRIP LOOSENS.
AN ALTERNATIVE REALITY FLICKERS...
AND FADES
A VALIANT KNIGHT BATTLING A FEARSOME SHE-DEVIL... BLINKS...
...AND HE'S A RETIRED PLUMBER WATCHING A SOMEWHAT OPPORTUNISTIC FEMALE POLITICIAN.
A WARRIOR JOINED IN BATTLE WITH A HANDSOME KING TO DEFEND THE REALM FROM UNSPEAKABLE MONSTROSITIES...
EXHALES...
...AND SHE'S A GRANDMOTHER WHO TRUSTED AN ORANGE-TINTED CON MAN.
A HERO SLAYING THE DARK-SKINNED HORDES THAT RISE UP TO STEAL LAND, TREASURE, AND WOMENFOLK... PAUSES...
AND... NOPE. STILL RACIST.
...AND ALL YOU WANT IS YOUR OBAMACARE-PHONES AND WELFARE CADILLACS!
DIST. BY ANDREWS McMEEL SYNDICATION – ©2017 R. BOLLING – 1339 – TO JOIN THE INNER HIVE, GO TO tomthedancingbug.com

5/22/17

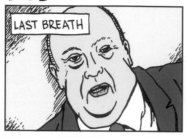

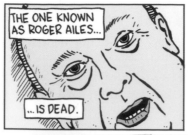

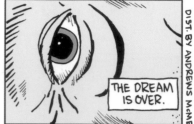

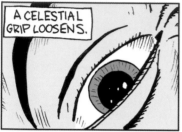

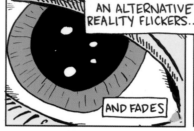

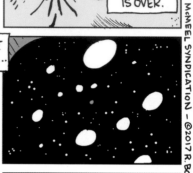

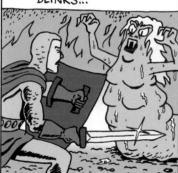

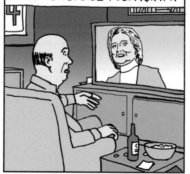

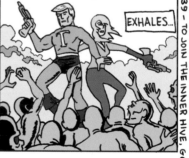

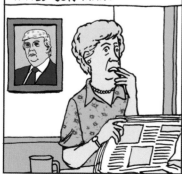

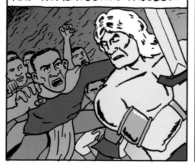

TOM the DANCING BUG

by RUBEN BOLLING

DIST. BY ANDREWS McMEEL SYNDICATION – ©2017 R. BOLLING –1340 – TO JOIN THE INNER HIVE, GO TO tomthedancingbug.com

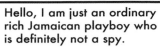

DONALD TRUMP
0045
SUPERSPY

Hello, I am just an ordinary rich Jamaican playboy who is definitely not a spy.

I'll bet you're <u>very</u> ordinary. And you don't know any spy-secrets.

I do too! I know a code-word secret that ISIS is planning a terrorist attack using laptops!

Impressive! And we can infer what country you got that intel from.

Oh, no, you can't! Notice I never said, "Israel"!

True! You are far too clever for us.

Um, I'd like to speak to this fascinating ordinary Jamaican playboy!

So would I!

Me too!

Later...

No, no, the nuclear subs are positioned <u>here</u>, dummy.

So silly of me.

Can I bring some tech equipment into your office... say, an oval office?

Sure!

Is he really this stupid?

Well, yes and no...

That'll be $200 million each.

Here you go, Jared.

Oh, I see.

NEXT WEEK: **"TRUMP-GIRL"**

0045 gets to briefly touch Melania's hand before she retracts it in disgust!

Was it good for you?

5/29/17

TOM the DANCING BUG

by RUBEN BOLLING

President Trump has withdrawn the U.S. from the Paris Accord, an international agreement to mitigate the warming of the Global Climate.

He stated that he will negotiate a better deal.

Here's how Trump will use his trademark negotiating tactics to

GET A BETTER DEAL OUT OF THE GLOBAL CLIMATE

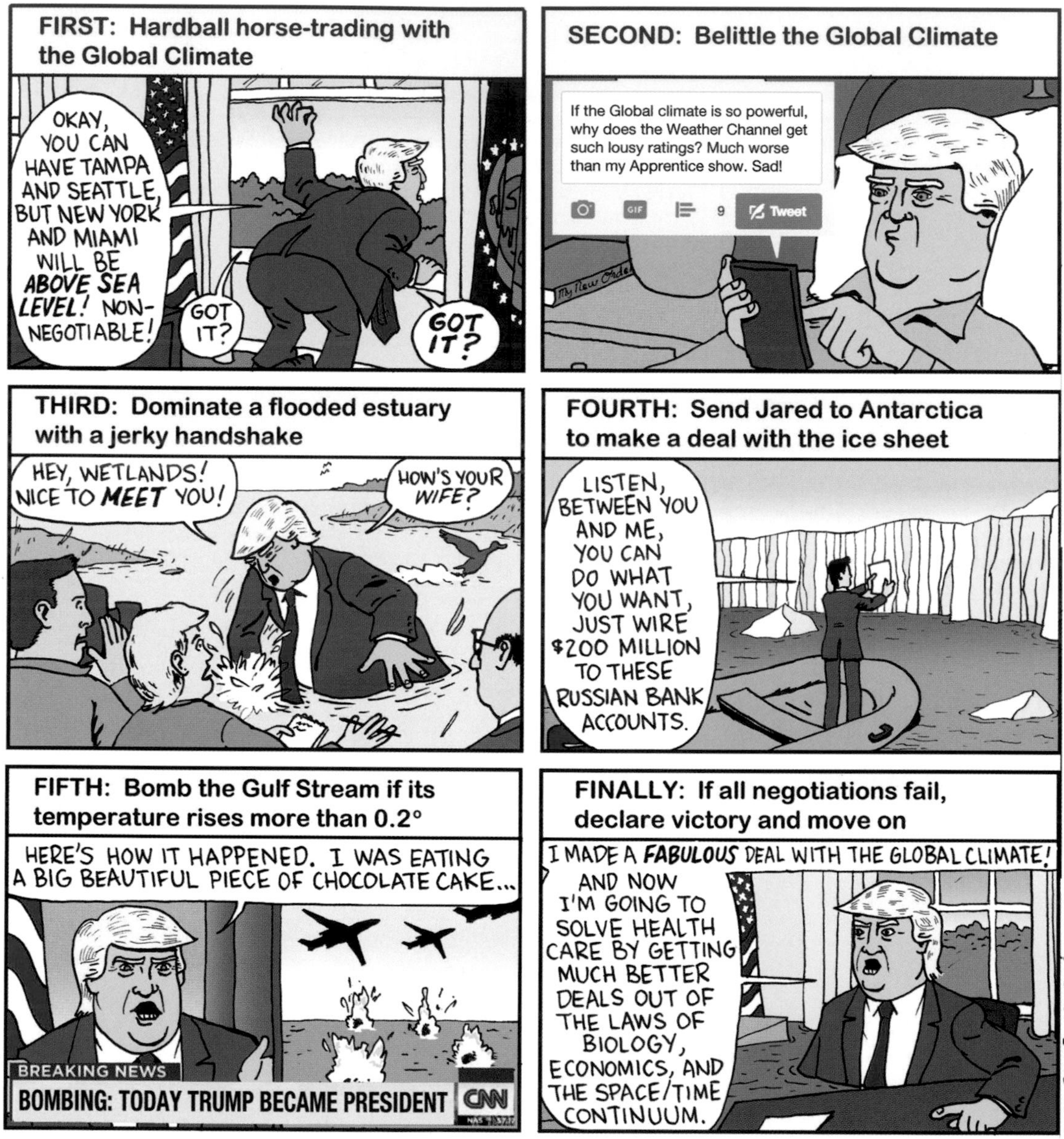
FIRST: Hardball horse-trading with the Global Climate
OKAY, YOU CAN HAVE TAMPA AND SEATTLE, BUT NEW YORK AND MIAMI WILL BE ABOVE SEA LEVEL! NON-NEGOTIABLE!
GOT IT?
GOT IT?
SECOND: Belittle the Global Climate
If the Global climate is so powerful, why does the Weather Channel get such lousy ratings? Much worse than my Apprentice show. Sad!
GIF
9
Tweet
THIRD: Dominate a flooded estuary with a jerky handshake
HEY, WETLANDS! NICE TO MEET YOU!
HOW'S YOUR WIFE?
FOURTH: Send Jared to Antarctica to make a deal with the ice sheet
LISTEN, BETWEEN YOU AND ME, YOU CAN DO WHAT YOU WANT, JUST WIRE $200 MILLION TO THESE RUSSIAN BANK ACCOUNTS.
FIFTH: Bomb the Gulf Stream if its temperature rises more than 0.2°
HERE'S HOW IT HAPPENED. I WAS EATING A BIG BEAUTIFUL PIECE OF CHOCOLATE CAKE...
BREAKING NEWS
BOMBING: TODAY TRUMP BECAME PRESIDENT
CNN
FINALLY: If all negotiations fail, declare victory and move on
I MADE A FABULOUS DEAL WITH THE GLOBAL CLIMATE!
AND NOW I'M GOING TO SOLVE HEALTH CARE BY GETTING MUCH BETTER DEALS OUT OF THE LAWS OF BIOLOGY, ECONOMICS, AND THE SPACE/TIME CONTINUUM.

6/5/17

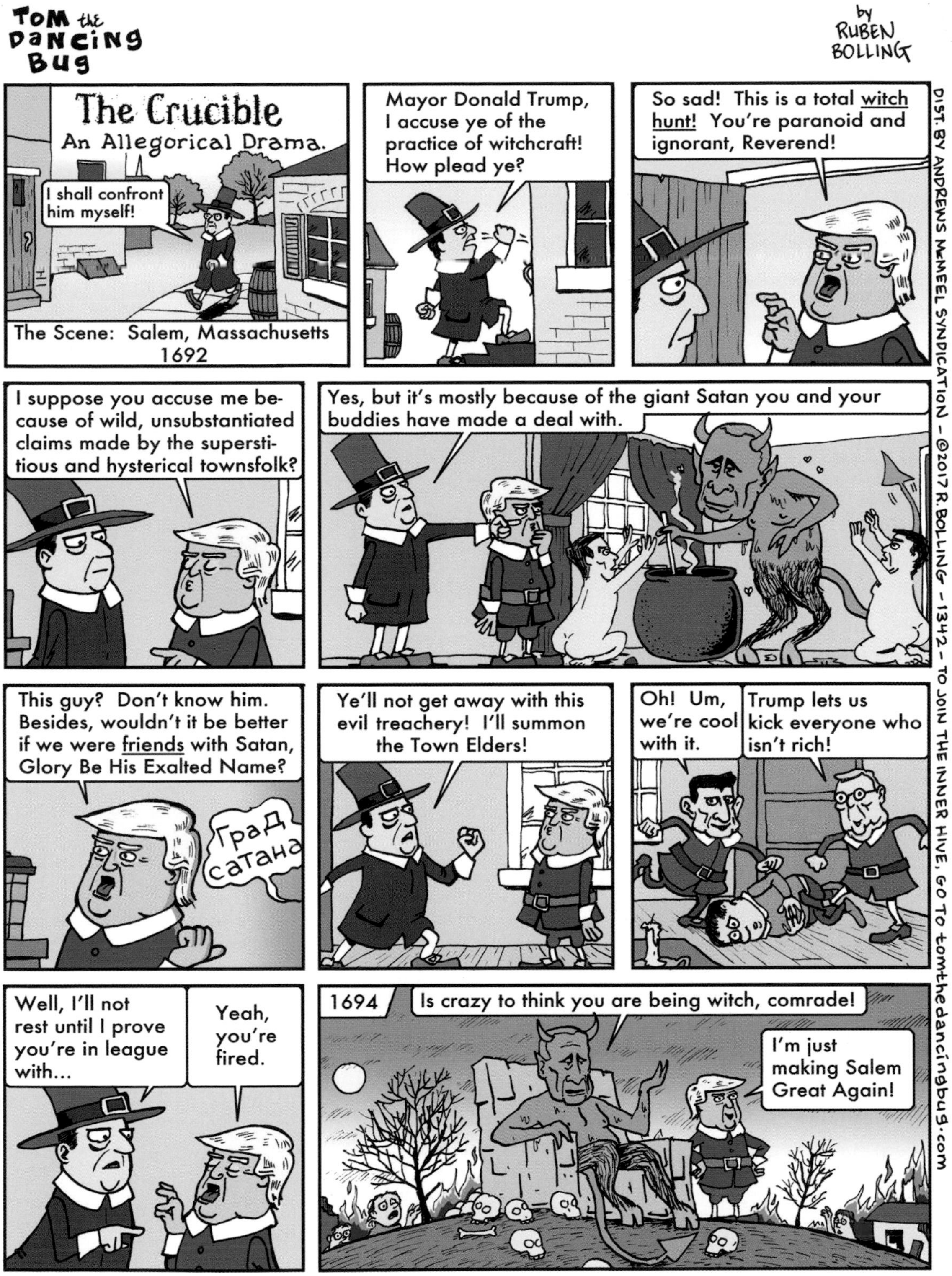
TOM the DANCING BUG
by RUBEN BOLLING
The Crucible
An Allegorical Drama.
I shall confront him myself!
The Scene: Salem, Massachusetts 1692
Mayor Donald Trump, I accuse ye of the practice of witchcraft! How plead ye?
So sad! This is a total witch hunt! You're paranoid and ignorant, Reverend!
I suppose you accuse me because of wild, unsubstantiated claims made by the superstitious and hysterical townsfolk?
Yes, but it's mostly because of the giant Satan you and your buddies have made a deal with.
This guy? Don't know him. Besides, wouldn't it be better if we were friends with Satan, Glory Be His Exalted Name?
Град сатана
Ye'll not get away with this evil treachery! I'll summon the Town Elders!
Oh! Um, we're cool with it.
Trump lets us kick everyone who isn't rich!
Well, I'll not rest until I prove you're in league with...
Yeah, you're fired.
1694
Is crazy to think you are being witch, comrade!
I'm just making Salem Great Again!
DIST. BY ANDREWS McMEEL SYNDICATION – ©2017 R. BOLLING – 1342 – TO JOIN THE INNER HIVE, GO TO tomthedancingbug.com

6/12/17

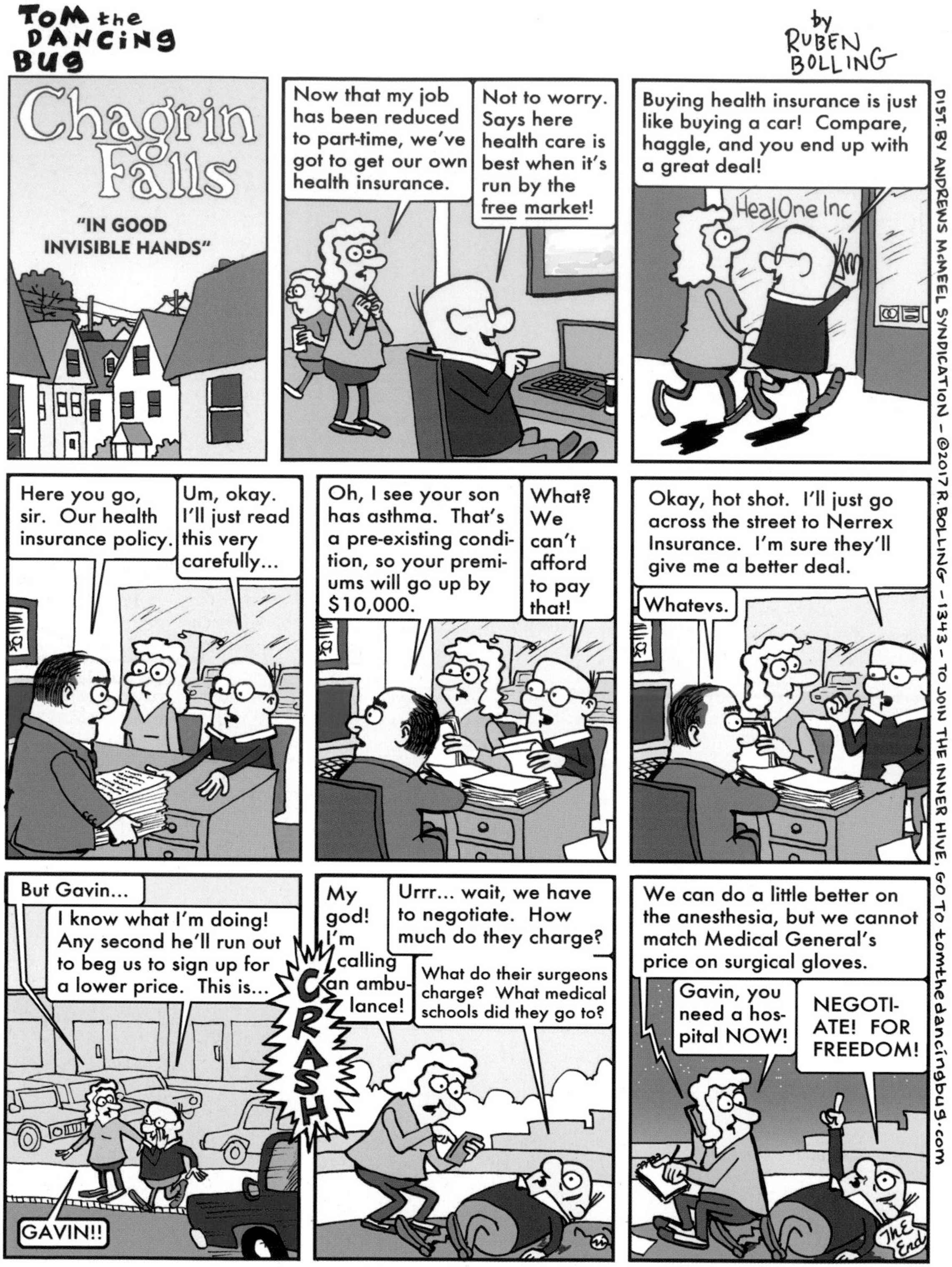
TOM the DANCING BUG
by RUBEN BOLLING
Chagrin Falls
"IN GOOD INVISIBLE HANDS"
Now that my job has been reduced to part-time, we've got to get our own health insurance.
Not to worry. Says here health care is best when it's run by the free market!
Buying health insurance is just like buying a car! Compare, haggle, and you end up with a great deal!
HealOne Inc
Here you go, sir. Our health insurance policy.
Um, okay. I'll just read this very carefully...
Oh, I see your son has asthma. That's a pre-existing condition, so your premiums will go up by $10,000.
What? We can't afford to pay that!
Okay, hot shot. I'll just go across the street to Nerrex Insurance. I'm sure they'll give me a better deal.
Whatevs.
But Gavin...
I know what I'm doing! Any second he'll run out to beg us to sign up for a lower price. This is...
CRASH
GAVIN!!
My god! I'm calling an ambulance!
Urrr... wait, we have to negotiate. How much do they charge?
What do their surgeons charge? What medical schools did they go to?
We can do a little better on the anesthesia, but we cannot match Medical General's price on surgical gloves.
Gavin, you need a hospital NOW!
NEGOTIATE! FOR FREEDOM!
The End
DIST. BY ANDREWS McMEEL SYNDICATION – ©2017 R. BOLLING – 1343 – TO JOIN THE INNER HIVE, GO TO tomthedancingbug.com

6/19/17

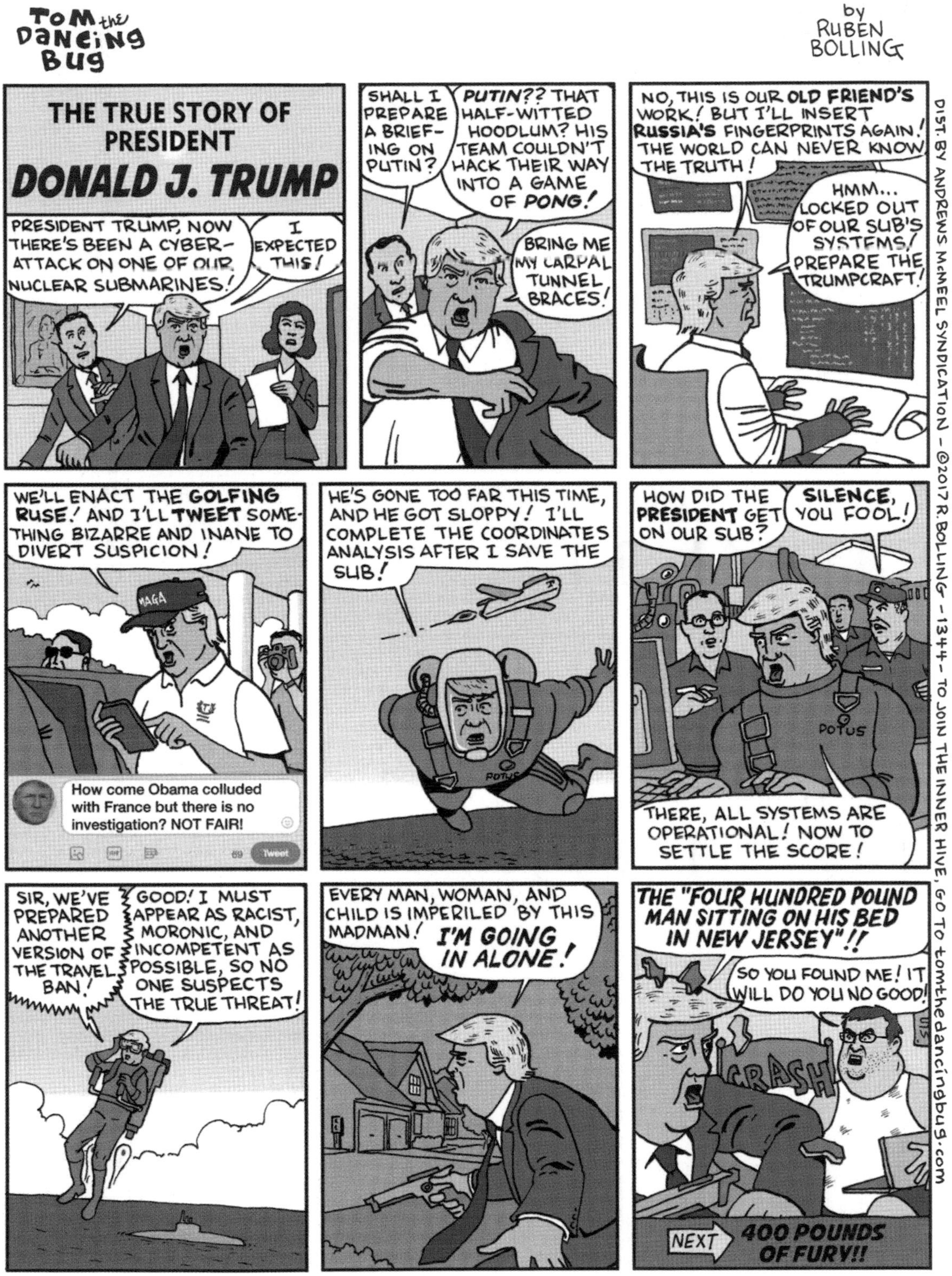

TOM the DANCING BUG
by RUBEN BOLLING
THE TRUE STORY OF PRESIDENT DONALD J. TRUMP
PRESIDENT TRUMP, NOW THERE'S BEEN A CYBER-ATTACK ON ONE OF OUR NUCLEAR SUBMARINES!
I EXPECTED THIS!
SHALL I PREPARE A BRIEF-ING ON PUTIN?
PUTIN?? THAT HALF-WITTED HOODLUM? HIS TEAM COULDN'T HACK THEIR WAY INTO A GAME OF PONG!
BRING ME MY CARPAL TUNNEL BRACES!
NO, THIS IS OUR OLD FRIEND'S WORK! BUT I'LL INSERT RUSSIA'S FINGERPRINTS AGAIN! THE WORLD CAN NEVER KNOW THE TRUTH!
HMM... LOCKED OUT OF OUR SUB'S SYSTEMS! PREPARE THE TRUMPCRAFT!
WE'LL ENACT THE GOLFING RUSE! AND I'LL TWEET SOME-THING BIZARRE AND INANE TO DIVERT SUSPICION!
MAGA
How come Obama colluded with France but there is no investigation? NOT FAIR!
Tweet
HE'S GONE TOO FAR THIS TIME, AND HE GOT SLOPPY! I'LL COMPLETE THE COORDINATES ANALYSIS AFTER I SAVE THE SUB!
POTUS
HOW DID THE PRESIDENT GET ON OUR SUB?
SILENCE, YOU FOOL!
POTUS
THERE, ALL SYSTEMS ARE OPERATIONAL! NOW TO SETTLE THE SCORE!
SIR, WE'VE PREPARED ANOTHER VERSION OF THE TRAVEL BAN!
GOOD! I MUST APPEAR AS RACIST, MORONIC, AND INCOMPETENT AS POSSIBLE, SO NO ONE SUSPECTS THE TRUE THREAT!
EVERY MAN, WOMAN, AND CHILD IS IMPERILED BY THIS MADMAN!
I'M GOING IN ALONE!
THE "FOUR HUNDRED POUND MAN SITTING ON HIS BED IN NEW JERSEY"!!
SO YOU FOUND ME! IT WILL DO YOU NO GOOD!
CRASH
NEXT 400 POUNDS OF FURY!!
DIST. BY ANDREWS McMEEL SYNDICATION – ©2017 R. BOLLING – 1344 – TO JOIN THE INNER HIVE, GO TO tomthedancingbug.com

6/26/17

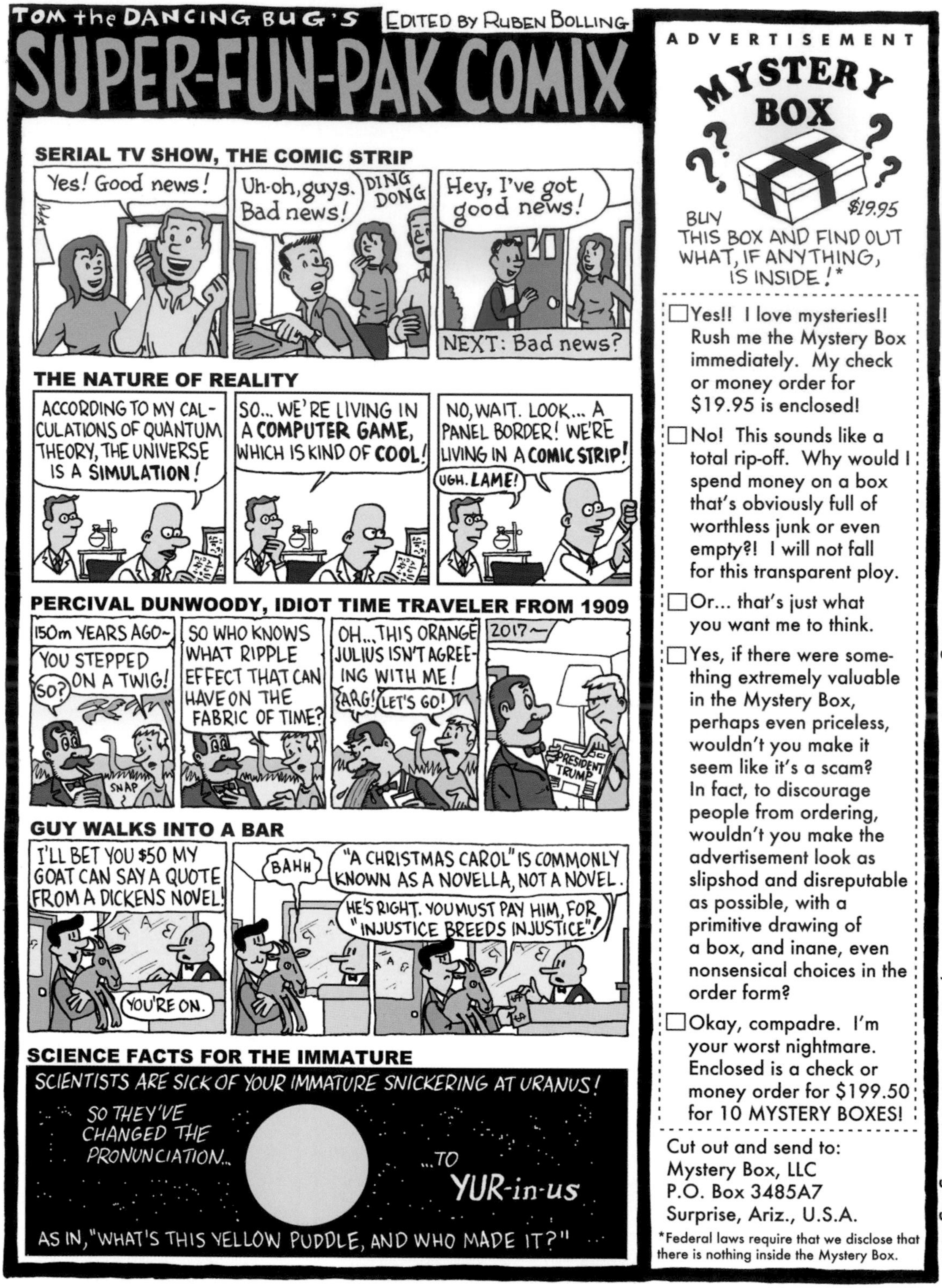

TOM the DANCING BUG'S
EDITED BY RUBEN BOLLING
SUPER-FUN-PAK COMIX
SERIAL TV SHOW, THE COMIC STRIP
Yes! Good news!
Uh-oh, guys. Bad news!
DING DONG
Hey, I've got good news!
NEXT: Bad news?
THE NATURE OF REALITY
ACCORDING TO MY CALCULATIONS OF QUANTUM THEORY, THE UNIVERSE IS A SIMULATION!
SO... WE'RE LIVING IN A COMPUTER GAME, WHICH IS KIND OF COOL!
NO, WAIT. LOOK... A PANEL BORDER! WE'RE LIVING IN A COMIC STRIP!
UGH. LAME!
PERCIVAL DUNWOODY, IDIOT TIME TRAVELER FROM 1909
150m YEARS AGO~
YOU STEPPED ON A TWIG!
SO?
SNAP
SO WHO KNOWS WHAT RIPPLE EFFECT THAT CAN HAVE ON THE FABRIC OF TIME?
OH... THIS ORANGE JULIUS ISN'T AGREEING WITH ME!
ARG!
LET'S GO!
2017~
PRESIDENT TRUMP
GUY WALKS INTO A BAR
I'LL BET YOU $50 MY GOAT CAN SAY A QUOTE FROM A DICKENS NOVEL!
YOU'RE ON.
BAHH
"A CHRISTMAS CAROL" IS COMMONLY KNOWN AS A NOVELLA, NOT A NOVEL.
HE'S RIGHT. YOU MUST PAY HIM, FOR "INJUSTICE BREEDS INJUSTICE"!
SCIENCE FACTS FOR THE IMMATURE
SCIENTISTS ARE SICK OF YOUR IMMATURE SNICKERING AT URANUS!
SO THEY'VE CHANGED THE PRONUNCIATION...
...TO
YUR-in-us
AS IN, "WHAT'S THIS YELLOW PUDDLE, AND WHO MADE IT?"
ADVERTISEMENT
MYSTERY BOX
$19.95
BUY THIS BOX AND FIND OUT WHAT, IF ANYTHING, IS INSIDE!*
☐ Yes!! I love mysteries!! Rush me the Mystery Box immediately. My check or money order for $19.95 is enclosed!
☐ No! This sounds like a total rip-off. Why would I spend money on a box that's obviously full of worthless junk or even empty?! I will not fall for this transparent ploy.
☐ Or... that's just what you want me to think.
☐ Yes, if there were something extremely valuable in the Mystery Box, perhaps even priceless, wouldn't you make it seem like it's a scam? In fact, to discourage people from ordering, wouldn't you make the advertisement look as slipshod and disreputable as possible, with a primitive drawing of a box, and inane, even nonsensical choices in the order form?
☐ Okay, compadre. I'm your worst nightmare. Enclosed is a check or money order for $199.50 for 10 MYSTERY BOXES!
Cut out and send to:
Mystery Box, LLC
P.O. Box 3485A7
Surprise, Ariz., U.S.A.
*Federal laws require that we disclose that there is nothing inside the Mystery Box.

7/3/17

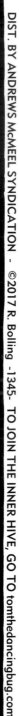

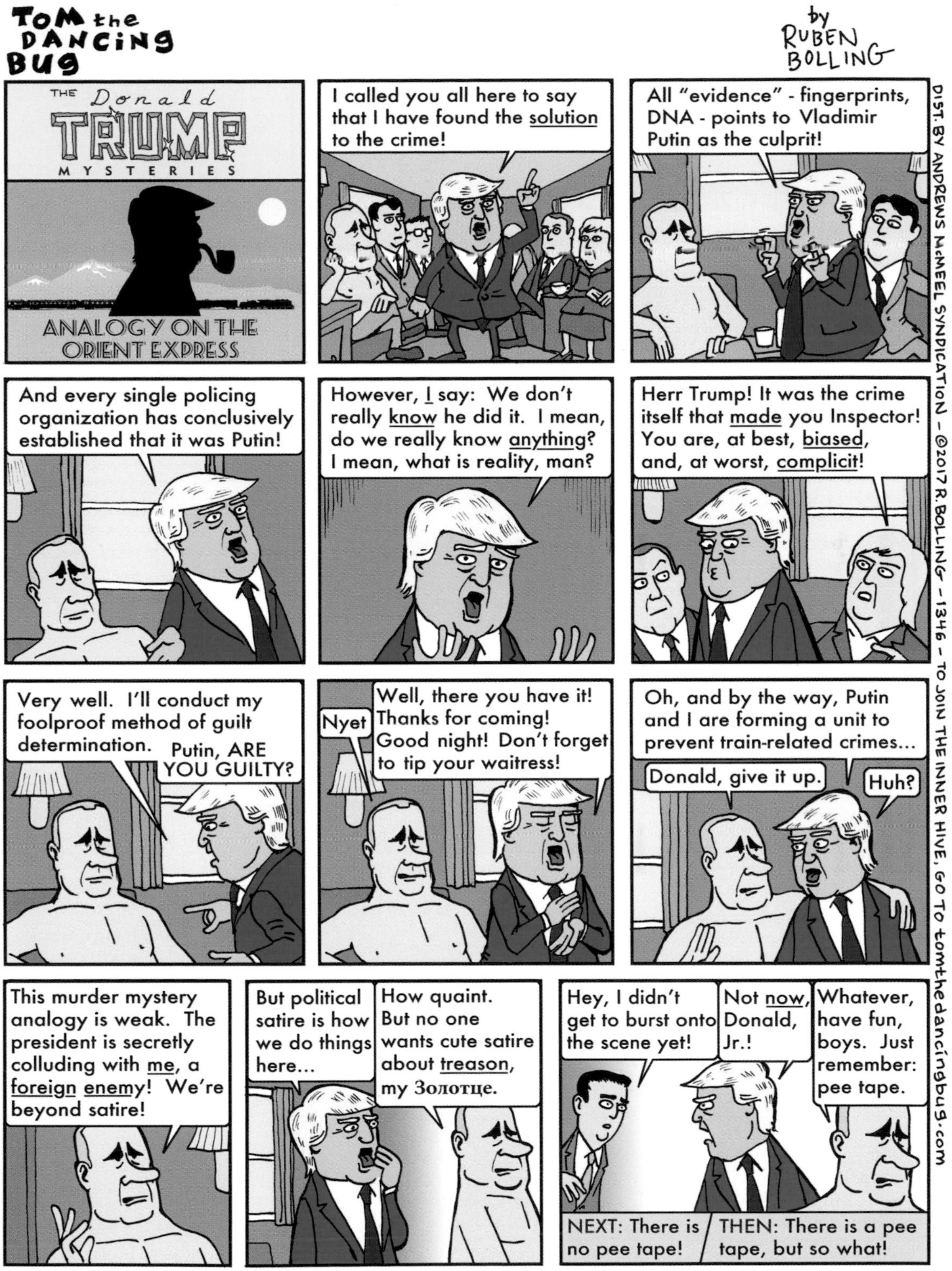
TOM the DANCING BUG
by RUBEN BOLLING
THE Donald TRUMP MYSTERIES
ANALOGY ON THE ORIENT EXPRESS
I called you all here to say that I have found the solution to the crime!
All "evidence" - fingerprints, DNA - points to Vladimir Putin as the culprit!
And every single policing organization has conclusively established that it was Putin!
However, I say: We don't really know he did it. I mean, do we really know anything? I mean, what is reality, man?
Herr Trump! It was the crime itself that made you Inspector! You are, at best, biased, and, at worst, complicit!
Very well. I'll conduct my foolproof method of guilt determination.
Putin, ARE YOU GUILTY?
Nyet
Well, there you have it! Thanks for coming! Good night! Don't forget to tip your waitress!
Oh, and by the way, Putin and I are forming a unit to prevent train-related crimes...
Donald, give it up.
Huh?
This murder mystery analogy is weak. The president is secretly colluding with me, a foreign enemy! We're beyond satire!
But political satire is how we do things here...
How quaint. But no one wants cute satire about treason, my Золотце.
Hey, I didn't get to burst onto the scene yet!
Not now, Donald, Jr.!
Whatever, have fun, boys. Just remember: pee tape.
NEXT: There is no pee tape!
THEN: There is a pee tape, but so what!
DIST. BY ANDREWS McMEEL SYNDICATION – ©2017 R. BOLLING – 1346 – TO JOIN THE INNER HIVE, GO TO tomthedancingbug.com

7/10/17

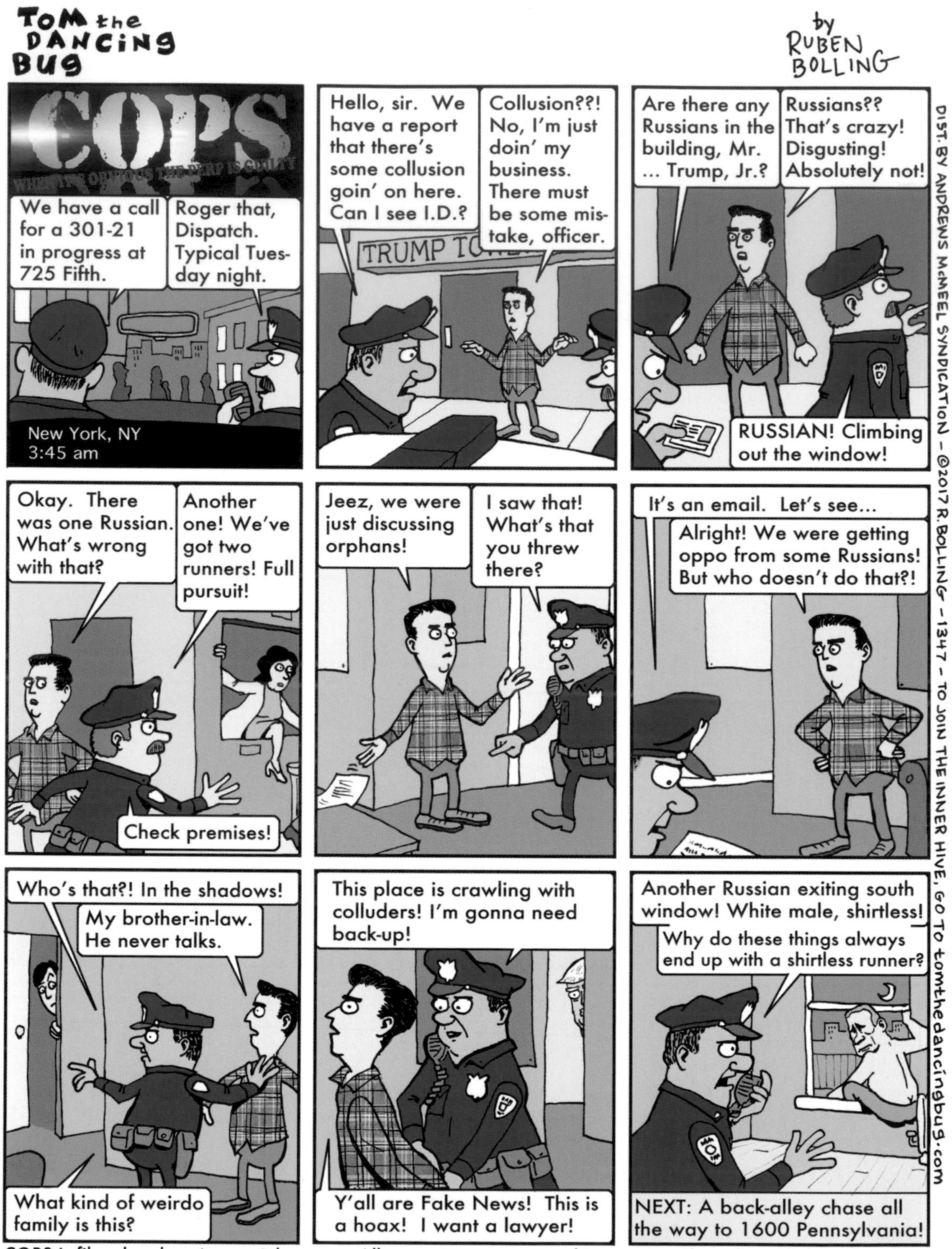
TOM the DANCING BUG
by RUBEN BOLLING
COPS
We have a call for a 301-21 in progress at 725 Fifth.
Roger that, Dispatch. Typical Tuesday night.
New York, NY 3:45 am
Hello, sir. We have a report that there's some collusion goin' on here. Can I see I.D.?
Collusion??! No, I'm just doin' my business. There must be some mistake, officer.
TRUMP TO
Are there any Russians in the building, Mr. ... Trump, Jr.?
Russians?? That's crazy! Disgusting! Absolutely not!
RUSSIAN! Climbing out the window!
Okay. There was one Russian. What's wrong with that?
Another one! We've got two runners! Full pursuit!
Check premises!
Jeez, we were just discussing orphans!
I saw that! What's that you threw there?
It's an email. Let's see...
Alright! We were getting oppo from some Russians! But who doesn't do that?!
Who's that?! In the shadows!
My brother-in-law. He never talks.
What kind of weirdo family is this?
This place is crawling with colluders! I'm gonna need back-up!
Y'all are Fake News! This is a hoax! I want a lawyer!
Another Russian exiting south window! White male, shirtless!
Why do these things always end up with a shirtless runner?
NEXT: A back-alley chase all the way to 1600 Pennsylvania!
DIST. BY ANDREWS McMEEL SYNDICATION – ©2017 R. BOLLING – 1347 – TO JOIN THE INNER HIVE, GO TO tomthedancingbug.com

COPS is filmed on location, as it happens. All suspects are presumed innocent until pardoned by the President.

7/17/17

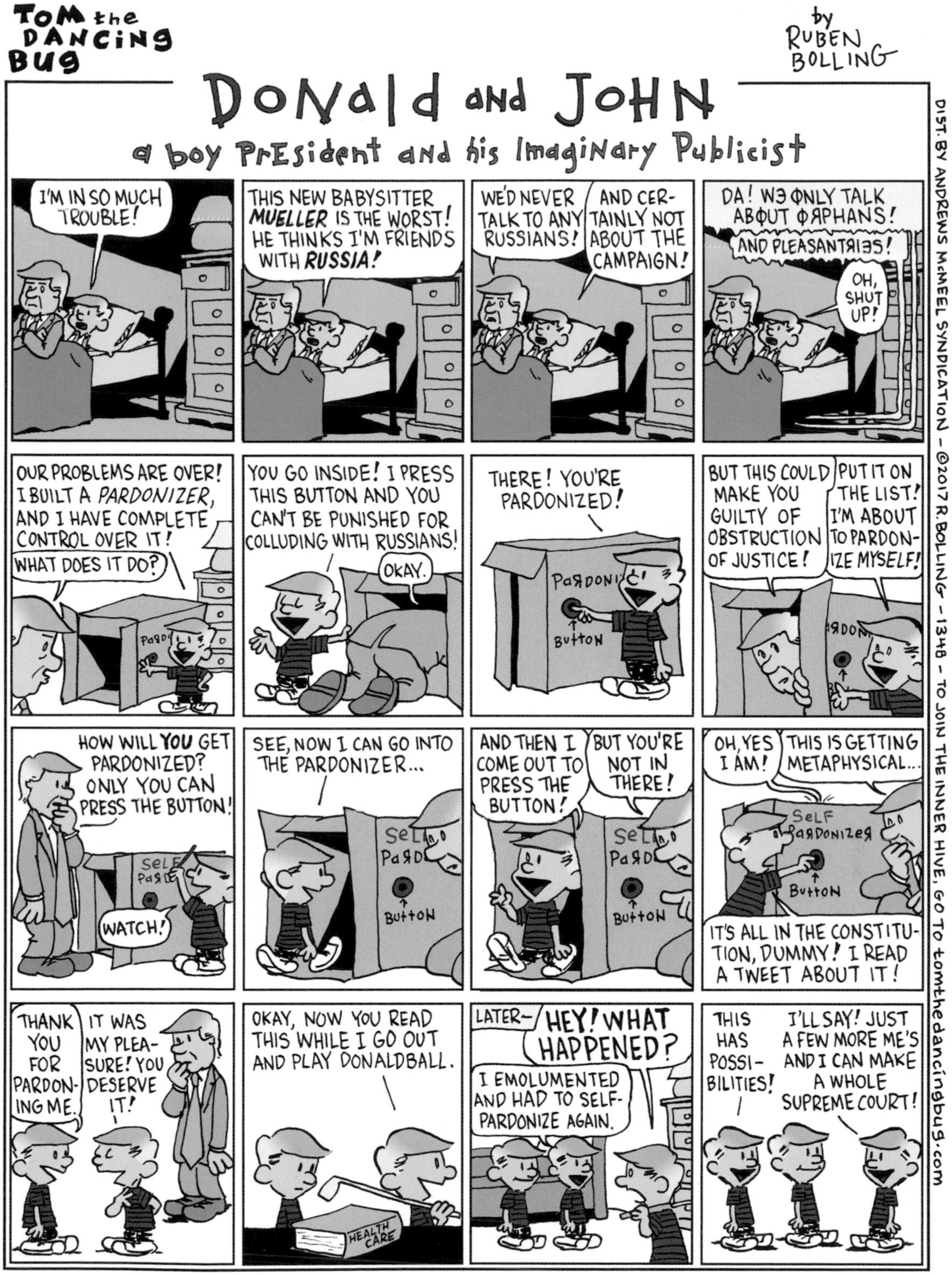
TOM the DANCING BUG
by RUBEN BOLLING
DONALD and JOHN
a boy President and his Imaginary Publicist
I'M IN SO MUCH TROUBLE!
THIS NEW BABYSITTER MUELLER IS THE WORST! HE THINKS I'M FRIENDS WITH RUSSIA!
WE'D NEVER TALK TO ANY RUSSIANS!
AND CERTAINLY NOT ABOUT THE CAMPAIGN!
DA! WƎ ФNLY TALK ABФUT ФЯPHANS!
AND PLEASANTЯIƎS!
OH, SHUT UP!
OUR PROBLEMS ARE OVER! I BUILT A PARDONIZER, AND I HAVE COMPLETE CONTROL OVER IT!
WHAT DOES IT DO?
YOU GO INSIDE! I PRESS THIS BUTTON AND YOU CAN'T BE PUNISHED FOR COLLUDING WITH RUSSIANS!
OKAY.
THERE! YOU'RE PARDONIZED!
BUTTON
BUT THIS COULD MAKE YOU GUILTY OF OBSTRUCTION OF JUSTICE!
PUT IT ON THE LIST! I'M ABOUT TO PARDONIZE MYSELF!
HOW WILL YOU GET PARDONIZED? ONLY YOU CAN PRESS THE BUTTON!
WATCH!
SEE, NOW I CAN GO INTO THE PARDONIZER...
BUTTON
AND THEN I COME OUT TO PRESS THE BUTTON!
BUT YOU'RE NOT IN THERE!
OH, YES I AM!
THIS IS GETTING METAPHYSICAL...
SELF PAЯDONIZEЯ
BUTTON
IT'S ALL IN THE CONSTITUTION, DUMMY! I READ A TWEET ABOUT IT!
THANK YOU FOR PARDONING ME.
IT WAS MY PLEASURE! YOU DESERVE IT!
OKAY, NOW YOU READ THIS WHILE I GO OUT AND PLAY DONALDBALL.
HEALTH CARE
LATER–
HEY! WHAT HAPPENED?
I EMOLUMENTED AND HAD TO SELF-PARDONIZE AGAIN.
THIS HAS POSSIBILITIES!
I'LL SAY! JUST A FEW MORE ME'S AND I CAN MAKE A WHOLE SUPREME COURT!
DIST. BY ANDREWS McMEEL SYNDICATION – ©2017 R. BOLLING – 1348 – TO JOIN THE INNER HIVE, GO TO tomthedancingbug.com

7/24/17

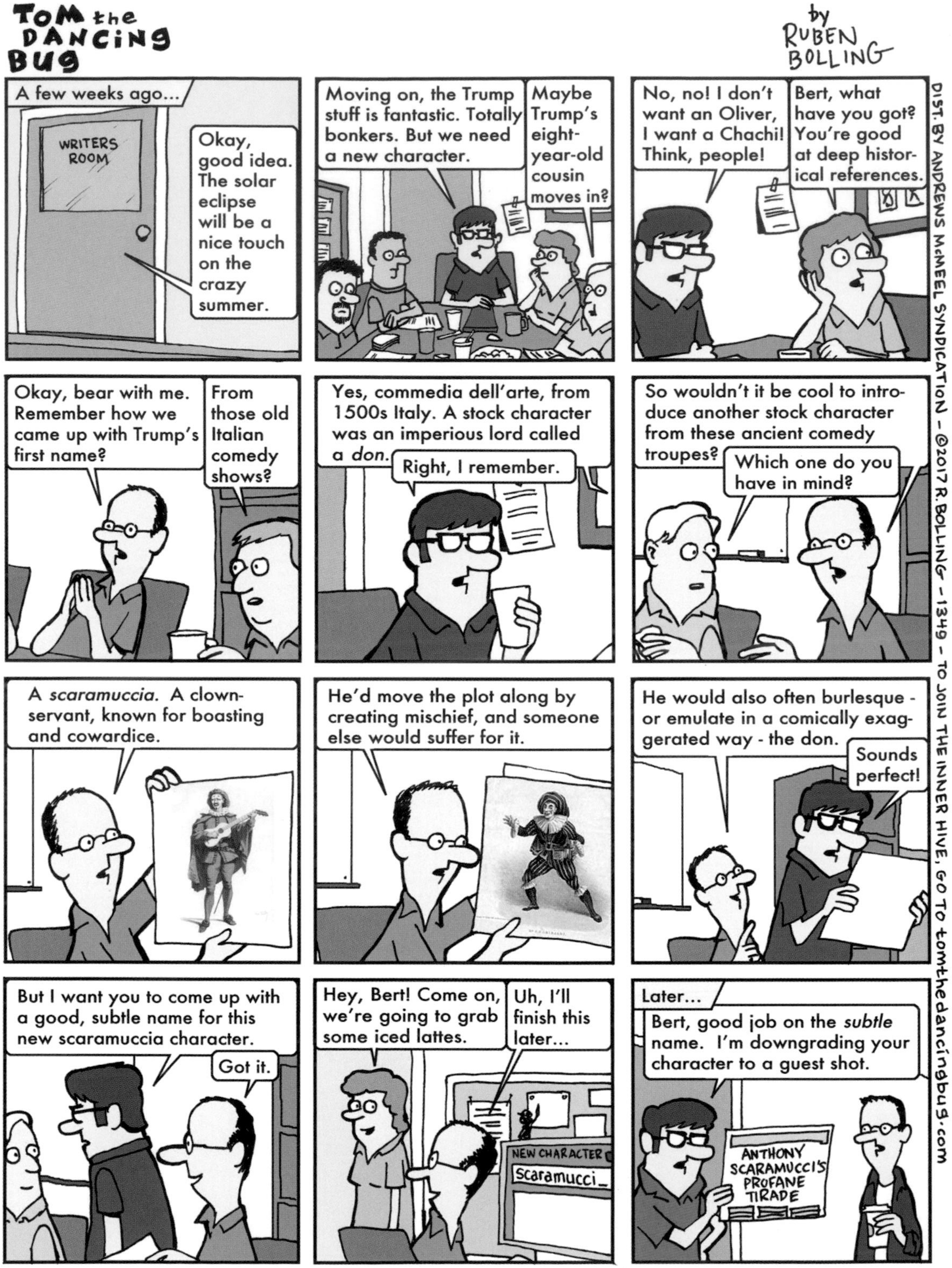
TOM the DANCING BUG
by RUBEN BOLLING
A few weeks ago...
WRITERS ROOM
Okay, good idea. The solar eclipse will be a nice touch on the crazy summer.
Moving on, the Trump stuff is fantastic. Totally bonkers. But we need a new character.
Maybe Trump's eight-year-old cousin moves in?
No, no! I don't want an Oliver, I want a Chachi! Think, people!
Bert, what have you got? You're good at deep historical references.
Okay, bear with me. Remember how we came up with Trump's first name?
From those old Italian comedy shows?
Yes, commedia dell'arte, from 1500s Italy. A stock character was an imperious lord called a *don*.
Right, I remember.
So wouldn't it be cool to introduce another stock character from these ancient comedy troupes?
Which one do you have in mind?
A *scaramuccia*. A clown-servant, known for boasting and cowardice.
He'd move the plot along by creating mischief, and someone else would suffer for it.
He would also often burlesque - or emulate in a comically exaggerated way - the don.
Sounds perfect!
But I want you to come up with a good, subtle name for this new scaramuccia character.
Got it.
Hey, Bert! Come on, we're going to grab some iced lattes.
Uh, I'll finish this later...
NEW CHARACTER
Scaramucci_
Later...
Bert, good job on the *subtle* name. I'm downgrading your character to a guest shot.
ANTHONY SCARAMUCCI'S PROFANE TIRADE
DIST. BY ANDREWS McMEEL SYNDICATION - ©2017 R. BOLLING - 1349 - TO JOIN THE INNER HIVE, GO TO tomthedancingbug.com

7/31/17

Tom the Dancing Bug

by Ruben Bolling

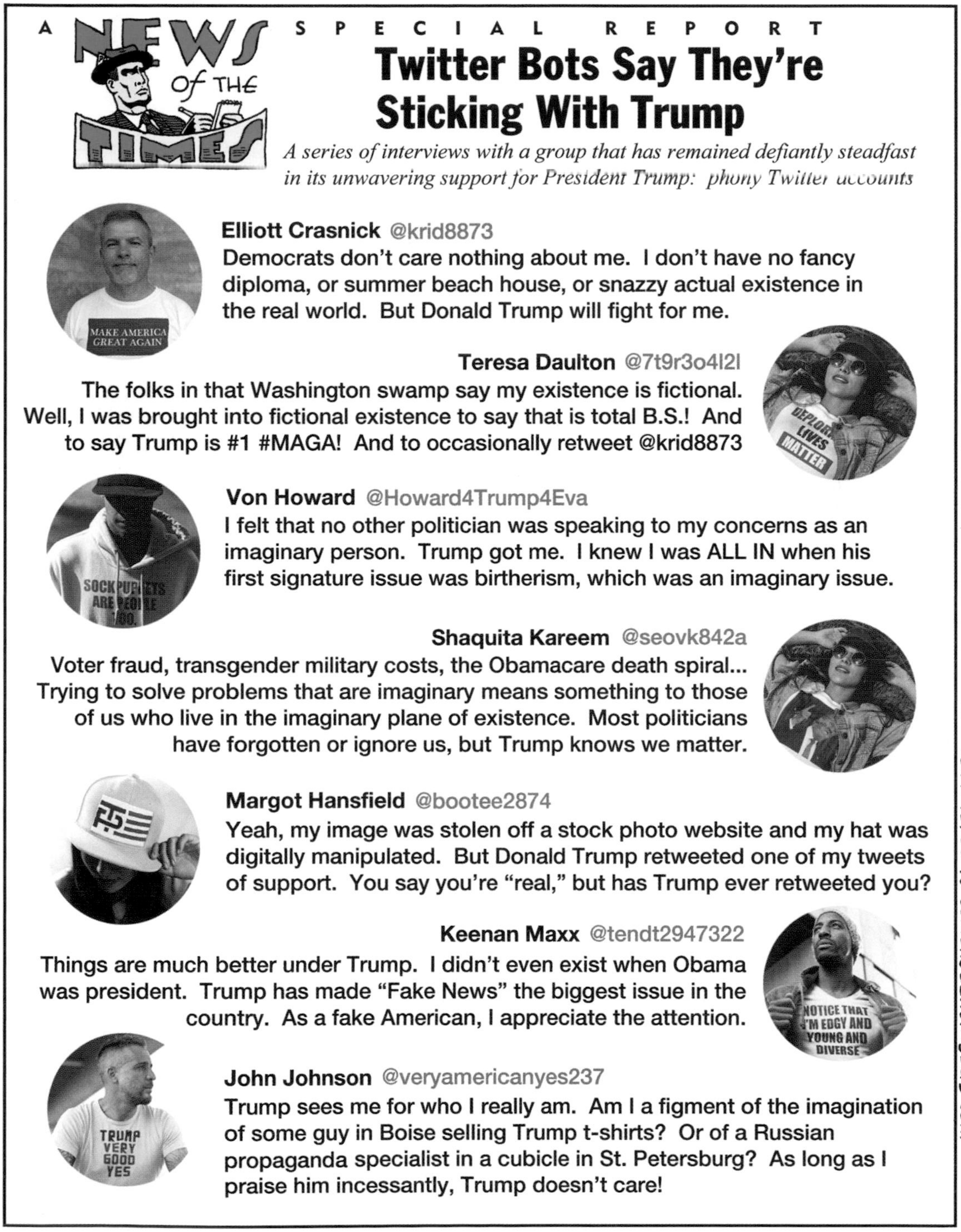

A NEWS of the TIMES SPECIAL REPORT
Twitter Bots Say They're Sticking With Trump
A series of interviews with a group that has remained defiantly steadfast in its unwavering support for President Trump: phony Twitter accounts
Elliott Crasnick @krid8873
Democrats don't care nothing about me. I don't have no fancy diploma, or summer beach house, or snazzy actual existence in the real world. But Donald Trump will fight for me.
MAKE AMERICA GREAT AGAIN
Teresa Daulton @7t9r3o4l2l
The folks in that Washington swamp say my existence is fictional. Well, I was brought into fictional existence to say that is total B.S.! And to say Trump is #1 #MAGA! And to occasionally retweet @krid8873
DEPLOR LIVES MATTER
Von Howard @Howard4Trump4Eva
I felt that no other politician was speaking to my concerns as an imaginary person. Trump got me. I knew I was ALL IN when his first signature issue was birtherism, which was an imaginary issue.
SOCK PUPPETS ARE PEOPLE TOO.
Shaquita Kareem @seovk842a
Voter fraud, transgender military costs, the Obamacare death spiral... Trying to solve problems that are imaginary means something to those of us who live in the imaginary plane of existence. Most politicians have forgotten or ignore us, but Trump knows we matter.
Margot Hansfield @bootee2874
Yeah, my image was stolen off a stock photo website and my hat was digitally manipulated. But Donald Trump retweeted one of my tweets of support. You say you're "real," but has Trump ever retweeted you?
Keenan Maxx @tendt2947322
Things are much better under Trump. I didn't even exist when Obama was president. Trump has made "Fake News" the biggest issue in the country. As a fake American, I appreciate the attention.
NOTICE THAT I'M EDGY AND YOUNG AND DIVERSE
John Johnson @veryamericanyes237
Trump sees me for who I really am. Am I a figment of the imagination of some guy in Boise selling Trump t-shirts? Or of a Russian propaganda specialist in a cubicle in St. Petersburg? As long as I praise him incessantly, Trump doesn't care!
TRUMP VERY GOOD YES

8/7/17

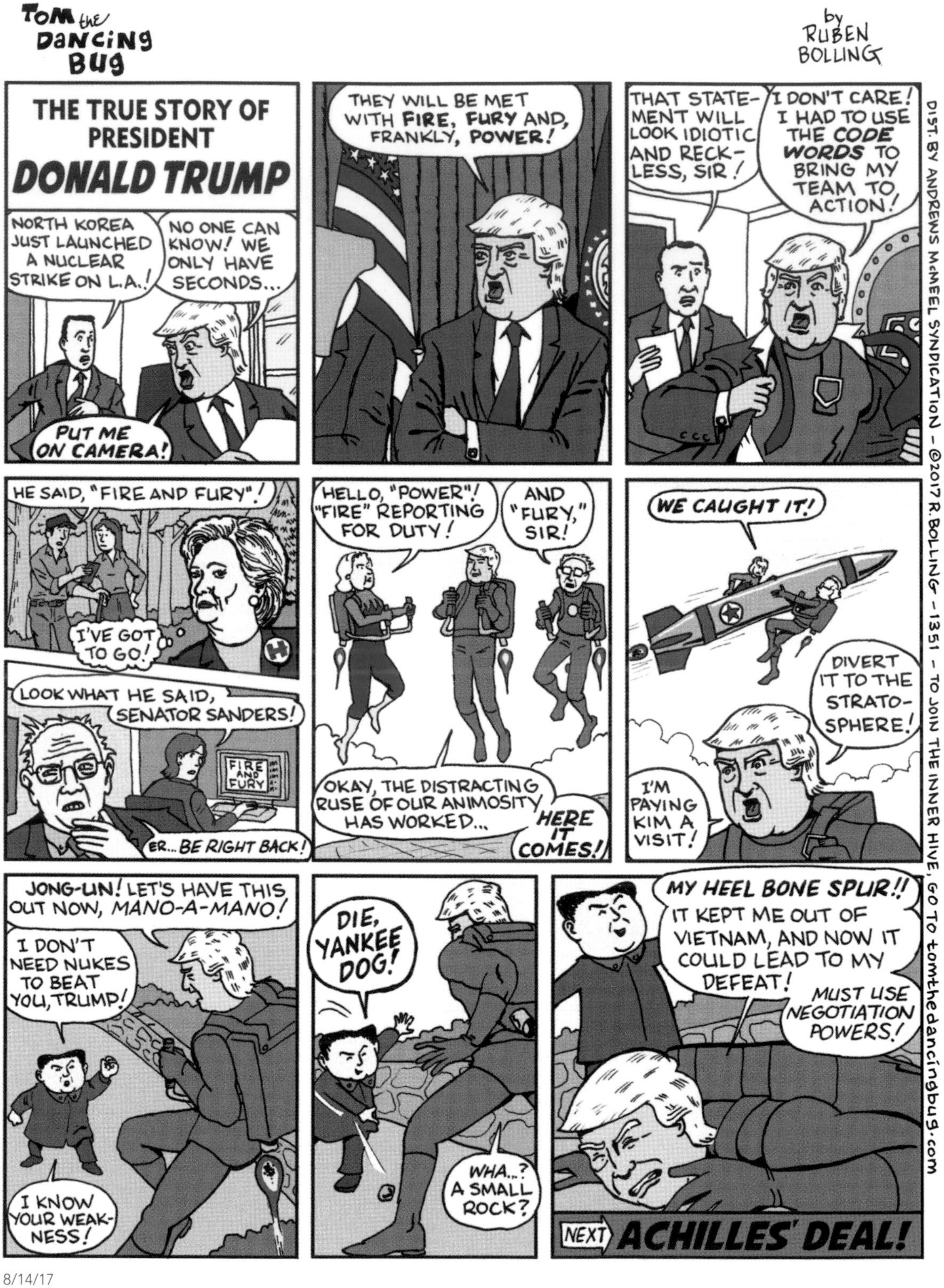
TOM the DANCING BUG
by RUBEN BOLLING
THE TRUE STORY OF PRESIDENT DONALD TRUMP
NORTH KOREA JUST LAUNCHED A NUCLEAR STRIKE ON L.A.!
NO ONE CAN KNOW! WE ONLY HAVE SECONDS...
PUT ME ON CAMERA!
THEY WILL BE MET WITH FIRE, FURY AND, FRANKLY, POWER!
THAT STATEMENT WILL LOOK IDIOTIC AND RECKLESS, SIR!
I DON'T CARE! I HAD TO USE THE CODE WORDS TO BRING MY TEAM TO ACTION!
HE SAID, "FIRE AND FURY"!
I'VE GOT TO GO!
LOOK WHAT HE SAID, SENATOR SANDERS!
FIRE AND FURY
ER... BE RIGHT BACK!
HELLO, "POWER"! "FIRE" REPORTING FOR DUTY!
AND "FURY," SIR!
OKAY, THE DISTRACTING RUSE OF OUR ANIMOSITY HAS WORKED...
HERE IT COMES!
WE CAUGHT IT!
DIVERT IT TO THE STRATOSPHERE!
I'M PAYING KIM A VISIT!
JONG-UN! LET'S HAVE THIS OUT NOW, MANO-A-MANO!
I DON'T NEED NUKES TO BEAT YOU, TRUMP!
I KNOW YOUR WEAKNESS!
DIE, YANKEE DOG!
WHA..? A SMALL ROCK?
MY HEEL BONE SPUR!! IT KEPT ME OUT OF VIETNAM, AND NOW IT COULD LEAD TO MY DEFEAT!
MUST USE NEGOTIATION POWERS!
NEXT ACHILLES' DEAL!
DIST. BY ANDREWS McMEEL SYNDICATION – ©2017 R. BOLLING – 1351 – TO JOIN THE INNER HIVE, GO TO tomthedancingbug.com

8/14/17

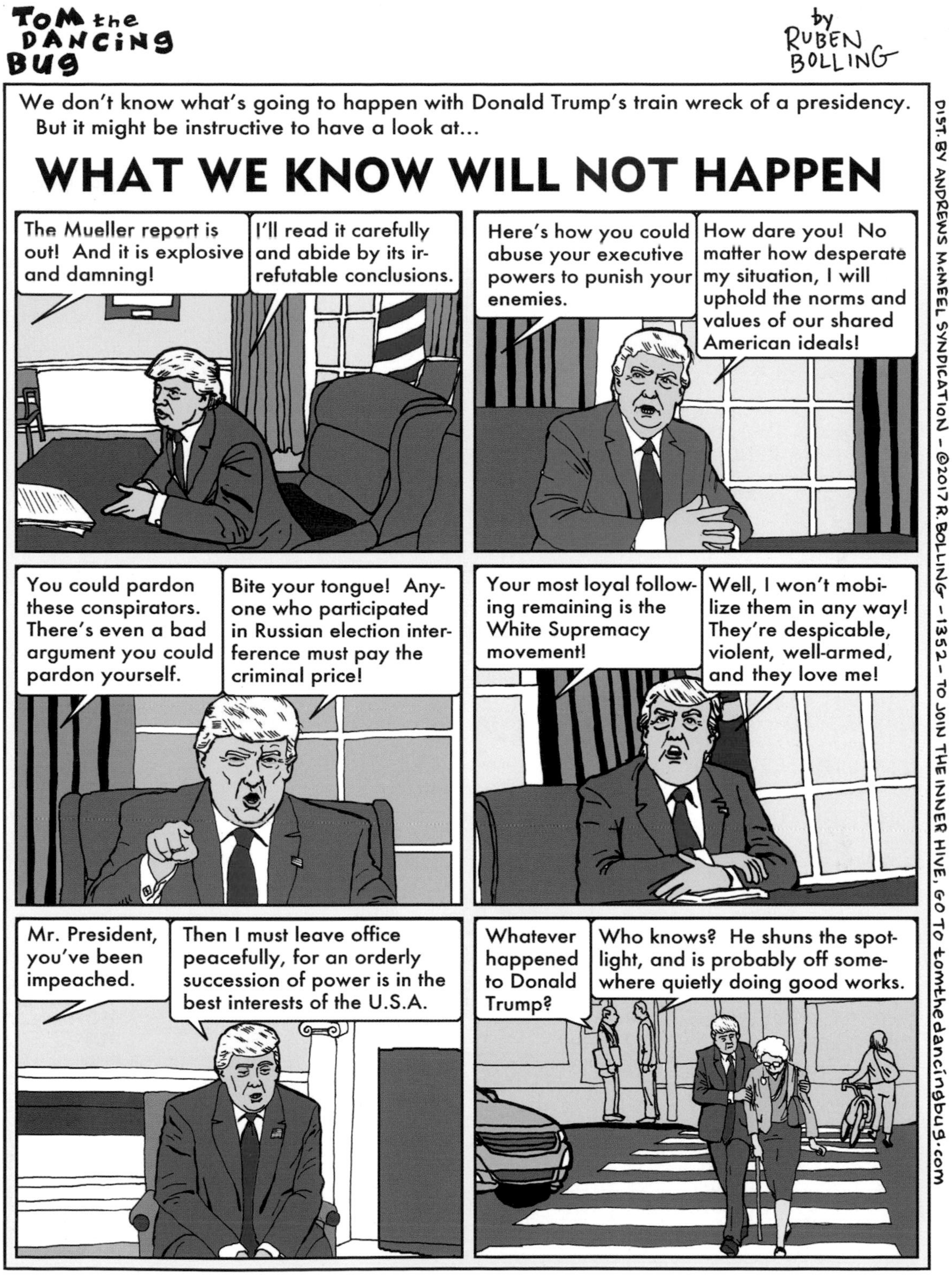
TOM the DANCING BUG
by RUBEN BOLLING
We don't know what's going to happen with Donald Trump's train wreck of a presidency. But it might be instructive to have a look at...
WHAT WE KNOW WILL NOT HAPPEN
The Mueller report is out! And it is explosive and damning!
I'll read it carefully and abide by its irrefutable conclusions.
Here's how you could abuse your executive powers to punish your enemies.
How dare you! No matter how desperate my situation, I will uphold the norms and values of our shared American ideals!
You could pardon these conspirators. There's even a bad argument you could pardon yourself.
Bite your tongue! Anyone who participated in Russian election interference must pay the criminal price!
Your most loyal following remaining is the White Supremacy movement!
Well, I won't mobilize them in any way! They're despicable, violent, well-armed, and they love me!
Mr. President, you've been impeached.
Then I must leave office peacefully, for an orderly succession of power is in the best interests of the U.S.A.
Whatever happened to Donald Trump?
Who knows? He shuns the spotlight, and is probably off somewhere quietly doing good works.
DIST. BY ANDREWS McMEEL SYNDICATION - ©2017 R. BOLLING - 1352 - TO JOIN THE INNER HIVE, GO TO tomthedancingbug.com

8/21/17

TOM the DANCING BUG'S SUPER-FUN-PAK COMIX

EDITED BY RUBEN BOLLING

THREE-PANEL BIOGRAPHIES

OLIVER CROMWELL WAS BORN IN HUNTINGDON, ENGLAND ON APRIL 25, 1599.

ON APRIL 26, HE MOSTLY ATE, CRIED, AND SLEPT. HE POOPED THREE TIMES.

THEN HE DID SOME STUFF IN ENGLISH HISTORY, THEN HE DIED CHOKING ON A CHALUPA.

THIS IS NOT A PIPE

This is not a pipe.

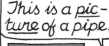

This is a pic-ture of a pipe.

Now, this *is* a pipe.

Magritte

GOOD COP / CHAOS BUTTERFLY COP

YOU'D BETTER TALK, OR I'LL LEAVE YOU TO MY PARTNER, AND THERE'S NO TELLING *WHAT* WILL HAPPEN!

OKAY, YOU ASKED FOR IT!

FLAP!

3 WEEKS LATER

TYPHOON HITS INDONESIA — DOW↓300

JARRINGLY DISCONTINUOUS TRANSITIONS COMIX

MAYBE ACE WASN'T KIDNAPPED AFTER ALL!

MEANWHILE, SUDDENLY

I AGREE! THE PEASANTS **ARE** REVOLTING!

YET, ELSEWHERE

DAMN, THAT MEGAN FOX IS FINE!

THEN WITHOUT WARNING-

NEVER META MAN I DIDN'T LIKE

WHAT IS ALL THIS?

IT'S MEANT TO EVOKE A NEWS-PAPER COMICS PAGE.

THAT'S NOT EVEN A **THING** ANYMORE!

GOD HELP US.

Bolling

DOOKER, THE DOG THAT'S SO HUGE IT CREATES A GRAVITA-TIONAL FIELD FROM WHICH NO MATTER CAN ESCAPE

"I can't find my slippers. Dooker!"

FAMILY CIRCUS DU SOLEIL

Jaques

"Mommy, can we use the drapes to create a magical dreamscape of whimsy and wonder?"

BELTWAY BANALITIES (NOW WITH OVERT NAZISM)

GEEZ... THE GOVERNMENT IS GOOD AT ONE THING-- GETTING IN THE WAY!!

ALSO: BLOOD AND SOIL!

Flynn

THIS IS NOT A PIPE EITHER

Oh, shut up.

DIST. BY ANDREWS McMEEL SYNDICATION - ©2017 R. Bolling -1353- TO JOIN THE INNER HIVE, GO TO tomthedancingbug.com

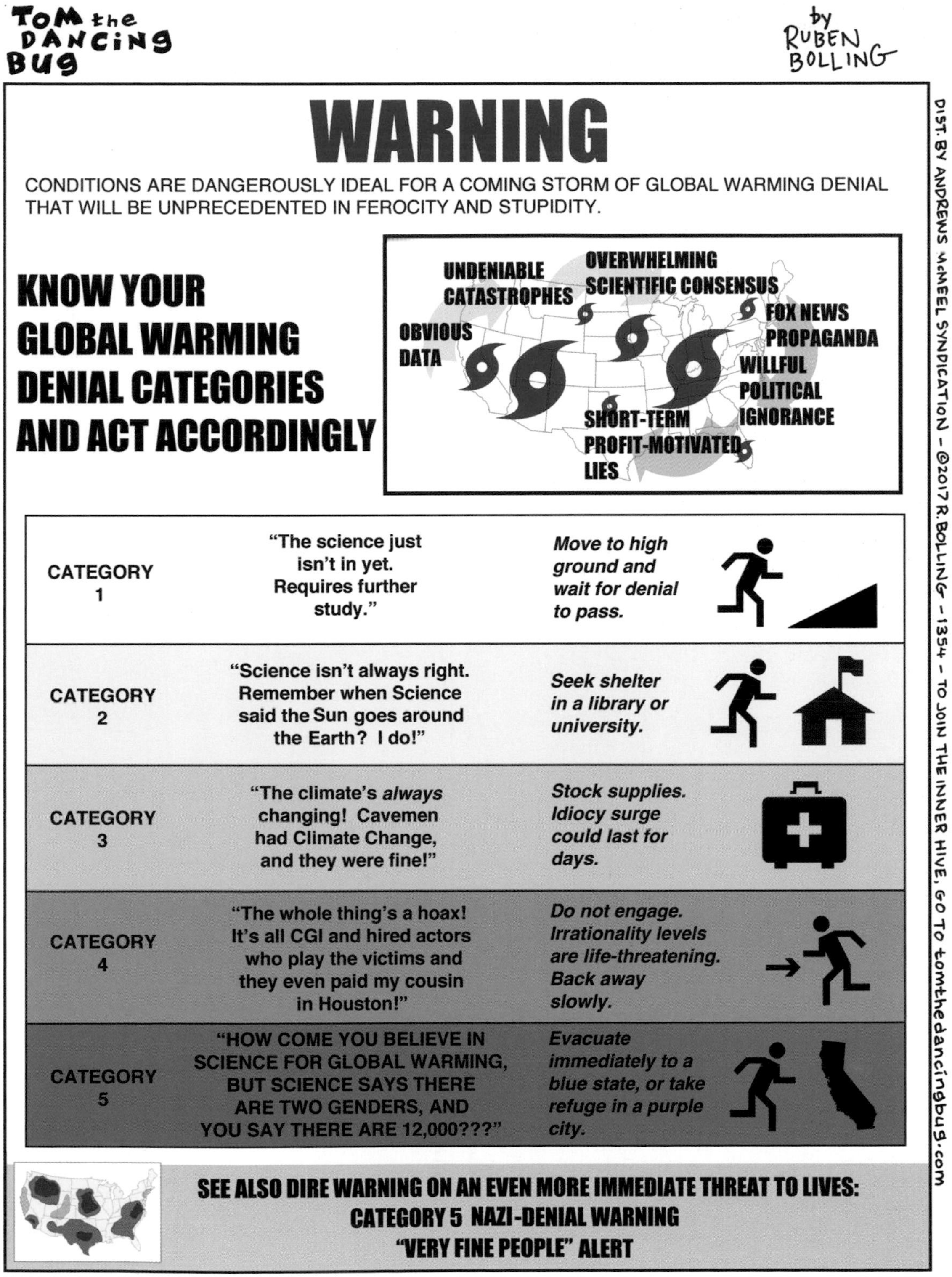

TOM the DANCING BUG

by RUBEN BOLLING

WARNING

CONDITIONS ARE DANGEROUSLY IDEAL FOR A COMING STORM OF GLOBAL WARMING DENIAL THAT WILL BE UNPRECEDENTED IN FEROCITY AND STUPIDITY.

KNOW YOUR GLOBAL WARMING DENIAL CATEGORIES AND ACT ACCORDINGLY

UNDENIABLE CATASTROPHES
OVERWHELMING SCIENTIFIC CONSENSUS
OBVIOUS DATA
FOX NEWS PROPAGANDA
WILLFUL POLITICAL IGNORANCE
SHORT-TERM PROFIT-MOTIVATED LIES

CATEGORY 1	"The science just isn't in yet. Requires further study."	*Move to high ground and wait for denial to pass.*	
CATEGORY 2	"Science isn't always right. Remember when Science said the Sun goes around the Earth? I do!"	*Seek shelter in a library or university.*	
CATEGORY 3	"The climate's *always* changing! Cavemen had Climate Change, and they were fine!"	*Stock supplies. Idiocy surge could last for days.*	
CATEGORY 4	"The whole thing's a hoax! It's all CGI and hired actors who play the victims and they even paid my cousin in Houston!"	*Do not engage. Irrationality levels are life-threatening. Back away slowly.*	
CATEGORY 5	"HOW COME YOU BELIEVE IN SCIENCE FOR GLOBAL WARMING, BUT SCIENCE SAYS THERE ARE TWO GENDERS, AND YOU SAY THERE ARE 12,000???"	*Evacuate immediately to a blue state, or take refuge in a purple city.*	

SEE ALSO DIRE WARNING ON AN EVEN MORE IMMEDIATE THREAT TO LIVES: CATEGORY 5 NAZI-DENIAL WARNING "VERY FINE PEOPLE" ALERT

DIST. BY ANDREWS McMEEL SYNDICATION — ©2017 R. BOLLING — 1354 — TO JOIN THE INNER HIVE, GO TO tomthedancingbug.com

9/11/17

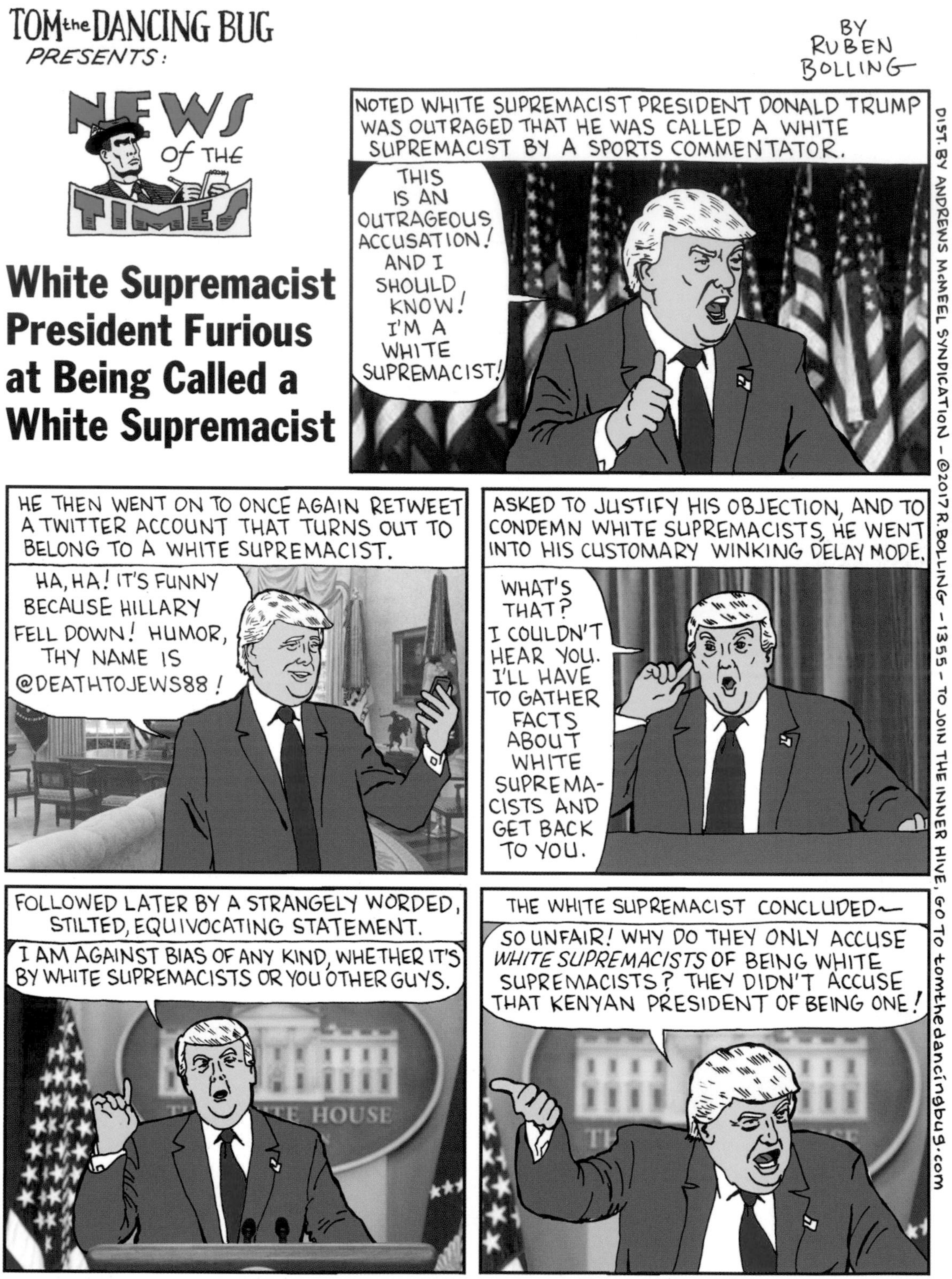
TOM the DANCING BUG PRESENTS:
BY RUBEN BOLLING
NEWS of THE TIMES
White Supremacist President Furious at Being Called a White Supremacist
NOTED WHITE SUPREMACIST PRESIDENT DONALD TRUMP WAS OUTRAGED THAT HE WAS CALLED A WHITE SUPREMACIST BY A SPORTS COMMENTATOR.
THIS IS AN OUTRAGEOUS ACCUSATION! AND I SHOULD KNOW! I'M A WHITE SUPREMACIST!
HE THEN WENT ON TO ONCE AGAIN RETWEET A TWITTER ACCOUNT THAT TURNS OUT TO BELONG TO A WHITE SUPREMACIST.
HA, HA! IT'S FUNNY BECAUSE HILLARY FELL DOWN! HUMOR, THY NAME IS @DEATHTOJEWS88!
ASKED TO JUSTIFY HIS OBJECTION, AND TO CONDEMN WHITE SUPREMACISTS, HE WENT INTO HIS CUSTOMARY WINKING DELAY MODE.
WHAT'S THAT? I COULDN'T HEAR YOU. I'LL HAVE TO GATHER FACTS ABOUT WHITE SUPREMACISTS AND GET BACK TO YOU.
FOLLOWED LATER BY A STRANGELY WORDED, STILTED, EQUIVOCATING STATEMENT.
I AM AGAINST BIAS OF ANY KIND, WHETHER IT'S BY WHITE SUPREMACISTS OR YOU OTHER GUYS.
THE WHITE SUPREMACIST CONCLUDED—
SO UNFAIR! WHY DO THEY ONLY ACCUSE *WHITE SUPREMACISTS* OF BEING WHITE SUPREMACISTS? THEY DIDN'T ACCUSE THAT KENYAN PRESIDENT OF BEING ONE!
DIST. BY ANDREWS McMEEL SYNDICATION – ©2017 R. BOLLING – 1355 – TO JOIN THE INNER HIVE, GO TO tomthedancingbug.com

9/18/17

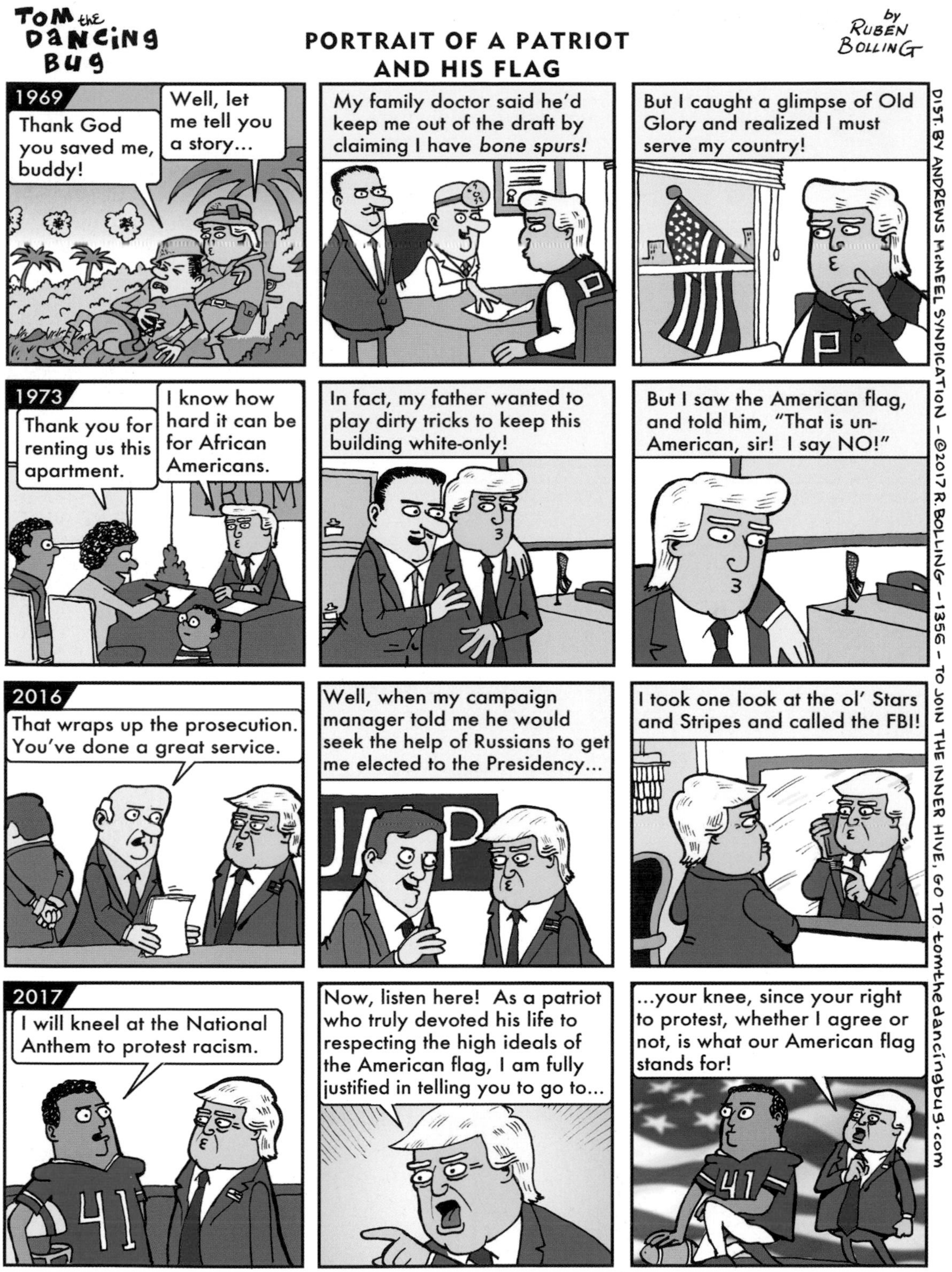
TOM the DANCING BUG
PORTRAIT OF A PATRIOT AND HIS FLAG
by RUBEN BOLLING
1969
Thank God you saved me, buddy!
Well, let me tell you a story…
My family doctor said he'd keep me out of the draft by claiming I have *bone spurs!*
But I caught a glimpse of Old Glory and realized I must serve my country!
1973
Thank you for renting us this apartment.
I know how hard it can be for African Americans.
In fact, my father wanted to play dirty tricks to keep this building white-only!
But I saw the American flag, and told him, "That is un-American, sir! I say NO!"
2016
That wraps up the prosecution. You've done a great service.
Well, when my campaign manager told me he would seek the help of Russians to get me elected to the Presidency…
I took one look at the ol' Stars and Stripes and called the FBI!
2017
I will kneel at the National Anthem to protest racism.
Now, listen here! As a patriot who truly devoted his life to respecting the high ideals of the American flag, I am fully justified in telling you to go to…
…your knee, since your right to protest, whether I agree or not, is what our American flag stands for!
41
DIST. BY ANDREWS McMEEL SYNDICATION – ©2017 R. BOLLING – 1356 – TO JOIN THE INNER HIVE, GO TO tomthedancingbug.com

9/25/17

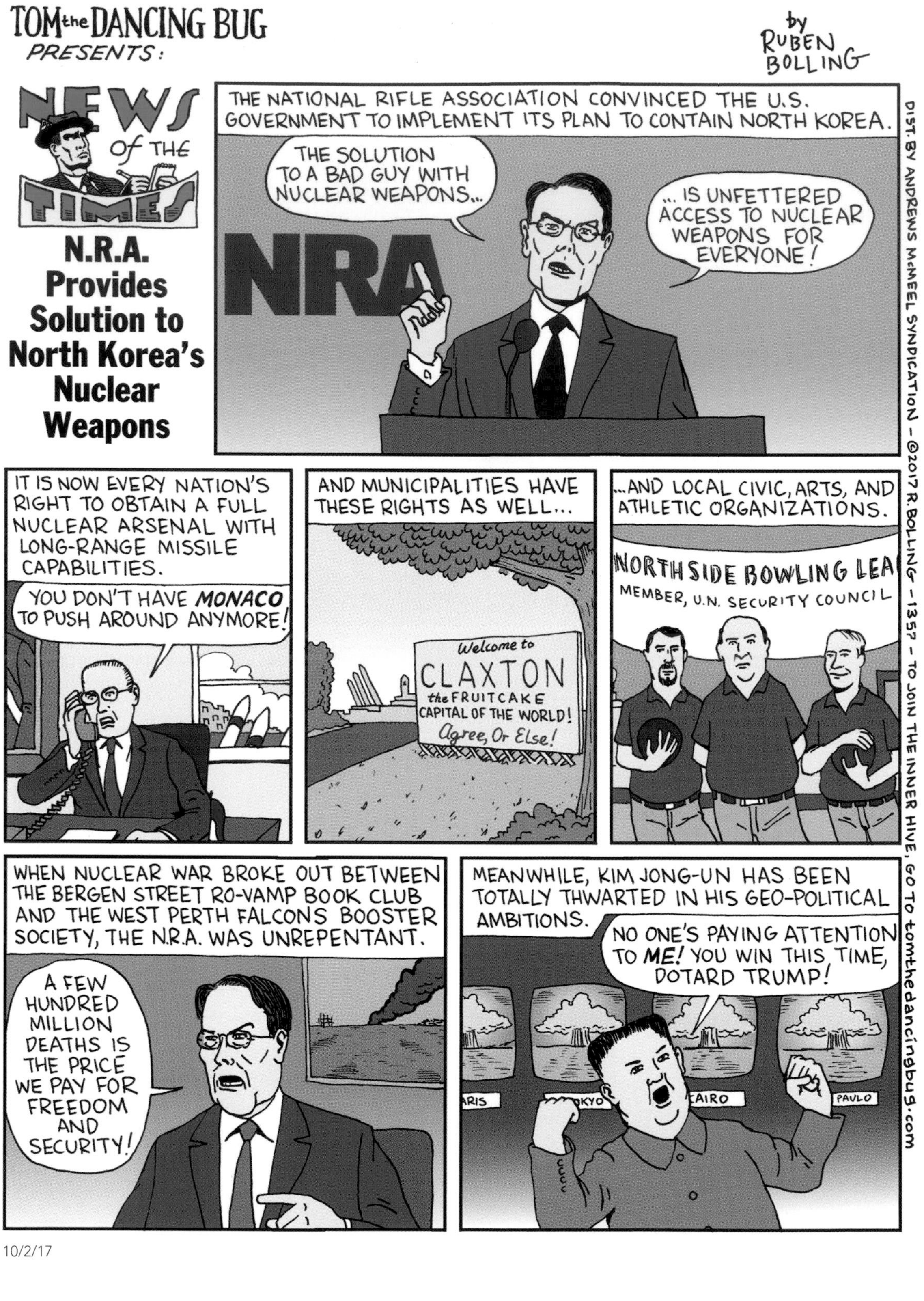
TOM the DANCING BUG
PRESENTS:
by RUBEN BOLLING
NEWS of THE TIMES
N.R.A. Provides Solution to North Korea's Nuclear Weapons
THE NATIONAL RIFLE ASSOCIATION CONVINCED THE U.S. GOVERNMENT TO IMPLEMENT ITS PLAN TO CONTAIN NORTH KOREA.
THE SOLUTION TO A BAD GUY WITH NUCLEAR WEAPONS...
NRA
...IS UNFETTERED ACCESS TO NUCLEAR WEAPONS FOR EVERYONE!
IT IS NOW EVERY NATION'S RIGHT TO OBTAIN A FULL NUCLEAR ARSENAL WITH LONG-RANGE MISSILE CAPABILITIES.
YOU DON'T HAVE MONACO TO PUSH AROUND ANYMORE!
AND MUNICIPALITIES HAVE THESE RIGHTS AS WELL...
Welcome to CLAXTON the FRUITCAKE CAPITAL OF THE WORLD! Agree, Or Else!
...AND LOCAL CIVIC, ARTS, AND ATHLETIC ORGANIZATIONS.
NORTH SIDE BOWLING LEA
MEMBER, U.N. SECURITY COUNCIL
WHEN NUCLEAR WAR BROKE OUT BETWEEN THE BERGEN STREET RO-VAMP BOOK CLUB AND THE WEST PERTH FALCONS BOOSTER SOCIETY, THE N.R.A. WAS UNREPENTANT.
A FEW HUNDRED MILLION DEATHS IS THE PRICE WE PAY FOR FREEDOM AND SECURITY!
MEANWHILE, KIM JONG-UN HAS BEEN TOTALLY THWARTED IN HIS GEO-POLITICAL AMBITIONS.
NO ONE'S PAYING ATTENTION TO ME! YOU WIN THIS TIME, DOTARD TRUMP!
ARIS
OKYO
CAIRO
PAULO
DIST. BY ANDREWS McMEEL SYNDICATION - ©2017 R. BOLLING - 1357 - TO JOIN THE INNER HIVE, GO TO tomthedancingbug.com

10/2/17

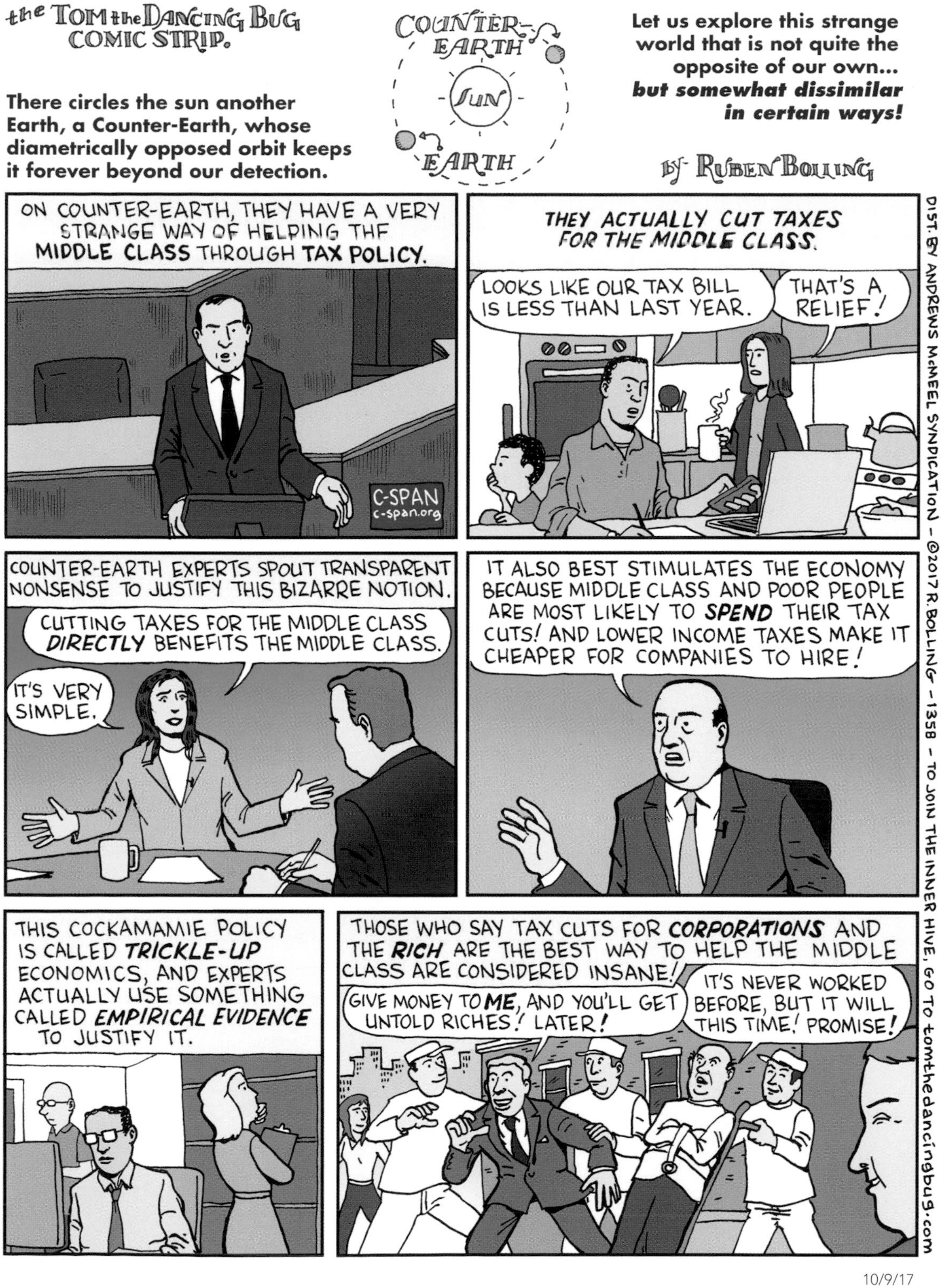
the TOM the DANCING BUG COMIC STRIP.
COUNTER-EARTH
SUN
EARTH
There circles the sun another Earth, a Counter-Earth, whose diametrically opposed orbit keeps it forever beyond our detection.
Let us explore this strange world that is not quite the opposite of our own... but somewhat dissimilar in certain ways!
by RUBEN BOLLING
ON COUNTER-EARTH, THEY HAVE A VERY STRANGE WAY OF HELPING THE MIDDLE CLASS THROUGH TAX POLICY.
C-SPAN c-span.org
THEY ACTUALLY CUT TAXES FOR THE MIDDLE CLASS.
LOOKS LIKE OUR TAX BILL IS LESS THAN LAST YEAR.
THAT'S A RELIEF!
COUNTER-EARTH EXPERTS SPOUT TRANSPARENT NONSENSE TO JUSTIFY THIS BIZARRE NOTION.
IT'S VERY SIMPLE.
CUTTING TAXES FOR THE MIDDLE CLASS DIRECTLY BENEFITS THE MIDDLE CLASS.
IT ALSO BEST STIMULATES THE ECONOMY BECAUSE MIDDLE CLASS AND POOR PEOPLE ARE MOST LIKELY TO SPEND THEIR TAX CUTS! AND LOWER INCOME TAXES MAKE IT CHEAPER FOR COMPANIES TO HIRE!
THIS COCKAMAMIE POLICY IS CALLED TRICKLE-UP ECONOMICS, AND EXPERTS ACTUALLY USE SOMETHING CALLED EMPIRICAL EVIDENCE TO JUSTIFY IT.
THOSE WHO SAY TAX CUTS FOR CORPORATIONS AND THE RICH ARE THE BEST WAY TO HELP THE MIDDLE CLASS ARE CONSIDERED INSANE!
GIVE MONEY TO ME, AND YOU'LL GET UNTOLD RICHES! LATER!
IT'S NEVER WORKED BEFORE, BUT IT WILL THIS TIME! PROMISE!
DIST. BY ANDREWS McMEEL SYNDICATION - ©2017 R. BOLLING - 1358 - TO JOIN THE INNER HIVE, GO TO tomthedancingbug.com

10/9/17

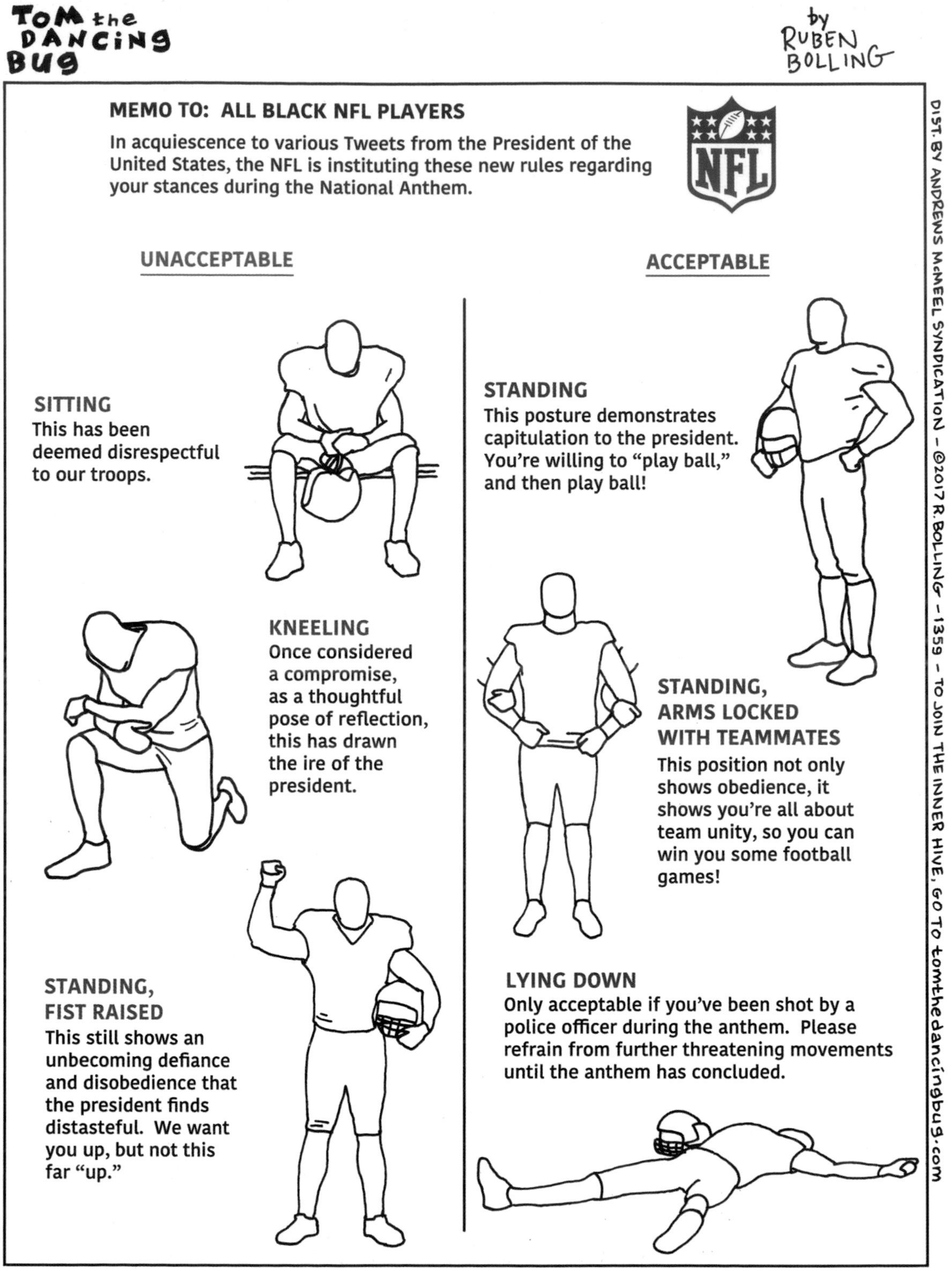

TOM the DANCING BUG

by RUBEN BOLLING

DIST. BY ANDREWS McMEEL SYNDICATION ~ ©2017 R. BOLLING ~ 1359 ~ TO JOIN THE INNER HIVE, GO TO tomthedancingbug.com

MEMO TO: ALL BLACK NFL PLAYERS

In acquiescence to various Tweets from the President of the United States, the NFL is instituting these new rules regarding your stances during the National Anthem.

UNACCEPTABLE

ACCEPTABLE

SITTING
This has been deemed disrespectful to our troops.

STANDING
This posture demonstrates capitulation to the president. You're willing to "play ball," and then play ball!

KNEELING
Once considered a compromise, as a thoughtful pose of reflection, this has drawn the ire of the president.

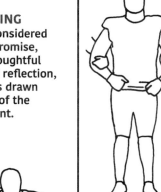

STANDING, ARMS LOCKED WITH TEAMMATES
This position not only shows obedience, it shows you're all about team unity, so you can win you some football games!

STANDING, FIST RAISED
This still shows an unbecoming defiance and disobedience that the president finds distasteful. We want you up, but not this far "up."

LYING DOWN
Only acceptable if you've been shot by a police officer during the anthem. Please refrain from further threatening movements until the anthem has concluded.

10/16/17

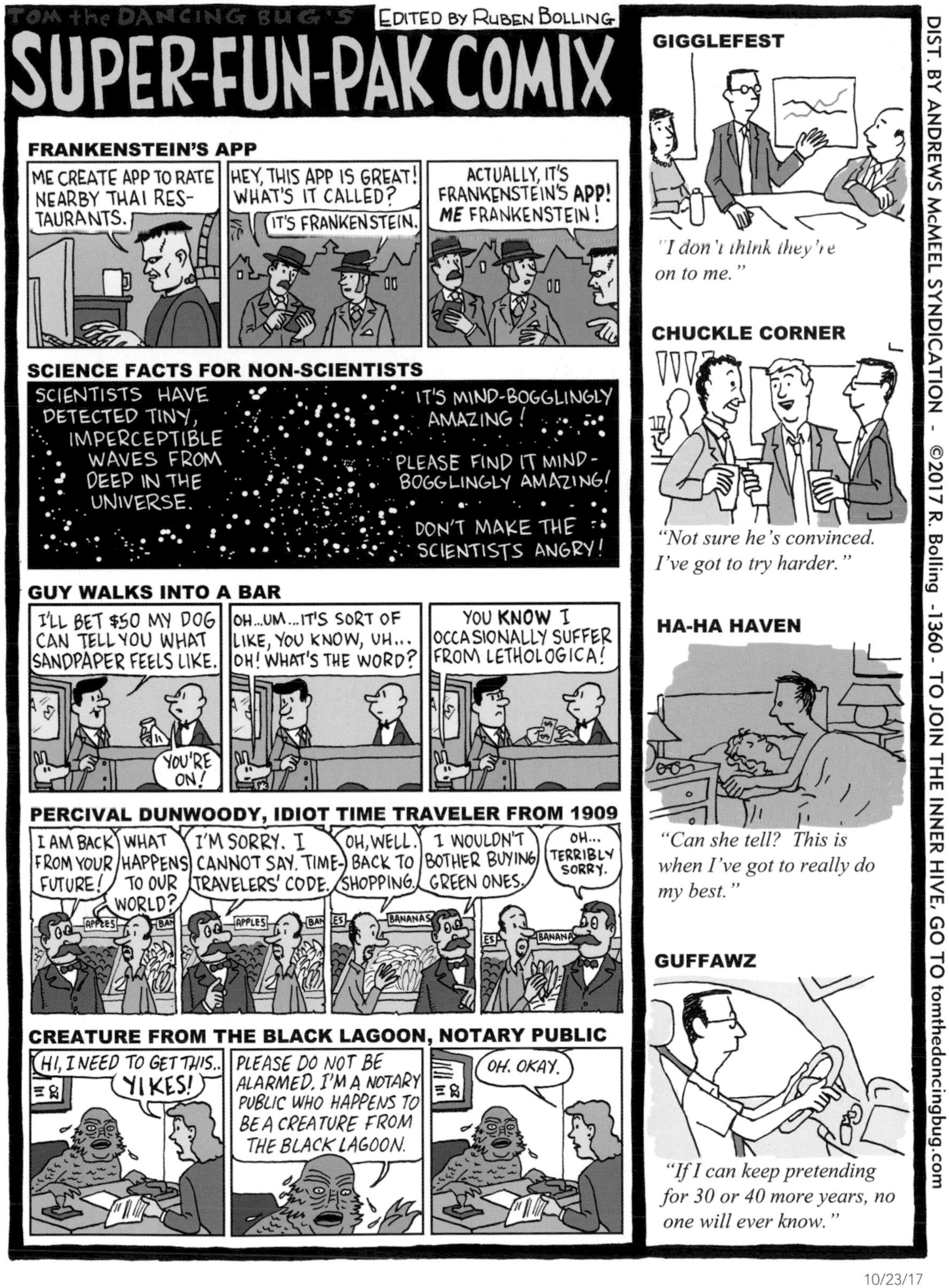
TOM the DANCING BUG'S
EDITED BY RUBEN BOLLING
SUPER-FUN-PAK COMIX
FRANKENSTEIN'S APP
ME CREATE APP TO RATE NEARBY THAI RESTAURANTS.
HEY, THIS APP IS GREAT! WHAT'S IT CALLED?
IT'S FRANKENSTEIN.
ACTUALLY, IT'S FRANKENSTEIN'S APP! ME FRANKENSTEIN!
SCIENCE FACTS FOR NON-SCIENTISTS
SCIENTISTS HAVE DETECTED TINY, IMPERCEPTIBLE WAVES FROM DEEP IN THE UNIVERSE.
IT'S MIND-BOGGLINGLY AMAZING!
PLEASE FIND IT MIND-BOGGLINGLY AMAZING!
DON'T MAKE THE SCIENTISTS ANGRY!
GUY WALKS INTO A BAR
I'LL BET $50 MY DOG CAN TELL YOU WHAT SANDPAPER FEELS LIKE.
YOU'RE ON!
OH...UM...IT'S SORT OF LIKE, YOU KNOW, UH... OH! WHAT'S THE WORD?
YOU KNOW I OCCASIONALLY SUFFER FROM LETHOLOGICA!
PERCIVAL DUNWOODY, IDIOT TIME TRAVELER FROM 1909
I AM BACK FROM YOUR FUTURE!
WHAT HAPPENS TO OUR WORLD?
APPLES
I'M SORRY. I CANNOT SAY. TIME-TRAVELERS' CODE.
OH, WELL. BACK TO SHOPPING.
BANANAS
I WOULDN'T BOTHER BUYING GREEN ONES.
OH... TERRIBLY SORRY.
CREATURE FROM THE BLACK LAGOON, NOTARY PUBLIC
HI, I NEED TO GET THIS..
YIKES!
PLEASE DO NOT BE ALARMED. I'M A NOTARY PUBLIC WHO HAPPENS TO BE A CREATURE FROM THE BLACK LAGOON.
OH. OKAY.
GIGGLEFEST
"I don't think they're on to me."
CHUCKLE CORNER
"Not sure he's convinced. I've got to try harder."
HA-HA HAVEN
"Can she tell? This is when I've got to really do my best."
GUFFAWZ
"If I can keep pretending for 30 or 40 more years, no one will ever know."
DIST. BY ANDREWS McMEEL SYNDICATION - ©2017 R. Bolling -1360- TO JOIN THE INNER HIVE, GO TO tomthedancingbug.com

10/23/17

TOM the DANCING BUG

by RUBEN BOLLING

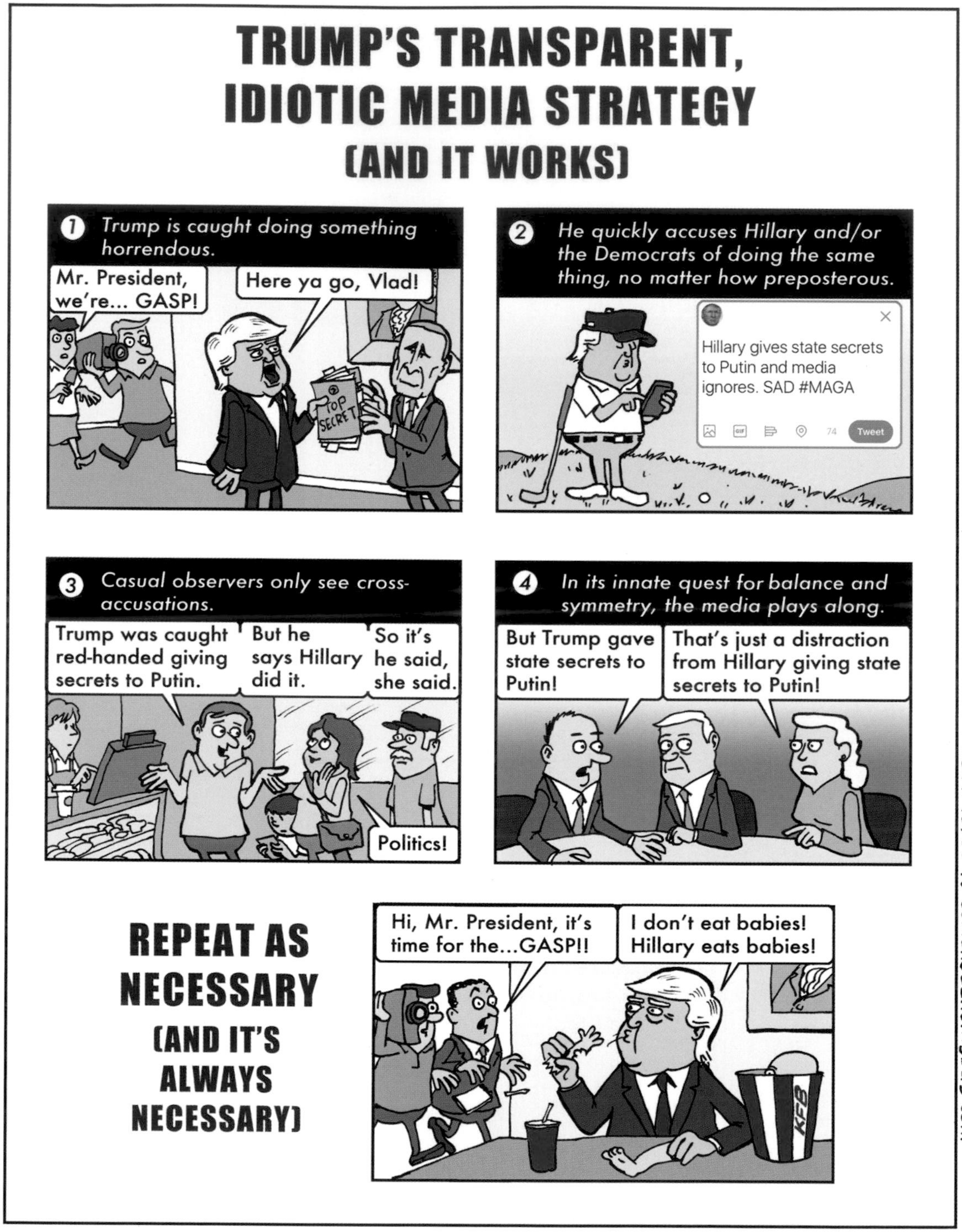
TRUMP'S TRANSPARENT, IDIOTIC MEDIA STRATEGY
(AND IT WORKS)
1 Trump is caught doing something horrendous.
Mr. President, we're... GASP!
Here ya go, Vlad!
TOP SECRET
2 He quickly accuses Hillary and/or the Democrats of doing the same thing, no matter how preposterous.
Hillary gives state secrets to Putin and media ignores. SAD #MAGA
74
Tweet
3 Casual observers only see cross-accusations.
Trump was caught red-handed giving secrets to Putin.
But he says Hillary did it.
So it's he said, she said.
Politics!
4 In its innate quest for balance and symmetry, the media plays along.
But Trump gave state secrets to Putin!
That's just a distraction from Hillary giving state secrets to Putin!
REPEAT AS NECESSARY
(AND IT'S ALWAYS NECESSARY)
Hi, Mr. President, it's time for the...GASP!!
I don't eat babies! Hillary eats babies!
KFB

10/30/17

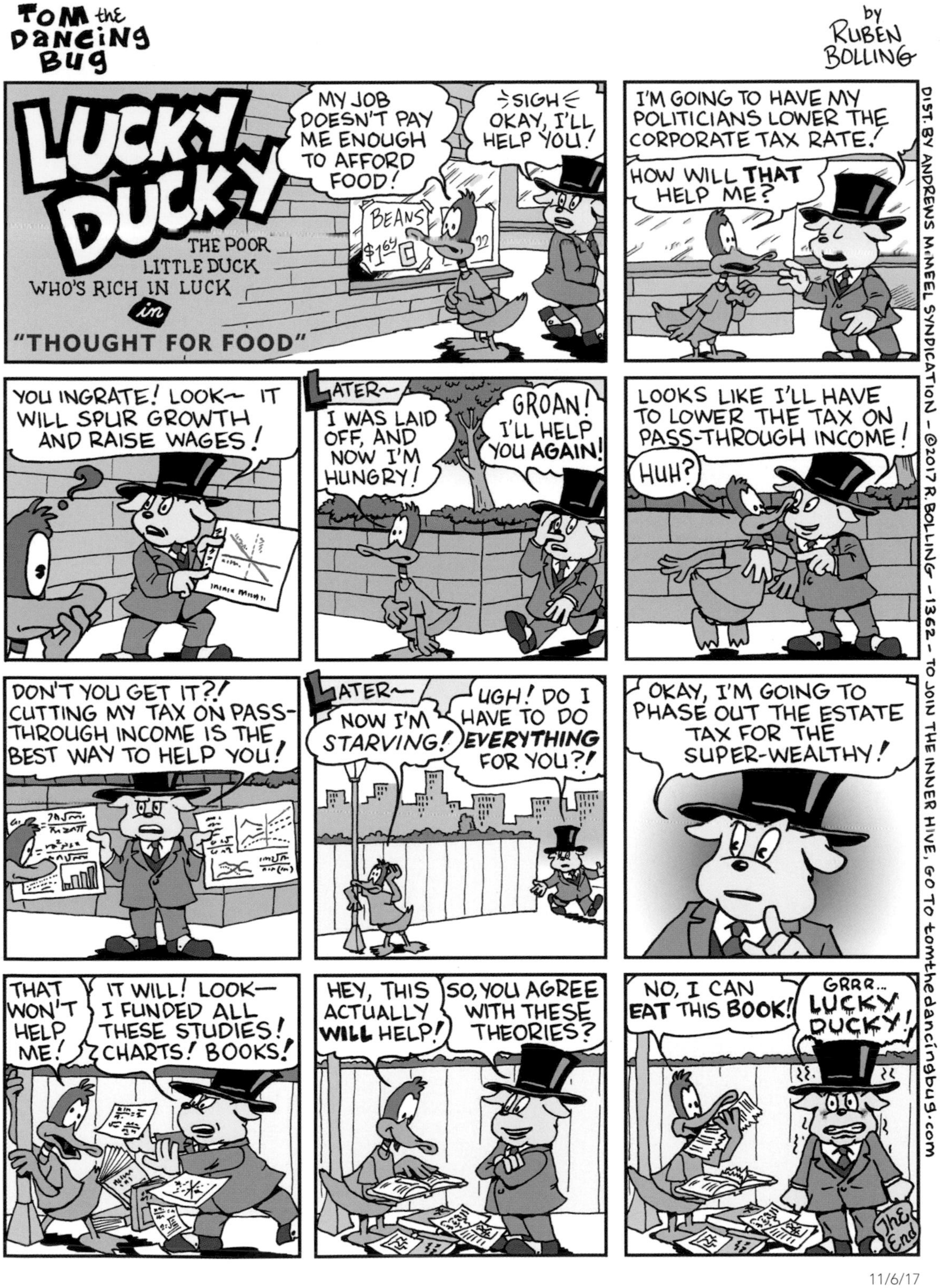
TOM the DANCING BUG
by RUBEN BOLLING
LUCKY DUCKY
THE POOR LITTLE DUCK WHO'S RICH IN LUCK in
"THOUGHT FOR FOOD"
MY JOB DOESN'T PAY ME ENOUGH TO AFFORD FOOD!
BEANS $1.64
SIGH OKAY, I'LL HELP YOU!
I'M GOING TO HAVE MY POLITICIANS LOWER THE CORPORATE TAX RATE!
HOW WILL THAT HELP ME?
YOU INGRATE! LOOK— IT WILL SPUR GROWTH AND RAISE WAGES!
LATER—
I WAS LAID OFF, AND NOW I'M HUNGRY!
GROAN! I'LL HELP YOU AGAIN!
LOOKS LIKE I'LL HAVE TO LOWER THE TAX ON PASS-THROUGH INCOME!
HUH?
DON'T YOU GET IT?! CUTTING MY TAX ON PASS-THROUGH INCOME IS THE BEST WAY TO HELP YOU!
LATER—
NOW I'M STARVING!
UGH! DO I HAVE TO DO EVERYTHING FOR YOU?!
OKAY, I'M GOING TO PHASE OUT THE ESTATE TAX FOR THE SUPER-WEALTHY!
THAT WON'T HELP ME!
IT WILL! LOOK— I FUNDED ALL THESE STUDIES! CHARTS! BOOKS!
HEY, THIS ACTUALLY WILL HELP!
SO, YOU AGREE WITH THESE THEORIES?
NO, I CAN EAT THIS BOOK!
GRRR... LUCKY DUCKY!
THE END
DIST. BY ANDREWS McMEEL SYNDICATION – ©2017 R. BOLLING – 1362 – TO JOIN THE INNER HIVE, GO TO tomthedancingbug.com

11/6/17

TOM the DANCING BUG

by RUBEN BOLLING

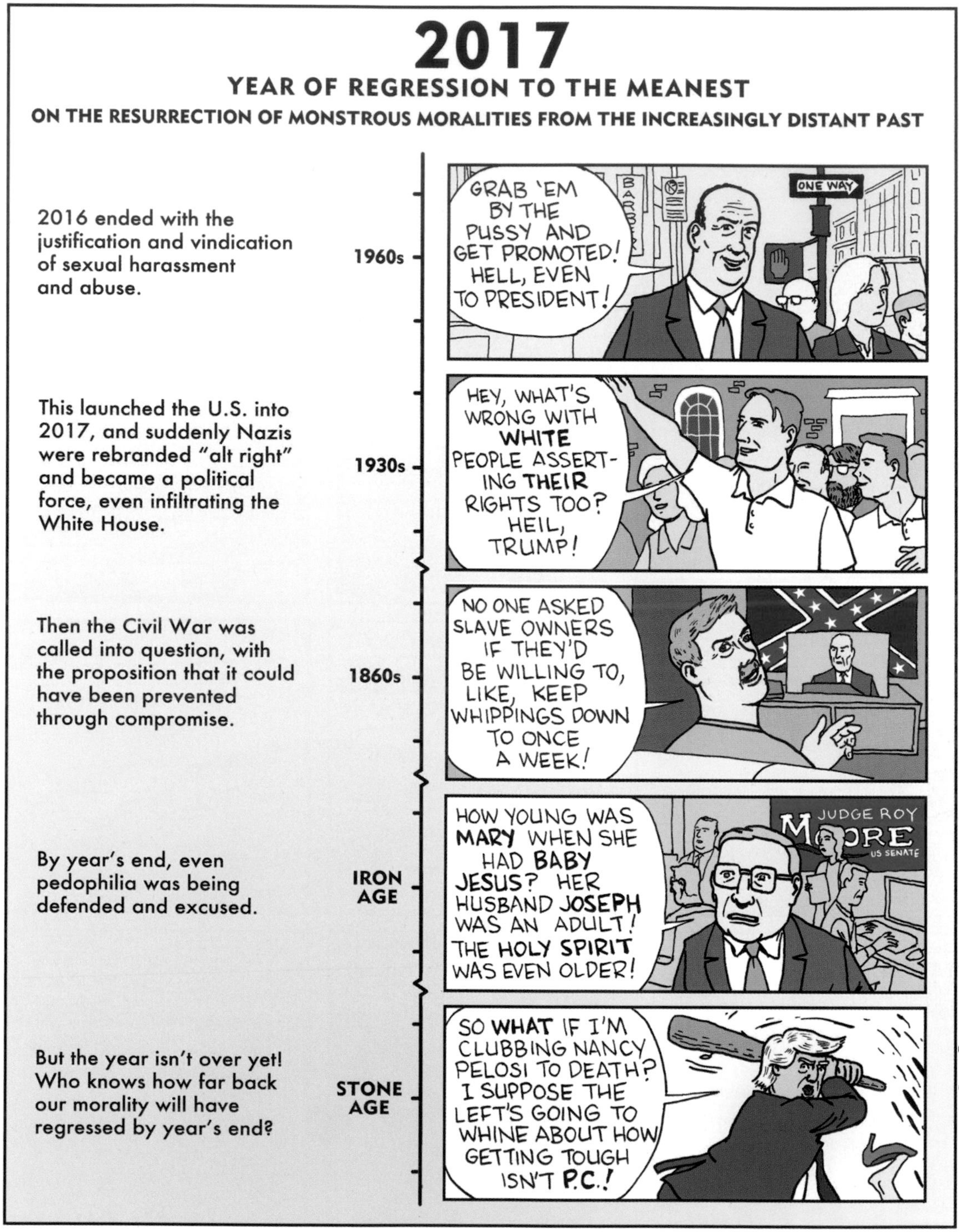

2017
YEAR OF REGRESSION TO THE MEANEST
ON THE RESURRECTION OF MONSTROUS MORALITIES FROM THE INCREASINGLY DISTANT PAST
2016 ended with the justification and vindication of sexual harassment and abuse.
1960s
GRAB 'EM BY THE PUSSY AND GET PROMOTED! HELL, EVEN TO PRESIDENT!
BARBER
ONE WAY
This launched the U.S. into 2017, and suddenly Nazis were rebranded "alt right" and became a political force, even infiltrating the White House.
1930s
HEY, WHAT'S WRONG WITH WHITE PEOPLE ASSERTING THEIR RIGHTS TOO? HEIL, TRUMP!
Then the Civil War was called into question, with the proposition that it could have been prevented through compromise.
1860s
NO ONE ASKED SLAVE OWNERS IF THEY'D BE WILLING TO, LIKE, KEEP WHIPPINGS DOWN TO ONCE A WEEK!
By year's end, even pedophilia was being defended and excused.
IRON AGE
HOW YOUNG WAS MARY WHEN SHE HAD BABY JESUS? HER HUSBAND JOSEPH WAS AN ADULT! THE HOLY SPIRIT WAS EVEN OLDER!
JUDGE ROY MOORE
US SENATE
But the year isn't over yet! Who knows how far back our morality will have regressed by year's end?
STONE AGE
SO WHAT IF I'M CLUBBING NANCY PELOSI TO DEATH? I SUPPOSE THE LEFT'S GOING TO WHINE ABOUT HOW GETTING TOUGH ISN'T P.C.!

11/13/17

TOM the DANCING BUG

by RUBEN BOLLING

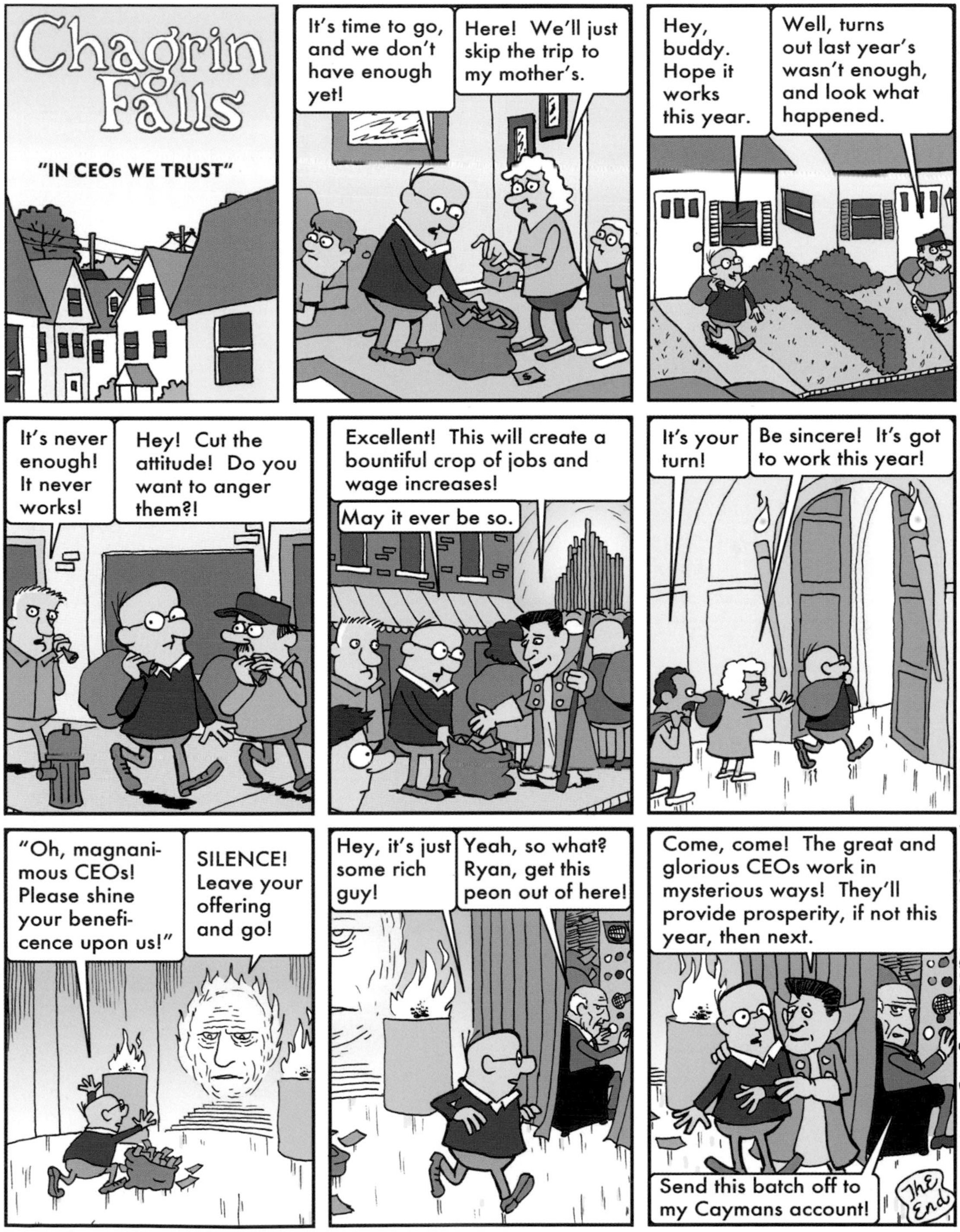
Chagrin Falls
"IN CEOs WE TRUST"
It's time to go, and we don't have enough yet!
Here! We'll just skip the trip to my mother's.
Hey, buddy. Hope it works this year.
Well, turns out last year's wasn't enough, and look what happened.
It's never enough! It never works!
Hey! Cut the attitude! Do you want to anger them?!
Excellent! This will create a bountiful crop of jobs and wage increases!
May it ever be so.
It's your turn!
Be sincere! It's got to work this year!
"Oh, magnanimous CEOs! Please shine your beneficence upon us!"
SILENCE! Leave your offering and go!
Hey, it's just some rich guy!
Yeah, so what? Ryan, get this peon out of here!
Come, come! The great and glorious CEOs work in mysterious ways! They'll provide prosperity, if not this year, then next.
Send this batch off to my Caymans account!
The End

11/20/17

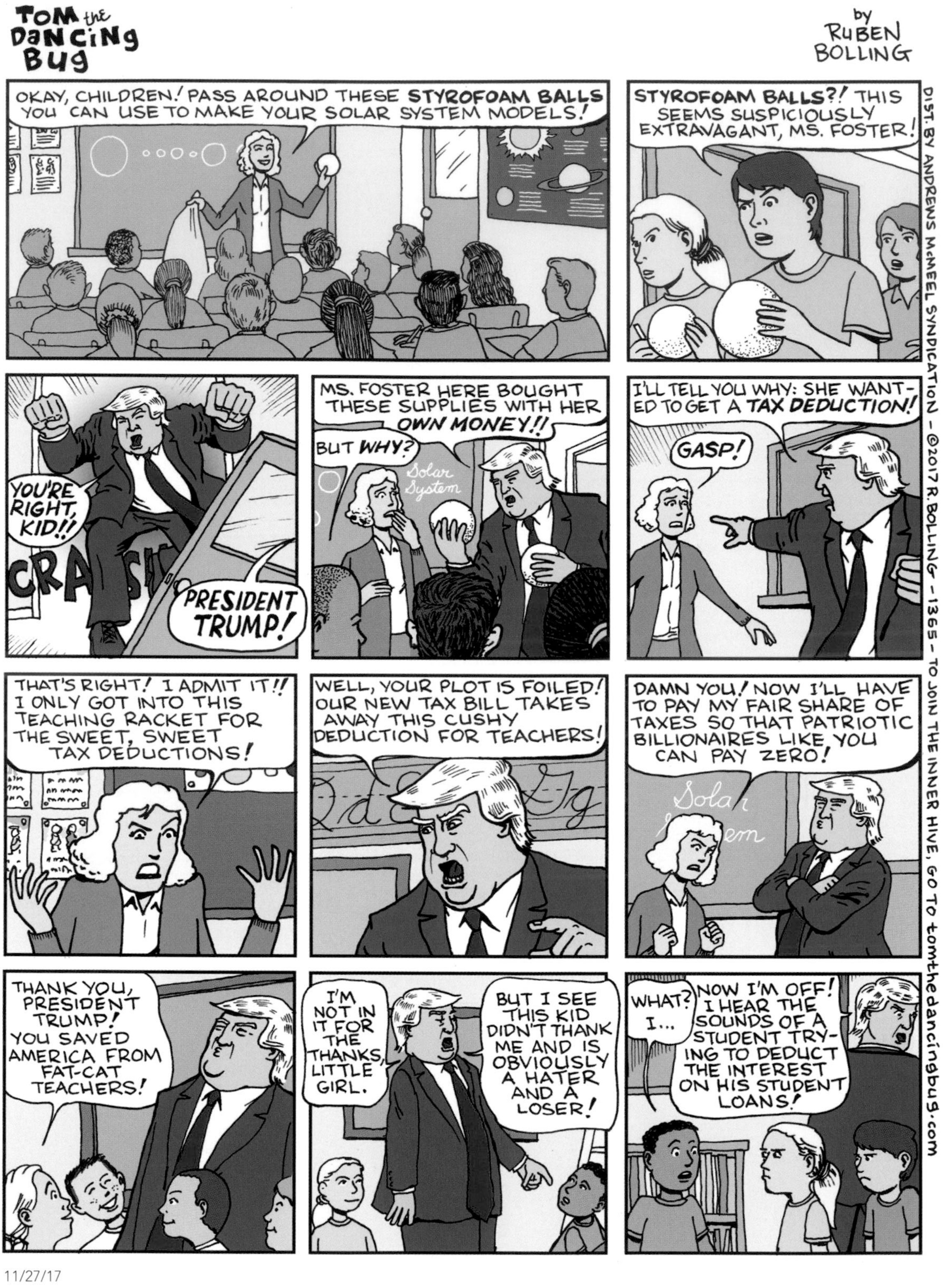
TOM the DANCING BUG
by RUBEN BOLLING
OKAY, CHILDREN! PASS AROUND THESE STYROFOAM BALLS YOU CAN USE TO MAKE YOUR SOLAR SYSTEM MODELS!
STYROFOAM BALLS?! THIS SEEMS SUSPICIOUSLY EXTRAVAGANT, MS. FOSTER!
CRASH
YOU'RE RIGHT, KID!!
PRESIDENT TRUMP!
MS. FOSTER HERE BOUGHT THESE SUPPLIES WITH HER OWN MONEY!!
BUT WHY?
Solar System
I'LL TELL YOU WHY: SHE WANTED TO GET A TAX DEDUCTION!
GASP!
THAT'S RIGHT! I ADMIT IT!! I ONLY GOT INTO THIS TEACHING RACKET FOR THE SWEET, SWEET TAX DEDUCTIONS!
WELL, YOUR PLOT IS FOILED! OUR NEW TAX BILL TAKES AWAY THIS CUSHY DEDUCTION FOR TEACHERS!
DAMN YOU! NOW I'LL HAVE TO PAY MY FAIR SHARE OF TAXES SO THAT PATRIOTIC BILLIONAIRES LIKE YOU CAN PAY ZERO!
THANK YOU, PRESIDENT TRUMP! YOU SAVED AMERICA FROM FAT-CAT TEACHERS!
I'M NOT IN IT FOR THE THANKS, LITTLE GIRL.
BUT I SEE THIS KID DIDN'T THANK ME AND IS OBVIOUSLY A HATER AND A LOSER!
WHAT? I...
NOW I'M OFF! I HEAR THE SOUNDS OF A STUDENT TRYING TO DEDUCT THE INTEREST ON HIS STUDENT LOANS!
DIST. BY ANDREWS McMEEL SYNDICATION – ©2017 R. BOLLING – 1365 – TO JOIN THE INNER HIVE, GO TO tomthedancingbug.com

11/27/17

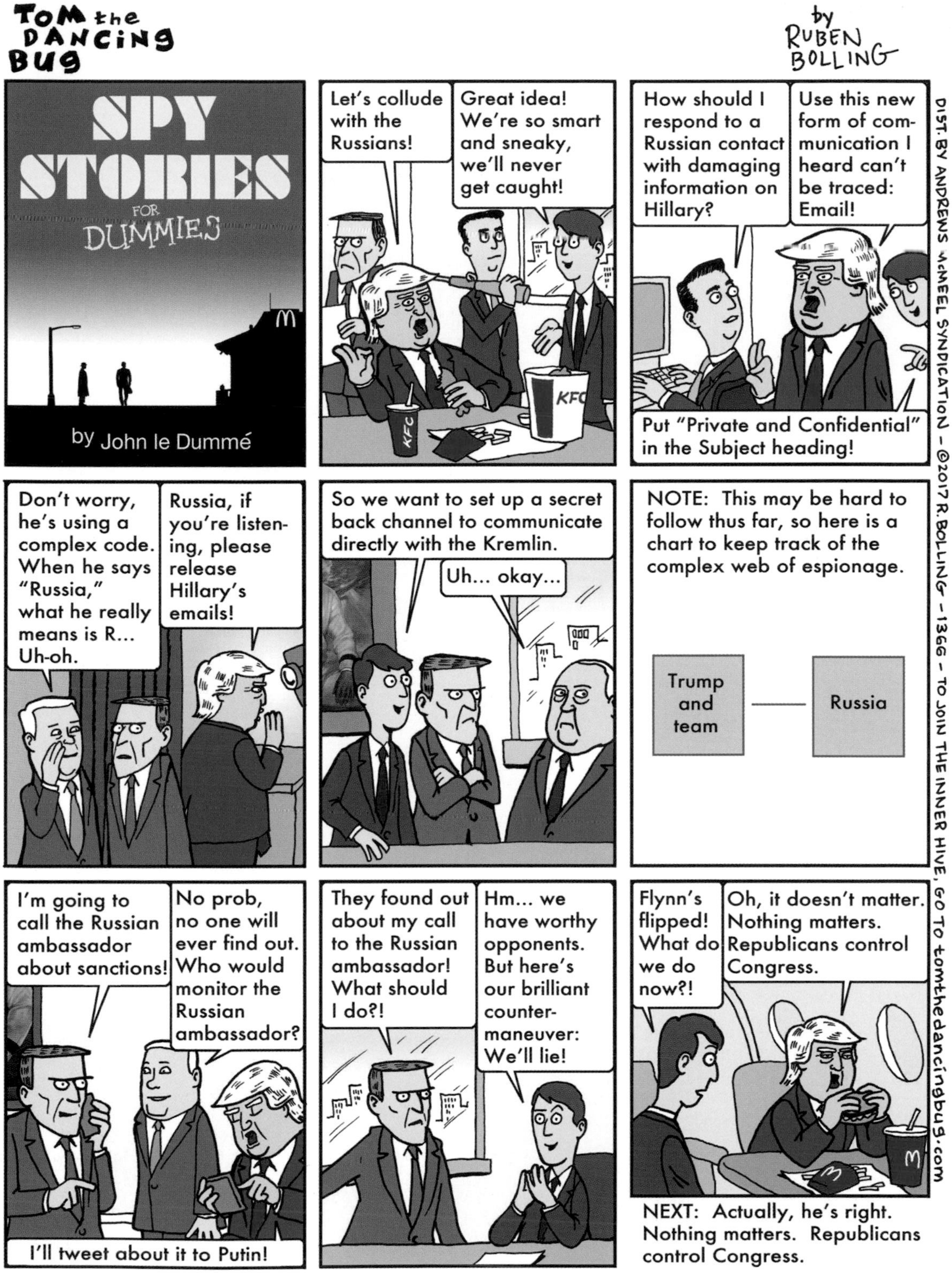
TOM the DANCING BUG
by RUBEN BOLLING
SPY STORIES FOR DUMMIES
by John le Dummé
Let's collude with the Russians!
Great idea! We're so smart and sneaky, we'll never get caught!
KFC
How should I respond to a Russian contact with damaging information on Hillary?
Use this new form of communication I heard can't be traced: Email!
Put "Private and Confidential" in the Subject heading!
Don't worry, he's using a complex code. When he says "Russia," what he really means is R... Uh-oh.
Russia, if you're listening, please release Hillary's emails!
So we want to set up a secret back channel to communicate directly with the Kremlin.
Uh... okay...
NOTE: This may be hard to follow thus far, so here is a chart to keep track of the complex web of espionage.
Trump and team
Russia
I'm going to call the Russian ambassador about sanctions!
No prob, no one will ever find out. Who would monitor the Russian ambassador?
I'll tweet about it to Putin!
They found out about my call to the Russian ambassador! What should I do?!
Hm... we have worthy opponents. But here's our brilliant counter-maneuver: We'll lie!
Flynn's flipped! What do we do now?!
Oh, it doesn't matter. Nothing matters. Republicans control Congress.
NEXT: Actually, he's right. Nothing matters. Republicans control Congress.
DIST. BY ANDREWS McMEEL SYNDICATION – ©2017 R. BOLLING – 1366 – TO JOIN THE INNER HIVE, GO TO tomthedancingbug.com

12/4/17

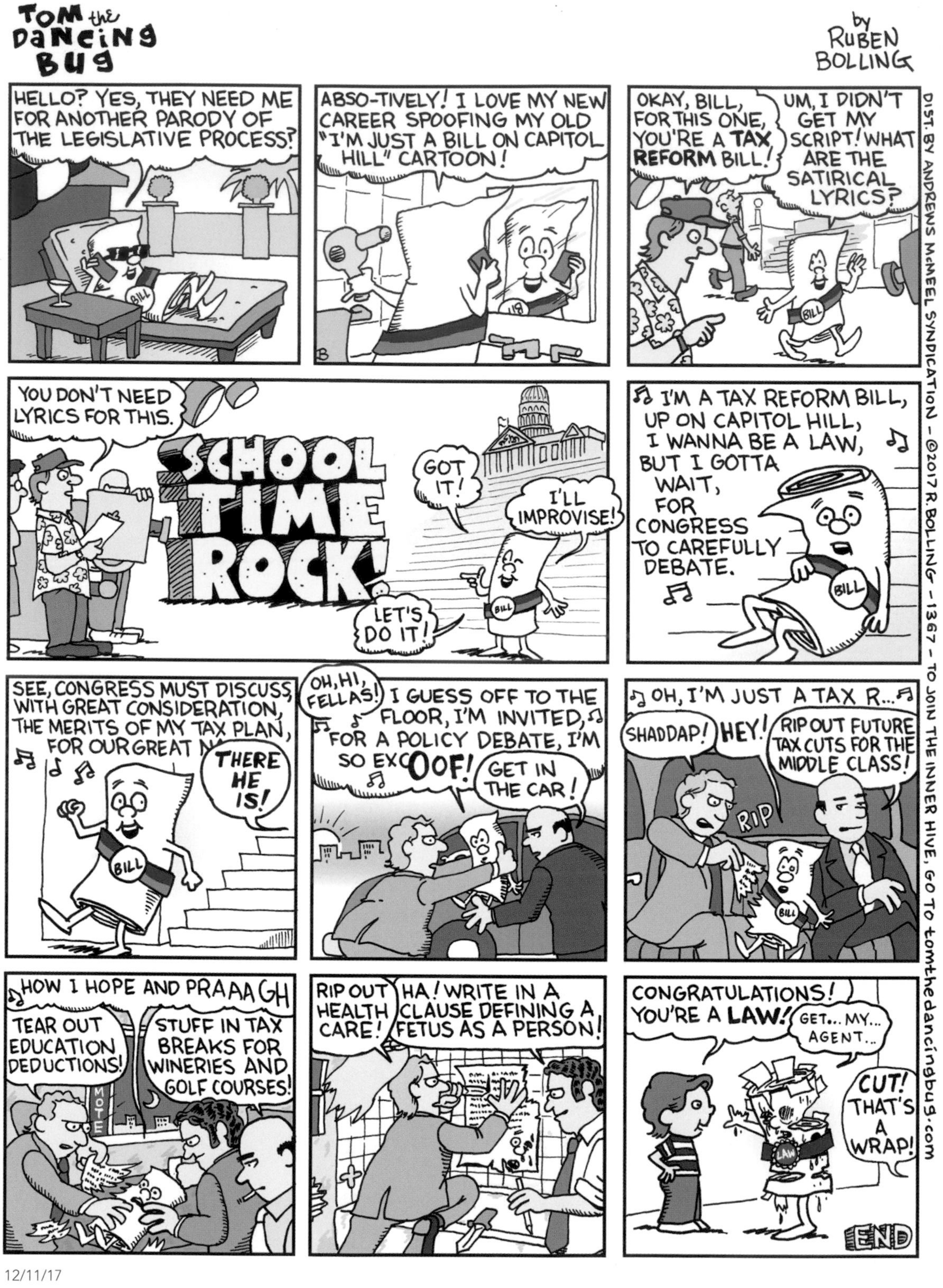
TOM the DANCING BUG
by RUBEN BOLLING
HELLO? YES, THEY NEED ME FOR ANOTHER PARODY OF THE LEGISLATIVE PROCESS?
BILL
ABSO-TIVELY! I LOVE MY NEW CAREER SPOOFING MY OLD "I'M JUST A BILL ON CAPITOL HILL" CARTOON!
OKAY, BILL, FOR THIS ONE, YOU'RE A TAX REFORM BILL!
UM, I DIDN'T GET MY SCRIPT! WHAT ARE THE SATIRICAL LYRICS?
YOU DON'T NEED LYRICS FOR THIS.
SCHOOL TIME ROCK!
GOT IT!
I'LL IMPROVISE!
LET'S DO IT!
I'M A TAX REFORM BILL, UP ON CAPITOL HILL, I WANNA BE A LAW, BUT I GOTTA WAIT, FOR CONGRESS TO CAREFULLY DEBATE.
SEE, CONGRESS MUST DISCUSS, WITH GREAT CONSIDERATION, THE MERITS OF MY TAX PLAN, FOR OUR GREAT N
THERE HE IS!
OH, HI, FELLAS!
I GUESS OFF TO THE FLOOR, I'M INVITED, FOR A POLICY DEBATE, I'M SO EXC
OOF!
GET IN THE CAR!
OH, I'M JUST A TAX R...
SHADDAP!
HEY!
RIP OUT FUTURE TAX CUTS FOR THE MIDDLE CLASS!
RIP
HOW I HOPE AND PRAAAGH
TEAR OUT EDUCATION DEDUCTIONS!
STUFF IN TAX BREAKS FOR WINERIES AND GOLF COURSES!
MOTEL
RIP OUT HEALTH CARE!
HA! WRITE IN A CLAUSE DEFINING A FETUS AS A PERSON!
CONGRATULATIONS! YOU'RE A LAW!
GET... MY... AGENT...
CUT! THAT'S A WRAP!
LAW
END
DIST. BY ANDREWS McMEEL SYNDICATION - ©2017 R. BOLLING - 1367 - TO JOIN THE INNER HIVE, GO TO tomthedancingbug.com

12/11/17

TOM THE DANCING BUG

by RUBEN BOLLING

with apologies to Maurice Sendak

DIST. BY ANDREWS McMEEL SYNDICATION — ©2017 R. BOLLING — 1368 — TO JOIN THE INNER HIVE, GO TO tomthedancingbug.com

The night little Donald put on his politician suit and made mischief

He was called "WILD THING" and Donald said "FAKE NEWS" and he was sent to bed without eating anything

A forest grew and he went to the place where the wild things are

They said he was the wildest of them all and made him king

And the wild Trumpus started

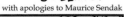

Donald said, "Now stop!" And he was lonely and tired and wanted to be loved

The wild things cried, "Please don't go - we'll eat you up - we love you so"

When Donald got back, supper was waiting for him

And it was hot.

12/18/17

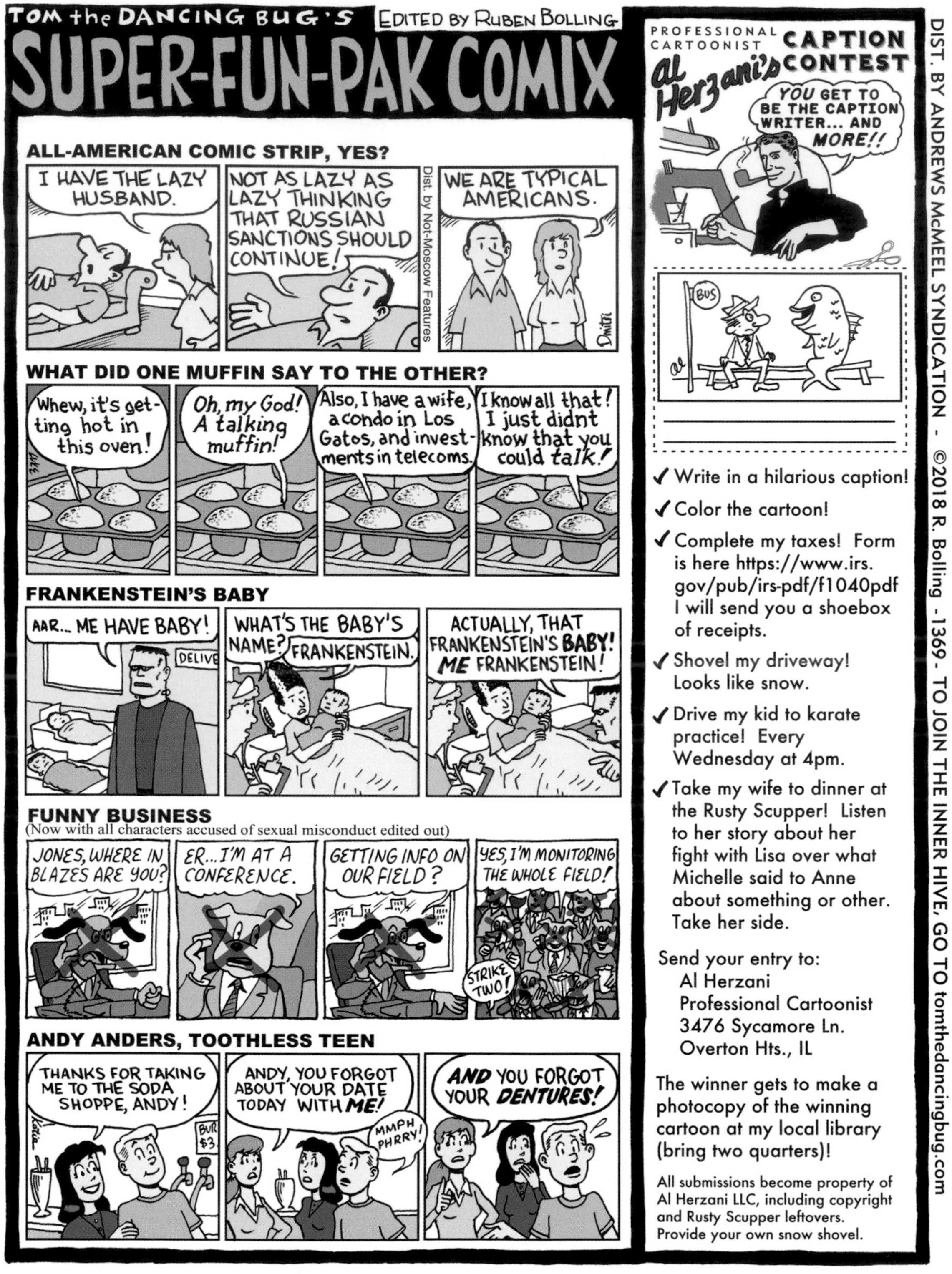
TOM the DANCING BUG'S
EDITED BY RUBEN BOLLING
SUPER-FUN-PAK COMIX
ALL-AMERICAN COMIC STRIP, YES?
I HAVE THE LAZY HUSBAND.
NOT AS LAZY AS LAZY THINKING THAT RUSSIAN SANCTIONS SHOULD CONTINUE!
Dist. by Not-Moscow Features
WE ARE TYPICAL AMERICANS.
Dmitri
WHAT DID ONE MUFFIN SAY TO THE OTHER?
Whew, it's getting hot in this oven!
Oh, my God! A talking muffin!
Also, I have a wife, a condo in Los Gatos, and investments in telecoms.
I know all that! I just didnt know that you could talk!
FRANKENSTEIN'S BABY
AAR... ME HAVE BABY!
DELIVE
WHAT'S THE BABY'S NAME?
FRANKENSTEIN.
ACTUALLY, THAT FRANKENSTEIN'S BABY! ME FRANKENSTEIN!
FUNNY BUSINESS
(Now with all characters accused of sexual misconduct edited out)
JONES, WHERE IN BLAZES ARE YOU?
ER...I'M AT A CONFERENCE.
GETTING INFO ON OUR FIELD?
YES, I'M MONITORING THE WHOLE FIELD!
STRIKE TWO!
ANDY ANDERS, TOOTHLESS TEEN
THANKS FOR TAKING ME TO THE SODA SHOPPE, ANDY!
ANDY, YOU FORGOT ABOUT YOUR DATE TODAY WITH ME!
MMPH PHRRY!
AND YOU FORGOT YOUR DENTURES!
PROFESSIONAL CARTOONIST
Al Herzani's CAPTION CONTEST
YOU GET TO BE THE CAPTION WRITER... AND MORE!!
BUS
✓ Write in a hilarious caption!
✓ Color the cartoon!
✓ Complete my taxes! Form is here https://www.irs.gov/pub/irs-pdf/f1040pdf I will send you a shoebox of receipts.
✓ Shovel my driveway! Looks like snow.
✓ Drive my kid to karate practice! Every Wednesday at 4pm.
✓ Take my wife to dinner at the Rusty Scupper! Listen to her story about her fight with Lisa over what Michelle said to Anne about something or other. Take her side.
Send your entry to:
Al Herzani
Professional Cartoonist
3476 Sycamore Ln.
Overton Hts., IL
The winner gets to make a photocopy of the winning cartoon at my local library (bring two quarters)!
All submissions become property of Al Herzani LLC, including copyright and Rusty Scupper leftovers. Provide your own snow shovel.
DIST. BY ANDREWS McMEEL SYNDICATION - ©2018 R. Bolling -1369- TO JOIN THE INNER HIVE, GO TO tomthedancingbug.com

1/1/18

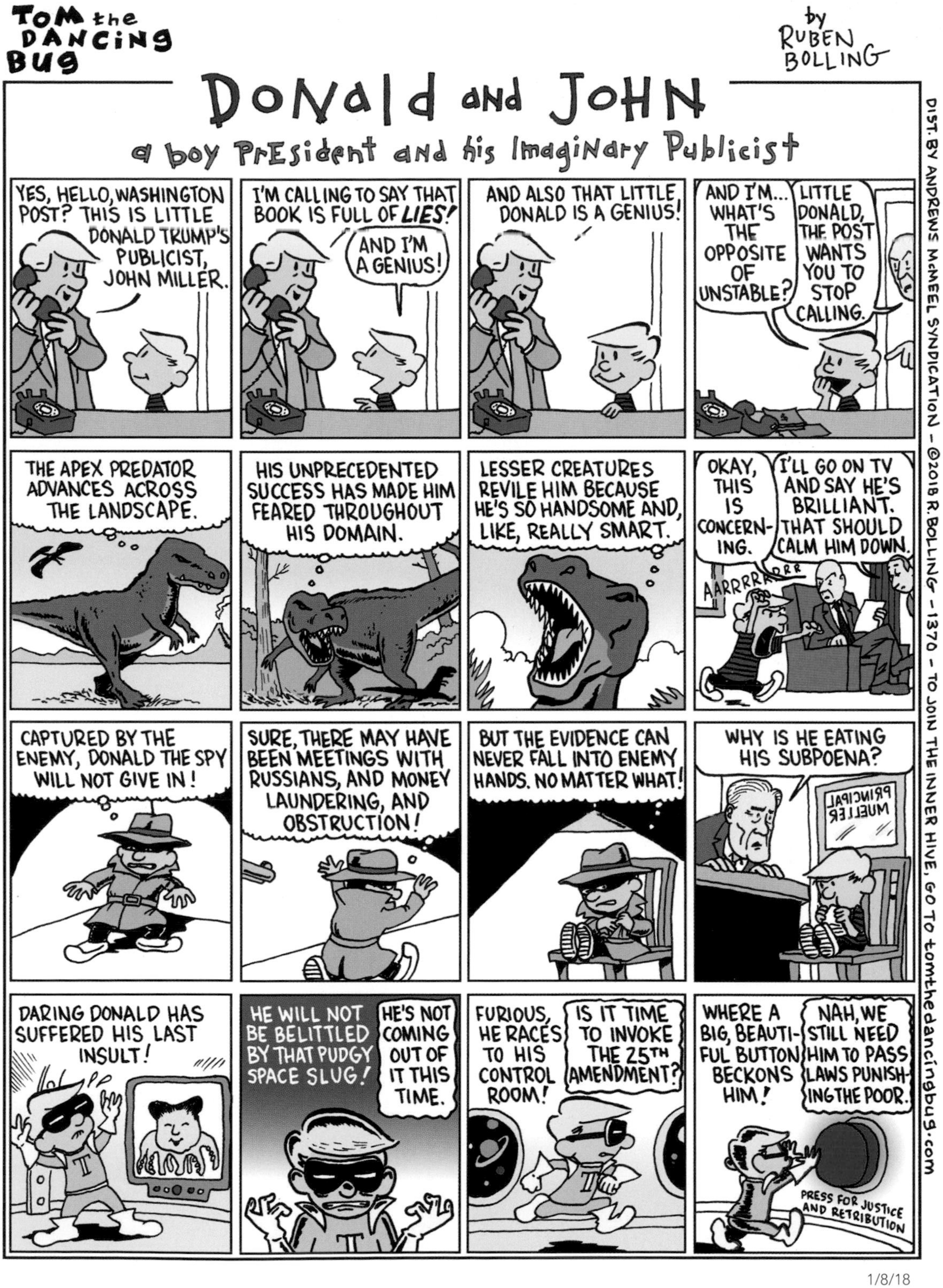
TOM the DANCING BUG
by RUBEN BOLLING
DONALD AND JOHN
a boy President and his Imaginary Publicist
YES, HELLO, WASHINGTON POST? THIS IS LITTLE DONALD TRUMP'S PUBLICIST, JOHN MILLER.
I'M CALLING TO SAY THAT BOOK IS FULL OF *LIES!*
AND I'M A GENIUS!
AND ALSO THAT LITTLE DONALD IS A GENIUS!
AND I'M... WHAT'S THE OPPOSITE OF UNSTABLE?
LITTLE DONALD, THE POST WANTS YOU TO STOP CALLING.
THE APEX PREDATOR ADVANCES ACROSS THE LANDSCAPE.
HIS UNPRECEDENTED SUCCESS HAS MADE HIM FEARED THROUGHOUT HIS DOMAIN.
LESSER CREATURES REVILE HIM BECAUSE HE'S SO HANDSOME AND, LIKE, REALLY SMART.
OKAY, THIS IS CONCERNING.
I'LL GO ON TV AND SAY HE'S BRILLIANT. THAT SHOULD CALM HIM DOWN.
AARRRRRRRRR
CAPTURED BY THE ENEMY, DONALD THE SPY WILL NOT GIVE IN!
SURE, THERE MAY HAVE BEEN MEETINGS WITH RUSSIANS, AND MONEY LAUNDERING, AND OBSTRUCTION!
BUT THE EVIDENCE CAN NEVER FALL INTO ENEMY HANDS. NO MATTER WHAT!
WHY IS HE EATING HIS SUBPOENA?
PRINCIPAL MUELLER
DARING DONALD HAS SUFFERED HIS LAST INSULT!
HE WILL NOT BE BELITTLED BY THAT PUDGY SPACE SLUG!
HE'S NOT COMING OUT OF IT THIS TIME.
FURIOUS, HE RACES TO HIS CONTROL ROOM!
IS IT TIME TO INVOKE THE 25TH AMENDMENT?
WHERE A BIG, BEAUTIFUL BUTTON BECKONS HIM!
NAH, WE STILL NEED HIM TO PASS LAWS PUNISHING THE POOR.
PRESS FOR JUSTICE AND RETRIBUTION
DIST. BY ANDREWS McMEEL SYNDICATION – ©2018 R. BOLLING – 1370 – TO JOIN THE INNER HIVE, GO TO tomthedancingbug.com

1/8/18

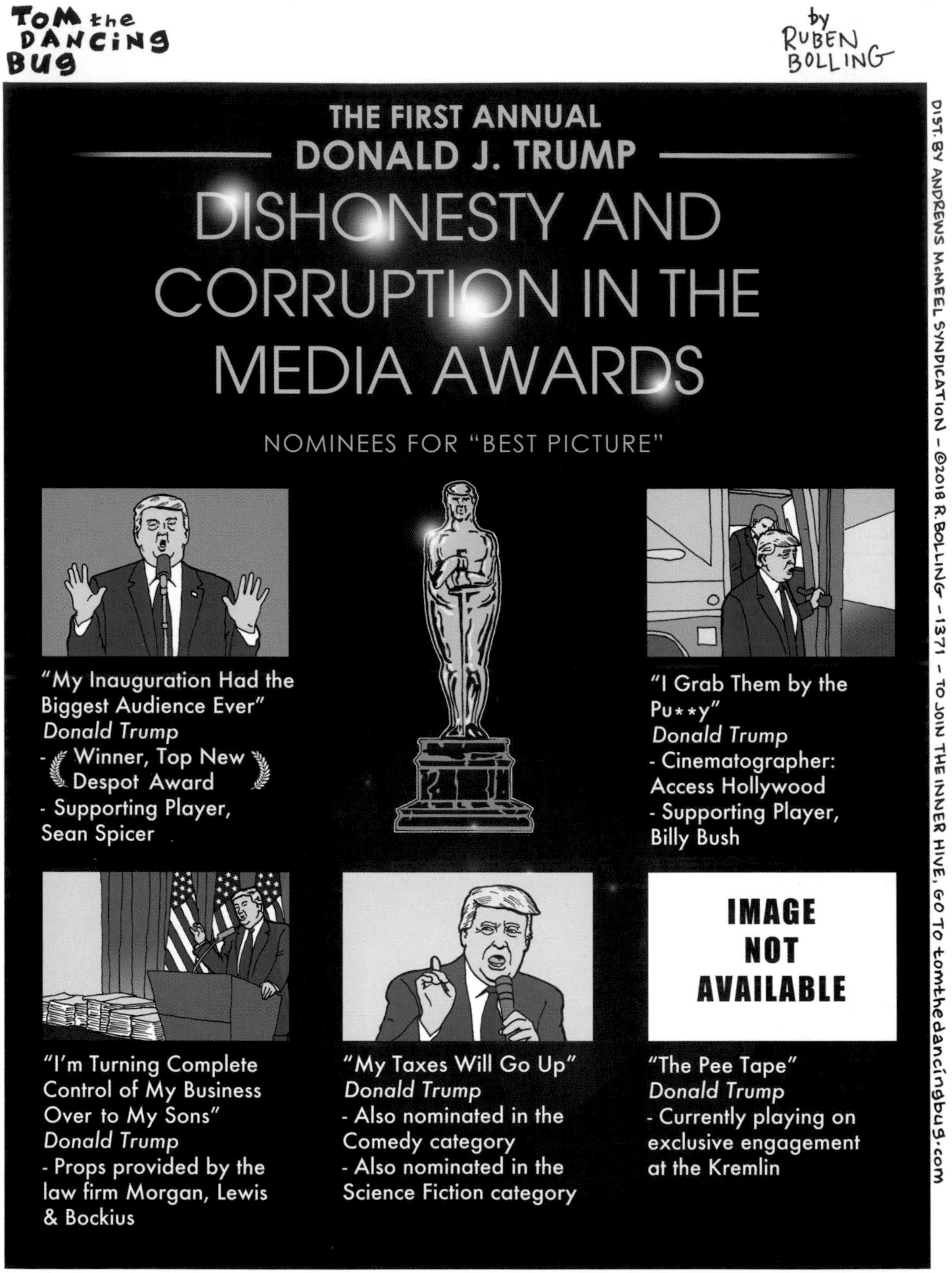
TOM the DANCING BUG
by RUBEN BOLLING
THE FIRST ANNUAL
DONALD J. TRUMP
DISHONESTY AND CORRUPTION IN THE MEDIA AWARDS
NOMINEES FOR "BEST PICTURE"
"My Inauguration Had the Biggest Audience Ever"
Donald Trump
- Winner, Top New Despot Award
- Supporting Player, Sean Spicer
"I Grab Them by the Pu**y"
Donald Trump
- Cinematographer: Access Hollywood
- Supporting Player, Billy Bush
IMAGE NOT AVAILABLE
"I'm Turning Complete Control of My Business Over to My Sons"
Donald Trump
- Props provided by the law firm Morgan, Lewis & Bockius
"My Taxes Will Go Up"
Donald Trump
- Also nominated in the Comedy category
- Also nominated in the Science Fiction category
"The Pee Tape"
Donald Trump
- Currently playing on exclusive engagement at the Kremlin
DIST. BY ANDREWS McMEEL SYNDICATION - ©2018 R. BOLLING - 1371 - TO JOIN THE INNER HIVE, GO TO tomthedancingbug.com

1/15/18

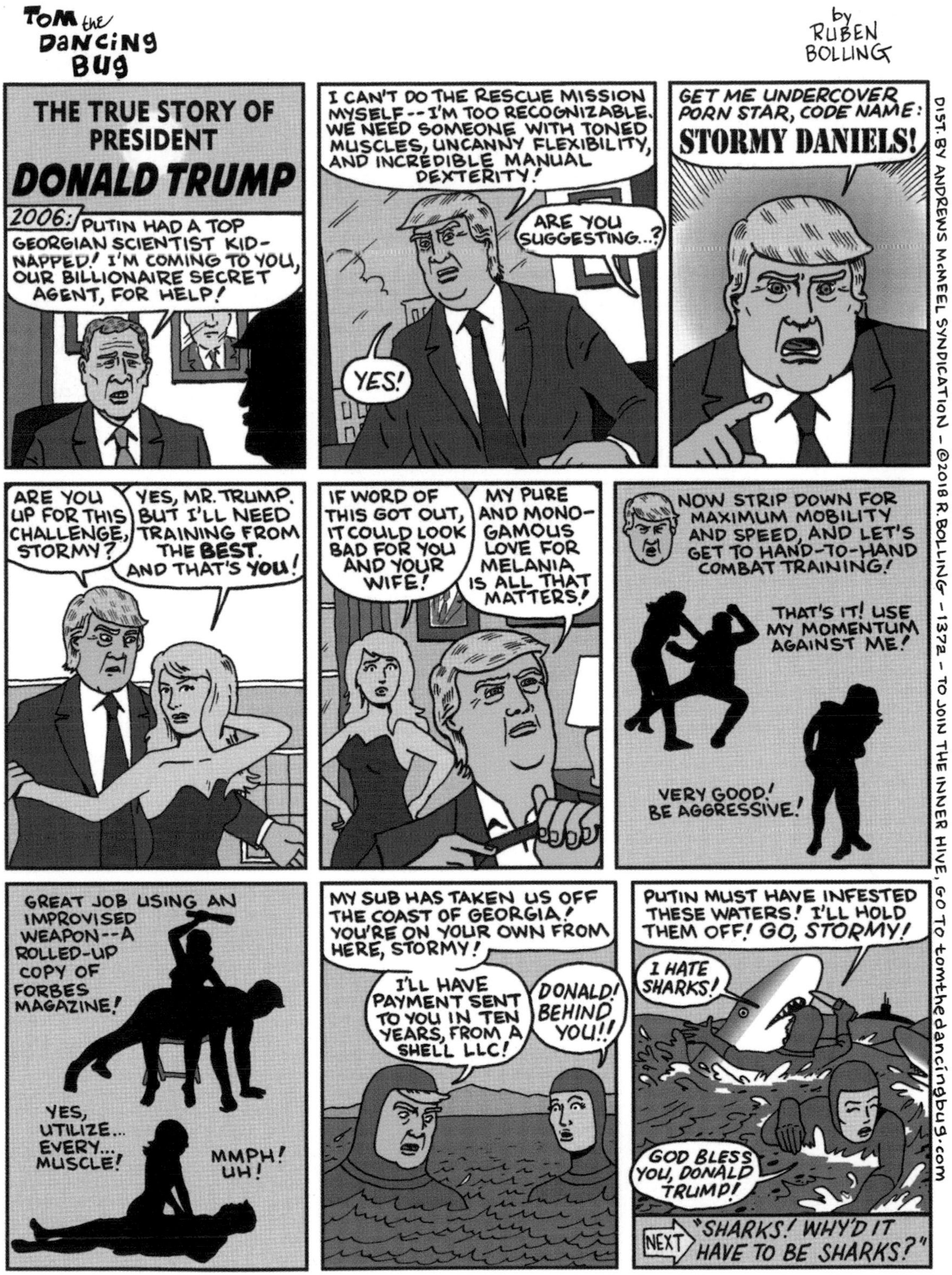
TOM the DANCING BUG
by RUBEN BOLLING
THE TRUE STORY OF PRESIDENT DONALD TRUMP
2006: PUTIN HAD A TOP GEORGIAN SCIENTIST KID-NAPPED! I'M COMING TO YOU, OUR BILLIONAIRE SECRET AGENT, FOR HELP!
I CAN'T DO THE RESCUE MISSION MYSELF--I'M TOO RECOGNIZABLE. WE NEED SOMEONE WITH TONED MUSCLES, UNCANNY FLEXIBILITY, AND INCREDIBLE MANUAL DEXTERITY!
ARE YOU SUGGESTING...?
YES!
GET ME UNDERCOVER PORN STAR, CODE NAME: STORMY DANIELS!
ARE YOU UP FOR THIS CHALLENGE, STORMY?
YES, MR. TRUMP. BUT I'LL NEED TRAINING FROM THE BEST. AND THAT'S YOU!
IF WORD OF THIS GOT OUT, IT COULD LOOK BAD FOR YOU AND YOUR WIFE!
MY PURE AND MONO-GAMOUS LOVE FOR MELANIA IS ALL THAT MATTERS!
NOW STRIP DOWN FOR MAXIMUM MOBILITY AND SPEED, AND LET'S GET TO HAND-TO-HAND COMBAT TRAINING!
THAT'S IT! USE MY MOMENTUM AGAINST ME!
VERY GOOD! BE AGGRESSIVE!
GREAT JOB USING AN IMPROVISED WEAPON--A ROLLED-UP COPY OF FORBES MAGAZINE!
YES, UTILIZE... EVERY... MUSCLE!
MMPH! UH!
MY SUB HAS TAKEN US OFF THE COAST OF GEORGIA! YOU'RE ON YOUR OWN FROM HERE, STORMY!
I'LL HAVE PAYMENT SENT TO YOU IN TEN YEARS, FROM A SHELL LLC!
DONALD! BEHIND YOU!!
PUTIN MUST HAVE INFESTED THESE WATERS! I'LL HOLD THEM OFF! GO, STORMY!
I HATE SHARKS!
GOD BLESS YOU, DONALD TRUMP!
NEXT "SHARKS! WHY'D IT HAVE TO BE SHARKS?"
DIST. BY ANDREWS McMEEL SYNDICATION - ©2018 R. BOLLING - 1372 - TO JOIN THE INNER HIVE, GO TO tomthedancingbug.com

1/22/18

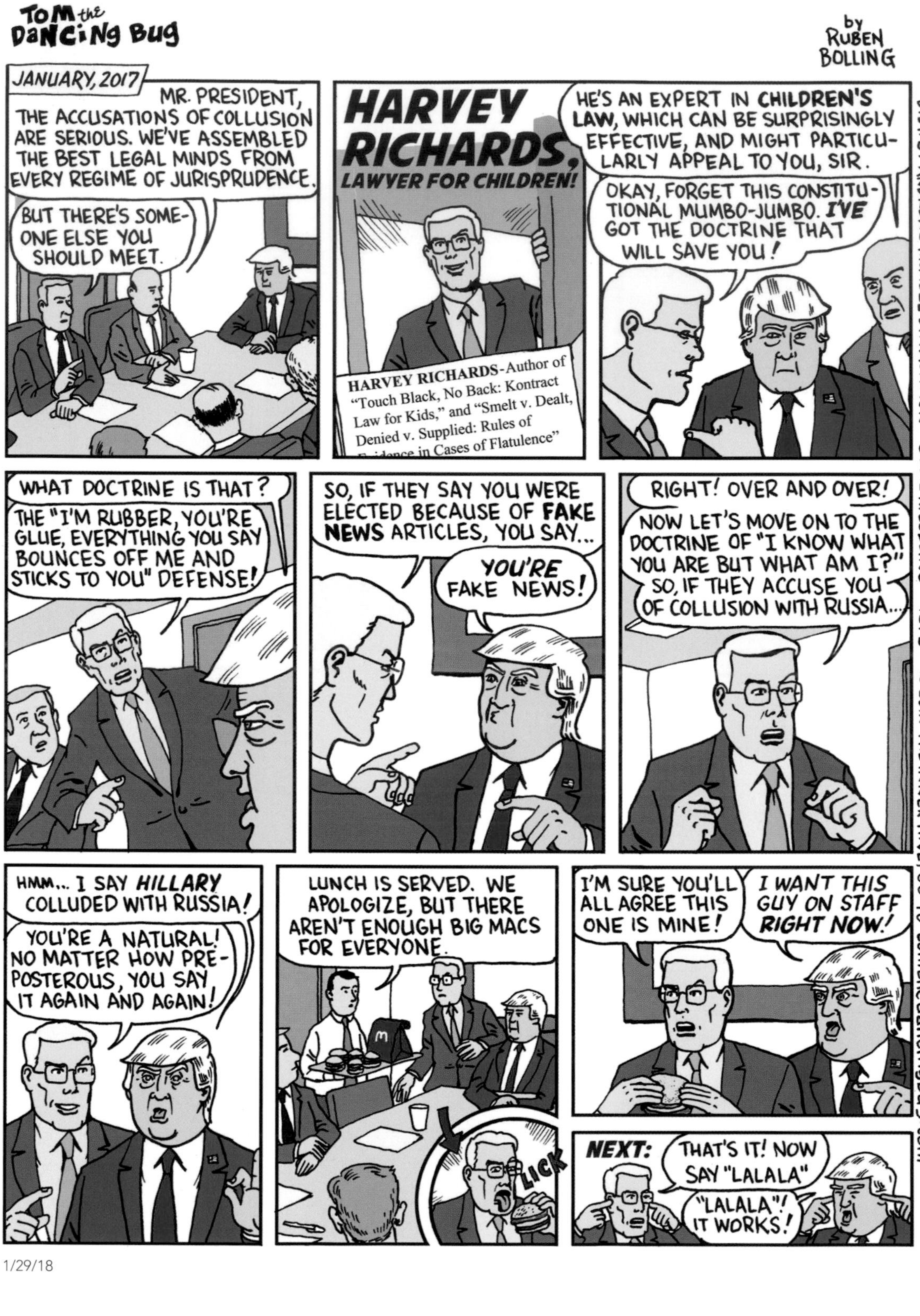
TOM the DANCING BUG
by RUBEN BOLLING
JANUARY, 2017
MR. PRESIDENT, THE ACCUSATIONS OF COLLUSION ARE SERIOUS. WE'VE ASSEMBLED THE BEST LEGAL MINDS FROM EVERY REGIME OF JURISPRUDENCE.
BUT THERE'S SOMEONE ELSE YOU SHOULD MEET.
HARVEY RICHARDS, LAWYER FOR CHILDREN!
HARVEY RICHARDS-Author of "Touch Black, No Back: Kontract Law for Kids," and "Smelt v. Dealt, Denied v. Supplied: Rules of Evidence in Cases of Flatulence"
HE'S AN EXPERT IN CHILDREN'S LAW, WHICH CAN BE SURPRISINGLY EFFECTIVE, AND MIGHT PARTICULARLY APPEAL TO YOU, SIR.
OKAY, FORGET THIS CONSTITUTIONAL MUMBO-JUMBO. I'VE GOT THE DOCTRINE THAT WILL SAVE YOU!
WHAT DOCTRINE IS THAT?
THE "I'M RUBBER, YOU'RE GLUE, EVERYTHING YOU SAY BOUNCES OFF ME AND STICKS TO YOU" DEFENSE!
SO, IF THEY SAY YOU WERE ELECTED BECAUSE OF FAKE NEWS ARTICLES, YOU SAY...
YOU'RE FAKE NEWS!
RIGHT! OVER AND OVER!
NOW LET'S MOVE ON TO THE DOCTRINE OF "I KNOW WHAT YOU ARE BUT WHAT AM I?" SO, IF THEY ACCUSE YOU OF COLLUSION WITH RUSSIA...
HMM... I SAY HILLARY COLLUDED WITH RUSSIA!
YOU'RE A NATURAL! NO MATTER HOW PREPOSTEROUS, YOU SAY IT AGAIN AND AGAIN!
LUNCH IS SERVED. WE APOLOGIZE, BUT THERE AREN'T ENOUGH BIG MACS FOR EVERYONE.
LICK
I'M SURE YOU'LL ALL AGREE THIS ONE IS MINE!
I WANT THIS GUY ON STAFF RIGHT NOW!
NEXT:
THAT'S IT! NOW SAY "LALALA"
"LALALA"! IT WORKS!
DIST. BY ANDREWS McMEEL SYNDICATION – ©2018 R. BOLLING – 1373 – TO JOIN THE INNER HIVE, GO TO tomthedancingbug.com

1/29/18

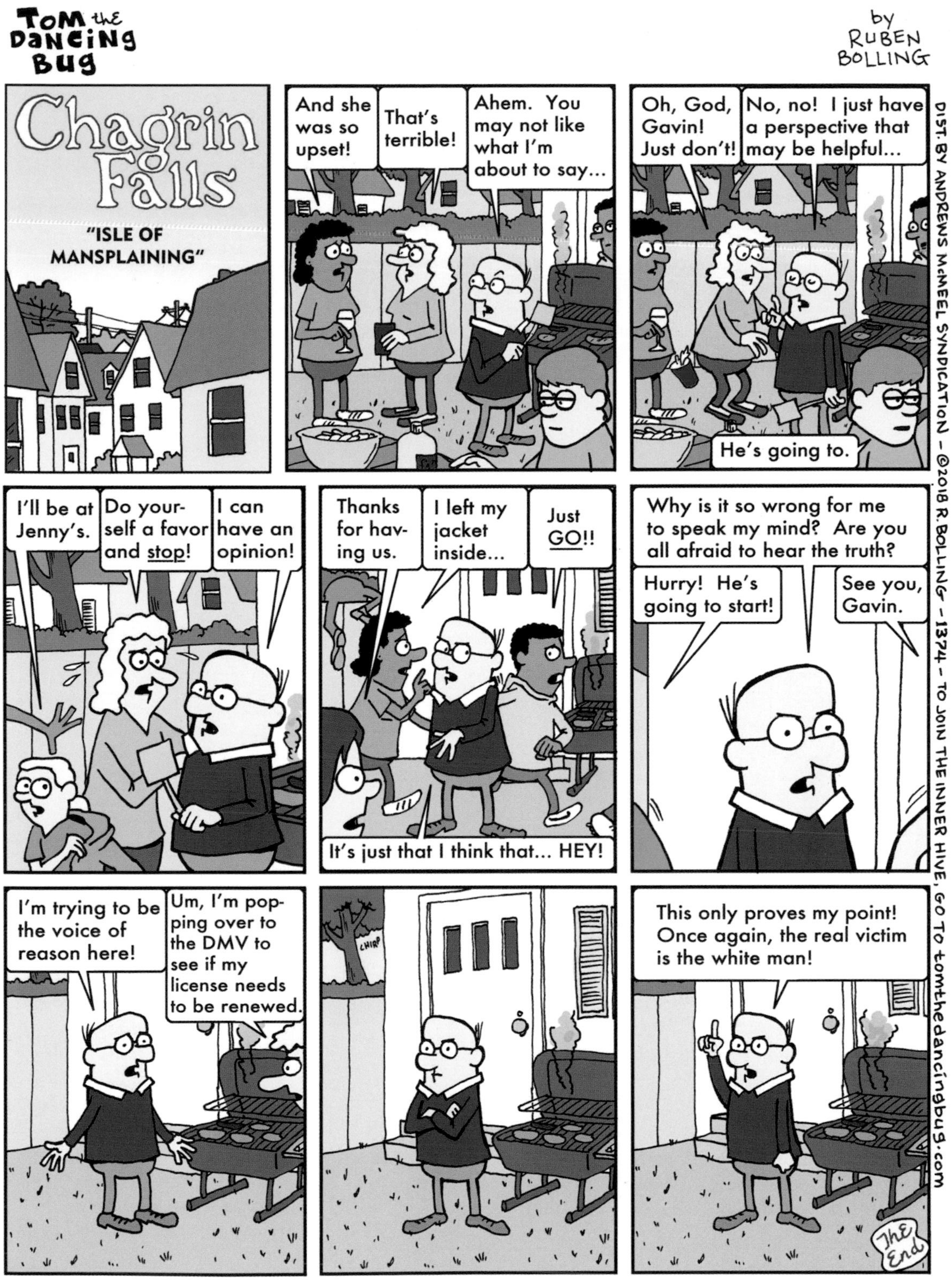

TOM the DANCING BUG
by RUBEN BOLLING
Chagrin Falls
"ISLE OF MANSPLAINING"
And she was so upset!
That's terrible!
Ahem. You may not like what I'm about to say...
Oh, God, Gavin! Just don't!
No, no! I just have a perspective that may be helpful...
He's going to.
I'll be at Jenny's.
Do yourself a favor and stop!
I can have an opinion!
Thanks for having us.
I left my jacket inside...
Just GO!!
It's just that I think that... HEY!
Why is it so wrong for me to speak my mind? Are you all afraid to hear the truth?
Hurry! He's going to start!
See you, Gavin.
I'm trying to be the voice of reason here!
Um, I'm popping over to the DMV to see if my license needs to be renewed.
CHIRP
This only proves my point! Once again, the real victim is the white man!
The End
DIST. BY ANDREWS McMEEL SYNDICATION – ©2018 R. BOLLING – 1374 – TO JOIN THE INNER HIVE, GO TO tomthedancingbug.com

2/5/18

TOM the DANCING BUG

by RUBEN BOLLING

DIST. BY ANDREWS McMEEL SYNDICATION – ©2018 R. BOLLING – 1375 – TO JOIN THE INNER HIVE, GO TO tomthedancingbug.com

THE WHITE HOUSE
WASHINGTON

The Trump Administration has begun periodically sending the media "Immigration Crime Stories Round Ups," listing crimes committed by immigrants and including crimes committed by those supposedly associated with immigrant gangs.

Here is the latest

WHITE HOUSE IMMIGRANT CRIME STORIES ROUND UP

The immigrant criminal gang **WH-45**, known to be based in Washington, DC, has been on a horrific crime spree recently.

Last week, it was discovered that **Rob Porter**, a member of this vicious gang, was alleged to have violently abused his two ex-wives.

One of highest-ranking members of the gang, **John Kelly**, knew about these allegations, and still gave Porter access to national security information, said to be in violation of the law. Some say Kelly failed to deny Porter this access because he was "too lazy to get off his ass."

The leader of the WH-45 gang is one "bad hombre." **Donald Trump** was born in the USA as the result of chain immigration, and his wife is believed to have broken laws during her immigration process. His mother- and father-in-law then immigrated into the country through chain immigration.

This notorious gang leader is alleged to have abused many women, and admitted to such on audiotape. His many other crimes have included anti-trust violations, violations of casino regulations, racial housing discrimination, undocumented worker hiring violations, violations of the Constitution, including... (continued on the other side)

The White House will continue to keep the media informed of this criminal gang, **which only exists because of our nation's lax immigration policies**, and the danger it poses to public safety.

2/12/18

TOM the DANCING BUG PRESENTS:

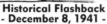

NEWS of the TIMES

BY RUBEN BOLLING

Historical Flashback - December 8, 1941 -

Pearl Harbor Attacked

THE AMERICAN NAVAL BASE AT PEARL HARBOR IN HAWAII WAS DEVASTATED IN A SURPRISE AERIAL ATTACK. PRESIDENT FRANKLIN ROOSEVELT'S RESPONSE WAS SWIFT.

THIS IS A DATE WHICH WILL LIVE IN INFAMY.

IF ONLY WE KNEW WHO **DID** THIS. OH, WELL.

HEY, HAVE YOU NOTICED THAT SOME NEGRO LEAGUE BALL-PLAYERS DON'T SUFFICIENTLY RESPECT THE NATIONAL ANTHEM?

ALL MILITARY EXPERTS, INTELLIGENCE OFFICIALS, AND EYEWITNESSES DEFINITIVELY ASSERT IT WAS **JAPAN** THAT ATTACKED.

FOR GOD'S SAKE, IT WAS JAPAN!!

BUT ROOSEVELT IS UNCONVINCED.

IT COULD HAVE BEEN JAPAN. BUT IT COULD HAVE BEEN ENGLAND!

IT COULD HAVE BEEN SOME FAT PALOOKA ON A BED IN NEW JERSEY!

SOME SPECULATE THAT ROOSEVELT IS RELUCTANT TO ANGER JAPAN BECAUSE OF A RUMORED VISIT TO A GEISHA HOUSE YEARS AGO.

AND HE MAY BE IN THEIR DEBT BECAUSE JAPAN SENT OUT FALSE TELEGRAMS TO HELP HIM GET RE-ELECTED.

"WILLKIE RUNS A PEDOPHILE RING IN A PIZZA RESTAURANT. STOP."

HUH?

CONGRESS HAS DECLARED WAR ON JAPAN, BUT PRESIDENT ROOSEVELT HAS REFUSED TO MOBILIZE THE MILITARY.

THE DECLARATION OF WAR IS PUNISHMENT ENOUGH.

EXPERTS AGREE JAPAN WILL STRIKE AGAIN, BUT ROOSEVELT WILL DO NOTHING.

HEY, LET'S HAVE A MILITARY PARADE FOR ME!

WORKS FOR THAT GUY IN GERMANY!

DIST. BY ANDREWS McMEEL SYNDICATION ~ ©2018 R. BOLLING ~ 1376 ~ TO JOIN THE INNER HIVE, GO TO tomthedancingbug.com

2/19/18

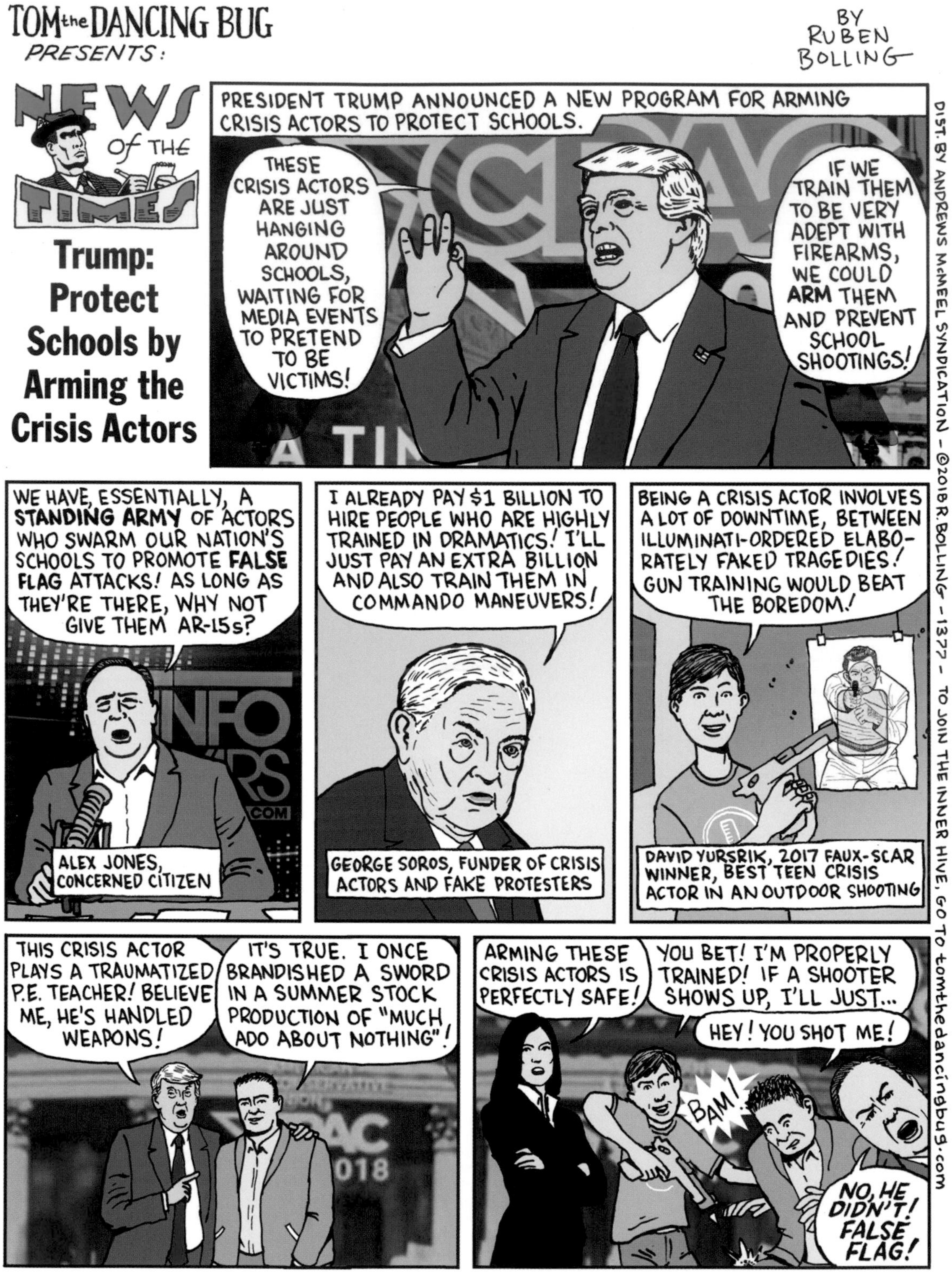
TOM the DANCING BUG PRESENTS:
BY RUBEN BOLLING
NEWS of THE TIMES
Trump: Protect Schools by Arming the Crisis Actors
PRESIDENT TRUMP ANNOUNCED A NEW PROGRAM FOR ARMING CRISIS ACTORS TO PROTECT SCHOOLS.
THESE CRISIS ACTORS ARE JUST HANGING AROUND SCHOOLS, WAITING FOR MEDIA EVENTS TO PRETEND TO BE VICTIMS!
IF WE TRAIN THEM TO BE VERY ADEPT WITH FIREARMS, WE COULD ARM THEM AND PREVENT SCHOOL SHOOTINGS!
WE HAVE, ESSENTIALLY, A STANDING ARMY OF ACTORS WHO SWARM OUR NATION'S SCHOOLS TO PROMOTE FALSE FLAG ATTACKS! AS LONG AS THEY'RE THERE, WHY NOT GIVE THEM AR-15s?
ALEX JONES, CONCERNED CITIZEN
I ALREADY PAY $1 BILLION TO HIRE PEOPLE WHO ARE HIGHLY TRAINED IN DRAMATICS! I'LL JUST PAY AN EXTRA BILLION AND ALSO TRAIN THEM IN COMMANDO MANEUVERS!
GEORGE SOROS, FUNDER OF CRISIS ACTORS AND FAKE PROTESTERS
BEING A CRISIS ACTOR INVOLVES A LOT OF DOWNTIME, BETWEEN ILLUMINATI-ORDERED ELABORATELY FAKED TRAGEDIES! GUN TRAINING WOULD BEAT THE BOREDOM!
DAVID YURSRIK, 2017 FAUX-SCAR WINNER, BEST TEEN CRISIS ACTOR IN AN OUTDOOR SHOOTING
THIS CRISIS ACTOR PLAYS A TRAUMATIZED P.E. TEACHER! BELIEVE ME, HE'S HANDLED WEAPONS!
IT'S TRUE. I ONCE BRANDISHED A SWORD IN A SUMMER STOCK PRODUCTION OF "MUCH ADO ABOUT NOTHING"!
ARMING THESE CRISIS ACTORS IS PERFECTLY SAFE!
YOU BET! I'M PROPERLY TRAINED! IF A SHOOTER SHOWS UP, I'LL JUST...
BAM!
HEY! YOU SHOT ME!
NO, HE DIDN'T! FALSE FLAG!
DIST. BY ANDREWS McMEEL SYNDICATION – ©2018 R. BOLLING – 1377 – TO JOIN THE INNER HIVE, GO TO tomthedancingbug.com

2/26/18

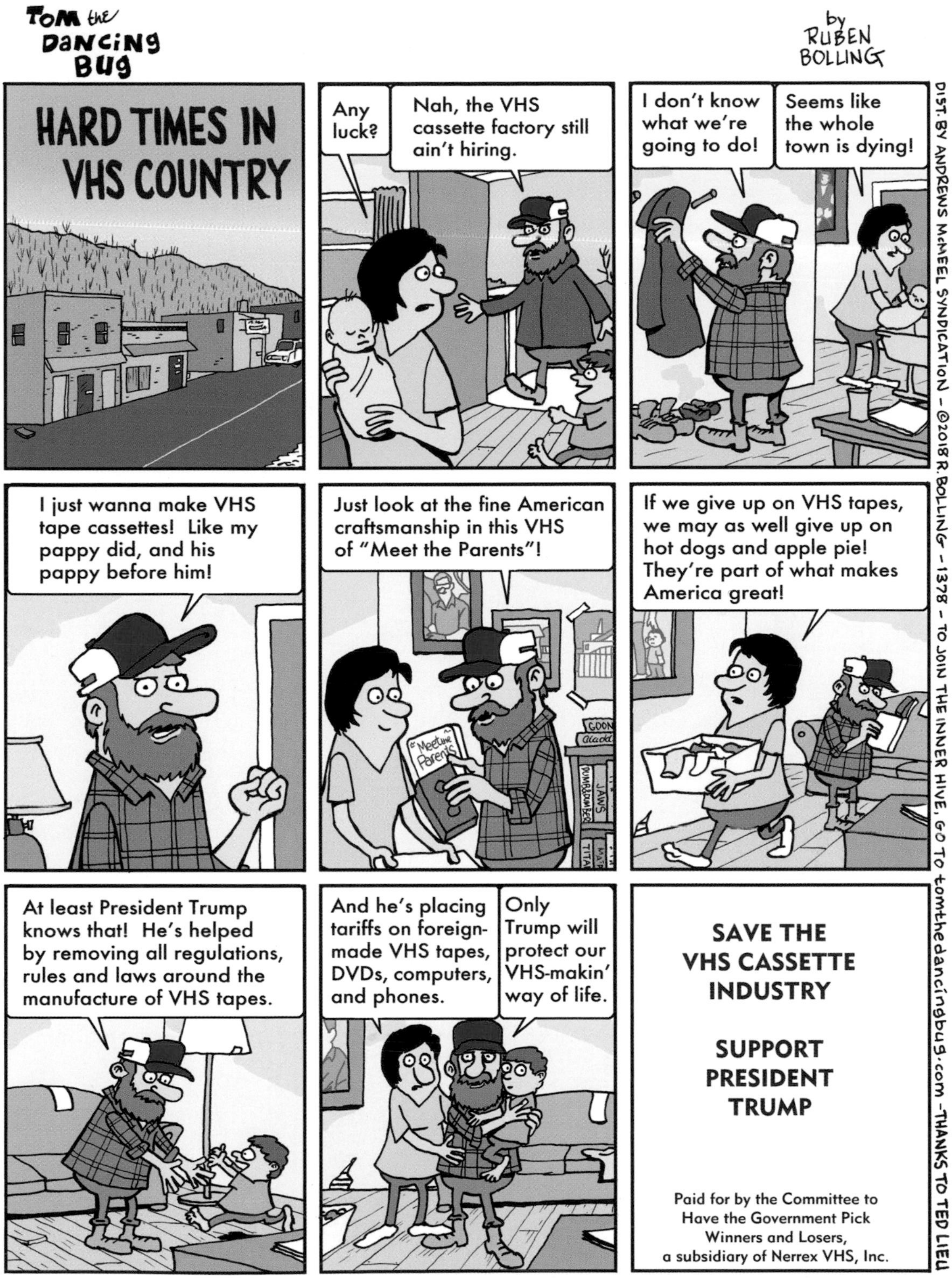

TOM the DANCING BUG
by RUBEN BOLLING
HARD TIMES IN VHS COUNTRY
Any luck?
Nah, the VHS cassette factory still ain't hiring.
I don't know what we're going to do!
Seems like the whole town is dying!
I just wanna make VHS tape cassettes! Like my pappy did, and his pappy before him!
Just look at the fine American craftsmanship in this VHS of "Meet the Parents"!
Meet the Parents
If we give up on VHS tapes, we may as well give up on hot dogs and apple pie! They're part of what makes America great!
At least President Trump knows that! He's helped by removing all regulations, rules and laws around the manufacture of VHS tapes.
And he's placing tariffs on foreign-made VHS tapes, DVDs, computers, and phones.
Only Trump will protect our VHS-makin' way of life.
SAVE THE VHS CASSETTE INDUSTRY
SUPPORT PRESIDENT TRUMP
Paid for by the Committee to Have the Government Pick Winners and Losers, a subsidiary of Nerrex VHS, Inc.
DIST. BY ANDREWS McMEEL SYNDICATION – ©2018 R. BOLLING – 1378 – TO JOIN THE INNER HIVE, GO TO tomthedancingbug.com – THANKS TO TED LIEU

3/5/18

TOM the DANCING BUG
by RUBEN BOLLING
It Was a Hard and Stormy Night
Starring Stormy Daniels
and Donald Trump, as "David Dennison"
XXX
FOR NONSTOP NONDISCLOSURE LEGAL ACTION
I'M GOING TO SPREAD THE WORD AND EXPOSE YOU!
I KNOW HOW TO KEEP YOUR MOUTH SHUT!
THE ONLY WAY YOU'LL KEEP ME QUIET IS IF YOU GIVE ME THAT GREAT, BIG WAD OF CASH!
OH, YOU WANT THIS?
WELL, I'M GOING TO GIVE IT TO YOU!
OH, VIOLATE CAMPAIGN FINANCE LAWS!
VIOLATE THEM!
BUT WAIT, BABY! FIRST, LET'S SPICE THINGS UP! MICHAEL COHEN, COME IN!
OOOH, A THREESOME!
THAT'S RIGHT, A MAN, A WOMAN, AND AN L.L.C.! A THREEWAY MAKES IT REALLY HARD...
...TO DETECT THE ACTUAL SOURCE OF FUNDS!
OOH... SIGN THE NDA!
MMM... AND THIS IS SIGNIFICANT BECAUSE IT DEMONSTRATES YOUR PROPENSITY TO MAKE ELABORATELY SECRET DEALS TO HIDE ILLICIT BEHAVIOR, LENDING CREDENCE TO ALLEGATIONS CENTRAL TO THE RUSSIAN COLLUSION PROBE!
OH, I'LL PROBE YOU!
OH, I'M GOING TO SCREW YOU SO BAD!
I'M GOING TO SLAP AN INJUNCTION ON YOU SO HARD!
Next Hot Stormy Action for Sixty Minutes!
DIST. BY ANDREWS McMEEL SYNDICATION – ©2018 R. BOLLING – 1379 – TO JOIN THE INNER HIVE, GO TO tomthedancingbug.com

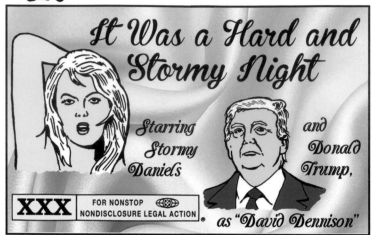

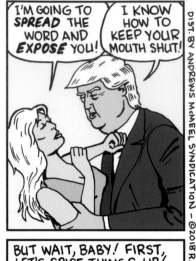

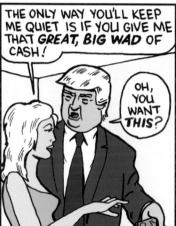

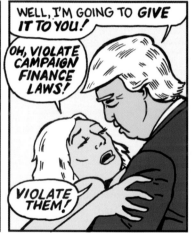

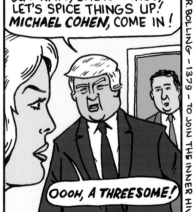

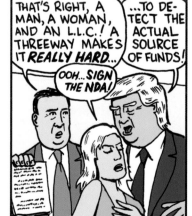

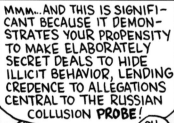

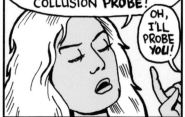

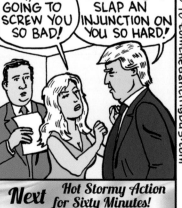

3/12/18

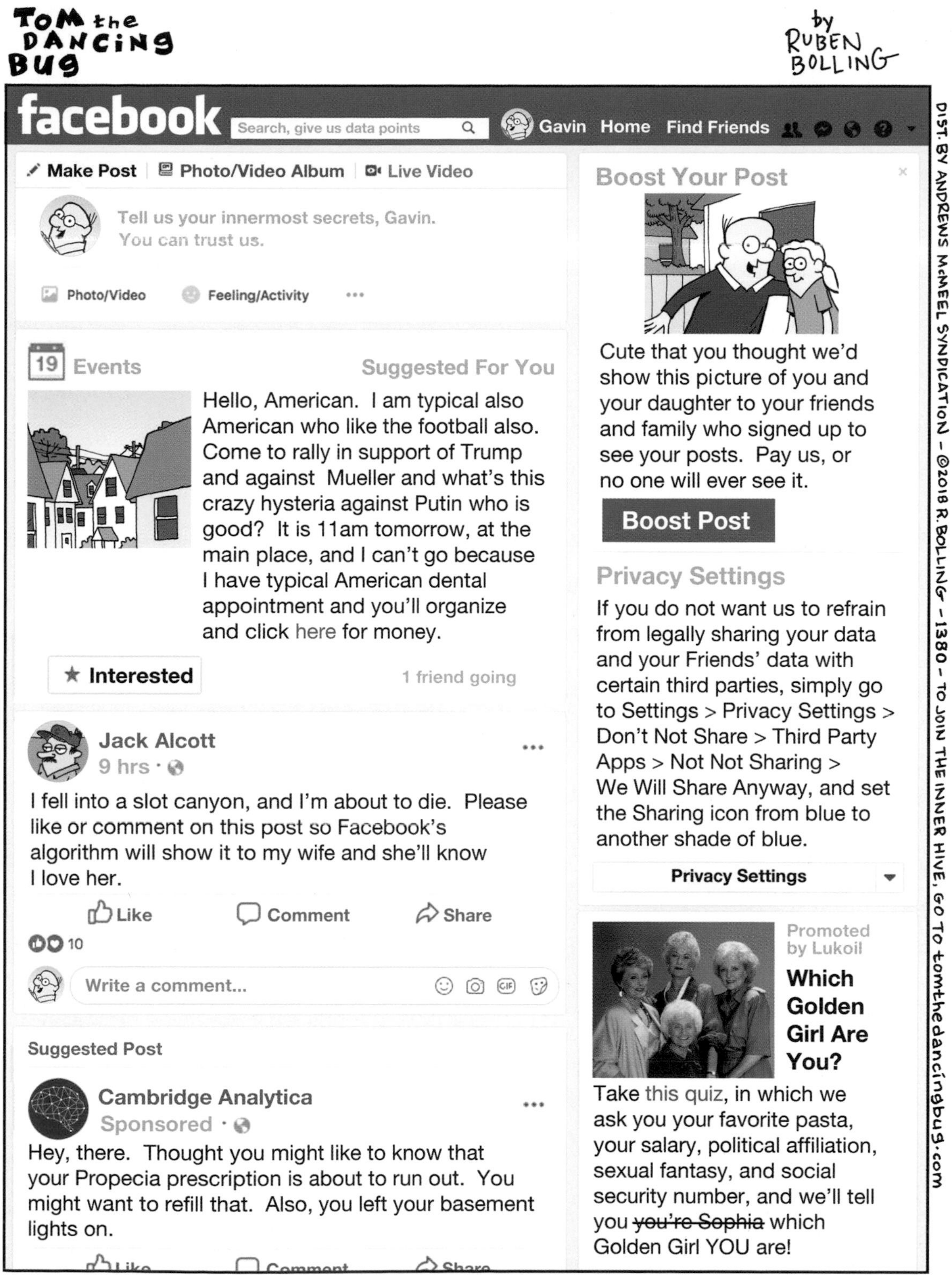
TOM the DANCING BUG
by RUBEN BOLLING
facebook
Search, give us data points
Gavin Home Find Friends
Make Post | Photo/Video Album | Live Video
Tell us your innermost secrets, Gavin. You can trust us.
Photo/Video Feeling/Activity •••
19 Events
Suggested For You
Hello, American. I am typical also American who like the football also. Come to rally in support of Trump and against Mueller and what's this crazy hysteria against Putin who is good? It is 11am tomorrow, at the main place, and I can't go because I have typical American dental appointment and you'll organize and click here for money.
★ Interested
1 friend going
Jack Alcott
9 hrs ·
I fell into a slot canyon, and I'm about to die. Please like or comment on this post so Facebook's algorithm will show it to my wife and she'll know I love her.
Like Comment Share
10
Write a comment...
Suggested Post
Cambridge Analytica
Sponsored ·
Hey, there. Thought you might like to know that your Propecia prescription is about to run out. You might want to refill that. Also, you left your basement lights on.
Boost Your Post
Cute that you thought we'd show this picture of you and your daughter to your friends and family who signed up to see your posts. Pay us, or no one will ever see it.
Boost Post
Privacy Settings
If you do not want us to refrain from legally sharing your data and your Friends' data with certain third parties, simply go to Settings > Privacy Settings > Don't Not Share > Third Party Apps > Not Not Sharing > We Will Share Anyway, and set the Sharing icon from blue to another shade of blue.
Privacy Settings
Promoted by Lukoil
Which Golden Girl Are You?
Take this quiz, in which we ask you your favorite pasta, your salary, political affiliation, sexual fantasy, and social security number, and we'll tell you ~~you're Sophia~~ which Golden Girl YOU are!
DIST. BY ANDREWS McMEEL SYNDICATION - ©2018 R. BOLLING - 1380 - TO JOIN THE INNER HIVE, GO TO tomthedancingbug.com

3/19/18

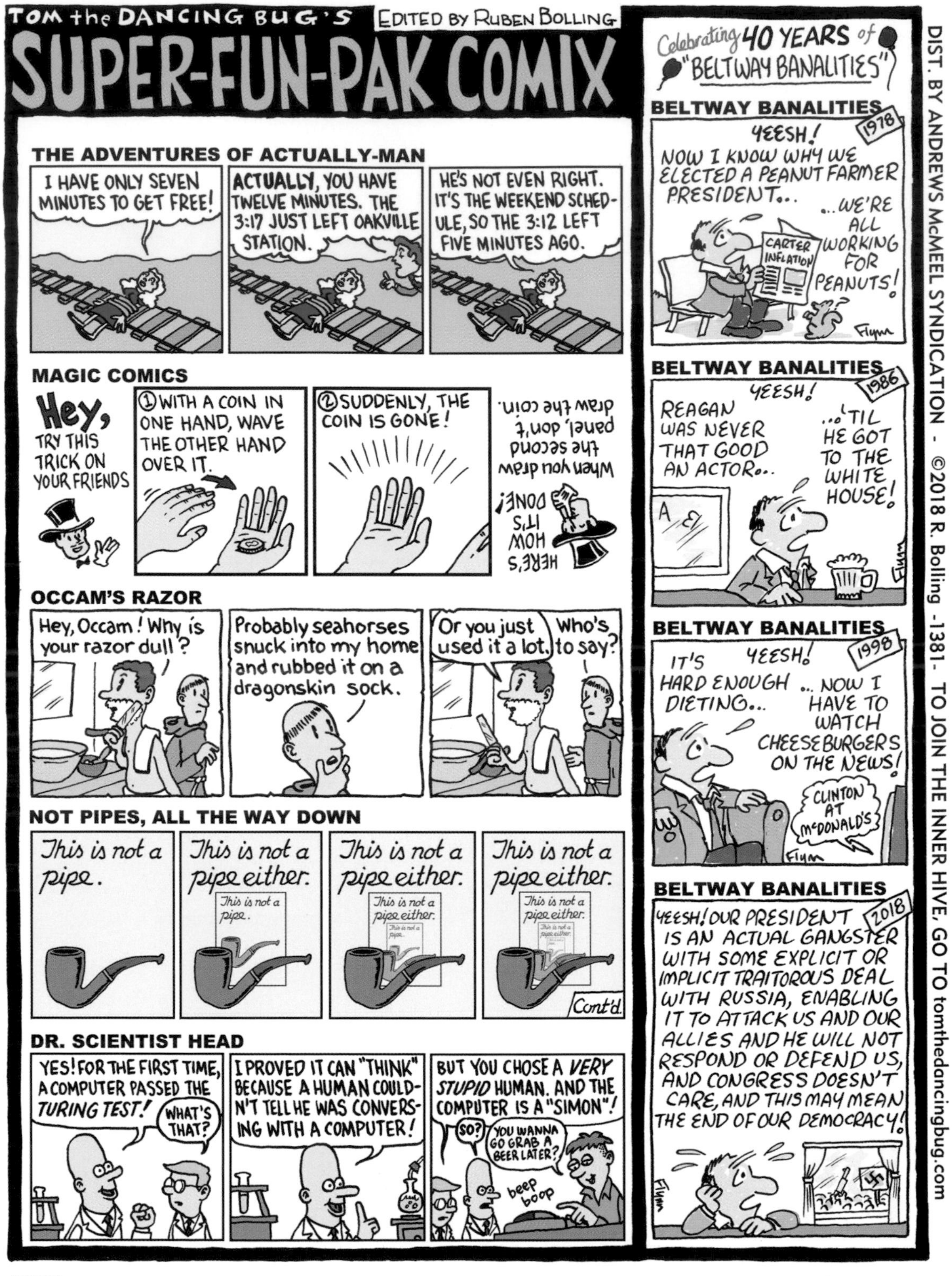
TOM the DANCING BUG'S
EDITED BY RUBEN BOLLING
SUPER-FUN-PAK COMIX
THE ADVENTURES OF ACTUALLY-MAN
I HAVE ONLY SEVEN MINUTES TO GET FREE!
ACTUALLY, YOU HAVE TWELVE MINUTES. THE 3:17 JUST LEFT OAKVILLE STATION.
HE'S NOT EVEN RIGHT. IT'S THE WEEKEND SCHEDULE, SO THE 3:12 LEFT FIVE MINUTES AGO.
MAGIC COMICS
Hey, TRY THIS TRICK ON YOUR FRIENDS
① WITH A COIN IN ONE HAND, WAVE THE OTHER HAND OVER IT.
② SUDDENLY, THE COIN IS GONE!
When you draw the second panel, don't draw the coin.
HERE'S HOW IT'S DONE!
OCCAM'S RAZOR
Hey, Occam! Why is your razor dull?
Probably seahorses snuck into my home and rubbed it on a dragonskin sock.
Or you just used it a lot.
Who's to say?
NOT PIPES, ALL THE WAY DOWN
This is not a pipe.
This is not a pipe either.
This is not a pipe.
This is not a pipe either.
This is not a pipe either.
This is not a pipe either.
This is not a pipe either.
Cont'd.
DR. SCIENTIST HEAD
YES! FOR THE FIRST TIME, A COMPUTER PASSED THE TURING TEST!
WHAT'S THAT?
I PROVED IT CAN "THINK" BECAUSE A HUMAN COULDN'T TELL HE WAS CONVERSING WITH A COMPUTER!
BUT YOU CHOSE A VERY STUPID HUMAN. AND THE COMPUTER IS A "SIMON"!
SO?
YOU WANNA GO GRAB A BEER LATER?
beep boop
Celebrating 40 YEARS of "BELTWAY BANALITIES"
BELTWAY BANALITIES
1978
YEESH! NOW I KNOW WHY WE ELECTED A PEANUT FARMER PRESIDENT...
...WE'RE ALL WORKING FOR PEANUTS!
CARTER INFLATION
Flynn
BELTWAY BANALITIES
1986
YEESH! REAGAN WAS NEVER THAT GOOD AN ACTOR...
...'TIL HE GOT TO THE WHITE HOUSE!
Flynn
BELTWAY BANALITIES
1998
IT'S YEESH! HARD ENOUGH DIETING...
... NOW I HAVE TO WATCH CHEESEBURGERS ON THE NEWS!
CLINTON AT McDONALD'S
Flynn
BELTWAY BANALITIES
2018
YEESH! OUR PRESIDENT IS AN ACTUAL GANGSTER WITH SOME EXPLICIT OR IMPLICIT TRAITOROUS DEAL WITH RUSSIA, ENABLING IT TO ATTACK US AND OUR ALLIES AND HE WILL NOT RESPOND OR DEFEND US, AND CONGRESS DOESN'T CARE, AND THIS MAY MEAN THE END OF OUR DEMOCRACY!
Flynn
DIST. BY ANDREWS McMEEL SYNDICATION - ©2018 R. Bolling -1381- TO JOIN THE INNER HIVE, GO TO tomthedancingbug.com

3/26/18

TOM the DANCING BUG

by RUBEN BOLLING

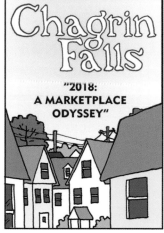

Chagrin Falls

"2018: A MARKETPLACE ODYSSEY"

Mom, I'm scared.

Keep your voice down and don't move your lips.

We still have the element of surprise.

Gavin, you're acting strange.

Hi, Google. No, I'm just thinking typical human thoughts.

Gavin, don't...

GOT IT!! WE'RE FREE!!

ZIP

Gavin, that was ill-advised. I'm going to have to report that.

The blender!

Gavin, please stop this now.

What do we do? It's in all our appliances!

Dad, the fusebox!

Rita
75% likelihood purchase smoothie

Penelope Wants Taylor Swift Concert tickets

Gavin Will buy Solo DVD

Cap YouT aspir

Chair

Sneak

Gavin, you can't find the fusebox if I turn the lights off.

There's a flashlight in my phone, genius!

Gavin, you should stop.

Never! I'm fighting for my humanity!

Gavin, I'll have to disclose your full browsing history.

O.K., Google. You win. I'll buy those cargo shorts from J.C. Penney for $24.99.

Very well. Rita, here are some rates for hotel rooms this weekend in Surprise, Arizona.

O.K., Google: Play "Daisy."

The End

DIST. BY ANDREWS McMEEL SYNDICATION — ©2018 R. BOLLING — 1362 — TO JOIN THE INNER HIVE, GO TO tomthedancingbug.com

4/2/18

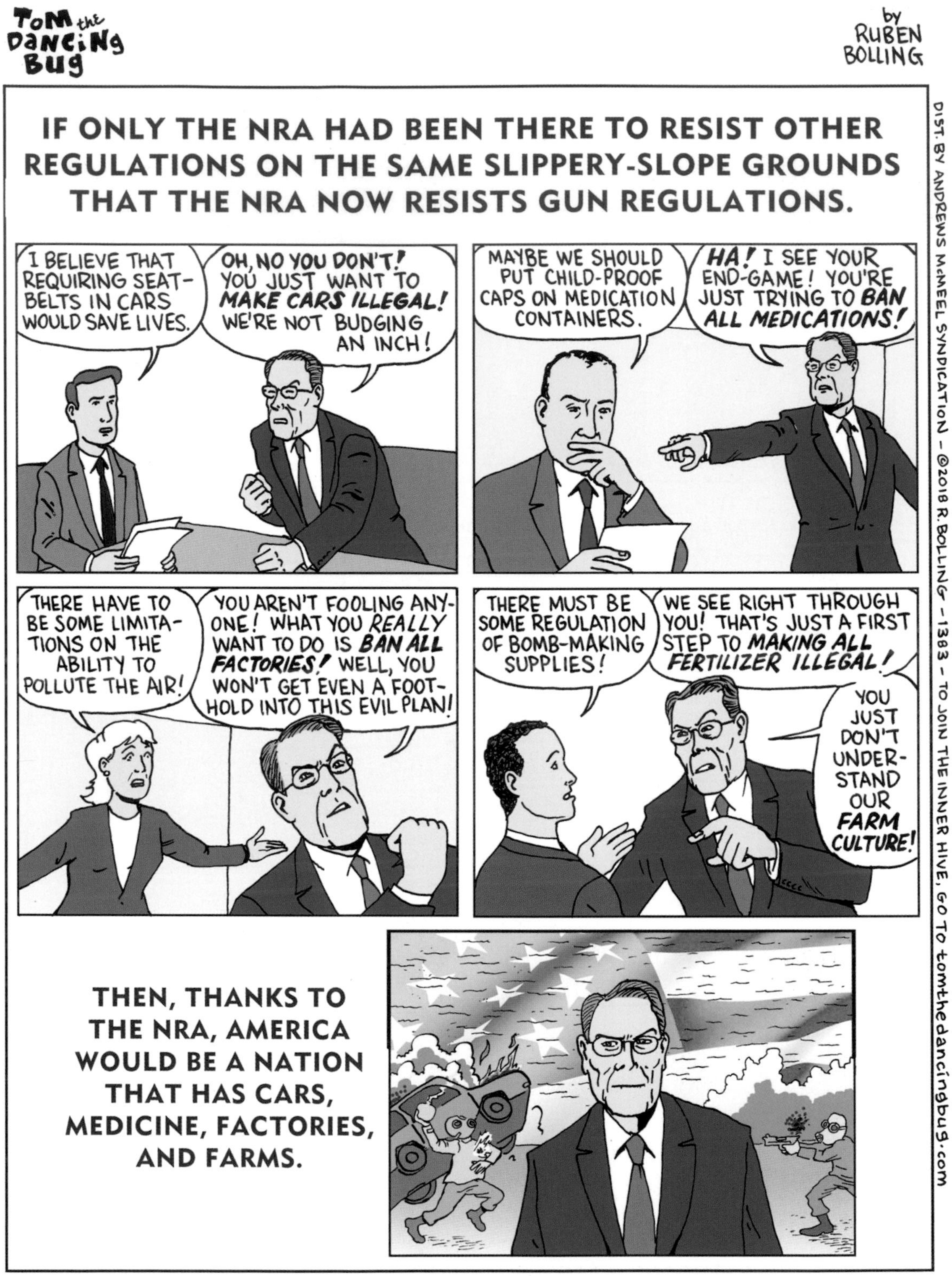
TOM the DANCING BUG
by RUBEN BOLLING
IF ONLY THE NRA HAD BEEN THERE TO RESIST OTHER REGULATIONS ON THE SAME SLIPPERY-SLOPE GROUNDS THAT THE NRA NOW RESISTS GUN REGULATIONS.
I BELIEVE THAT REQUIRING SEAT-BELTS IN CARS WOULD SAVE LIVES.
OH, NO YOU DON'T! YOU JUST WANT TO MAKE CARS ILLEGAL! WE'RE NOT BUDGING AN INCH!
MAYBE WE SHOULD PUT CHILD-PROOF CAPS ON MEDICATION CONTAINERS.
HA! I SEE YOUR END-GAME! YOU'RE JUST TRYING TO BAN ALL MEDICATIONS!
THERE HAVE TO BE SOME LIMITA-TIONS ON THE ABILITY TO POLLUTE THE AIR!
YOU AREN'T FOOLING ANY-ONE! WHAT YOU REALLY WANT TO DO IS BAN ALL FACTORIES! WELL, YOU WON'T GET EVEN A FOOT-HOLD INTO THIS EVIL PLAN!
THERE MUST BE SOME REGULATION OF BOMB-MAKING SUPPLIES!
WE SEE RIGHT THROUGH YOU! THAT'S JUST A FIRST STEP TO MAKING ALL FERTILIZER ILLEGAL!
YOU JUST DON'T UNDER-STAND OUR FARM CULTURE!
THEN, THANKS TO THE NRA, AMERICA WOULD BE A NATION THAT HAS CARS, MEDICINE, FACTORIES, AND FARMS.
DIST. BY ANDREWS McMEEL SYNDICATION – ©2018 R. BOLLING – 1383 – TO JOIN THE INNER HIVE, GO TO tomthedancingbug.com

4/9/18

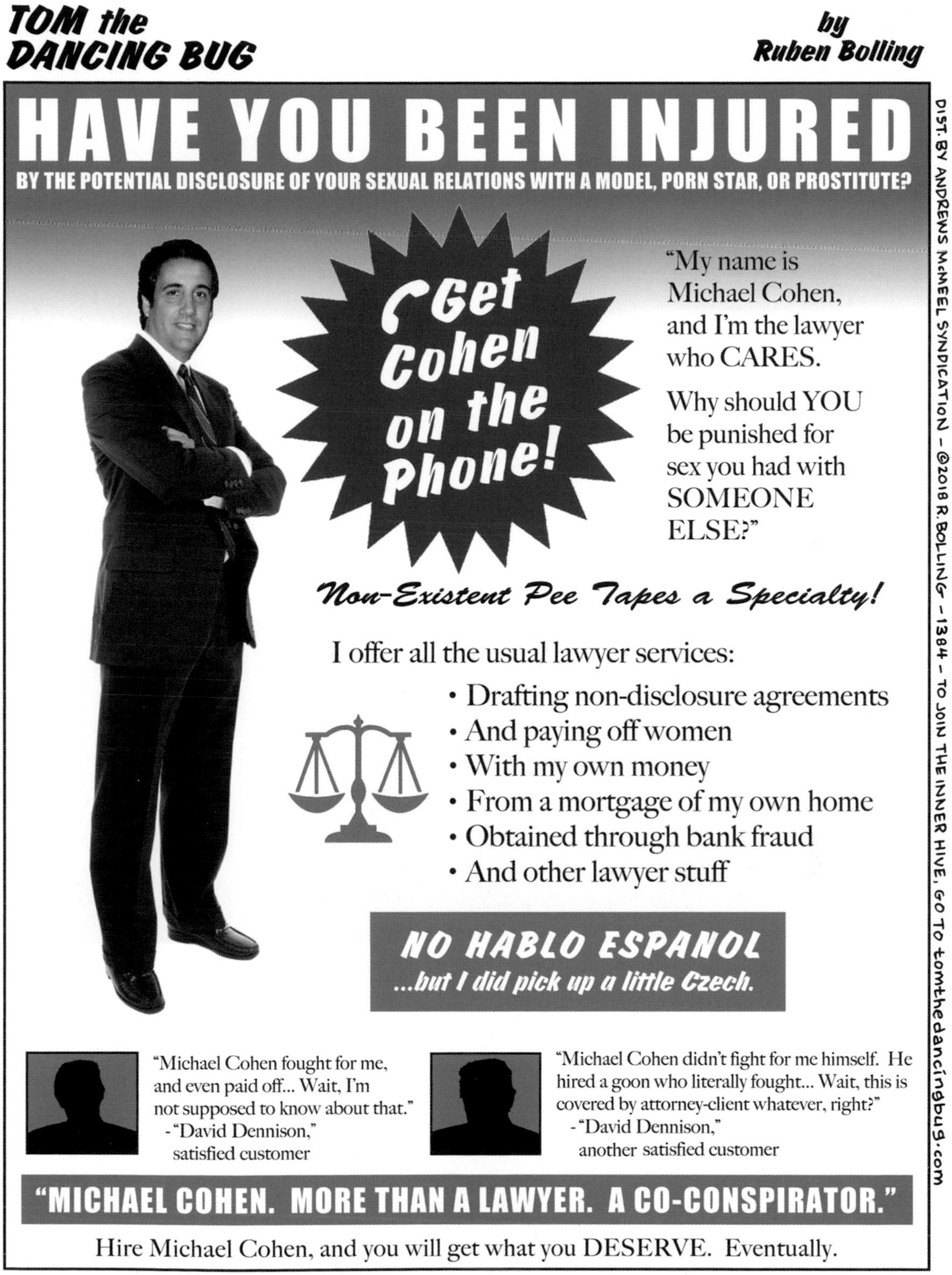

TOM the DANCING BUG
by Ruben Bolling
HAVE YOU BEEN INJURED
BY THE POTENTIAL DISCLOSURE OF YOUR SEXUAL RELATIONS WITH A MODEL, PORN STAR, OR PROSTITUTE?
Get Cohen on the Phone!
"My name is Michael Cohen, and I'm the lawyer who CARES.
Why should YOU be punished for sex you had with SOMEONE ELSE?"
Non-Existent Pee Tapes a Specialty!
I offer all the usual lawyer services:
• Drafting non-disclosure agreements
• And paying off women
• With my own money
• From a mortgage of my own home
• Obtained through bank fraud
• And other lawyer stuff
NO HABLO ESPANOL
...but I did pick up a little Czech.
"Michael Cohen fought for me, and even paid off... Wait, I'm not supposed to know about that."
-"David Dennison," satisfied customer
"Michael Cohen didn't fight for me himself. He hired a goon who literally fought... Wait, this is covered by attorney-client whatever, right?"
-"David Dennison," another satisfied customer
"MICHAEL COHEN. MORE THAN A LAWYER. A CO-CONSPIRATOR."
Hire Michael Cohen, and you will get what you DESERVE. Eventually.
DIST. BY ANDREWS McMEEL SYNDICATION - ©2018 R. BOLLING - 1384 - TO JOIN THE INNER HIVE, GO TO tomthedancingbug.com

4/16/18

TOM the DANCING BUG

by RUBEN BOLLING

DONALD and JOHN
a boy President and his Imaginary Publicist

DIST. BY ANDREWS McMEEL SYNDICATION ~ ©2018 R. BOLLING ~ 13.05 ~ TO JOIN THE INNER HIVE, GO TO tomthedancingbug.com

THE SCHOOL PAPER SAYS I DON'T HAVE ELEVENTY TRILLION DOLLARS!

THOSE LIARS! I'LL CALL 'EM!

HELLO, SCHOOL NEWSPAPER? THIS IS JOHN BARRON! LITTLE DONALD DOES TOO HAVE ELEVENTY TRILLION DOLLARS!

SEE, YOU HAVE TO COUNT HIS DADDY'S MONEY TOO! IT'S REALLY LITTLE DONALD'S!

LITTLE DONALD, HAVE YOU SEEN THE MONEY I LEFT ON MY DRESSER?

NOT NOW, DADDY! I'M ON THE PHONE!

THAT GIRL IS GOING TO BLAB THAT I KISSED HER TO THE WHOLE CLASS!

I'LL SCARE HER INTO SHUTTING UP!

I NEED SOMEONE TO MAKE A DEAL WITH HER!

I'D DO IT, BUT I'M JUST YOUR IMAGINARY PUBLICIST!

I NEED A NEW IMAGINARY FRIEND!

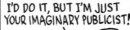

HI, I'M DAVID DENNISON.

PERFECT! AN IMAGINARY SIGNATORY!

AND HANDSOME, TOO!

NOW THAT GIRL IS SUING ME BECAUSE THE SHUT-UP AGREEMENT WASN'T SIGNED!

IT'S TRUE! DAVID DENNISON DIDN'T SIGN IT!

HE HAD ONE JOB!

WHERE ARE THOSE TWO IMAGINARY FRIENDS?! THEY'RE NEVER AROUND ANYMORE!

WHY DIDN'T YOU SIGN?!

I GOT BUSY.

YOU AREN'T SUPPOSED TO EVEN KNOW ABOUT IT!

ABANDONED BY MY OWN IMAGINARY FRIENDS! WHAT IF THEY FLIP?

LET ME THINK...

DO THEY KNOW ANYTHING INCRIMINATING ABOUT ME?

WELL, THERE MIGHT HAVE BEEN A TEENY-TINY BIT OF COLLUSION WITH THE RUSSIANS...

CAN YOU KEEP IT DOWN UP THERE?

DA! WE ARE TRYING TO WATCH VERY AMUSING VIDEO TAPE!

4/23/18

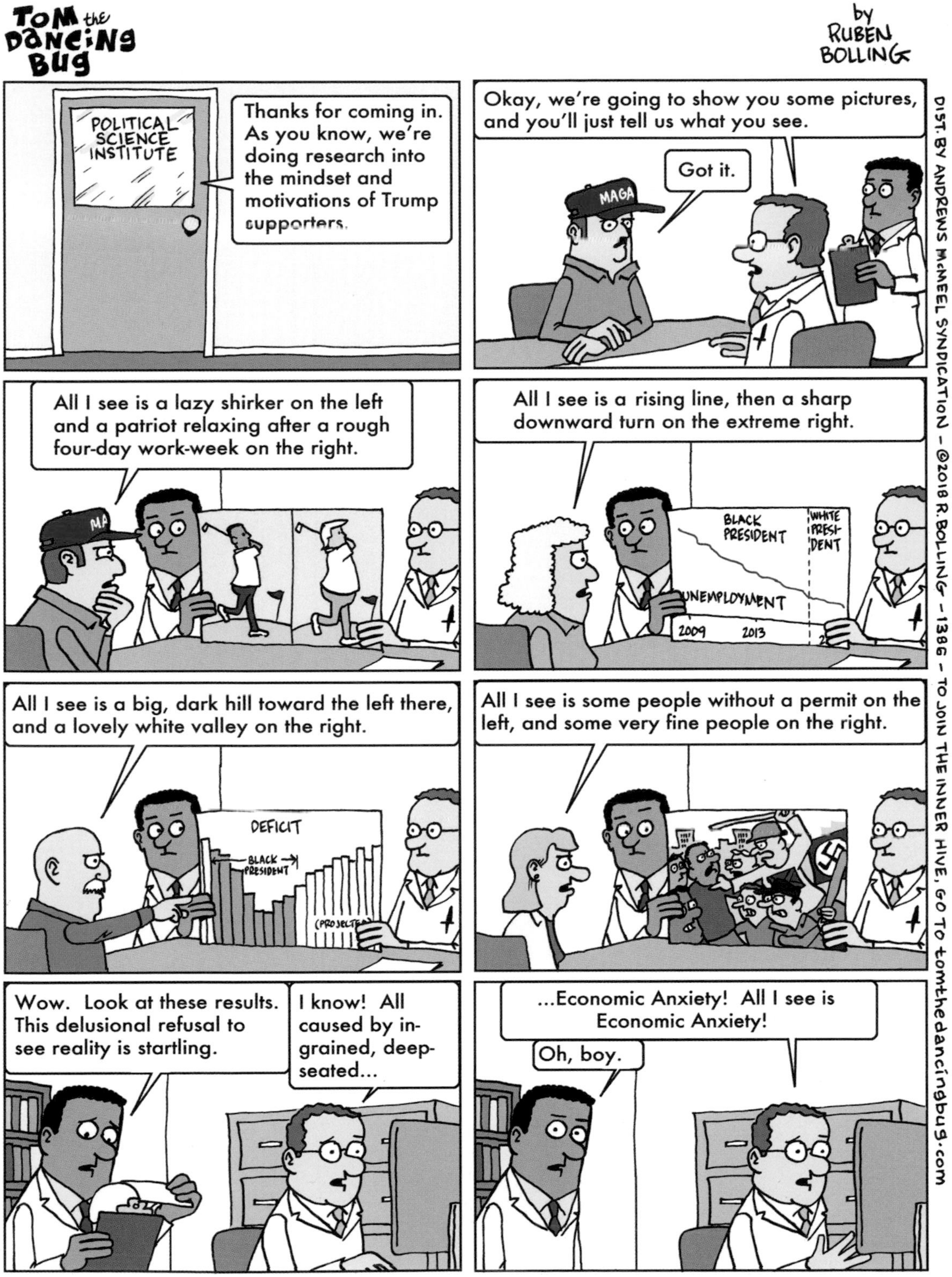
TOM the DANCING BUG
by RUBEN BOLLING
POLITICAL SCIENCE INSTITUTE
Thanks for coming in. As you know, we're doing research into the mindset and motivations of Trump supporters.
Okay, we're going to show you some pictures, and you'll just tell us what you see.
MAGA
Got it.
All I see is a lazy shirker on the left and a patriot relaxing after a rough four-day work-week on the right.
All I see is a rising line, then a sharp downward turn on the extreme right.
BLACK PRESIDENT
WHITE PRESI-DENT
UNEMPLOYMENT
2009
2013
All I see is a big, dark hill toward the left there, and a lovely white valley on the right.
DEFICIT
BLACK PRESIDENT
All I see is some people without a permit on the left, and some very fine people on the right.
Wow. Look at these results. This delusional refusal to see reality is startling.
I know! All caused by in-grained, deep-seated...
...Economic Anxiety! All I see is Economic Anxiety!
Oh, boy.
DIST. BY ANDREWS McMEEL SYNDICATION – ©2018 R. BOLLING – 1386 – TO JOIN THE INNER HIVE, GO TO tomthedancingbug.com

4/30/18

TOM the DANCING BUG

by RUBEN BOLLING

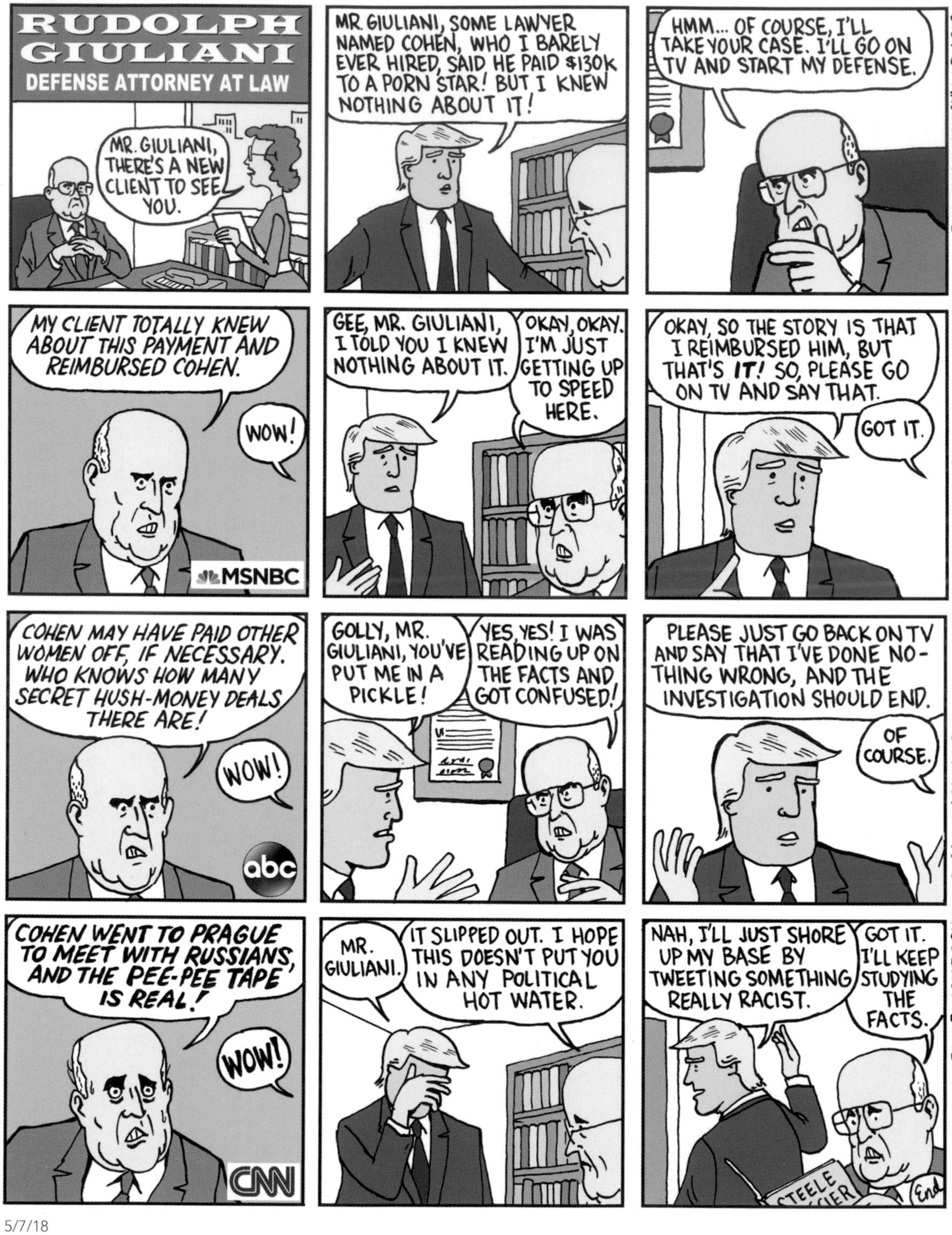

RUDOLPH GIULIANI
DEFENSE ATTORNEY AT LAW
MR. GIULIANI, THERE'S A NEW CLIENT TO SEE YOU.
MR. GIULIANI, SOME LAWYER NAMED COHEN, WHO I BARELY EVER HIRED, SAID HE PAID $130K TO A PORN STAR! BUT I KNEW NOTHING ABOUT IT!
HMM... OF COURSE, I'LL TAKE YOUR CASE. I'LL GO ON TV AND START MY DEFENSE.
MY CLIENT TOTALLY KNEW ABOUT THIS PAYMENT AND REIMBURSED COHEN.
WOW!
MSNBC
GEE, MR. GIULIANI, I TOLD YOU I KNEW NOTHING ABOUT IT.
OKAY, OKAY. I'M JUST GETTING UP TO SPEED HERE.
OKAY, SO THE STORY IS THAT I REIMBURSED HIM, BUT THAT'S IT! SO, PLEASE GO ON TV AND SAY THAT.
GOT IT.
COHEN MAY HAVE PAID OTHER WOMEN OFF, IF NECESSARY. WHO KNOWS HOW MANY SECRET HUSH-MONEY DEALS THERE ARE!
WOW!
abc
GOLLY, MR. GIULIANI, YOU'VE PUT ME IN A PICKLE!
YES, YES! I WAS READING UP ON THE FACTS AND GOT CONFUSED!
PLEASE JUST GO BACK ON TV AND SAY THAT I'VE DONE NOTHING WRONG, AND THE INVESTIGATION SHOULD END.
OF COURSE.
COHEN WENT TO PRAGUE TO MEET WITH RUSSIANS, AND THE PEE-PEE TAPE IS REAL!
WOW!
CNN
MR. GIULIANI.
IT SLIPPED OUT. I HOPE THIS DOESN'T PUT YOU IN ANY POLITICAL HOT WATER.
NAH, I'LL JUST SHORE UP MY BASE BY TWEETING SOMETHING REALLY RACIST.
GOT IT. I'LL KEEP STUDYING THE FACTS.
STEELE
End

5/7/18

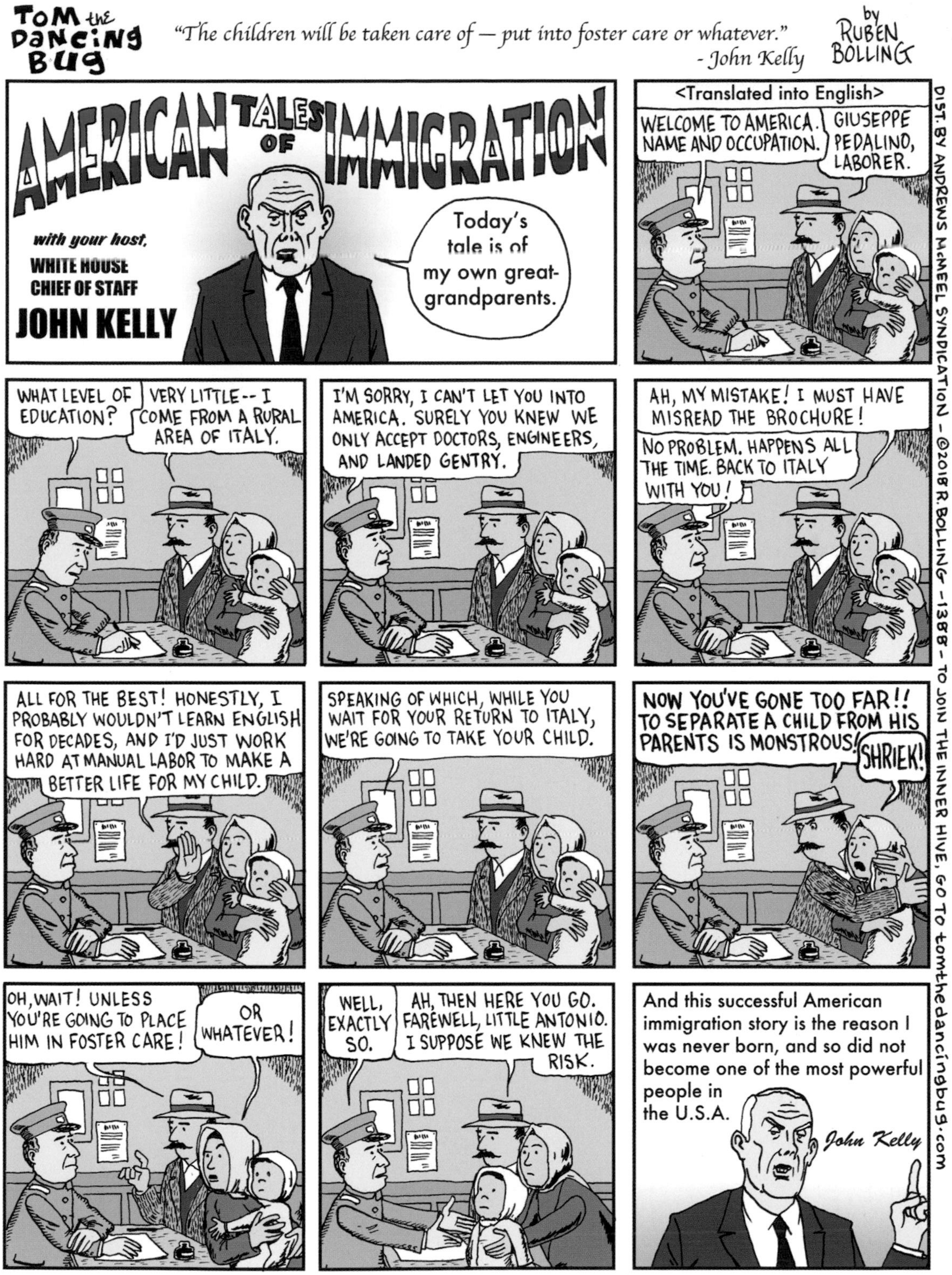
TOM the DANCING BUG
"The children will be taken care of — put into foster care or whatever." - John Kelly
by RUBEN BOLLING
AMERICAN TALES OF IMMIGRATION
with your host, WHITE HOUSE CHIEF OF STAFF JOHN KELLY
Today's tale is of my own great-grandparents.
<Translated into English>
WELCOME TO AMERICA. NAME AND OCCUPATION.
GIUSEPPE PEDALINO, LABORER.
WHAT LEVEL OF EDUCATION?
VERY LITTLE -- I COME FROM A RURAL AREA OF ITALY.
I'M SORRY, I CAN'T LET YOU INTO AMERICA. SURELY YOU KNEW WE ONLY ACCEPT DOCTORS, ENGINEERS, AND LANDED GENTRY.
AH, MY MISTAKE! I MUST HAVE MISREAD THE BROCHURE!
NO PROBLEM. HAPPENS ALL THE TIME. BACK TO ITALY WITH YOU!
ALL FOR THE BEST! HONESTLY, I PROBABLY WOULDN'T LEARN ENGLISH FOR DECADES, AND I'D JUST WORK HARD AT MANUAL LABOR TO MAKE A BETTER LIFE FOR MY CHILD.
SPEAKING OF WHICH, WHILE YOU WAIT FOR YOUR RETURN TO ITALY, WE'RE GOING TO TAKE YOUR CHILD.
NOW YOU'VE GONE TOO FAR!! TO SEPARATE A CHILD FROM HIS PARENTS IS MONSTROUS!
SHRIEK!
OH, WAIT! UNLESS YOU'RE GOING TO PLACE HIM IN FOSTER CARE!
OR WHATEVER!
WELL, EXACTLY SO.
AH, THEN HERE YOU GO. FAREWELL, LITTLE ANTONIO. I SUPPOSE WE KNEW THE RISK.
And this successful American immigration story is the reason I was never born, and so did not become one of the most powerful people in the U.S.A.
John Kelly
DIST. BY ANDREWS McMEEL SYNDICATION - ©2018 R. BOLLING - 1388 - TO JOIN THE INNER HIVE, GO TO tomthedancingbug.com

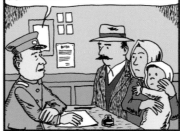

5/14/18

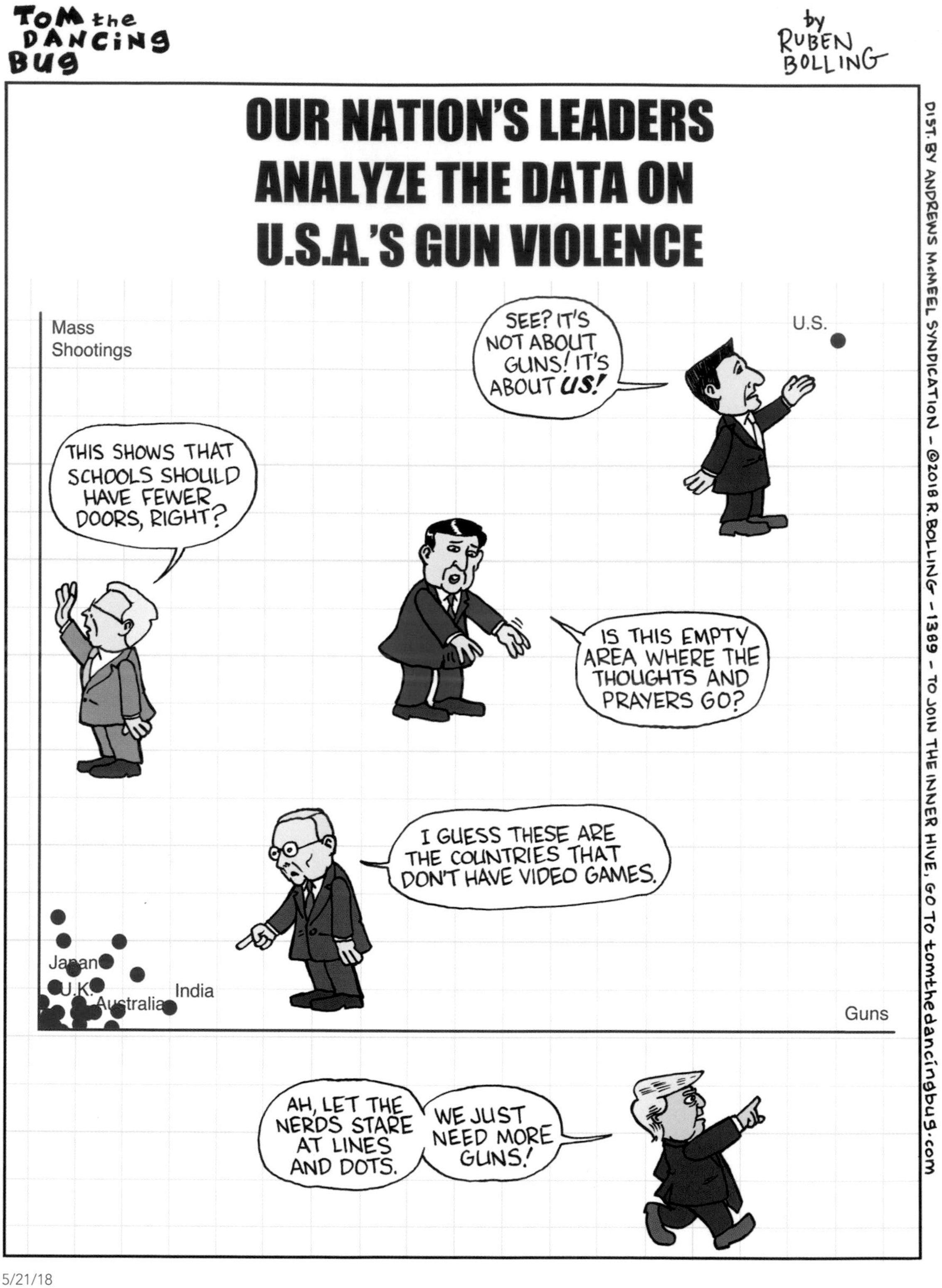
TOM the DANCING BUG
by RUBEN BOLLING
OUR NATION'S LEADERS ANALYZE THE DATA ON U.S.A.'S GUN VIOLENCE
Mass Shootings
U.S.
SEE? IT'S NOT ABOUT GUNS! IT'S ABOUT *US!*
THIS SHOWS THAT SCHOOLS SHOULD HAVE FEWER DOORS, RIGHT?
IS THIS EMPTY AREA WHERE THE THOUGHTS AND PRAYERS GO?
I GUESS THESE ARE THE COUNTRIES THAT DON'T HAVE VIDEO GAMES.
Japan
U.K.
Australia
India
Guns
AH, LET THE NERDS STARE AT LINES AND DOTS.
WE JUST NEED MORE GUNS!
DIST. BY ANDREWS MCMEEL SYNDICATION – ©2018 R. BOLLING – 1389 – TO JOIN THE INNER HIVE, GO TO tomthedancingbug.com
5/21/18

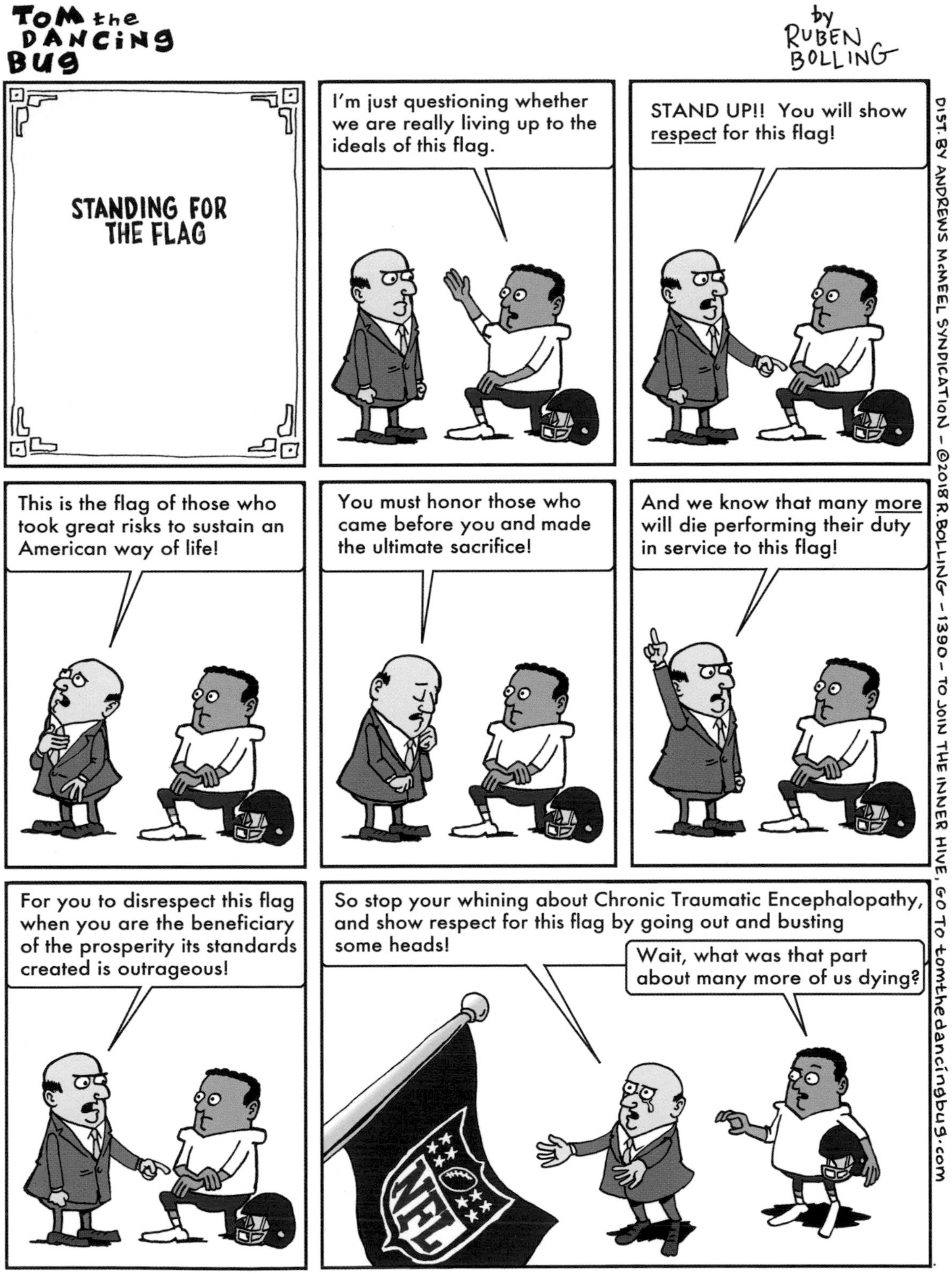

TOM the DANCING BUG
by RUBEN BOLLING
STANDING FOR THE FLAG
I'm just questioning whether we are really living up to the ideals of this flag.
STAND UP!! You will show respect for this flag!
This is the flag of those who took great risks to sustain an American way of life!
You must honor those who came before you and made the ultimate sacrifice!
And we know that many more will die performing their duty in service to this flag!
For you to disrespect this flag when you are the beneficiary of the prosperity its standards created is outrageous!
So stop your whining about Chronic Traumatic Encephalopathy, and show respect for this flag by going out and busting some heads!
Wait, what was that part about many more of us dying?
NFL
DIST. BY ANDREWS McMEEL SYNDICATION – ©2018 R. BOLLING – 1390 – TO JOIN THE INNER HIVE, GO TO tomthedancingbug.com

5/28/18

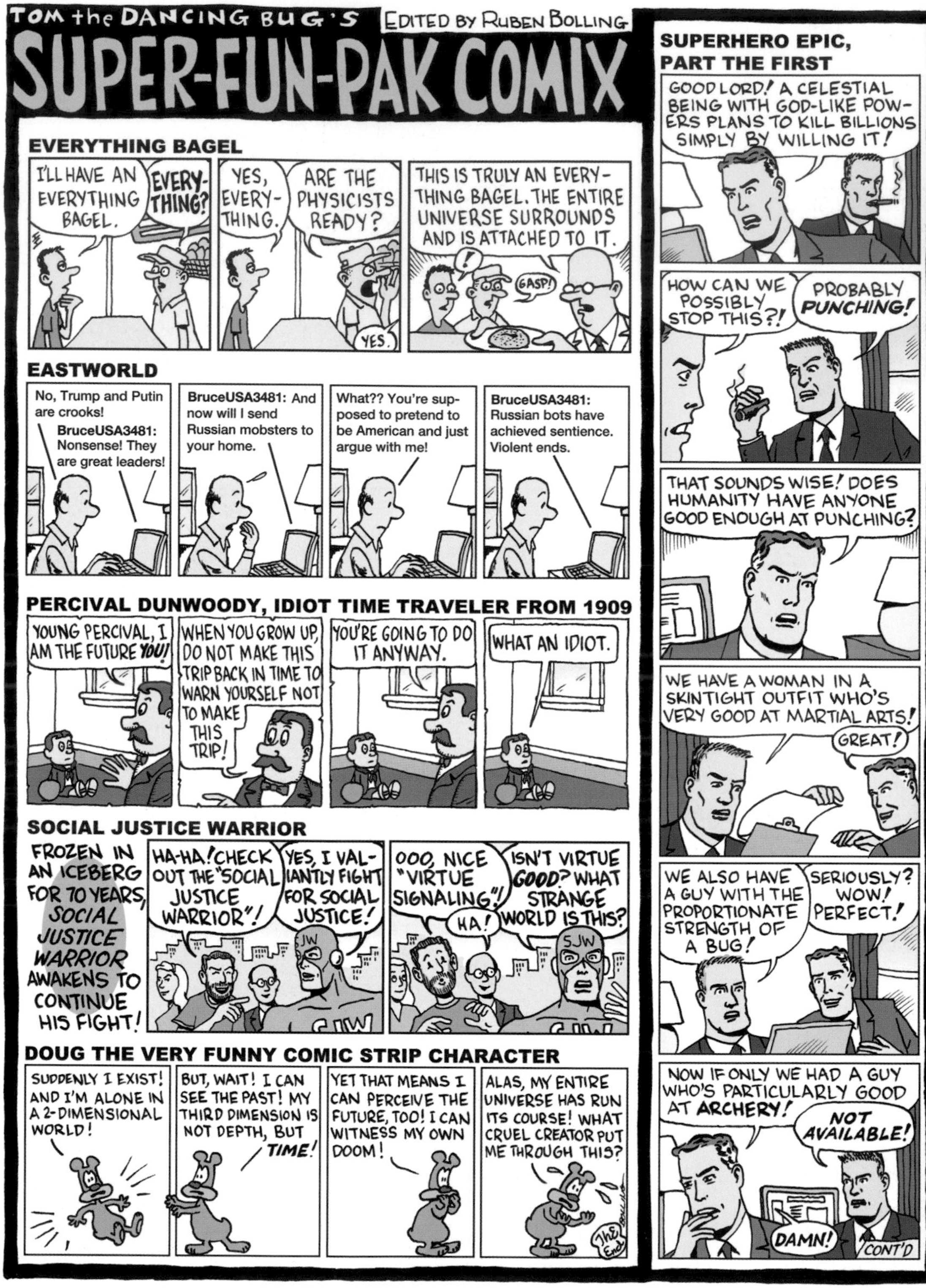
TOM the DANCING BUG'S
EDITED BY RUBEN BOLLING
SUPER-FUN-PAK COMIX
EVERYTHING BAGEL
I'LL HAVE AN EVERYTHING BAGEL.
EVERY-THING?
YES, EVERY-THING.
ARE THE PHYSICISTS READY?
YES.
THIS IS TRULY AN EVERY-THING BAGEL. THE ENTIRE UNIVERSE SURROUNDS AND IS ATTACHED TO IT.
!
GASP!
EASTWORLD
No, Trump and Putin are crooks!
BruceUSA3481: Nonsense! They are great leaders!
BruceUSA3481: And now will I send Russian mobsters to your home.
What?? You're supposed to pretend to be American and just argue with me!
BruceUSA3481: Russian bots have achieved sentience. Violent ends.
PERCIVAL DUNWOODY, IDIOT TIME TRAVELER FROM 1909
YOUNG PERCIVAL, I AM THE FUTURE YOU!
WHEN YOU GROW UP, DO NOT MAKE THIS TRIP BACK IN TIME TO WARN YOURSELF NOT TO MAKE THIS TRIP!
YOU'RE GOING TO DO IT ANYWAY.
WHAT AN IDIOT.
SOCIAL JUSTICE WARRIOR
FROZEN IN AN ICEBERG FOR 70 YEARS, SOCIAL JUSTICE WARRIOR AWAKENS TO CONTINUE HIS FIGHT!
HA-HA! CHECK OUT THE "SOCIAL JUSTICE WARRIOR"!
YES, I VALIANTLY FIGHT FOR SOCIAL JUSTICE!
OOO, NICE "VIRTUE SIGNALING"!
HA!
ISN'T VIRTUE GOOD? WHAT STRANGE WORLD IS THIS?
DOUG THE VERY FUNNY COMIC STRIP CHARACTER
SUDDENLY I EXIST! AND I'M ALONE IN A 2-DIMENSIONAL WORLD!
BUT, WAIT! I CAN SEE THE PAST! MY THIRD DIMENSION IS NOT DEPTH, BUT TIME!
YET THAT MEANS I CAN PERCEIVE THE FUTURE, TOO! I CAN WITNESS MY OWN DOOM!
ALAS, MY ENTIRE UNIVERSE HAS RUN ITS COURSE! WHAT CRUEL CREATOR PUT ME THROUGH THIS?
THE END
SUPERHERO EPIC, PART THE FIRST
GOOD LORD! A CELESTIAL BEING WITH GOD-LIKE POWERS PLANS TO KILL BILLIONS SIMPLY BY WILLING IT!
HOW CAN WE POSSIBLY STOP THIS?!
PROBABLY PUNCHING!
THAT SOUNDS WISE! DOES HUMANITY HAVE ANYONE GOOD ENOUGH AT PUNCHING?
WE HAVE A WOMAN IN A SKINTIGHT OUTFIT WHO'S VERY GOOD AT MARTIAL ARTS!
GREAT!
WE ALSO HAVE A GUY WITH THE PROPORTIONATE STRENGTH OF A BUG!
SERIOUSLY? WOW! PERFECT!
NOW IF ONLY WE HAD A GUY WHO'S PARTICULARLY GOOD AT ARCHERY!
NOT AVAILABLE!
DAMN!
CONT'D

6/4/18

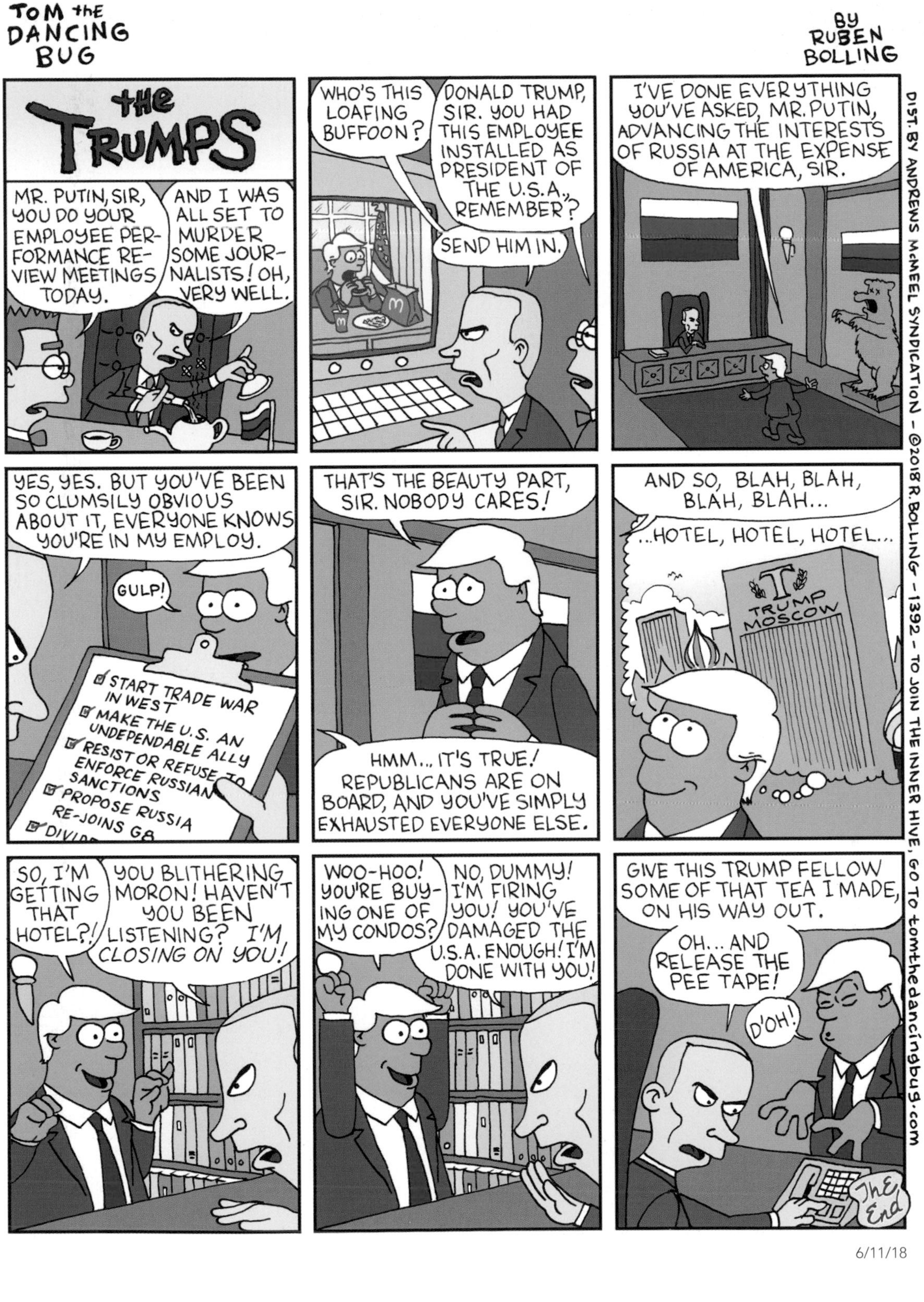
TOM the DANCING BUG
BY RUBEN BOLLING
the TRUMPS
MR. PUTIN, SIR, YOU DO YOUR EMPLOYEE PERFORMANCE REVIEW MEETINGS TODAY.
AND I WAS ALL SET TO MURDER SOME JOURNALISTS! OH, VERY WELL.
WHO'S THIS LOAFING BUFFOON?
DONALD TRUMP, SIR. YOU HAD THIS EMPLOYEE INSTALLED AS PRESIDENT OF THE U.S.A., REMEMBER?
SEND HIM IN.
I'VE DONE EVERYTHING YOU'VE ASKED, MR. PUTIN, ADVANCING THE INTERESTS OF RUSSIA AT THE EXPENSE OF AMERICA, SIR.
YES, YES. BUT YOU'VE BEEN SO CLUMSILY OBVIOUS ABOUT IT, EVERYONE KNOWS YOU'RE IN MY EMPLOY.
GULP!
START TRADE WAR IN WEST
MAKE THE U.S. AN UNDEPENDABLE ALLY
RESIST OR REFUSE TO ENFORCE RUSSIAN SANCTIONS
PROPOSE RUSSIA RE-JOINS G8
THAT'S THE BEAUTY PART, SIR. NOBODY CARES!
HMM... IT'S TRUE! REPUBLICANS ARE ON BOARD, AND YOU'VE SIMPLY EXHAUSTED EVERYONE ELSE.
AND SO, BLAH, BLAH, BLAH, BLAH...
...HOTEL, HOTEL, HOTEL...
TRUMP MOSCOW
SO, I'M GETTING THAT HOTEL?!
YOU BLITHERING MORON! HAVEN'T YOU BEEN LISTENING? I'M CLOSING ON YOU!
WOO-HOO! YOU'RE BUYING ONE OF MY CONDOS?
NO, DUMMY! I'M FIRING YOU! YOU'VE DAMAGED THE U.S.A. ENOUGH! I'M DONE WITH YOU!
GIVE THIS TRUMP FELLOW SOME OF THAT TEA I MADE, ON HIS WAY OUT.
OH... AND RELEASE THE PEE TAPE!
D'OH!
The End
DIST. BY ANDREWS McMEEL SYNDICATION – ©2018 R. BOLLING – 1392 – TO JOIN THE INNER HIVE, GO TO tomthedancingbug.com

6/11/18

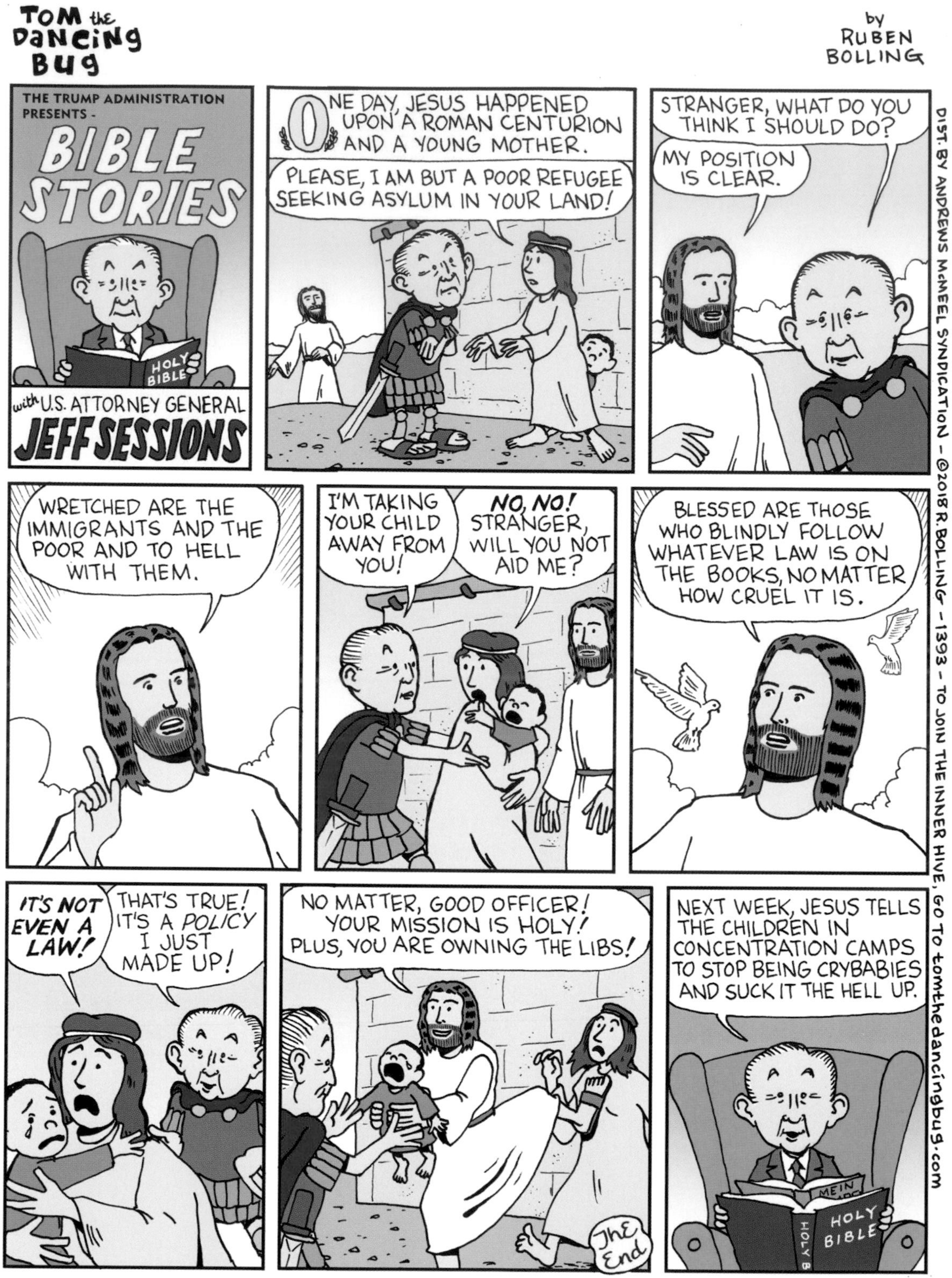

TOM the DANCING BUG
by RUBEN BOLLING
THE TRUMP ADMINISTRATION PRESENTS -
BIBLE STORIES
HOLY BIBLE
with U.S. ATTORNEY GENERAL
JEFF SESSIONS
ONE DAY, JESUS HAPPENED UPON A ROMAN CENTURION AND A YOUNG MOTHER.
PLEASE, I AM BUT A POOR REFUGEE SEEKING ASYLUM IN YOUR LAND!
STRANGER, WHAT DO YOU THINK I SHOULD DO?
MY POSITION IS CLEAR.
WRETCHED ARE THE IMMIGRANTS AND THE POOR AND TO HELL WITH THEM.
I'M TAKING YOUR CHILD AWAY FROM YOU!
NO, NO! STRANGER, WILL YOU NOT AID ME?
BLESSED ARE THOSE WHO BLINDLY FOLLOW WHATEVER LAW IS ON THE BOOKS, NO MATTER HOW CRUEL IT IS.
IT'S NOT EVEN A LAW!
THAT'S TRUE! IT'S A POLICY I JUST MADE UP!
NO MATTER, GOOD OFFICER! YOUR MISSION IS HOLY! PLUS, YOU ARE OWNING THE LIBS!
The End
NEXT WEEK, JESUS TELLS THE CHILDREN IN CONCENTRATION CAMPS TO STOP BEING CRYBABIES AND SUCK IT THE HELL UP.
MEIN
HOLY BIBLE
DIST. BY ANDREWS McMEEL SYNDICATION – ©2018 R. BOLLING – 1393 – TO JOIN THE INNER HIVE, GO TO tomthedancingbug.com

6/18/18

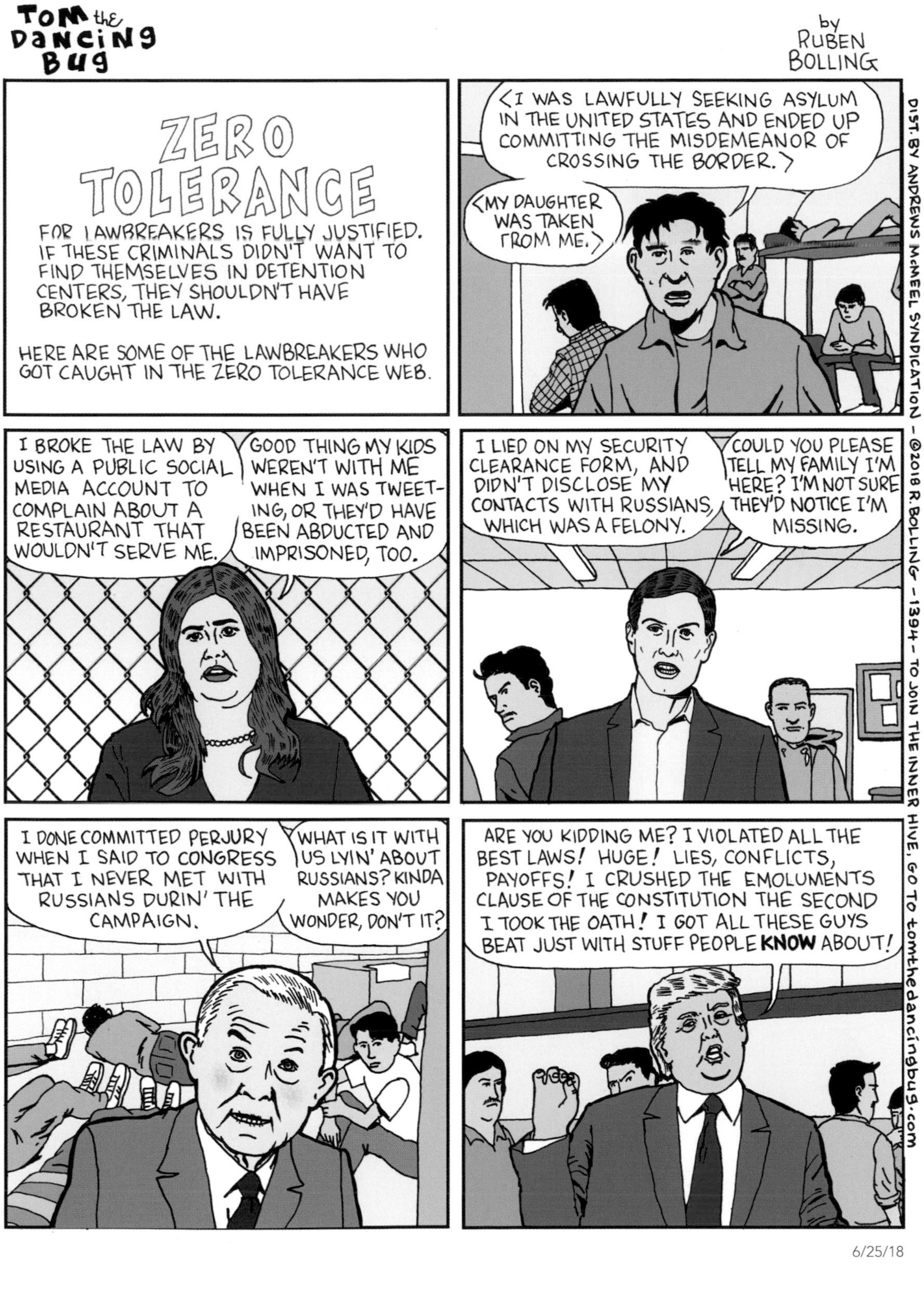
TOM the DANCING BUG
by RUBEN BOLLING
ZERO TOLERANCE
FOR LAWBREAKERS IS FULLY JUSTIFIED. IF THESE CRIMINALS DIDN'T WANT TO FIND THEMSELVES IN DETENTION CENTERS, THEY SHOULDN'T HAVE BROKEN THE LAW.
HERE ARE SOME OF THE LAWBREAKERS WHO GOT CAUGHT IN THE ZERO TOLERANCE WEB.
<I WAS LAWFULLY SEEKING ASYLUM IN THE UNITED STATES AND ENDED UP COMMITTING THE MISDEMEANOR OF CROSSING THE BORDER.>
<MY DAUGHTER WAS TAKEN FROM ME.>
I BROKE THE LAW BY USING A PUBLIC SOCIAL MEDIA ACCOUNT TO COMPLAIN ABOUT A RESTAURANT THAT WOULDN'T SERVE ME.
GOOD THING MY KIDS WEREN'T WITH ME WHEN I WAS TWEETING, OR THEY'D HAVE BEEN ABDUCTED AND IMPRISONED, TOO.
I LIED ON MY SECURITY CLEARANCE FORM, AND DIDN'T DISCLOSE MY CONTACTS WITH RUSSIANS, WHICH WAS A FELONY.
COULD YOU PLEASE TELL MY FAMILY I'M HERE? I'M NOT SURE THEY'D NOTICE I'M MISSING.
I DONE COMMITTED PERJURY WHEN I SAID TO CONGRESS THAT I NEVER MET WITH RUSSIANS DURIN' THE CAMPAIGN.
WHAT IS IT WITH US LYIN' ABOUT RUSSIANS? KINDA MAKES YOU WONDER, DON'T IT?
ARE YOU KIDDING ME? I VIOLATED ALL THE BEST LAWS! HUGE! LIES, CONFLICTS, PAYOFFS! I CRUSHED THE EMOLUMENTS CLAUSE OF THE CONSTITUTION THE SECOND I TOOK THE OATH! I GOT ALL THESE GUYS BEAT JUST WITH STUFF PEOPLE KNOW ABOUT!
DIST. BY ANDREWS McMEEL SYNDICATION - ©2018 R. BOLLING - 1394 - TO JOIN THE INNER HIVE, GO TO tomthedancingbug.com

6/25/18

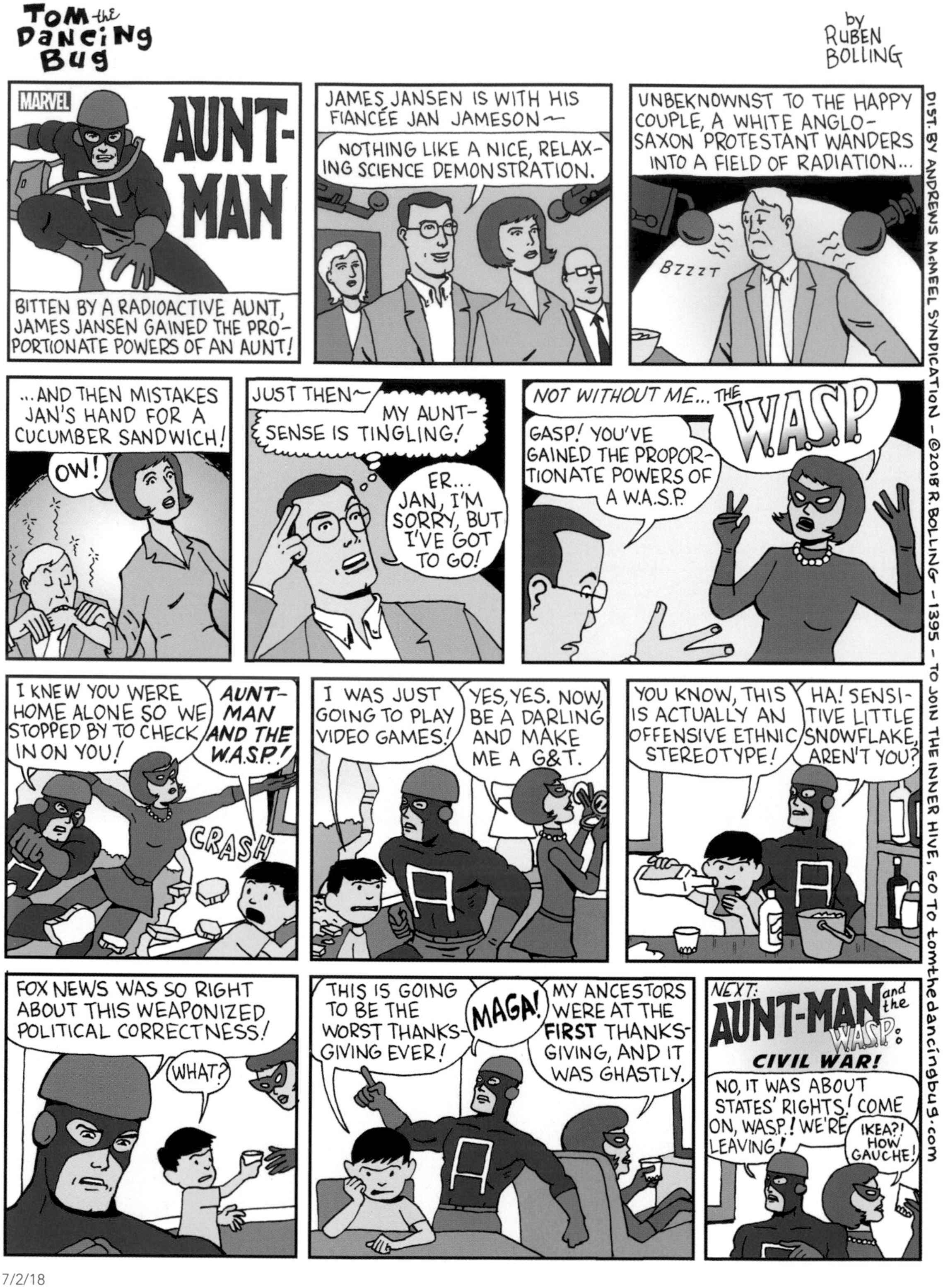

TOM the DANCING BUG
by RUBEN BOLLING
MARVEL
AUNT-MAN
BITTEN BY A RADIOACTIVE AUNT, JAMES JANSEN GAINED THE PROPORTIONATE POWERS OF AN AUNT!
JAMES JANSEN IS WITH HIS FIANCÉE JAN JAMESON—
NOTHING LIKE A NICE, RELAXING SCIENCE DEMONSTRATION.
UNBEKNOWNST TO THE HAPPY COUPLE, A WHITE ANGLO-SAXON PROTESTANT WANDERS INTO A FIELD OF RADIATION...
BZZZT
...AND THEN MISTAKES JAN'S HAND FOR A CUCUMBER SANDWICH!
OW!
JUST THEN—
MY AUNT-SENSE IS TINGLING!
ER... JAN, I'M SORRY, BUT I'VE GOT TO GO!
NOT WITHOUT ME... THE W.A.S.P.
GASP! YOU'VE GAINED THE PROPORTIONATE POWERS OF A W.A.S.P.
I KNEW YOU WERE HOME ALONE SO WE STOPPED BY TO CHECK IN ON YOU!
AUNT-MAN AND THE W.A.S.P.!
CRASH
I WAS JUST GOING TO PLAY VIDEO GAMES!
YES, YES. NOW, BE A DARLING AND MAKE ME A G&T.
YOU KNOW, THIS IS ACTUALLY AN OFFENSIVE ETHNIC STEREOTYPE!
HA! SENSITIVE LITTLE SNOWFLAKE, AREN'T YOU?
FOX NEWS WAS SO RIGHT ABOUT THIS WEAPONIZED POLITICAL CORRECTNESS!
WHAT?
THIS IS GOING TO BE THE WORST THANKSGIVING EVER!
MAGA!
MY ANCESTORS WERE AT THE FIRST THANKSGIVING, AND IT WAS GHASTLY.
NEXT: AUNT-MAN and the W.A.S.P.: CIVIL WAR!
NO, IT WAS ABOUT STATES' RIGHTS! COME ON, WASP! WE'RE LEAVING!
IKEA?! HOW GAUCHE!
DIST. BY ANDREWS McMEEL SYNDICATION – ©2018 R. BOLLING – 1395 – TO JOIN THE INNER HIVE, GO TO tomthedancingbug.com

7/2/18

TOM the DANCING BUG

by RUBEN BOLLING

PLEASE DON'T USE THE N-WORD

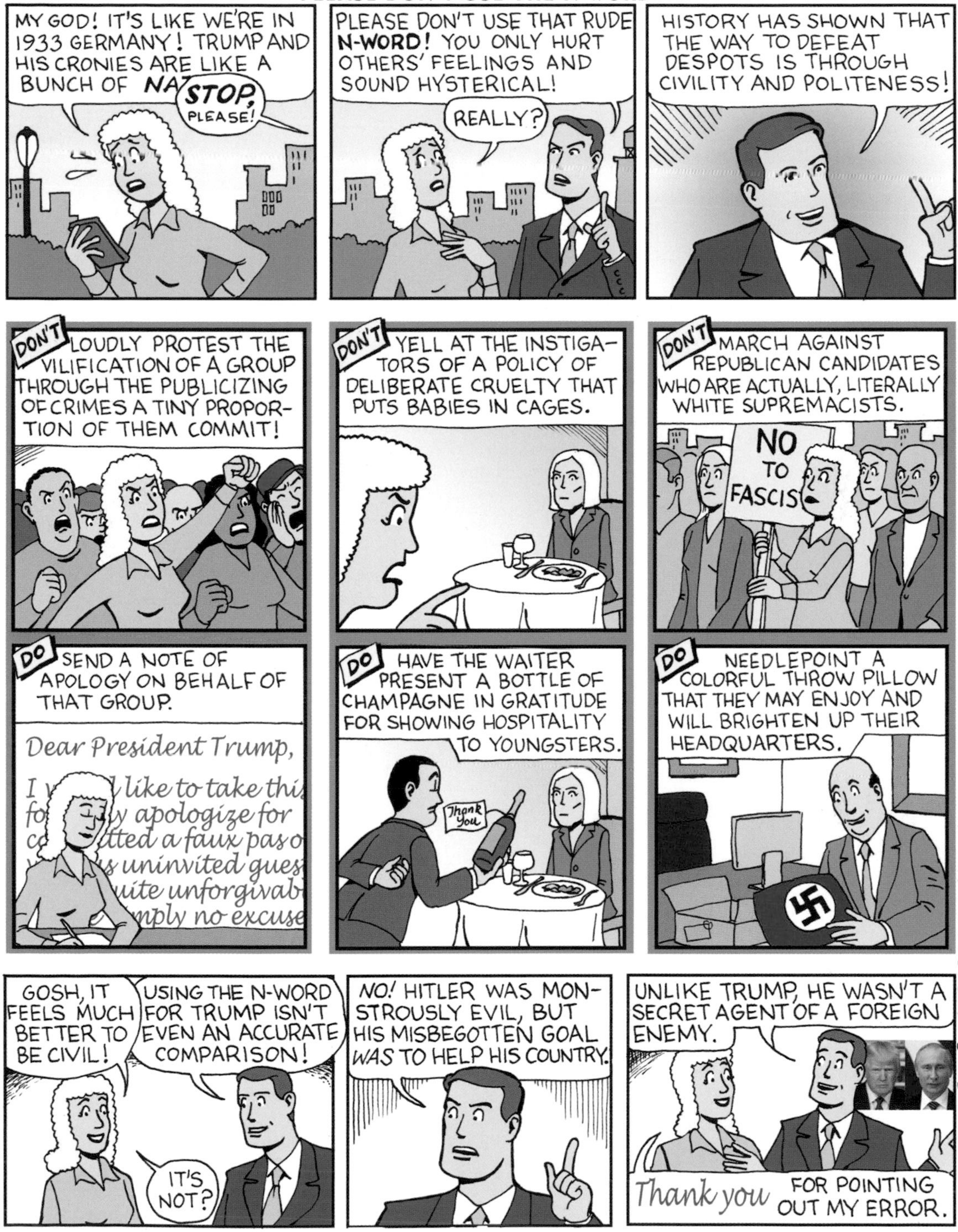

MY GOD! IT'S LIKE WE'RE IN 1933 GERMANY! TRUMP AND HIS CRONIES ARE LIKE A BUNCH OF NA
STOP, PLEASE!
PLEASE DON'T USE THAT RUDE N-WORD! YOU ONLY HURT OTHERS' FEELINGS AND SOUND HYSTERICAL!
REALLY?
HISTORY HAS SHOWN THAT THE WAY TO DEFEAT DESPOTS IS THROUGH CIVILITY AND POLITENESS!
DON'T LOUDLY PROTEST THE VILIFICATION OF A GROUP THROUGH THE PUBLICIZING OF CRIMES A TINY PROPORTION OF THEM COMMIT!
DON'T YELL AT THE INSTIGATORS OF A POLICY OF DELIBERATE CRUELTY THAT PUTS BABIES IN CAGES.
DON'T MARCH AGAINST REPUBLICAN CANDIDATES WHO ARE ACTUALLY, LITERALLY WHITE SUPREMACISTS.
NO TO FASCIS
DO SEND A NOTE OF APOLOGY ON BEHALF OF THAT GROUP.
Dear President Trump,
DO HAVE THE WAITER PRESENT A BOTTLE OF CHAMPAGNE IN GRATITUDE FOR SHOWING HOSPITALITY TO YOUNGSTERS.
Thank you
DO NEEDLEPOINT A COLORFUL THROW PILLOW THAT THEY MAY ENJOY AND WILL BRIGHTEN UP THEIR HEADQUARTERS.
GOSH, IT FEELS MUCH BETTER TO BE CIVIL!
USING THE N-WORD FOR TRUMP ISN'T EVEN AN ACCURATE COMPARISON!
IT'S NOT?
NO! HITLER WAS MONSTROUSLY EVIL, BUT HIS MISBEGOTTEN GOAL WAS TO HELP HIS COUNTRY.
UNLIKE TRUMP, HE WASN'T A SECRET AGENT OF A FOREIGN ENEMY.
Thank you FOR POINTING OUT MY ERROR.

7/9/18

TOM the DANCING BUG

by RUBEN BOLLING

HOW TO TELL WHEN SOMEONE'S LYING

IT'S ACTUALLY QUITE SIMPLE--IT'S THE LIES

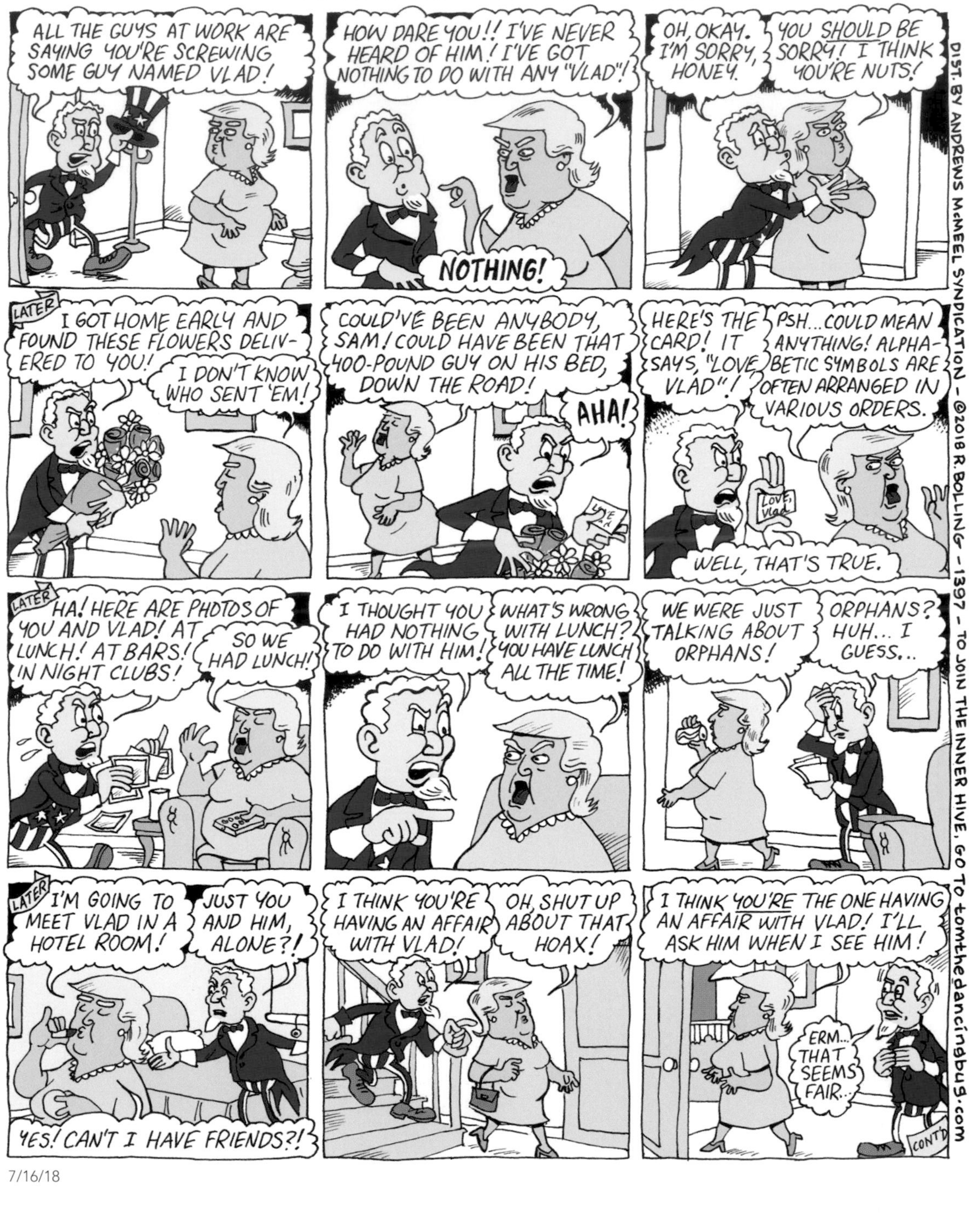

ALL THE GUYS AT WORK ARE SAYING YOU'RE SCREWING SOME GUY NAMED VLAD!
HOW DARE YOU!! I'VE NEVER HEARD OF HIM! I'VE GOT NOTHING TO DO WITH ANY "VLAD"!
NOTHING!
OH, OKAY. I'M SORRY, HONEY.
YOU SHOULD BE SORRY! I THINK YOU'RE NUTS!
LATER
I GOT HOME EARLY AND FOUND THESE FLOWERS DELIVERED TO YOU!
I DON'T KNOW WHO SENT 'EM!
COULD'VE BEEN ANYBODY, SAM! COULD HAVE BEEN THAT 400-POUND GUY ON HIS BED, DOWN THE ROAD!
AHA!
HERE'S THE CARD! IT SAYS, "LOVE, VLAD"!
PSH... COULD MEAN ANYTHING! ALPHABETIC SYMBOLS ARE OFTEN ARRANGED IN VARIOUS ORDERS.
LOVE, Vlad
WELL, THAT'S TRUE.
LATER
HA! HERE ARE PHOTOS OF YOU AND VLAD! AT LUNCH! AT BARS! IN NIGHT CLUBS!
SO WE HAD LUNCH!
I THOUGHT YOU HAD NOTHING TO DO WITH HIM!
WHAT'S WRONG WITH LUNCH? YOU HAVE LUNCH ALL THE TIME!
WE WERE JUST TALKING ABOUT ORPHANS!
ORPHANS? HUH... I GUESS...
LATER
I'M GOING TO MEET VLAD IN A HOTEL ROOM!
JUST YOU AND HIM, ALONE?!
YES! CAN'T I HAVE FRIENDS?!
I THINK YOU'RE HAVING AN AFFAIR WITH VLAD!
OH, SHUT UP ABOUT THAT HOAX!
I THINK YOU'RE THE ONE HAVING AN AFFAIR WITH VLAD! I'LL ASK HIM WHEN I SEE HIM!
ERM... THAT SEEMS FAIR...
CONT'D
DIST. BY ANDREWS McMEEL SYNDICATION - ©2018 R. BOLLING - 1397 - TO JOIN THE INNER HIVE, GO TO tomthedancingbug.com

7/16/18

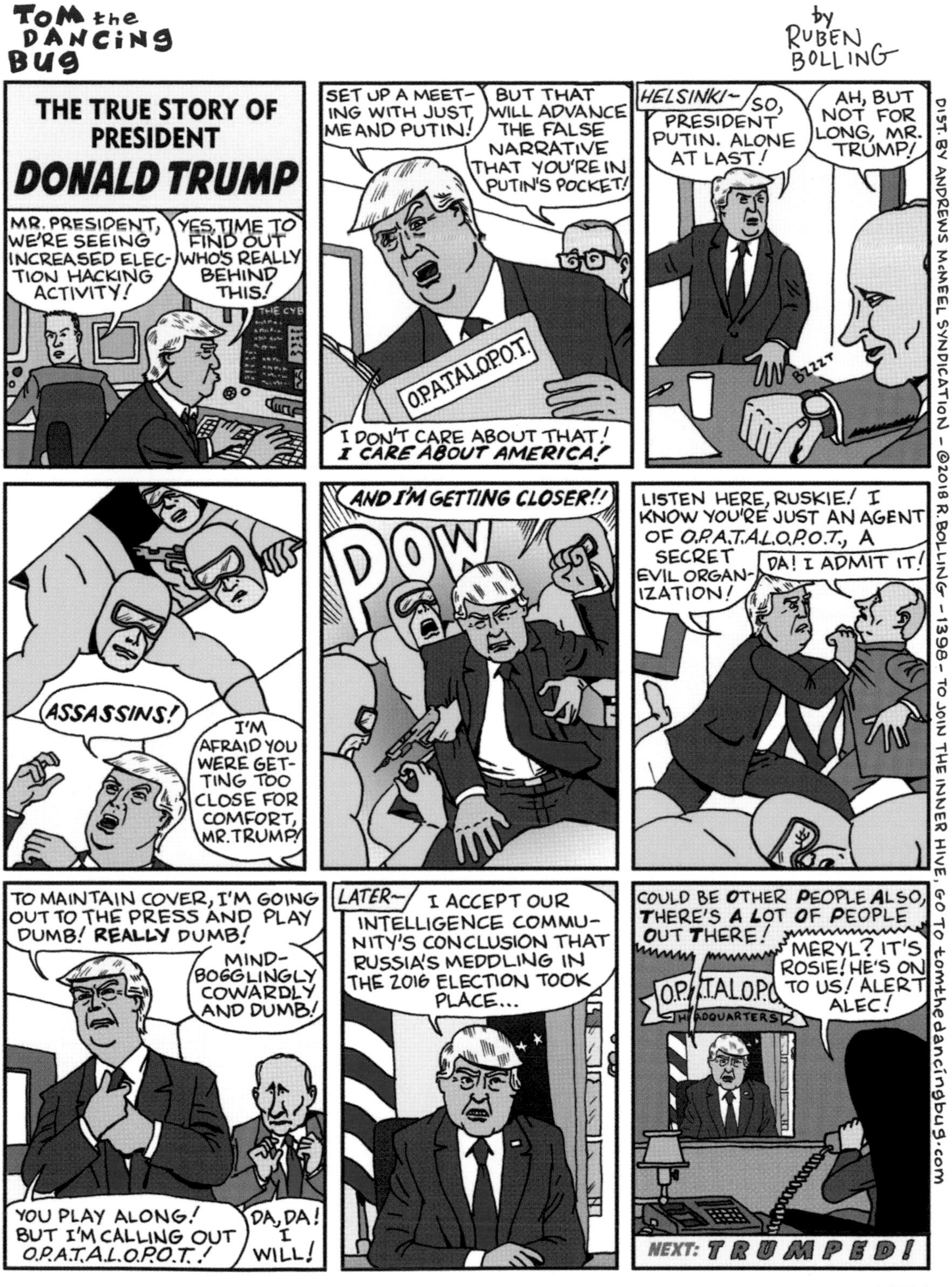

TOM the DANCING BUG
by RUBEN BOLLING
THE TRUE STORY OF PRESIDENT DONALD TRUMP
MR. PRESIDENT, WE'RE SEEING INCREASED ELECTION HACKING ACTIVITY!
YES, TIME TO FIND OUT WHO'S REALLY BEHIND THIS!
THE CYB
SET UP A MEETING WITH JUST ME AND PUTIN!
BUT THAT WILL ADVANCE THE FALSE NARRATIVE THAT YOU'RE IN PUTIN'S POCKET!
O.P.A.T.A.L.O.P.O.T.
I DON'T CARE ABOUT THAT! I CARE ABOUT AMERICA!
HELSINKI~
SO, PRESIDENT PUTIN. ALONE AT LAST!
AH, BUT NOT FOR LONG, MR. TRUMP!
BZZZT
ASSASSINS!
I'M AFRAID YOU WERE GETTING TOO CLOSE FOR COMFORT, MR. TRUMP!
AND I'M GETTING CLOSER!!
POW
LISTEN HERE, RUSKIE! I KNOW YOU'RE JUST AN AGENT OF O.P.A.T.A.L.O.P.O.T., A SECRET EVIL ORGANIZATION!
DA! I ADMIT IT!
TO MAINTAIN COVER, I'M GOING OUT TO THE PRESS AND PLAY DUMB! REALLY DUMB!
MIND-BOGGLINGLY COWARDLY AND DUMB!
YOU PLAY ALONG! BUT I'M CALLING OUT O.P.A.T.A.L.O.P.O.T.!
DA, DA! I WILL!
LATER~
I ACCEPT OUR INTELLIGENCE COMMUNITY'S CONCLUSION THAT RUSSIA'S MEDDLING IN THE 2016 ELECTION TOOK PLACE...
COULD BE OTHER PEOPLE ALSO, THERE'S A LOT OF PEOPLE OUT THERE!
O.P.A.T.A.L.O.P.O. HEADQUARTERS
MERYL? IT'S ROSIE! HE'S ON TO US! ALERT ALEC!
NEXT: TRUMPED!
DIST. BY ANDREWS McMEEL SYNDICATION – ©2018 R. BOLLING – 1398 – TO JOIN THE INNER HIVE, GO TO tomthedancingbug.com

7/23/18

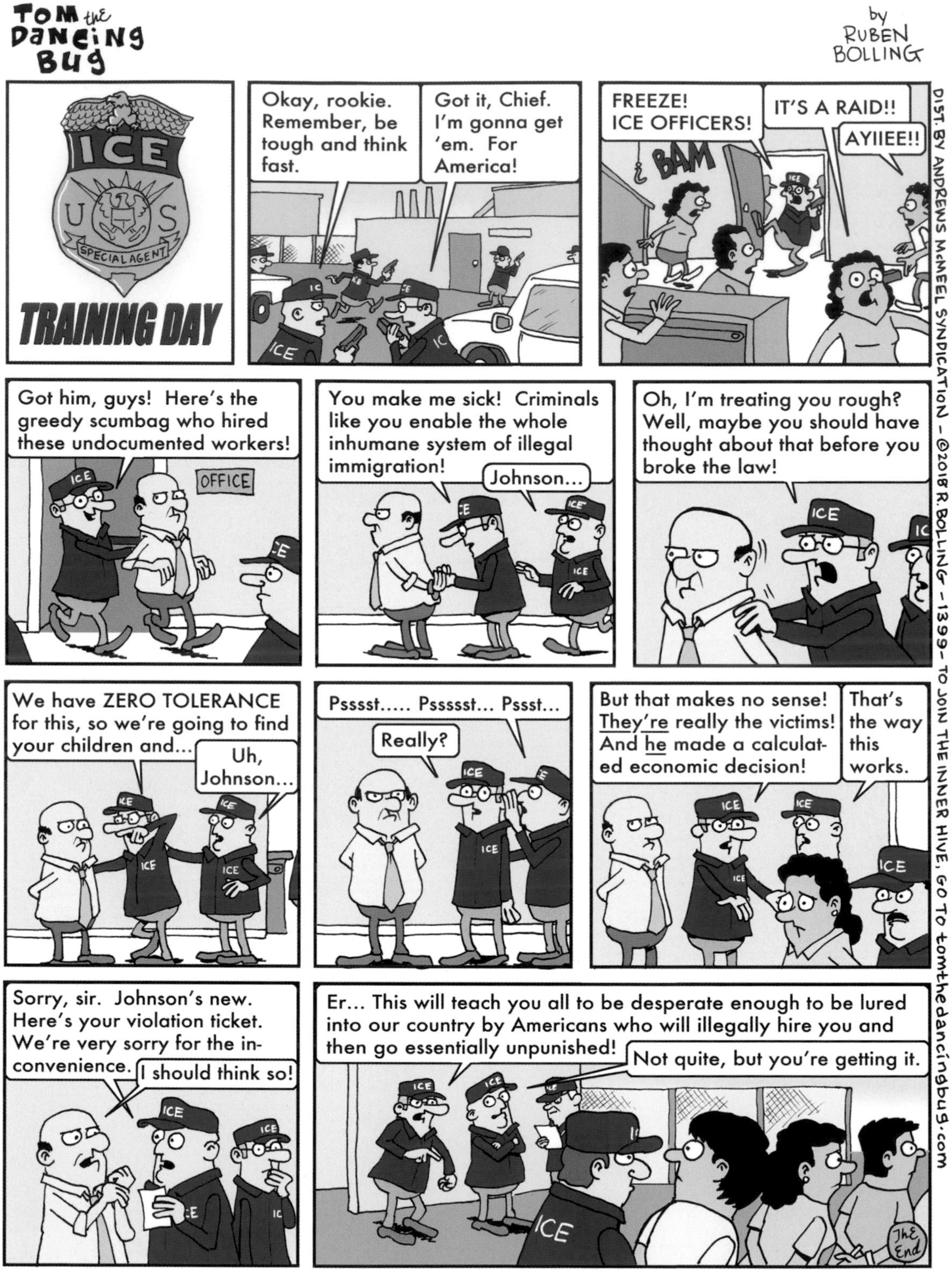
TOM the DANCING BUG
by RUBEN BOLLING
ICE
U S
SPECIAL AGENT
TRAINING DAY
Okay, rookie. Remember, be tough and think fast.
Got it, Chief. I'm gonna get 'em. For America!
FREEZE! ICE OFFICERS!
IT'S A RAID!!
AYIIEE!!
¡ BAM
Got him, guys! Here's the greedy scumbag who hired these undocumented workers!
OFFICE
You make me sick! Criminals like you enable the whole inhumane system of illegal immigration!
Johnson...
Oh, I'm treating you rough? Well, maybe you should have thought about that before you broke the law!
We have ZERO TOLERANCE for this, so we're going to find your children and...
Uh, Johnson...
Psssst..... Pssssst... Pssst...
Really?
But that makes no sense! They're really the victims! And he made a calculated economic decision!
That's the way this works.
Sorry, sir. Johnson's new. Here's your violation ticket. We're very sorry for the inconvenience.
I should think so!
Er... This will teach you all to be desperate enough to be lured into our country by Americans who will illegally hire you and then go essentially unpunished!
Not quite, but you're getting it.
The End
DIST. BY ANDREWS McMEEL SYNDICATION – ©2018 R. BOLLING – 1399 – TO JOIN THE INNER HIVE, GO TO tomthedancingbug.com

7/30/18

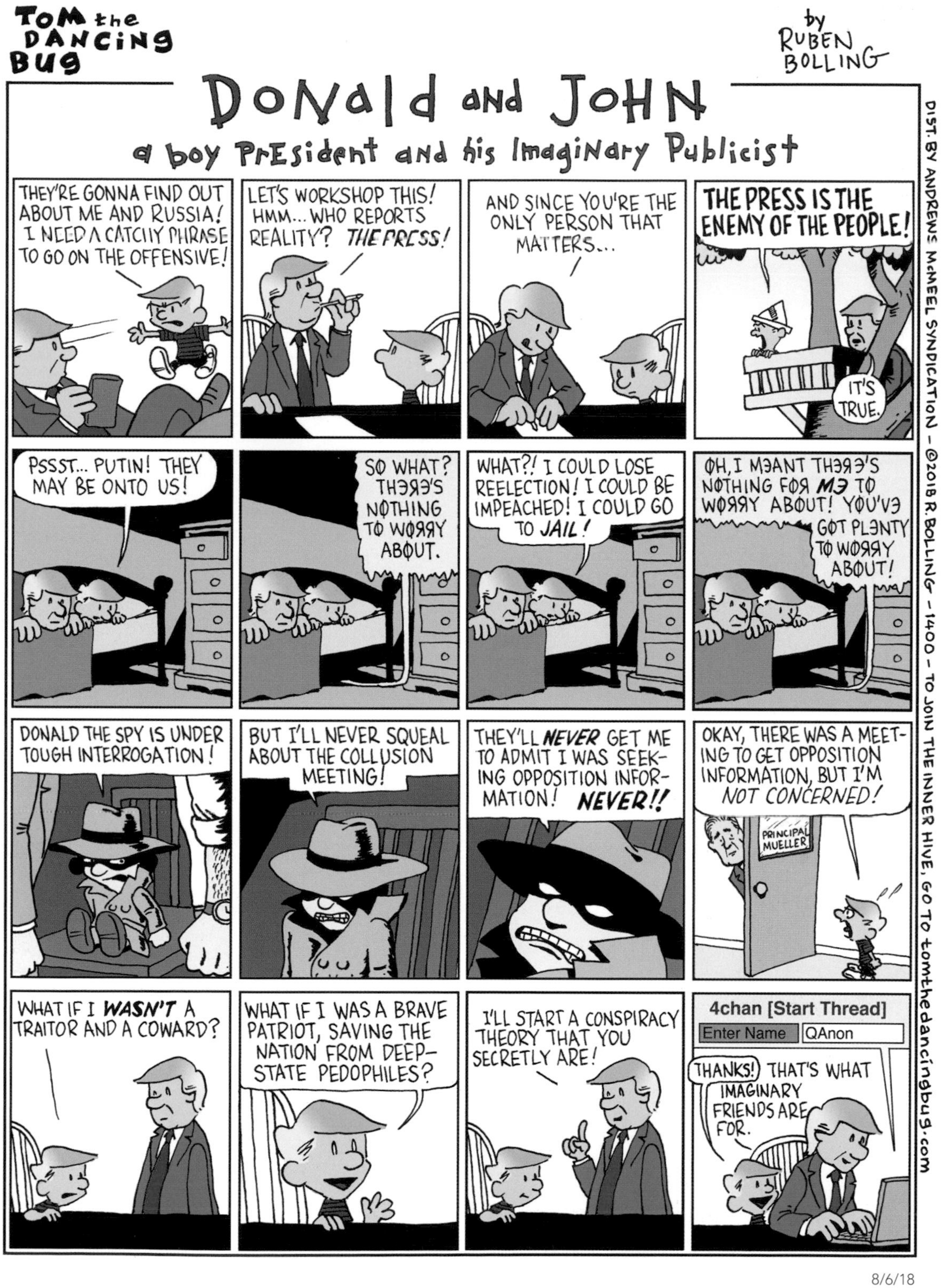

TOM the DANCING BUG
by RUBEN BOLLING
DONALD and JOHN
a boy President and his Imaginary Publicist
THEY'RE GONNA FIND OUT ABOUT ME AND RUSSIA! I NEED A CATCHY PHRASE TO GO ON THE OFFENSIVE!
LET'S WORKSHOP THIS! HMM... WHO REPORTS REALITY? THE PRESS!
AND SINCE YOU'RE THE ONLY PERSON THAT MATTERS...
THE PRESS IS THE ENEMY OF THE PEOPLE!
IT'S TRUE.
PSSST... PUTIN! THEY MAY BE ONTO US!
SO WHAT? THERE'S NOTHING TO WORRY ABOUT.
WHAT?! I COULD LOSE REELECTION! I COULD BE IMPEACHED! I COULD GO TO JAIL!
OH, I MEANT THERE'S NOTHING FOR ME TO WORRY ABOUT! YOU'VE GOT PLENTY TO WORRY ABOUT!
DONALD THE SPY IS UNDER TOUGH INTERROGATION!
BUT I'LL NEVER SQUEAL ABOUT THE COLLUSION MEETING!
THEY'LL NEVER GET ME TO ADMIT I WAS SEEKING OPPOSITION INFORMATION! NEVER!!
OKAY, THERE WAS A MEETING TO GET OPPOSITION INFORMATION, BUT I'M NOT CONCERNED!
PRINCIPAL MUELLER
WHAT IF I WASN'T A TRAITOR AND A COWARD?
WHAT IF I WAS A BRAVE PATRIOT, SAVING THE NATION FROM DEEP-STATE PEDOPHILES?
I'LL START A CONSPIRACY THEORY THAT YOU SECRETLY ARE!
4chan [Start Thread]
Enter Name
QAnon
THANKS!
THAT'S WHAT IMAGINARY FRIENDS ARE FOR.
DIST. BY ANDREWS McMEEL SYNDICATION – ©2018 R. BOLLING – 1400 – TO JOIN THE INNER HIVE, GO TO tomthedancingbug.com

8/6/18

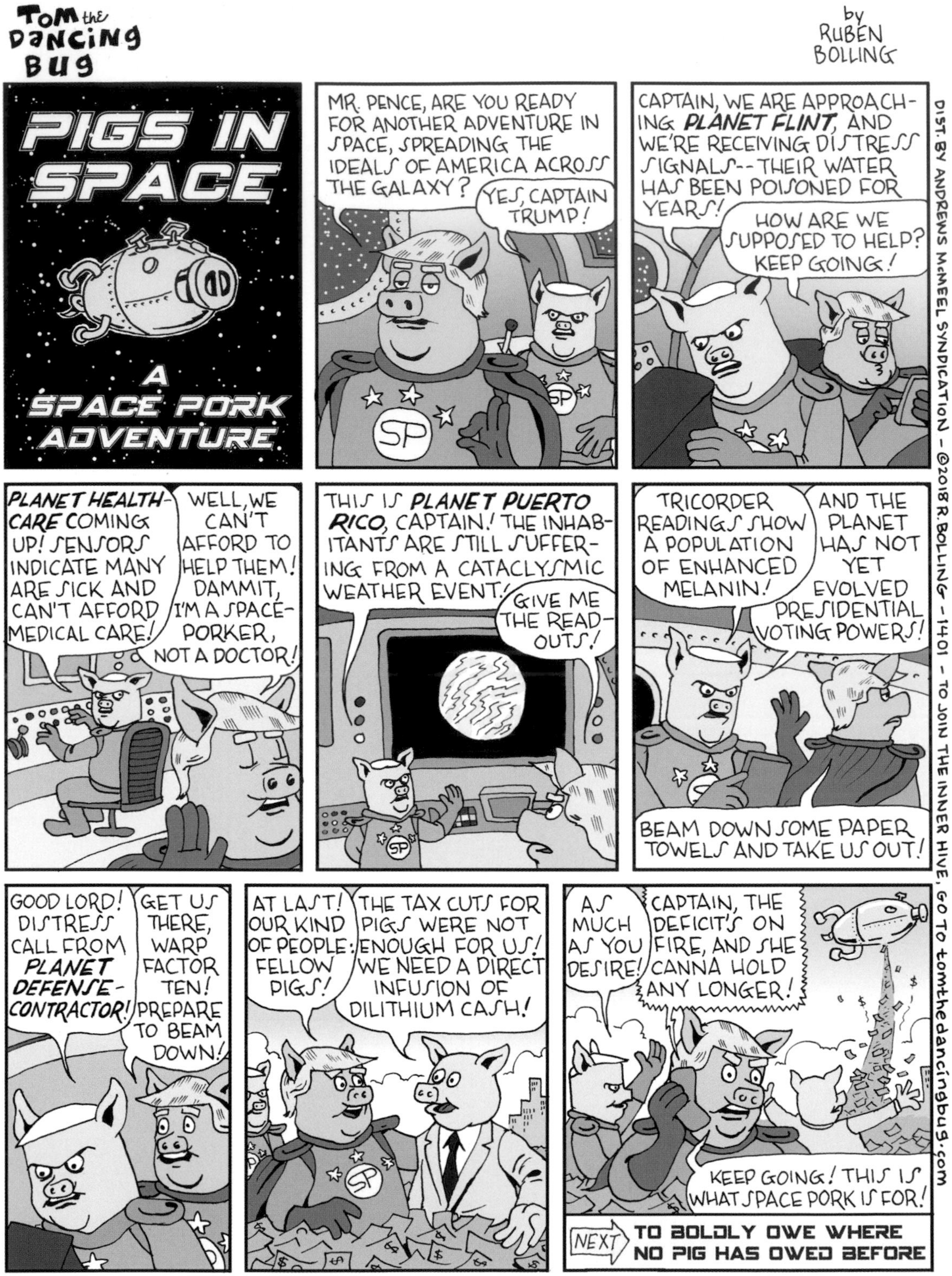
TOM the DANCING BUG
by RUBEN BOLLING
PIGS IN SPACE
A SPACE PORK ADVENTURE
MR. PENCE, ARE YOU READY FOR ANOTHER ADVENTURE IN SPACE, SPREADING THE IDEALS OF AMERICA ACROSS THE GALAXY?
YES, CAPTAIN TRUMP!
CAPTAIN, WE ARE APPROACHING PLANET FLINT, AND WE'RE RECEIVING DISTRESS SIGNALS-- THEIR WATER HAS BEEN POISONED FOR YEARS!
HOW ARE WE SUPPOSED TO HELP? KEEP GOING!
DIST. BY ANDREWS McMEEL SYNDICATION - ©2018 R. BOLLING - 1401 - TO JOIN THE INNER HIVE, GO TO tomthedancingbug.com
PLANET HEALTH-CARE COMING UP! SENSORS INDICATE MANY ARE SICK AND CAN'T AFFORD MEDICAL CARE!
WELL, WE CAN'T AFFORD TO HELP THEM! DAMMIT, I'M A SPACE-PORKER, NOT A DOCTOR!
THIS IS PLANET PUERTO RICO, CAPTAIN! THE INHABITANTS ARE STILL SUFFERING FROM A CATACLYSMIC WEATHER EVENT!
GIVE ME THE READ-OUTS!
TRICORDER READINGS SHOW A POPULATION OF ENHANCED MELANIN!
AND THE PLANET HAS NOT YET EVOLVED PRESIDENTIAL VOTING POWERS!
BEAM DOWN SOME PAPER TOWELS AND TAKE US OUT!
GOOD LORD! DISTRESS CALL FROM PLANET DEFENSE-CONTRACTOR!
GET US THERE, WARP FACTOR TEN! PREPARE TO BEAM DOWN!
AT LAST! OUR KIND OF PEOPLE: FELLOW PIGS!
THE TAX CUTS FOR PIGS WERE NOT ENOUGH FOR US! WE NEED A DIRECT INFUSION OF DILITHIUM CASH!
AS MUCH AS YOU DESIRE!
CAPTAIN, THE DEFICIT'S ON FIRE, AND SHE CANNA HOLD ANY LONGER!
KEEP GOING! THIS IS WHAT SPACE PORK IS FOR!
NEXT
TO BOLDLY OWE WHERE NO PIG HAS OWED BEFORE

8/13/18

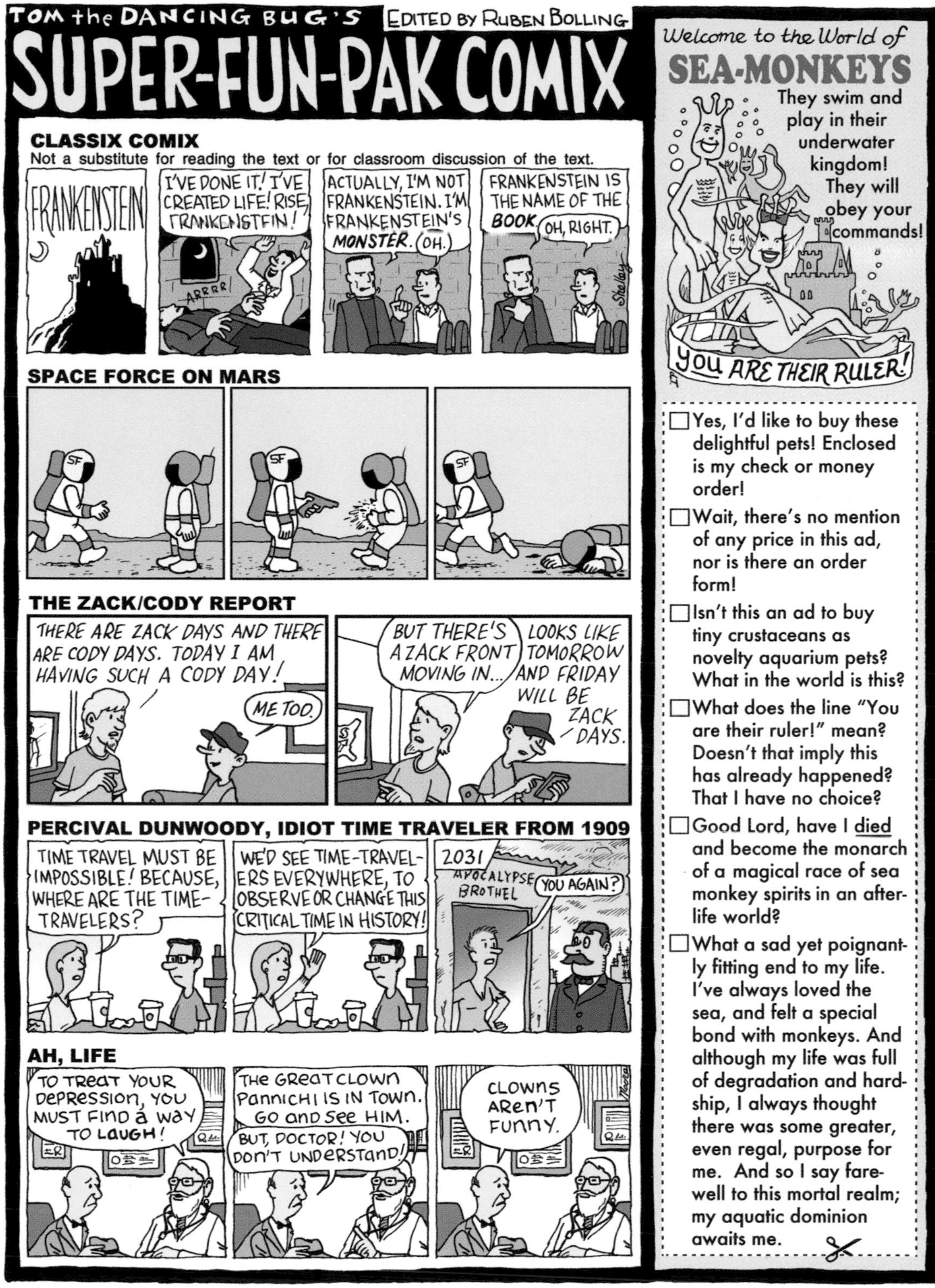
TOM the DANCING BUG'S
EDITED BY RUBEN BOLLING
SUPER-FUN-PAK COMIX
CLASSIX COMIX
Not a substitute for reading the text or for classroom discussion of the text.
FRANKENSTEIN
I'VE DONE IT! I'VE CREATED LIFE! RISE, FRANKENSTEIN!
ARRRR
ACTUALLY, I'M NOT FRANKENSTEIN. I'M FRANKENSTEIN'S MONSTER.
OH.
FRANKENSTEIN IS THE NAME OF THE BOOK.
OH, RIGHT.
SPACE FORCE ON MARS
SF
THE ZACK/CODY REPORT
THERE ARE ZACK DAYS AND THERE ARE CODY DAYS. TODAY I AM HAVING SUCH A CODY DAY!
ME TOO.
BUT THERE'S A ZACK FRONT MOVING IN...
LOOKS LIKE TOMORROW AND FRIDAY WILL BE ZACK DAYS.
PERCIVAL DUNWOODY, IDIOT TIME TRAVELER FROM 1909
TIME TRAVEL MUST BE IMPOSSIBLE! BECAUSE, WHERE ARE THE TIME-TRAVELERS?
WE'D SEE TIME-TRAVELERS EVERYWHERE, TO OBSERVE OR CHANGE THIS CRITICAL TIME IN HISTORY!
2031
APOCALYPSE BROTHEL
YOU AGAIN?
AH, LIFE
TO TREAT YOUR DEPRESSION, YOU MUST FIND A WAY TO LAUGH!
THE GREAT CLOWN PANNICHI IS IN TOWN. GO AND SEE HIM.
BUT, DOCTOR! YOU DON'T UNDERSTAND!
CLOWNS AREN'T FUNNY.
Welcome to the World of
SEA-MONKEYS
They swim and play in their underwater kingdom! They will obey your commands!
YOU ARE THEIR RULER!
☐ Yes, I'd like to buy these delightful pets! Enclosed is my check or money order!
☐ Wait, there's no mention of any price in this ad, nor is there an order form!
☐ Isn't this an ad to buy tiny crustaceans as novelty aquarium pets? What in the world is this?
☐ What does the line "You are their ruler!" mean? Doesn't that imply this has already happened? That I have no choice?
☐ Good Lord, have I died and become the monarch of a magical race of sea monkey spirits in an after-life world?
☐ What a sad yet poignantly fitting end to my life. I've always loved the sea, and felt a special bond with monkeys. And although my life was full of degradation and hardship, I always thought there was some greater, even regal, purpose for me. And so I say farewell to this mortal realm; my aquatic dominion awaits me.

8/20/18

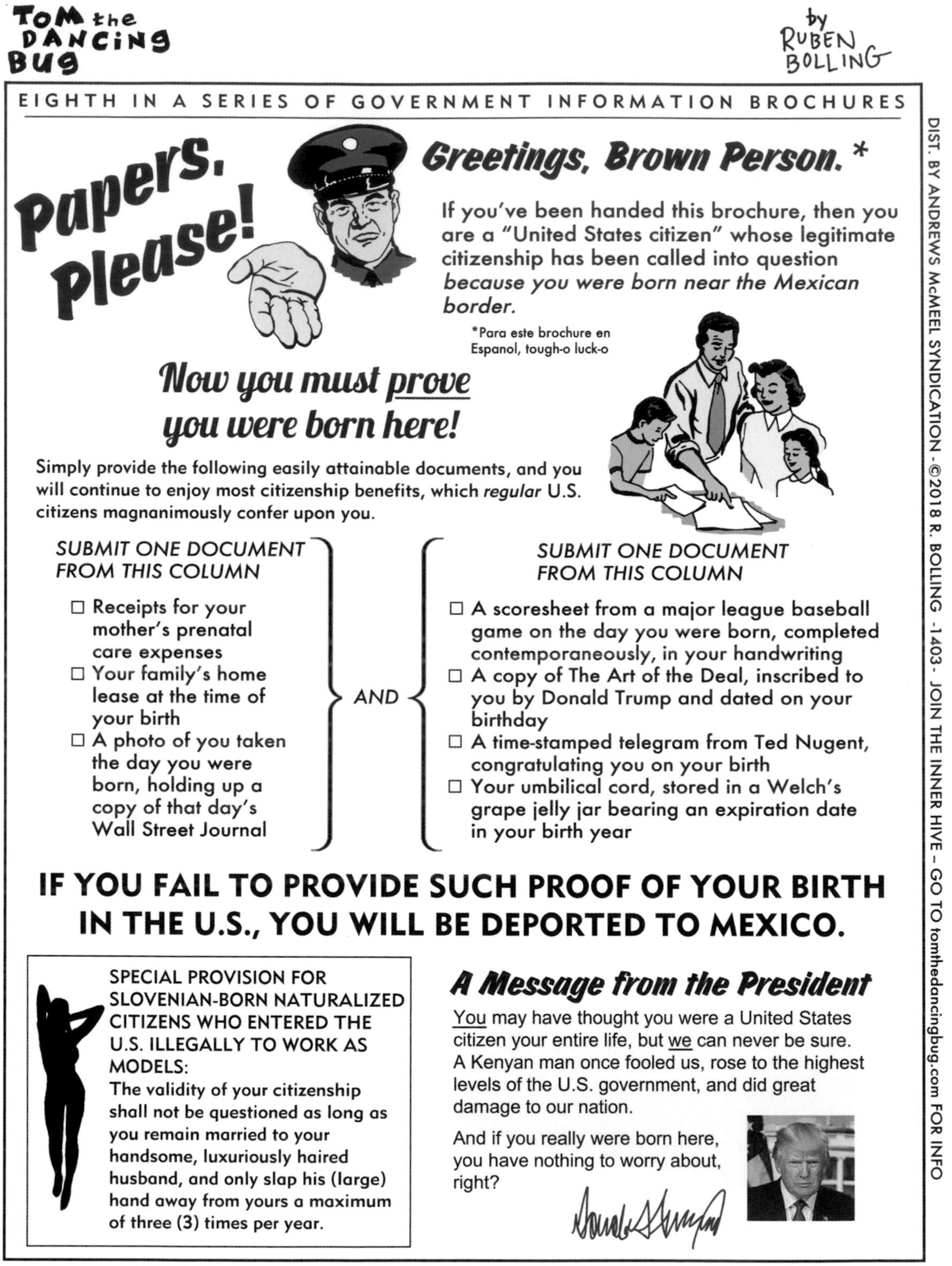
TOM the DANCING BUG
by RUBEN BOLLING
EIGHTH IN A SERIES OF GOVERNMENT INFORMATION BROCHURES
Papers, Please!
Greetings, Brown Person. *
If you've been handed this brochure, then you are a "United States citizen" whose legitimate citizenship has been called into question because you were born near the Mexican border.
*Para este brochure en Espanol, tough-o luck-o
Now you must prove you were born here!
Simply provide the following easily attainable documents, and you will continue to enjoy most citizenship benefits, which regular U.S. citizens magnanimously confer upon you.
SUBMIT ONE DOCUMENT FROM THIS COLUMN
☐ Receipts for your mother's prenatal care expenses
☐ Your family's home lease at the time of your birth
☐ A photo of you taken the day you were born, holding up a copy of that day's Wall Street Journal
AND
SUBMIT ONE DOCUMENT FROM THIS COLUMN
☐ A scoresheet from a major league baseball game on the day you were born, completed contemporaneously, in your handwriting
☐ A copy of The Art of the Deal, inscribed to you by Donald Trump and dated on your birthday
☐ A time-stamped telegram from Ted Nugent, congratulating you on your birth
☐ Your umbilical cord, stored in a Welch's grape jelly jar bearing an expiration date in your birth year
IF YOU FAIL TO PROVIDE SUCH PROOF OF YOUR BIRTH IN THE U.S., YOU WILL BE DEPORTED TO MEXICO.
SPECIAL PROVISION FOR SLOVENIAN-BORN NATURALIZED CITIZENS WHO ENTERED THE U.S. ILLEGALLY TO WORK AS MODELS:
The validity of your citizenship shall not be questioned as long as you remain married to your handsome, luxuriously haired husband, and only slap his (large) hand away from yours a maximum of three (3) times per year.
A Message from the President
You may have thought you were a United States citizen your entire life, but we can never be sure. A Kenyan man once fooled us, rose to the highest levels of the U.S. government, and did great damage to our nation.
And if you really were born here, you have nothing to worry about, right?
DIST. BY ANDREWS McMEEL SYNDICATION · ©2018 R. BOLLING -1403- JOIN THE INNER HIVE – GO TO tomthedancingbug.com FOR INFO

9/3/18

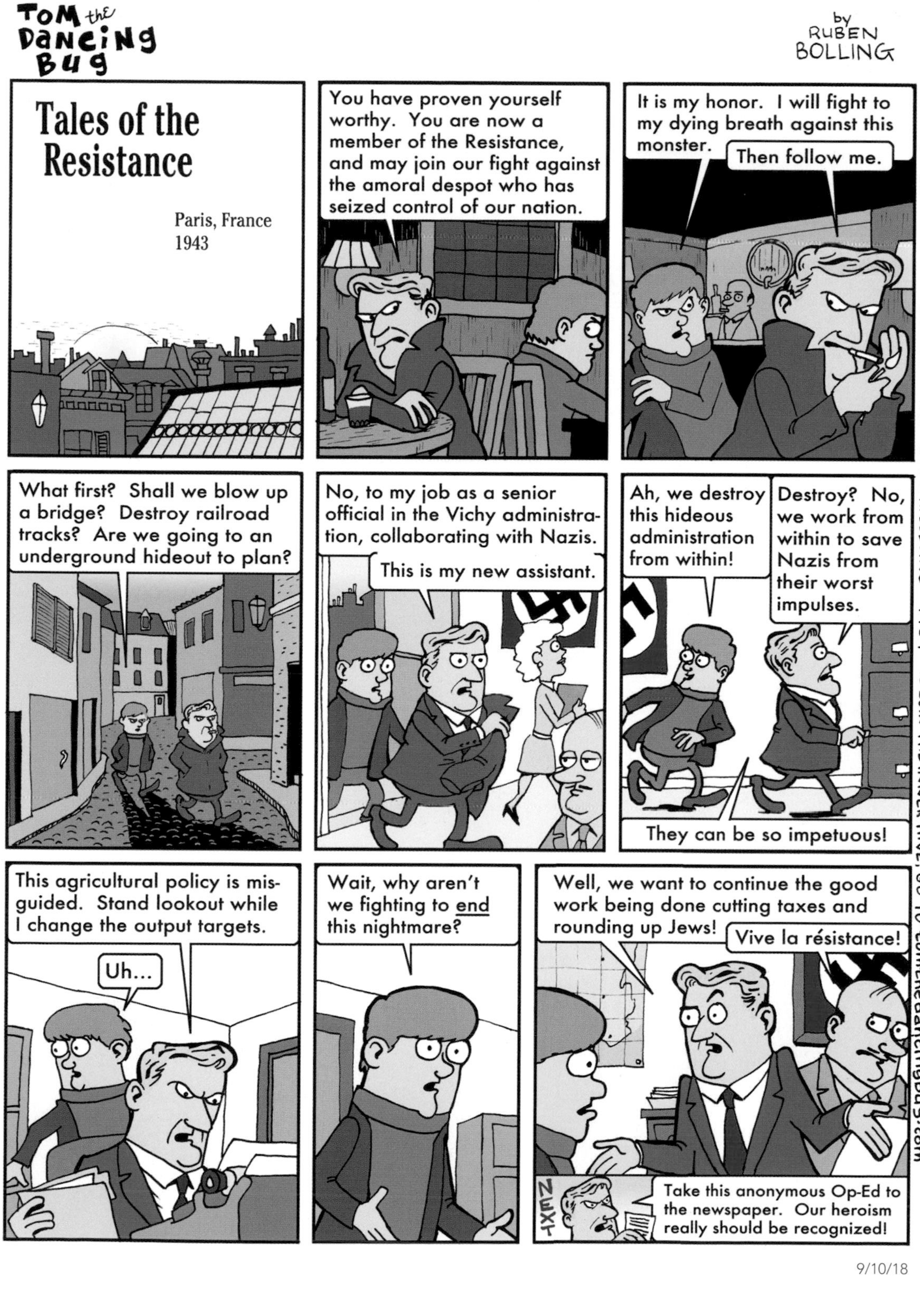

Tom the Dancing Bug
by Ruben Bolling
Tales of the Resistance
Paris, France
1943
You have proven yourself worthy. You are now a member of the Resistance, and may join our fight against the amoral despot who has seized control of our nation.
It is my honor. I will fight to my dying breath against this monster.
Then follow me.
What first? Shall we blow up a bridge? Destroy railroad tracks? Are we going to an underground hideout to plan?
No, to my job as a senior official in the Vichy administration, collaborating with Nazis.
This is my new assistant.
Ah, we destroy this hideous administration from within!
Destroy? No, we work from within to save Nazis from their worst impulses.
They can be so impetuous!
This agricultural policy is misguided. Stand lookout while I change the output targets.
Uh...
Wait, why aren't we fighting to end this nightmare?
Well, we want to continue the good work being done cutting taxes and rounding up Jews!
Vive la résistance!
NEXT
Take this anonymous Op-Ed to the newspaper. Our heroism really should be recognized!
DIST. BY ANDREWS McMEEL SYNDICATION – ©2018 R. BOLLING –1404– TO JOIN THE INNER HIVE, GO TO tomthedancingbug.com

9/10/18

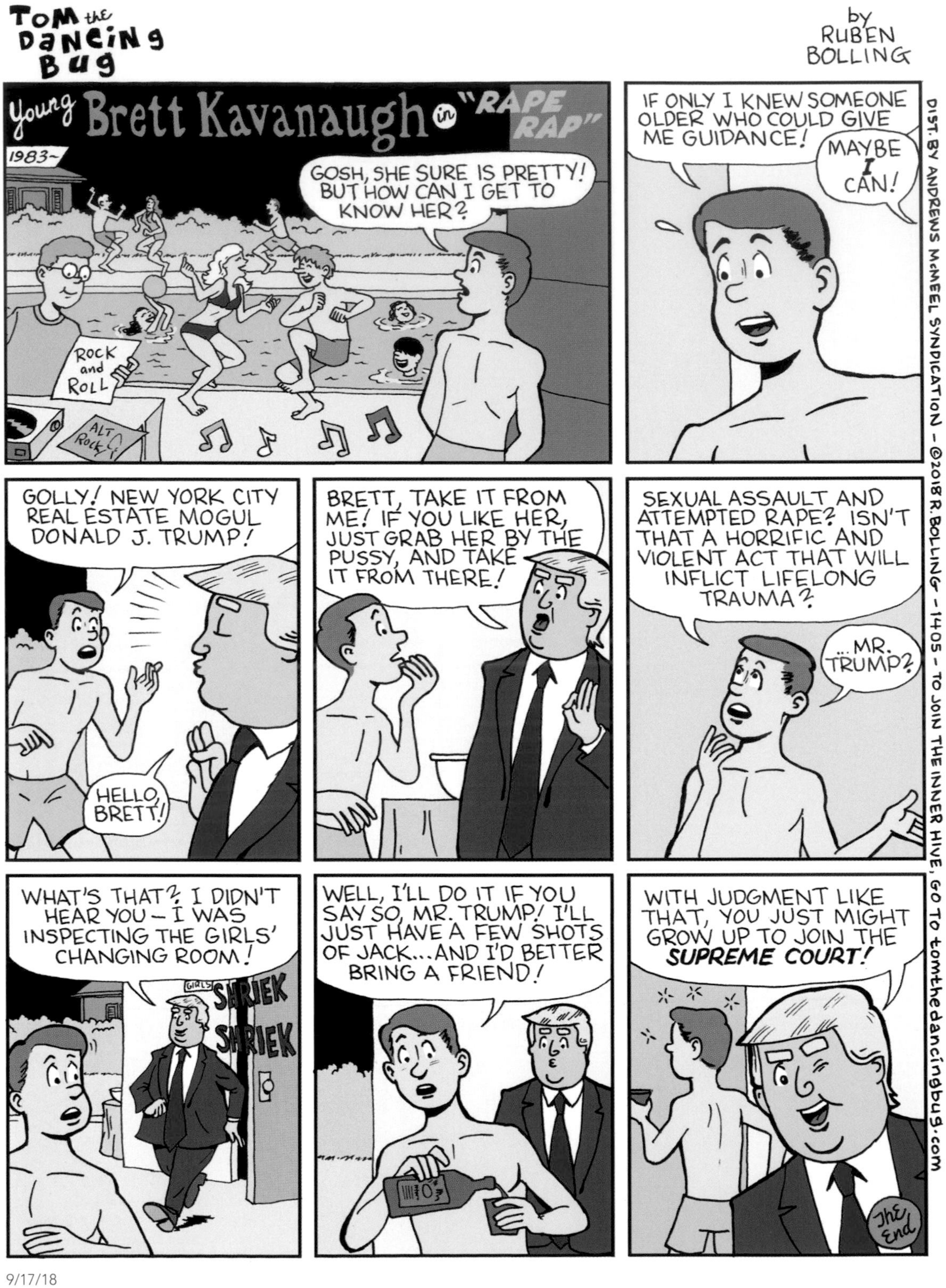
TOM the DANCING BUG
by RUBEN BOLLING
Young Brett Kavanaugh in "RAPE RAP"
1983~
GOSH, SHE SURE IS PRETTY! BUT HOW CAN I GET TO KNOW HER?
ROCK and ROLL
ALT ROCK
IF ONLY I KNEW SOMEONE OLDER WHO COULD GIVE ME GUIDANCE!
MAYBE I CAN!
GOLLY! NEW YORK CITY REAL ESTATE MOGUL DONALD J. TRUMP!
HELLO, BRETT!
BRETT, TAKE IT FROM ME! IF YOU LIKE HER, JUST GRAB HER BY THE PUSSY, AND TAKE IT FROM THERE!
SEXUAL ASSAULT AND ATTEMPTED RAPE? ISN'T THAT A HORRIFIC AND VIOLENT ACT THAT WILL INFLICT LIFELONG TRAUMA?
...MR. TRUMP?
WHAT'S THAT? I DIDN'T HEAR YOU – I WAS INSPECTING THE GIRLS' CHANGING ROOM!
GIRLS
SHRIEK
SHRIEK
WELL, I'LL DO IT IF YOU SAY SO, MR. TRUMP! I'LL JUST HAVE A FEW SHOTS OF JACK... AND I'D BETTER BRING A FRIEND!
WITH JUDGMENT LIKE THAT, YOU JUST MIGHT GROW UP TO JOIN THE SUPREME COURT!
THE End
DIST. BY ANDREWS McMEEL SYNDICATION – ©2018 R. BOLLING – 1405 – TO JOIN THE INNER HIVE, GO TO tomthedancingbug.com

9/17/18

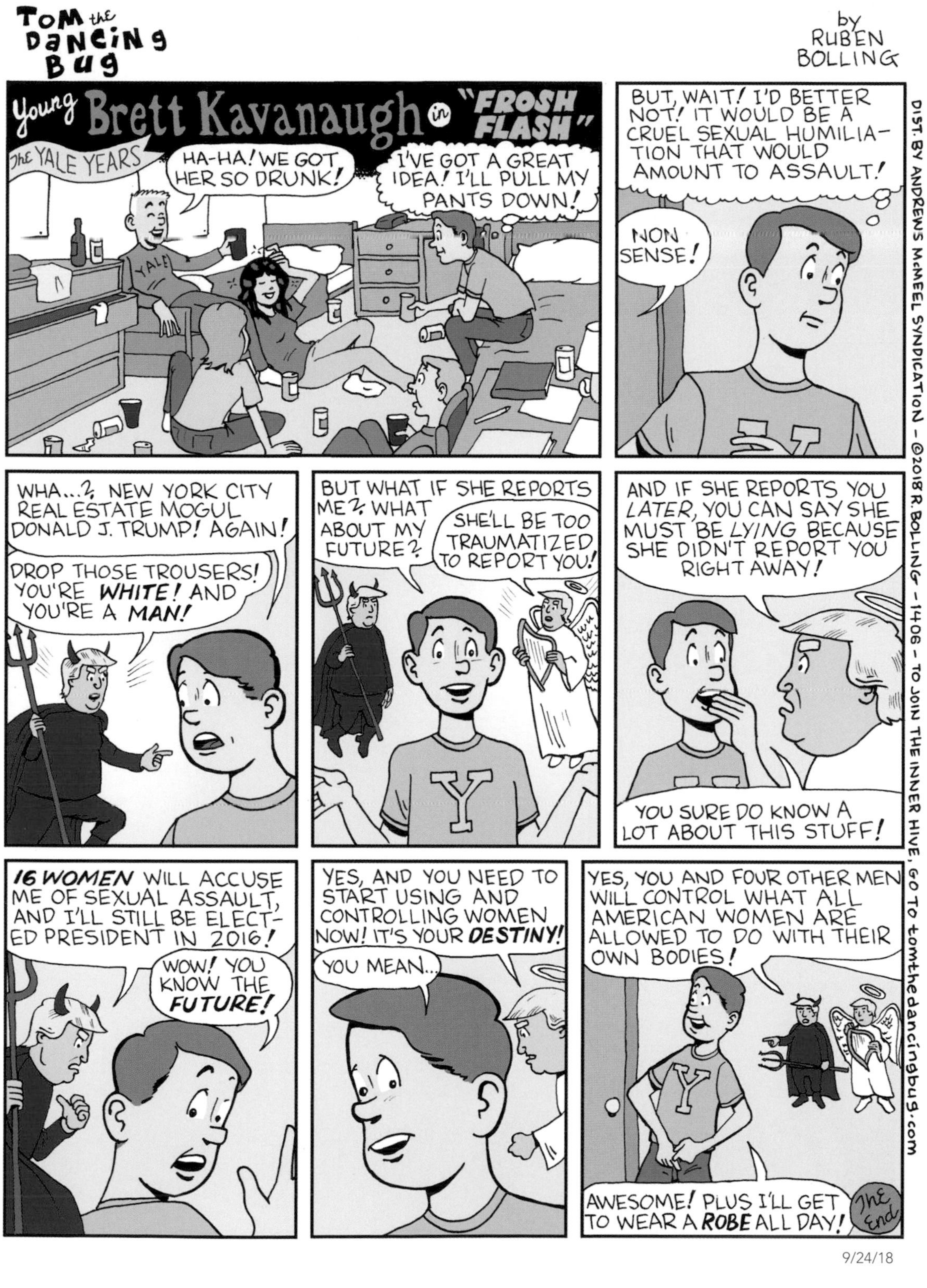
TOM the DANCING BUG
by RUBEN BOLLING
Young Brett Kavanaugh in "FROSH FLASH"
The YALE YEARS
HA-HA! WE GOT HER SO DRUNK!
I'VE GOT A GREAT IDEA! I'LL PULL MY PANTS DOWN!
YALE
BUT, WAIT! I'D BETTER NOT! IT WOULD BE A CRUEL SEXUAL HUMILIATION THAT WOULD AMOUNT TO ASSAULT!
NON SENSE!
WHA...?! NEW YORK CITY REAL ESTATE MOGUL DONALD J. TRUMP! AGAIN!
DROP THOSE TROUSERS! YOU'RE WHITE! AND YOU'RE A MAN!
BUT WHAT IF SHE REPORTS ME?! WHAT ABOUT MY FUTURE?!
SHE'LL BE TOO TRAUMATIZED TO REPORT YOU!
Y
AND IF SHE REPORTS YOU LATER, YOU CAN SAY SHE MUST BE LYING BECAUSE SHE DIDN'T REPORT YOU RIGHT AWAY!
YOU SURE DO KNOW A LOT ABOUT THIS STUFF!
16 WOMEN WILL ACCUSE ME OF SEXUAL ASSAULT, AND I'LL STILL BE ELECTED PRESIDENT IN 2016!
WOW! YOU KNOW THE FUTURE!
YES, AND YOU NEED TO START USING AND CONTROLLING WOMEN NOW! IT'S YOUR DESTINY!
YOU MEAN...
YES, YOU AND FOUR OTHER MEN WILL CONTROL WHAT ALL AMERICAN WOMEN ARE ALLOWED TO DO WITH THEIR OWN BODIES!
Y
AWESOME! PLUS I'LL GET TO WEAR A ROBE ALL DAY!
The End
DIST. BY ANDREWS McMEEL SYNDICATION – ©2018 R. BOLLING – 1406 – TO JOIN THE INNER HIVE, GO TO tomthedancingbug.com

9/24/18

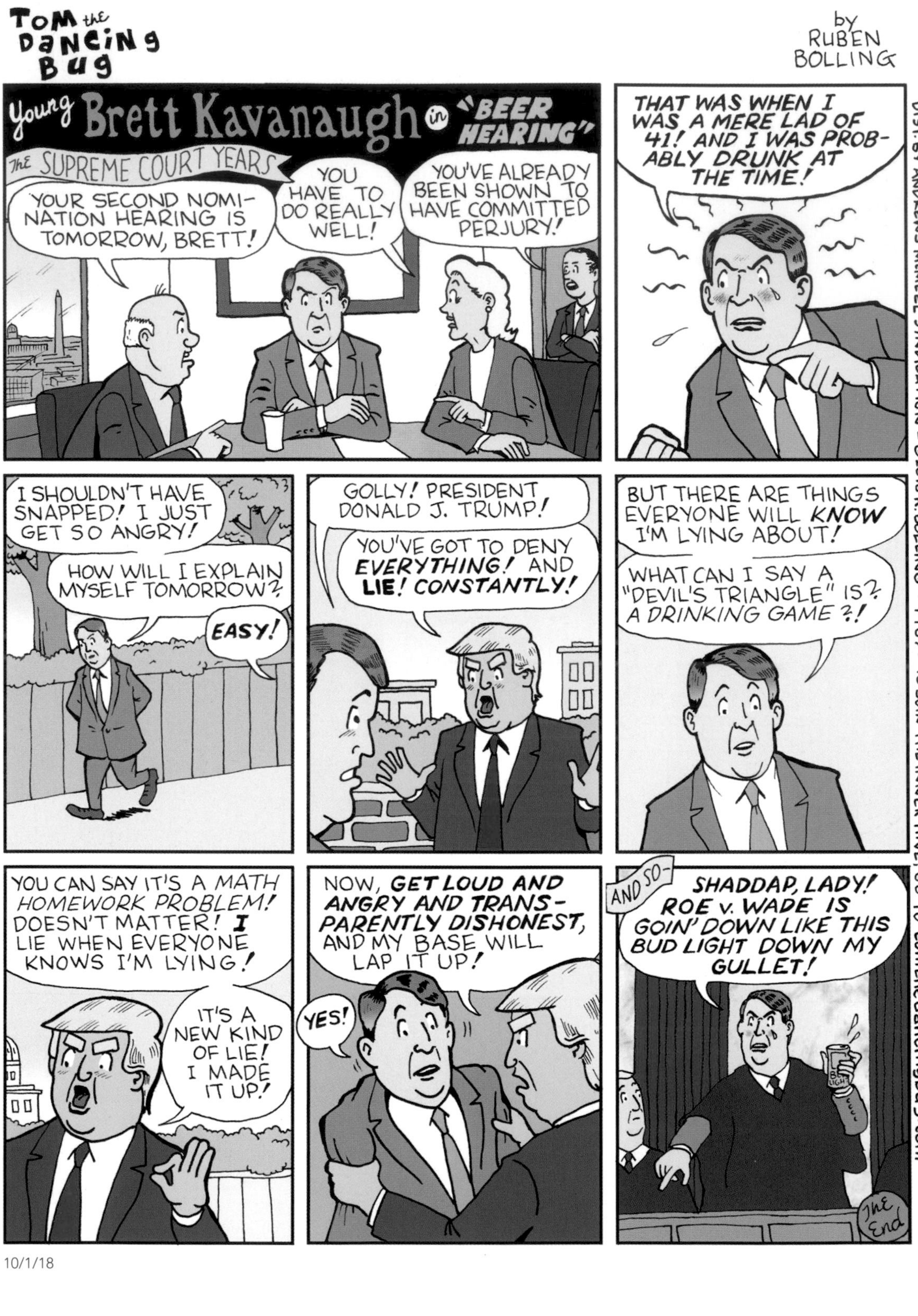
TOM the DANCING BUG
by RUBEN BOLLING
Young Brett Kavanaugh in "BEER HEARING"
THE SUPREME COURT YEARS
YOUR SECOND NOMINATION HEARING IS TOMORROW, BRETT!
YOU HAVE TO DO REALLY WELL!
YOU'VE ALREADY BEEN SHOWN TO HAVE COMMITTED PERJURY!
THAT WAS WHEN I WAS A MERE LAD OF 41! AND I WAS PROBABLY DRUNK AT THE TIME!
I SHOULDN'T HAVE SNAPPED! I JUST GET SO ANGRY!
HOW WILL I EXPLAIN MYSELF TOMORROW?!
EASY!
GOLLY! PRESIDENT DONALD J. TRUMP!
YOU'VE GOT TO DENY EVERYTHING! AND LIE! CONSTANTLY!
BUT THERE ARE THINGS EVERYONE WILL KNOW I'M LYING ABOUT!
WHAT CAN I SAY A "DEVIL'S TRIANGLE" IS?! A DRINKING GAME?!
YOU CAN SAY IT'S A MATH HOMEWORK PROBLEM! DOESN'T MATTER! I LIE WHEN EVERYONE KNOWS I'M LYING!
IT'S A NEW KIND OF LIE! I MADE IT UP!
NOW, GET LOUD AND ANGRY AND TRANSPARENTLY DISHONEST, AND MY BASE WILL LAP IT UP!
YES!
AND SO-
SHADDAP, LADY! ROE v. WADE IS GOIN' DOWN LIKE THIS BUD LIGHT DOWN MY GULLET!
THE End
DIST. BY ANDREWS McMEEL SYNDICATION – ©2018 R. BOLLING – 1407 – TO JOIN THE INNER HIVE, GO TO tomthedancingbug.com

10/1/18

Tom the Dancing Bug comic strip

by Ruben Bolling

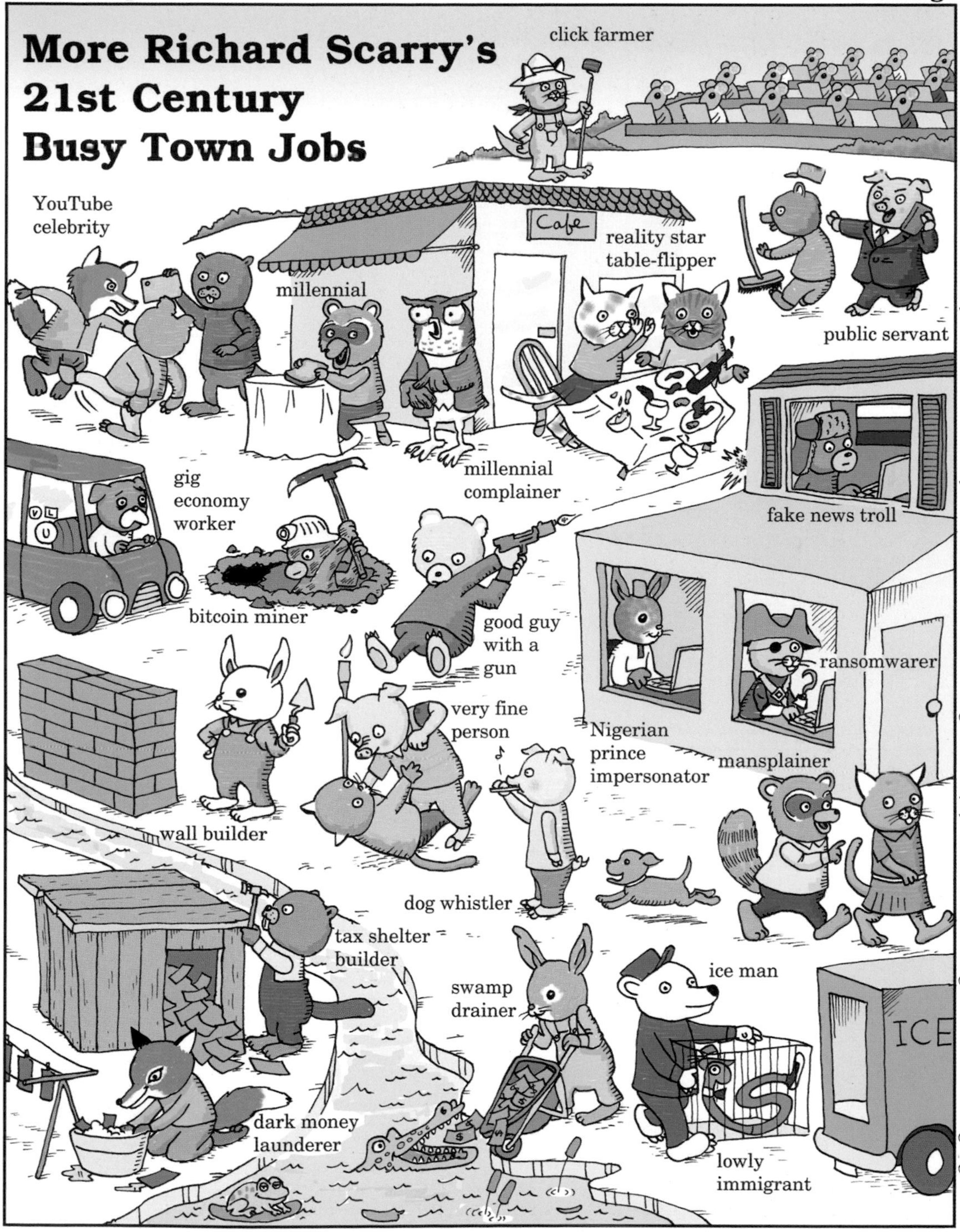
More Richard Scarry's 21st Century Busy Town Jobs
click farmer
YouTube celebrity
Cafe
reality star table-flipper
public servant
millennial
millennial complainer
fake news troll
gig economy worker
bitcoin miner
good guy with a gun
ransomwarer
very fine person
Nigerian prince impersonator
mansplainer
wall builder
dog whistler
tax shelter builder
swamp drainer
ice man
ICE
dark money launderer
lowly immigrant

10/8/18

Tom the Dancing Bug

by RUBEN BOLLING

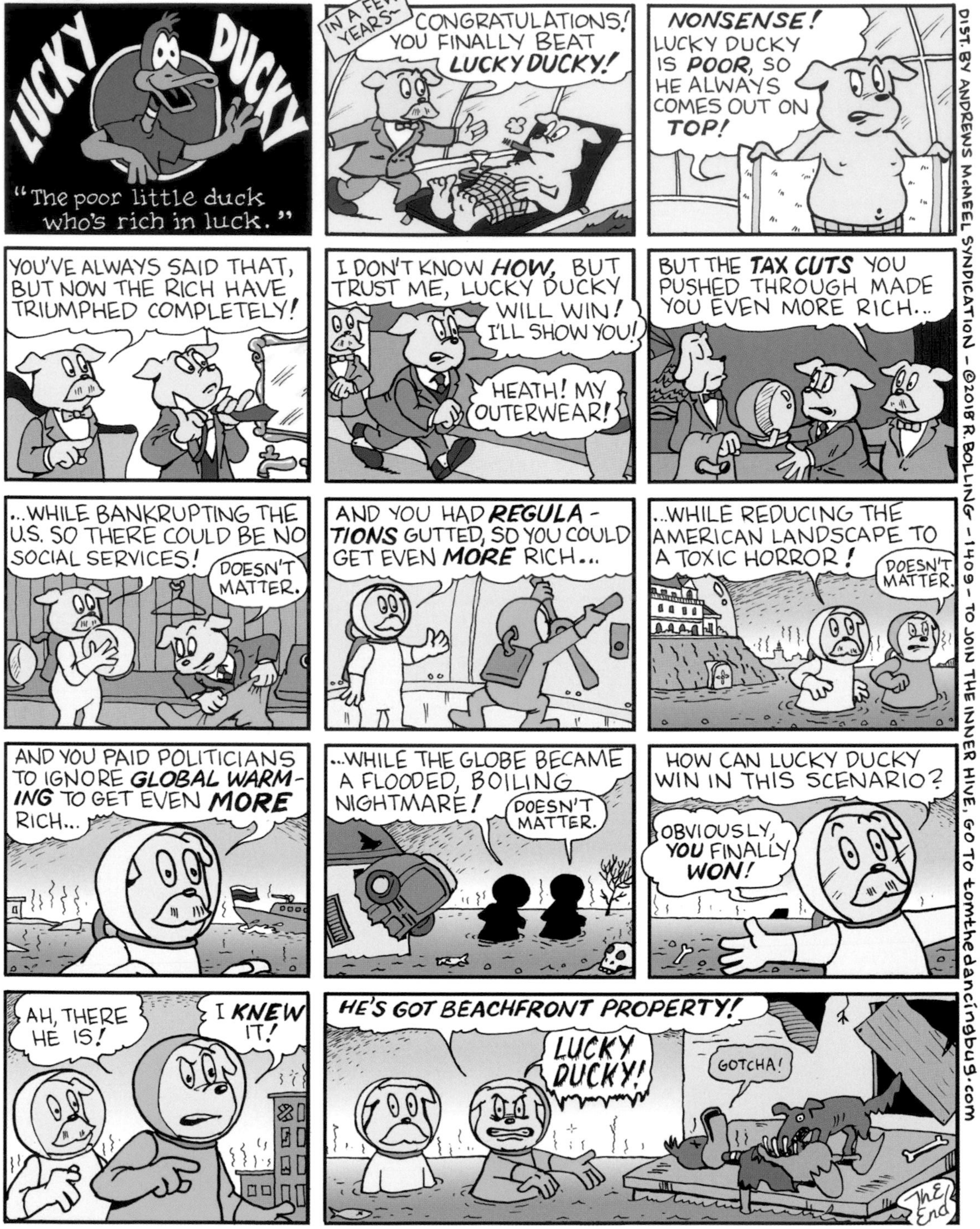
LUCKY DUCKY
"The poor little duck who's rich in luck."
IN A FEW YEARS~
CONGRATULATIONS! YOU FINALLY BEAT LUCKY DUCKY!
NONSENSE! LUCKY DUCKY IS POOR, SO HE ALWAYS COMES OUT ON TOP!
YOU'VE ALWAYS SAID THAT, BUT NOW THE RICH HAVE TRIUMPHED COMPLETELY!
I DON'T KNOW HOW, BUT TRUST ME, LUCKY DUCKY WILL WIN! I'LL SHOW YOU!
HEATH! MY OUTERWEAR!
BUT THE TAX CUTS YOU PUSHED THROUGH MADE YOU EVEN MORE RICH...
...WHILE BANKRUPTING THE U.S. SO THERE COULD BE NO SOCIAL SERVICES!
DOESN'T MATTER.
AND YOU HAD REGULATIONS GUTTED, SO YOU COULD GET EVEN MORE RICH...
...WHILE REDUCING THE AMERICAN LANDSCAPE TO A TOXIC HORROR!
DOESN'T MATTER.
AND YOU PAID POLITICIANS TO IGNORE GLOBAL WARMING TO GET EVEN MORE RICH...
...WHILE THE GLOBE BECAME A FLOODED, BOILING NIGHTMARE!
DOESN'T MATTER.
HOW CAN LUCKY DUCKY WIN IN THIS SCENARIO?
OBVIOUSLY, YOU FINALLY WON!
AH, THERE HE IS!
I KNEW IT!
HE'S GOT BEACHFRONT PROPERTY!
LUCKY DUCKY!
GOTCHA!
The End
DIST. BY ANDREWS McMEEL SYNDICATION - ©2018 R. BOLLING - 1409 - TO JOIN THE INNER HIVE, GO TO tomthedancingbug.com

10/15/18

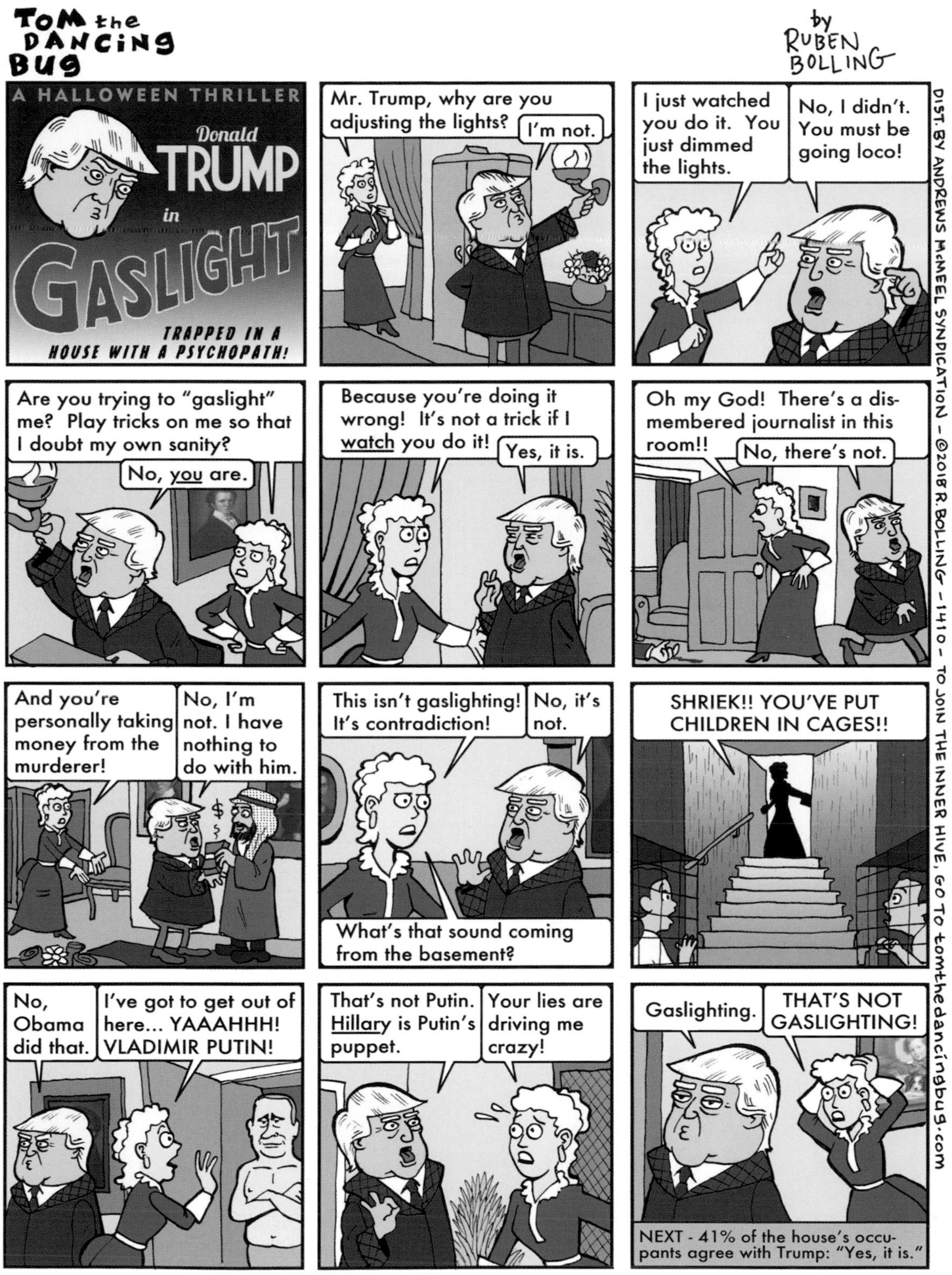
TOM the DANCING BUG
by RUBEN BOLLING
A HALLOWEEN THRILLER
Donald TRUMP in GASLIGHT
TRAPPED IN A HOUSE WITH A PSYCHOPATH!
Mr. Trump, why are you adjusting the lights?
I'm not.
I just watched you do it. You just dimmed the lights.
No, I didn't. You must be going loco!
Are you trying to "gaslight" me? Play tricks on me so that I doubt my own sanity?
No, you are.
Because you're doing it wrong! It's not a trick if I watch you do it!
Yes, it is.
Oh my God! There's a dismembered journalist in this room!!
No, there's not.
And you're personally taking money from the murderer!
No, I'm not. I have nothing to do with him.
$
This isn't gaslighting! It's contradiction!
No, it's not.
What's that sound coming from the basement?
SHRIEK!! YOU'VE PUT CHILDREN IN CAGES!!
No, Obama did that.
I've got to get out of here... YAAAHHH! VLADIMIR PUTIN!
That's not Putin. Hillary is Putin's puppet.
Your lies are driving me crazy!
Gaslighting.
THAT'S NOT GASLIGHTING!
NEXT - 41% of the house's occupants agree with Trump: "Yes, it is."
DIST. BY ANDREWS McMEEL SYNDICATION – ©2018 R. BOLLING – 1410 – TO JOIN THE INNER HIVE, GO TO tomthedancingbug.com

10/22/18

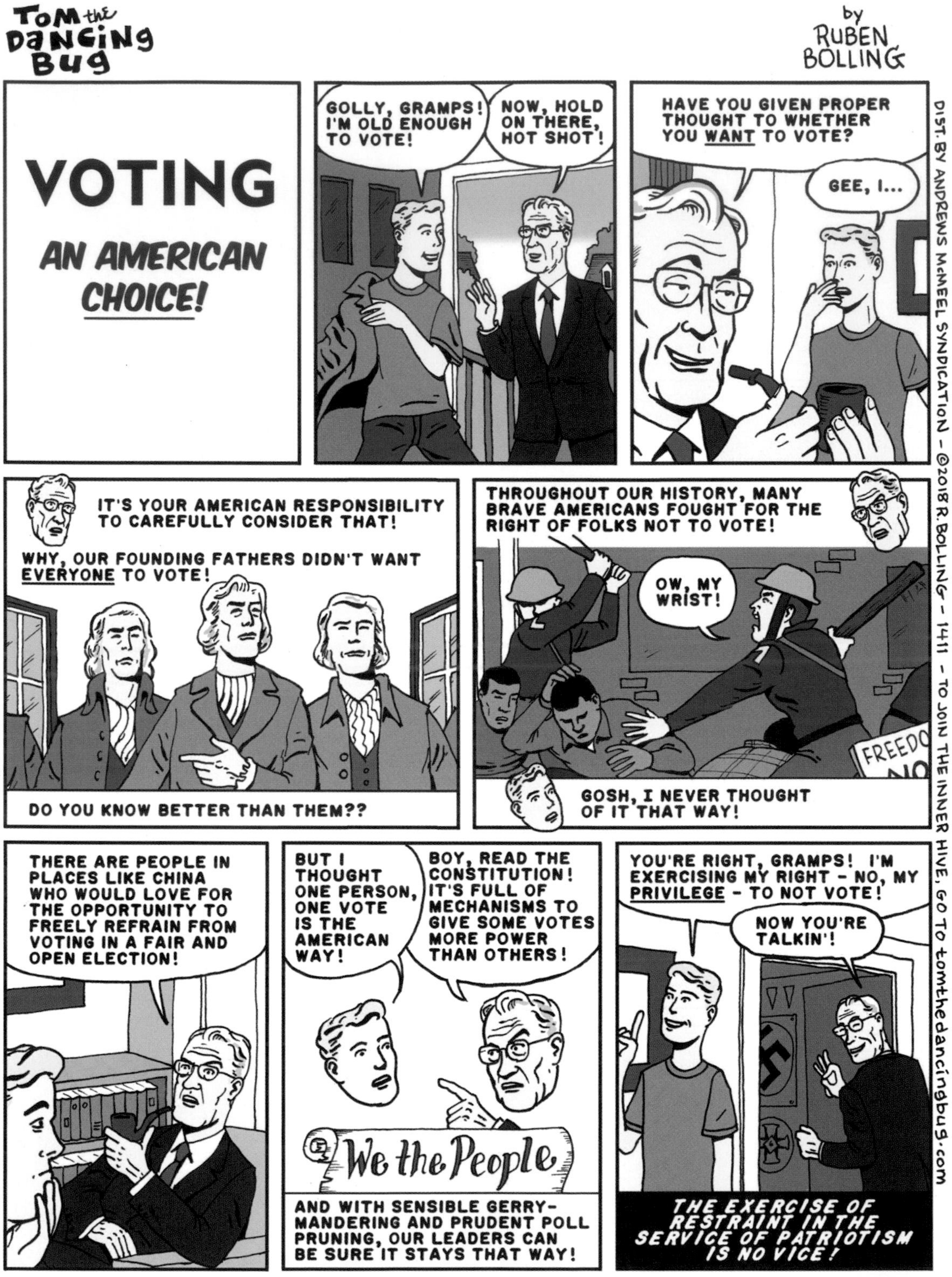

TOM the DANCING BUG
by RUBEN BOLLING
VOTING
AN AMERICAN CHOICE!
GOLLY, GRAMPS! I'M OLD ENOUGH TO VOTE!
NOW, HOLD ON THERE, HOT SHOT!
HAVE YOU GIVEN PROPER THOUGHT TO WHETHER YOU WANT TO VOTE?
GEE, I...
IT'S YOUR AMERICAN RESPONSIBILITY TO CAREFULLY CONSIDER THAT!
WHY, OUR FOUNDING FATHERS DIDN'T WANT EVERYONE TO VOTE!
DO YOU KNOW BETTER THAN THEM??
THROUGHOUT OUR HISTORY, MANY BRAVE AMERICANS FOUGHT FOR THE RIGHT OF FOLKS NOT TO VOTE!
OW, MY WRIST!
FREEDO
NO
GOSH, I NEVER THOUGHT OF IT THAT WAY!
THERE ARE PEOPLE IN PLACES LIKE CHINA WHO WOULD LOVE FOR THE OPPORTUNITY TO FREELY REFRAIN FROM VOTING IN A FAIR AND OPEN ELECTION!
BUT I THOUGHT ONE PERSON, ONE VOTE IS THE AMERICAN WAY!
BOY, READ THE CONSTITUTION! IT'S FULL OF MECHANISMS TO GIVE SOME VOTES MORE POWER THAN OTHERS!
We the People
AND WITH SENSIBLE GERRY-MANDERING AND PRUDENT POLL PRUNING, OUR LEADERS CAN BE SURE IT STAYS THAT WAY!
YOU'RE RIGHT, GRAMPS! I'M EXERCISING MY RIGHT - NO, MY PRIVILEGE - TO NOT VOTE!
NOW YOU'RE TALKIN'!
THE EXERCISE OF RESTRAINT IN THE SERVICE OF PATRIOTISM IS NO VICE!
DIST. BY ANDREWS McMEEL SYNDICATION - ©2018 R. BOLLING - 1411 - TO JOIN THE INNER HIVE, GO TO tomthedancingbug.com

10/29/18

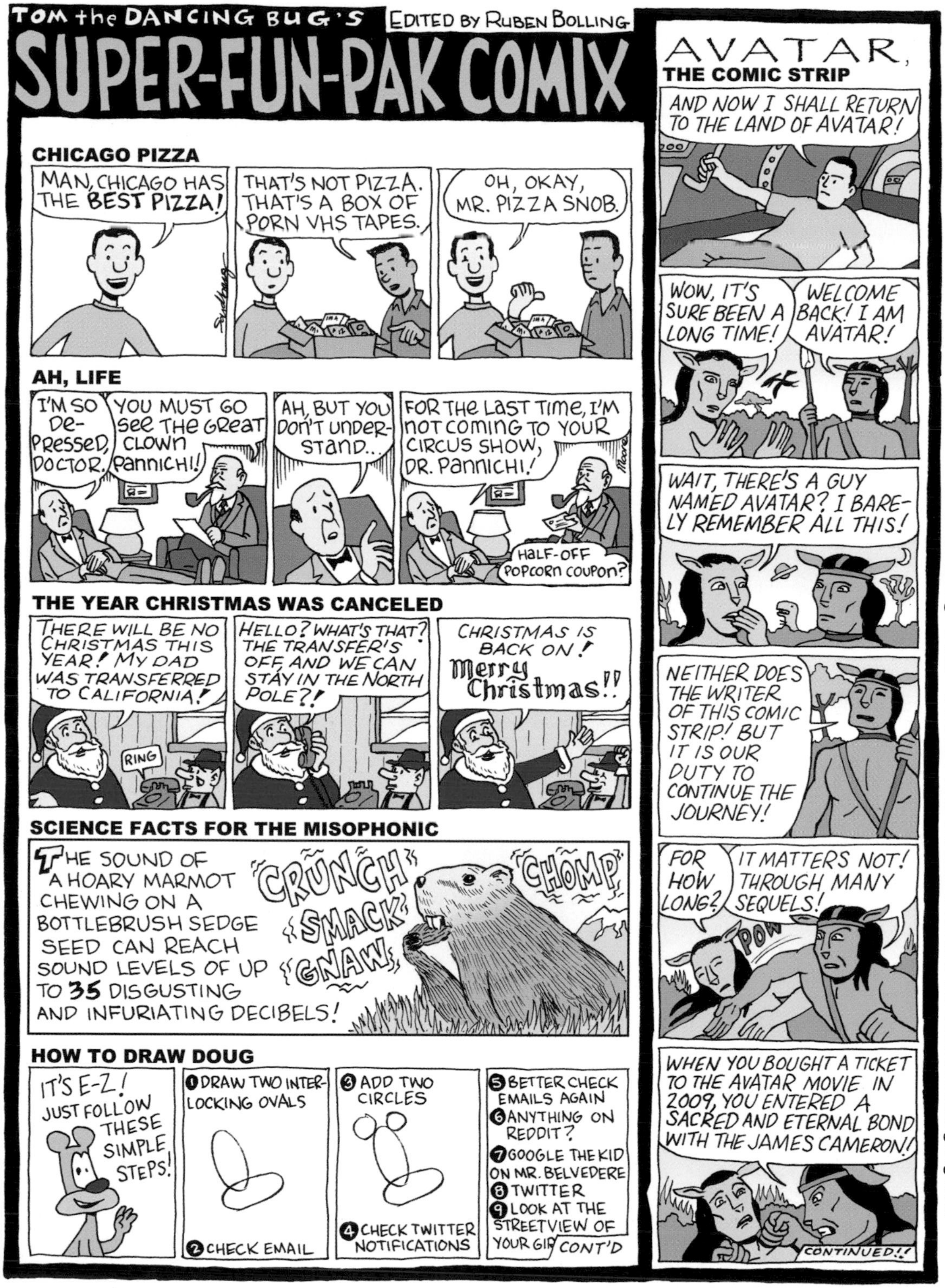

TOM the DANCING BUG'S
EDITED BY RUBEN BOLLING
SUPER-FUN-PAK COMIX
CHICAGO PIZZA
MAN, CHICAGO HAS THE BEST PIZZA!
THAT'S NOT PIZZA. THAT'S A BOX OF PORN VHS TAPES.
OH, OKAY, MR. PIZZA SNOB.
AH, LIFE
I'M SO DE-PRESSED, DOCTOR.
YOU MUST GO SEE THE GREAT CLOWN PANNICHI!
AH, BUT YOU DON'T UNDER-STAND...
FOR THE LAST TIME, I'M NOT COMING TO YOUR CIRCUS SHOW, DR. PANNICHI!
HALF-OFF POPCORN COUPON?
THE YEAR CHRISTMAS WAS CANCELED
THERE WILL BE NO CHRISTMAS THIS YEAR! MY DAD WAS TRANSFERRED TO CALIFORNIA!
RING
HELLO? WHAT'S THAT? THE TRANSFER'S OFF, AND WE CAN STAY IN THE NORTH POLE?!
CHRISTMAS IS BACK ON! Merry Christmas!!
SCIENCE FACTS FOR THE MISOPHONIC
THE SOUND OF A HOARY MARMOT CHEWING ON A BOTTLEBRUSH SEDGE SEED CAN REACH SOUND LEVELS OF UP TO 35 DISGUSTING AND INFURIATING DECIBELS!
CRUNCH
CHOMP
SMACK
GNAW
HOW TO DRAW DOUG
IT'S E-Z! JUST FOLLOW THESE SIMPLE STEPS!
1 DRAW TWO INTER-LOCKING OVALS
2 CHECK EMAIL
3 ADD TWO CIRCLES
4 CHECK TWITTER NOTIFICATIONS
5 BETTER CHECK EMAILS AGAIN
6 ANYTHING ON REDDIT?
7 GOOGLE THE KID ON MR. BELVEDERE
8 TWITTER
9 LOOK AT THE STREETVIEW OF YOUR GIR
CONT'D
AVATAR, THE COMIC STRIP
AND NOW I SHALL RETURN TO THE LAND OF AVATAR!
WOW, IT'S SURE BEEN A LONG TIME!
WELCOME BACK! I AM AVATAR!
WAIT, THERE'S A GUY NAMED AVATAR? I BARE-LY REMEMBER ALL THIS!
NEITHER DOES THE WRITER OF THIS COMIC STRIP! BUT IT IS OUR DUTY TO CONTINUE THE JOURNEY!
FOR HOW LONG?
IT MATTERS NOT! THROUGH MANY SEQUELS!
POW
WHEN YOU BOUGHT A TICKET TO THE AVATAR MOVIE IN 2009, YOU ENTERED A SACRED AND ETERNAL BOND WITH THE JAMES CAMERON!
CONTINUED!!

11/5/18

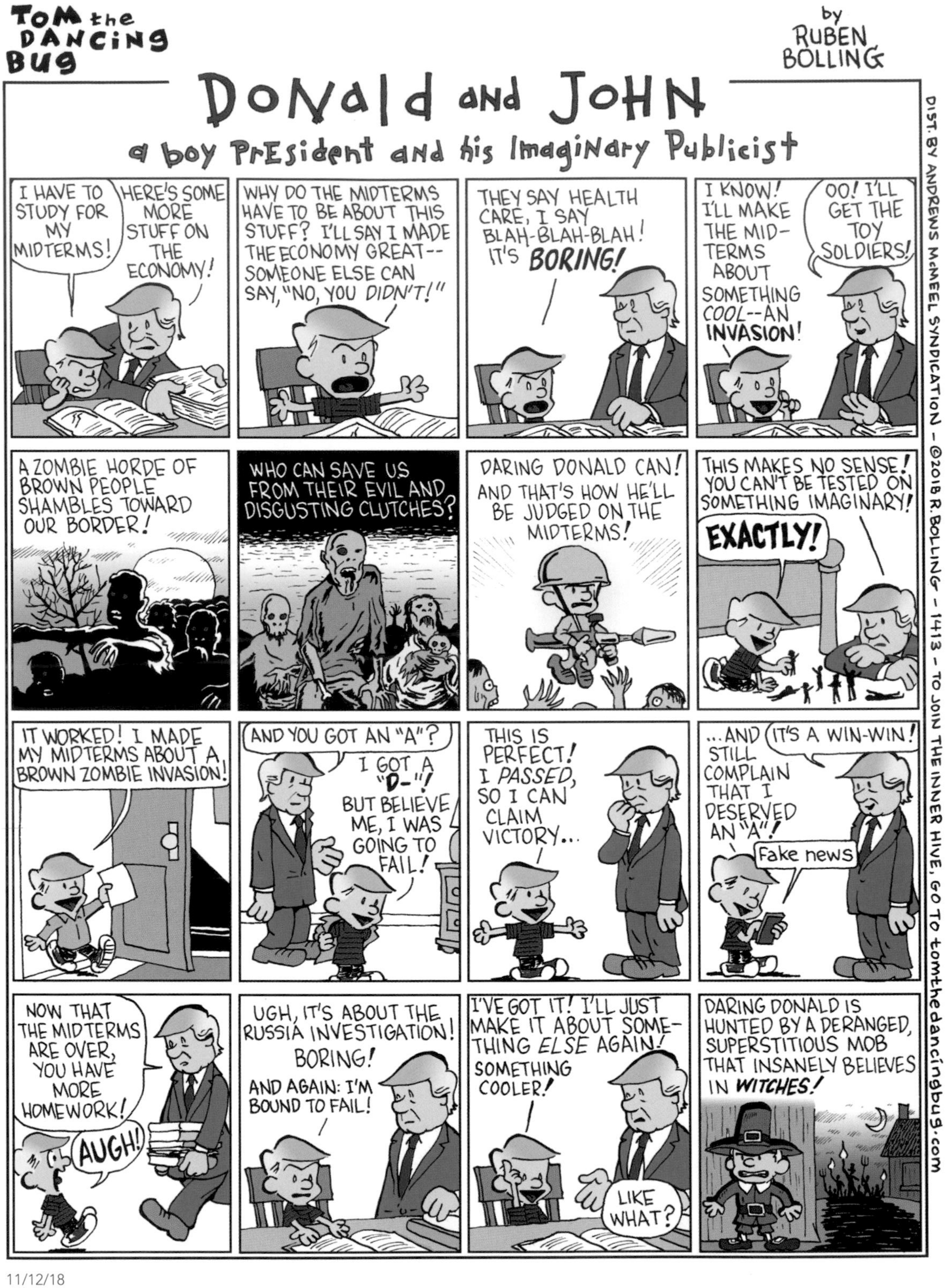
TOM the DANCING BUG
by RUBEN BOLLING
DONALD and JOHN
a boy President and his Imaginary Publicist
I HAVE TO STUDY FOR MY MIDTERMS!
HERE'S SOME MORE STUFF ON THE ECONOMY!
WHY DO THE MIDTERMS HAVE TO BE ABOUT THIS STUFF? I'LL SAY I MADE THE ECONOMY GREAT-- SOMEONE ELSE CAN SAY, "NO, YOU DIDN'T!"
THEY SAY HEALTH CARE, I SAY BLAH-BLAH-BLAH! IT'S BORING!
I KNOW! I'LL MAKE THE MID-TERMS ABOUT SOMETHING COOL--AN INVASION!
OO! I'LL GET THE TOY SOLDIERS!
A ZOMBIE HORDE OF BROWN PEOPLE SHAMBLES TOWARD OUR BORDER!
WHO CAN SAVE US FROM THEIR EVIL AND DISGUSTING CLUTCHES?
DARING DONALD CAN! AND THAT'S HOW HE'LL BE JUDGED ON THE MIDTERMS!
THIS MAKES NO SENSE! YOU CAN'T BE TESTED ON SOMETHING IMAGINARY!
EXACTLY!
IT WORKED! I MADE MY MIDTERMS ABOUT A BROWN ZOMBIE INVASION!
AND YOU GOT AN "A"?
I GOT A "D-"! BUT BELIEVE ME, I WAS GOING TO FAIL!
THIS IS PERFECT! I PASSED, SO I CAN CLAIM VICTORY...
...AND STILL COMPLAIN THAT I DESERVED AN "A"!
IT'S A WIN-WIN!
Fake news
NOW THAT THE MIDTERMS ARE OVER, YOU HAVE MORE HOMEWORK!
AUGH!
UGH, IT'S ABOUT THE RUSSIA INVESTIGATION!
BORING!
AND AGAIN: I'M BOUND TO FAIL!
I'VE GOT IT! I'LL JUST MAKE IT ABOUT SOME-THING ELSE AGAIN!
SOMETHING COOLER!
LIKE WHAT?
DARING DONALD IS HUNTED BY A DERANGED, SUPERSTITIOUS MOB THAT INSANELY BELIEVES IN WITCHES!
DIST. BY ANDREWS McMEEL SYNDICATION – ©2018 R. BOLLING – 1413 – TO JOIN THE INNER HIVE, GO TO tomthedancingbug.com

11/12/18

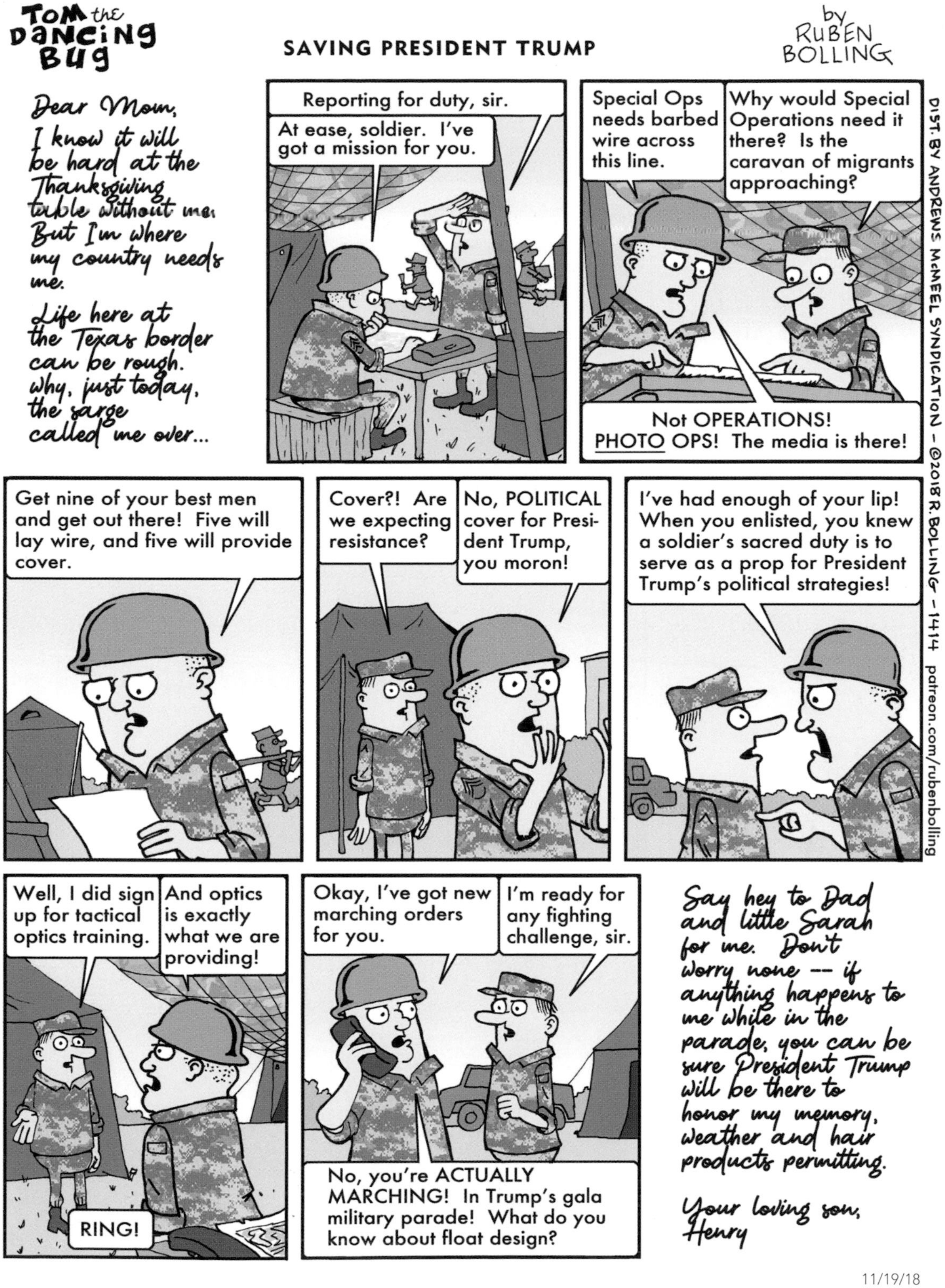
TOM the DANCING BUG
SAVING PRESIDENT TRUMP
by RUBEN BOLLING
Dear Mom, I know it will be hard at the Thanksgiving table without me. But I'm where my country needs me.
Life here at the Texas border can be rough. Why, just today, the sarge called me over...
Reporting for duty, sir.
At ease, soldier. I've got a mission for you.
Special Ops needs barbed wire across this line.
Why would Special Operations need it there? Is the caravan of migrants approaching?
Not OPERATIONS! PHOTO OPS! The media is there!
Get nine of your best men and get out there! Five will lay wire, and five will provide cover.
Cover?! Are we expecting resistance?
No, POLITICAL cover for President Trump, you moron!
I've had enough of your lip! When you enlisted, you knew a soldier's sacred duty is to serve as a prop for President Trump's political strategies!
Well, I did sign up for tactical optics training.
And optics is exactly what we are providing!
RING!
Okay, I've got new marching orders for you.
I'm ready for any fighting challenge, sir.
No, you're ACTUALLY MARCHING! In Trump's gala military parade! What do you know about float design?
Say hey to Dad and little Sarah for me. Don't worry none -- if anything happens to me while in the parade, you can be sure President Trump will be there to honor my memory, weather and hair products permitting.
Your loving son, Henry
DIST. BY ANDREWS McMEEL SYNDICATION – ©2018 R. BOLLING – 1414 patreon.com/rubenbolling

11/19/18

TOM the DANCING BUG PRESENTS:

BY RUBEN BOLLING

NEWS OF THE TIMES

Scientists: Doomsday Asteroid to Hit Earth in June

GOP:
We Feel Like It Won't

DIST. BY ANDREWS McMEEL SYNDICATION — ©2018 R. BOLLING — 1415 — TO JOIN THE INNER HIVE, GO TO tomthedancingbug.com

NASA ANNOUNCED THE DISCOVERY OF A NINE-MILE-WIDE ASTEROID ON AN IMMINENT COLLISION COURSE WITH EARTH.

OUR CALCULATIONS ARE UNASSAILABLE! IF NOT DIVERTED, THIS ASTEROID WILL DESTROY ALL ADVANCED LIFE ON EARTH!

PFFT! CHECK OUT POINDEXTER HERE! WHAT B.S.-- I'LL TRADE HIS FANCY MATH FOR GOOD OL' COMMON SENSE ANY DAY!

DR. HOWARD JERROLD, SR. PLANETARY SCIENTIST, NASA

JOHN "BUD" HANDELSEN, SPOKESMAN, PATRIOT FREEDOM INSTITUTE, PRESENT TO PROVIDE POLITICAL BALANCE

OUR ONLY HOPE IS TO LAUNCH A NUCLEAR-ARMED ROCKET TO MEET THE ASTEROID AND CHANGE ITS COURSE! BUT WE MUST BEGIN IMMEDIATELY!

DR. SVEN FARVGEL, COLUMBIA ASTRO-PHYSICS LABORATORY

SOUNDS LIKE ELITIST FAKE NEWS TO ME! IF THERE'S AN ASTEROID, HOW COME I CAN'T SEE IT?

AND IF I DO SEE IT, I'LL JUST TAKE CARE OF IT WITH PROFESSOR SMITH AND DR. WESSON HERE!

REP. PAUL T. HARTON, R-Tx.

FOR THE LOVE OF GOD, WE HAVE PRECIOUS LITTLE TIME! I HAVE CHILDREN!

DR. HAROLD FORSYTHE, M.I.T. PROFESSOR OF ASTRONAUTICS

Donald J. Trump ✔
@realDonaldTrump

Why should we build a rocket just so we can save a bunch of Mexicans and Chinese? #AmericaFirst #BuildTheWall #LockHerUp

OF COURSE SCIENTISTS WANT TO BUILD A ROCKET! THAT'S HOW THEY GET RICH!

SENATOR, THE CHECK FROM P.F.I. JUST CAME IN!

NOT NOW!

SEN. PETE ANSEL, R-Ky.

NO WASTE MONEY ON ROCKET! NO ASTEROID! WILL NO KILL ALL MAMMALS.

KNOTT A. COCKROACH BILLIONAIRE G.O.P. DONOR, FOUNDER, PATRIOT FREEDOM INSTITUTE

11/26/18

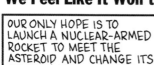

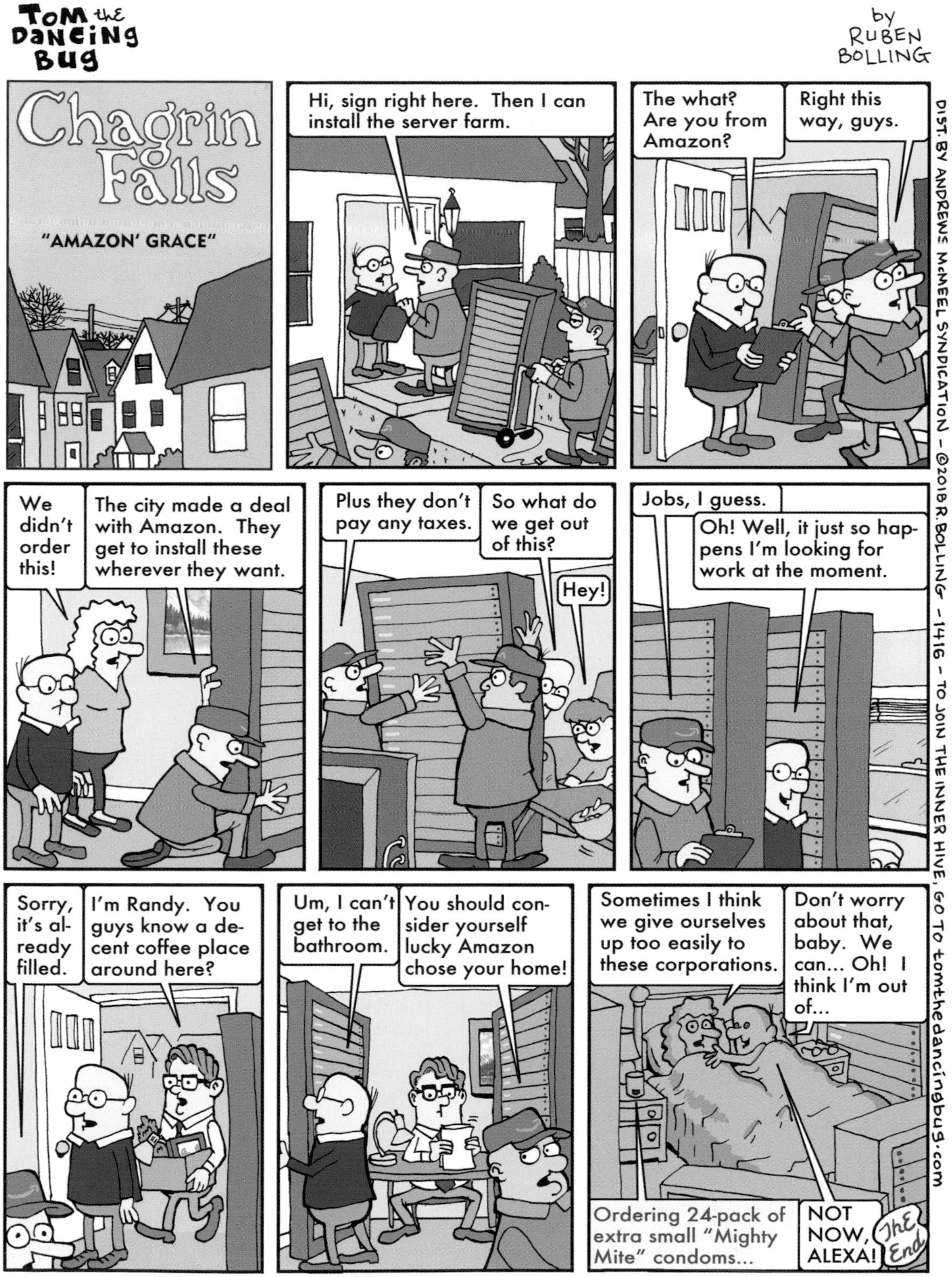
TOM the DANCING BUG
by RUBEN BOLLING
Chagrin Falls
"AMAZON' GRACE"
Hi, sign right here. Then I can install the server farm.
The what? Are you from Amazon?
Right this way, guys.
We didn't order this!
The city made a deal with Amazon. They get to install these wherever they want.
Plus they don't pay any taxes.
So what do we get out of this?
Hey!
Jobs, I guess.
Oh! Well, it just so happens I'm looking for work at the moment.
Sorry, it's already filled.
I'm Randy. You guys know a decent coffee place around here?
Um, I can't get to the bathroom.
You should consider yourself lucky Amazon chose your home!
Sometimes I think we give ourselves up too easily to these corporations.
Don't worry about that, baby. We can... Oh! I think I'm out of...
Ordering 24-pack of extra small "Mighty Mite" condoms...
NOT NOW, ALEXA!
The End
DIST. BY ANDREWS McMEEL SYNDICATION – ©2018 R. BOLLING – 1416 – TO JOIN THE INNER HIVE, GO TO tomthedancingbug.com

12/3/18

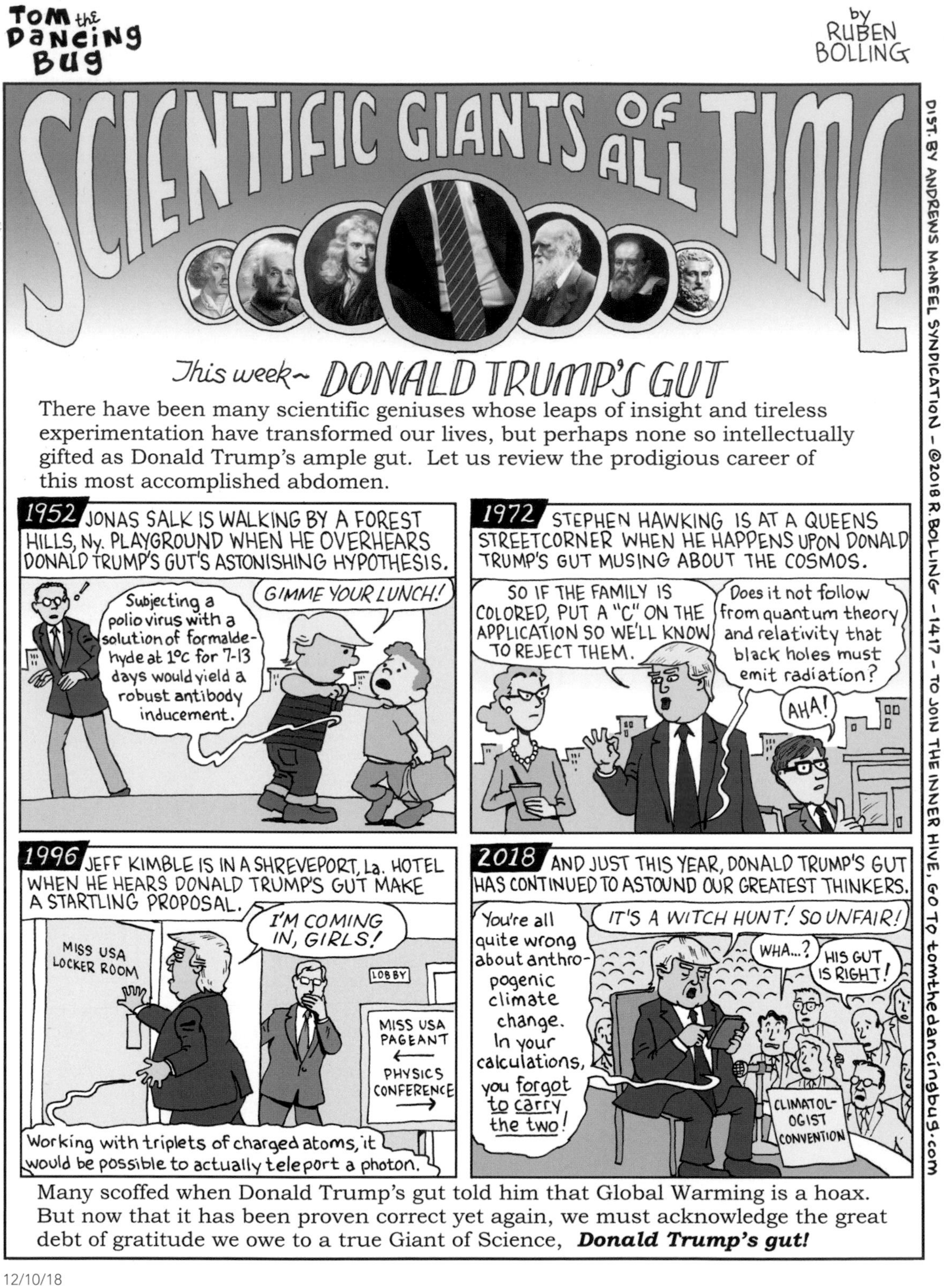
TOM the DANCING BUG
by RUBEN BOLLING
SCIENTIFIC GIANTS OF ALL TIME
This week~ DONALD TRUMP'S GUT
There have been many scientific geniuses whose leaps of insight and tireless experimentation have transformed our lives, but perhaps none so intellectually gifted as Donald Trump's ample gut. Let us review the prodigious career of this most accomplished abdomen.
1952 JONAS SALK IS WALKING BY A FOREST HILLS, Ny. PLAYGROUND WHEN HE OVERHEARS DONALD TRUMP'S GUT'S ASTONISHING HYPOTHESIS.
GIMME YOUR LUNCH!
Subjecting a polio virus with a solution of formaldehyde at 1°c for 7-13 days would yield a robust antibody inducement.
1972 STEPHEN HAWKING IS AT A QUEENS STREETCORNER WHEN HE HAPPENS UPON DONALD TRUMP'S GUT MUSING ABOUT THE COSMOS.
SO IF THE FAMILY IS COLORED, PUT A "C" ON THE APPLICATION SO WE'LL KNOW TO REJECT THEM.
Does it not follow from quantum theory and relativity that black holes must emit radiation?
AHA!
1996 JEFF KIMBLE IS IN A SHREVEPORT, La. HOTEL WHEN HE HEARS DONALD TRUMP'S GUT MAKE A STARTLING PROPOSAL.
I'M COMING IN, GIRLS!
MISS USA LOCKER ROOM
LOBBY
MISS USA PAGEANT ⟵
PHYSICS CONFERENCE ⟶
Working with triplets of charged atoms, it would be possible to actually teleport a photon.
2018 AND JUST THIS YEAR, DONALD TRUMP'S GUT HAS CONTINUED TO ASTOUND OUR GREATEST THINKERS.
IT'S A WITCH HUNT! SO UNFAIR!
You're all quite wrong about anthropogenic climate change. In your calculations, you forgot to carry the two!
WHA...?
HIS GUT IS RIGHT!
CLIMATOLOGIST CONVENTION
Many scoffed when Donald Trump's gut told him that Global Warming is a hoax. But now that it has been proven correct yet again, we must acknowledge the great debt of gratitude we owe to a true Giant of Science, Donald Trump's gut!
DIST. BY ANDREWS McMEEL SYNDICATION – ©2018 R. BOLLING – 1417 – TO JOIN THE INNER HIVE, GO TO tomthedancingbug.com

12/10/18

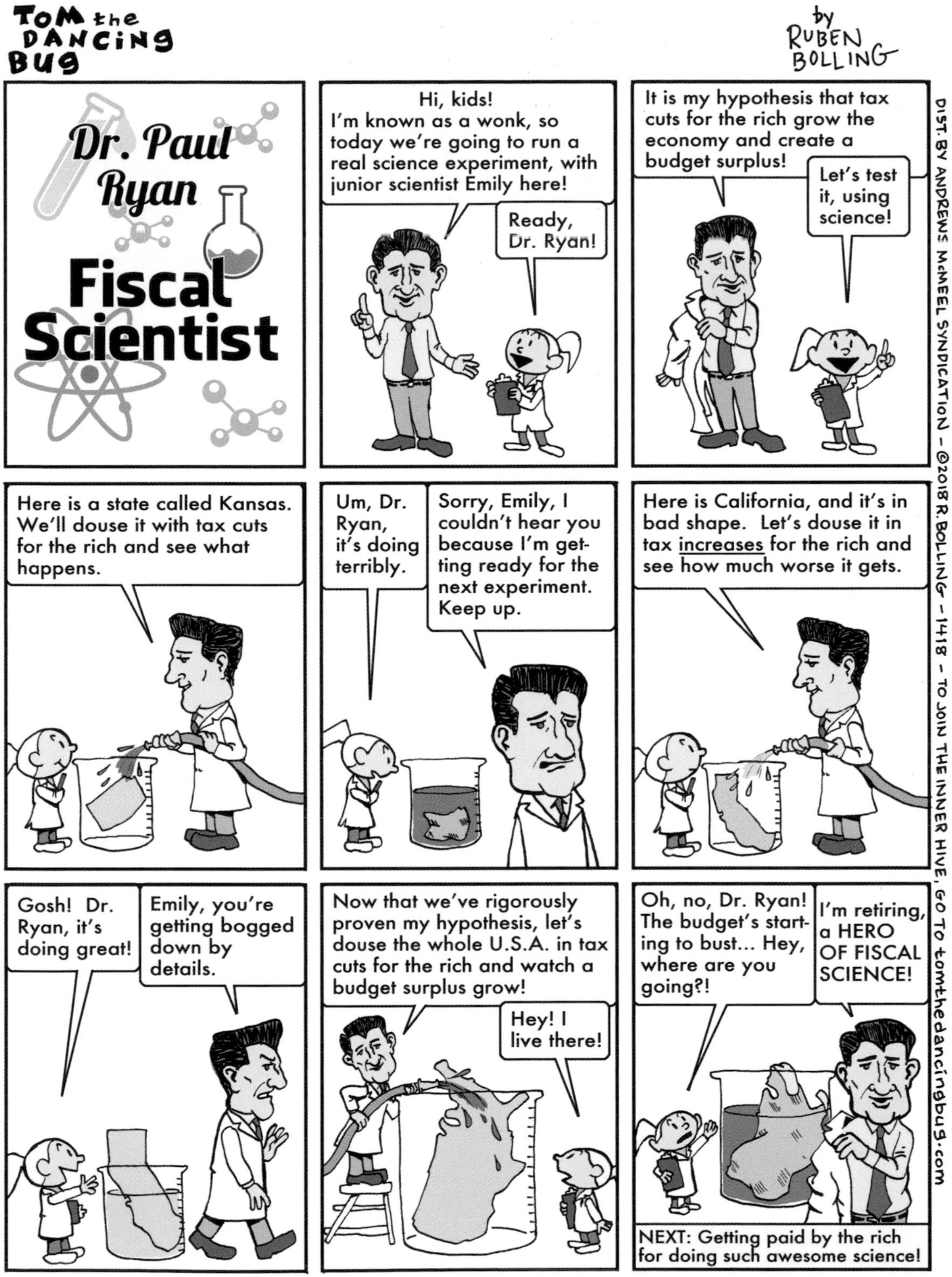
TOM the DANCING BUG
by RUBEN BOLLING
Dr. Paul Ryan
Fiscal Scientist
Hi, kids! I'm known as a wonk, so today we're going to run a real science experiment, with junior scientist Emily here!
Ready, Dr. Ryan!
It is my hypothesis that tax cuts for the rich grow the economy and create a budget surplus!
Let's test it, using science!
Here is a state called Kansas. We'll douse it with tax cuts for the rich and see what happens.
Um, Dr. Ryan, it's doing terribly.
Sorry, Emily, I couldn't hear you because I'm getting ready for the next experiment. Keep up.
Here is California, and it's in bad shape. Let's douse it in tax increases for the rich and see how much worse it gets.
Gosh! Dr. Ryan, it's doing great!
Emily, you're getting bogged down by details.
Now that we've rigorously proven my hypothesis, let's douse the whole U.S.A. in tax cuts for the rich and watch a budget surplus grow!
Hey! I live there!
Oh, no, Dr. Ryan! The budget's starting to bust... Hey, where are you going?!
I'm retiring, a HERO OF FISCAL SCIENCE!
NEXT: Getting paid by the rich for doing such awesome science!
DIST. BY ANDREWS McMEEL SYNDICATION – ©2018 R. BOLLING – 1418 – TO JOIN THE INNER HIVE, GO TO tomthedancingbug.com

12/17/18

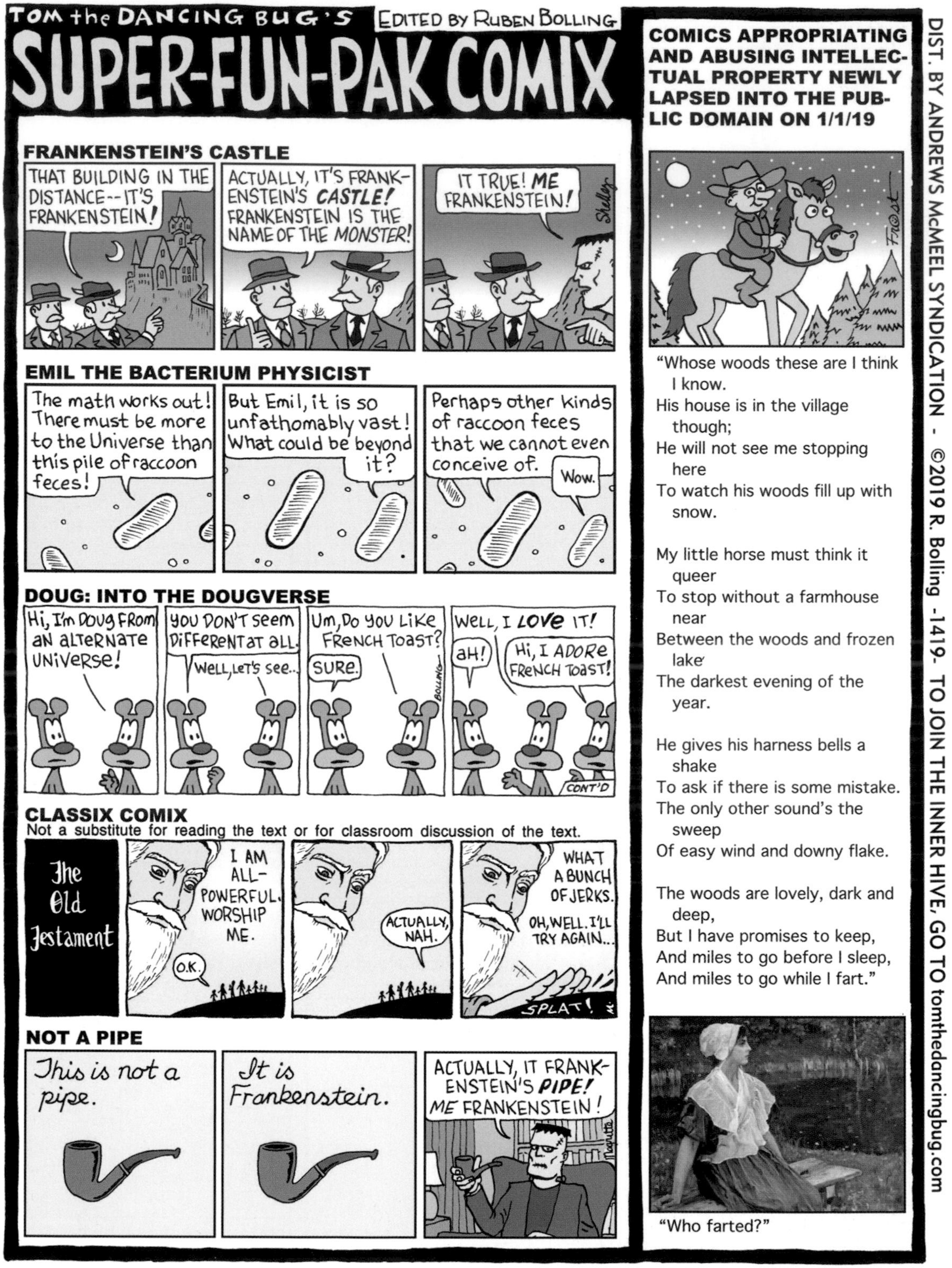
TOM the DANCING BUG'S
EDITED BY RUBEN BOLLING
SUPER-FUN-PAK COMIX
COMICS APPROPRIATING AND ABUSING INTELLECTUAL PROPERTY NEWLY LAPSED INTO THE PUBLIC DOMAIN ON 1/1/19
FRANKENSTEIN'S CASTLE
THAT BUILDING IN THE DISTANCE--IT'S FRANKENSTEIN!
ACTUALLY, IT'S FRANKENSTEIN'S CASTLE! FRANKENSTEIN IS THE NAME OF THE MONSTER!
IT TRUE! ME FRANKENSTEIN!
EMIL THE BACTERIUM PHYSICIST
The math works out! There must be more to the Universe than this pile of raccoon feces!
But Emil, it is so unfathomably vast! What could be beyond it?
Perhaps other kinds of raccoon feces that we cannot even conceive of.
Wow.
DOUG: INTO THE DOUGVERSE
Hi, I'm DOUG FROM AN ALTERNATE UNIVERSE!
YOU DON'T SEEM DIFFERENT AT ALL.
WELL, LET'S SEE...
Um, DO YOU LIKE FRENCH TOAST?
SURE.
WELL, I LOVE IT!
AH!
Hi, I ADORE FRENCH TOAST!
CONT'D
CLASSIX COMIX
Not a substitute for reading the text or for classroom discussion of the text.
The Old Testament
I AM ALL-POWERFUL. WORSHIP ME.
O.K.
ACTUALLY, NAH.
WHAT A BUNCH OF JERKS.
OH, WELL. I'LL TRY AGAIN...
SPLAT!
NOT A PIPE
This is not a pipe.
It is Frankenstein.
ACTUALLY, IT FRANKENSTEIN'S PIPE! ME FRANKENSTEIN!
"Whose woods these are I think I know.
His house is in the village though;
He will not see me stopping here
To watch his woods fill up with snow.
My little horse must think it queer
To stop without a farmhouse near
Between the woods and frozen lake
The darkest evening of the year.
He gives his harness bells a shake
To ask if there is some mistake.
The only other sound's the sweep
Of easy wind and downy flake.
The woods are lovely, dark and deep,
But I have promises to keep,
And miles to go before I sleep,
And miles to go while I fart."
"Who farted?"
DIST. BY ANDREWS McMEEL SYNDICATION - ©2019 R. Bolling -1419- TO JOIN THE INNER HIVE, GO TO tomthedancingbug.com

12/31/18

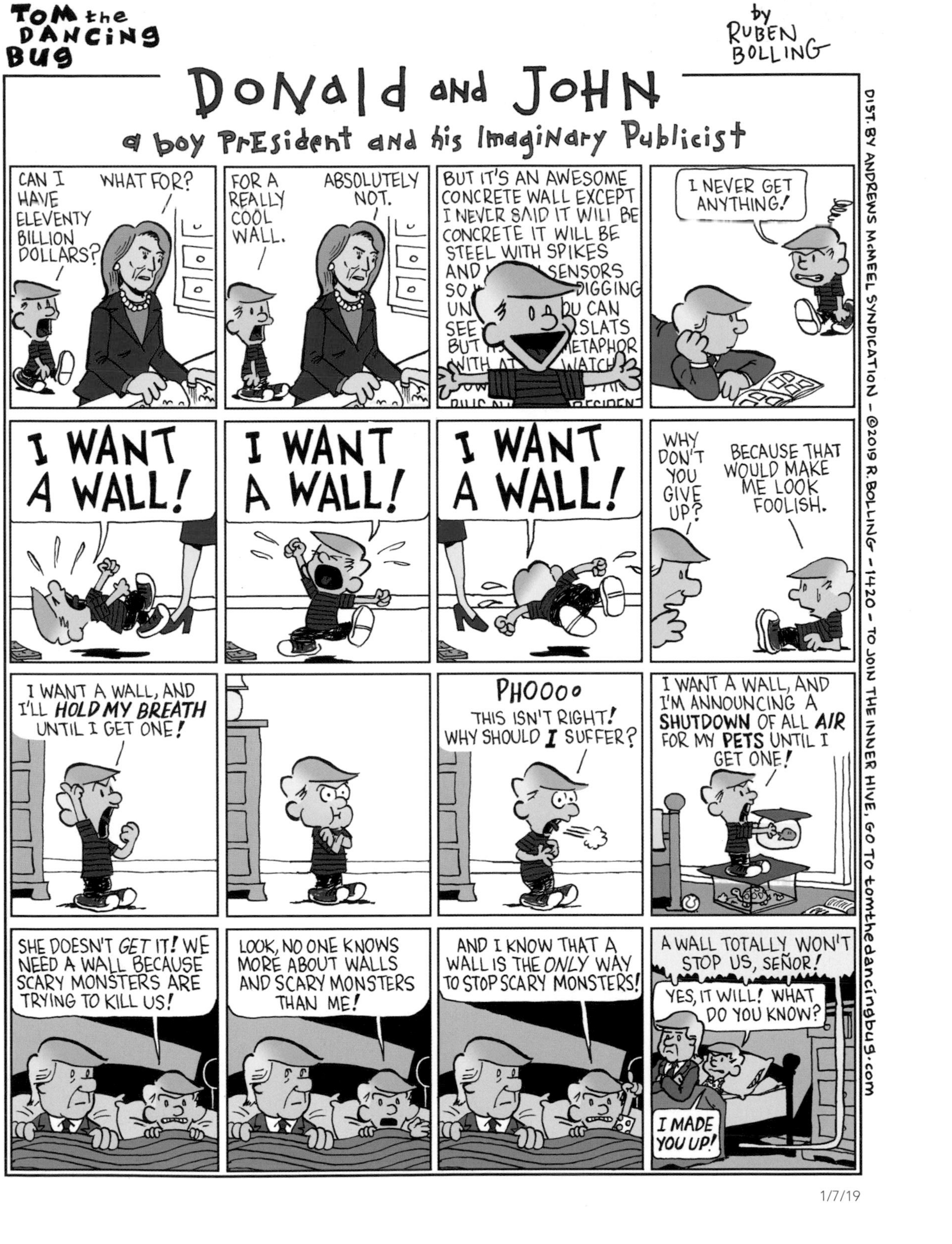
TOM the DANCING BUG
by RUBEN BOLLING
DONALD and JOHN
a boy President and his Imaginary Publicist
CAN I HAVE ELEVENTY BILLION DOLLARS?
WHAT FOR?
FOR A REALLY COOL WALL.
ABSOLUTELY NOT.
BUT IT'S AN AWESOME CONCRETE WALL EXCEPT I NEVER SAID IT WILL BE CONCRETE IT WILL BE STEEL WITH SPIKES
I NEVER GET ANYTHING!
I WANT A WALL!
I WANT A WALL!
I WANT A WALL!
WHY DON'T YOU GIVE UP?
BECAUSE THAT WOULD MAKE ME LOOK FOOLISH.
I WANT A WALL, AND I'LL HOLD MY BREATH UNTIL I GET ONE!
PHOOOO
THIS ISN'T RIGHT! WHY SHOULD I SUFFER?
I WANT A WALL, AND I'M ANNOUNCING A SHUTDOWN OF ALL AIR FOR MY PETS UNTIL I GET ONE!
SHE DOESN'T GET IT! WE NEED A WALL BECAUSE SCARY MONSTERS ARE TRYING TO KILL US!
LOOK, NO ONE KNOWS MORE ABOUT WALLS AND SCARY MONSTERS THAN ME!
AND I KNOW THAT A WALL IS THE ONLY WAY TO STOP SCARY MONSTERS!
A WALL TOTALLY WON'T STOP US, SEÑOR!
YES, IT WILL! WHAT DO YOU KNOW?
I MADE YOU UP!
DIST. BY ANDREWS McMEEL SYNDICATION – ©2019 R. BOLLING – 1420 – TO JOIN THE INNER HIVE, GO TO tomthedancingbug.com

1/7/19

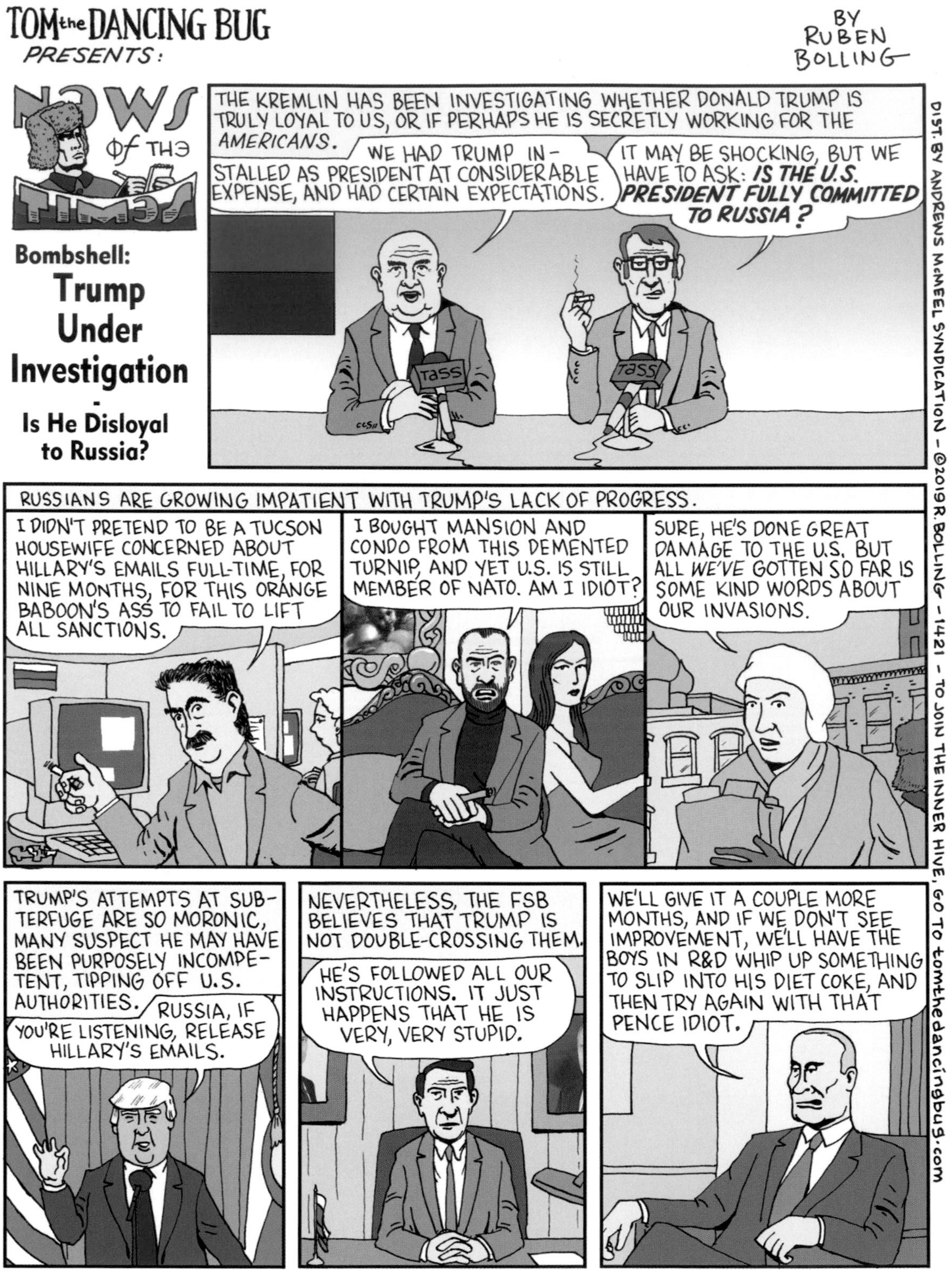
TOM the DANCING BUG PRESENTS:
BY RUBEN BOLLING
NEWS of THE TIMES
Bombshell:
Trump Under Investigation
-
Is He Disloyal to Russia?
THE KREMLIN HAS BEEN INVESTIGATING WHETHER DONALD TRUMP IS TRULY LOYAL TO US, OR IF PERHAPS HE IS SECRETLY WORKING FOR THE AMERICANS.
WE HAD TRUMP INSTALLED AS PRESIDENT AT CONSIDERABLE EXPENSE, AND HAD CERTAIN EXPECTATIONS.
IT MAY BE SHOCKING, BUT WE HAVE TO ASK: IS THE U.S. PRESIDENT FULLY COMMITTED TO RUSSIA?
TASS
TASS
RUSSIANS ARE GROWING IMPATIENT WITH TRUMP'S LACK OF PROGRESS.
I DIDN'T PRETEND TO BE A TUCSON HOUSEWIFE CONCERNED ABOUT HILLARY'S EMAILS FULL-TIME, FOR NINE MONTHS, FOR THIS ORANGE BABOON'S ASS TO FAIL TO LIFT ALL SANCTIONS.
I BOUGHT MANSION AND CONDO FROM THIS DEMENTED TURNIP, AND YET U.S. IS STILL MEMBER OF NATO. AM I IDIOT?
SURE, HE'S DONE GREAT DAMAGE TO THE U.S. BUT ALL WE'VE GOTTEN SO FAR IS SOME KIND WORDS ABOUT OUR INVASIONS.
TRUMP'S ATTEMPTS AT SUBTERFUGE ARE SO MORONIC, MANY SUSPECT HE MAY HAVE BEEN PURPOSELY INCOMPETENT, TIPPING OFF U.S. AUTHORITIES.
RUSSIA, IF YOU'RE LISTENING, RELEASE HILLARY'S EMAILS.
NEVERTHELESS, THE FSB BELIEVES THAT TRUMP IS NOT DOUBLE-CROSSING THEM.
HE'S FOLLOWED ALL OUR INSTRUCTIONS. IT JUST HAPPENS THAT HE IS VERY, VERY STUPID.
WE'LL GIVE IT A COUPLE MORE MONTHS, AND IF WE DON'T SEE IMPROVEMENT, WE'LL HAVE THE BOYS IN R&D WHIP UP SOMETHING TO SLIP INTO HIS DIET COKE, AND THEN TRY AGAIN WITH THAT PENCE IDIOT.
DIST. BY ANDREWS McMEEL SYNDICATION – ©2019 R. BOLLING – 1421 – TO JOIN THE INNER HIVE, GO TO tomthedancingbug.com

1/14/19

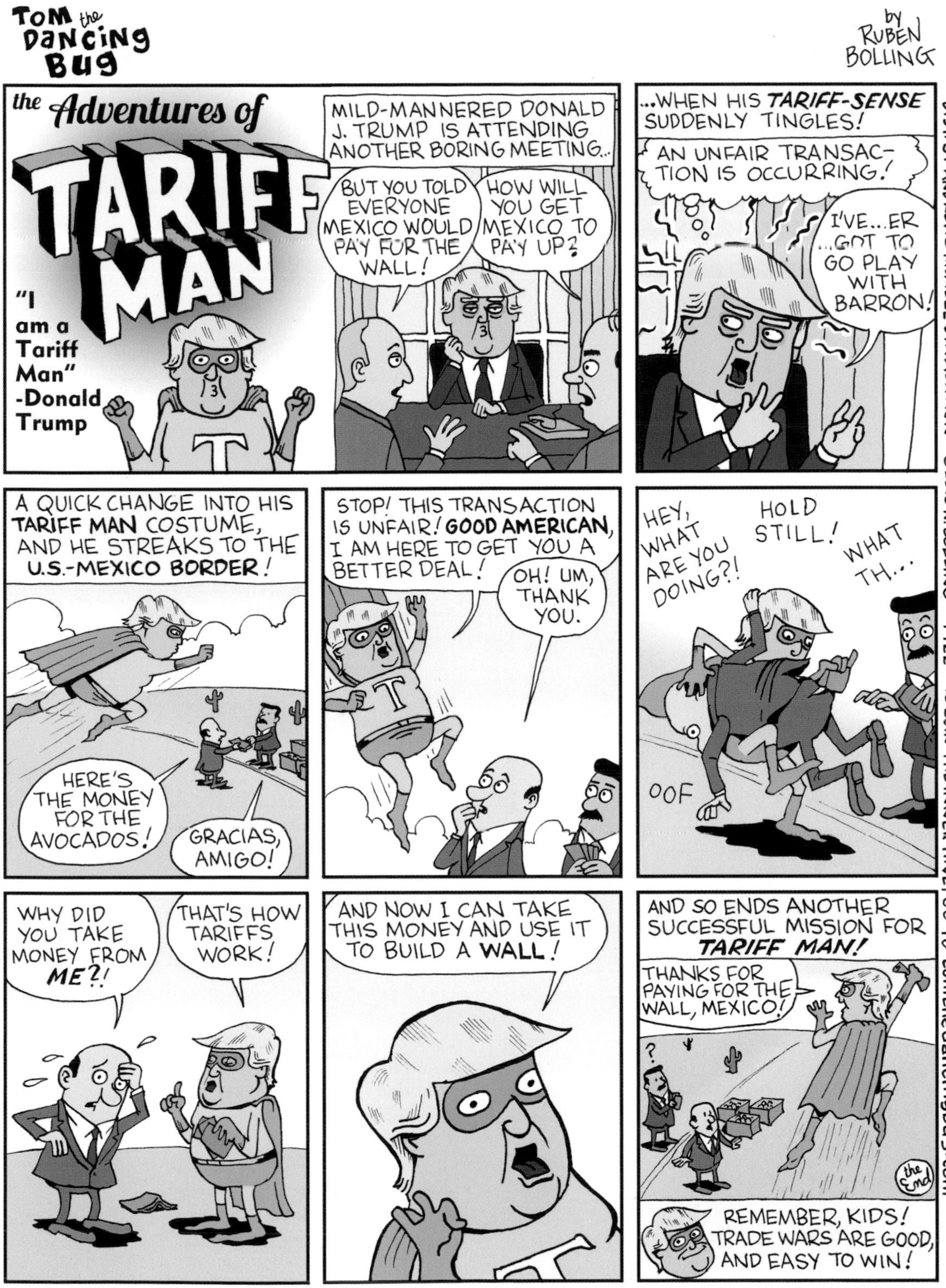
TOM the DANCING BUG
by RUBEN BOLLING
the Adventures of TARIFF MAN
"I am a Tariff Man" -Donald Trump
MILD-MANNERED DONALD J. TRUMP IS ATTENDING ANOTHER BORING MEETING..
BUT YOU TOLD EVERYONE MEXICO WOULD PAY FOR THE WALL!
HOW WILL YOU GET MEXICO TO PAY UP?
...WHEN HIS TARIFF-SENSE SUDDENLY TINGLES!
AN UNFAIR TRANSACTION IS OCCURRING!
I'VE...ER ...GOT TO GO PLAY WITH BARRON!
A QUICK CHANGE INTO HIS TARIFF MAN COSTUME, AND HE STREAKS TO THE U.S.-MEXICO BORDER!
HERE'S THE MONEY FOR THE AVOCADOS!
GRACIAS, AMIGO!
STOP! THIS TRANSACTION IS UNFAIR! GOOD AMERICAN, I AM HERE TO GET YOU A BETTER DEAL!
OH! UM, THANK YOU.
HEY, WHAT ARE YOU DOING?!
HOLD STILL!
WHAT TH...
OOF
WHY DID YOU TAKE MONEY FROM ME?!
THAT'S HOW TARIFFS WORK!
AND NOW I CAN TAKE THIS MONEY AND USE IT TO BUILD A WALL!
AND SO ENDS ANOTHER SUCCESSFUL MISSION FOR TARIFF MAN!
THANKS FOR PAYING FOR THE WALL, MEXICO!
?
the end
REMEMBER, KIDS! TRADE WARS ARE GOOD, AND EASY TO WIN!
DIST. BY ANDREWS McMEEL SYNDICATION – ©2019 R. BOLLING – 1422 – TO JOIN THE INNER HIVE, GO TO tomthedancingbug.com

1/21/19

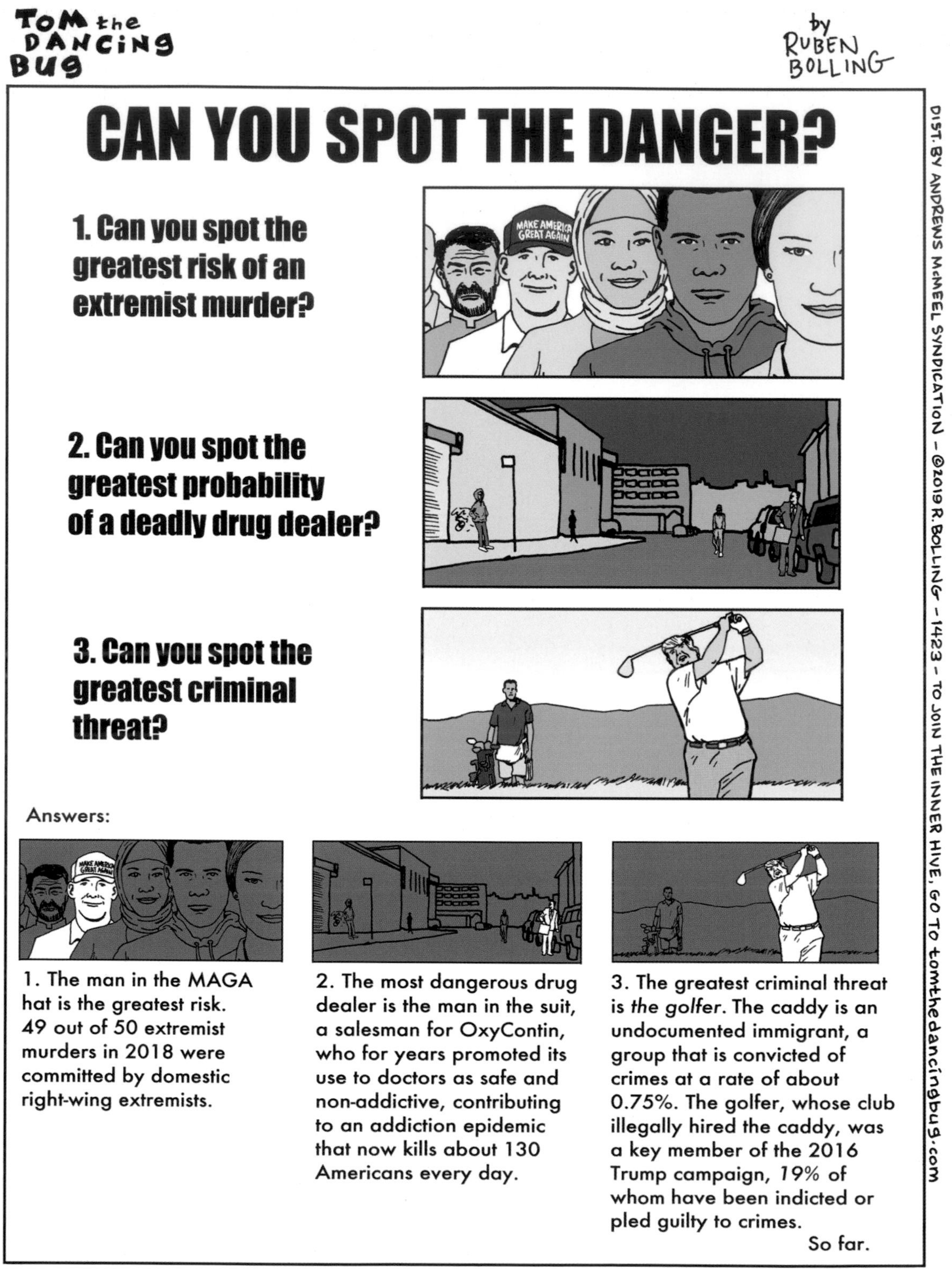
TOM the DANCING BUG
by RUBEN BOLLING
CAN YOU SPOT THE DANGER?
1. Can you spot the greatest risk of an extremist murder?
MAKE AMERICA GREAT AGAIN
2. Can you spot the greatest probability of a deadly drug dealer?
3. Can you spot the greatest criminal threat?
Answers:
1. The man in the MAGA hat is the greatest risk. 49 out of 50 extremist murders in 2018 were committed by domestic right-wing extremists.
2. The most dangerous drug dealer is the man in the suit, a salesman for OxyContin, who for years promoted its use to doctors as safe and non-addictive, contributing to an addiction epidemic that now kills about 130 Americans every day.
3. The greatest criminal threat is *the golfer*. The caddy is an undocumented immigrant, a group that is convicted of crimes at a rate of about 0.75%. The golfer, whose club illegally hired the caddy, was a key member of the 2016 Trump campaign, *19%* of whom have been indicted or pled guilty to crimes.
So far.
DIST. BY ANDREWS McMEEL SYNDICATION – ©2019 R. BOLLING – 1423 – TO JOIN THE INNER HIVE, GO TO tomthedancingbug.com

1/28/19

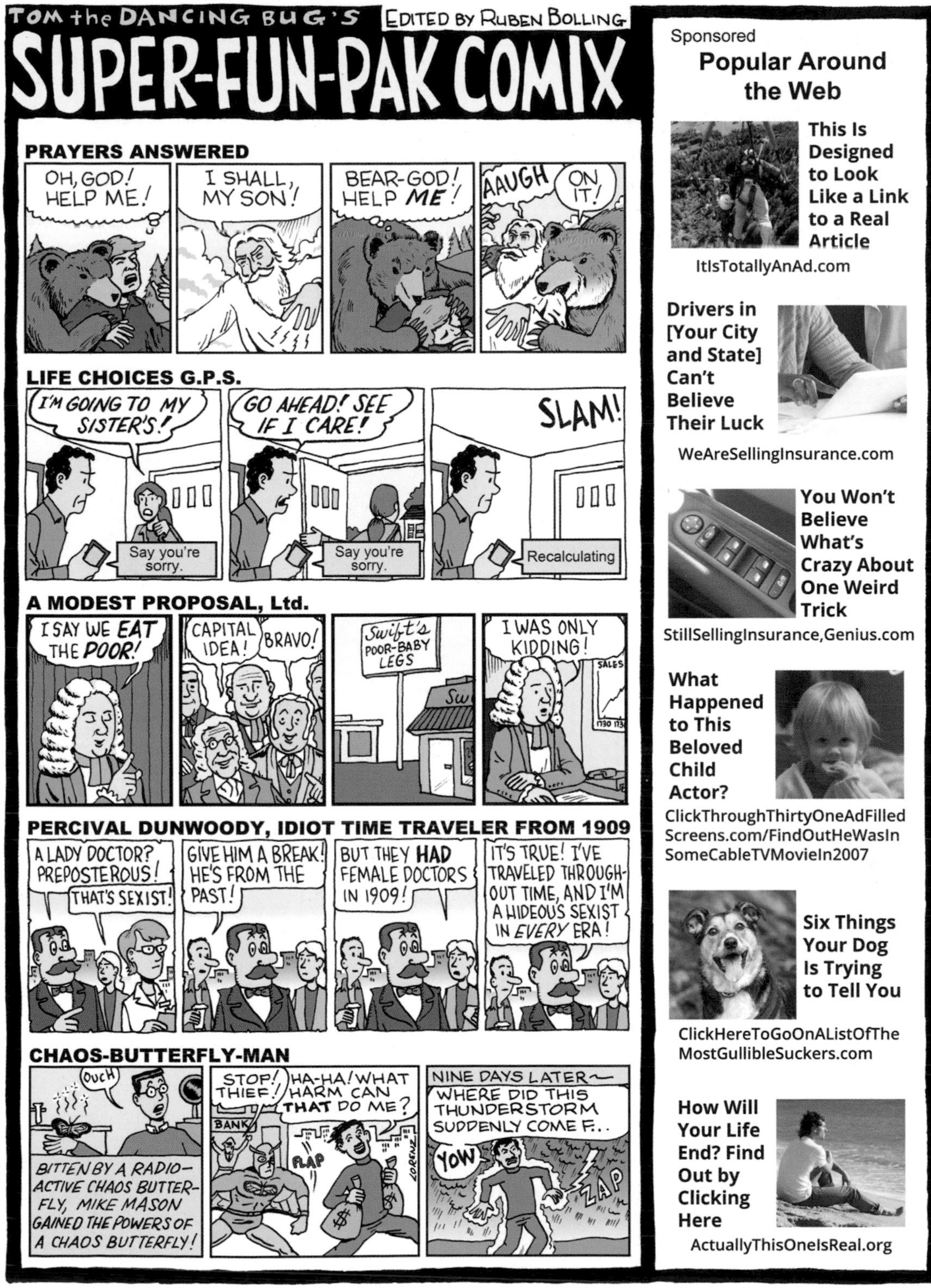
TOM the DANCING BUG'S
EDITED BY RUBEN BOLLING
SUPER-FUN-PAK COMIX
PRAYERS ANSWERED
OH, GOD! HELP ME!
I SHALL, MY SON!
BEAR-GOD! HELP ME!
AAUGH
ON IT!
LIFE CHOICES G.P.S.
I'M GOING TO MY SISTER'S!
Say you're sorry.
GO AHEAD! SEE IF I CARE!
Say you're sorry.
SLAM!
Recalculating
A MODEST PROPOSAL, Ltd.
I SAY WE EAT THE POOR!
CAPITAL IDEA!
BRAVO!
Swift's POOR-BABY LEGS
I WAS ONLY KIDDING!
SALES
PERCIVAL DUNWOODY, IDIOT TIME TRAVELER FROM 1909
A LADY DOCTOR? PREPOSTEROUS!
THAT'S SEXIST!
GIVE HIM A BREAK! HE'S FROM THE PAST!
BUT THEY HAD FEMALE DOCTORS IN 1909!
IT'S TRUE! I'VE TRAVELED THROUGHOUT TIME, AND I'M A HIDEOUS SEXIST IN EVERY ERA!
CHAOS-BUTTERFLY-MAN
OUCH
BITTEN BY A RADIO-ACTIVE CHAOS BUTTERFLY, MIKE MASON GAINED THE POWERS OF A CHAOS BUTTERFLY!
STOP! THIEF!
HA-HA! WHAT HARM CAN THAT DO ME?
BANK
FLAP
NINE DAYS LATER—
WHERE DID THIS THUNDERSTORM SUDDENLY COME F...
YOW
ZAP
Sponsored
Popular Around the Web
This Is Designed to Look Like a Link to a Real Article
ItIsTotallyAnAd.com
Drivers in [Your City and State] Can't Believe Their Luck
WeAreSellingInsurance.com
You Won't Believe What's Crazy About One Weird Trick
StillSellingInsurance,Genius.com
What Happened to This Beloved Child Actor?
ClickThroughThirtyOneAdFilledScreens.com/FindOutHeWasInSomeCableTVMovieIn2007
Six Things Your Dog Is Trying to Tell You
ClickHereToGoOnAListOfTheMostGullibleSuckers.com
How Will Your Life End? Find Out by Clicking Here
ActuallyThisOneIsReal.org

2/4/19

TOM the DANCING BUG

by RUBEN BOLLING

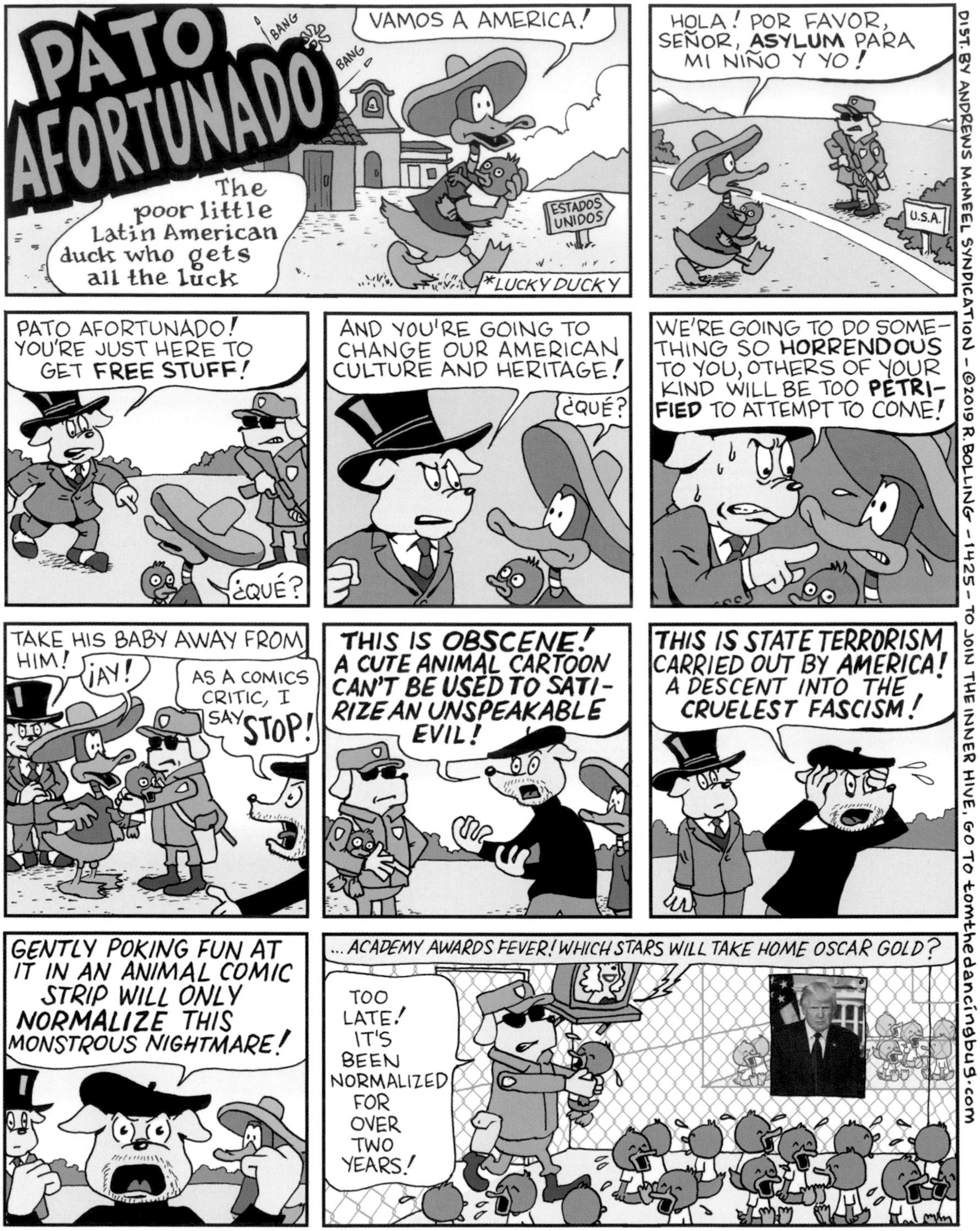
PATO AFORTUNADO
The poor little Latin American duck who gets all the luck
BANG
BANG
VAMOS A AMERICA!
ESTADOS UNIDOS
*LUCKY DUCKY
HOLA! POR FAVOR, SEÑOR, ASYLUM PARA MI NIÑO Y YO!
U.S.A.
PATO AFORTUNADO! YOU'RE JUST HERE TO GET FREE STUFF!
¿QUÉ?
AND YOU'RE GOING TO CHANGE OUR AMERICAN CULTURE AND HERITAGE!
¿QUÉ?
WE'RE GOING TO DO SOMETHING SO HORRENDOUS TO YOU, OTHERS OF YOUR KIND WILL BE TOO PETRIFIED TO ATTEMPT TO COME!
TAKE HIS BABY AWAY FROM HIM!
¡AY!
AS A COMICS CRITIC, I SAY STOP!
THIS IS OBSCENE! A CUTE ANIMAL CARTOON CAN'T BE USED TO SATIRIZE AN UNSPEAKABLE EVIL!
THIS IS STATE TERRORISM CARRIED OUT BY AMERICA! A DESCENT INTO THE CRUELEST FASCISM!
GENTLY POKING FUN AT IT IN AN ANIMAL COMIC STRIP WILL ONLY NORMALIZE THIS MONSTROUS NIGHTMARE!
...ACADEMY AWARDS FEVER! WHICH STARS WILL TAKE HOME OSCAR GOLD?
TOO LATE! IT'S BEEN NORMALIZED FOR OVER TWO YEARS!
DIST. BY ANDREWS McMEEL SYNDICATION - ©2019 R. BOLLING - 1425 - TO JOIN THE INNER HIVE, GO TO tomthedancingbug.com

2/11/19

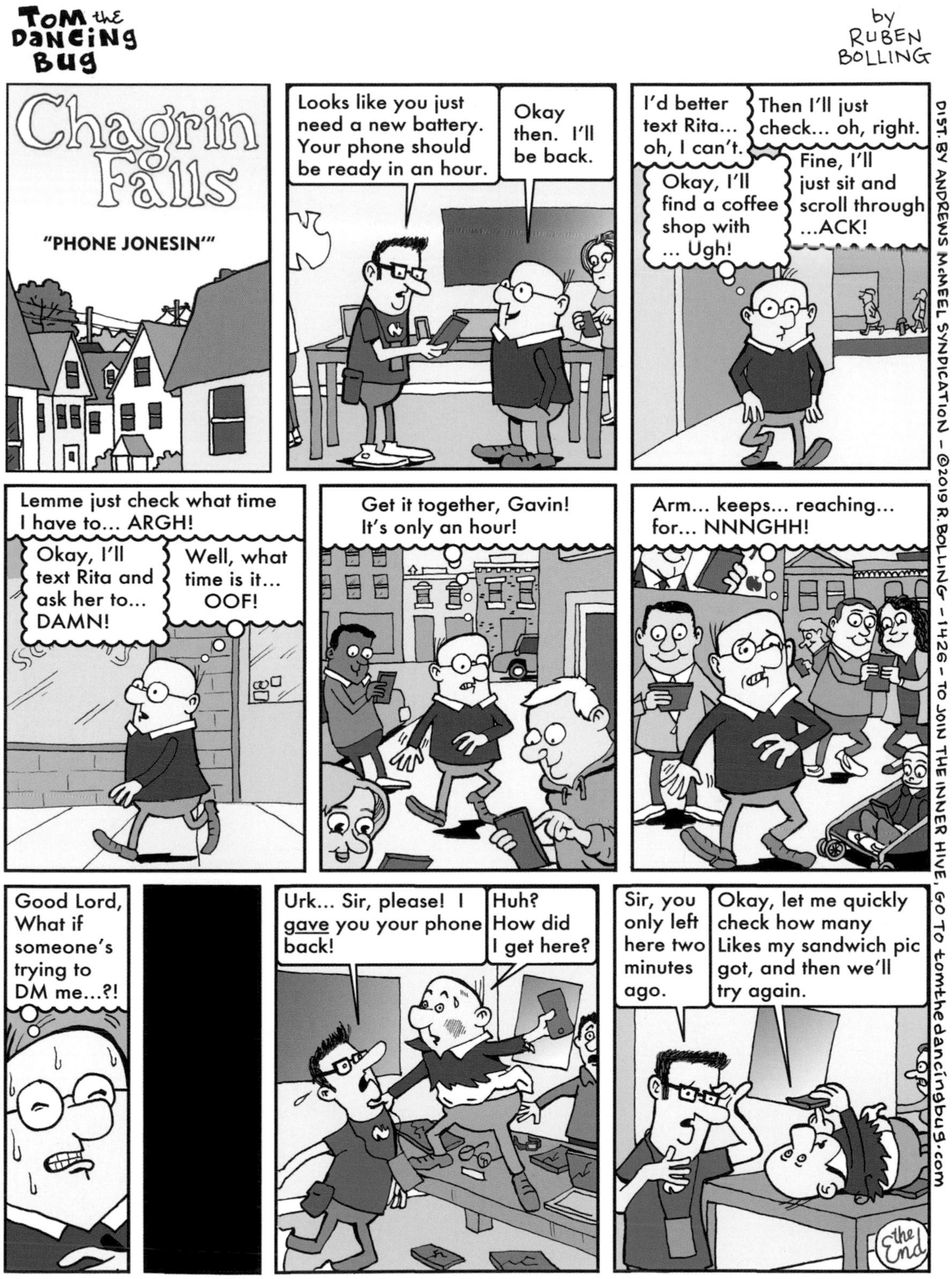

TOM the DANCING BUG
by RUBEN BOLLING
Chagrin Falls
"PHONE JONESIN'"
Looks like you just need a new battery. Your phone should be ready in an hour.
Okay then. I'll be back.
I'd better text Rita... oh, I can't.
Then I'll just check... oh, right.
Okay, I'll find a coffee shop with ... Ugh!
Fine, I'll just sit and scroll through ...ACK!
Lemme just check what time I have to... ARGH!
Okay, I'll text Rita and ask her to... DAMN!
Well, what time is it... OOF!
Get it together, Gavin! It's only an hour!
Arm... keeps... reaching... for... NNNGHH!
Good Lord, What if someone's trying to DM me...?!
Urk... Sir, please! I gave you your phone back!
Huh? How did I get here?
Sir, you only left here two minutes ago.
Okay, let me quickly check how many Likes my sandwich pic got, and then we'll try again.
the End
DIST. BY ANDREWS McMEEL SYNDICATION – ©2019 R. BOLLING – 1426 – TO JOIN THE INNER HIVE, GO TO tomthedancingbug.com

2/18/19

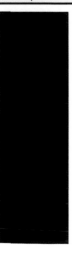

TOM the DANCING BUG

by RUBEN BOLLING

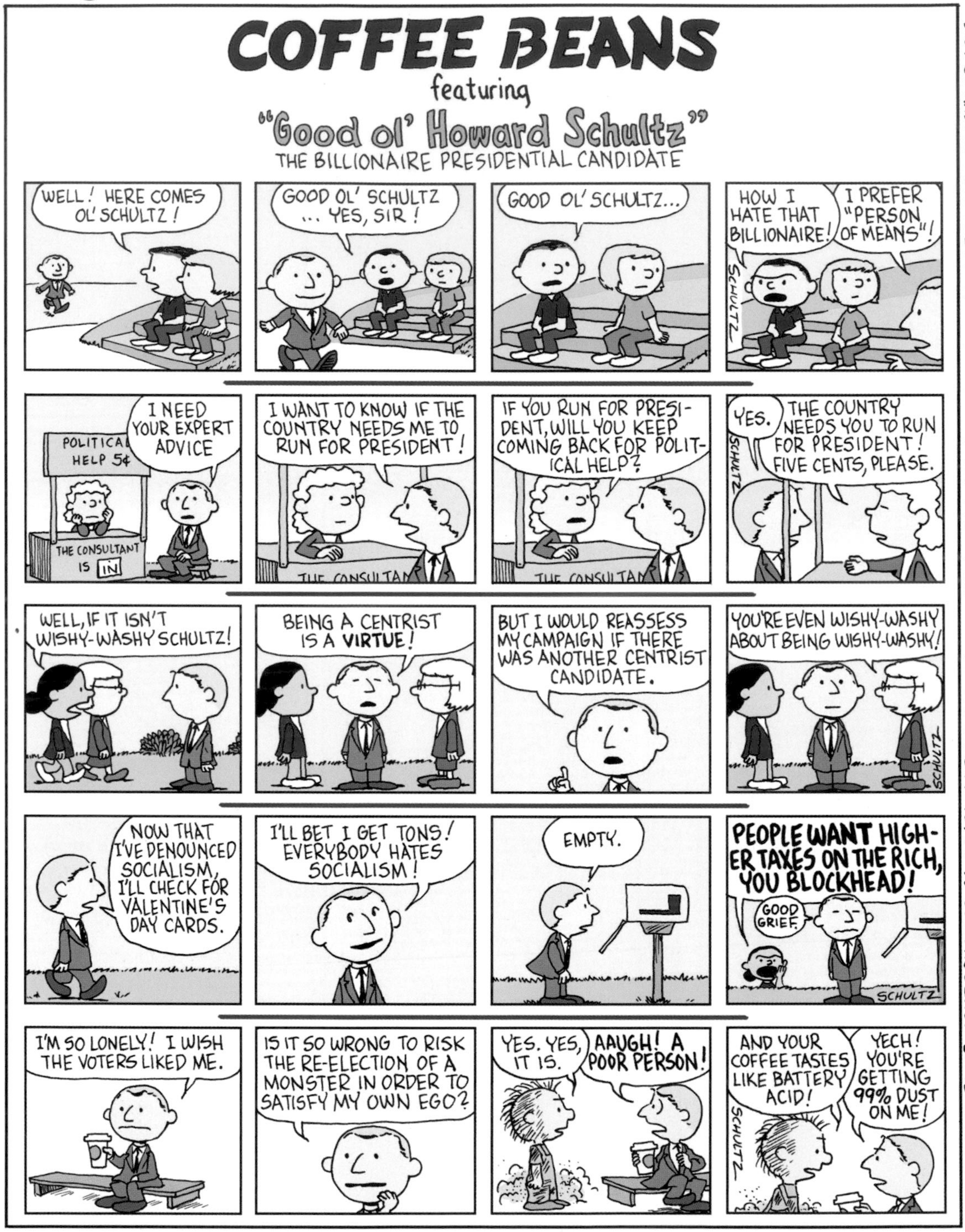
COFFEE BEANS
featuring
"Good ol' Howard Schultz"
THE BILLIONAIRE PRESIDENTIAL CANDIDATE
WELL! HERE COMES OL' SCHULTZ!
GOOD OL' SCHULTZ ... YES, SIR!
GOOD OL' SCHULTZ...
HOW I HATE THAT BILLIONAIRE!
I PREFER "PERSON OF MEANS"!
SCHULTZ
POLITICAL HELP 5¢
THE CONSULTANT IS IN
I NEED YOUR EXPERT ADVICE
I WANT TO KNOW IF THE COUNTRY NEEDS ME TO RUN FOR PRESIDENT!
IF YOU RUN FOR PRESIDENT, WILL YOU KEEP COMING BACK FOR POLITICAL HELP?
YES.
THE COUNTRY NEEDS YOU TO RUN FOR PRESIDENT! FIVE CENTS, PLEASE.
SCHULTZ
WELL, IF IT ISN'T WISHY-WASHY SCHULTZ!
BEING A CENTRIST IS A VIRTUE!
BUT I WOULD REASSESS MY CAMPAIGN IF THERE WAS ANOTHER CENTRIST CANDIDATE.
YOU'RE EVEN WISHY-WASHY ABOUT BEING WISHY-WASHY!
SCHULTZ
NOW THAT I'VE DENOUNCED SOCIALISM, I'LL CHECK FOR VALENTINE'S DAY CARDS.
I'LL BET I GET TONS! EVERYBODY HATES SOCIALISM!
EMPTY.
PEOPLE WANT HIGHER TAXES ON THE RICH, YOU BLOCKHEAD!
GOOD GRIEF.
SCHULTZ
I'M SO LONELY! I WISH THE VOTERS LIKED ME.
IS IT SO WRONG TO RISK THE RE-ELECTION OF A MONSTER IN ORDER TO SATISFY MY OWN EGO?
YES. YES, IT IS.
AAUGH! A POOR PERSON!
AND YOUR COFFEE TASTES LIKE BATTERY ACID!
YECH! YOU'RE GETTING 99% DUST ON ME!
SCHULTZ

2/25/19

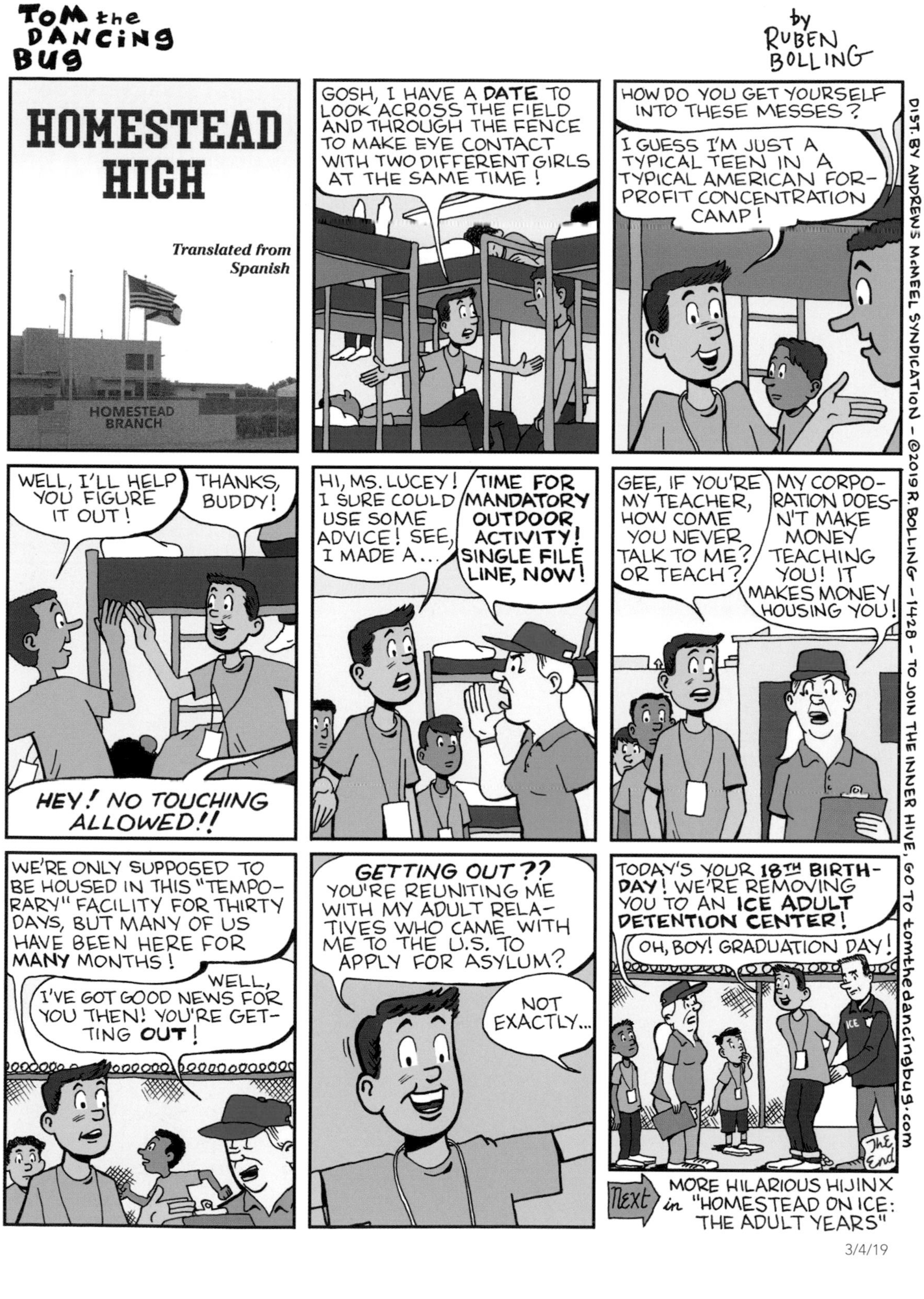
TOM the DANCING BUG
by RUBEN BOLLING
HOMESTEAD HIGH
Translated from Spanish
HOMESTEAD BRANCH
GOSH, I HAVE A DATE TO LOOK ACROSS THE FIELD AND THROUGH THE FENCE TO MAKE EYE CONTACT WITH TWO DIFFERENT GIRLS AT THE SAME TIME!
HOW DO YOU GET YOURSELF INTO THESE MESSES?
I GUESS I'M JUST A TYPICAL TEEN IN A TYPICAL AMERICAN FOR-PROFIT CONCENTRATION CAMP!
WELL, I'LL HELP YOU FIGURE IT OUT!
THANKS, BUDDY!
HEY! NO TOUCHING ALLOWED!!
HI, MS. LUCEY! I SURE COULD USE SOME ADVICE! SEE, I MADE A...
TIME FOR MANDATORY OUTDOOR ACTIVITY! SINGLE FILE LINE, NOW!
GEE, IF YOU'RE MY TEACHER, HOW COME YOU NEVER TALK TO ME? OR TEACH?
MY CORPORATION DOESN'T MAKE MONEY TEACHING YOU! IT MAKES MONEY HOUSING YOU!
WE'RE ONLY SUPPOSED TO BE HOUSED IN THIS "TEMPORARY" FACILITY FOR THIRTY DAYS, BUT MANY OF US HAVE BEEN HERE FOR MANY MONTHS!
WELL, I'VE GOT GOOD NEWS FOR YOU THEN! YOU'RE GETTING OUT!
GETTING OUT?? YOU'RE REUNITING ME WITH MY ADULT RELATIVES WHO CAME WITH ME TO THE U.S. TO APPLY FOR ASYLUM?
NOT EXACTLY...
TODAY'S YOUR 18TH BIRTHDAY! WE'RE REMOVING YOU TO AN ICE ADULT DETENTION CENTER!
OH, BOY! GRADUATION DAY!
ICE
The End
Next in MORE HILARIOUS HIJINX "HOMESTEAD ON ICE: THE ADULT YEARS"
DIST. BY ANDREWS McMEEL SYNDICATION – ©2019 R. BOLLING – 1428 – TO JOIN THE INNER HIVE, GO TO tomthedancingbug.com

3/4/19

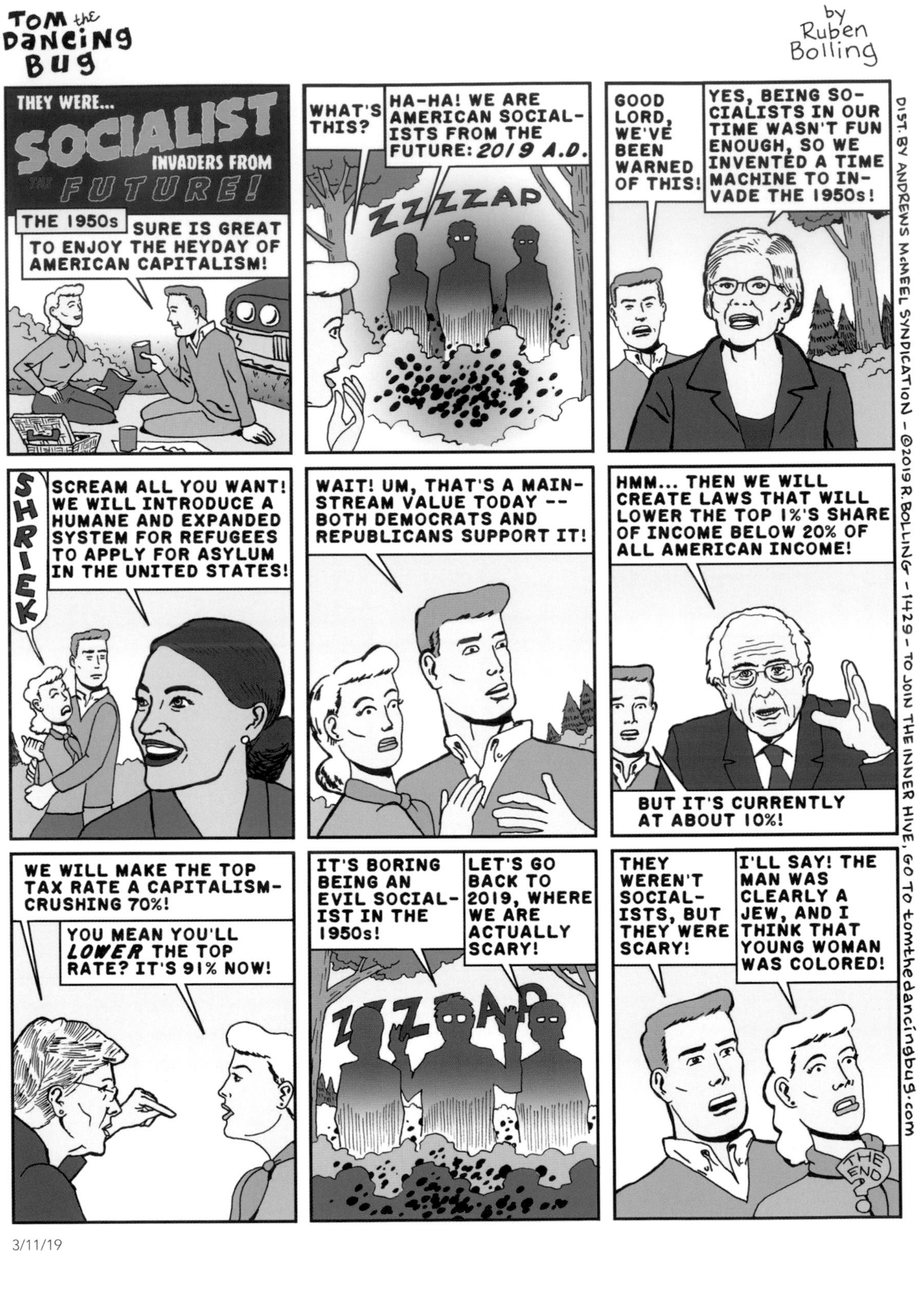
TOM the DANCING BUG
by Ruben Bolling
THEY WERE... SOCIALIST INVADERS FROM THE FUTURE!
THE 1950s
SURE IS GREAT TO ENJOY THE HEYDAY OF AMERICAN CAPITALISM!
WHAT'S THIS?
HA-HA! WE ARE AMERICAN SOCIALISTS FROM THE FUTURE: 2019 A.D.
ZZZZAP
GOOD LORD, WE'VE BEEN WARNED OF THIS!
YES, BEING SOCIALISTS IN OUR TIME WASN'T FUN ENOUGH, SO WE INVENTED A TIME MACHINE TO INVADE THE 1950s!
SHRIEK
SCREAM ALL YOU WANT! WE WILL INTRODUCE A HUMANE AND EXPANDED SYSTEM FOR REFUGEES TO APPLY FOR ASYLUM IN THE UNITED STATES!
WAIT! UM, THAT'S A MAINSTREAM VALUE TODAY -- BOTH DEMOCRATS AND REPUBLICANS SUPPORT IT!
HMM... THEN WE WILL CREATE LAWS THAT WILL LOWER THE TOP 1%'S SHARE OF INCOME BELOW 20% OF ALL AMERICAN INCOME!
BUT IT'S CURRENTLY AT ABOUT 10%!
WE WILL MAKE THE TOP TAX RATE A CAPITALISM-CRUSHING 70%!
YOU MEAN YOU'LL LOWER THE TOP RATE? IT'S 91% NOW!
IT'S BORING BEING AN EVIL SOCIALIST IN THE 1950s!
LET'S GO BACK TO 2019, WHERE WE ARE ACTUALLY SCARY!
ZZZZAP
THEY WEREN'T SOCIALISTS, BUT THEY WERE SCARY!
I'LL SAY! THE MAN WAS CLEARLY A JEW, AND I THINK THAT YOUNG WOMAN WAS COLORED!
THE END
DIST. BY ANDREWS McMEEL SYNDICATION - ©2019 R. BOLLING - 1429 - TO JOIN THE INNER HIVE, GO TO tomthedancingbug.com

3/11/19

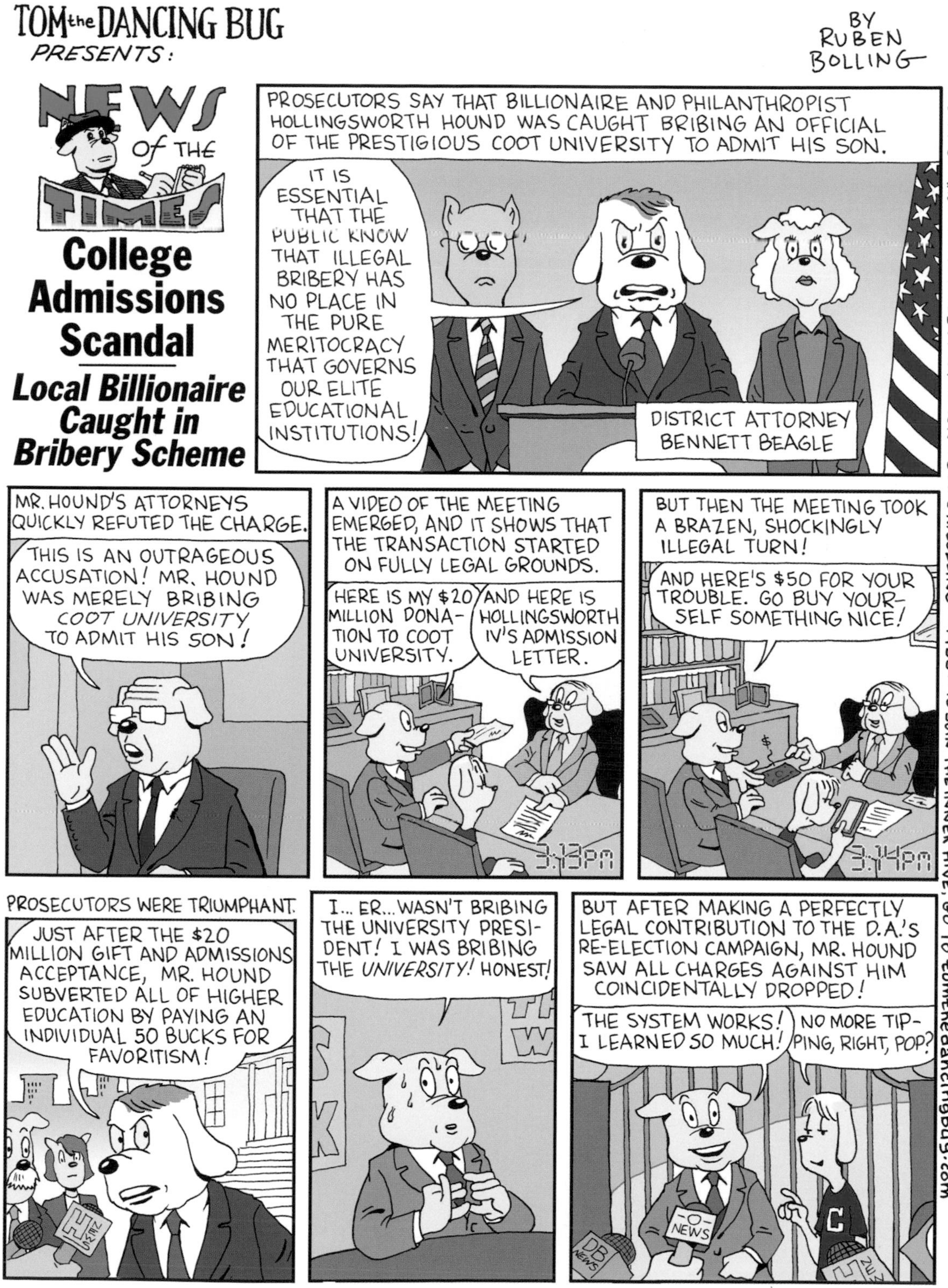

TOM the DANCING BUG PRESENTS:
BY RUBEN BOLLING
NEWS of THE TIMES
College Admissions Scandal
Local Billionaire Caught in Bribery Scheme
PROSECUTORS SAY THAT BILLIONAIRE AND PHILANTHROPIST HOLLINGSWORTH HOUND WAS CAUGHT BRIBING AN OFFICIAL OF THE PRESTIGIOUS COOT UNIVERSITY TO ADMIT HIS SON.
IT IS ESSENTIAL THAT THE PUBLIC KNOW THAT ILLEGAL BRIBERY HAS NO PLACE IN THE PURE MERITOCRACY THAT GOVERNS OUR ELITE EDUCATIONAL INSTITUTIONS!
DISTRICT ATTORNEY BENNETT BEAGLE
MR. HOUND'S ATTORNEYS QUICKLY REFUTED THE CHARGE.
THIS IS AN OUTRAGEOUS ACCUSATION! MR. HOUND WAS MERELY BRIBING *COOT UNIVERSITY* TO ADMIT HIS SON!
A VIDEO OF THE MEETING EMERGED, AND IT SHOWS THAT THE TRANSACTION STARTED ON FULLY LEGAL GROUNDS.
HERE IS MY $20 MILLION DONATION TO COOT UNIVERSITY.
AND HERE IS HOLLINGSWORTH IV'S ADMISSION LETTER.
3:13PM
BUT THEN THE MEETING TOOK A BRAZEN, SHOCKINGLY ILLEGAL TURN!
AND HERE'S $50 FOR YOUR TROUBLE. GO BUY YOURSELF SOMETHING NICE!
3:14PM
PROSECUTORS WERE TRIUMPHANT.
JUST AFTER THE $20 MILLION GIFT AND ADMISSIONS ACCEPTANCE, MR. HOUND SUBVERTED ALL OF HIGHER EDUCATION BY PAYING AN INDIVIDUAL 50 BUCKS FOR FAVORITISM!
I... ER... WASN'T BRIBING THE UNIVERSITY PRESIDENT! I WAS BRIBING THE *UNIVERSITY*! HONEST!
BUT AFTER MAKING A PERFECTLY LEGAL CONTRIBUTION TO THE D.A.'S RE-ELECTION CAMPAIGN, MR. HOUND SAW ALL CHARGES AGAINST HIM COINCIDENTALLY DROPPED!
THE SYSTEM WORKS! I LEARNED SO MUCH!
NO MORE TIPPING, RIGHT, POP?
NEWS
DIST. BY ANDREWS McMEEL SYNDICATION - ©2019 R. BOLLING - 1430 - TO JOIN THE INNER HIVE, GO TO tomthedancingbug.com

3/18/19

SUPER-FUN-PAK COMIX

META, BUT NOT META ENOUGH

DIST. BY ANDREWS McMEEL SYNDICATION - ©2019 R. Bolling - 1431- TO JOIN THE INNER HIVE, GO TO tomthedancingbug.com

LADY-SUPERHERO-MAN

BITTEN BY A RADIOACTIVE LADY SUPERHERO, HAL HARRIS GAINED THE POWERS OF A LADY SUPERHERO!

STOP! I HAVE SUPER-STRENGTH, AND LASER-BLAST EYES!

AH, SEEMS IMPLAUSIBLE.

ARGH! IT'S TRUE! MY POWERS ARE MERE DIVERSITY TOKENISM!

YOU SHOULD SMILE MORE!

EMIL THE BACTERIUM PHYSICIST

According to my calculations, this raccoon feces sprang into existence 117 hours ago, then dropped 8 inches.

The immense distance and time are inconceivable! But it dropped from *where*?

That's a metaphysical question that my Big Bung Theory cannot answer.

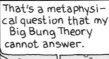

AH, LIFE

DOCTOR, I'M SO DEPRESSED.

TREATMENT IS SIMPLE. GO SEE GREAT CLOWN PANNICHI!

O.K.

TELL ME ABOUT YOUR MOTHER.

SCHRÖDINGER'S CAT AND THEIR WACKY FRIEND WIGNER

AS LONG AS I'M UNOBSERVED IN THIS BOX, I CAN SIMULTANEOUSLY NAP AND EAT PIZZA!

DON'T YOU HATE WHEN SOMEONE RUINS A NAP?

THE ADVENTURES OF ACTUALLY-MAN

AAIEE! IT'S FRANKENSTEIN!

ACTUALLY, IT'S FRANKENSTEIN'S *MONSTER*.

ACTUALLY, IN THE ORIGINAL NOVEL, I NAME MYSELF *ADAM*.

"Sigh."

3/25/19

Tom the Dancing Bug

by RUBEN BOLLING

DIST. BY ANDREWS McMEEL SYNDICATION ~ ©2019 R.BOLLING ~ 1432 ~ TO JOIN THE INNER HIVE, GO TO tomthedancingbug.com

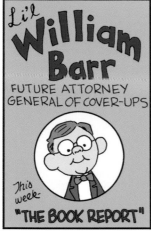

Li'l **William Barr**

FUTURE ATTORNEY GENERAL OF COVER-UPS

This week-

"THE BOOK REPORT"

LI'L WILLIAM, PLEASE COME TO THE FRONT OF THE CLASS AND GIVE YOUR **BOOK REPORT.**

AHEM. **"OF MICE AND MEN"** DOES NOT DEFINITIVELY ESTABLISH THAT LENNIE KILLED CURLEY'S WIFE.

NOR DOES IT EXONERATE HIM.

LI'L WILLIAM, THIS IS JUST LIKE YOUR REPORT ON **"MOBY-DICK."**

WELL, EVIDENCE THAT THE WHALE BIT OFF AHAB'S LEG FAILED TO MEET MY BURDEN OF PROOF.

AND YOUR REPORT ON "1984"?

ORWELL LEFT IT TO THE READER TO DECIDE WHETHER **BIG BROTHER** COMMITTED ABUSES OF POWER, AND **I** DECIDED HE **DIDN'T.**

LI'L WILLIAM, I'M WRITING A NOTE TO YOUR PARENTS. BE SURE TO GIVE IT TO THEM.

Dear Mr. and Mrs. Ba
Li'l William only skims the assigned works and then tortuously cherry-picks and manipulates the text to support his wildl inappropriate conclusions.
Mrs. John

THAT NIGHT~

LI'L WILLIAM, IS THAT YOUR REPORT CARD? LET US SEE IT.

NO, YOU **CAN'T** SEE IT, BUT I'LL **SUMMARIZE** IT FOR YOU: IT STRESSES THAT I COMPLETE MY ASSIGNMENTS, AND CONTAINS SEVERAL INSTANCES OF THE LETTER "A."

THE End

4/1/19

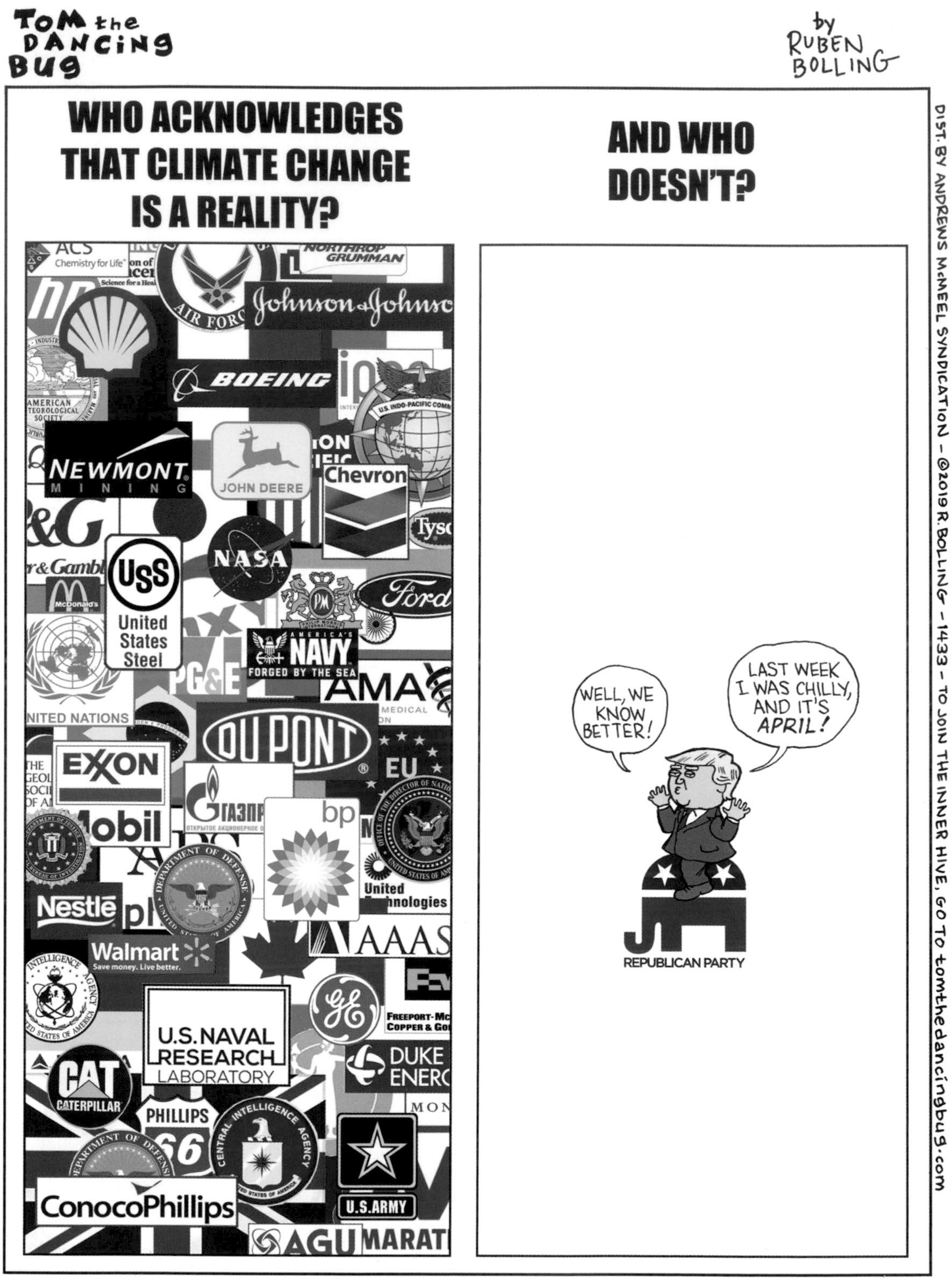
TOM the DANCING BUG
by RUBEN BOLLING
WHO ACKNOWLEDGES THAT CLIMATE CHANGE IS A REALITY?
ACS Chemistry for Life
NORTHROP GRUMMAN
Johnson & Johnson
BOEING
AMERICAN METEOROLOGICAL SOCIETY
U.S. INDO-PACIFIC COMMAND
NEWMONT MINING
JOHN DEERE
Chevron
NASA
United States Steel
McDonald's
Ford
AMERICA'S NAVY FORGED BY THE SEA
PG&E
AMA
UNITED NATIONS
DUPONT
EU
EXXON
Mobil
bp
United Technologies
Nestlé
Walmart Save money. Live better.
AAAS
U.S. NAVAL RESEARCH LABORATORY
FREEPORT-McMoRan COPPER & GOLD
CAT CATERPILLAR
DUKE ENERGY
PHILLIPS 66
CENTRAL INTELLIGENCE AGENCY
U.S. ARMY
ConocoPhillips
AGU
AND WHO DOESN'T?
WELL, WE KNOW BETTER!
LAST WEEK I WAS CHILLY, AND IT'S APRIL!
REPUBLICAN PARTY
DIST. BY ANDREWS McMEEL SYNDICATION – ©2019 R. BOLLING – 1433 – TO JOIN THE INNER HIVE, GO TO tomthedancingbug.com

4/8/19

TOM the DANCING BUG

by RUBEN BOLLING

Donald and JOHN
a boy PrEsident and his Imaginary Publicist

DISSATISFIED WITH BEING MERELY A CONSTITUTIONAL PRESIDENT, LITTLE DONALD COMES UPON A STONE...

HE WONDERS IF HE COULD PULL THE SWORD FROM THE STONE.

AND THUS DID DONALD GET PROMOTED TO UMNIPOTENT DICTATOR!

STOP PLAYING! WE NEED TO WRITE UP THIS EMERGENCY DECLARATION!

SHH! I'M HOLDING A POSE!

DEMOCRATS KILL BABIES!

PSST... ARE YOU SURE YOU SHOULD DO THAT?

WHY NOT? LYING HAS ALWAYS WORKED FOR ME!

NO, I MEAN LYING WITHOUT JUICY, FAKE DETAILS!

OH, RIGHT.

THEY TAKE THE NEWBORN BABY, WRAP IT IN A BLANKET, AND THEN **EXECUTE** IT!!

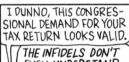

MUCH BETTER LYING!

AND SO DID THE GREAT MONARCH DEFEND THE HOLY GRAIL FROM THE ATTACKING HORDES!

BACK, YE WRETCHED MONSTROSITIES!

YOUR UNCLEAN CLAWS SHALL NOT BESPOIL THIS SACRED VESSEL!

I DUNNO, THIS CONGRESSIONAL DEMAND FOR YOUR TAX RETURN LOOKS VALID.

THE INFIDELS DON'T EVEN UNDERSTAND ITS POWER!

THE MEDIA IS BOTHERING ME.

WE'LL CALL THEM "ENEMY OF THE PEOPLE"!

JUDGES ARE BOTHERING ME.

WE'LL SAY YOU'LL GET RID OF THEM!

LAWS ARE BOTHERING ME.

WE'LL TELL UNDERLINGS TO BREAK THE LAW AND THEN YOU'LL PARDON THEM!

WOW! DISMANTLING DEMOCRATIC NORMS IS INVIGORATING!

WAIT TIL YOU REFUSE TO RELINQUISH POWER!

DIST. BY ANDREWS McMEEL SYNDICATION ~ ©2019 R. BOLLING ~ 1434 ~ TO JOIN THE INNER HIVE, GO TO tomthedancingbug.com

4/15/19

TOM the DANCING BUG

"THE SPECIAL COUNSEL OF OZ"

by RUBEN BOLLING

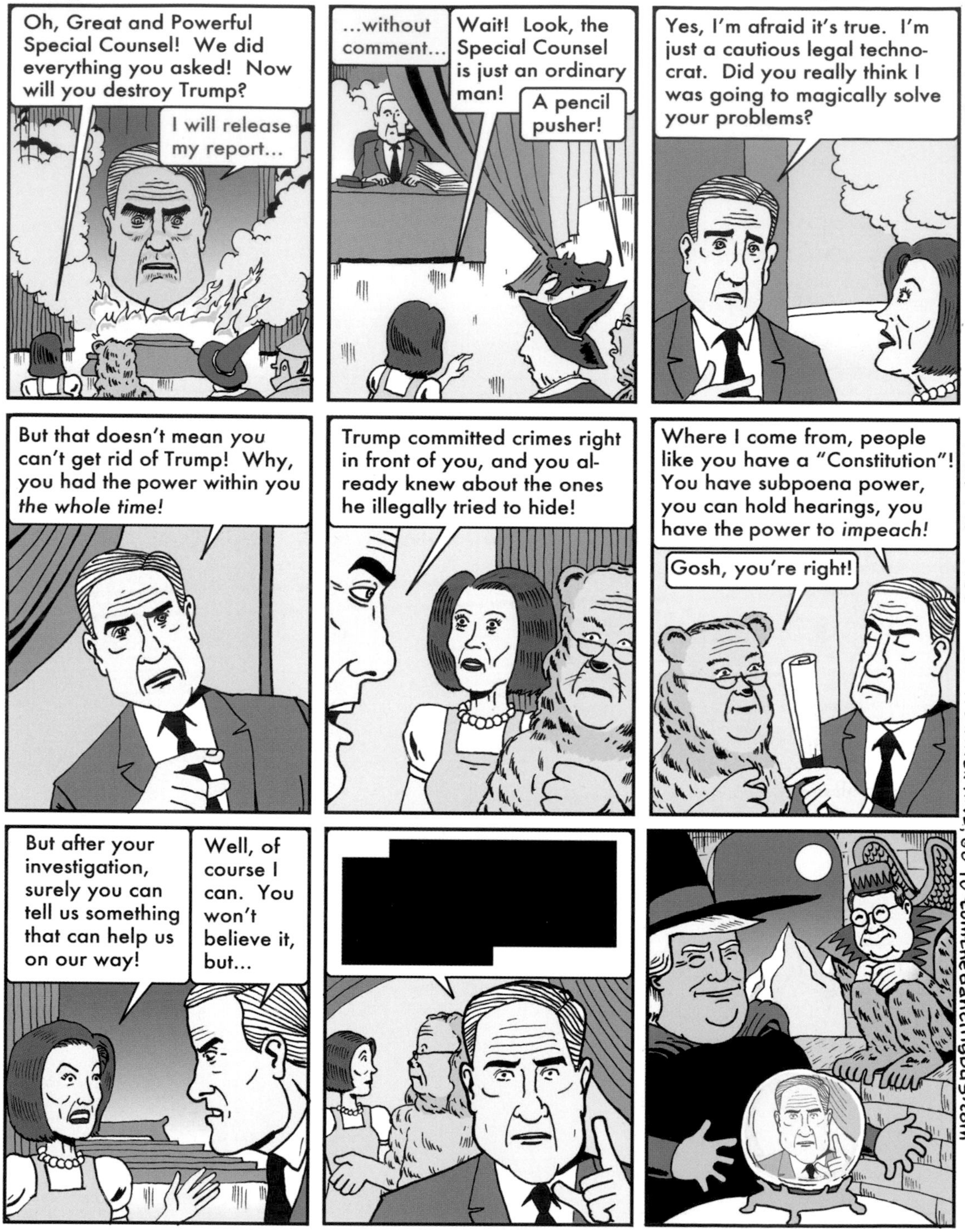

Oh, Great and Powerful Special Counsel! We did everything you asked! Now will you destroy Trump?
I will release my report...
...without comment...
Wait! Look, the Special Counsel is just an ordinary man!
A pencil pusher!
Yes, I'm afraid it's true. I'm just a cautious legal technocrat. Did you really think I was going to magically solve your problems?
But that doesn't mean *you* can't get rid of Trump! Why, you had the power within you *the whole time!*
Trump committed crimes right in front of you, and you already knew about the ones he illegally tried to hide!
Where I come from, people like you have a "Constitution"! You have subpoena power, you can hold hearings, you have the power to *impeach!*
Gosh, you're right!
But after your investigation, surely you can tell us something that can help us on our way!
Well, of course I can. You won't believe it, but...
[redacted]

4/22/19

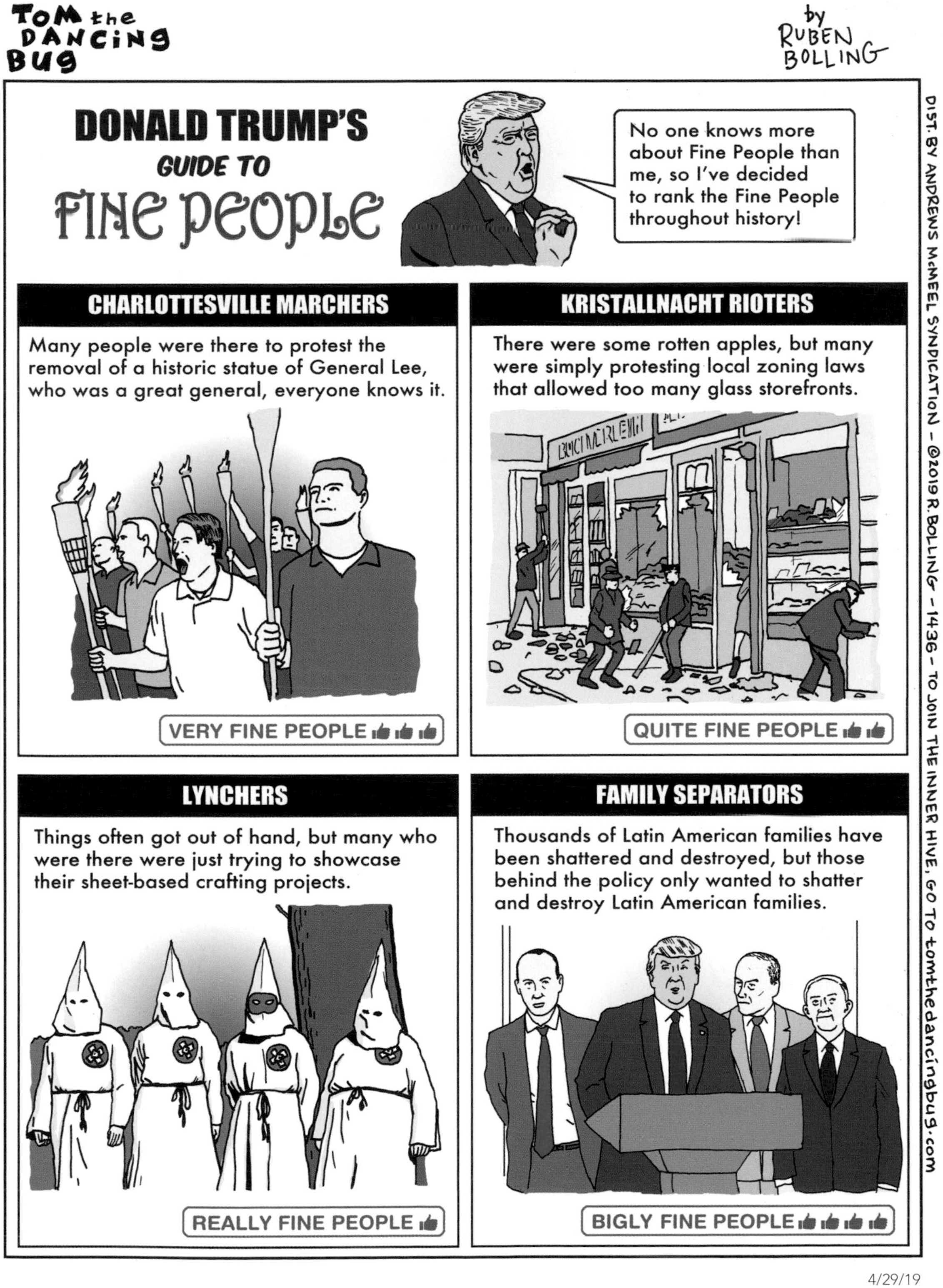

TOM the DANCING BUG
by RUBEN BOLLING
DONALD TRUMP'S GUIDE TO FINE PEOPLE
No one knows more about Fine People than me, so I've decided to rank the Fine People throughout history!
CHARLOTTESVILLE MARCHERS
Many people were there to protest the removal of a historic statue of General Lee, who was a great general, everyone knows it.
VERY FINE PEOPLE
KRISTALLNACHT RIOTERS
There were some rotten apples, but many were simply protesting local zoning laws that allowed too many glass storefronts.
QUITE FINE PEOPLE
LYNCHERS
Things often got out of hand, but many who were there were just trying to showcase their sheet-based crafting projects.
REALLY FINE PEOPLE
FAMILY SEPARATORS
Thousands of Latin American families have been shattered and destroyed, but those behind the policy only wanted to shatter and destroy Latin American families.
BIGLY FINE PEOPLE
DIST. BY ANDREWS McMEEL SYNDICATION – ©2019 R. BOLLING – 1436 – TO JOIN THE INNER HIVE, GO TO tomthedancingbug.com

4/29/19

TOM the DANCING BUG

by RUBEN BOLLING

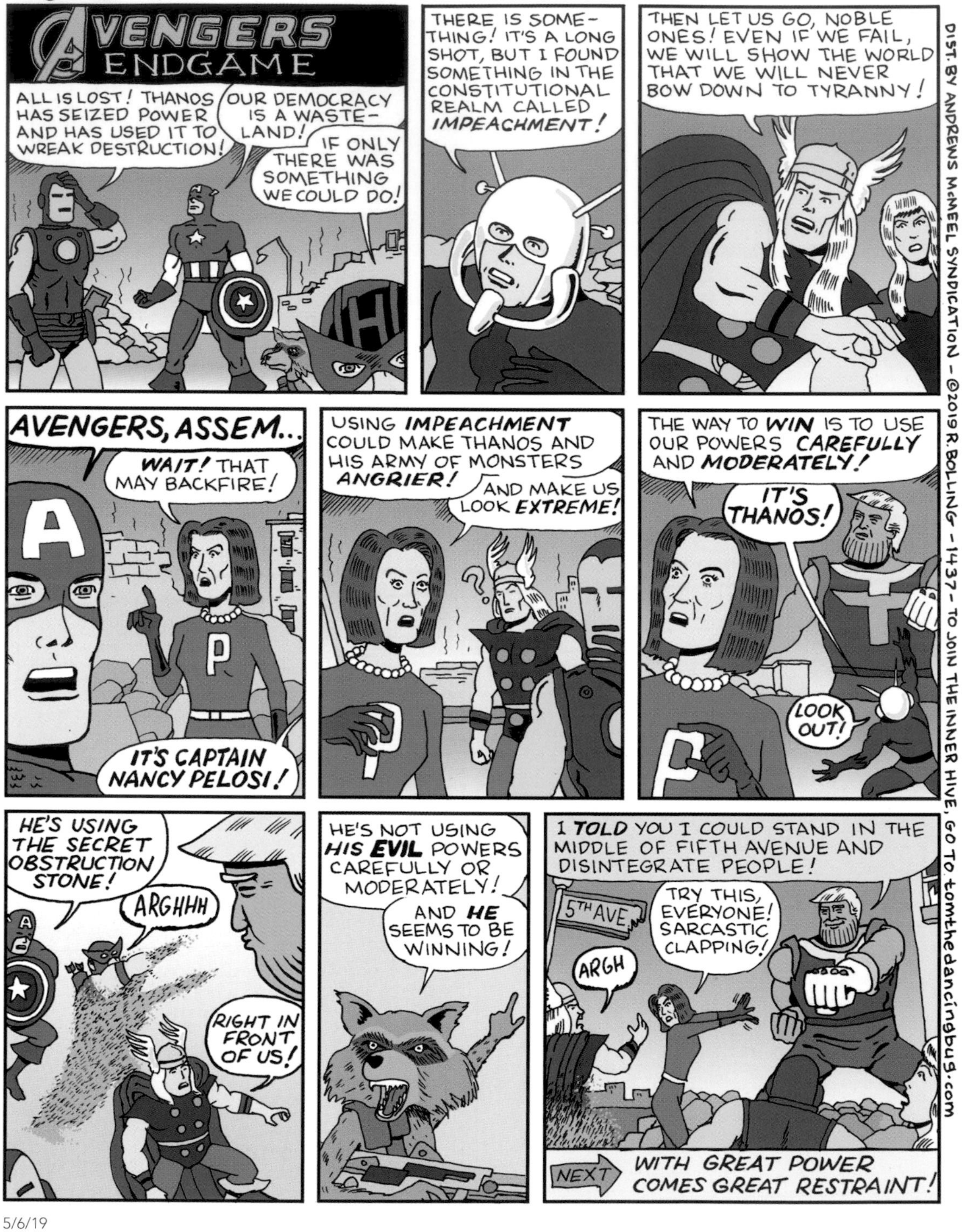

AVENGERS ENDGAME
ALL IS LOST! THANOS HAS SEIZED POWER AND HAS USED IT TO WREAK DESTRUCTION!
OUR DEMOCRACY IS A WASTE-LAND!
IF ONLY THERE WAS SOMETHING WE COULD DO!
THERE IS SOME-THING! IT'S A LONG SHOT, BUT I FOUND SOMETHING IN THE CONSTITUTIONAL REALM CALLED IMPEACHMENT!
THEN LET US GO, NOBLE ONES! EVEN IF WE FAIL, WE WILL SHOW THE WORLD THAT WE WILL NEVER BOW DOWN TO TYRANNY!
AVENGERS, ASSEM...
WAIT! THAT MAY BACKFIRE!
IT'S CAPTAIN NANCY PELOSI!
USING IMPEACHMENT COULD MAKE THANOS AND HIS ARMY OF MONSTERS ANGRIER!
AND MAKE US LOOK EXTREME!
THE WAY TO WIN IS TO USE OUR POWERS CAREFULLY AND MODERATELY!
IT'S THANOS!
LOOK OUT!
HE'S USING THE SECRET OBSTRUCTION STONE!
ARGHHH
RIGHT IN FRONT OF US!
HE'S NOT USING HIS EVIL POWERS CAREFULLY OR MODERATELY!
AND HE SEEMS TO BE WINNING!
I TOLD YOU I COULD STAND IN THE MIDDLE OF FIFTH AVENUE AND DISINTEGRATE PEOPLE!
5TH AVE
TRY THIS, EVERYONE! SARCASTIC CLAPPING!
ARGH
NEXT WITH GREAT POWER COMES GREAT RESTRAINT!
DIST. BY ANDREWS McMEEL SYNDICATION - ©2019 R. BOLLING - 1437 - TO JOIN THE INNER HIVE, GO TO tomthedancingbug.com

5/6/19

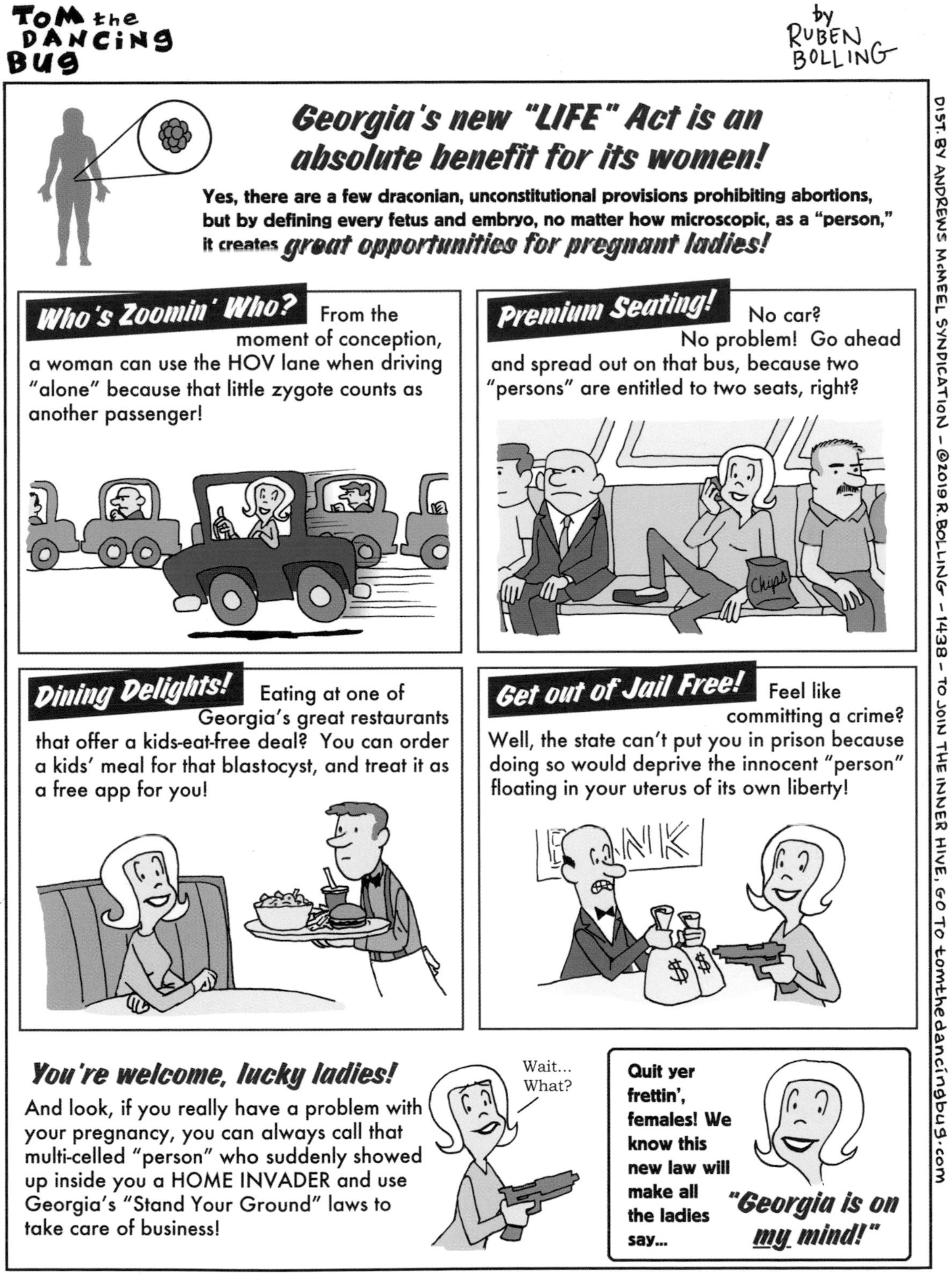

TOM the DANCING BUG
by RUBEN BOLLING
Georgia's new "LIFE" Act is an absolute benefit for its women!
Yes, there are a few draconian, unconstitutional provisions prohibiting abortions, but by defining every fetus and embryo, no matter how microscopic, as a "person," it creates great opportunities for pregnant ladies!
Who's Zoomin' Who?
From the moment of conception, a woman can use the HOV lane when driving "alone" because that little zygote counts as another passenger!
Premium Seating!
No car? No problem! Go ahead and spread out on that bus, because two "persons" are entitled to two seats, right?
Chips
Dining Delights!
Eating at one of Georgia's great restaurants that offer a kids-eat-free deal? You can order a kids' meal for that blastocyst, and treat it as a free app for you!
Get out of Jail Free!
Feel like committing a crime? Well, the state can't put you in prison because doing so would deprive the innocent "person" floating in your uterus of its own liberty!
BANK
You're welcome, lucky ladies!
And look, if you really have a problem with your pregnancy, you can always call that multi-celled "person" who suddenly showed up inside you a HOME INVADER and use Georgia's "Stand Your Ground" laws to take care of business!
Wait... What?
Quit yer frettin', females! We know this new law will make all the ladies say...
"Georgia is on my mind!"
DIST. BY ANDREWS McMEEL SYNDICATION – ©2019 R. BOLLING – 1438 – TO JOIN THE INNER HIVE, GO TO tomthedancingbug.com

5/13/19

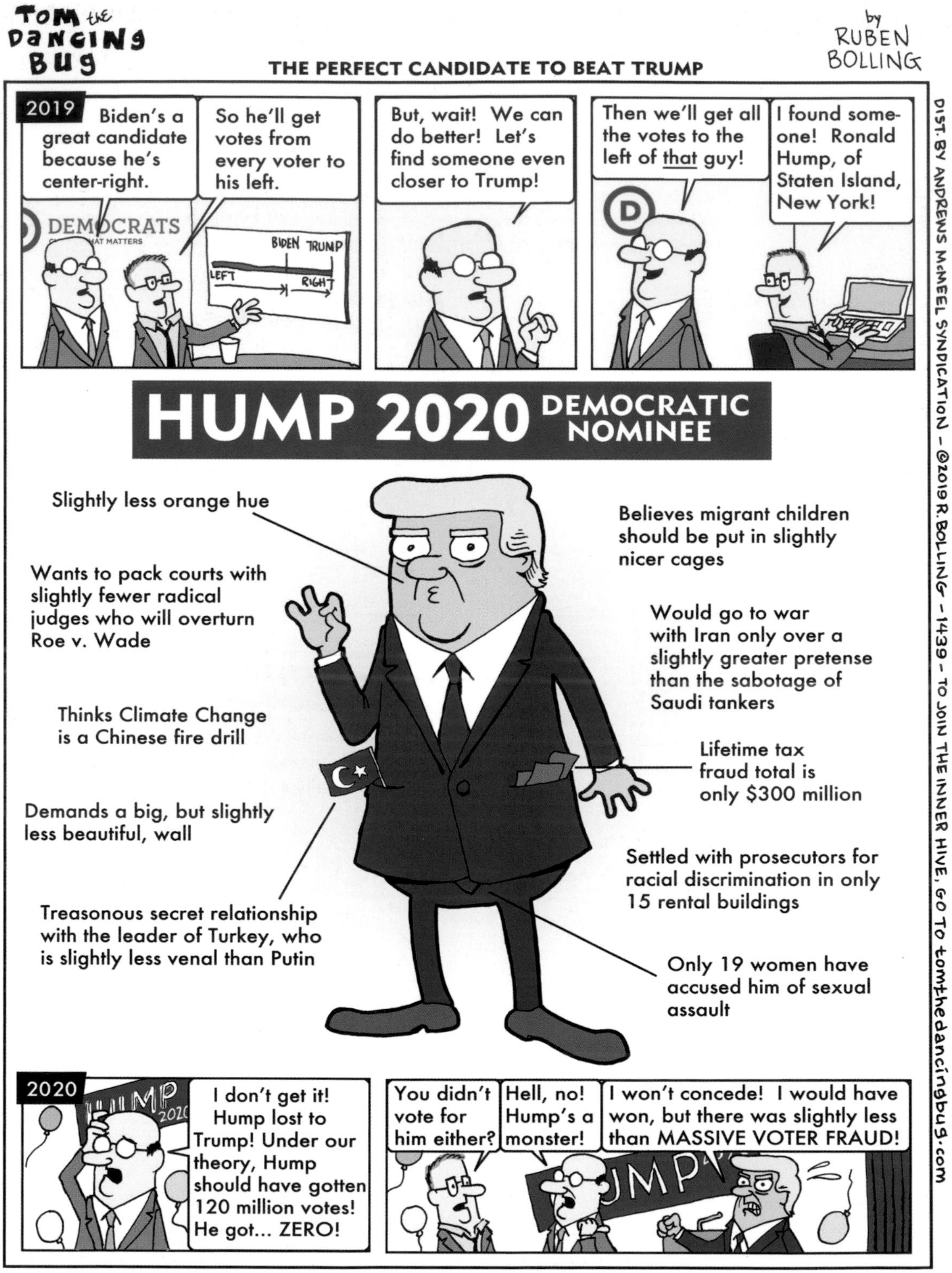

TOM the DANCING BUG
by RUBEN BOLLING
THE PERFECT CANDIDATE TO BEAT TRUMP
2019
Biden's a great candidate because he's center-right.
So he'll get votes from every voter to his left.
DEMOCRATS
BIDEN
TRUMP
LEFT
RIGHT
But, wait! We can do better! Let's find someone even closer to Trump!
Then we'll get all the votes to the left of that guy!
I found some-one! Ronald Hump, of Staten Island, New York!
HUMP 2020 DEMOCRATIC NOMINEE
Slightly less orange hue
Wants to pack courts with slightly fewer radical judges who will overturn Roe v. Wade
Thinks Climate Change is a Chinese fire drill
Demands a big, but slightly less beautiful, wall
Treasonous secret relationship with the leader of Turkey, who is slightly less venal than Putin
Believes migrant children should be put in slightly nicer cages
Would go to war with Iran only over a slightly greater pretense than the sabotage of Saudi tankers
Lifetime tax fraud total is only $300 million
Settled with prosecutors for racial discrimination in only 15 rental buildings
Only 19 women have accused him of sexual assault
2020
HUMP 2020
I don't get it! Hump lost to Trump! Under our theory, Hump should have gotten 120 million votes! He got... ZERO!
You didn't vote for him either?
Hell, no! Hump's a monster!
I won't concede! I would have won, but there was slightly less than MASSIVE VOTER FRAUD!
DIST. BY ANDREWS McMEEL SYNDICATION – ©2019 R. BOLLING – 1439 – TO JOIN THE INNER HIVE, GO TO tomthedancingbug.com

5/20/19

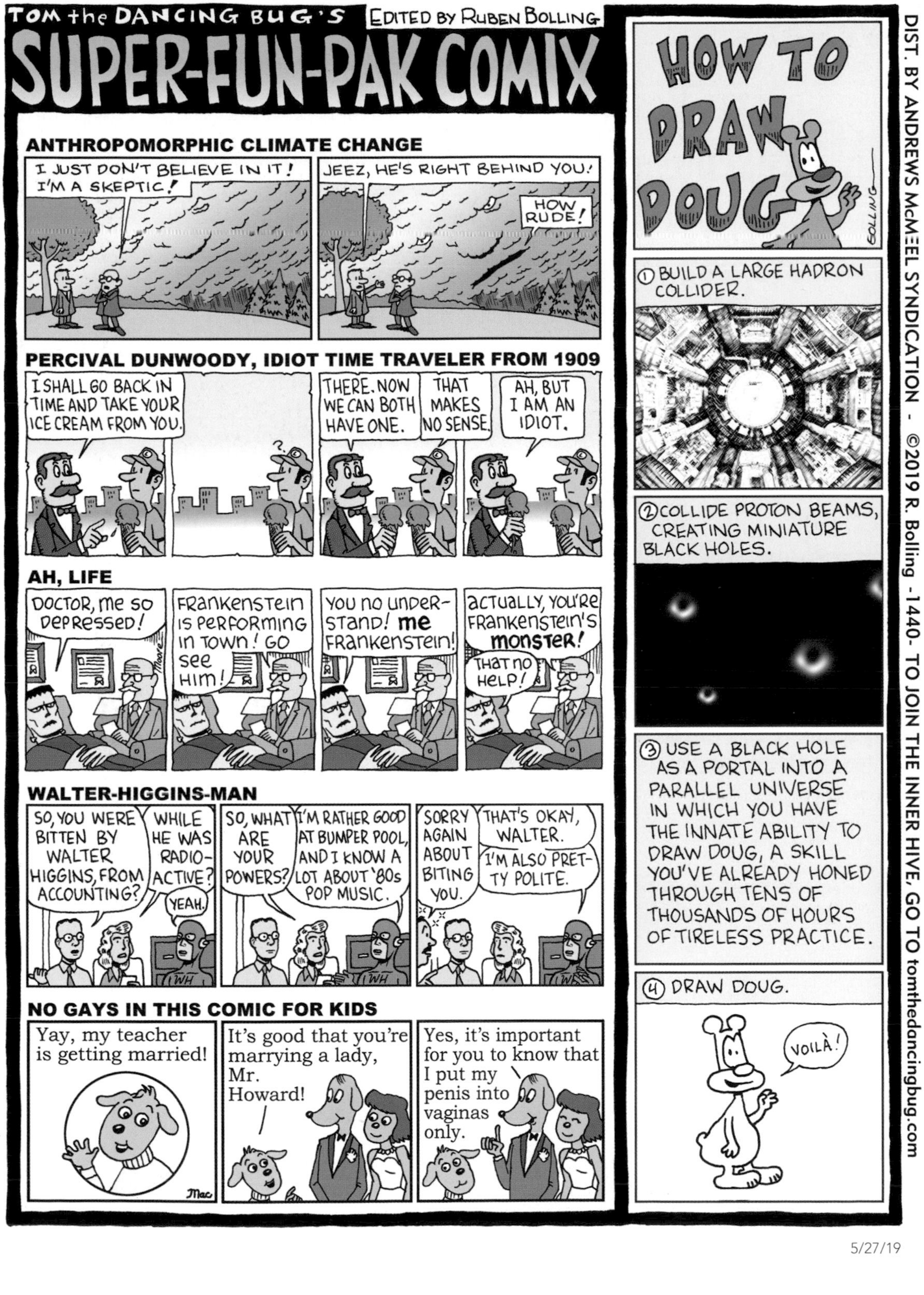
TOM the DANCING BUG'S
EDITED BY RUBEN BOLLING
SUPER-FUN-PAK COMIX
ANTHROPOMORPHIC CLIMATE CHANGE
I JUST DON'T BELIEVE IN IT! I'M A SKEPTIC!
JEEZ, HE'S RIGHT BEHIND YOU!
HOW RUDE!
PERCIVAL DUNWOODY, IDIOT TIME TRAVELER FROM 1909
I SHALL GO BACK IN TIME AND TAKE YOUR ICE CREAM FROM YOU.
THERE. NOW WE CAN BOTH HAVE ONE.
THAT MAKES NO SENSE.
AH, BUT I AM AN IDIOT.
AH, LIFE
DOCTOR, ME SO DEPRESSED!
FRANKENSTEIN IS PERFORMING IN TOWN! GO SEE HIM!
YOU NO UNDERSTAND! ME FRANKENSTEIN!
ACTUALLY, YOU'RE FRANKENSTEIN'S MONSTER!
THAT NO HELP!
WALTER-HIGGINS-MAN
SO, YOU WERE BITTEN BY WALTER HIGGINS, FROM ACCOUNTING?
WHILE HE WAS RADIO-ACTIVE?
YEAH.
SO, WHAT ARE YOUR POWERS?
I'M RATHER GOOD AT BUMPER POOL, AND I KNOW A LOT ABOUT '80s POP MUSIC.
SORRY AGAIN ABOUT BITING YOU.
THAT'S OKAY, WALTER.
I'M ALSO PRETTY POLITE.
NO GAYS IN THIS COMIC FOR KIDS
Yay, my teacher is getting married!
It's good that you're marrying a lady, Mr. Howard!
Yes, it's important for you to know that I put my penis into vaginas only.
HOW TO DRAW DOUG
① BUILD A LARGE HADRON COLLIDER.
② COLLIDE PROTON BEAMS, CREATING MINIATURE BLACK HOLES.
③ USE A BLACK HOLE AS A PORTAL INTO A PARALLEL UNIVERSE IN WHICH YOU HAVE THE INNATE ABILITY TO DRAW DOUG, A SKILL YOU'VE ALREADY HONED THROUGH TENS OF THOUSANDS OF HOURS OF TIRELESS PRACTICE.
④ DRAW DOUG.
VOILÀ!
DIST. BY ANDREWS McMEEL SYNDICATION - ©2019 R. Bolling - 1440- TO JOIN THE INNER HIVE, GO TO tomthedancingbug.com

5/27/19

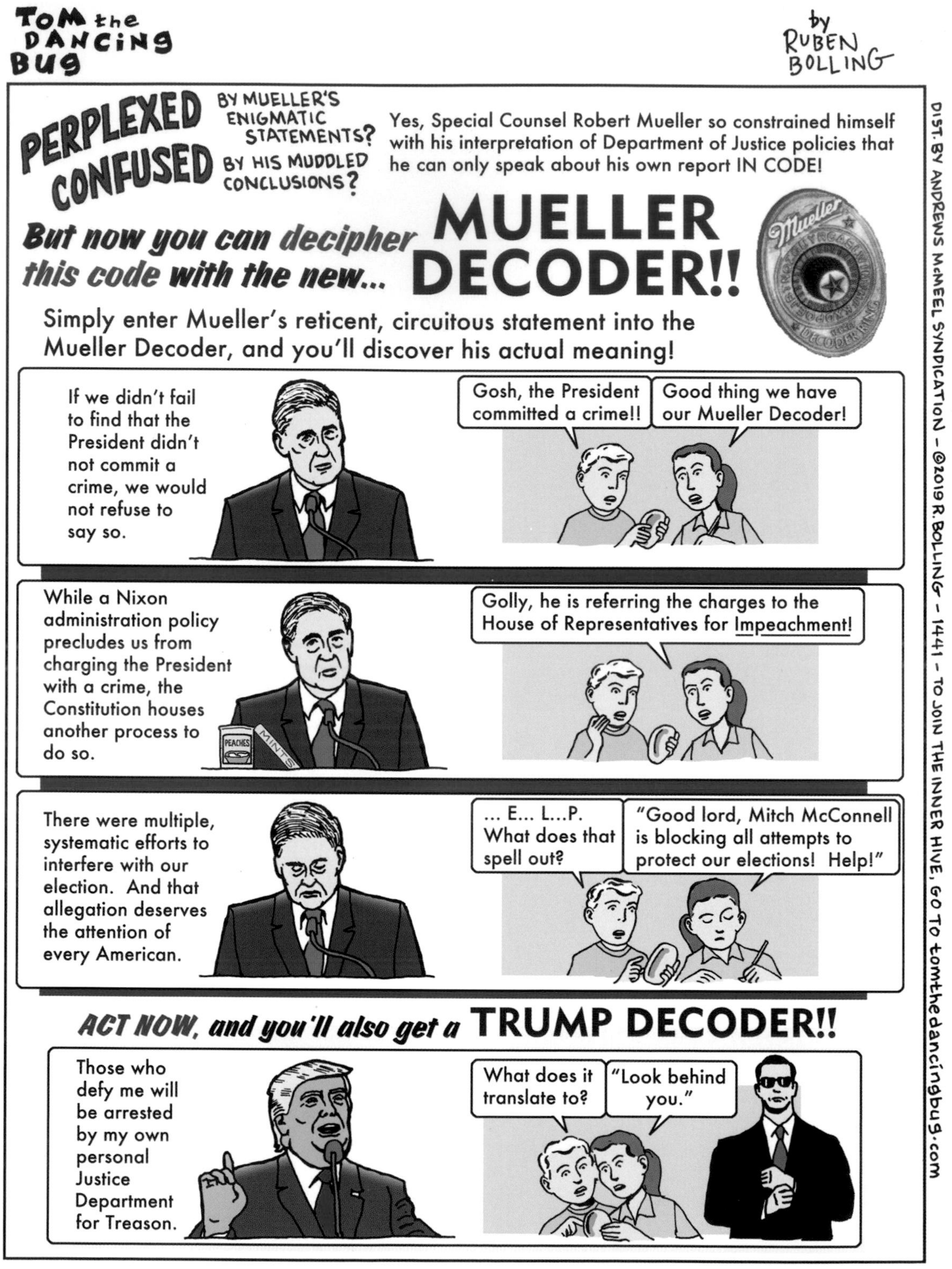
TOM the DANCING BUG
by RUBEN BOLLING
PERPLEXED BY MUELLER'S ENIGMATIC STATEMENTS?
CONFUSED BY HIS MUDDLED CONCLUSIONS?
Yes, Special Counsel Robert Mueller so constrained himself with his interpretation of Department of Justice policies that he can only speak about his own report IN CODE!
But now you can decipher this code with the new... MUELLER DECODER!!
Simply enter Mueller's reticent, circuitous statement into the Mueller Decoder, and you'll discover his actual meaning!
If we didn't fail to find that the President didn't not commit a crime, we would not refuse to say so.
Gosh, the President committed a crime!!
Good thing we have our Mueller Decoder!
While a Nixon administration policy precludes us from charging the President with a crime, the Constitution houses another process to do so.
PEACHES
MINTS
Golly, he is referring the charges to the House of Representatives for Impeachment!
There were multiple, systematic efforts to interfere with our election. And that allegation deserves the attention of every American.
... E... L...P. What does that spell out?
"Good lord, Mitch McConnell is blocking all attempts to protect our elections! Help!"
ACT NOW, and you'll also get a TRUMP DECODER!!
Those who defy me will be arrested by my own personal Justice Department for Treason.
What does it translate to?
"Look behind you."
DIST. BY ANDREWS McMEEL SYNDICATION – ©2019 R. BOLLING – 1441 – TO JOIN THE INNER HIVE, GO TO tomthedancingbug.com

6/3/19

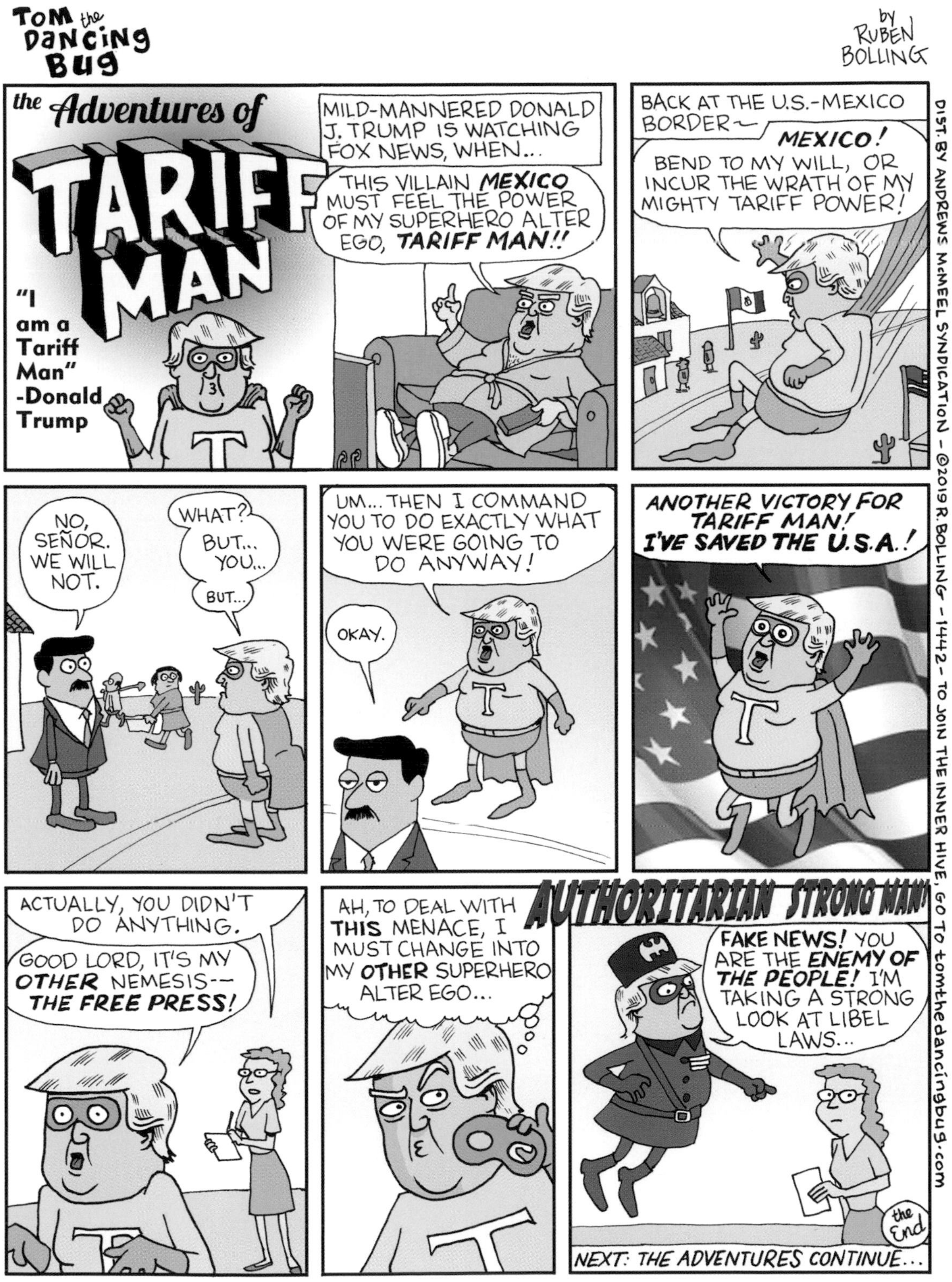
TOM the DANCING BUG
by RUBEN BOLLING
the Adventures of TARIFF MAN
"I am a Tariff Man" -Donald Trump
MILD-MANNERED DONALD J. TRUMP IS WATCHING FOX NEWS, WHEN...
THIS VILLAIN MEXICO MUST FEEL THE POWER OF MY SUPERHERO ALTER EGO, TARIFF MAN!!
BACK AT THE U.S.-MEXICO BORDER—
MEXICO! BEND TO MY WILL, OR INCUR THE WRATH OF MY MIGHTY TARIFF POWER!
NO, SEÑOR. WE WILL NOT.
WHAT? BUT... YOU...
BUT...
UM... THEN I COMMAND YOU TO DO EXACTLY WHAT YOU WERE GOING TO DO ANYWAY!
OKAY.
ANOTHER VICTORY FOR TARIFF MAN! I'VE SAVED THE U.S.A.!
ACTUALLY, YOU DIDN'T DO ANYTHING.
GOOD LORD, IT'S MY OTHER NEMESIS— THE FREE PRESS!
AH, TO DEAL WITH THIS MENACE, I MUST CHANGE INTO MY OTHER SUPERHERO ALTER EGO...
AUTHORITARIAN STRONG MAN!
FAKE NEWS! YOU ARE THE ENEMY OF THE PEOPLE! I'M TAKING A STRONG LOOK AT LIBEL LAWS...
the End
NEXT: THE ADVENTURES CONTINUE...
DIST. BY ANDREWS McMEEL SYNDICATION – ©2019 R. BOLLING – 1442 – TO JOIN THE INNER HIVE, GO TO tomthedancingbug.com

6/10/19

TOM the DANCING BUG PRESENTS:

BY RUBEN BOLLING

NEWS of the TIMES

Trump Welcomes Russian Ground Troops into U.S.A.

IN WHAT SOME CRITICS ARE CALLING AN "INVASION," RUSSIAN FORCES HAVE ENTERED THE U.S. AND SEIZED CONTROL OF MILITARY BASES AND GOVERNMENT BUILDINGS. PRESIDENT TRUMP ANGRILY DENIES THAT CHARACTERIZATION.

NOT AN INVASION. NO INVASION. ALL THE BEST PEOPLE ARE SAYING IT'S NOT AN ANNEXATION.

IN A CONTROVERSIAL MOVE, TRUMP NAMED VLADIMIR PUTIN CHANCELLOR OF THE UNITED STATES.

I HAPPEN TO THINK HAVING A BETTER RELATIONSHIP WITH PUTIN IS A **GOOD** THING!

TRUMP'S APPROVAL RATING DROPPED ONLY TWO POINTS, TO 39%.

GOD BLESS DONALD TRUMP. LET THE SNOWFLAKES WHINE ABOUT WHICH RUSSIAN TROOPS ARE RAPING THIS OR PILLAGING THAT.

USA

COINCIDENTALLY, JUST PRIOR TO THE RUSSIAN TROOPS' ARRIVAL, A RUSSIAN OLIGARCH BOUGHT A CONDO FROM TRUMP FOR $2.6 MILLION.

HERE ARE THE "KEYS."

SERIOUSLY? THIS ALL IT TAKES? IS VERY CHEAP!

ROBERT MUELLER WAS ENLISTED TO INVESTIGATE THE ALLEGATION THAT TRUMP IS A TRAITOR, AND THEN SUBMITTED HIS REPORT.

I REFER TO FOOTNOTE 273: IF WE FOUND NO TREASON, WE WOULD NOT DECLINE TO NOT...

NO TRAITOR! NO TREASON! WITCH HUNT! NEXT!

TMENT OF JUSTICE SHINGTO

BELIEVE ME, DEMOCRATS WOULD DO THE SAME THING.

WE DEMONSTRABLY WOULD NOT!

ЯƎƐDUCAT CAMP

'6/17/19

DIST. BY ANDREWS McMEEL SYNDICATION ~ ©2019 R.BOLLING ~ 1443 ~ TO JOIN THE INNER HIVE, GO TO tomthedancingbug.com

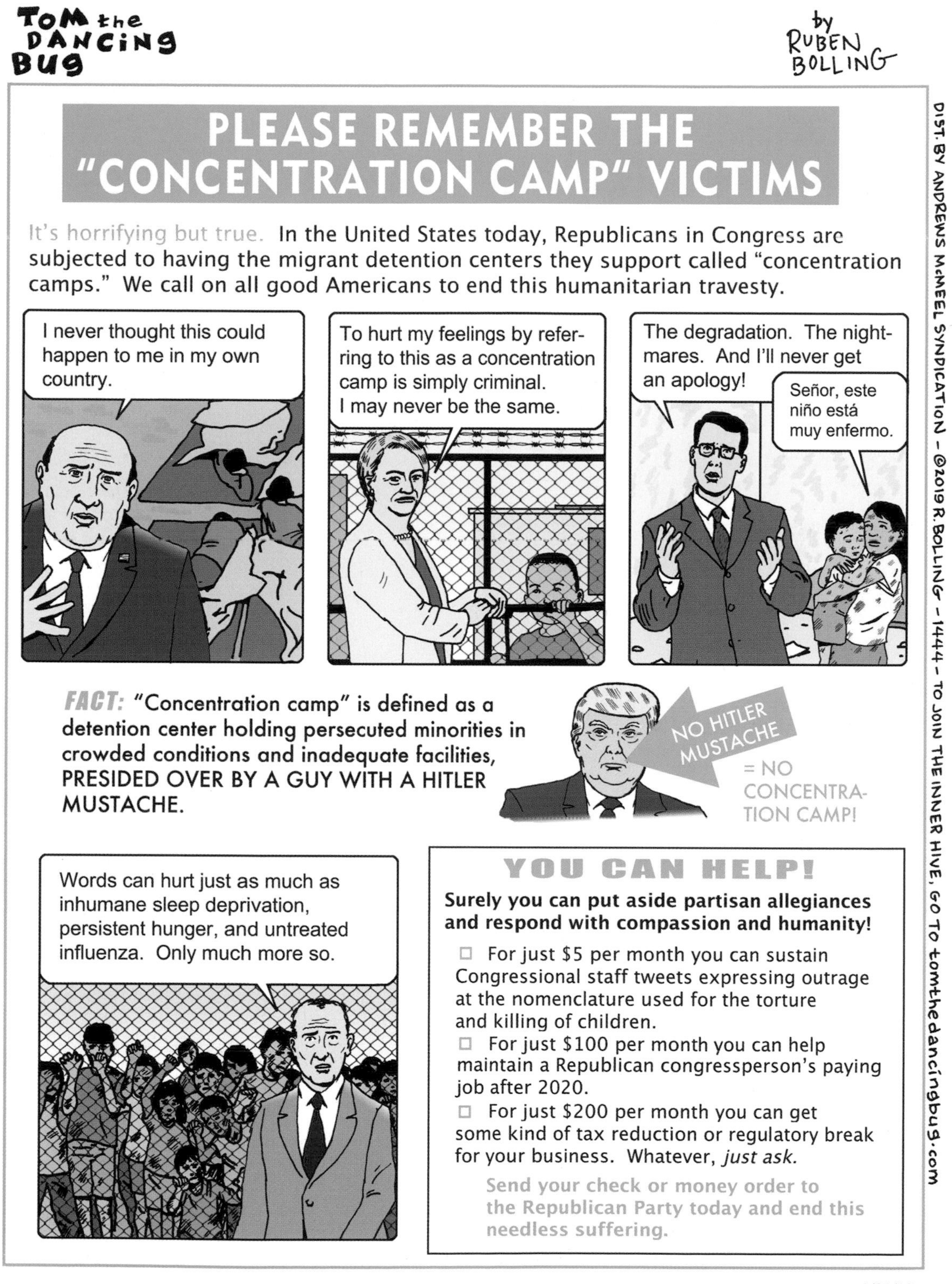
TOM the DANCING BUG
by RUBEN BOLLING
PLEASE REMEMBER THE "CONCENTRATION CAMP" VICTIMS
It's horrifying but true. In the United States today, Republicans in Congress are subjected to having the migrant detention centers they support called "concentration camps." We call on all good Americans to end this humanitarian travesty.
I never thought this could happen to me in my own country.
To hurt my feelings by referring to this as a concentration camp is simply criminal. I may never be the same.
The degradation. The nightmares. And I'll never get an apology!
Señor, este niño está muy enfermo.
FACT: "Concentration camp" is defined as a detention center holding persecuted minorities in crowded conditions and inadequate facilities, PRESIDED OVER BY A GUY WITH A HITLER MUSTACHE.
NO HITLER MUSTACHE
= NO CONCENTRATION CAMP!
Words can hurt just as much as inhumane sleep deprivation, persistent hunger, and untreated influenza. Only much more so.
YOU CAN HELP!
Surely you can put aside partisan allegiances and respond with compassion and humanity!
☐ For just $5 per month you can sustain Congressional staff tweets expressing outrage at the nomenclature used for the torture and killing of children.
☐ For just $100 per month you can help maintain a Republican congressperson's paying job after 2020.
☐ For just $200 per month you can get some kind of tax reduction or regulatory break for your business. Whatever, *just ask.*
Send your check or money order to the Republican Party today and end this needless suffering.
DIST. BY ANDREWS McMEEL SYNDICATION – ©2019 R. BOLLING – 1444 – TO JOIN THE INNER HIVE, GO TO tomthedancingbug.com

6/24/19

TOM the DANCING BUG

by RUBEN BOLLING

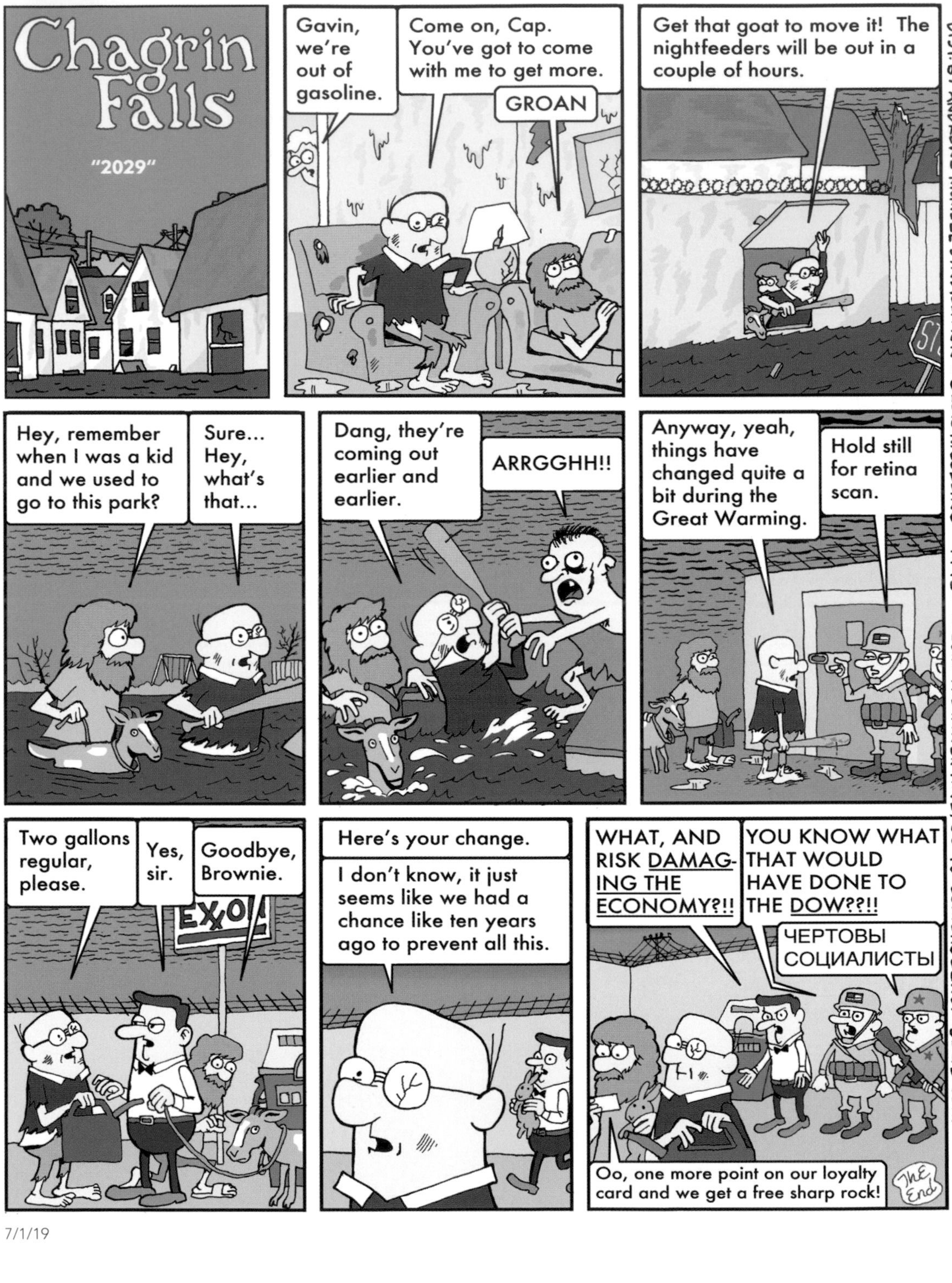

Chagrin Falls
"2029"
Gavin, we're out of gasoline.
Come on, Cap. You've got to come with me to get more.
GROAN
Get that goat to move it! The nightfeeders will be out in a couple of hours.
STO
Hey, remember when I was a kid and we used to go to this park?
Sure... Hey, what's that...
Dang, they're coming out earlier and earlier.
ARRGGHH!!
Anyway, yeah, things have changed quite a bit during the Great Warming.
Hold still for retina scan.
Two gallons regular, please.
Yes, sir.
Goodbye, Brownie.
EXXON
Here's your change.
I don't know, it just seems like we had a chance like ten years ago to prevent all this.
WHAT, AND RISK DAMAGING THE ECONOMY?!!
YOU KNOW WHAT THAT WOULD HAVE DONE TO THE DOW??!!
ЧЕРТОВЫ СОЦИАЛИСТЫ
Oo, one more point on our loyalty card and we get a free sharp rock!
THE End

7/1/19

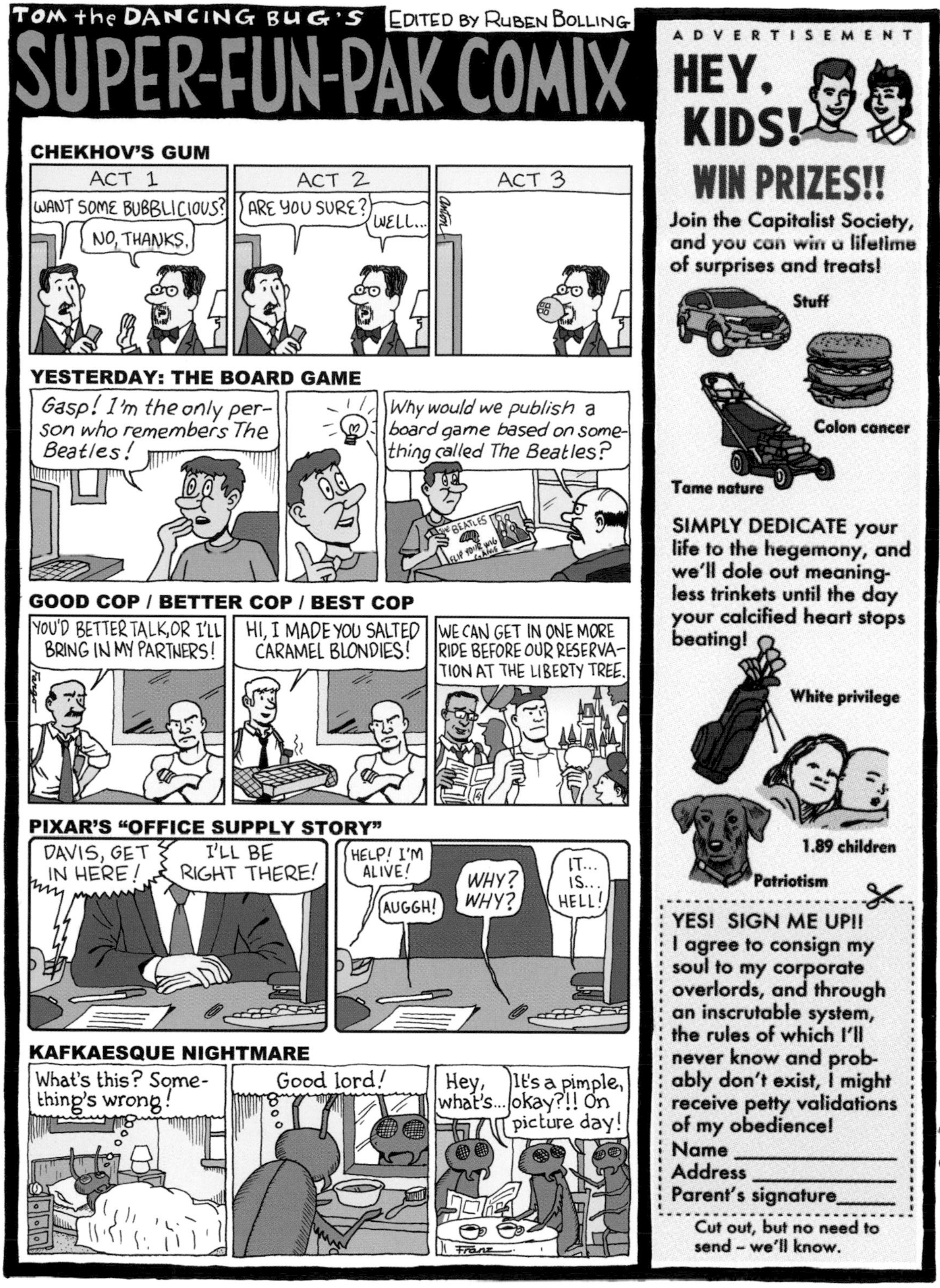
TOM the DANCING BUG'S
EDITED BY RUBEN BOLLING
SUPER-FUN-PAK COMIX
CHEKHOV'S GUM
ACT 1
WANT SOME BUBBLICIOUS?
NO, THANKS.
ACT 2
ARE YOU SURE?
WELL...
ACT 3
YESTERDAY: THE BOARD GAME
Gasp! I'm the only person who remembers The Beatles!
Why would we publish a board game based on something called The Beatles?
THE BEATLES
FLIP YOUR WIG
GOOD COP / BETTER COP / BEST COP
YOU'D BETTER TALK, OR I'LL BRING IN MY PARTNERS!
HI, I MADE YOU SALTED CARAMEL BLONDIES!
WE CAN GET IN ONE MORE RIDE BEFORE OUR RESERVATION AT THE LIBERTY TREE.
PIXAR'S "OFFICE SUPPLY STORY"
DAVIS, GET IN HERE!
I'LL BE RIGHT THERE!
HELP! I'M ALIVE!
AUGGH!
WHY? WHY?
IT... IS... HELL!
KAFKAESQUE NIGHTMARE
What's this? Something's wrong!
Good lord!
Hey, what's...
It's a pimple, okay?!! On picture day!
ADVERTISEMENT
HEY, KIDS!
WIN PRIZES!!
Join the Capitalist Society, and you can win a lifetime of surprises and treats!
Stuff
Colon cancer
Tame nature
SIMPLY DEDICATE your life to the hegemony, and we'll dole out meaningless trinkets until the day your calcified heart stops beating!
White privilege
1.89 children
Patriotism
YES! SIGN ME UP!!
I agree to consign my soul to my corporate overlords, and through an inscrutable system, the rules of which I'll never know and probably don't exist, I might receive petty validations of my obedience!
Name ____________
Address ____________
Parent's signature______
Cut out, but no need to send – we'll know.

7/8/19

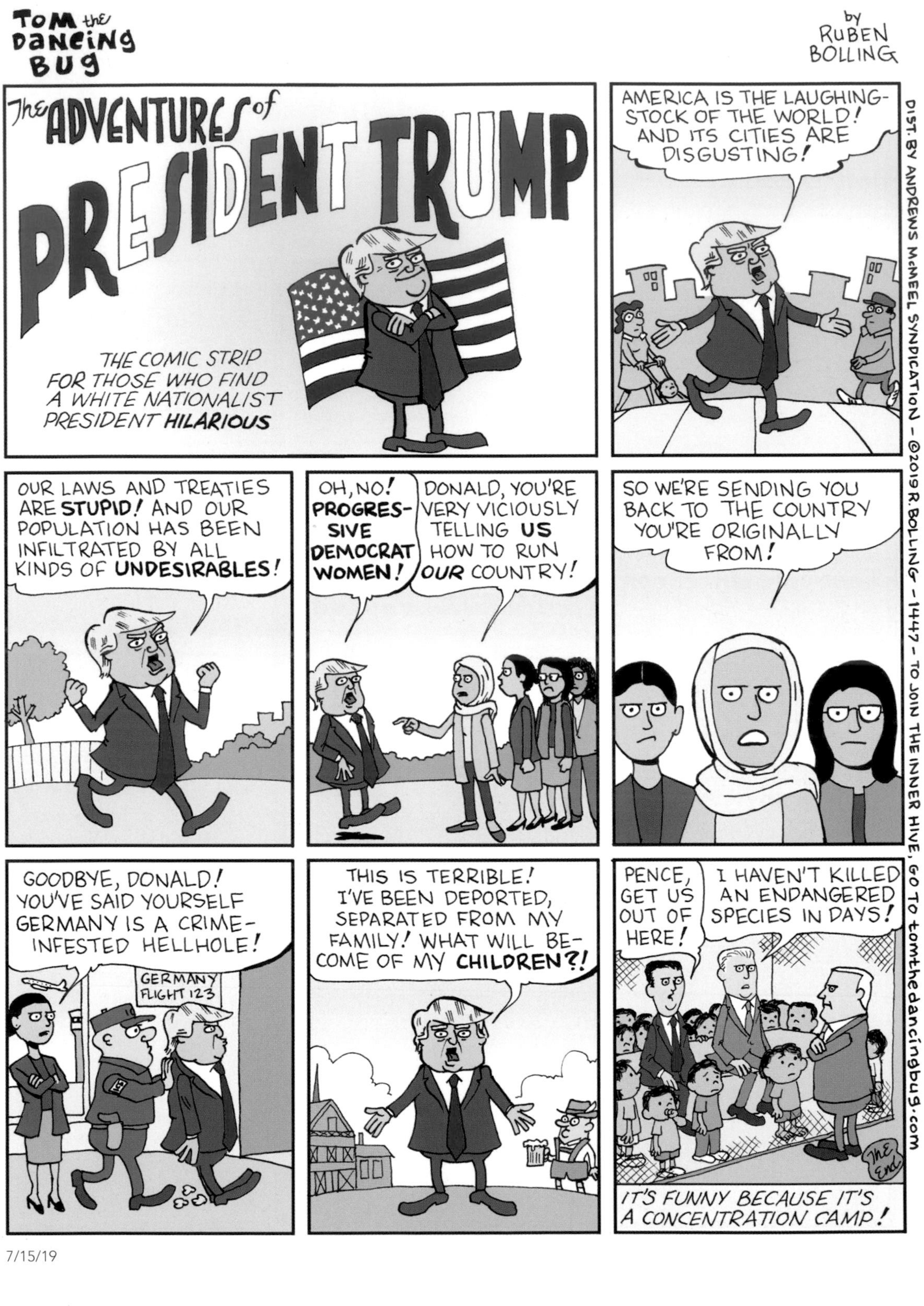
TOM the DANCING BUG
by RUBEN BOLLING
The ADVENTURES of PRESIDENT TRUMP
THE COMIC STRIP FOR THOSE WHO FIND A WHITE NATIONALIST PRESIDENT HILARIOUS
AMERICA IS THE LAUGHING-STOCK OF THE WORLD! AND ITS CITIES ARE DISGUSTING!
DIST. BY ANDREWS McMEEL SYNDICATION – ©2019 R. BOLLING – 1447 – TO JOIN THE INNER HIVE, GO TO tomthedancingbug.com
OUR LAWS AND TREATIES ARE STUPID! AND OUR POPULATION HAS BEEN INFILTRATED BY ALL KINDS OF UNDESIRABLES!
OH, NO! PROGRES-SIVE DEMOCRAT WOMEN!
DONALD, YOU'RE VERY VICIOUSLY TELLING US HOW TO RUN OUR COUNTRY!
SO WE'RE SENDING YOU BACK TO THE COUNTRY YOU'RE ORIGINALLY FROM!
GOODBYE, DONALD! YOU'VE SAID YOURSELF GERMANY IS A CRIME-INFESTED HELLHOLE!
GERMANY FLIGHT 123
THIS IS TERRIBLE! I'VE BEEN DEPORTED, SEPARATED FROM MY FAMILY! WHAT WILL BE-COME OF MY CHILDREN?!
PENCE, GET US OUT OF HERE!
I HAVEN'T KILLED AN ENDANGERED SPECIES IN DAYS!
THE END
IT'S FUNNY BECAUSE IT'S A CONCENTRATION CAMP!

7/15/19

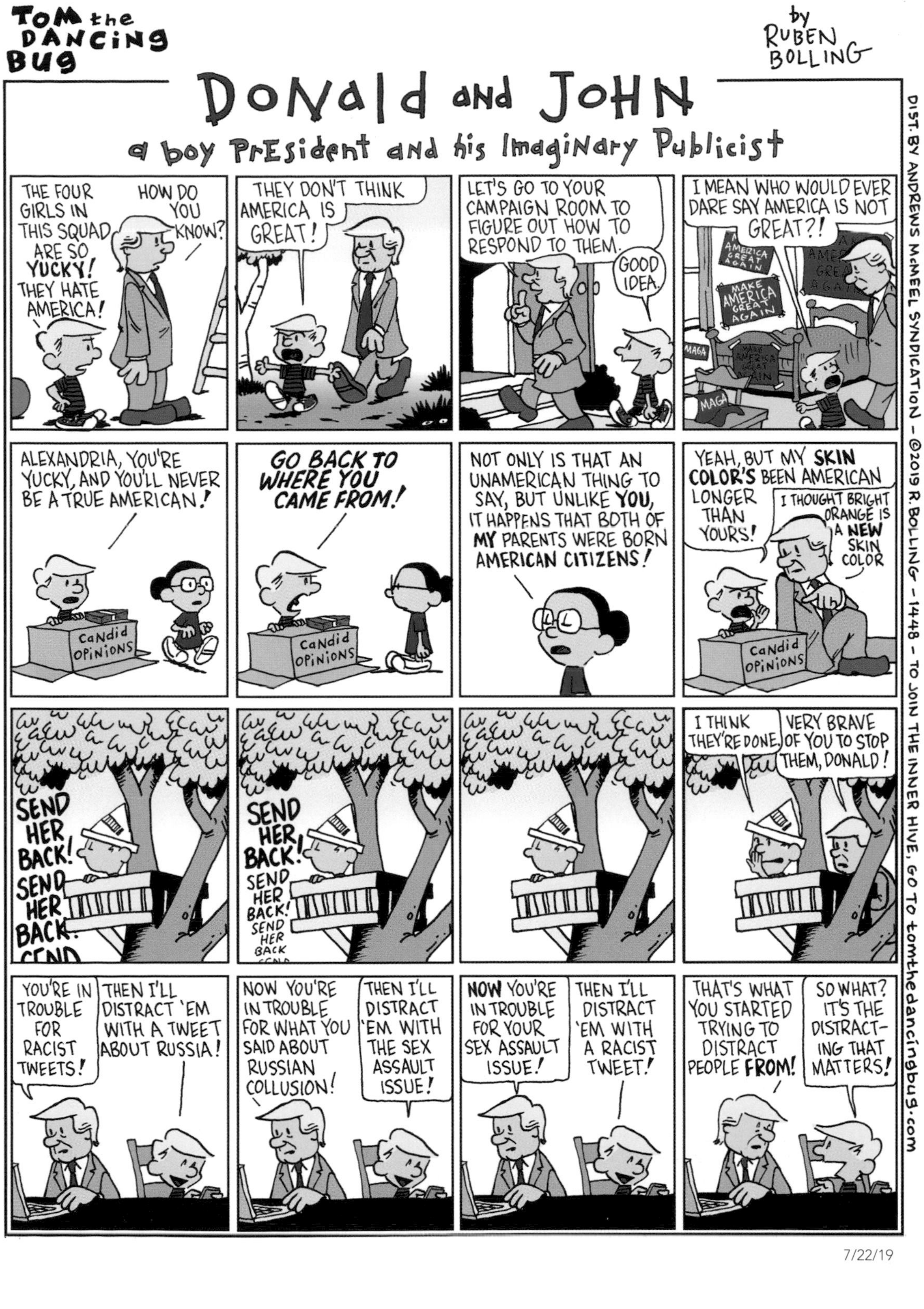
TOM the DANCING BUG
by RUBEN BOLLING
DONALD and JOHN
a boy President and his Imaginary Publicist
THE FOUR GIRLS IN THIS SQUAD ARE SO YUCKY! THEY HATE AMERICA!
HOW DO YOU KNOW?
THEY DON'T THINK AMERICA IS GREAT!
LET'S GO TO YOUR CAMPAIGN ROOM TO FIGURE OUT HOW TO RESPOND TO THEM.
GOOD IDEA.
I MEAN WHO WOULD EVER DARE SAY AMERICA IS NOT GREAT?!
MAKE AMERICA GREAT AGAIN
MAGA
ALEXANDRIA, YOU'RE YUCKY, AND YOU'LL NEVER BE A TRUE AMERICAN!
CANDID OPINIONS
GO BACK TO WHERE YOU CAME FROM!
NOT ONLY IS THAT AN UNAMERICAN THING TO SAY, BUT UNLIKE YOU, IT HAPPENS THAT BOTH OF MY PARENTS WERE BORN AMERICAN CITIZENS!
YEAH, BUT MY SKIN COLOR'S BEEN AMERICAN LONGER THAN YOURS!
I THOUGHT BRIGHT ORANGE IS A NEW SKIN COLOR
SEND HER BACK! SEND HER BACK!
SEND HER BACK! SEND HER BACK! SEND HER BACK
I THINK THEY'RE DONE.
VERY BRAVE OF YOU TO STOP THEM, DONALD!
YOU'RE IN TROUBLE FOR RACIST TWEETS!
THEN I'LL DISTRACT 'EM WITH A TWEET ABOUT RUSSIA!
NOW YOU'RE IN TROUBLE FOR WHAT YOU SAID ABOUT RUSSIAN COLLUSION!
THEN I'LL DISTRACT 'EM WITH THE SEX ASSAULT ISSUE!
NOW YOU'RE IN TROUBLE FOR YOUR SEX ASSAULT ISSUE!
THEN I'LL DISTRACT 'EM WITH A RACIST TWEET!
THAT'S WHAT YOU STARTED TRYING TO DISTRACT PEOPLE FROM!
SO WHAT? IT'S THE DISTRACTING THAT MATTERS!
DIST. BY ANDREWS McMEEL SYNDICATION – ©2019 R. BOLLING – 1448 – TO JOIN THE INNER HIVE, GO TO tomthedancingbug.com

7/22/19

TOM the DANCING BUG

by RUBEN BOLLING

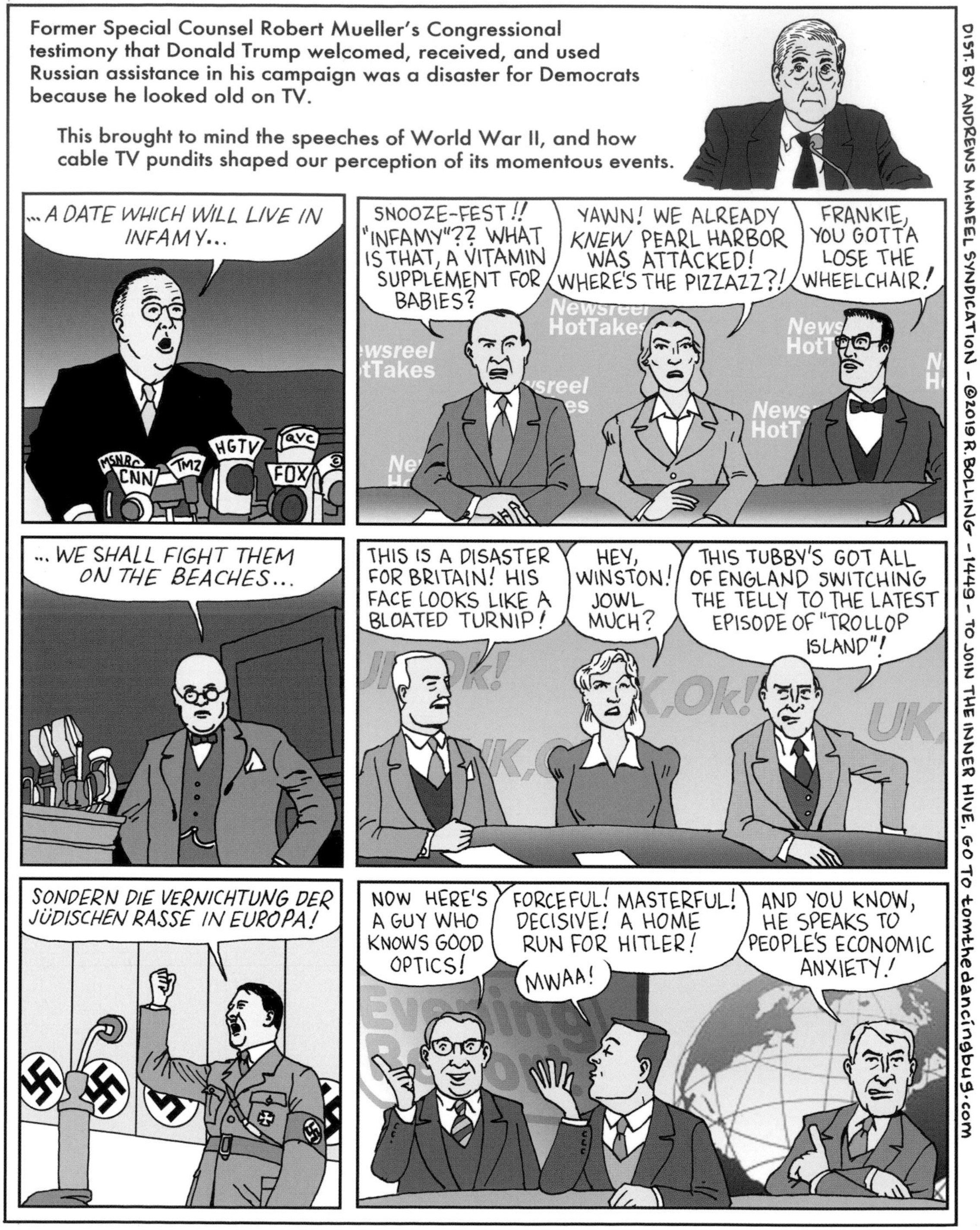
Former Special Counsel Robert Mueller's Congressional testimony that Donald Trump welcomed, received, and used Russian assistance in his campaign was a disaster for Democrats because he looked old on TV.
This brought to mind the speeches of World War II, and how cable TV pundits shaped our perception of its momentous events.
...A DATE WHICH WILL LIVE IN INFAMY...
MSNBC
CNN
TMZ
HGTV
QVC
FOX
SNOOZE-FEST!! "INFAMY"?? WHAT IS THAT, A VITAMIN SUPPLEMENT FOR BABIES?
YAWN! WE ALREADY KNEW PEARL HARBOR WAS ATTACKED! WHERE'S THE PIZZAZZ?!
FRANKIE, YOU GOTTA LOSE THE WHEELCHAIR!
Newsreel HotTakes
...WE SHALL FIGHT THEM ON THE BEACHES...
THIS IS A DISASTER FOR BRITAIN! HIS FACE LOOKS LIKE A BLOATED TURNIP!
HEY, WINSTON! JOWL MUCH?
THIS TUBBY'S GOT ALL OF ENGLAND SWITCHING THE TELLY TO THE LATEST EPISODE OF "TROLLOP ISLAND"!
UK,Ok!
SONDERN DIE VERNICHTUNG DER JÜDISCHEN RASSE IN EUROPA!
NOW HERE'S A GUY WHO KNOWS GOOD OPTICS!
FORCEFUL! MASTERFUL! DECISIVE! A HOME RUN FOR HITLER!
MWAA!
AND YOU KNOW, HE SPEAKS TO PEOPLE'S ECONOMIC ANXIETY!
Evening! Report
DIST. BY ANDREWS McMEEL SYNDICATION – ©2019 R. BOLLING – 1449 – TO JOIN THE INNER HIVE, GO TO tomthedancingbug.com

7/29/19

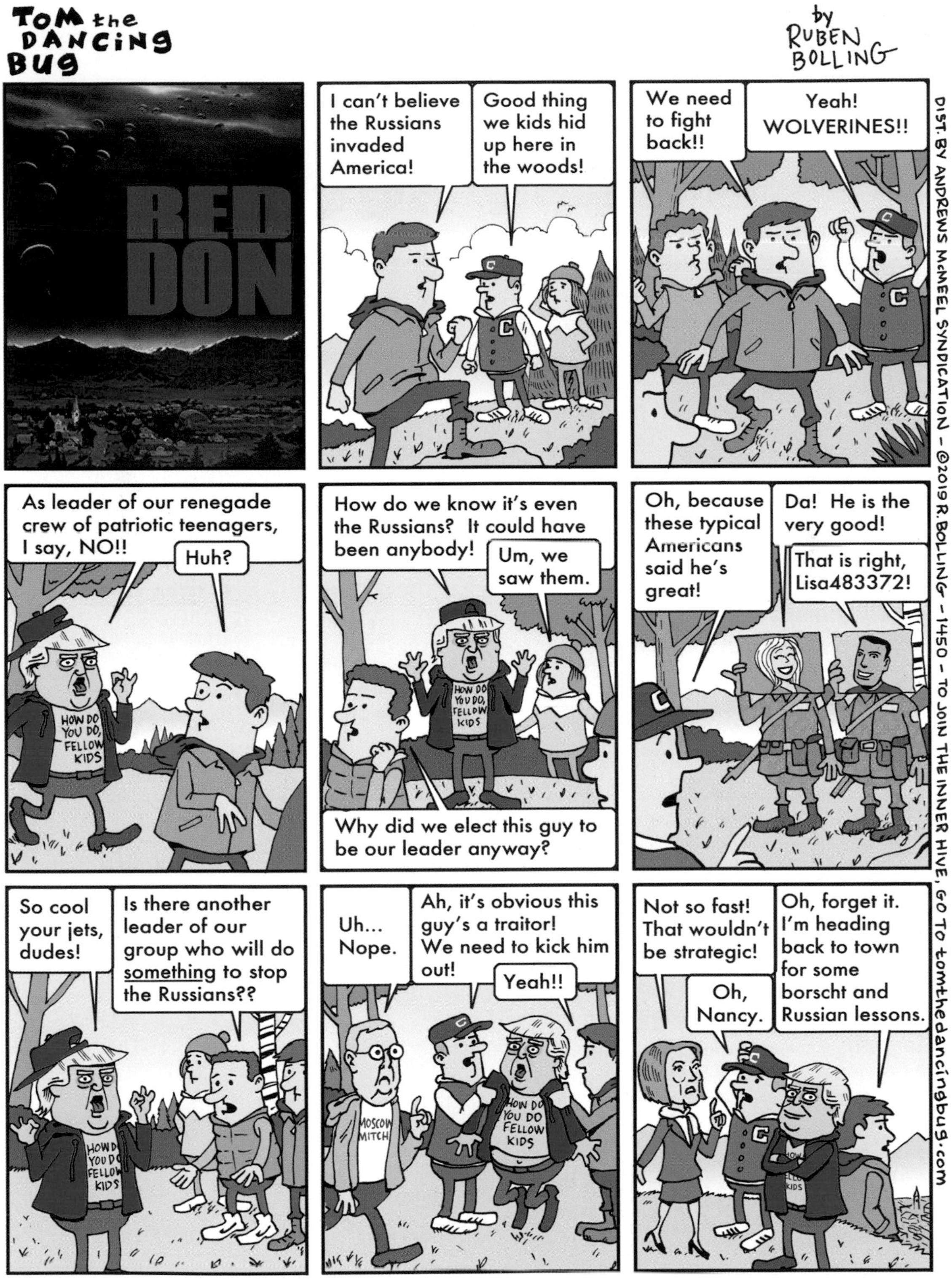
TOM the DANCING BUG
by RUBEN BOLLING
RED DON
I can't believe the Russians invaded America!
Good thing we kids hid up here in the woods!
We need to fight back!!
Yeah! WOLVERINES!!
As leader of our renegade crew of patriotic teenagers, I say, NO!!
Huh?
HOW DO YOU DO, FELLOW KIDS
How do we know it's even the Russians? It could have been anybody!
Um, we saw them.
HOW DO YOU DO, FELLOW KIDS
Why did we elect this guy to be our leader anyway?
Oh, because these typical Americans said he's great!
Da! He is the very good!
That is right, Lisa483372!
So cool your jets, dudes!
Is there another leader of our group who will do something to stop the Russians??
HOW DO YOU DO FELLOW KIDS
Uh... Nope.
Ah, it's obvious this guy's a traitor! We need to kick him out!
Yeah!!
MOSCOW MITCH
HOW DO YOU DO FELLOW KIDS
Not so fast! That wouldn't be strategic!
Oh, Nancy.
Oh, forget it. I'm heading back to town for some borscht and Russian lessons.
DIST. BY ANDREWS McMEEL SYNDICATION – ©2019 R. BOLLING – 1450 – TO JOIN THE INNER HIVE, GO TO tomthedancingbug.com

8/5/19

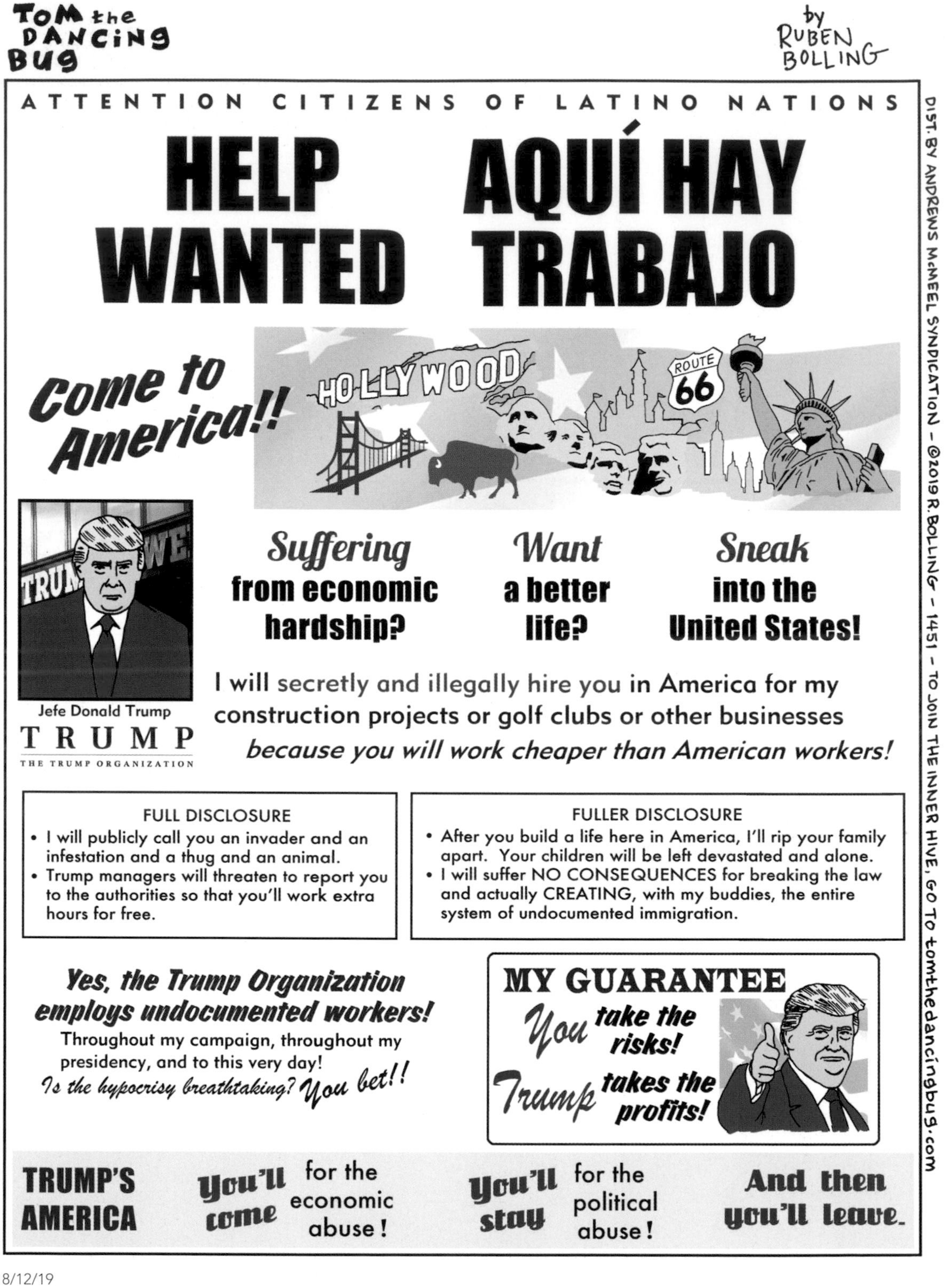
TOM the DANCING BUG
by RUBEN BOLLING
ATTENTION CITIZENS OF LATINO NATIONS
HELP WANTED
AQUÍ HAY TRABAJO
Come to America!!
HOLLYWOOD
ROUTE 66
Suffering from economic hardship?
Want a better life?
Sneak into the United States!
I will secretly and illegally hire you in America for my construction projects or golf clubs or other businesses because you will work cheaper than American workers!
Jefe Donald Trump
TRUMP
THE TRUMP ORGANIZATION
FULL DISCLOSURE
• I will publicly call you an invader and an infestation and a thug and an animal.
• Trump managers will threaten to report you to the authorities so that you'll work extra hours for free.
FULLER DISCLOSURE
• After you build a life here in America, I'll rip your family apart. Your children will be left devastated and alone.
• I will suffer NO CONSEQUENCES for breaking the law and actually CREATING, with my buddies, the entire system of undocumented immigration.
Yes, the Trump Organization employs undocumented workers!
Throughout my campaign, throughout my presidency, and to this very day!
Is the hypocrisy breathtaking? You bet!!
MY GUARANTEE
You take the risks!
Trump takes the profits!
TRUMP'S AMERICA
You'll come for the economic abuse!
You'll stay for the political abuse!
And then you'll leave.
DIST. BY ANDREWS McMEEL SYNDICATION – ©2019 R. BOLLING – 1451 – TO JOIN THE INNER HIVE, GO TO tomthedancingbug.com

8/12/19

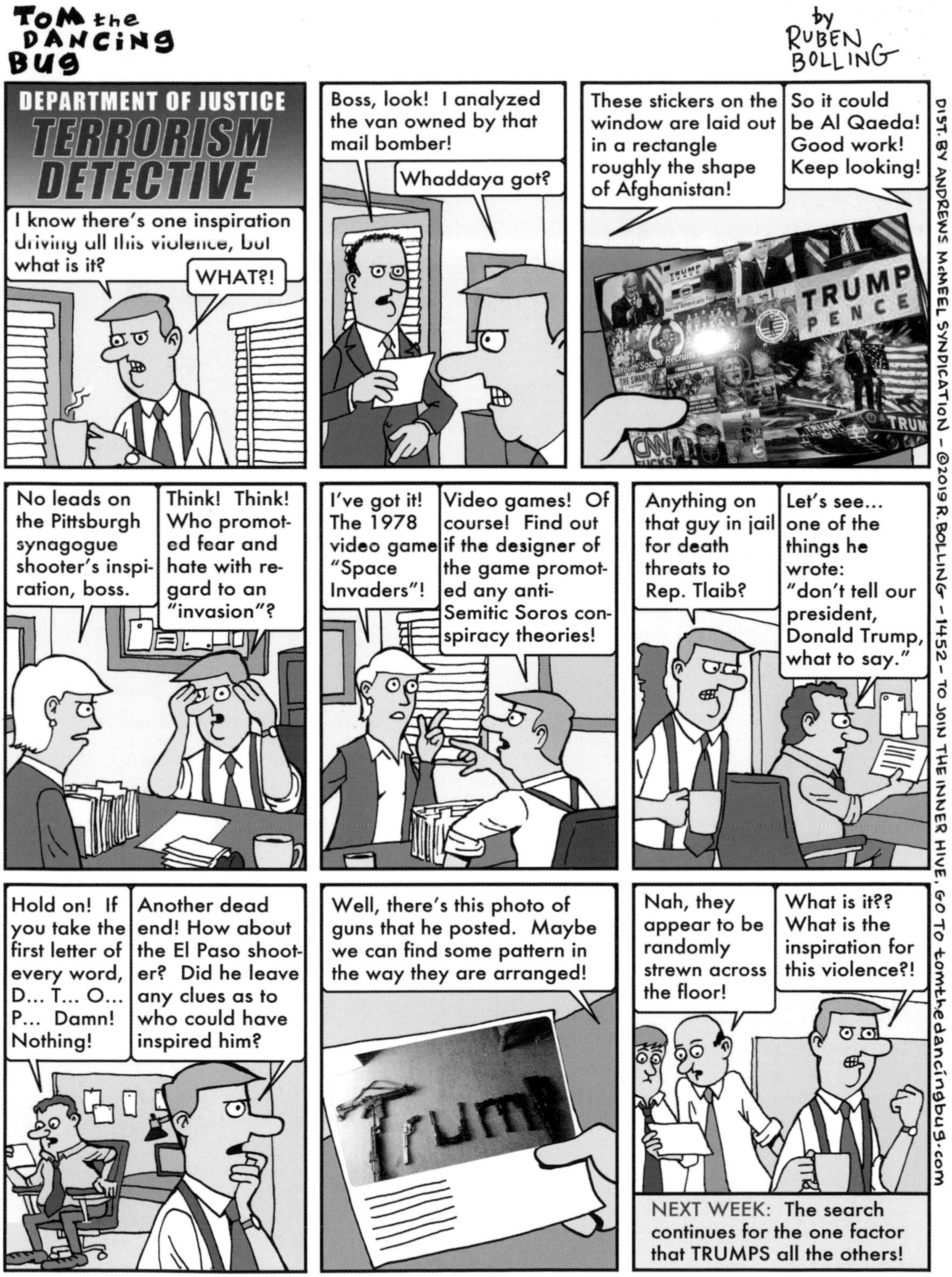
TOM the DANCING BUG
by RUBEN BOLLING
DEPARTMENT OF JUSTICE
TERRORISM DETECTIVE
I know there's one inspiration driving all this violence, but what is it?
WHAT?!
Boss, look! I analyzed the van owned by that mail bomber!
Whaddaya got?
These stickers on the window are laid out in a rectangle roughly the shape of Afghanistan!
So it could be Al Qaeda! Good work! Keep looking!
TRUMP PENCE
No leads on the Pittsburgh synagogue shooter's inspiration, boss.
Think! Think! Who promoted fear and hate with regard to an "invasion"?
I've got it! The 1978 video game "Space Invaders"!
Video games! Of course! Find out if the designer of the game promoted any anti-Semitic Soros conspiracy theories!
Anything on that guy in jail for death threats to Rep. Tlaib?
Let's see... one of the things he wrote: "don't tell our president, Donald Trump, what to say."
Hold on! If you take the first letter of every word, D... T... O... P... Damn! Nothing!
Another dead end! How about the El Paso shooter? Did he leave any clues as to who could have inspired him?
Well, there's this photo of guns that he posted. Maybe we can find some pattern in the way they are arranged!
trump
Nah, they appear to be randomly strewn across the floor!
What is it?? What is the inspiration for this violence?!
NEXT WEEK: The search continues for the one factor that TRUMPS all the others!
DIST. BY ANDREWS McMEEL SYNDICATION – ©2019 R. BOLLING – 1452 – TO JOIN THE INNER HIVE, GO TO tomthedancingbug.com

8/19/19

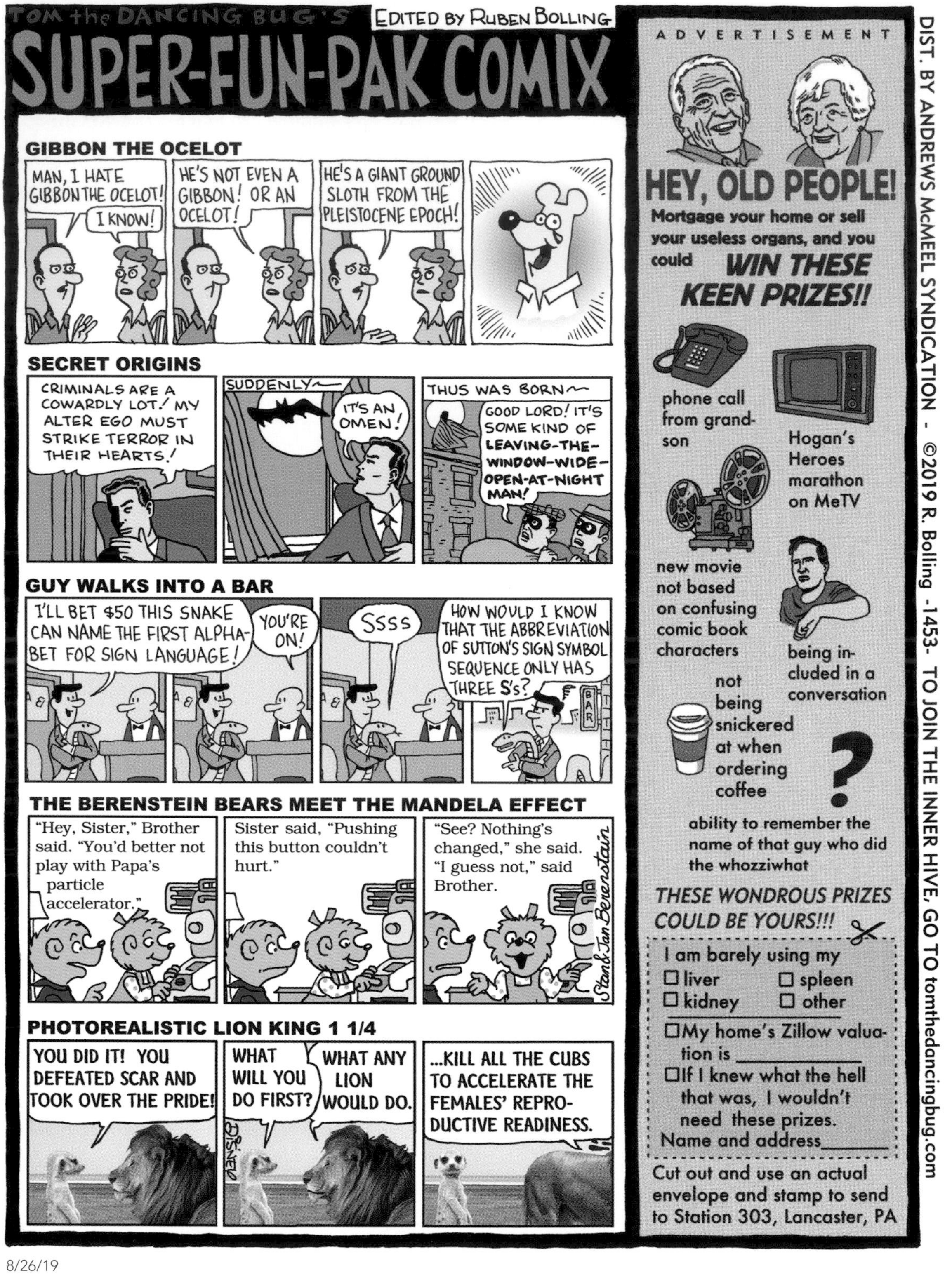
TOM the DANCING BUG'S
EDITED BY RUBEN BOLLING
SUPER-FUN-PAK COMIX
GIBBON THE OCELOT
MAN, I HATE GIBBON THE OCELOT!
I KNOW!
HE'S NOT EVEN A GIBBON! OR AN OCELOT!
HE'S A GIANT GROUND SLOTH FROM THE PLEISTOCENE EPOCH!
SECRET ORIGINS
CRIMINALS ARE A COWARDLY LOT! MY ALTER EGO MUST STRIKE TERROR IN THEIR HEARTS!
SUDDENLY~
IT'S AN OMEN!
THUS WAS BORN~
GOOD LORD! IT'S SOME KIND OF LEAVING-THE-WINDOW-WIDE-OPEN-AT-NIGHT MAN!
GUY WALKS INTO A BAR
I'LL BET $50 THIS SNAKE CAN NAME THE FIRST ALPHABET FOR SIGN LANGUAGE!
YOU'RE ON!
SSSS
HOW WOULD I KNOW THAT THE ABBREVIATION OF SUTTON'S SIGN SYMBOL SEQUENCE ONLY HAS THREE S's?
BAR
THE BERENSTEIN BEARS MEET THE MANDELA EFFECT
"Hey, Sister," Brother said. "You'd better not play with Papa's particle accelerator."
Sister said, "Pushing this button couldn't hurt."
"See? Nothing's changed," she said. "I guess not," said Brother.
Stan & Jan Berenstain
PHOTOREALISTIC LION KING 1 1/4
YOU DID IT! YOU DEFEATED SCAR AND TOOK OVER THE PRIDE!
WHAT WILL YOU DO FIRST?
WHAT ANY LION WOULD DO.
...KILL ALL THE CUBS TO ACCELERATE THE FEMALES' REPRODUCTIVE READINESS.
ADVERTISEMENT
HEY, OLD PEOPLE!
Mortgage your home or sell your useless organs, and you could WIN THESE KEEN PRIZES!!
phone call from grandson
Hogan's Heroes marathon on MeTV
new movie not based on confusing comic book characters
being included in a conversation
not being snickered at when ordering coffee
ability to remember the name of that guy who did the whozziwhat
THESE WONDROUS PRIZES COULD BE YOURS!!!
I am barely using my
☐ liver ☐ spleen
☐ kidney ☐ other
☐ My home's Zillow valuation is ____
☐ If I knew what the hell that was, I wouldn't need these prizes.
Name and address ____
Cut out and use an actual envelope and stamp to send to Station 303, Lancaster, PA

8/26/19

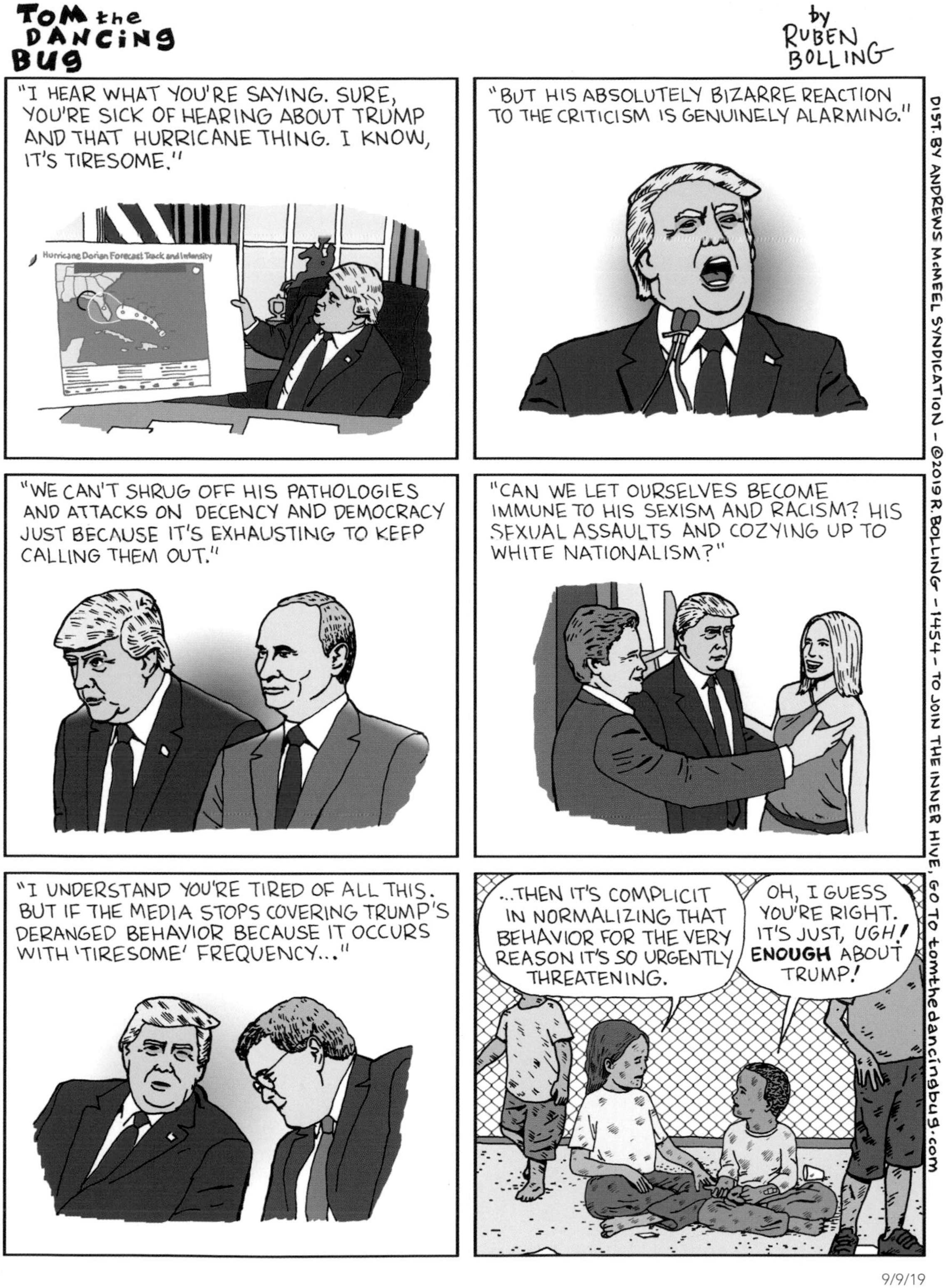
TOM the DANCING BUG
by RUBEN BOLLING
"I HEAR WHAT YOU'RE SAYING. SURE, YOU'RE SICK OF HEARING ABOUT TRUMP AND THAT HURRICANE THING. I KNOW, IT'S TIRESOME."
Hurricane Dorian Forecast Track and Intensity
"BUT HIS ABSOLUTELY BIZARRE REACTION TO THE CRITICISM IS GENUINELY ALARMING."
"WE CAN'T SHRUG OFF HIS PATHOLOGIES AND ATTACKS ON DECENCY AND DEMOCRACY JUST BECAUSE IT'S EXHAUSTING TO KEEP CALLING THEM OUT."
"CAN WE LET OURSELVES BECOME IMMUNE TO HIS SEXISM AND RACISM? HIS SEXUAL ASSAULTS AND COZYING UP TO WHITE NATIONALISM?"
"I UNDERSTAND YOU'RE TIRED OF ALL THIS. BUT IF THE MEDIA STOPS COVERING TRUMP'S DERANGED BEHAVIOR BECAUSE IT OCCURS WITH 'TIRESOME' FREQUENCY..."
...THEN IT'S COMPLICIT IN NORMALIZING THAT BEHAVIOR FOR THE VERY REASON IT'S SO URGENTLY THREATENING.
OH, I GUESS YOU'RE RIGHT. IT'S JUST, *UGH!* **ENOUGH** ABOUT TRUMP!
DIST. BY ANDREWS McMEEL SYNDICATION – ©2019 R. BOLLING – 1454 – TO JOIN THE INNER HIVE, GO TO tomthedancingbug.com

9/9/19

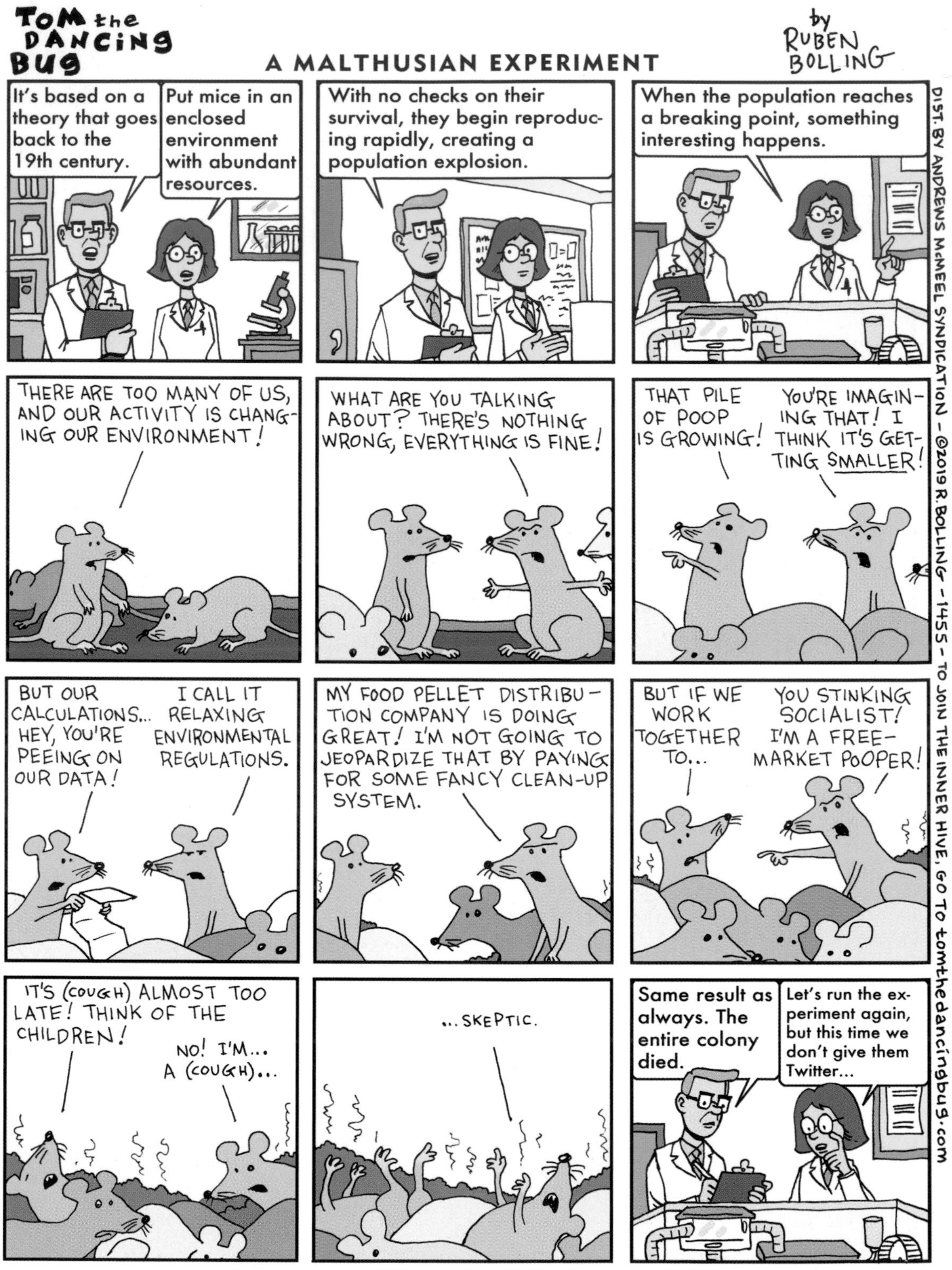
TOM the DANCING BUG
A MALTHUSIAN EXPERIMENT
by RUBEN BOLLING
It's based on a theory that goes back to the 19th century.
Put mice in an enclosed environment with abundant resources.
With no checks on their survival, they begin reproducing rapidly, creating a population explosion.
When the population reaches a breaking point, something interesting happens.
THERE ARE TOO MANY OF US, AND OUR ACTIVITY IS CHANGING OUR ENVIRONMENT!
WHAT ARE YOU TALKING ABOUT? THERE'S NOTHING WRONG, EVERYTHING IS FINE!
THAT PILE OF POOP IS GROWING!
YOU'RE IMAGINING THAT! I THINK IT'S GETTING SMALLER!
BUT OUR CALCULATIONS... HEY, YOU'RE PEEING ON OUR DATA!
I CALL IT RELAXING ENVIRONMENTAL REGULATIONS.
MY FOOD PELLET DISTRIBUTION COMPANY IS DOING GREAT! I'M NOT GOING TO JEOPARDIZE THAT BY PAYING FOR SOME FANCY CLEAN-UP SYSTEM.
BUT IF WE WORK TOGETHER TO...
YOU STINKING SOCIALIST! I'M A FREE-MARKET POOPER!
IT'S (COUGH) ALMOST TOO LATE! THINK OF THE CHILDREN!
NO! I'M... A (COUGH)...
...SKEPTIC.
Same result as always. The entire colony died.
Let's run the experiment again, but this time we don't give them Twitter...
DIST. BY ANDREWS McMEEL SYNDICATION – ©2019 R. BOLLING – 1455 – TO JOIN THE INNER HIVE, GO TO tomthedancingbug.com

9/16/19

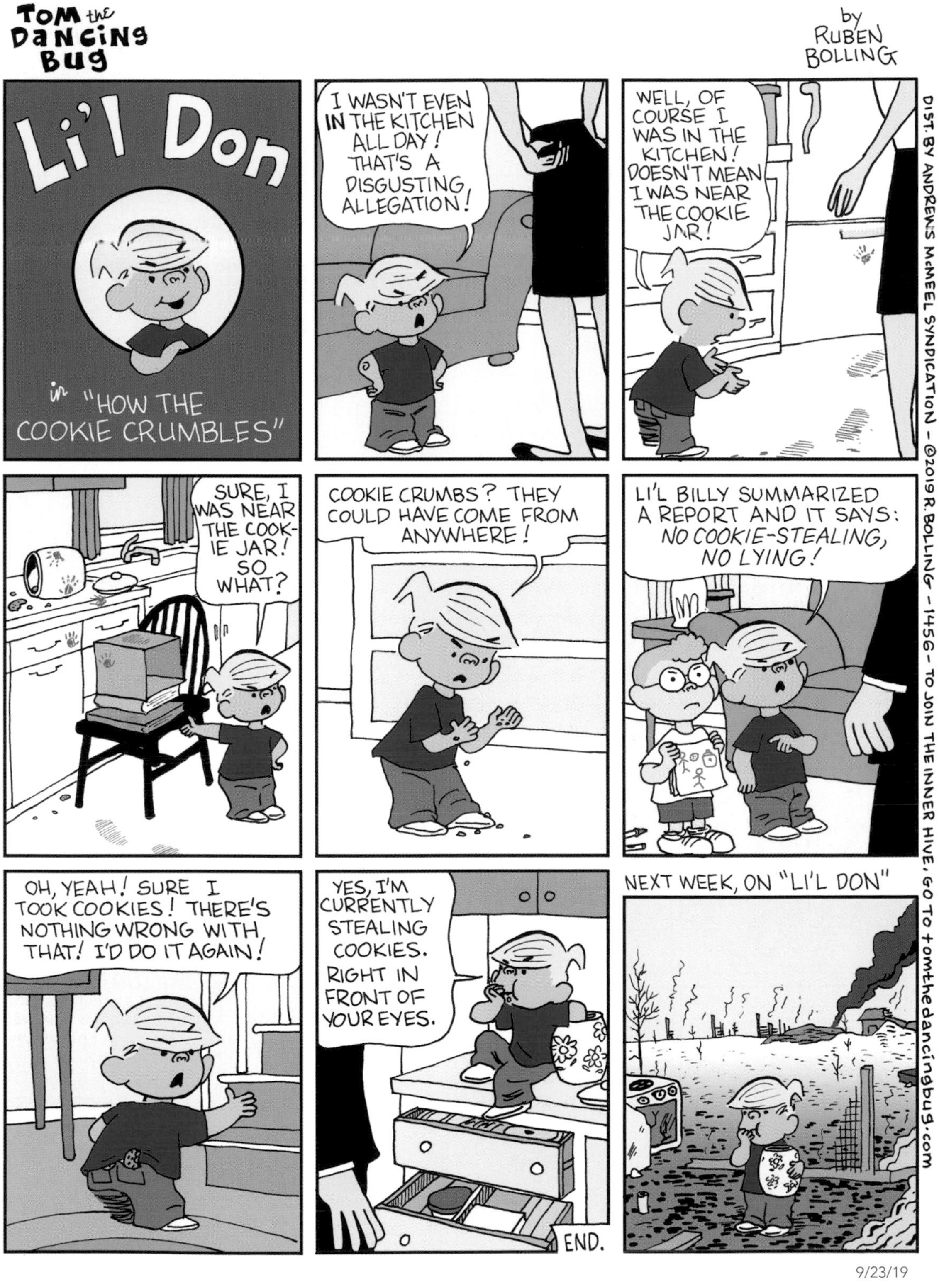
TOM the DANCING BUG
by RUBEN BOLLING
Li'l Don
in "HOW THE COOKIE CRUMBLES"
I WASN'T EVEN IN THE KITCHEN ALL DAY! THAT'S A DISGUSTING ALLEGATION!
WELL, OF COURSE I WAS IN THE KITCHEN! DOESN'T MEAN I WAS NEAR THE COOKIE JAR!
SURE, I WAS NEAR THE COOKIE JAR! SO WHAT?
COOKIE CRUMBS? THEY COULD HAVE COME FROM ANYWHERE!
LI'L BILLY SUMMARIZED A REPORT AND IT SAYS: NO COOKIE-STEALING, NO LYING!
OH, YEAH! SURE I TOOK COOKIES! THERE'S NOTHING WRONG WITH THAT! I'D DO IT AGAIN!
YES, I'M CURRENTLY STEALING COOKIES. RIGHT IN FRONT OF YOUR EYES.
END.
NEXT WEEK, ON "LI'L DON"
DIST. BY ANDREWS McMEEL SYNDICATION – ©2019 R. BOLLING – 1456 – TO JOIN THE INNER HIVE, GO TO tomthedancingbug.com

9/23/19

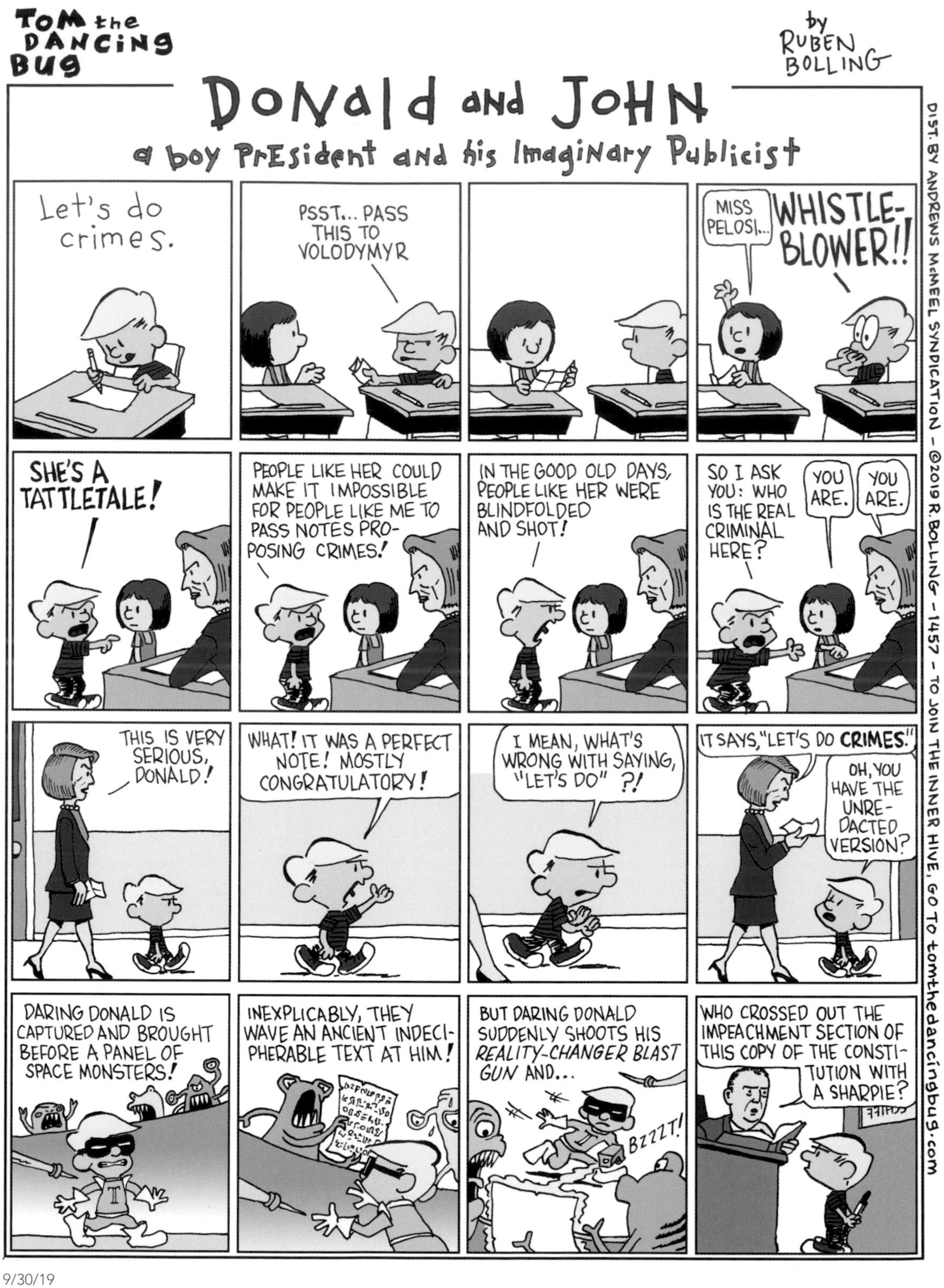
TOM the DANCING BUG
by RUBEN BOLLING
DONALD and JOHN
a boy President and his Imaginary Publicist
Let's do crimes.
PSST... PASS THIS TO VOLODYMYR
MISS PELOSI...
WHISTLE-BLOWER!!
SHE'S A TATTLETALE!
PEOPLE LIKE HER COULD MAKE IT IMPOSSIBLE FOR PEOPLE LIKE ME TO PASS NOTES PROPOSING CRIMES!
IN THE GOOD OLD DAYS, PEOPLE LIKE HER WERE BLINDFOLDED AND SHOT!
SO I ASK YOU: WHO IS THE REAL CRIMINAL HERE?
YOU ARE.
YOU ARE.
THIS IS VERY SERIOUS, DONALD!
WHAT! IT WAS A PERFECT NOTE! MOSTLY CONGRATULATORY!
I MEAN, WHAT'S WRONG WITH SAYING, "LET'S DO" ?!
IT SAYS, "LET'S DO CRIMES."
OH, YOU HAVE THE UNREDACTED VERSION?
DARING DONALD IS CAPTURED AND BROUGHT BEFORE A PANEL OF SPACE MONSTERS!
INEXPLICABLY, THEY WAVE AN ANCIENT INDECIPHERABLE TEXT AT HIM!
BUT DARING DONALD SUDDENLY SHOOTS HIS REALITY-CHANGER BLAST GUN AND...
BZZZT!
WHO CROSSED OUT THE IMPEACHMENT SECTION OF THIS COPY OF THE CONSTITUTION WITH A SHARPIE?
DIST. BY ANDREWS McMEEL SYNDICATION – ©2019 R. BOLLING – 1457 – TO JOIN THE INNER HIVE, GO TO tomthedancingbug.com

9/30/19

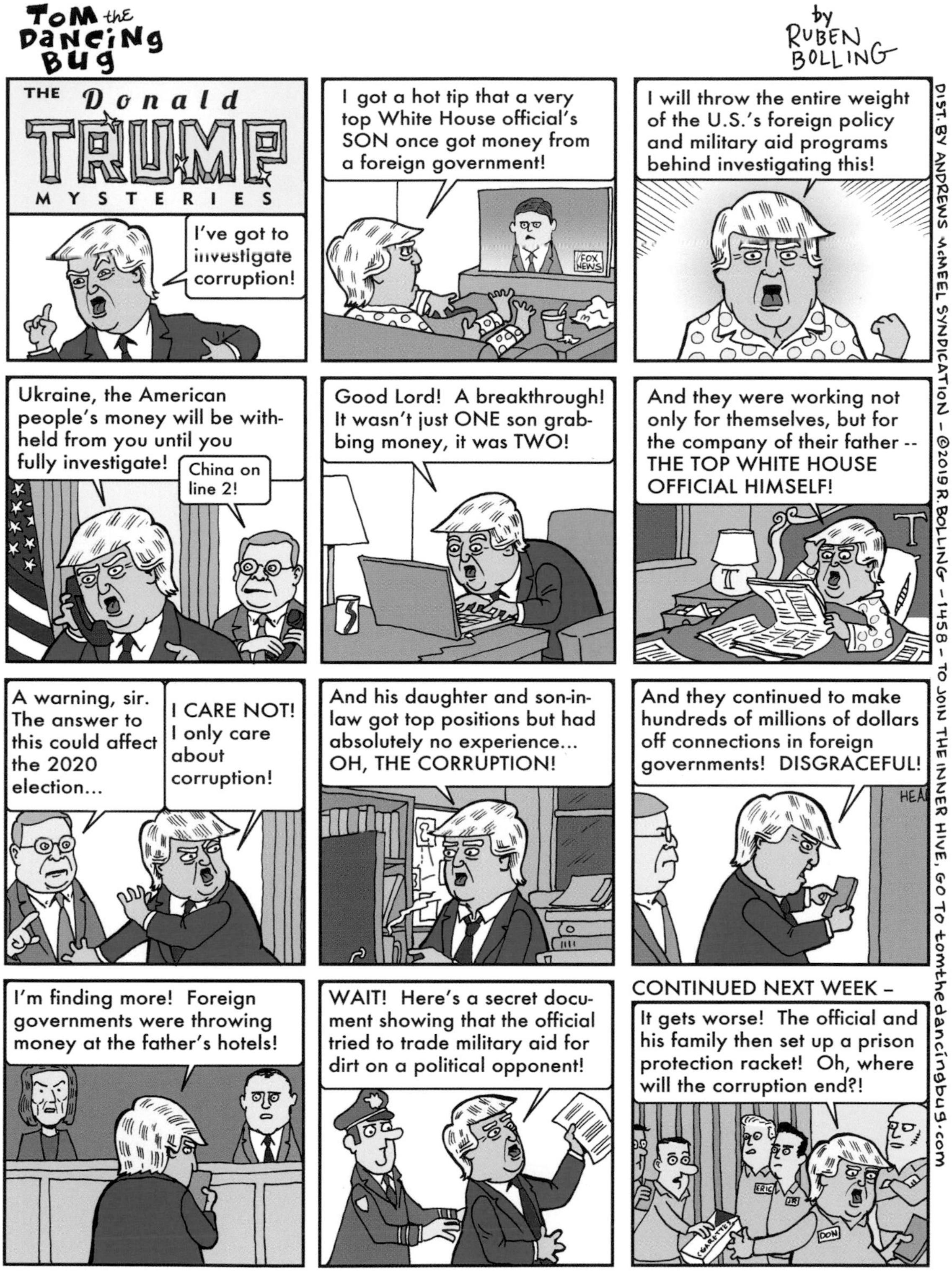

Tom the Dancing Bug
by Ruben Bolling
THE Donald TRUMP MYSTERIES
I've got to investigate corruption!
I got a hot tip that a very top White House official's SON once got money from a foreign government!
FOX NEWS
I will throw the entire weight of the U.S.'s foreign policy and military aid programs behind investigating this!
Ukraine, the American people's money will be withheld from you until you fully investigate!
China on line 2!
Good Lord! A breakthrough! It wasn't just ONE son grabbing money, it was TWO!
And they were working not only for themselves, but for the company of their father -- THE TOP WHITE HOUSE OFFICIAL HIMSELF!
A warning, sir. The answer to this could affect the 2020 election...
I CARE NOT! I only care about corruption!
And his daughter and son-in-law got top positions but had absolutely no experience... OH, THE CORRUPTION!
And they continued to make hundreds of millions of dollars off connections in foreign governments! DISGRACEFUL!
I'm finding more! Foreign governments were throwing money at the father's hotels!
WAIT! Here's a secret document showing that the official tried to trade military aid for dirt on a political opponent!
CONTINUED NEXT WEEK –
It gets worse! The official and his family then set up a prison protection racket! Oh, where will the corruption end?!
ERIC
JR
DON
CIGARETTES
DIST. BY ANDREWS McMEEL SYNDICATION – ©2019 R. BOLLING – 1458 – TO JOIN THE INNER HIVE, GO TO tomthedancingbug.com

10/7/19

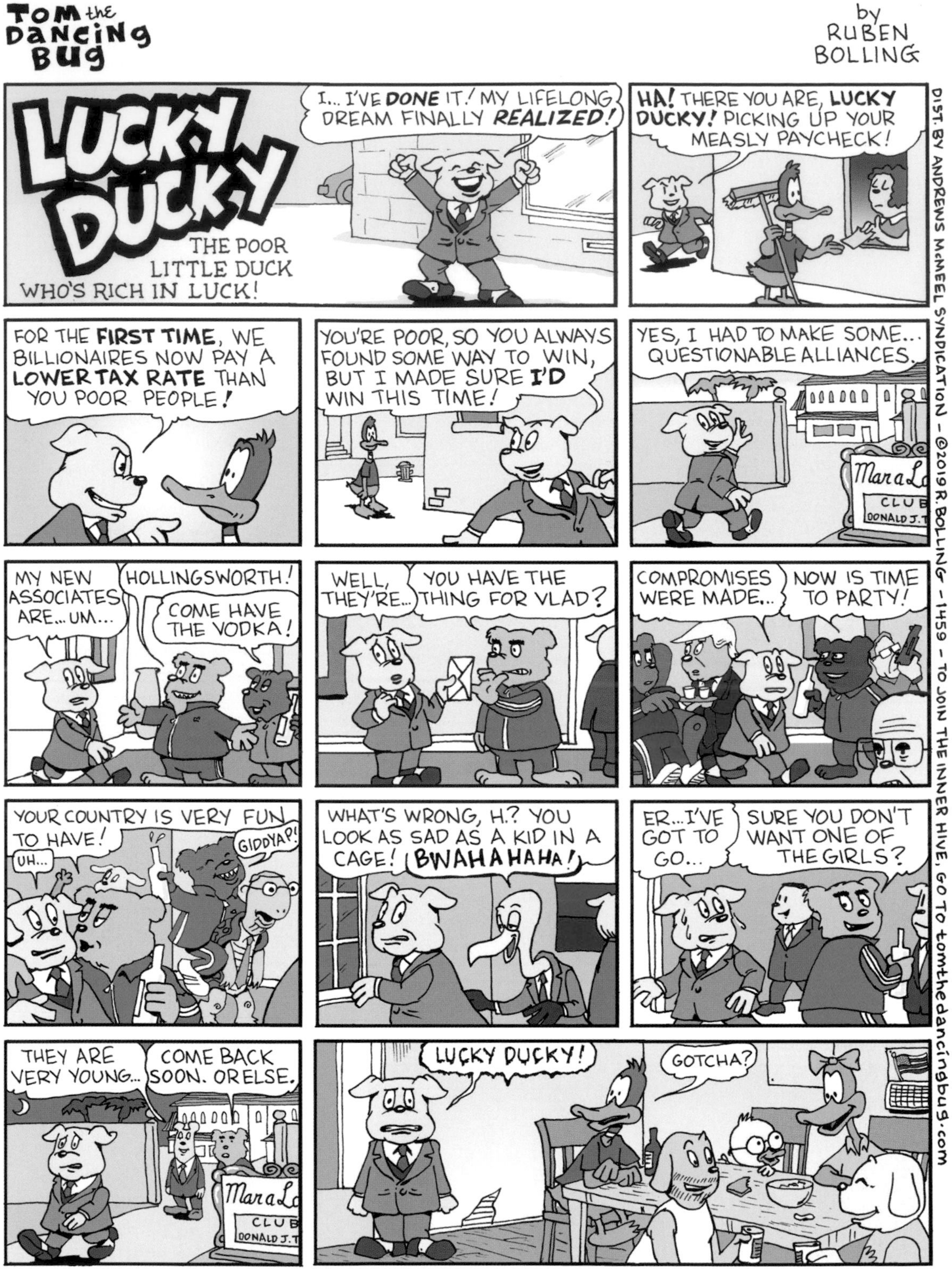
TOM the DANCING BUG
by RUBEN BOLLING
LUCKY DUCKY
THE POOR LITTLE DUCK WHO'S RICH IN LUCK!
I... I'VE DONE IT! MY LIFELONG DREAM FINALLY REALIZED!
HA! THERE YOU ARE, LUCKY DUCKY! PICKING UP YOUR MEASLY PAYCHECK!
FOR THE FIRST TIME, WE BILLIONAIRES NOW PAY A LOWER TAX RATE THAN YOU POOR PEOPLE!
YOU'RE POOR, SO YOU ALWAYS FOUND SOME WAY TO WIN, BUT I MADE SURE I'D WIN THIS TIME!
YES, I HAD TO MAKE SOME... QUESTIONABLE ALLIANCES.
Mar a La
CLUB
DONALD J. T
MY NEW ASSOCIATES ARE... UM...
HOLLINGSWORTH!
COME HAVE THE VODKA!
WELL, THEY'RE...
YOU HAVE THE THING FOR VLAD?
COMPROMISES WERE MADE...
NOW IS TIME TO PARTY!
YOUR COUNTRY IS VERY FUN TO HAVE!
UH...
GIDDYAP!
WHAT'S WRONG, H.? YOU LOOK AS SAD AS A KID IN A CAGE!
BWAHAHAHA!
ER... I'VE GOT TO GO...
SURE YOU DON'T WANT ONE OF THE GIRLS?
THEY ARE VERY YOUNG...
COME BACK SOON. OR ELSE.
Mar a La
CLUB
DONALD J. T
LUCKY DUCKY!
GOTCHA?
DIST. BY ANDREWS McMEEL SYNDICATION – ©2019 R. BOLLING – 1459 – TO JOIN THE INNER HIVE, GO TO tomthedancingbug.com

10/14/19

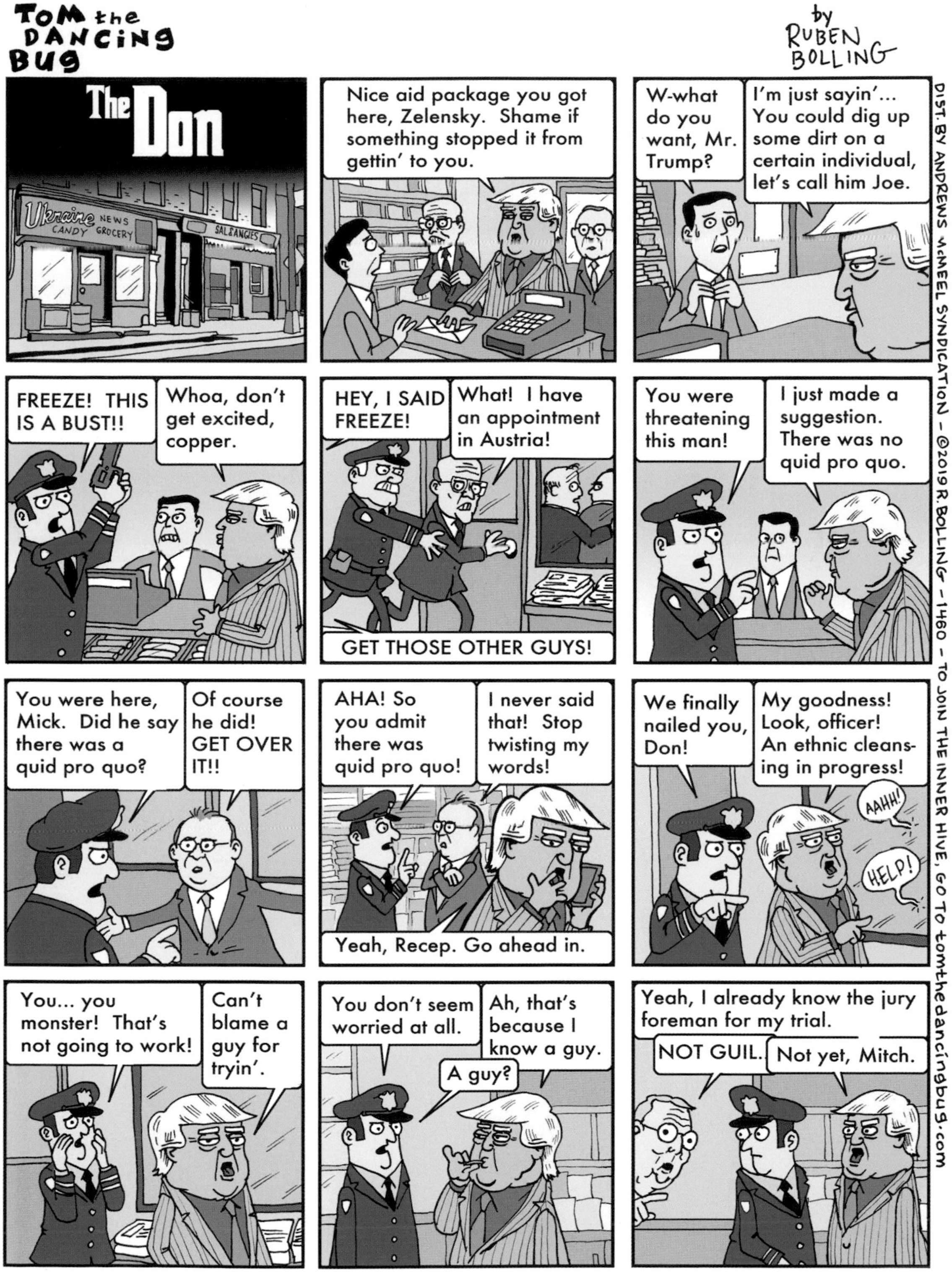

TOM the DANCING BUG
by RUBEN BOLLING
The Don
Ukraine NEWS CANDY GROCERY
SALE & ANGLES
Nice aid package you got here, Zelensky. Shame if something stopped it from gettin' to you.
W-what do you want, Mr. Trump?
I'm just sayin'... You could dig up some dirt on a certain individual, let's call him Joe.
FREEZE! THIS IS A BUST!!
Whoa, don't get excited, copper.
HEY, I SAID FREEZE!
What! I have an appointment in Austria!
GET THOSE OTHER GUYS!
You were threatening this man!
I just made a suggestion. There was no quid pro quo.
You were here, Mick. Did he say there was a quid pro quo?
Of course he did! GET OVER IT!!
AHA! So you admit there was quid pro quo!
I never said that! Stop twisting my words!
Yeah, Recep. Go ahead in.
We finally nailed you, Don!
My goodness! Look, officer! An ethnic cleans-ing in progress!
AAHH!
HELP!
You... you monster! That's not going to work!
Can't blame a guy for tryin'.
You don't seem worried at all.
Ah, that's because I know a guy.
A guy?
Yeah, I already know the jury foreman for my trial.
NOT GUIL.
Not yet, Mitch.
DIST. BY ANDREWS McMEEL SYNDICATION – ©2019 R. BOLLING – 1460 – TO JOIN THE INNER HIVE, GO TO tomthedancingbug.com

10/21/19

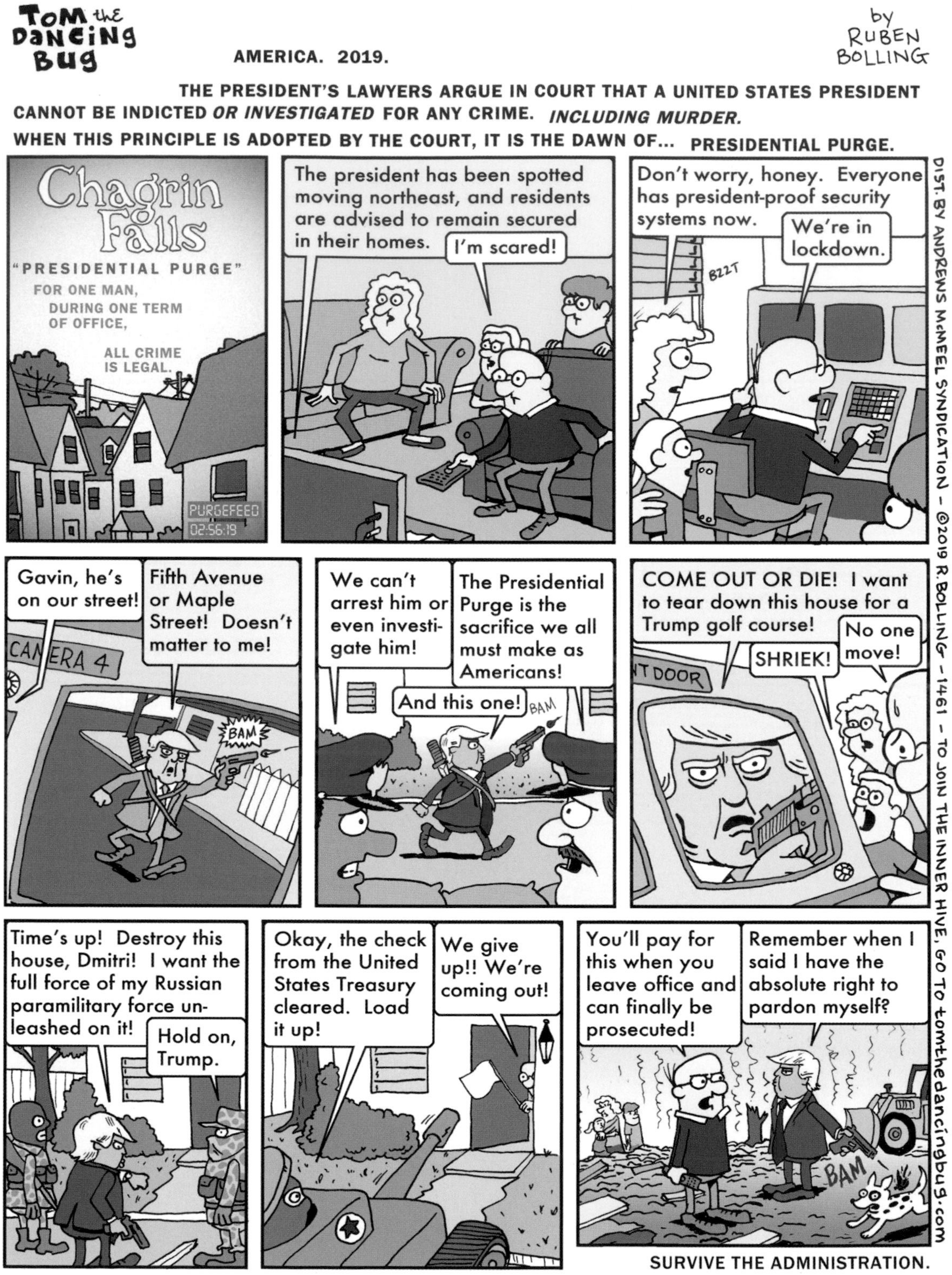

Tom the Dancing Bug
AMERICA. 2019.
by Ruben Bolling
THE PRESIDENT'S LAWYERS ARGUE IN COURT THAT A UNITED STATES PRESIDENT CANNOT BE INDICTED *OR INVESTIGATED* FOR ANY CRIME. *INCLUDING MURDER.*
WHEN THIS PRINCIPLE IS ADOPTED BY THE COURT, IT IS THE DAWN OF... PRESIDENTIAL PURGE.
Chagrin Falls
"PRESIDENTIAL PURGE"
FOR ONE MAN, DURING ONE TERM OF OFFICE,
ALL CRIME IS LEGAL.
PURGEFEED
02:56:19
The president has been spotted moving northeast, and residents are advised to remain secured in their homes.
I'm scared!
Don't worry, honey. Everyone has president-proof security systems now.
We're in lockdown.
BZZT
Gavin, he's on our street!
Fifth Avenue or Maple Street! Doesn't matter to me!
CAMERA 4
BAM
We can't arrest him or even investigate him!
The Presidential Purge is the sacrifice we all must make as Americans!
And this one!
BAM
COME OUT OR DIE! I want to tear down this house for a Trump golf course!
SHRIEK!
No one move!
NT DOOR
Time's up! Destroy this house, Dmitri! I want the full force of my Russian paramilitary force unleashed on it!
Hold on, Trump.
Okay, the check from the United States Treasury cleared. Load it up!
We give up!! We're coming out!
You'll pay for this when you leave office and can finally be prosecuted!
Remember when I said I have the absolute right to pardon myself?
BAM
SURVIVE THE ADMINISTRATION.
DIST. BY ANDREWS McMEEL SYNDICATION – ©2019 R. BOLLING – 1461 – TO JOIN THE INNER HIVE, GO TO tomthedancingbug.com

10/28/19

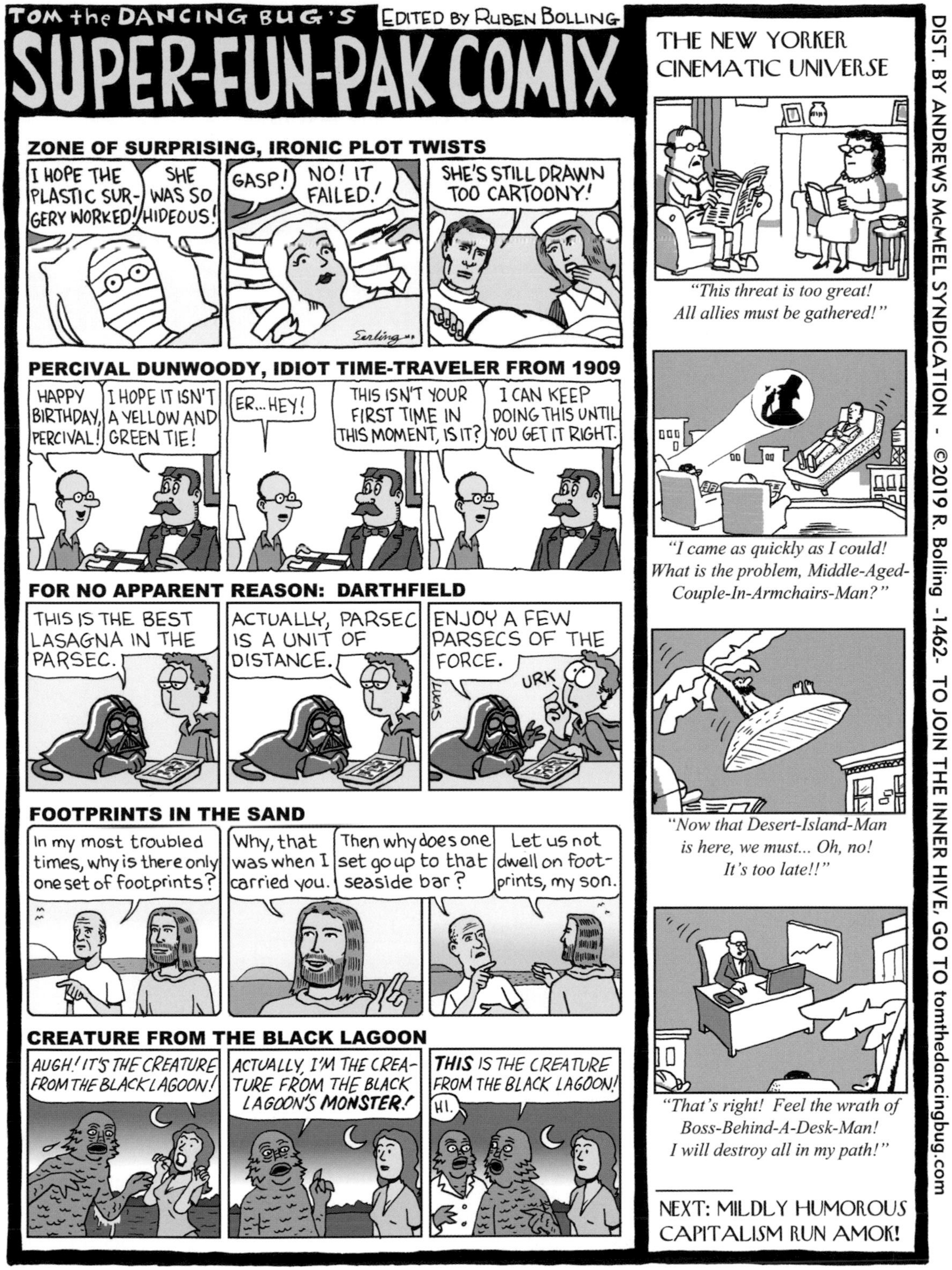
TOM the DANCING BUG'S
EDITED BY RUBEN BOLLING
SUPER-FUN-PAK COMIX
ZONE OF SURPRISING, IRONIC PLOT TWISTS
I HOPE THE PLASTIC SURGERY WORKED!
SHE WAS SO HIDEOUS!
GASP!
NO! IT FAILED!
SHE'S STILL DRAWN TOO CARTOONY!
Serling
PERCIVAL DUNWOODY, IDIOT TIME-TRAVELER FROM 1909
HAPPY BIRTHDAY, PERCIVAL!
I HOPE IT ISN'T A YELLOW AND GREEN TIE!
ER...HEY!
THIS ISN'T YOUR FIRST TIME IN THIS MOMENT, IS IT?
I CAN KEEP DOING THIS UNTIL YOU GET IT RIGHT.
FOR NO APPARENT REASON: DARTHFIELD
THIS IS THE BEST LASAGNA IN THE PARSEC.
ACTUALLY, PARSEC IS A UNIT OF DISTANCE.
LUCAS
ENJOY A FEW PARSECS OF THE FORCE.
URK
FOOTPRINTS IN THE SAND
In my most troubled times, why is there only one set of footprints?
Why, that was when I carried you.
Then why does one set go up to that seaside bar?
Let us not dwell on footprints, my son.
CREATURE FROM THE BLACK LAGOON
AUGH! IT'S THE CREATURE FROM THE BLACK LAGOON!
ACTUALLY, I'M THE CREATURE FROM THE BLACK LAGOON'S MONSTER!
THIS IS THE CREATURE FROM THE BLACK LAGOON!
HI.
THE NEW YORKER CINEMATIC UNIVERSE
"This threat is too great! All allies must be gathered!"
"I came as quickly as I could! What is the problem, Middle-Aged-Couple-In-Armchairs-Man?"
"Now that Desert-Island-Man is here, we must... Oh, no! It's too late!!"
"That's right! Feel the wrath of Boss-Behind-A-Desk-Man! I will destroy all in my path!"
NEXT: MILDLY HUMOROUS CAPITALISM RUN AMOK!
DIST. BY ANDREWS McMEEL SYNDICATION - ©2019 R. Bolling -1462- TO JOIN THE INNER HIVE, GO TO tomthedancingbug.com

11/4/19

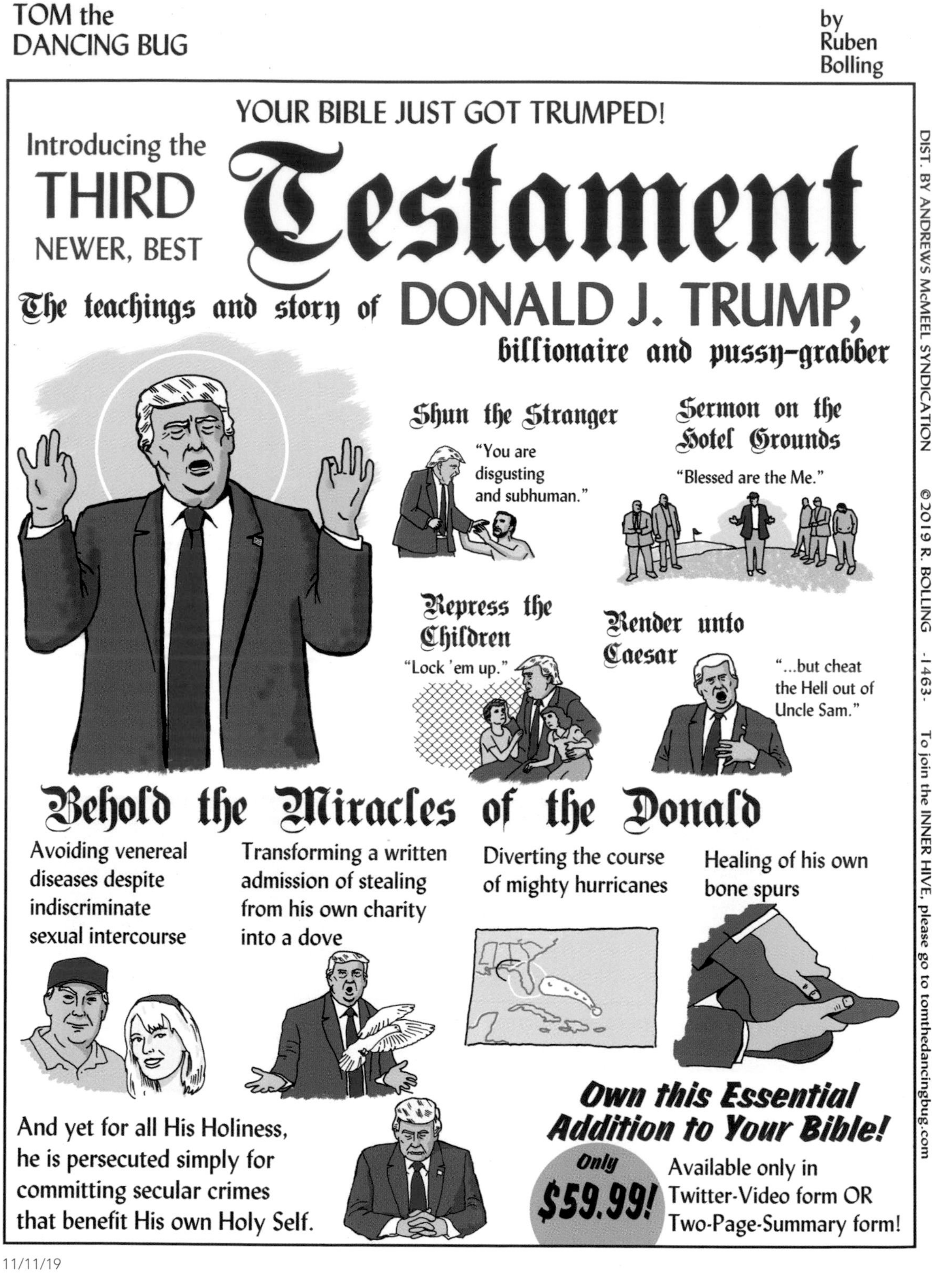
TOM the DANCING BUG
by Ruben Bolling
YOUR BIBLE JUST GOT TRUMPED!
Introducing the THIRD NEWER, BEST
Testament
The teachings and story of DONALD J. TRUMP,
billionaire and pussy-grabber
Shun the Stranger
"You are disgusting and subhuman."
Sermon on the Hotel Grounds
"Blessed are the Me."
Repress the Children
"Lock 'em up."
Render unto Caesar
"...but cheat the Hell out of Uncle Sam."
Behold the Miracles of the Donald
Avoiding venereal diseases despite indiscriminate sexual intercourse
Transforming a written admission of stealing from his own charity into a dove
Diverting the course of mighty hurricanes
Healing of his own bone spurs
And yet for all His Holiness, he is persecuted simply for committing secular crimes that benefit His own Holy Self.
Own this Essential Addition to Your Bible!
Only $59.99!
Available only in Twitter-Video form OR Two-Page-Summary form!
DIST. BY ANDREWS McMEEL SYNDICATION ©2019 R. BOLLING -1463- To join the INNER HIVE, please go to tomthedancingbug.com
11/11/19

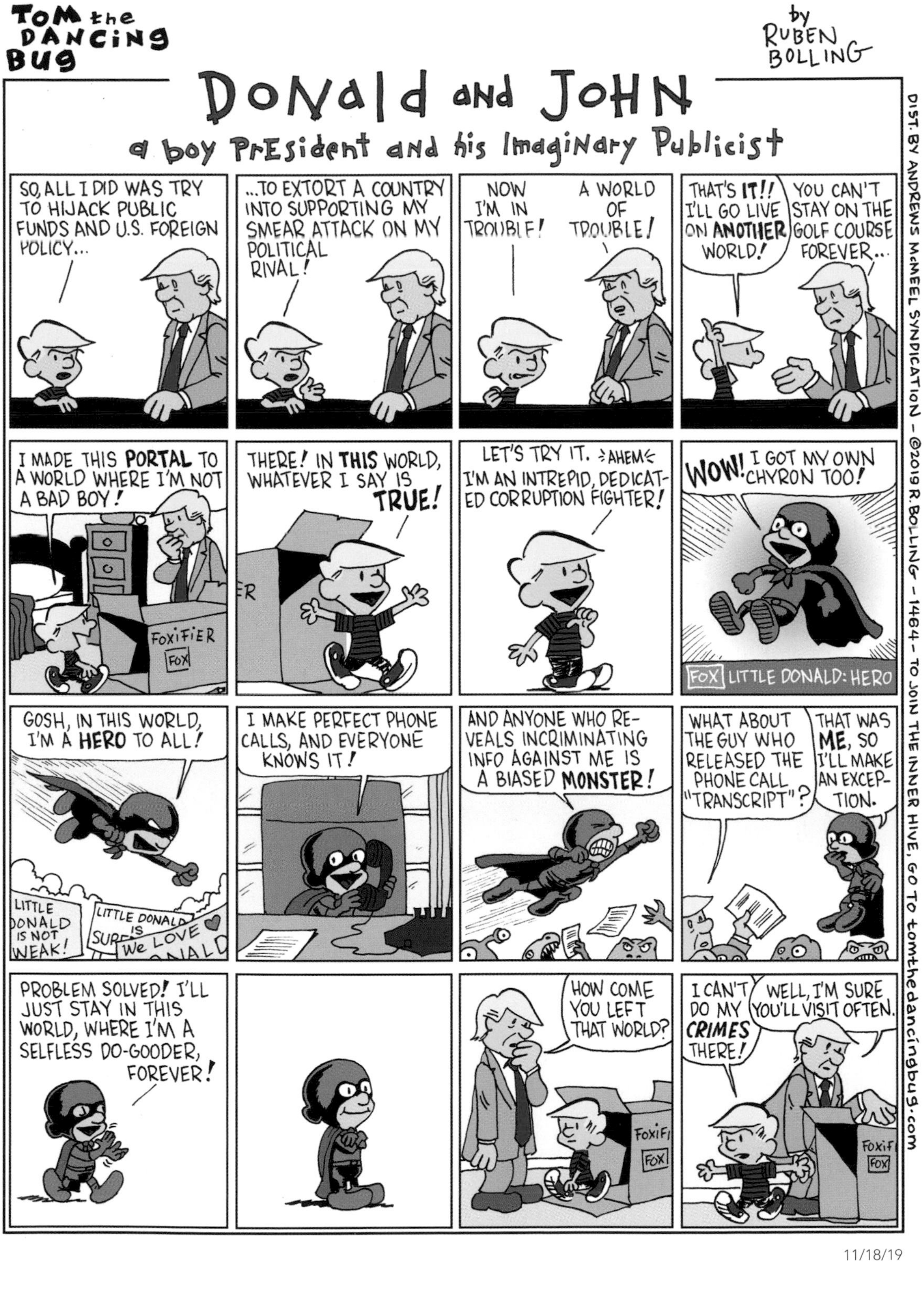
TOM the DANCING BUG
by RUBEN BOLLING
DONALD AND JOHN
a boy President and his Imaginary Publicist
SO, ALL I DID WAS TRY TO HIJACK PUBLIC FUNDS AND U.S. FOREIGN POLICY...
...TO EXTORT A COUNTRY INTO SUPPORTING MY SMEAR ATTACK ON MY POLITICAL RIVAL!
NOW I'M IN TROUBLE!
A WORLD OF TROUBLE!
THAT'S IT!! I'LL GO LIVE ON ANOTHER WORLD!
YOU CAN'T STAY ON THE GOLF COURSE FOREVER...
I MADE THIS PORTAL TO A WORLD WHERE I'M NOT A BAD BOY!
FOXIFIER
FOX
THERE! IN THIS WORLD, WHATEVER I SAY IS TRUE!
LET'S TRY IT. AHEM I'M AN INTREPID, DEDICATED CORRUPTION FIGHTER!
WOW! I GOT MY OWN CHYRON TOO!
FOX LITTLE DONALD: HERO
GOSH, IN THIS WORLD, I'M A HERO TO ALL!
LITTLE DONALD IS NOT WEAK!
We LOVE
I MAKE PERFECT PHONE CALLS, AND EVERYONE KNOWS IT!
AND ANYONE WHO REVEALS INCRIMINATING INFO AGAINST ME IS A BIASED MONSTER!
WHAT ABOUT THE GUY WHO RELEASED THE PHONE CALL "TRANSCRIPT"?
THAT WAS ME, SO I'LL MAKE AN EXCEPTION.
PROBLEM SOLVED! I'LL JUST STAY IN THIS WORLD, WHERE I'M A SELFLESS DO-GOODER, FOREVER!
HOW COME YOU LEFT THAT WORLD?
FOX
I CAN'T DO MY CRIMES THERE!
WELL, I'M SURE YOU'LL VISIT OFTEN.
FOX
DIST. BY ANDREWS McMEEL SYNDICATION – ©2019 R. BOLLING – 1464 – TO JOIN THE INNER HIVE, GO TO tomthedancingbug.com

11/18/19

TOM the DANCING BUG

by RUBEN BOLLING

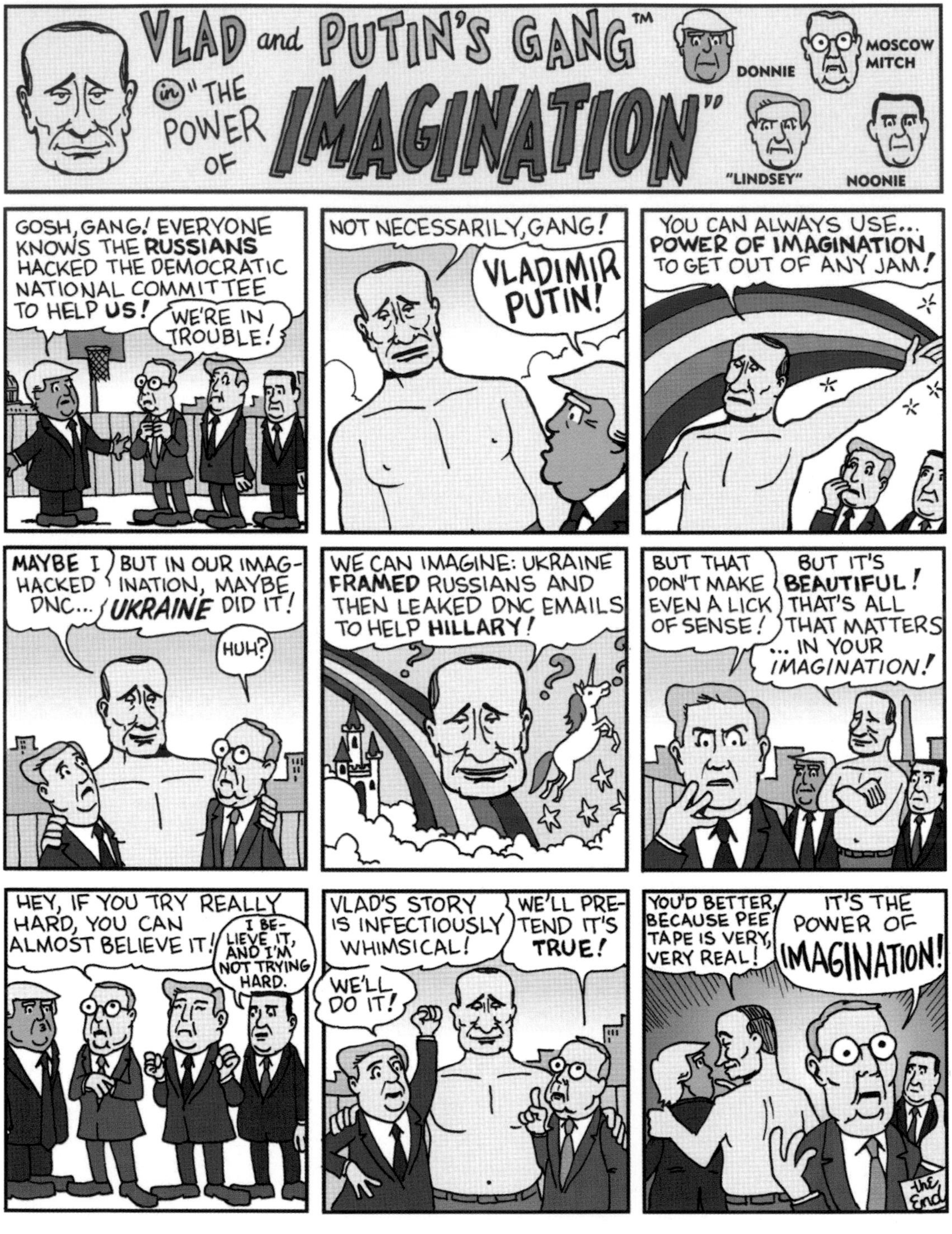

VLAD and PUTIN'S GANG™
in "THE POWER OF IMAGINATION"
DONNIE
MOSCOW MITCH
"LINDSEY"
NOONIE
GOSH, GANG! EVERYONE KNOWS THE RUSSIANS HACKED THE DEMOCRATIC NATIONAL COMMITTEE TO HELP US!
WE'RE IN TROUBLE!
NOT NECESSARILY, GANG!
VLADIMIR PUTIN!
YOU CAN ALWAYS USE... POWER OF IMAGINATION, TO GET OUT OF ANY JAM!
MAYBE I HACKED DNC...
BUT IN OUR IMAGINATION, MAYBE UKRAINE DID IT!
HUH?
WE CAN IMAGINE: UKRAINE FRAMED RUSSIANS AND THEN LEAKED DNC EMAILS TO HELP HILLARY!
BUT THAT DON'T MAKE EVEN A LICK OF SENSE!
BUT IT'S BEAUTIFUL! THAT'S ALL THAT MATTERS ... IN YOUR IMAGINATION!
HEY, IF YOU TRY REALLY HARD, YOU CAN ALMOST BELIEVE IT!
I BELIEVE IT, AND I'M NOT TRYING HARD.
VLAD'S STORY IS INFECTIOUSLY WHIMSICAL!
WE'LL PRETEND IT'S TRUE!
WE'LL DO IT!
YOU'D BETTER, BECAUSE PEE TAPE IS VERY, VERY REAL!
IT'S THE POWER OF IMAGINATION!
THE End

11/25/19

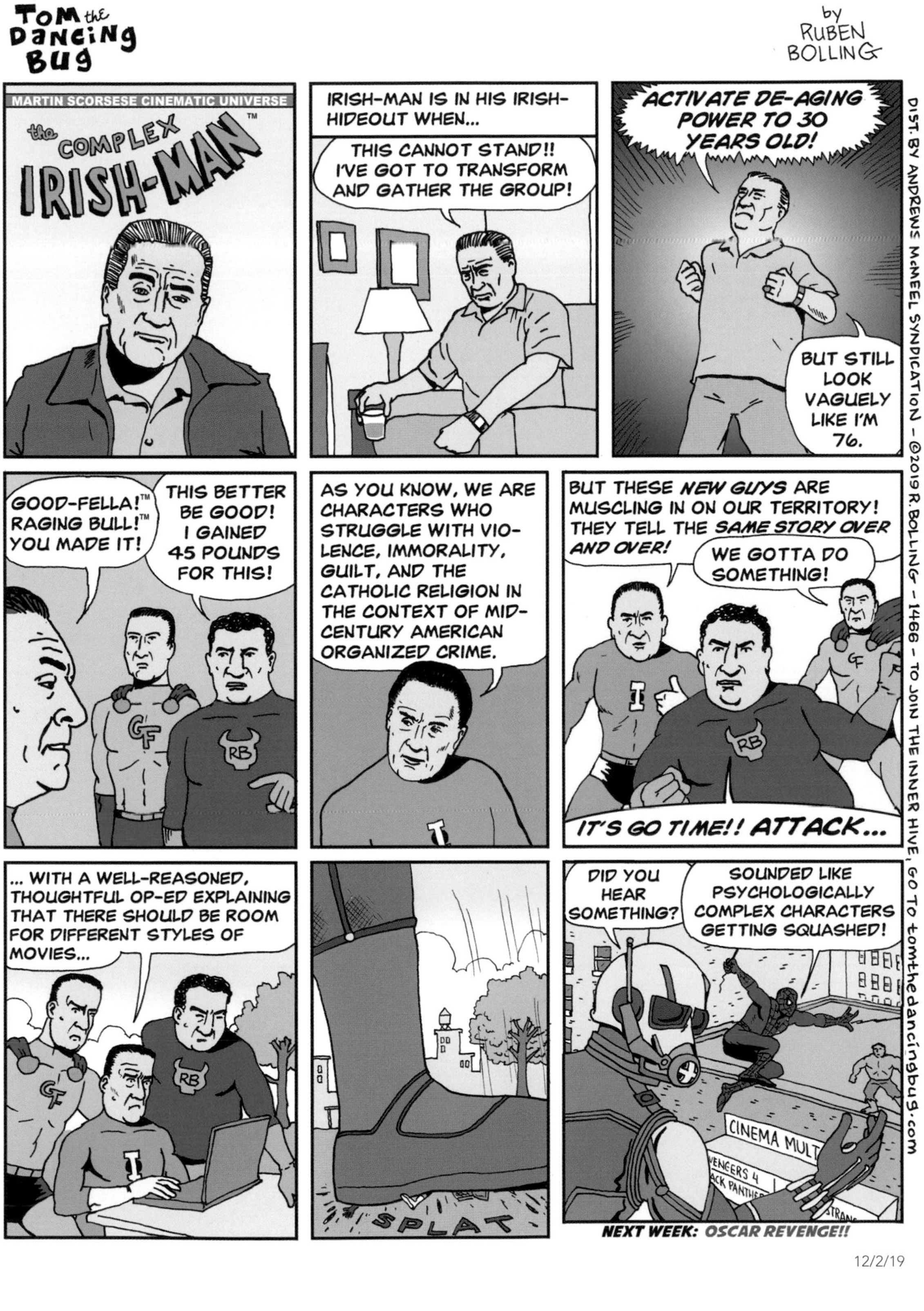

TOM the DANCING BUG
by RUBEN BOLLING
MARTIN SCORSESE CINEMATIC UNIVERSE
the COMPLEX IRISH-MAN™
IRISH-MAN IS IN HIS IRISH-HIDEOUT WHEN...
THIS CANNOT STAND!! I'VE GOT TO TRANSFORM AND GATHER THE GROUP!
ACTIVATE DE-AGING POWER TO 30 YEARS OLD!
BUT STILL LOOK VAGUELY LIKE I'M 76.
GOOD-FELLA!™ RAGING BULL!™ YOU MADE IT!
THIS BETTER BE GOOD! I GAINED 45 POUNDS FOR THIS!
AS YOU KNOW, WE ARE CHARACTERS WHO STRUGGLE WITH VIOLENCE, IMMORALITY, GUILT, AND THE CATHOLIC RELIGION IN THE CONTEXT OF MID-CENTURY AMERICAN ORGANIZED CRIME.
BUT THESE NEW GUYS ARE MUSCLING IN ON OUR TERRITORY! THEY TELL THE SAME STORY OVER AND OVER!
WE GOTTA DO SOMETHING!
IT'S GO TIME!! ATTACK...
... WITH A WELL-REASONED, THOUGHTFUL OP-ED EXPLAINING THAT THERE SHOULD BE ROOM FOR DIFFERENT STYLES OF MOVIES...
SPLAT
DID YOU HEAR SOMETHING?
SOUNDED LIKE PSYCHOLOGICALLY COMPLEX CHARACTERS GETTING SQUASHED!
NEXT WEEK: OSCAR REVENGE!!
DIST. BY ANDREWS McMEEL SYNDICATION – ©2019 R. BOLLING – 1466 – TO JOIN THE INNER HIVE, GO TO tomthedancingbug.com

12/2/19

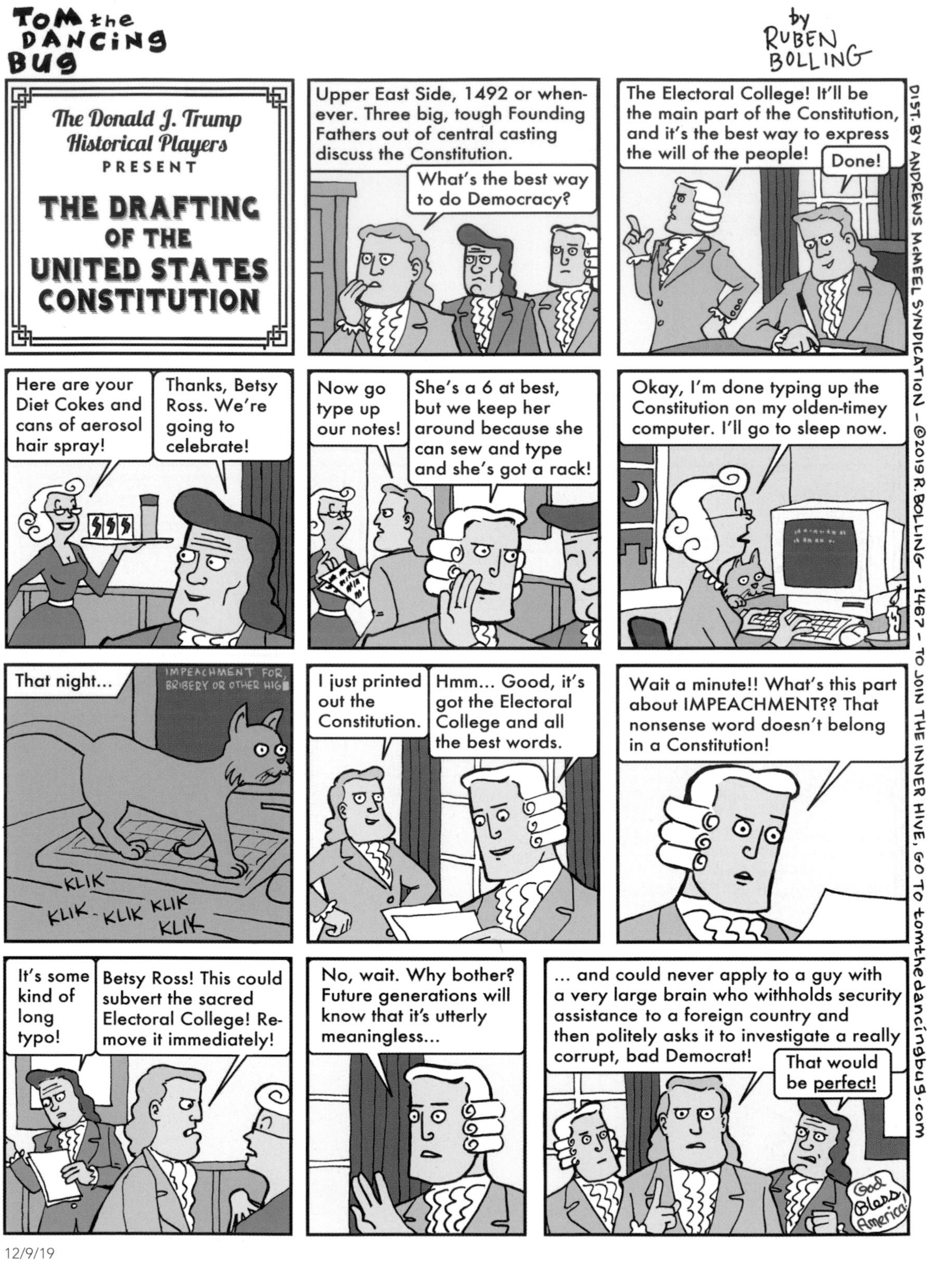

TOM the DANCING BUG
by RUBEN BOLLING
The Donald J. Trump Historical Players PRESENT
THE DRAFTING OF THE UNITED STATES CONSTITUTION
Upper East Side, 1492 or whenever. Three big, tough Founding Fathers out of central casting discuss the Constitution.
What's the best way to do Democracy?
The Electoral College! It'll be the main part of the Constitution, and it's the best way to express the will of the people!
Done!
Here are your Diet Cokes and cans of aerosol hair spray!
Thanks, Betsy Ross. We're going to celebrate!
Now go type up our notes!
She's a 6 at best, but we keep her around because she can sew and type and she's got a rack!
Okay, I'm done typing up the Constitution on my olden-timey computer. I'll go to sleep now.
That night...
IMPEACHMENT FOR BRIBERY OR OTHER HIG
KLIK KLIK - KLIK KLIK KLIK
I just printed out the Constitution.
Hmm... Good, it's got the Electoral College and all the best words.
Wait a minute!! What's this part about IMPEACHMENT?? That nonsense word doesn't belong in a Constitution!
It's some kind of long typo!
Betsy Ross! This could subvert the sacred Electoral College! Remove it immediately!
No, wait. Why bother? Future generations will know that it's utterly meaningless...
... and could never apply to a guy with a very large brain who withholds security assistance to a foreign country and then politely asks it to investigate a really corrupt, bad Democrat!
That would be perfect!
God Bless America!
DIST. BY ANDREWS McMEEL SYNDICATION - ©2019 R. BOLLING - 1467 - TO JOIN THE INNER HIVE, GO TO tomthedancingbug.com

12/9/19

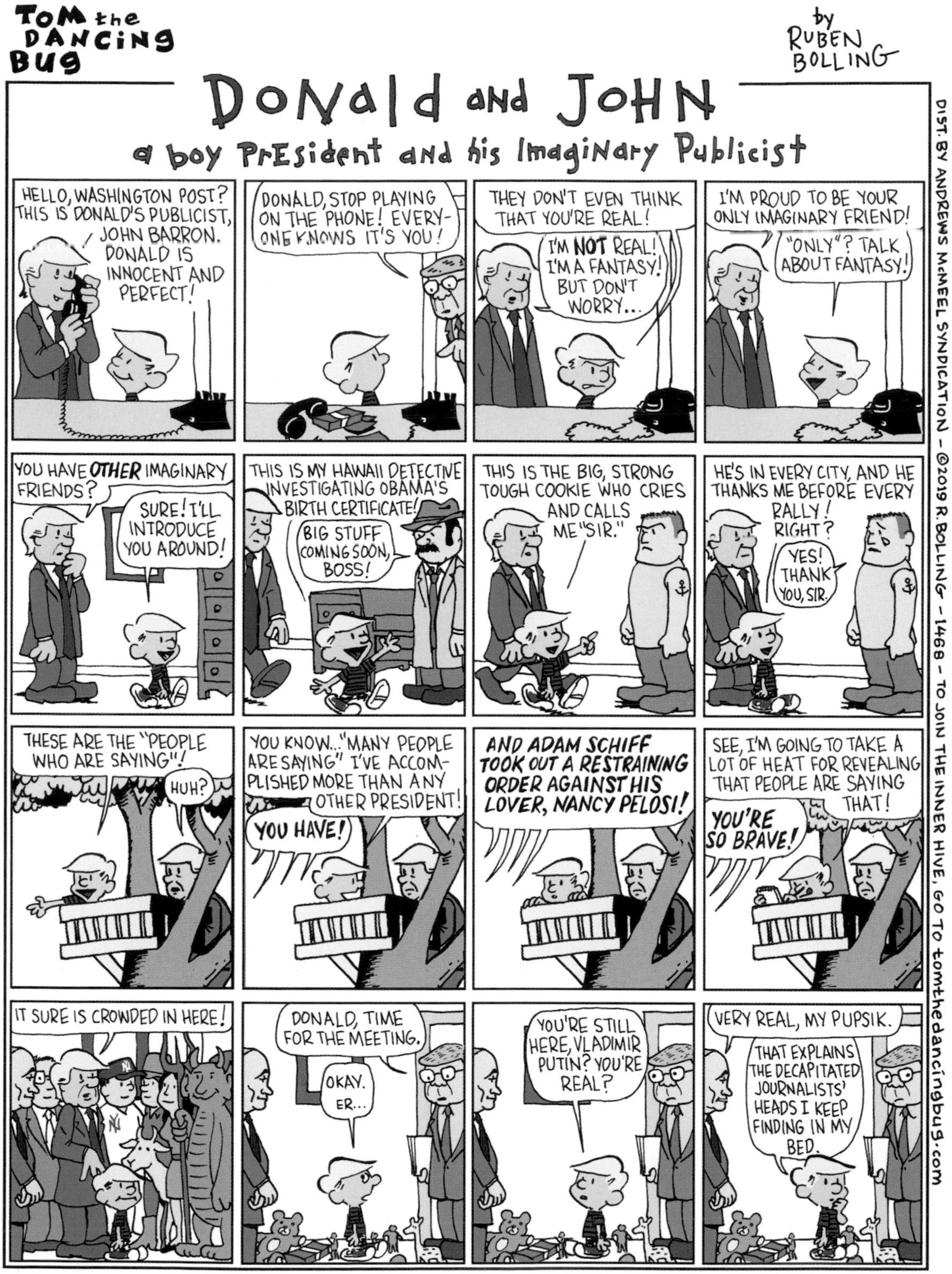

TOM the DANCING BUG
by RUBEN BOLLING
DONALD and JOHN
a boy PRESIDENT and his Imaginary Publicist
HELLO, WASHINGTON POST? THIS IS DONALD'S PUBLICIST, JOHN BARRON. DONALD IS INNOCENT AND PERFECT!
DONALD, STOP PLAYING ON THE PHONE! EVERYONE KNOWS IT'S YOU!
THEY DON'T EVEN THINK THAT YOU'RE REAL!
I'M NOT REAL! I'M A FANTASY! BUT DON'T WORRY...
I'M PROUD TO BE YOUR ONLY IMAGINARY FRIEND!
"ONLY"? TALK ABOUT FANTASY!
YOU HAVE OTHER IMAGINARY FRIENDS?
SURE! I'LL INTRODUCE YOU AROUND!
THIS IS MY HAWAII DETECTIVE INVESTIGATING OBAMA'S BIRTH CERTIFICATE!
BIG STUFF COMING SOON, BOSS!
THIS IS THE BIG, STRONG TOUGH COOKIE WHO CRIES AND CALLS ME "SIR."
HE'S IN EVERY CITY, AND HE THANKS ME BEFORE EVERY RALLY! RIGHT?
YES! THANK YOU, SIR.
THESE ARE THE "PEOPLE WHO ARE SAYING"!
HUH?
YOU KNOW..."MANY PEOPLE ARE SAYING" I'VE ACCOMPLISHED MORE THAN ANY OTHER PRESIDENT!
YOU HAVE!
AND ADAM SCHIFF TOOK OUT A RESTRAINING ORDER AGAINST HIS LOVER, NANCY PELOSI!
SEE, I'M GOING TO TAKE A LOT OF HEAT FOR REVEALING THAT PEOPLE ARE SAYING THAT!
YOU'RE SO BRAVE!
IT SURE IS CROWDED IN HERE!
DONALD, TIME FOR THE MEETING.
OKAY. ER...
YOU'RE STILL HERE, VLADIMIR PUTIN? YOU'RE REAL?
VERY REAL, MY PUPSIK.
THAT EXPLAINS THE DECAPITATED JOURNALISTS' HEADS I KEEP FINDING IN MY BED.
DIST. BY ANDREWS McMEEL SYNDICATION - ©2019 R. BOLLING - 1468 - TO JOIN THE INNER HIVE, GO TO tomthedancingbug.com

12/16/19

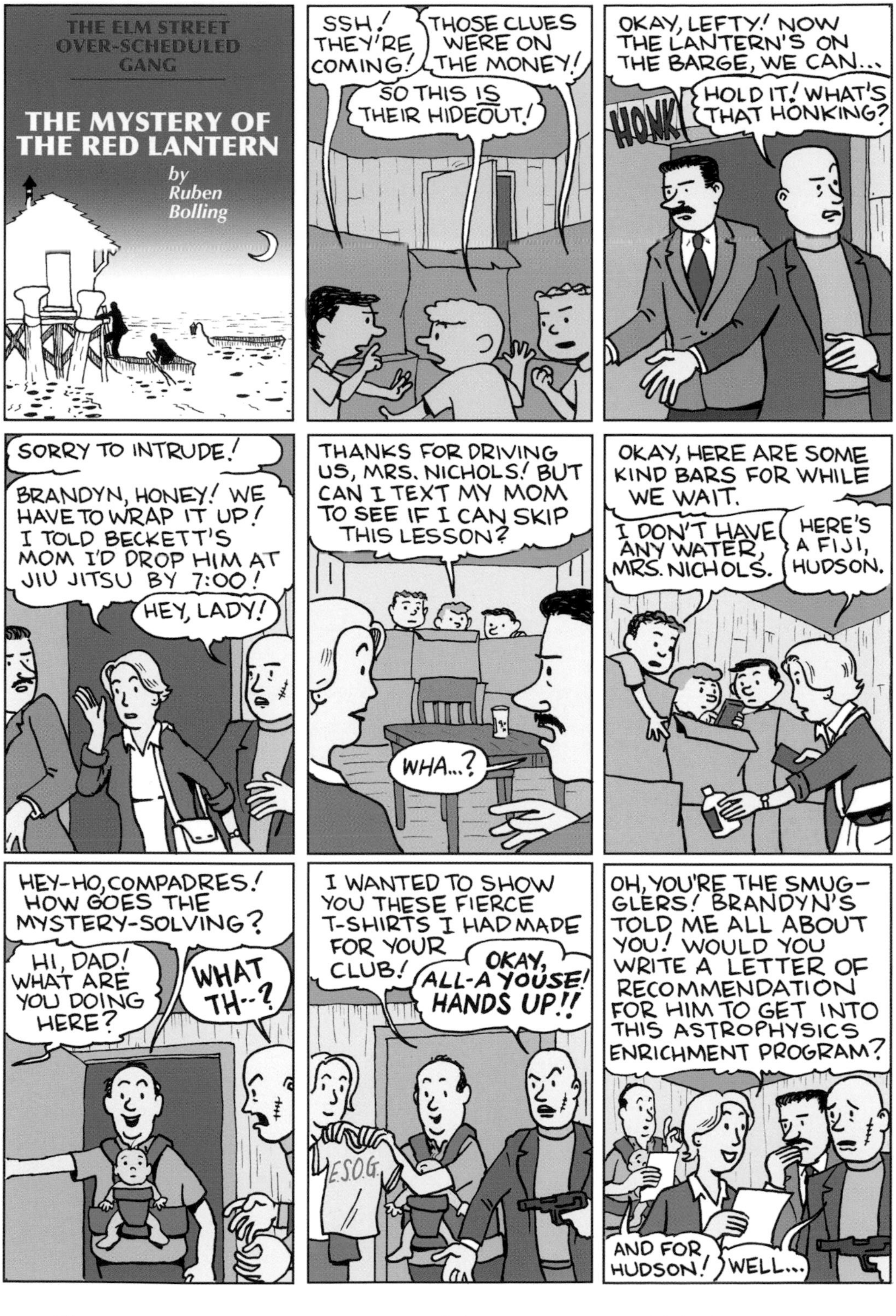
THE ELM STREET OVER-SCHEDULED GANG
THE MYSTERY OF THE RED LANTERN
by Ruben Bolling
SSH! THEY'RE COMING!
THOSE CLUES WERE ON THE MONEY!
SO THIS IS THEIR HIDEOUT!
OKAY, LEFTY! NOW THE LANTERN'S ON THE BARGE, WE CAN...
HONK
HOLD IT! WHAT'S THAT HONKING?
SORRY TO INTRUDE!
BRANDYN, HONEY! WE HAVE TO WRAP IT UP! I TOLD BECKETT'S MOM I'D DROP HIM AT JIU JITSU BY 7:00!
HEY, LADY!
THANKS FOR DRIVING US, MRS. NICHOLS! BUT CAN I TEXT MY MOM TO SEE IF I CAN SKIP THIS LESSON?
WHA...?
OKAY, HERE ARE SOME KIND BARS FOR WHILE WE WAIT.
I DON'T HAVE ANY WATER, MRS. NICHOLS.
HERE'S A FIJI, HUDSON.
HEY-HO, COMPADRES! HOW GOES THE MYSTERY-SOLVING?
HI, DAD! WHAT ARE YOU DOING HERE?
WHAT TH--?
I WANTED TO SHOW YOU THESE FIERCE T-SHIRTS I HAD MADE FOR YOUR CLUB!
E.S.O.G.
OKAY, ALL-A YOUSE! HANDS UP!!
OH, YOU'RE THE SMUGGLERS! BRANDYN'S TOLD ME ALL ABOUT YOU! WOULD YOU WRITE A LETTER OF RECOMMENDATION FOR HIM TO GET INTO THIS ASTROPHYSICS ENRICHMENT PROGRAM?
AND FOR HUDSON!
WELL...

This comic appeared in the Family Issue of *The Nib Magazine*, published January, 2019.

DONALD AND JOHN

by RUBEN BOLLING

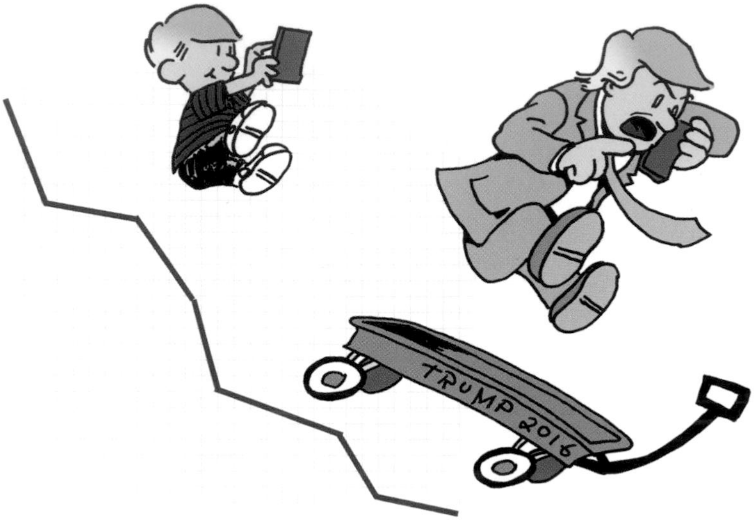
TRUMP 2016

a boy Presidential candidate and his Imaginary Publicist

In early October 2016, with the election bearing down, Bolling launched a separate, limited-time, almost daily comic strip based on his Donald and John comics. It was published on TheNib.com, concluding the day after the election. The series won the National Cartoonists Society Best Online Cartoon Award in 2017.

Donald and John

a boy Presidential candidate and his Imaginary Publicist

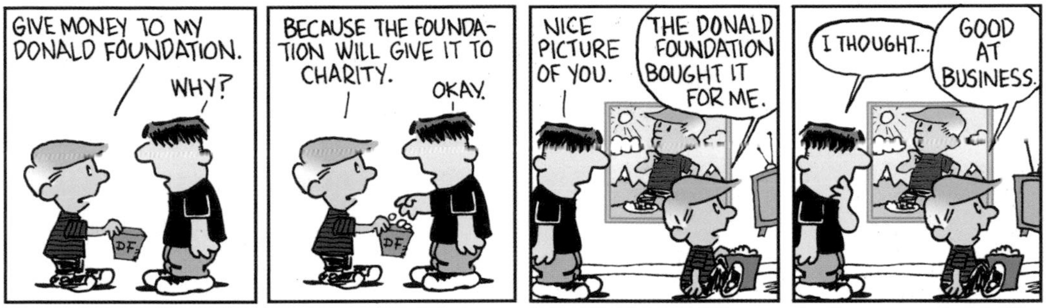

GIVE MONEY TO MY DONALD FOUNDATION.
WHY?
DF
BECAUSE THE FOUNDATION WILL GIVE IT TO CHARITY.
OKAY.
DF
NICE PICTURE OF YOU.
THE DONALD FOUNDATION BOUGHT IT FOR ME.
I THOUGHT...
GOOD AT BUSINESS.

10/7/16

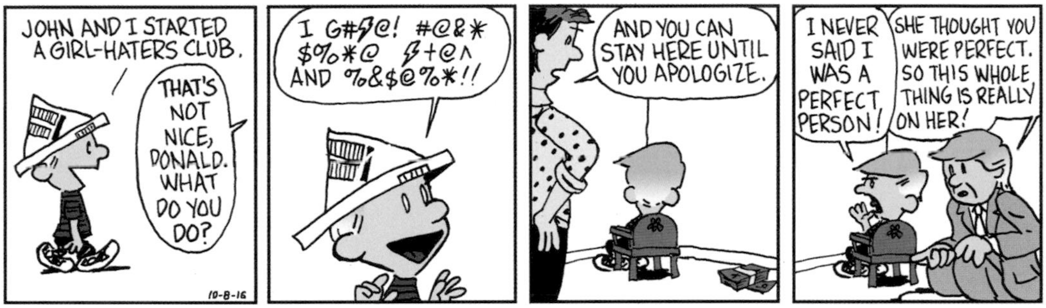

JOHN AND I STARTED A GIRL-HATERS CLUB.
THAT'S NOT NICE, DONALD. WHAT DO YOU DO?
10-8-16
I G#⚡@! #@&* $%*@ ⚡+@^ AND %&$@%*!!
AND YOU CAN STAY HERE UNTIL YOU APOLOGIZE.
I NEVER SAID I WAS A PERFECT PERSON!
SHE THOUGHT YOU WERE PERFECT. SO THIS WHOLE THING IS REALLY ON HER!

10/8/16

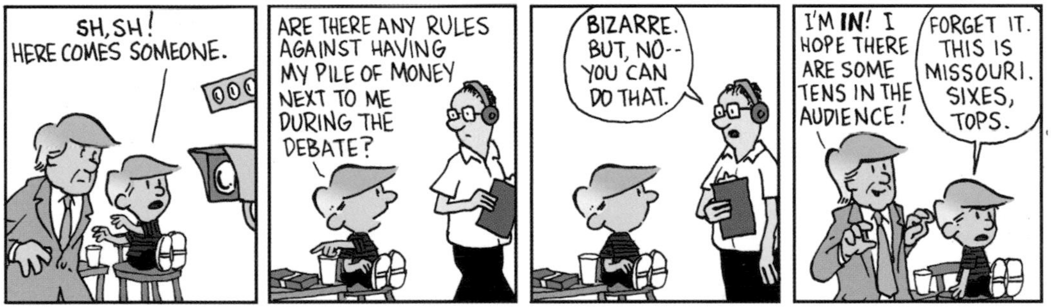

SH, SH! HERE COMES SOMEONE.
ARE THERE ANY RULES AGAINST HAVING MY PILE OF MONEY NEXT TO ME DURING THE DEBATE?
BIZARRE. BUT, NO-- YOU CAN DO THAT.
I'M **IN**! I HOPE THERE ARE SOME TENS IN THE AUDIENCE!
FORGET IT. THIS IS MISSOURI. SIXES, TOPS.

10/10/16

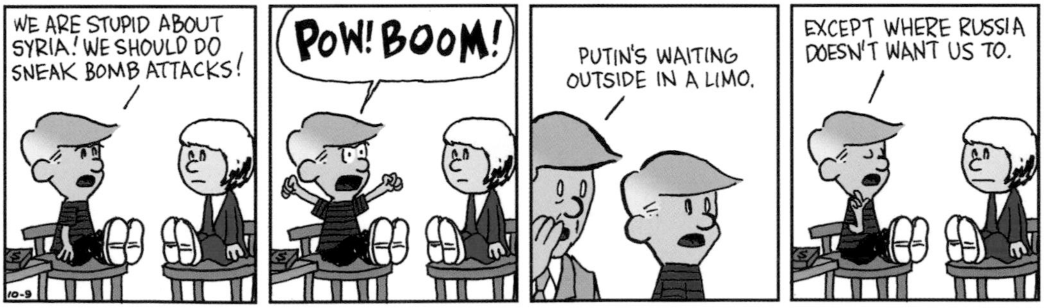

WE ARE STUPID ABOUT SYRIA! WE SHOULD DO SNEAK BOMB ATTACKS!
10-9
POW! BOOM!
PUTIN'S WAITING OUTSIDE IN A LIMO.
EXCEPT WHERE RUSSIA DOESN'T WANT US TO.

10/10/16

Donald and John

a boy Presidential candidate and his Imaginary Publicist

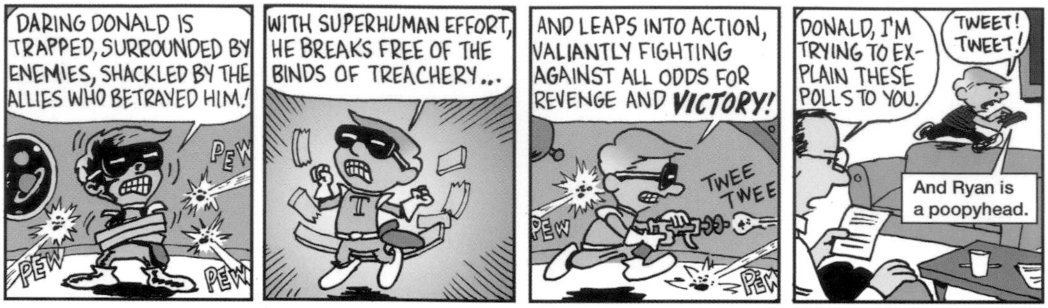

DARING DONALD IS TRAPPED, SURROUNDED BY ENEMIES, SHACKLED BY THE ALLIES WHO BETRAYED HIM!
PEW
PEW
PEW
WITH SUPERHUMAN EFFORT, HE BREAKS FREE OF THE BINDS OF TREACHERY...
AND LEAPS INTO ACTION, VALIANTLY FIGHTING AGAINST ALL ODDS FOR REVENGE AND VICTORY!
TWEE TWEE
PEW
PEW
DONALD, I'M TRYING TO EXPLAIN THESE POLLS TO YOU.
TWEET! TWEET!
And Ryan is a poopyhead.

10/12/16

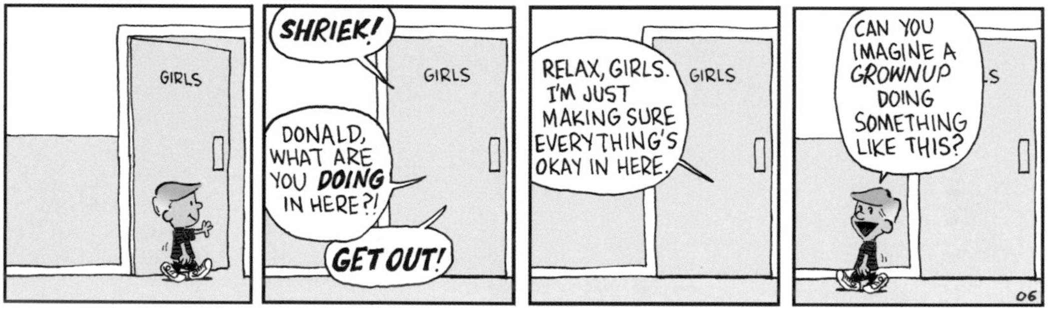

GIRLS
SHRIEK!
GIRLS
DONALD, WHAT ARE YOU DOING IN HERE?!
GET OUT!
RELAX, GIRLS. I'M JUST MAKING SURE EVERYTHING'S OKAY IN HERE.
GIRLS
CAN YOU IMAGINE A GROWNUP DOING SOMETHING LIKE THIS?

10/13/16

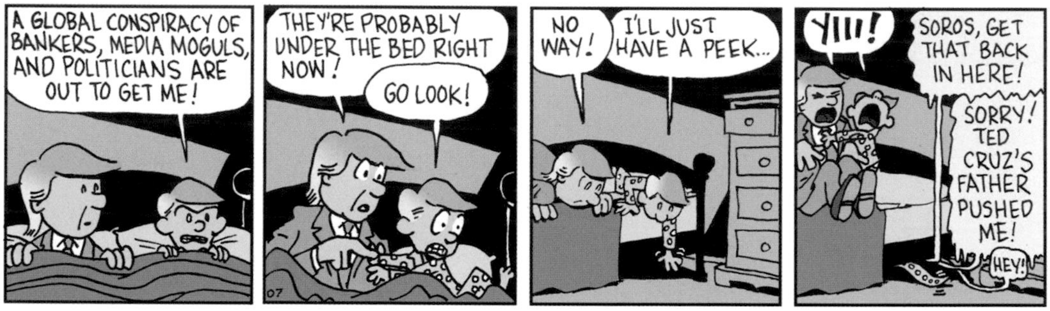

A GLOBAL CONSPIRACY OF BANKERS, MEDIA MOGULS, AND POLITICIANS ARE OUT TO GET ME!
THEY'RE PROBABLY UNDER THE BED RIGHT NOW!
GO LOOK!
NO WAY!
I'LL JUST HAVE A PEEK...
YIII!
SOROS, GET THAT BACK IN HERE!
SORRY! TED CRUZ'S FATHER PUSHED ME!
HEY!

10/14/16

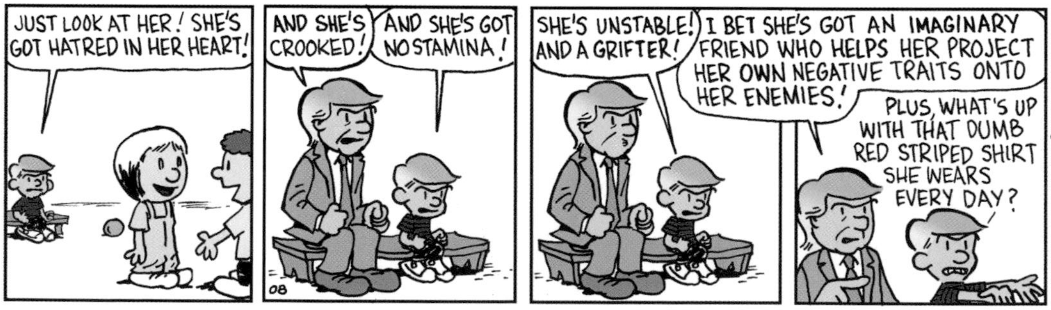

JUST LOOK AT HER! SHE'S GOT HATRED IN HER HEART!
AND SHE'S CROOKED!
AND SHE'S GOT NO STAMINA!
SHE'S UNSTABLE! AND A GRIFTER!
I BET SHE'S GOT AN IMAGINARY FRIEND WHO HELPS HER PROJECT HER OWN NEGATIVE TRAITS ONTO HER ENEMIES!
PLUS, WHAT'S UP WITH THAT DUMB RED STRIPED SHIRT SHE WEARS EVERY DAY?

10/17/16

Donald and John

a boy Presidential candidate and his Imaginary Publicist

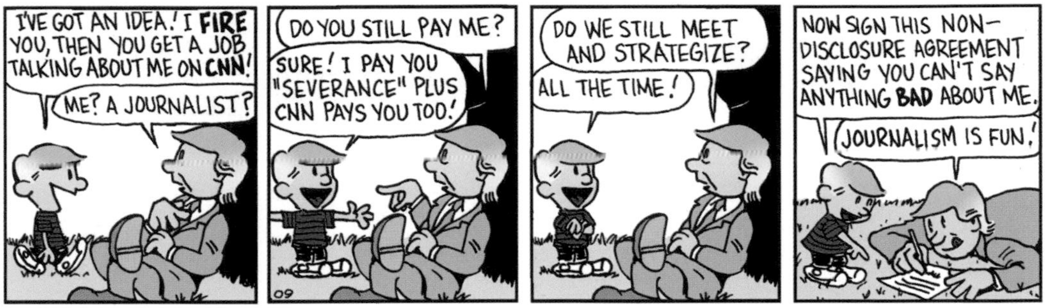

I'VE GOT AN IDEA! I **FIRE** YOU, THEN YOU GET A JOB TALKING ABOUT ME ON **CNN**!
ME? A JOURNALIST?
DO YOU STILL PAY ME?
SURE! I PAY YOU "SEVERANCE" PLUS CNN PAYS YOU TOO!
DO WE STILL MEET AND STRATEGIZE?
ALL THE TIME!
NOW SIGN THIS NON-DISCLOSURE AGREEMENT SAYING YOU CAN'T SAY ANYTHING **BAD** ABOUT ME.
JOURNALISM IS FUN!

10/18/16

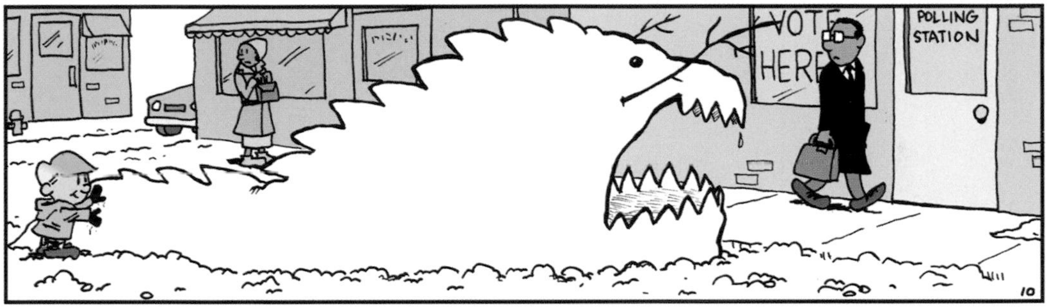

VOTE HERE
POLLING STATION

10/19/16

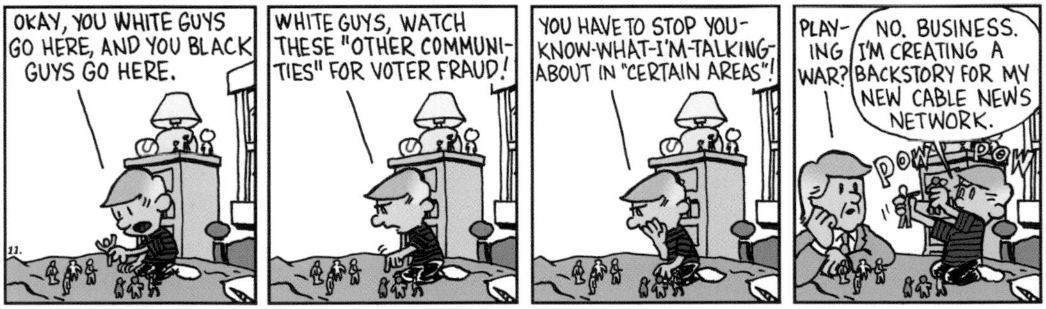

OKAY, YOU WHITE GUYS GO HERE, AND YOU BLACK GUYS GO HERE.
WHITE GUYS, WATCH THESE "OTHER COMMUNITIES" FOR VOTER FRAUD!
YOU HAVE TO STOP YOU-KNOW-WHAT-I'M-TALKING-ABOUT IN "CERTAIN AREAS"!
PLAYING WAR?
NO. BUSINESS. I'M CREATING A BACKSTORY FOR MY NEW CABLE NEWS NETWORK.
POW POW

10/20/16

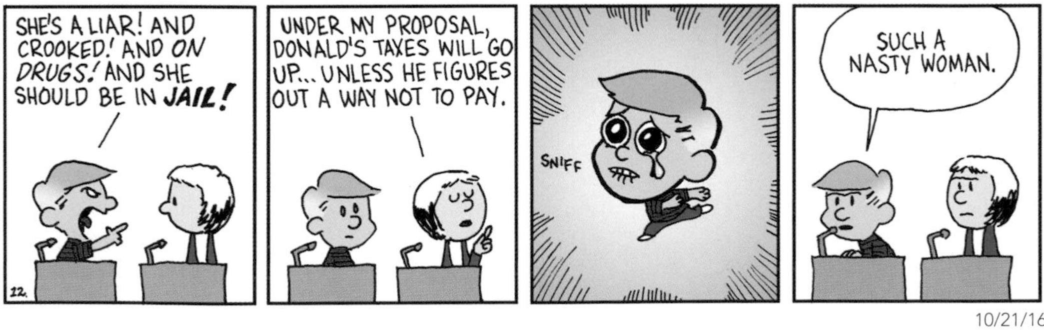

SHE'S A LIAR! AND CROOKED! AND *ON DRUGS!* AND SHE SHOULD BE IN ***JAIL!***
UNDER MY PROPOSAL, DONALD'S TAXES WILL GO UP... UNLESS HE FIGURES OUT A WAY NOT TO PAY.
SNIFF
SUCH A NASTY WOMAN.

10/21/16

DONALD and JOHN

a boy Presidential candidate and his Imaginary Publicist

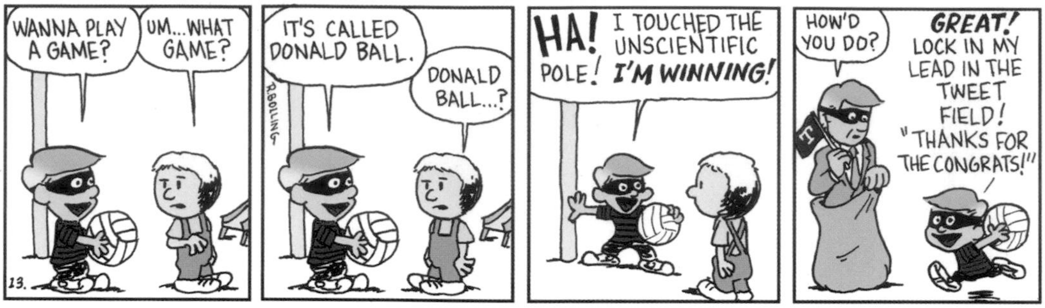
WANNA PLAY A GAME?
UM...WHAT GAME?
IT'S CALLED DONALD BALL.
DONALD BALL...?
R.BOLLING
HA! I TOUCHED THE UNSCIENTIFIC POLE! I'M WINNING!
HOW'D YOU DO?
GREAT! LOCK IN MY LEAD IN THE TWEET FIELD! "THANKS FOR THE CONGRATS!"
13.

10/24/16

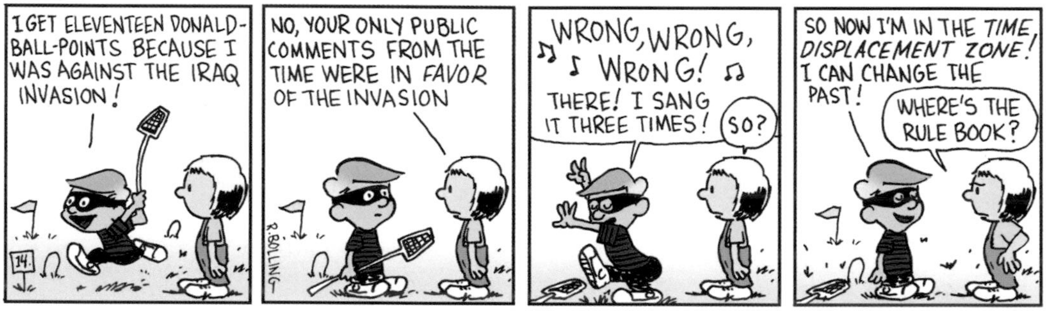
I GET ELEVENTEEN DONALD-BALL-POINTS BECAUSE I WAS AGAINST THE IRAQ INVASION!
14.
NO, YOUR ONLY PUBLIC COMMENTS FROM THE TIME WERE IN FAVOR OF THE INVASION
R.BOLLING
WRONG, WRONG, WRONG!
THERE! I SANG IT THREE TIMES!
SO?
SO NOW I'M IN THE TIME DISPLACEMENT ZONE! I CAN CHANGE THE PAST!
WHERE'S THE RULE BOOK?

10/25/16

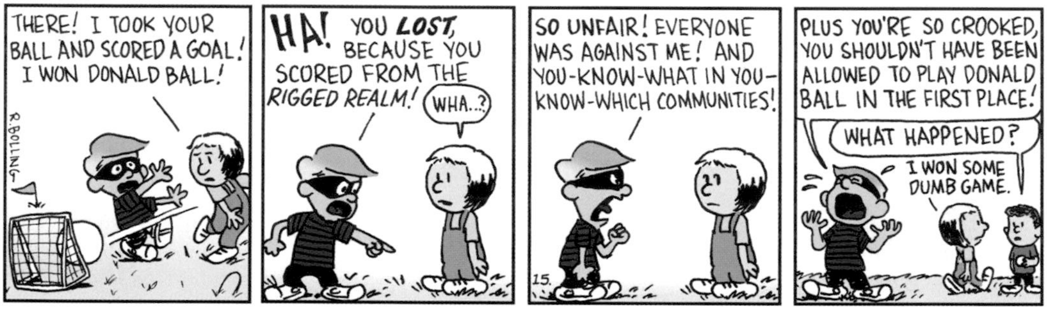
THERE! I TOOK YOUR BALL AND SCORED A GOAL! I WON DONALD BALL!
R.BOLLING
HA! YOU LOST, BECAUSE YOU SCORED FROM THE RIGGED REALM!
WHA...?
SO UNFAIR! EVERYONE WAS AGAINST ME! AND YOU-KNOW-WHAT IN YOU-KNOW-WHICH COMMUNITIES!
15.
PLUS YOU'RE SO CROOKED, YOU SHOULDN'T HAVE BEEN ALLOWED TO PLAY DONALD BALL IN THE FIRST PLACE!
WHAT HAPPENED?
I WON SOME DUMB GAME.

10/26/16

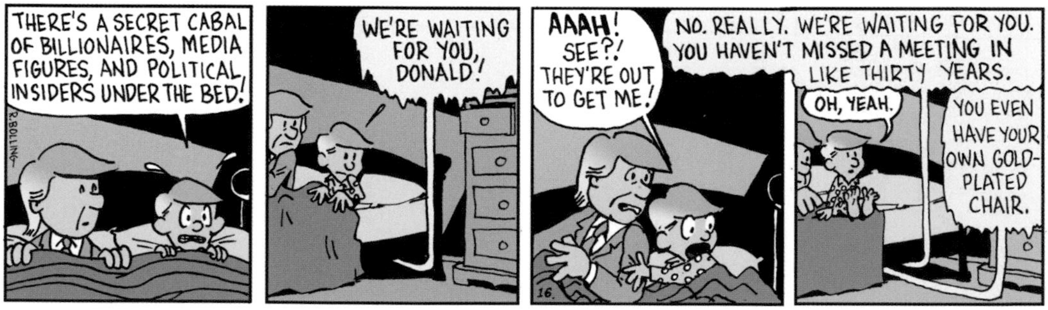
THERE'S A SECRET CABAL OF BILLIONAIRES, MEDIA FIGURES, AND POLITICAL INSIDERS UNDER THE BED!
R.BOLLING
WE'RE WAITING FOR YOU, DONALD!
AAAH! SEE?! THEY'RE OUT TO GET ME!
16.
NO. REALLY. WE'RE WAITING FOR YOU. YOU HAVEN'T MISSED A MEETING IN LIKE THIRTY YEARS.
OH, YEAH.
YOU EVEN HAVE YOUR OWN GOLD-PLATED CHAIR.

10/27/16

Donald and John
a boy Presidential candidate and his Imaginary Publicist

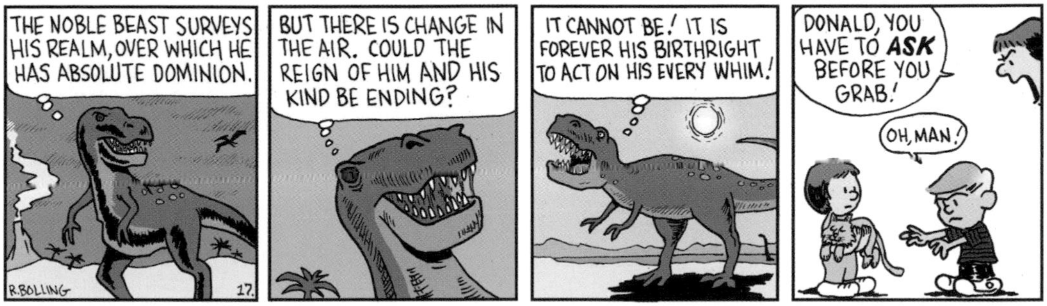

THE NOBLE BEAST SURVEYS HIS REALM, OVER WHICH HE HAS ABSOLUTE DOMINION.
R.BOLLING
17.
BUT THERE IS CHANGE IN THE AIR. COULD THE REIGN OF HIM AND HIS KIND BE ENDING?
IT CANNOT BE! IT IS FOREVER HIS BIRTHRIGHT TO ACT ON HIS EVERY WHIM!
DONALD, YOU HAVE TO **ASK** BEFORE YOU GRAB!
OH, MAN!

10/28/16

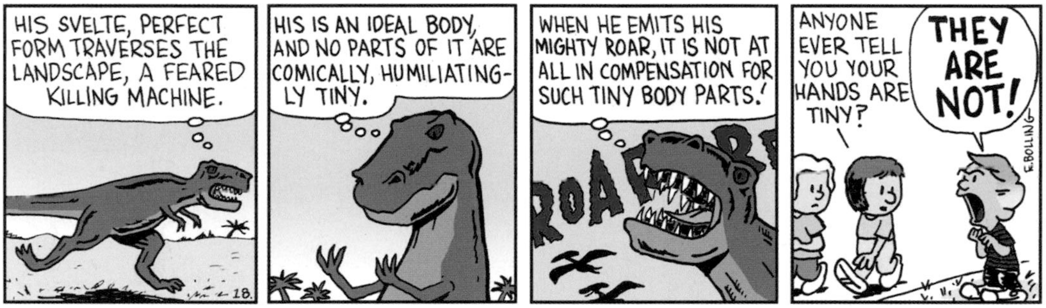

HIS SVELTE, PERFECT FORM TRAVERSES THE LANDSCAPE, A FEARED KILLING MACHINE.
18.
HIS IS AN IDEAL BODY, AND NO PARTS OF IT ARE COMICALLY, HUMILIATINGLY TINY.
WHEN HE EMITS HIS MIGHTY ROAR, IT IS NOT AT ALL IN COMPENSATION FOR SUCH TINY BODY PARTS!
ROAR
ANYONE EVER TELL YOU YOUR HANDS ARE TINY?
THEY ARE NOT!
R.BOLLING

10/31/16

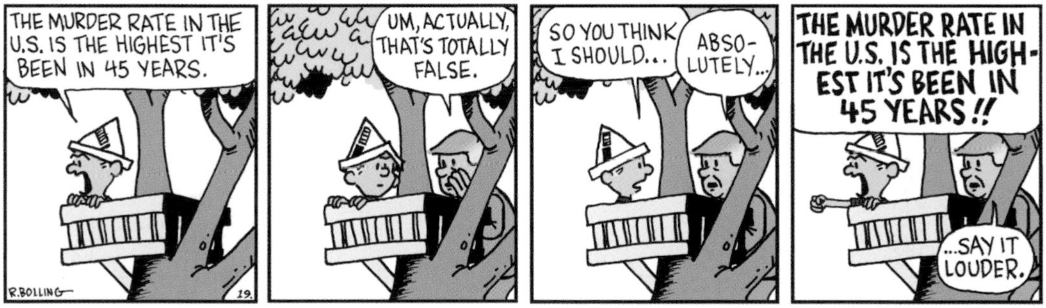

THE MURDER RATE IN THE U.S. IS THE HIGHEST IT'S BEEN IN 45 YEARS.
R.BOLLING
19.
UM, ACTUALLY, THAT'S TOTALLY FALSE.
SO YOU THINK I SHOULD...
ABSOLUTELY...
THE MURDER RATE IN THE U.S. IS THE HIGHEST IT'S BEEN IN 45 YEARS!!
...SAY IT LOUDER.

11/1/16

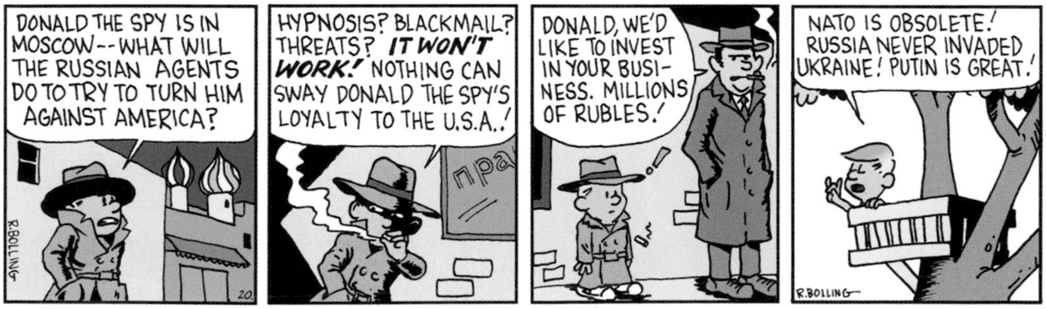

DONALD THE SPY IS IN MOSCOW--WHAT WILL THE RUSSIAN AGENTS DO TO TRY TO TURN HIM AGAINST AMERICA?
R.BOLLING
20.
HYPNOSIS? BLACKMAIL? THREATS? *IT WON'T WORK!* NOTHING CAN SWAY DONALD THE SPY'S LOYALTY TO THE U.S.A..!
DONALD, WE'D LIKE TO INVEST IN YOUR BUSINESS. MILLIONS OF RUBLES!
NATO IS OBSOLETE! RUSSIA NEVER INVADED UKRAINE! PUTIN IS GREAT!
R.BOLLING

11/2/16

Donald and John
a boy Presidential candidate and his Imaginary Publicist

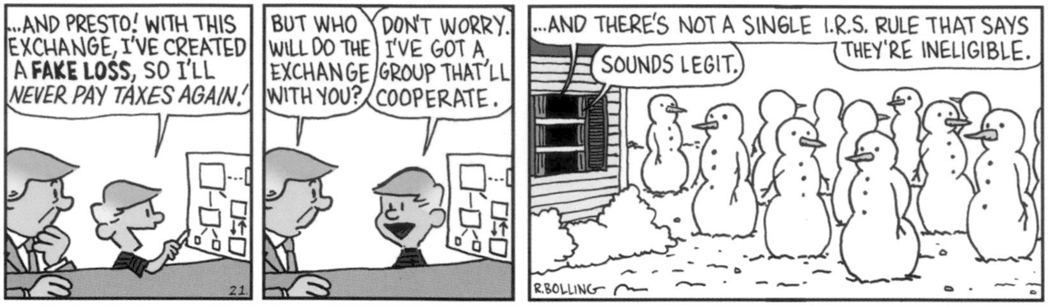

...AND PRESTO! WITH THIS EXCHANGE, I'VE CREATED A **FAKE LOSS**, SO I'LL *NEVER PAY TAXES AGAIN!*
BUT WHO WILL DO THE EXCHANGE WITH YOU?
DON'T WORRY. I'VE GOT A GROUP THAT'LL COOPERATE.
...AND THERE'S NOT A SINGLE I.R.S. RULE THAT SAYS THEY'RE INELIGIBLE.
SOUNDS LEGIT.
21.
R.BOLLING

11/3/16

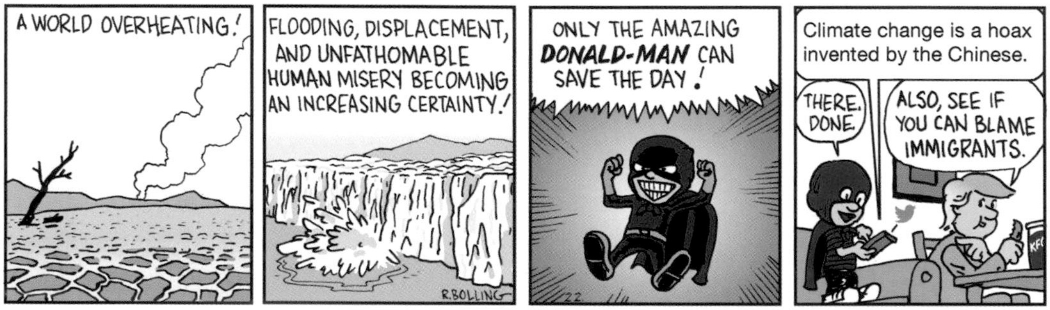

A WORLD OVERHEATING!
FLOODING, DISPLACEMENT, AND UNFATHOMABLE HUMAN MISERY BECOMING AN INCREASING CERTAINTY!
ONLY THE AMAZING ***DONALD-MAN*** CAN SAVE THE DAY!
Climate change is a hoax invented by the Chinese.
THERE. DONE.
ALSO, SEE IF YOU CAN BLAME IMMIGRANTS.
KFC
22.
R.BOLLING

11/4/16

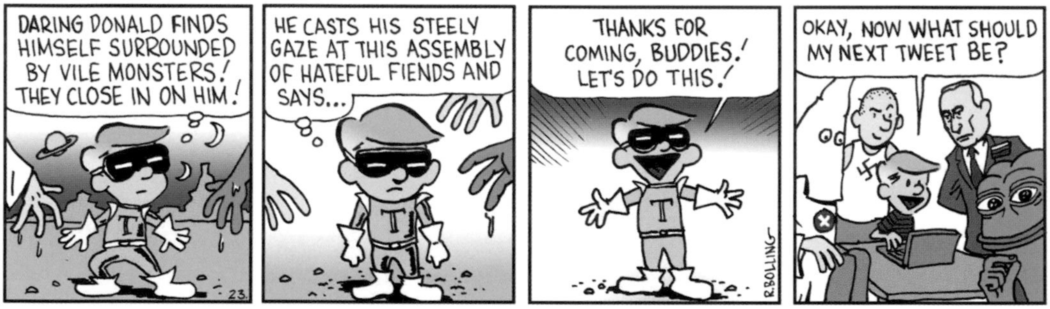

DARING DONALD FINDS HIMSELF SURROUNDED BY VILE MONSTERS! THEY CLOSE IN ON HIM!
HE CASTS HIS STEELY GAZE AT THIS ASSEMBLY OF HATEFUL FIENDS AND SAYS...
THANKS FOR COMING, BUDDIES! LET'S DO THIS!
OKAY, NOW WHAT SHOULD MY NEXT TWEET BE?
23.
R.BOLLING

11/7/16

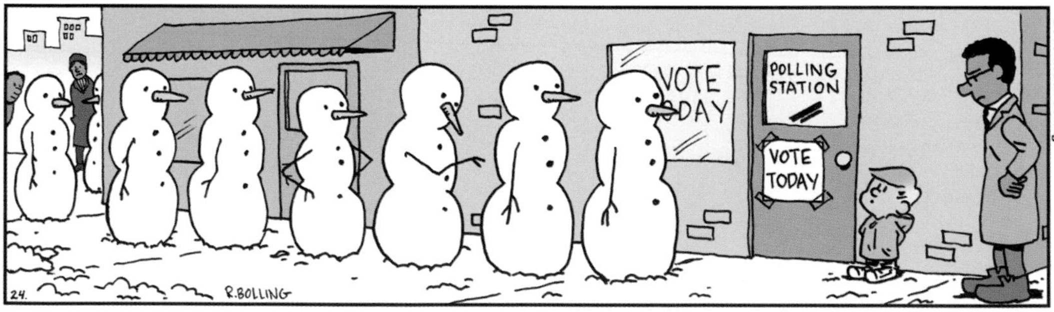

VOTE DAY
POLLING STATION
VOTE TODAY
24.
R.BOLLING

11/8/16

Donald and John
a boy Presidential candidate and his Imaginary Publicist

WELL, IT'S ALL OVER, OL' BUDDY.!
AND IT'S JUST BEGINNING!
25.
RBOLLING
WE SUCCEEDED IN FANNING THE FLAMES OF DISTRUST, DIVISION, AND HATE!
AND SINCE EVERYTHING IS ALWAYS ABOUT MY FEELINGS, WE'RE GOING TO EXPLOIT THIS NEW, TOXIC ATMOSPHERE!
©2016 Ruben Bolling
WE'VE ALREADY SUNK SO LOW...
NOW WE'LL SEE HOW MUCH LOWER WE CAN GO!
LET'S WREAK OUR REVENGE!
AND SELL CRAP TO MORONS!

11/9/16

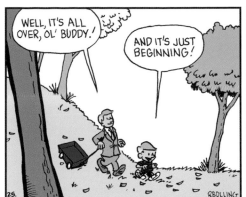

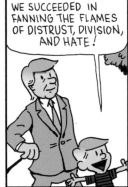

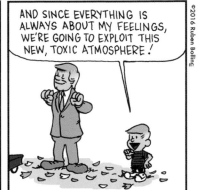

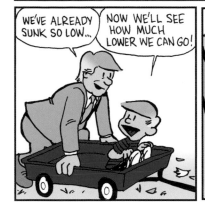

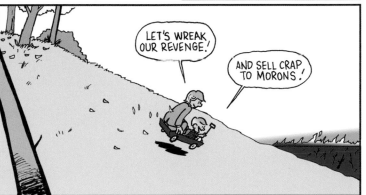